COMPETITION LAW AND POLICY IN LATIN AMERICA

This book offers an unparalleled analysis of the emerging law and economics of competition policy in Latin America. Nearly all Latin American countries now have competition laws and agencies to enforce them. Yet these laws and agencies are relatively young. The relative youth of Latin American competition agencies and the institutional and political environment in which they operate limit the ability of agencies to address anti-competitive conduct effectively. Competition policy is a tool to overcome anti-market traditions in Latin America. Effective competition policy is critical to assisting in the growth of Latin American economies and their global competitiveness, and to improving the welfare of domestic consumers. This book provides new region-specific insights into how better to achieve these aims.

This authoritative volume will be of particular interest to competition agencies, academics in law, economics and Latin American studies, practitioners around the world in the areas of antitrust and competition policy, policymakers, and journalists.

Competition Law and Policy in Latin America

Edited by
Eleanor M Fox
and
D Daniel Sokol

•HART•
PUBLISHING
OXFORD AND PORTLAND, OREGON
2009

Published in North America (US and Canada) by
Hart Publishing
c/o International Specialized Book Services
920 NE 58th Avenue, Suite 300
Portland, OR 97213-3786
USA
Tel: +1 503 287 3093 or toll-free: (1) 800 944 6190
Fax: +1 503 280 8832
E-mail: orders@isbs.com
Website: http://www.isbs.com

Hart Publishing Ltd, 16C Worcester Place, Oxford, OX1 2JW
Telephone: +44 (0)1865 517530 Fax: +44 (0)1865 510710
E-mail: mail@hartpub.co.uk
Website: http://www.hartpub.co.uk

British Library Cataloguing in Publication Data
Data Available

ISBN: 978-1-84113-882-4

Typeset by Compuscript Ltd, Shannon
Printed and bound in Great Britain by
TJ International Ltd, Padstow, Cornwall

TABLE OF CONTENTS

TABLE OF CASES

Andean Community

Argentina

Brazil

Canada

Chile

Colombia

European Commission

European Court of Justice and Court of First Instance

Italy

Mexico

Panama

Peru

Spain

United Kingdom

United States

Venezuela

TABLE OF LEGISLATION

Andean Community

Argentina

Barbados

Belgium

Bolivia

Brazil

Chile

China

Colombia

Costa Rica

Dominican Republic

Ecuador

El Salvador

European Union

Regulations

Germany

Honduras

Jamaica

Mercosur

Mexico

Nicaragua

Panama

Peru

Spain

Trinidad and Tobago

United States

Uruguay

Venezuela

TABLE OF AGREEMENTS, CONVENTIONS, TREATIES, etc

Chapter I

Introduction

ELEANOR M FOX* AND D DANIEL SOKOL**

I. Overview

In Latin America, competition law (known in the United States as antitrust) has become increasingly important. However, a lack of academic literature focusing on Latin America's specific competition policy[1] has left many fundamental questions unanswered. A number of general assumptions on how markets function and about how to combat anti-competitive conduct seem not to resonate as strongly in the specific Latin American context. The chapters in this book stem largely from papers presented at a Latin American competition policy conference held on 4 April 2008 in Sao Paolo, Brazil, at Fundação Getulio Vargas Law School.

The book has a particular focus on enforcement against what is often regarded as the most harmful private restraint (cartels), as well as the role of competition agencies in detecting and advocating against the most harmful government restraints (competition advocacy). Both efforts are particularly challenging in Latin American countries, given larger political economy considerations as well as issues of institutional design. The book also elucidates the competition policy systems of the largest countries in the region, and treats issues of region-wide impact such as merger control, the interface between trade agreements and competition policy, and the growing influence of civil society upon Latin American competition policy. We focus primarily on cartels and advocacy, though we note that some important vertical restraint and merger cases have been undertaken by antitrust authorities in the region. The chapters that focus on particular countries provide some detail into these other areas and the circumstances in which Latin American agencies have embraced US and European approaches to address certain types of potentially anti-competitive behavior.

* Walter J Derenberg Professor of Trade Regulation, New York University School of Law.
** Assistant Professor of Law, University of Florida College of Law.

[1] Competition policy is broader than competition law, and includes competition analysis such as competition advocacy.

Each of the book's chapters analyzes antitrust issues in the Latin American context. This is critical given the common tendency of many scholars to think in terms of universal, rather than regional or local, standards. Scholarship—and indeed policy—applying universal standards may or may not fit the context. This question of global versus a local tailored inquiry is one of the important themes of the book. The introductory chapters develop these themes and help to focus the issues as part of the broader context for the subsequent chapters.

Issues of capacity constraints internal both to each antitrust institution and to each country's other set of institutions (judiciary, legislature, sector regulators and non-government institutions) play a central role in the shape of competition policy enforcement in the region. Presently, nearly all Latin American countries have competition laws and agencies to enforce them. Yet these laws and agencies are relatively young. The institutional and political environment in which Latin American competition agencies operate limits the ability of agencies to address anti-competitive conduct effectively. Competition policy is a tool to overcome anti-market traditions in Latin America. Indeed, competition policy is critical to assisting in the growth of Latin American economies and their global competitiveness, and to improving the welfare of domestic consumers.[2] This book provides new insights into how better to achieve these goals.

Market distortions based on a lack of competition significantly harm Latin American economic development. Cartels or monopolists may control many of the entry points into a given country's economy. The government may provide incumbent companies a tilted playing field through discriminatory regulation, and may immunize certain behavior from antitrust coverage. A country may choose not to enforce its own antitrust laws for political reasons, such as the desire to create 'national champions'. Collectively, these restraints can be used against foreign firms to limit their entry into a market.

We highlight the institutional differences and market problems unique to Latin America in light of the various stages of economic development for countries in the region. Latin America went through a period of significant economic liberalization and privatization in the 1980s and 1990s. Competition policy was one of a number of policies to promote economic liberalization, a process which was more successful in some countries than others. However, issues of social inequity still haunt the region and every country. Competition policy works in the shadow of the larger ideological, political and economic battles regarding social inequality and economic liberalization.

Competition agencies interact with institutions such as legislatures, courts, and other administrative agencies in complex ways.[3] In Latin America, domestic

[2] Eleanor M Fox, 'Economic Development, Poverty, and Antitrust: The Other Path', 13 *Southwestern Journal of Law and Trade in the Americas* 211 (2007).

[3] Jean-Jacques Laffont, 'Competition, Information, and Development', in Boris Pleskovic and Joseph E Stiglitz (eds), *Annual World Bank Conference on Development Economies* 237 (Washington, DC, World Bank, 1999).

antitrust institutions (primarily competition agencies and courts, as opposed to regional or international institutions, which are relatively weak on competition policy) face considerable problems. These institutional constraints limit the effectiveness of competition policy in any given Latin American country. A number of the subsequent chapters point to how weak domestic institutions reduce the effectiveness of antitrust to combat anti-competitive conduct. Moreover, there are significant limits on the ability of domestic Latin American antitrust institutions adequately to address increasingly international antitrust issues. A number of the chapters in this book explore the limitations of Latin American domestic antitrust in combating international cartels.

In recent years, many Latin American countries have shifted towards governments that embrace greater populism. Some of the new populist regimes remain open to market forces and economic freedoms. Others regimes have taken a far more statist view of economic organization. Thus far, we have not seen a significant variation between Chavez-styled antitrust (where the Venezuelan competition agency has not been particularly active in years) and antitrust in populist market-oriented countries such as Brazil, or even in non-populist market-oriented countries such as Chile. For the most part, antitrust has been technocratic and not an area in which political elites have pushed to change it directly to reflect other agendas. Nevertheless, larger political-economy influences impact indirectly on Latin American competition policy. Corruption remains a serious problem in most of Latin America, both in countries ruled by populist regimes and in market-oriented ones. Corruption affects both competition and competition policy enforcement, as it weakens the institutions needed to assist in effective competition policy. Politics is a factor that reduces the ability of antitrust regulation to operate effectively. Agency independence and prosecutorial discretion remain tenuous in such circumstances. Part of this process is the result of capture, which in turn limits the effectiveness of Latin American antitrust. Capture works at a number of different levels within government.[4] An agency may serve as a revolving door that shuffles agency staff into positions with high-stakes players.[5] Agency staff may try to prosecute certain cases that advance their careers within the agency or government, or that lead to opportunities outside of government.[6] Capture as a response to political backlash may chill the behavior of antitrust agencies in enforcement priorities and decision-making. Special interest groups may respond to antitrust enforcement by pushing legislators to

[4] William C Mitchell, 'Interest Groups: Economic Perspectives and Contributions', 2 *Journal of Theoretical Politics* 85 (1990); Robert D Tollison, 'Public Choice and Legislation', 74 *Virginia Law Review* 339 (1988).

[5] Jonathan R Macey, 'Promoting Public-Regarding Legislation through Statutory Interpretation: An Interest Group Model', 86 *Columbia Law Review* 223 (1986); George J Stigler, 'The Theory of Economic Regulation', 2 *Bell Journal of Economics & Management Sciences* 3 (1971).

[6] William Shugart, Robert Tollison and Brian Goff, 'Bureaucratic Structure and Congressional Control', 52 *Southern Economic Journal* 962 (1986).

create legislative antitrust immunities for certain companies or sectors. Capture across other parts of government also may effect antitrust's ability to remedy anti-competitive conduct. For example, sector regulators may fear a loss of their own budgetary resources and prestige if antitrust was to take the lead in regulating business conduct rather than their own agency.

The overview chapter by Daniel Sokol addresses the human capacity constraints of Latin American competition policy agencies. The development of human capital is not an instant process; it takes time to develop staff and train officials to undertake economic analysis, and to identify, investigate and prosecute cases. Together, these traits are the building blocks for the greater effectiveness of an antitrust agency. Antitrust must draw the future members of antitrust agencies from a larger set of economists and lawyers. This requires teaching industrial organization in economics departments and business schools, and regulation and antitrust in the law schools of a given country's universities.[7] Because most of Latin America's antitrust agencies are young (even the older agencies have only recently become effective), human capital in competition policy remains underdeveloped and will remain so in the near term. This underdevelopment exists with respect to the capacity and technical expertise of agencies, private lawyers and economists, and academics. With few educators and practitioners devoted to this area, it is difficult for agencies to recruit staff specifically trained in antitrust law and economics. A well-staffed agency full of competition specialists is less likely to undertake misguided prosecutions or the non-prosecution of anti-competitive behavior. This chapter includes the first study to track the teaching of industrial organization and competition economics in Latin American economic departments and business schools, and competition law in Latin American law schools. It examines some of the various forms of agency training of staff and leadership that occurs vis-à-vis international organizations. Outside of the agency context, this study tracks the increased specialization in Latin American competition policy across law firms and economic consulting firms. The chapter concludes that the human element of Latin American competition policy is in a growth phase, and that demands from practitioners and an increased supply of well-trained instructors will increase the level of sophistication of teaching and practice of competition policy.

A series of chapters provides an introduction to the three major competition policy systems in the region. The first focuses on the changing competition policy of Brazil. In a relatively short time, Brazil has become the greatest success story of competition policy in the region. The chapter by Elizabeth Farina and Patricia Agra Araújo details the rise of the Conselho Administrativo de Defesa Econômica (CADE) and how CADE has tackled institutional issues within a three-agency

[7] William E Kovacic, 'Institutional Foundations for Economic Legal Reform in Transition Economies: The Case of Competition Policy and Antitrust Enforcement', 77 *Chicago Kent Law Review* 265 (2001).

antitrust system, along with relations with other parts of government. The chapter highlights some of the areas of enforcement emphasized by Brazilian competition authorities, and the relative success in enforcement.

Marcos Avalos Bracho provides an overview of Mexico's competition policy. His chapter examines the principles underpinning Mexican merger control and abuse of dominance. He provides a statistical overview of Mexican competition policy between 1993 and 2004, examining where the Comisión Federal de Competencia (CFC) has spent its resources in terms of cases and the types of industries affected. Thereafter, the chapter provides a statistical analysis of Mexican merger control from 1997 to 2001. The author calls for improvements in how the CFC handles abuse of dominance cases, including issues of information gathering and monitoring of firm behavior. In mergers, Avalos calls for greater transparency in evaluation criteria of the agency.

The last major antitrust system of Latin America is that of Argentina. Germán Coloma offers a historical triptych of Argentine antitrust from 1933 to the present. In doing so, he examines the impact of US and EU competition policies on the Argentine system. The chapter then proceeds with a review of the seminal Argentine antitrust cases across a number of substantive areas. Coloma concludes with a summary of the current state of play in Argentine competition policy, including an identification of those areas of competition policy that remain in need of greater clarification.

II. Cartels

The second set of chapters focuses on cartels. The major target of enforcement in Latin American competition agencies is cartels. The reason for this focus on cartel enforcement is that early efforts are relatively easy. Successful cartel enforcement requires less analytical expertise and yields a potentially higher payoff in terms of successful enforcement actions. The determination of what practices constitute anti-competitive behavior (price fixing, output restrictions, market allocation and bid rigging) seems to be clear. Domestic emphasis on cartel enforcement has been buttressed by global antitrust norms on increased cartel enforcement. For example, the Organisation for Economic Co-operation and Development has stated that cartels are 'the most egregious violations of competition law'.[8] Moreover, cartel enforcement is where the 'action' is in Latin American competition policy, and perhaps where it should be in terms of enforcement priorities, given the relative age of the region's antitrust agencies and their relative capabilities. Nevertheless, numerous problems with cartel enforcement continue to affect

[8] OECD Council, *Recommendation of the Council Concerning Effective Action Against Hard Core Cartels* (1998).

the region, as a number of the chapters illustrate. Particularly problematic are addressing potential tacit collusion and the importation of successful anti-cartel techniques from other jurisdictions (such as leniency programs for cartel members who blow the whistle on the cartel and/or provide evidence on the cartel), which may be difficult to transplant given the existing legal framework in Latin America.

We organize the cartel chapters by related themes. The first theme addresses the institutional issues of competition policy and cartel enforcement, which require effective and credible institutions, and how institutional design can be optimized to make competition policy institutions more credible to combat cartels. Leopoldo Pagotto addresses the institutional design and transplant effect of Brazil's leniency program. He argues that the transplant of the US-inspired leniency program to the Brazilian legal system is problematic given the institutional design of Brazilian competition policy. Similarly, he finds that the conventional wisdom of the utility of consent decrees does not hold in the Brazilian context because of administrability problems and the lack of resources.

Leonor Cordovil focuses her chapter on the difficulty of transplanting to the Brazilian context rules against a pre-merger strategy called gun jumping: the parties to a planned merger may try to use the merger plan as a shield to engage in anti-competitive behavior. After more than a decade of debate, it is expected that the Brazilian legislature will pass and implement a new competition law. What limits will be imposed on companies regarding pre-merger coordination remains unclear under the proposed law. The lack of clarity in Brazilian law may allow merger control to be abused by pre-merger collusion. Cordovil's chapter analyzes how a firm can determine whether certain exchanges of information are reasonable, and how to best structure such exchanges of information to reduce the possibility of collusion, taking into account emerging antitrust global 'best practices'.

In his chapter, Mauro Grinberg addresses a number of the legal problems raised by the Brazilian leniency program. This analysis includes a discussion that challenges the theory that the leniency program is unconstitutional under Brazilian law. However, Grinberg notes that the implications of leniency remain untested in Brazil, which suggests that Brazilian cartel enforcement will operate with a certain level of unpredictability.

The second cartel theme of the book is that of tacit collusion among parties. By tacit collusion we mean that the 'smoking gun' of an explicit agreement is not present. This does not mean, however, that in every case tacit collusion amounts to mere oligopoly through what is referred to as 'conscious parallelism'. Rather, by tacit collusion we mean some amount of coordinated conduct that is concerted, for which we may not have direct evidence of an agreement. Chapters within this theme examine the circumstances under which tacit collusion should be enough to prove the existence of a cartel. Moreover, they address the appropriate normative threshold for a tacit collusion claim. This is an important policy question, as firms react to initial enforcement efforts against cartels by moving from explicit to tacit collusion.

The first chapter on tacit collusion ties together themes of institutional design with problems specific to tacit collusion. Sebastian Zarate and Elina Cruz focus their chapter on the lack of confidence by the Chilean judiciary in Chilean competition policy. Chilean competition policy reflects this lack of confidence in two different ways: (a) in cartel enforcement regarding tacit collusion, and (b) in the institutional design of Chilean competition policy. Zarate and Cruz examine Chilean collusion-related case law between 1980 and 2007. From the case law analysis, they argue that almost no collusion-based claims have been successful in Chile, though the 2003 modifications to the Chilean competition law have led to some new developments. Under the 2003 modifications, cases before the newly-created Chilean Competition Tribunal have a route of direct appeal to the Chilean Supreme Court. Given the lack of knowledge of the Supreme Court justices of competition law specifically and economic reasoning more generally, Zarate and Cruz suggest that this institutional framework can only be interpreted as a sign of distrust of competition law and economic reasoning. Recently, this distrust has resulted in a number of what they argue are misguided decisions by the Chilean Supreme Court, particularly in the area of tacit collusion. Together with descriptions of the new Chilean antitrust judicial institutions and an analysis of these recent cartel cases, the authors explore the constitutional consequences of the changes as they relate to Chilean civil procedure. Zarate and Cruz also provide some solutions to correct what they perceive to be an institutional flaw. First, they suggest that Chilean antitrust be understood as administrative law, and that this new understanding would improve the standard of judicial review before the Supreme Court. Secondly, they advocate improved communication across Chilean legal institutions.

Aldo González takes a different approach to how Chilean courts view tacit collusion. He analyzes the three most recent Chilean cartel cases, all of which are based on claims of tacit collusion in which there was only circumstantial evidence. In two of the cases, the Chilean Competition Tribunal condemned the behavior in question, only to have the rulings reversed by the Chilean Supreme Court. In the third case, the Tribunal, in a divided decision, dismissed the cartel case based on the criteria used by the Supreme Court. González argues that the Supreme Court's required standard to prove tacit collusion makes establishing the guilt of parties based on behavioral evidence nearly impossible. As Chile introduces a leniency program and the power to obtain direct evidence into its competition law, Chilean antitrust enforcers will be better able to overcome the high threshold for tacit collusion by introducing more cases that have direct evidence.

Juan David Gutiérrez undertakes a cross-country regional analysis of tacit collusion. He analyzes the case law on tacit collusion of each Latin American jurisdiction. Gutiérrez describes each jurisdiction's antitrust system, as well as the prohibition on horizontal agreements established by the law. On tacit collusion, he includes for each jurisdiction: (a) the burden and standard of proof applied; (b) attributes of successful defenses and prosecutions; and (c) evolution of the case law. He then compares and contrasts the different features of the jurisdictions' competition policy.

William Comanor examines how Latin American courts decide between competing economic models in tacit collusion. This problem is particularly relevant for the judicial determination of cartel activity. There are two competing models which are relevant for determining whether or not a cartel is present. In order to evaluate the observed behavior of firms in a well-defined market, courts first need to determine how firms in the market would be expected to act in the absence of a cartel. The two models are the Turner model and the Posner model. Each model leads to a very different view of cartel detection. Comanor suggests that workable rules need to be fashioned in situations in which both Turner and Posner could be correct. As Comanor interprets the recent *Twombly* decision,[9] ambivalence remains in the text of the decision as to each of these two models. This ambivalence suggests that antitrust may not yet have overcome how to apply economic principles in a legal context.

The final set of cartel-related chapters focuses on enforcement issues. Víctor Pavón-Villamayor provides an analysis of the implications of technological convergence for competition policy enforcement. First, he develops a location-type model that helps explore the nature of competition between technologies that, due to technological progress, converge over time. Secondly, his chapter discusses the extent that converging technologies facilitate cartel formation within a dynamic setting. Lastly, he applies these lessons to Latin American competition policy on how better to design and implement enforcement where cartels and technological innovation intersect.

Increasingly, international cartels are active in Latin America. How to address them is the focus of the next two chapters. One of the chapters focuses on public enforcement, while the other advocates an increased role for private enforcement. John Connor undertakes an empirical analysis of the impact of international cartels in Latin America. He focuses his empirical work on the largest jurisdictions in the region. In these jurisdictions, most Latin American efforts center on domestic price-fixing and bid-rigging schemes. Allegations regarding illegal price-fixing are most likely because the injured parties can find evidence of suspicious changes in local prices compared with price changes in other domestic localities, or compared with imported good prices. Moreover, competition authorities may shy away from the additional challenges of international price-fixing investigations that derive from evidentiary hurdles, which a number of the chapters in this book identify. Connor argues that the harm imposed on Latin American

[9] *Bell Atlantic Corp v Twombly*, 127 S Ct 1955 (2007).

economies from international cartels is substantial.[10] He analyzes the injuries associated with known private international cartels in Latin America, and assesses the effectiveness of prosecutions of such cartels in the past decade. He compares these measures of effectiveness with cartel enforcement in other jurisdictions. Overall, Connor concludes that Latin America under-deters international cartels relative to other jurisdictions (such as North America and Europe), but that Brazil is much more effective than other Latin American countries in its anti-cartel efforts. He explains the reasons behind Brazil's success, and suggests steps that the other Latin American antitrust agencies can take to improve the quality of their cartel enforcement.

Daniel Crane explores the need for enhanced private anti-cartel enforcement in Latin America in light of *Empagran*[11] and contemporaneous economic scholarship. He argues for limited private enforcement that need not extend beyond cartels as it opens a 'Pandora's box' of private antitrust litigation abuses. First, Crane analyzes the *Empagran* decision, paying particular attention to the role of *amicus curiae* briefs by foreign governments. Thereafter, Crane considers the challenges facing private enforcement in Latin America, ranging from the lack of private rights of action to enforce anti-cartel laws to various administrative, procedural, evidentiary and cultural hurdles. Crane then compares the state of Latin American private enforcement with private enforcement reforms in the European Union, and considers Latin American reforms in the direction of greater private enforcement.

III. Competition Advocacy

Whereas the second grouping of chapters focuses on cartel enforcement, the third grouping addresses issues of competition advocacy. Competition advocacy is the process through which antitrust agencies make speeches, present reports, and intervene in the legislative and regulatory processes by making submissions suggesting pro-competitive reforms. Advocacy may be used against the passage of anti-competitive legislation. Advocacy also is used to argue against actions by another part of government that might create anti-competitive effects.[12] It also involves agencies undertaking retrospective reviews of competition in certain

[10] International cartels are those with corporate members that have headquarters in two or more countries, or those that are explicitly aimed at exploiting overseas markets; the latter include export cartels. Private cartels are those that do not operate under the protection of international treaties; hence, they are potentially indictable for antitrust offenses.

[11] *F Hoffman-La Roche Ltd v Empagran S A*, 542 US 155 (2004).

[12] James C Cooper, Paul A Pautler and Todd J Zywicki, 'The Theory and Practice of Competition Advocacy at the FTC', 72 *Antitrust Law Journal* 1091 (2005); ICN, *Consumer Outreach by ICN Members—A Report on Outreach Undertaken and Lessons Learned* (2005).

sectors (and agency enforcement in these sectors).[13] Competition advocacy enhances legitimacy in competition policy, in part because of increased transparency.[14] Without public understanding and support, economic liberalization may create a public backlash.[15]

Todd Zywicki and James Cooper provide an overview of the importance and effects of competition advocacy. They argue that fostering a vigorous competition advocacy program can be especially valuable in Latin American countries that historically have had heavily-regulated economies and a weak culture of competition. They draw upon the experience of the competition advocacy program of the United States Federal Trade Commission during the past 30 years to provide lessons for Latin American competition authorities seeking to build competition advocacy programs.

The final chapters in this section address three specific business sectors that require competition advocacy. Roy Costilla and Javier Velozo look at the effect of competition in the Chilean airline sector. LAN CHILE and Lan Express (previously Ladeco) are airline companies that merged in 1995 and cover many of the national Chilean routes. The combined firm maintains a market share of nearly 80 per cent. Costilla assembled a database for the years 2000–07 to consider the existing degree of pass-through of profits in this market. The data derive from monthly figures of the number of passengers and prices of flights for all the airlines and destinations within Chile during that period. Based on these data, Costilla and Velozo conclude, among other findings, that in markets with little competition, companies have taken advantage of their market power to increase price levels in the inelastic demand segment.

In their chapter, Andres Gómez-Lobo and Aldo González discuss competition in the Chilean supermarket industry. Technological changes and economic forces have generated a trend towards larger retail outlets, and a general higher concentration in the supermarket industry in Chile and other countries in Latin America. Gómez-Lobo and González examine the effects of concentration on prices, using a monthly panel database of retail food prices and supermarket market share data for 24 cities in Chile between 1998 and 2006. In particular, the chapter analyzes whether past mergers in this industry are associated with higher retail food prices, or if the increase in concentration has generated efficiency gains which ultimately benefit consumers through lower prices. They find no evidence

[13] William E Kovacic, 'Using Ex Post Evaluations to Improve the Performance of Competition Policy Authorities', 31 *Journal of Corporate Law* 503 (2006).

[14] Transparency increases the accountability of organizations to stakeholders. It allows stakeholders to improve the effectiveness of their influence on decision-making by antitrust authorities domestically and in international organizations. Francesca Bignami, 'Three Generations of Participation Rights Before the European Commission', 68 *Law and Contemporary Problems* 61 (2004).

[15] Guillermo Ortiz, 'Latin America and the Washington Consensus: Overcoming Reform Fatigue', 40 *Finance and Development* 14 (2003); Susan C Stokes, *Public Support for Market Reforms in New Democracies* (Cambridge, Cambridge University Press, 2001).

that past mergers by the two main supermarket chains have led to lower consumer prices. Rather, they find evidence that higher levels of concentration are associated with higher prices.

Agriculture more broadly defined is the focus of the final chapter by Ricardo Arguello and María Clara Lozano Ortiz de Zarate. The authors analyze competition policy in the Colombian agricultural sector. They examine the legal and institutional relationships between competition law and agricultural policy, as well as the role of competition policy in agricultural development. Thereafter, the chapter examines a number of cases investigated by the Colombian competition agency, to illustrate the main issues involved in implementing competition policy in the agricultural sector.

IV. Regional Issues

From the perspective of international counsel, merger control is an issue which many view regionally—how one gets a deal through multiple enforcers for a transaction that impacts an entire region. To understand this process, Joe Krauss compares the process of getting a deal through in Latin America with the processes in the United States and the European Union. To provide context for this analysis, the chapter reviews specific case studies in which companies faced competition review by Latin American authorities. It also focuses on the need for and the possibility of procedural convergence in the merger process among US, Latin American and European competition agencies.

Because of the growing number of trade agreements in Latin America, trade policy offers a way to improve competition policy capacity in countries that lack national competition laws. Francisco Marcos chronicles attempts by Ecuador and Bolivia (which lack national competition laws) to 'download' antitrust through regional competition available to them via the Andean Community. He notes that while this option is not free of problems, it provides a solution to the institutional and political deadlock found in these countries that has prevented the adoption of national competition laws.

The final chapter among regional issues, by Julián Peña, addresses the role of the private sector in the development of competition policy in the region. The author illustrates the various country- and region-wide efforts of the private sector to engage with government enforcers to improve the quality of competition policy. Part of the recipe for success of the creation of a greater competition culture is an engaged agency that is transparent in its competition policy. A second element to greater success is better interaction and engagement between lawyers and economists in the region. An improved competition culture can overcome some of the shortcomings of the unrealized promise of liberalization schemes in Latin America.

V. Conclusion

This book illustrates the importance of the context in which Latin American competition policy operates. It identifies the particular challenges in Latin America regionally, and in individual countries and competition policy systems that are themselves different from one another. However, some common themes emerge as to the quality of institutions, the types of legal and economic tools, and the quality of agency decision-making that provides lessons valuable to other countries and regions of the world.

Chapter II

The Development of Human Capital in Latin American Competition Policy

D DANIEL SOKOL*

I. Introduction

A common theme to Latin American competition policy is its limited effectiveness in addressing anti-competitive behavior, whether in terms of enforcement in the cases of mergers or cartels, or in abuse of dominance cases. Outside of cases, competition advocacy has also been uneven across Latin American agencies. Indeed, no Latin American agency ranks among the top tier of agencies in survey data ranking competition agencies produced by either the World Economic Forum's Global Competitiveness Report or the Global Competition Review. Such relatively low rankings are attributable to a number of factors that limit the effectiveness of competition agencies or, for that matter, any agency. These include issues of effective resources—financial, political, and human[1]—the lack of which may lead to greater errors in enforcement.

This chapter focuses on the development of human capital as an effective resource in competition agencies. Because the majority of Latin America's competition agencies are young (and even older ones have only relatively recently become effective), human capital is under-developed and will remain so for the near term in this region. Such under-development exists in agencies, among private lawyers and economists, and among the professoriate. With few professors and practitioners devoted to the area, it is difficult for agencies to recruit staff specifically trained in competition law and economics. Yet it is the well-staffed agency, full of competition specialists, that is less likely to create errors of misguided prosecution (type I errors) or errors of non-prosecution of anti-competitive behavior (type II errors).

The development of human capital is not an instant process; rather, it takes time to develop and train officials to identify, investigate and prosecute cases,

* Assistant Professor of Law, University of Florida Levin College of Law.

[1] Timothy J Muris, 'Principles for a Successful Competition Agency', 72 *University of Chicago Law Review* 165 (2005); Tomás Serebrisky, 'What Do We Know About Competition Agencies in Emerging and Transition Countries? Evidence on Workload, Personnel, Priority Sectors and Training Needs', 27 *World Competition* 651 (2004).

and to undertake economic analysis. Together, these traits comprise the building blocks of an effective competition agency. Competition policy must draw upon a larger set of economists and lawyers to become future members of competition agencies. However, the pool must be increased; this requires that faculties should teach industrial organization in economics departments and business schools, as well as regulation and competition law in the law schools in a given country's universities.[2] Outside of universities, human capital for an agency can be developed through technical assistance missions, international antitrust organizations, interactions with private law firms and economics firms, as well as through competition law and economics associations for practitioners.

This chapter addresses the human element of competition enforcement through an examination of its various components. First, it examines the training of current agency leadership and staff through various technical assistance and capacity building projects. Next, it analyzes long-term training and development through the teaching of competition law and economics. Lastly, it provides an assessment of norm diffusion and development at the non-agency practitioner level across the Latin American region. Overall, the chapter will conclude that human capital remains under-developed across all levels, but long-term changes are underway that suggest the development of human capacity will improve throughout the region.

II. Current Training

A. Knowledge Generally

As an individual learns, so does an organization. Since the focus of this chapter is improvement of the intellectual capacity of competition agencies, it begins with a focus on organization-learning and the various inputs into that process. Organizations learn in incremental steps,[3] as the transfer of knowledge throughout an organization is a difficult process. Generally, knowledge is not centralized or easy to access; rather, it may be found in various members within the organization. Nor is knowledge transfer something easily accomplished through preparing an antitrust handbook on running cartel cases (though it would help). Instead, much of antitrust knowledge is tacit or soft, rather than tangible or hard.[4] Over

[2] William E Kovacic, 'Institutional Foundations for Economic Legal Reform in Transition Economies: The Case of Competition Policy and Antitrust Enforcement', 77 *Chicago Kent Law Review* 265, 306 (2001).

[3] James H Lebovic, 'How Organizations Learn: US Government Estimates of Foreign Military Spending', 39 *American Journal of Political Science* 835, 836 (1995).

[4] L Argote and P Ingram, 'Knowledge Transfer: A Basis for Competitive Advantage in Firms', 82 *Organizational Behavior and Human Decision Processes* 150 (2000); Joanna Chataway and David Wield, 'Industrialization, Innovation and Development: What Does Development Management Change?', 12 *Journal of International Development* 803, 803–05 (2000).

time, the process of knowledge transfer creates routine and learning through the creation of institutional memory, which helps guide future behavior within an organization.[5] The process of routine shapes the organization (eg, a competition agency) in terms of the orientation of prevailing thought as to what constitutes anti-competitive behavior, enforcement priorities and resource allocation within the agency.

We have a sense of how this process plays out broadly within the context of Latin American competition agencies. For example, in 2004 a World Bank survey analyzed the needs of competition agencies in the developing world, finding that competition agencies in East Asia had a staff size four times as large as competition agencies in Latin America. However, the overall workload in terms of the number of cases was not four times as much. Does this mean that Latin American agencies are more effective? The answer is unclear, because the mandate of a given agency may be broader than mere antitrust and may include consumer protection. Moreover, unlike Latin America, administrative staff make up over 60 per cent of agency staff in East Asia and the Pacific Rim. The breakdown percentages of personnel by professional type in Latin American agencies, among permanent staff, are roughly: 21 per cent lawyers, 24 per cent economists, 19 per cent 'temporary' workers (not further classified by type), 31 per cent administrative and 5 per cent accountants.[6]

B. Technical Assistance Programs

Some antitrust learning comes from foreign sources, and must be transmitted and transplanted through technical assistance and capacity building. Technical assistance may occur at a number of different levels—outside experts may come to an agency and provide short-term advice as to particular issues, or may provide training to agency staff, the judiciary, or sector regulators in a country. The learning process may require that agency leadership or staff attend training programs abroad. Alternatively, technical assistance may mean that an outside person must spend a significant amount of time (eg, a year) in the agency to provide advice on case analysis and enforcement priorities.

Some of my previous work analyzes the various elements of successful technical assistance in developing-world competition agencies, including those in Latin America. Such research suggests that to improve the capacity of agencies to meet the needs of improved knowledge, both donors and recipients need to be involved in the design of technical assistance. Moreover, technical assistance seemed to be effective when the assistance improved the output of agencies by enabling them

[5] Barbara Levitt and James G March, 'Organizational Learning', 14 *Annual Review of Sociology* 319 (1988).

[6] Serebrisky, see above n 1. Latin American agencies preferred that training programs included other parts of government—particularly regulatory agencies and the judiciary—and seemed more reluctant to open up training programs to NGOs or private sector lawyers and economists.

to perform new tasks that they could not do on their own.[7] Yet without enough knowledge, agency staff cannot absorb technical assistance.[8] The lack of absorptive capacity means that the agency cannot assimilate new knowledge.

Separately, I have examined the role of long- and short-term advising in technical assistance. Long- and short-term work focus on three key areas: setting up and starting the assistance project, helping the agency with its operations, and helping in the management component of the agency. Overall, long-term and short-term advisers to new competition agencies seem to play an important role in the transmission of knowledge and in the creation of improved human capacity. Studies reveal that long-term advisers seem better equipped than short-term advisers in creating the capacity to take on a greater workload than an agency could handle prior to the adviser's arrival. Additionally, political economy issues seem to affect the absorption of technical assistance and the building of human capacity. For example, agencies absorbed teaching better when the agency was independent and headed by someone with a rank of minister or higher. Finally, bilateral (agency to agency) technical assistance to developing-world competition agencies was more effective than multilateral (eg, World Bank, UNCTAD, OECD) efforts.[9]

One method of technical assistance is the reverse of using long- and short-term advisers; instead of inviting advisers in, a country will send its staff elsewhere for training. A number of agencies around the world have internship arrangements where foreign staffers may spend a number of months working at a more mature competition agency. For example, arrangements exist at the Federal Trade Commission (FTC), the Directorate-General for Competition (DG Competition) and UK agencies, as well as in Switzerland, Canada and Australia, among others. This experience provides hands-on learning for the agency staff of young competition agencies, and also provides an opportunity to apply theoretical knowledge in a sophisticated setting. In reality, however, the real limiting factor is language. A staffer for the internship needs to be fluent enough in the working language of the hosting agency to follow along in day-to-day operations.

C. International Organizations

One must note that learning and capacity building need not be limited to formal technical assistance programs. Instead, learning within antitrust agencies can occur by means of norm diffusion across international competition policy organizations. Of course, international norms influence domestic processes.[10] It

[7] Michael Nicholson, D Daniel Sokol and Kyle W Stiegert, 'Technical Assistance for Law and Economics: An Empirical Analysis in Antitrust/Competition Policy', University of Wisconsin Legal Studies Research Paper No 1025.

[8] OECD, *Evaluation of the Actions and Resources of Competition Authorities. Evaluation of the Actions and Resources of Competition Authorities*, DAF/COMP(2005)30.

[9] D Daniel Sokol and Kyle W Stiegert, 'An Empirical Evaluation of Long Term Advisors and Short Term Interventions in Technical Assistance and Capacity Building', University of Missouri School of Law Legal Studies Research Paper No 2008-03.

[10] Andrew P Cortell and James W Davis, Jr, 'Understanding the Domestic Impact of International Norms: A Research Agenda', 2 *International Studies Review* 65 (2000).

is no different in the area of competition, where emerging international norms are transforming competition policy by creating additional points of norm diffusion through educational opportunities. This occurs both formally through training and degree programs for agency staff and leadership, and more informally through norm diffusion from the private sector and international antitrust organizations. One mechanism through which agencies and their staffs increase core understanding of competition policy is interaction with other agencies in a variety of international fora. Several international competition policy organizations allow for interaction at both the agency leadership and case handler levels, including the ICN, UNCTD and the OECD.

1. *International Competition Network*

The International Competition Network (ICN) is the youngest of the global fora for competition agencies. Nevertheless, it is perhaps the most effective because of the active involvement of competition agencies and non-governmental advisers from the private sector, civil society and academia. Each year, the ICN hosts a conference to review the product of its working groups. ICN working groups initially create various outputs to identify current law and practice in competition policy across a number of different areas (eg, cartels, mergers, regulated industries, and unilateral conduct). Thereafter, the groups identify better practices for agency adoption; the improved practices are generalized enough for implementation in any given agency's larger political and economic system. Besides the annual conference, additional outputs from the ICN include training manuals and templates for younger agencies, which allow for increased implementation of better practices as well as norm diffusion across Latin American competition agencies.[11] Increasingly, the ICN has moved towards more active norm diffusion through the creation of merger and cartel workshops for agency staff. El Salvador hosted the first such cartel workshop, with additional programs on cartels planned in the future.

2. *United Nations Conference on Trade and Development*

The United Nations Conference on Trade and Development (UNCTAD) also serves as a forum by holding a number of conferences and also by distributing topical publications. For example, it holds a yearly meeting entitled 'Intergovernmental Group of Experts on Competition Law', during which mostly developing-world agencies discuss issues of concern. The publications and conferences try to reflect the greater theme of UNCTAD: to ensure that developing-world issues and priorities have a voice in international debate.

Additionally, UNCTAD has been active in the realm of technical assistance in Latin America through its COMPAL project. The COMPAL program's purpose is to assist the agencies in Nicaragua, Costa Rica, El Salvador, Peru and Bolivia in their competition policy and consumer protection missions. Still another UNCTAD

[11] D Daniel Sokol, 'Order Without (Enforceable) Law: Why Countries Enter into Non-Enforceable Competition Policy Chapters in Free Trade Agreements,' 83 *Chicago Kent Law Review* 231 (2008).

project has focused Latin American competition agencies on the intersection of international trade and competition policy.

3. *Organisation for Economic Co-operation and Development*

The Organisation for Economic Co-operation and Development (OECD) Competition Law and Policy Committee is the oldest of the international competition policy organizations. It provides a forum for OECD member countries and observers to discuss competition policy at a senior level. Though most Latin American countries and agencies are not OECD members or observers, the OECD remains active in Latin American competition policy. The OECD hosts a yearly Latin American Competition Forum in which Latin American competition agencies discuss topical issues along with OECD member agencies. These meetings encourage norm diffusion to Latin American agencies, and also provide a learning opportunity through discussions with both similarly situated and developed-world agencies that have enforcement experience. The annual forum also provides an opportunity for agencies to learn about each other's institutional structures and larger political-economic concerns. Peer review plays an important signaling role for competition agencies; it is peer review recommendation that encourages agencies to go to their national legislatures and push for change. It also transforms the agency itself as other agency heads with similar experiences have an opportunity to weigh in during the peer review discussions to offer contextualized comments about similar institutional successes or malfunctions in their own countries and the ways in which the other agencies have addressed similar issues.

One recent innovation on the part of the OECD has been the creation of regional competition centers, one in Korea and another in Hungary. The OECD does not provide a formal training program in Latin America through a regional competition center the way it does in Europe or Asia; this has yet to be replicated in the region. However, a new OECD competition policy initiative for Latin America is in its pilot stage in Mexico. A team of 12 OECD staffers will work directly with the Chair of Mexico's competition agency to create a more competitive regulatory environment by working to eliminate anti-competitive restrictions in Mexican laws and regulations across a number of sectors. Additionally, another Latin American-specific project involves OECD assistance to agencies on the issue of government bid-rigging.

III. Long-term Training

A. Importance of Law and Economic Analysis

A second level of human capacity building occurs before agency staff and leadership ever set foot into competition agencies—at the university level. It begins with a general understanding of law and economics; after all, grasping the economic analysis of law is a fundamental analytical building block of competition law and policy. Law and economics provide a critical toolset for organizing law based on an understanding of how incentives shape human behavior. This approach has a profound impact on the structure of law, including contractual and property rights, as well as laws and institutions that facilitate a market-based system. In addition to greater analytical rigor, the economic analysis of law offers greater predictability which, in turn, reduces transaction costs for doing business in a given country. Thanks to the pioneering work of Henry Manne and others such as the Olin Foundation, the economic analysis of law has played an increasingly important role in the legislature, courts, regulatory agencies and academia.[12]

In Latin America, the economic analysis of law outside of competition policy remains nascent. Though there is a Latin American Law and Economics Association (ALACDE), it has not yet been widely embraced by the Latin American legal academy, which primarily remains wedded in analytical approach to a civil code-based doctrinal analysis. The lack of espousal of law and economics in Latin America may be due to the demand, supply, and market structure for education in Latin America not being conducive to a robust law and economics field. For this reason, Latin America looks more like Europe (low penetration) rather than the United States (high penetration) in terms of the importance of law and economics scholarship out of all law-faculty research and scholarship.[13]

Latin America lacks an education system similar to that of the United States, which features well-endowed universities with full-time and high-paying faculty positions. As a result of low pay at Latin American universities, there are far fewer full-time professors. Those who are full-time frequently spend time consulting away from class. Because adjunct faculty do significant amounts of teaching, part of the problem may indeed be this lack of law faculty who are full-time professors. Perhaps there are not the same sorts of incentives for scholarship in law and economics as there are in other regions of the world.[14] However, adjunct law professors who teach business law-related classes may themselves have been trained in economic analysis of law in the United States, and thus may be transmitting this education to law students in their home countries. Unfortunately, an education system in this state leaves Latin America with judges who grapple with issues using a set of formalistic-approach analytical

[12] Henry G Manne, 'How Law and Economics was Marketed in a Hostile World: A Very Personal History', in Francesco Parisi and Charles Kershaw Rowley (eds), *The Origins of Law and Economics: Essays by the Founding Fathers* (Cheltenham, UK, Edward Elgar Publishing, 2005); John J Miller, *A Gift of Freedom: How the John M Olin Foundation Changed America* (San Francisco, Encounter Books, 2005).

[13] Kenneth G Dau-Schmidt and Carmen L Brun, 'Lost in Translation: The Economic Analysis of Law in the United States and Europe', 44 *Columbia Journal of Transnational Law* 602 (2006); Nuno Garoupa and Thomas S Ulen, 'The Market for Legal Innovation: Law and Economics in Europe and the United States', University of Illinois Law and Economics Research Paper No LE07-009 (2007).

[14] Oren Gazal-Ayal, 'Economic Analysis of Law in North America, Europe and Israel', 3 *Review of Law and Economics* 485 (2007).

tools, much in need of the improvement a law and economics perspective could provide. Nevertheless, there has been some change over time to this situation in Latin America as more US-trained academics return to the region. Indeed, there has been an increase in the instruction of law and economics.

Still, antitrust education needs to be expanded upon so that it impacts not only future members of competition agencies, but also future members of the judiciary. Over time, a robust teaching of competition law (based on economics) in Latin American law schools should stimulate a generational transformation in thinking, akin to the scientific revolution brought about by Copernicus. As Kuhn explained, when Copernicus taught that the planets revolved around the sun, his idea took over as the older generation of scientists, trained in the previous system, were replaced with a younger group of professors who had received training in the Copernican view.[15]

B. Teaching Competition Law and Economics in Latin American Universities

If competition law and economics is the equivalent of the Copernican Revolution, the state of teaching this new system within Latin America must be examined in order to determine how rapidly the new framework will spread. There has been a long history of teaching economics in Latin America. In Mexico, for example, the origin of economics teaching was in 1929 when a specialized division of economics was set up within the law school of the National Autonomous University of Mexico (UNAM); it was perhaps the first law and economics department. By 1935, there was a separate economics department at UNAM. Similarly, Chile witnessed the development of economics at a roughly equivalent time, with the establishment of the Department of Commerce and Economics Science at the Catholic University of Chile in 1924 and the Department of Commerce and Industrial Economics at the University of Chile 10 years later. Argentina, however, was (surprisingly) a latecomer to the formalized study of economics, with an undergraduate degree program in economics not established until 1953. Overall, the only study examining undergraduate economics teaching in the region finds that the study of economics in Latin America does not focus heavily on quantitative methods, though more than half the classes are within the area of microeconomics.[16] Such de-emphasis on quantitative methods is problematic as antitrust econometrics becomes more important in case analysis.

In Latin America, the teaching of law has traditionally been based on formalistic reading of the civil code and has excluded significant economic analysis

[15] Thomas Kuhn, *The Structure of Scientific Revolutions* (University of Chicago Press, Chicago, 1962).

[16] Eduardo Lora and Hugo Ñopo, 'La Enseñanza de Economía en América Latina', mimeo.

until recently. Several factors explain this change. First of all, a number of Latin American law professors have been trained in the economic analysis of law through LLM programs in the United States. This is particularly so for those trained at elite universities in the United States (those most likely to teach at the elite Latin American universities), where the concentration of scholars in law and economics is particularly strong in business fields, including competition policy. Over time, this transformation has created some of the essential components of a potential transformation of economic analysis in Latin American law and, more generally, of that economic analysis directly relevant to competition policy.

A growing number of Latin American competition practitioners have received advanced degrees in economics or law from the United States. As a result of their visa status, some LLM-trained lawyers have the opportunity to spend a year working for law firms based in the United States. Doing so enables them to augment classroom learning with real world experience and to increase their hands-on experience with competition policy issues. Additionally, US firms spend significant time and financial resources to train their associates through meetings and workshops. While exact numbers of LLM-trained lawyers are exceedingly difficult to determine,[17] the *Global Competition Review* (under 'Who's Who of Competition Lawyers') lists 37 competition law practitioners as among the top in their areas across Latin America. This ranking is a rough proxy of who is a sophisticated and well-regarded legal practitioner in competition law. Though the rankings may have a number of flaws, they are created through discussions with clients, many of whom run international operations and thus have a comparative sense of the strength of competition lawyers and economists. Hence, they serve as the least-bad indirect proxy based on available sources. Of these attorneys, 24 have advanced degrees in law (and in one case economics) from US or European universities; of the 24, all but 3 studied in the US or UK. A handful of these attorneys had work experience in US law firms or with the European Commission. Furthermore, of the nine professional economists listed on 'Who's Who of Competition Economists', eight of nine obtained their PhDs from US graduate programs. Over time, the number of LLMs and PhDs in Latin America will increase, a gradual process that will in turn increase the analytic toolset of practitioners. For LLM students from countries only now introducing competition laws, the current cohort of US-trained LLMs may see the antitrust field as one in which they can develop early expertise and create a niche for themselves in their countries. This seems to be the trend in other Latin American countries, and indeed Europe itself.

On another level, the heavy emphasis in Latin America on adjunct teaching means that there is less room for scholarship. Furthermore, what scholarship

[17] Carole Silver, 'Local Matters: Internationalizing Strategies for US Law Firms', 14 *Indiana Journal of Global Legal Studies* 67, 83 (2007).

there is gets shaped by the demands of clients and would-be clients, as professors respond to the incentives of outside consulting. Among law faculty, competition scholarship tends to be descriptive and to focus heavily on case analysis; Latin American empirical competition law scholarship is rare. Among economists, output tends to focus on expert testimony-funded work and other studies funded by international donors or others. As a result, many important topics go unstudied.

So far, this chapter has focused on the supply-side factors involved in the teaching of competition law. In terms of the demand-side, there is neither a clear sense of the total enrollment in competition law and economics classes nor a sense of the profile of the average student in such programs. However, it is clear that demand has increased, as the total number of classes offered is now greater than ever before. Demand seems to come from both the private and public sectors. Among economists and lawyers, a new generation may be willing to move to new competition agencies in order to be a part of the early generation of agency staff. Although these economists and lawyers might previously have gone to sector regulators, the potential reward for early advancement may be larger in a newly-emerged competition agency. Furthermore, as sophisticated merger control becomes a larger part of competition practice in the private sector, there will be a need for more competition specialists for filings and for cases. As agencies develop the capacity to bring more cases, the number of lawyers and economists needed from the private sector to represent parties will also increase.

C. Where to Find Competition Law and Economics Teaching in Latin America

Competition law teaching in Latin America has spread across the region. The following chart provides some background as to where competition law is taught in Latin America.

COUNTRY	Number of Universities Offering Courses on Competition Law
Argentina	7
Bahamas	0
Barbados	0
Belize	0
Bolivia	2
Brazil	4
Cayman Islands	0
Chile	4

(continued)

COUNTRY	Number of Universities Offering Courses on Competition Law
Colombia	4
Costa Rica	0
Dominican Republic	3
Ecuador	3
El Salvador	1
Guatemala	0
Guyana	0
Haiti	0
Honduras	0
Jamaica	1
Mexico	6
Nicaragua	2
Panama	0
Paraguay	0
Peru	3
Suriname	0
Trinidad & Tobago	0
Uruguay	2
Venezuela	1

The foregoing chart summarizes the number of universities in a given country that offer courses focusing on competition law or related subjects at either the graduate or undergraduate level. The data were compiled by noting the relevant courses as listed on each university's law or economics faculty webpage or online list of available courses. The chart thus demonstrates the paucity of such classes in Latin American universities overall, especially if one were to compare these numbers with those in universities in the US or EU.

Those countries without any university offering competition law include The Bahamas, Barbados, Belize, the Cayman Islands, Costa Rica, Guatemala, Guyana, Haiti, Honduras, Panama, Paraguay, Suriname, and Trinidad & Tobago. Still, the majority of those Latin American countries offering competition law courses do so in a limited fashion (ranging from one to three universities). These include Bolivia with two, Dominican Republic with three, Ecuador with three, El Salvador with one, Jamaica with one, Nicaragua with two, Peru with three, Uruguay with two, and Venezuela with one. A few countries even boast four universities where students can access competition law courses—these include Brazil, Chile and Colombia. Lastly, those countries that by far offer the most are Mexico and Argentina, who respectively feature six and seven universities that teach competition law. Of these last two country groups, a number of universities have more than one such course in competition law.

There is also an increasingly wide number of countries and universities that teach industrial organization and specialized courses in competition policy economics, as summarized in the chart below.

COUNTRY	Number of Universities Offering Courses on International Organization
Argentina	5
Bahamas	0
Barbados	1
Belize	0
Bolivia	1
Brazil	4
Cayman Islands	0
Chile	4
Colombia	4
Costa Rica	0
Dominican Republic	1
Ecuador	2
El Salvador	0
Guatemala	0
Guyana	0
Haiti	0
Honduras	0
Jamaica	0
Mexico	4
Nicaragua	1
Panama	0
Paraguay	1
Peru	4
Suriname	0
Trinidad & Tobago	0
Uruguay	2
Venezuela	1

The foregoing chart summarizes the number of universities in a given country that offer courses focusing on industrial organizations or competition economics at either the graduate or undergraduate level. Again, the data were compiled by noting the relevant courses as listed on each university's law or economics faculty webpage or online list of available courses. While the numbers for these universities are meager, they are still indicative of a growing availability in Latin American universities.

As indicated by the chart, nearly half of Latin American countries do not have a university offering courses in industrial organization including the Bahamas, Belize, the Cayman Islands, Costa Rica, El Salvador, Guatemala, Guyana, Haiti,

Honduras, Jamaica, Panama, Suriname, and Trinidad and Tobago. Still, several countries have at least one university, if not two, that offers such courses—those with one university are Barbados, Bolivia, the Dominican Republic, Nicaragua, Paraguay, and Venezuela, while those with two are Ecuador and Uruguay. Overall, one-third of those Latin American countries listed boast at least four universities with courses in industrial organization including Brazil, Chile, Colombia, Mexico and Peru. Once again, Argentina is in the lead, with five universities offering such curricula. As with law, the countries that have the greatest number of courses in industrial organization are more likely to also have multiple courses in this area including specialized competition economics courses.

D. Learning From the Private Sector

The private sector is also critically important in improving the quality of Latin American competition agencies. With a sophisticated private sector involved in competition policy, the overall quality of agency staff increases because expectations are higher and competition more fierce. Moreover, a well-developed private sector of lawyers and economists allows for increased lateral movement from government to firms and vice versa. Those most likely to take senior agency positions will be younger partners at law firms or economists. These individuals may see an agency leadership position as a way to enhance their profile and long-term career prospects, by either returning to the private sector after a stint in government or moving up within the government.

IV. Formal Norm Diffusion and Development of Non-agency Practitioners

A. International Practitioner Associations

This chapter has thus far focused on formal training through technical assistance and university education, as well as informal norm diffusion through international competition policy organizations. An additional pillar of learning for practitioners and agency officials is through practitioner organizations. Indeed, there is a number of avenues for knowledge diffusion available to agencies and competition practitioners in Latin America via professional organizations. For example, the American Bar Association (ABA) features an Antitrust Section, which is one of its most sophisticated sections. To call the ABA Antitrust Section merely a US phenomenon overlooks the significant number of practitioners and academics outside the United States who are active members.[18] In any given month, the

[18] Similar to the ABA is the International Bar Association, which has a much larger contingent of European practitioners. However, its programming is far less extensive than that of the ABA.

Antitrust Section hosts brown-bag luncheons, with talks on any given issue from a number of committees, accessible via conference call or podcast on the Internet. Each substantive committee produces either a seasonal or a monthly newsletter. The Antitrust Section itself authors numerous books and issues a monthly online publication, a quarterly magazine and a peer-reviewed journal, all of which address topical matters of antitrust analysis and some of which are international in nature. Additionally, the Section organizes four major conferences each year, of which the Spring Meeting alone attracts over 1,000 attendees for three days of substantive programs on antitrust. Most speakers at the conferences are US-based practitioners, agency officials or academics, but a number of speakers and an even larger number of attendees are not US-based. There is always double-digit participation from Latin America, a number that seems to be growing long-term. As Latin American private sector lawyers and economists seek greater knowledge of the latest developments in US antitrust thought (both in law and economics) to analogize to Latin American practice, the ABA Antitrust Section affords them an opportunity to do so relatively cheaply. The Section also facilitates contact with practitioners outside of one's own country who are interested in the same area of law, which is important both for work-referral and strengthening any weak local interest.

Another venue that encourages competition policy norm diffusion is the Fordham Competition Law Institute, which hosts an annual conference on international competition policy. For many years, attendance at Fordham has been the venue for a practitioner to be viewed as 'the' international expert of his or her jurisdiction. Consequently, attending the Fordham conference may have financial advantages for practitioners from countries with young competition laws. By making contacts at Fordham, a young lawyer might learn something about the newest developments in international competition policy. Or he might get potential business; he may be the only 'known' person who is an expert on competition law from his country, at least in the eyes of a US or European practitioner. However, as the number of Latin American lawyers trained in competition law has increased, this first-mover advantage has eroded, as there are more contenders among those providing competition law counseling in Latin America.

B. Local Practitioner Associations

Another avenue for developing increased human capacity for competition policy practice in general is through local practitioner associations, such as bar associations or economics associations. In most countries, however, such associations that focus on competition policy are small or non-existent. In some cases, this might be a result of a small practitioner base in competition policy. After all, in a small economy there may never be more than a handful of people interested in or experienced in competition policy matters. Yet in the mid-size to larger countries of Latin America, critical mass is more possible. Even countries that lack critical mass have the Internet to create a virtual regional competition policy association that connects like-minded practitioners and academics across countries.

The oldest, and perhaps most successful, national association for competition policy in the region is Brazil's Institute of Studies on Competition, Consumer Affairs and International Trade (IBRAC), which dates back to 1992, a time before most Latin American countries had competition laws. The Institute sponsors conferences, courses and other events specific to competition law and policy. It also brings in speakers from around the world to complement its domestic-based activities and events. To promote greater academic interest in competition policy, IBRAC has sponsored an annual competition for undergraduate and graduate students and professionals for the best paper in competition policy. Furthermore, as part of a greater knowledge diffusion, its members produce a newsletter that describes and analyzes the latest developments in Brazilian competition policy. Other national organizations in the region are not as well-developed as IBRAC.

A rather unique private sector organization that promotes norm diffusion of competition policy is the ForoCompetencia. ForoCompetencia is a virtual competition organization that has a listserve for competition policy specialists in government, private practice and academia in the region. The listserve and its sister announcement listserve generate lively traffic when people post items regarding particular questions. Perhaps the most important development of the listserve has been the ability of practitioners across jurisdictions to compare experiences as well as application of competition law and economics in their jurisdictions. Furthermore, ForoCompetencia is not entirely virtual; it holds biennial conferences in Argentina, during which participants from six to eight jurisdictions across Latin America make presentions.

Still, there is no regional academic organization that is specific to competition policy. As discussed earlier, ALACDE exists as a vehicle for law and economics scholarship. There is also a Latin America and Caribbean Law and Economics Association. However, competition law and economics academics are not very active in either group. Various European and North American donors and international lending organizations (eg, World Bank or Inter-American Development Bank) have undertaken a number of efforts to improve capacity at the university level, but these efforts have yet to create a sustained and stand-alone regional group of competition law experts in academia who formally meet and collaborate as do similar groups in Europe, the United States or East Asia.

C. Internal Human Capacity Development

1. *Law Firms*

As organizations, law firms train their lawyers in the latest procedural and substantive techniques in competition law. Firms with international offices offer even more of an advantage—they provide, or at least purport to provide, seamless service across jurisdictions. As firms provide such services, they spend a significant amount of resources training their associates through practice group meetings, where attorneys review key legal developments and lessons learned from various case work. This enables the assimilation of knowledge across offices, as well as mentorship opportunities, providing additional training in competition law for practitioners in jurisdictions lacking the deal flow of the United States or United Kingdom.

Of those law firms listed on the *Global Competition Review's* Global 100 of top competition practices, most US and European law firms lack a Latin American presence. Even among those firms that do exist in the region, few have an antitrust presence. Baker & McKenzie is one international law firm that has an antitrust footprint in a number of countries. Another, Hogan & Hartson, has an antitrust presence in Venezuela that it uses as a platform (along with DC practitioners) to cover the entire region. Still another international law firm with a Latin American competition practice is White & Case. Much of its regional antitrust work is handled out of Mexico City, where the firm has three partners in its competition practice. The Mexican partners work closely with the Washington, New York, Brussels and Miami practices (the last of which has a mergers and acquisitions practice but no antitrust specialists). For example, with a global deal, the White & Case Mexico City office will often handle the merger control analysis for all of Latin America. The Mexican partners are in contact with non-Latin American partners for assistance with any analogies to US or EU practice, or assistance with law that might be relevant to their Latin American competition practice. The Mexican partners are also able to participate in practice group meetings; thus, their association with an international firm affords them both formal and informal training.

2. *Economic Consultancies*

A number of economics consulting firms have undertaken merger and conduct work in Latin America. However, in terms of creating local capacity, either the demand seems non-existent or global economic consulting firms have yet to create a large-scale Latin American-based capacity. The *Global Competition Review* ranks 20 economic consulting firms around the world as among the best in competition economics. Of those ranked, only one firm has its headquarters in Latin America, the Brazil-based Tendencias. Among international firms, LECG does have a presence in Latin America, although its actual footprint is quite small, with only two antitrust specialists located in Argentina.

Because economics is central to the antitrust endeavor, the lack of private sector economists has large repercussions on the strength of competition policy in a given jurisdiction. A recent article by Damien Neven suggests that a key cause of the rise of economic analysis in the European Union is due to the 1990 Merger Regulations and the rise of economic consulting firms to feed this demand.[19] No commentator, even those generally critical of EU competition decisions and policy, disputes that EU economic analysis has improved in the last 10 to 15 years.

[19] Damien J Neven, 'Competition Economics and Antitrust in Europe', 21 *Economic Policy* 741 (2006).

Some of that improvement can be attributed to the presence of economists. Yet how much can be attributed to direct causation remains an open question.

Early on, the EU did not have economists in its Directorate-General of Competition (DG Competition), DG Competition lawyers being wedded to formalistic thinking based on German ordoliberal thought; thus, efficiency was not considered the primary purpose of the EU. Rather, EU law was based on political concerns of economic integration in which efficiency concerns played a secondary role. Moreover, lawyers running DG Competition did not even believe in economics. Change came with the 1990 Merger Regulations, however, which created a demand for more sophisticated analysis. Consequently, larger politics may have forced the demand for sophisticated competition economics to arise in the EU. Universities may have had to play catch-up to meet this demand, which meant that the EU had a supply problem, both in competition economics and in economics-based competition law. By the mid-1980s, there were only a few law schools that taught competition law in Europe. Indeed, one of the most preeminent law schools teaching EU competition law was Fordham Law School in New York, not in Europe. The demand for increased knowledge and advanced degree programs came from young lawyers who wanted to make a name for themselves in an area becoming a critical part to any deal work and in which there was not an already existing group of lawyers.

Three reasons explain why this EU experience has not been replicated in Latin America. First, parties do not think to involve economic consultants until late in the process, if at all, when handling competition policy cases. Conversations with a number of Latin American-based competition lawyers have revealed a possible fear in these lawyers that if they bring in an economist early in their contact with Latin American competition agencies, it will be perceived by agency staff as indicative of a serious problem with the proposed transaction. Consequently, Latin American law firms err on the side of keeping an economist either out or on the sidelines for much longer than would be the case in the US or EU.

Secondly, the consultancies such as LECG have very limited Latin American practices, in part because the costs of such practices may be too high. When an economist provides advice on a deal, he is generally a local economist—one who has some connection to the people in the agency. These economists are generally academics and tend to be cheaper than US- or EU- based consulting firms; as a result, the percentage of economic consulting costs as to the total of the entire cost of a particular matter stays low if a US or European law firm runs a deal that requires a cross-country merger review.[20]

At present, it may make economic sense for a US or UK law firm to hire only local economists in a Latin American country because they are cheaper. These local (perhaps less sophisticated) economists may also be the minimum necessary

[20] Only recently has the percentage of economic consultants in EU competition cases reached US levels of roughly 15% of legal fees. *Ibid*, at 749. This suggests that economic analysis has been embraced in European competition cases.

to get the job done. Eventually, however, more enforcement officials in Latin American countries will want more than the current quality and caliber of local economists, who may lack competition policy specialization. At that point, multinational law firms and their multinational clients will have to pay more for high quality economic analysis. Only then will it be possible for international consultancies to be price competitive. It remains unclear whether this means the local economist will have to: (1) become better educated; (2) join a body like CRA, NERA or LECG; or (3) both 1 and 2. Otherwise, consultancies such as CRA and LECG will have to open more offices. Regardless, the trend of looking for more sophisticated economists is gaining momentum.

A final reason why Latin America has not experienced what the EU did is that the EU was easier to 'switch'. That is, not only did EU members literally speak the language (English) and a specific part of that language (economics), but they had been doing competition law at a high level for years. Sending US lawyers and economists to Europe made competition agency staff much more comfortable with the economic tools available. This caused agency staff to demand sound economic presentations from the parties, which led to increased demand for the Lexecons and LECGs of the world. And when the EU committed to having a Chief Economist, it institutionalized the increased dependence on economics (still, a number of US practitioners question whether or not the EU is nearly as far along in terms of reliance on economics as is the US). It was a long process with the first staff exchange with the EU occurring in 1990. However, causing a major shift like this takes time. Meetings among high level officials to discuss sophisticated economic issues cause some movement, but the movement really takes off when staff at the various agencies begin to interact.

Fortunately, it seems possible for Latin American agencies to reach a level of greater reliance on economists in agency decision-making without a crisis like *GE/Honeywell*.[21] After all, more companies, both US- and EU-based, are spending more time and money in such countries. My own sense is that the economics-based education is beginning to stick in Latin America—maybe not completely, but more than before. Perhaps the use of economists tracks the willingness of agencies to listen to economists. Agencies in the US heed the advice of economists; those in Europe sometimes do; and those in Latin American rarely do, despite the fact that within a number of Latin American agencies there is a Chief Economist. Of course, this assumes that larger politics within certain Latin American countries even allow the use of an efficiency-oriented competition policy.

Two larger points need to be made. First, the EU story is not a tale of complete success. One might argue that the EU uses economists most when it is concerned that the lack of economic based reasoning will lead to court reversals. Put differently, losses in cases such as *Airtours*, *Schneider* or *Tetra Pack* may have taught the

[21] Case T-209/01, *Honeywell Int'l Inc v Commission* [2006] OJ C48/26.

Commission to back up its claims with economic analysis.[22] A stronger claim can presently be made for the use of economic scrutiny in merger analysis in the EU. Overall, the move to greater economics in the EU has been solidified through the creation in 2003 of the Chief Economist position at the Commission.

Secondly, the EU is not a real comparison with Latin America. In the EU, there was real political and economic integration that necessitated increased competition policy at the community level, which in turn stimulated increased demand at the national level. MERCOSUR, the Central American Common Market and the Andean Community have not yet reached that same level of integration as has the EU. In terms of economic thought, it took the EU 40 years to begin to take economics seriously in competition policy. Moreover, if Latin America has already introduced, for the most part, merger control, the demand for creation of antitrust experts may not be as strong as it was in Europe.

V. Conclusion

It is increasingly apparent that academics and competition agencies need to spend more time on the human dimension of competition policy in Latin America. This new emphasis requires a sense of how best to utilize both formal and informal learning to improve the analytical skills of competition agencies. Admittedly, this chapter cannot prove causation as to which elements lead to the most effective development of human resources, but it does show that each element identified in this chapter seems to affect the human capacity of agencies positively, and that progress in each of the areas seems to be correlated. As Latin American markets become more integrated with each other and the United States through a series of free trade agreements, the number of cross-country mergers, and potentially cartels, will increase. Such changes will necessitate increased learning about the various Latin American competition policy regimes, and increased coordination in law and economics competition policy-related work. To meet these needs, one suggestion is the creation of a Latin American competition law and economics association. Additionally, universities must provide greater teaching in this area to respond to the increased demand for training. Finally, clients will demand more of their counsel as agencies become more economically sophisticated. A comparable push will encourage growth in the sophistication of human capital in Latin American competition agencies through international organizations, as well as local law and economics associations for practitioners.

[22] Case T-342/99, *Airtours v Commission* [2002] ECR II-2585; Case T-310/01, *Schneider Elec v Commission* [2002] ECR II-4071; Case T-5/02, *Tetra Laval v Commission* [2002] ECR II-4381, aff'd in part, Case C-12/03P, [2005] OJ C82/1 (ECJ).

Chapter III

The Recent Development of the Brazilian Competition Policy System

ELIZABETH MMQ FARINA* AND PATRICIA AGRA ARAÚJO**

I. Introduction

This chapter offers an abridged analysis of the institutional development of the Conselho Administrativo de Defesa Econômica (CADE), focusing on the 2004–08 period. Created in 1962, CADE has experienced great progress since 1994, when Law 8.884 was promulgated. The Law enlarged CADE's regulatory reach to include mandatory merger review. It also gave CADE autonomy, transformed it into a federal independent agency, and provided it with a wider range of instruments to enforce its decisions.

Since the Law's passage, some specific and relevant reforms have been promoted in the legislation, especially in 2000, with Law 10.149. Law 10.149 provided the Brazilian Competition Policy System (BCPS) with modern investigative instruments necessary to protect consumers against illegal conduct, particularly by cartels. These instruments included the creation of a leniency program and the ability of competition authorities to carry out dawn raids and inspections. The same law also established objective criteria for mandatory merger reviews, based on the merging firms' turnovers. More recently, in 2007, Law 11.482 authorized CADE to allow for settlements in cartel cases.

By July 2004, there was a widely accepted analysis of the quality of the BCPS among the Brazilian antitrust community of lawyers, economists and academics. Merger review procedures were too slow, conduct infractions had not received due priority, and CADE decisions were not enforced and therefore were ineffective. The Secretary of Economic Law (SDE) had already started to react to address

* Professor at the School of Economics at the University of São Paulo, Brazil. From July 2004 to July 2008, she was the President of CADE.

** LLM in Intellectual Property Law (Boston University). From 2004 to 2008, she was the legal advisor of the president of the CADE, as well as the international advisor of the Tribunal.

those negative aspects at that time, and CADE joined these efforts. CADE adopted the following objectives to reform the BCPS:

a) celerity in decisions;
b) efficiency;
c) effectiveness;
d) transparency of procedures and decisions;
e) enhancement of internal and external communication;
f) improvement in international antitrust networking across agencies, implementation of global antitrust recommended practices; and
g) improvements to competition advocacy efforts to the judiciary and public prosecutors.

Given the constraints of the Brazilian legal system, the BCPS authorities have made every effort towards administrative and procedural modernization by the adoption of legal measures. One example is the introduction of the fast track procedure in merger review. Between 2005 and 2008, CADE analyzed approximately 80 per cent of merger review cases under this procedure. The use of the fast track saves the tangible and intangible resources of CADE and of the business community, without sacrificing any attention to the public interest involved in each case. It releases resources to enable a faster and more careful analysis of the complex merger reviews and anti-competitive conduct cases.

Other measures have been taken by CADE to achieve the above-mentioned objectives: the strong commitment of all Commissioners[3] and the Attorney-General to speed up decisions; the reform of CADE's bylaws; the reform of administrative procedures within CADE; efforts towards obtaining a permanent technical staff (which was achieved in August 2005); the creation of '*Súmulas*' ('understanding briefs' issued by the Plenary of CADE, based on recurrent decisions); the issuance of Understanding Brief 1, which restricted the notification threshold to BRL 400 million for companies' turnover in Brazil; the CADE Attorney's office reorganization in order closely to follow those decisions that are under judicial review; the creation of the Social Communication Coordination; the Internet transmission of CADE's public decision sessions; the creation of

[3] Commissioners from August 2004 to July 2008: Roberto Augusto Castellanos Pfeiffer (Doctor in Law from University of São Paulo and member of the State of São Paulo Attorney Office), Luiz Alberto Scallope (Public Prosecuter from Mato Grosso State), Ricardo Villas Boas Cueva (Doctor in Law from Johann Wolfgang Goethe Universität, Germany, Attorney of the Federal Tax Attorney's Office), Luis Carlos Prado (Doctor in Economics from the University of London, Queen Mary & Westfield College, and Full Professor at the Federal University of Rio de Janeiro State), Luis Fernando Rigato (Doctor in Economics from the Getúlio Vargas Foundation of São Paulo), Luis Fernando Schuartz (Doctor in Law from Johann Wolfgang Goethe Universität, Germany, and Full Professor at Getúlio Vargas Foundation of Rio de Janeiro), Abraham B Sicsú (Doctor in Economics from the State University of Campinas, Full Professor at Joaquim Nabuco Foundation and Associate Professor of the Federal University of Pernambuco State), Luis Fernando Furlan (Doctor in Political Science from Sorbonne University, France), Paulo Furquim de Azevedo (Doctor in Economics from University of São Paulo and Full Professor at Getúlio Vargas Foundation).

CADE's newsletter; and the availability of updated data on CADE's decisions on the website, among others.

Despite the efforts of the SDE, SEAE[4] and CADE to improve the BCPS and to adopt international recommended practices, the legal changes and other administrative arrangements can only be preserved within a new legal framework for competition policy in Brazil. This new framework would lead to greater legal certainty and predictability, as well as a sustainable improvement in efficiency and decision effectiveness.

Acknowledging the need for a reform of the BCPS, the President of Brazil included a Bill for its reform (among the priorities of the Growth Acceleration Program (PAC)) in January 2007, as an instrument to improve the business environment. Among the main changes that are expected to be introduced into the BCPS with the new Law are a pre-notification merger review system (adopted in almost every country in which the control of mergers is mandatory); more objective criteria for mandatory notification; and the unification of the BCPS under an independent autarchy, which will speed up the conduct cases and the merger reviews, providing more independence to the investigations conducted today by the SDE and SEAE.

The BCPS has long benefited from an increase in its international network through international antitrust organizations, which has provided a valuable platform for discussion, apprenticeship and experience, and information exchange. Maintaining this relationship requires continuous participation and involvement. This has led CADE to invest its resources in active participation in fora and meetings promoted by organizations such as the Organisation for Economic Co-operation and Development (OECD), the International Competition Network (ICN) and the United Nations Conference on Trade and Development (UNCTAD). In 2007, the BCPS maintained its position as observer in the Competition Committee of the OECD, and CADE joined the 'Steering Group' of the ICN, both until 2009.

Lastly, the work of CADE's Public Attorney's Office has been essential to guaranteeing the enforcement of Council decisions. Because parties have the right to appeal decisions to a judicial court, as laid down in the Federal Constitution, most CADE decisions are routed into courts, where the cases can last 10 years. Considering the economic timing of the competition law decisions, a preliminary injunction that can last for a long time may make the decision totally ineffective. On the other hand, CADE's records show that although the judiciary has granted a number of preliminary injunctions suspending CADE's decisions, it has mostly confirmed the same decisions afterwards.

[4] The SDE (Secretary of Economic Law of the Ministry of Justice) and the SEAE (Secretary for Economic Monitoring of the Ministry of Finance) are responsible for the investigation and preparation of the cases, which are adjudicated by CADE. CADE may conduct complementary investigations as well.

Some of CADE's objectives have not been achieved in full and cannot be taken for granted. This suggests both a continuous effort to get the new Bill approved and an insistence on building the capacity of new generations of judges, agency staff and the private lawyers.

II. In Search of Effectiveness

The main objective of any competition authority is to make effective decisions. That is, decisions which are enforced in a timely manner and produce the expected effects on the market. *Market outcomes* are the main target: more competitive markets must be achieved. However, market outcomes are not produced without the competition authorities' *outputs*: number of decisions, fines collected, and competition advocacy reports, among others. No market effect can be produced if the decisions are not made in a timely manner and enforced: remedies must be adopted; fines paid; and illegal profits seized.

As with any other organization, competition authorities face budgetary constraints and have to use scarce resources efficiently. Scarcity is a relative concept. Tangible and intangible resources are scarce if they are not sufficient to reach a pre-determined set of objectives. Therefore, the objectives chosen by the competition authorities must be in line with the resources available. Some jurisdictions have more flexibility than others to define their objectives, but prioritization is always possible and must be adopted, in order to guarantee resource allocation to cases that show a higher probability of producing the desired market outcomes.

A recent survey conducted by the ICN[5] showed that for most competition authorities, law establishes the objectives of the agency, leaving very little discretion to the agencies. The law typically includes merger review, prohibited conduct and competition advocacy. Law also establishes the threshold for mandatory notification of mergers. In many jurisdictions such authorities are responsible for consumer protection as well. Nevertheless, the resources available to achieve so many objectives are scant, especially in developing countries.

The comparison between the US and Brazil is striking. The US Federal Trade Commission has 70 PhDs in Economics, and the US Department of Justice Antitrust Division has another 55 PhDs. This is more than any university's Department of Economics in Brazil. The BCPS has no more than two PhDs in Economics among the technical staff.

[5] www.internationalcompetitionnetwork.org.

III. Defining Priorities and Strategy

Three primary substantive areas exist in antitrust policy:

a) merger reviews;
b) deterrence of illegal conduct; and
c) competition advocacy.

A. Merger Review

Merger review can be extremely resource-consuming and very demanding on technical expertise. Nevertheless, most of the young jurisdictions adopt mandatory merger notifications, which result in a high number of filings to the competition authorities. Brazil has very rich experience in this subject. Since 1994, under Law 8.884, merger notification has been mandatory for

> acts and agreements (generally considered to include mergers, acquisitions and joint venture, among any kind of contracts) that may limit or otherwise restrain open competition, or that result in the control of relevant markets for certain products or services.[6]

The wording of Law 8.884 is too broad and can be applied to contracts with suppliers or distributors, or even contracts with no overlapping activities at all. The result is too many notifications.

Law 10.149 of 2000 included the third paragraph of Article 54, which oriented the definition towards a more objective criterion, as recommended by ICN and the OECD, including the OECD peer review of Brazil in 2000. According to paragraph 3, notifications are mandatory for 'concentration transactions' in which one of the parties has a gross revenue equal to or greater than BRL 400 million, or where the transaction results in a party gaining more than 20 per cent of a relevant market.[7]

Even after the objective criterion was applied, there was recognition among CADE's Commissioners and the Brazilian antitrust community that the BCPS reviewed too many cases with no or very low probability of harming competition, due to the overly broad definition of Article 54 of Law 8884/94. Indeed, fewer than 7 per cent of mergers are approved with some restriction. CADE adopted legal measures to attack the merger review system's weaknesses, when feasible. First, as from January 2005, CADE began to apply a turnover criteria threshold relating

[6] Law 8884.

[7] The reference to 'a relevant market' is tricky for defining the notification criteria. As most companies are multiproduct companies, if they have 20% or more in any of the relevant markets in which they participate, the notification will be mandatory—even if they have less than 20% in the target market. Some Commissioners have recently adopted a more restrictive understanding of the Law, but it is not the CADE understanding so far.

only to Brazilian territory. This understanding was consolidated by Understanding Brief 1 in October 2005. The consequence was a sensible reduction in the number of analyzed and notified mergers (the number of merger reviews dropped 46 per cent in 2005), releasing human resources to speed up complex merger reviews and to address conduct cases.

Secondly, in August 2007, CADE issued Understanding Brief 2, which restricts mandatory notification filings by stating that minority share acquisitions by a partner that already has a majority share need not be submitted if the following hypothetical situation occurs:

(i) the seller does not hold corporate powers, derived from the law, bylaws or an agreement to:
    (i.a) appoint a manager;
    (i.b) determine the commercial policy of the company; or
    (i.c) reject any corporate matter; and
(ii) the documents do not contain any clause
    (ii.a) of 'non-competition' valid for more than 5 years or for territorial scope beyond the company's activities; and
    (ii.b) derives any kind of control between the parties after the operation.

Thirdly, in 2003 the SDE and SEAE formally adopted the fast track procedure to speed up merger review analysis and the issuance of their opinions.[8] CADE later adopted the same procedure. Currently more than 75 per cent of the cases are completed under the fast track procedure.

Under the limits of the Law, CADE has continued to consider further measures to reduce the number of submissions that have no or very low likelihood of negatively affecting competition. Reducing the number of mandatory notifications is part of the prioritization process necessitated by the institutional constraints caused by the overly broad wording of the Law.

Regarding complex merger cases, the biggest challenge is to overcome the limitations imposed by the Brazilian post-notification system. That is, companies are allowed to conclude a transaction while the BCPS analyzes the competition effects. It is widely recognized that after a consummated fact, the costs of a decision that blocks the transaction or imposes structural remedies are too high for everybody concerned—the competition authority, the company, and the market. Moreover, the process tends to take longer due to the lack of incentives for the parties to provide information for the analysis.

In order to remedy this weakness of the law, in 2002 CADE issued Ordinance No 28, regulating the imposition of preliminary injunctions[9] and Agreements to Preserve the Reversibility of Transactions (APROs). An APRO, created and regulated by this Ordinance, has two main goals. First, it aims to preserve the

[8] Later, the Secretariats created a joint analysis procedure for complex cases, when the two staffs jointly analyze the case and issue only one opinion.

[9] The first interim measures to suspend the effects of a transaction's conclusion were taken in 2000.

enforcement of a further blocking of the merger or a divestiture decision by CADE, in order to get approval for the transaction. Secondly, it seeks to inform society at large and the market that these restrictions may be imposed.

The major challenge in this case is to guarantee that, while under analysis, the companies' management teams remain independent and that the value of the assets is protected. This is a very difficult task to accomplish, and requires a lot of negotiation and imagination, including, in some cases, the intervention of a trustee. However, an APRO will be useful only if the analysis does not take too long. This is a real challenge for CADE. An example is illustrative of the difficulties that can arise. For instance, in more than one case involving supermarket mergers, an APRO was signed. During the SDE and SEAE analysis of the merger, the APRO had to be amended more than once in order to authorize the sale or closure of some stores (authorized because of a change in the business environment or because they had no impact in the market). At the time of the decision by CADE, few stores were left to be sold.

In order to speed up the analysis, the SDE and SEAE issued a joint ordinance to establish joint merger analysis in 2006. The objective was to use human resources better and to reach a common conclusion to send to CADE. Moreover, the joint analysis avoids differences of opinion between the two bodies that are often exploited by the parties when they challenge potential restrictions to the merger. This is a good example of how to manage the resources of the competition authorities more effectively under legal constraints. However, despite the efforts of the SDE, SEAE and CADE to improve the BCPS, significant improvement requires a new legal framework. Such a new framework could lead to greater legal security and predictability, as well as to a sustainable improvement in the efficiency and effectiveness of decisions.

Recognizing these needs, the new proposed law introduces the following changes:

a) the pre-notification merger review system;
b) more objective criteria for mandatory notification;
c) the unification of the BCPS under an independent authority, which will speed up the conduct cases and the merger reviews; and
d) an increase in the number of technical staff.

The new proposed law also changes the notification criteria, including a minimum turnover threshold for the acquired firm, and restricts mandatory notification to transactions that increase concentration. Moreover, the 20 per cent market share criterion is excluded. This change corresponds to giving priority to the combat of illegal conduct without abandoning the merger review.

B. Deterrence of Anticompetitive Conduct

To put an end to, punish and deter illegal conduct is the primary focus of any competition authority. Therefore most resources should be applied to this course of action.

1. *Cartels*

It is widely recognized that hard-core cartels represent the most harmful conduct of all, because they cannot be justified on the grounds of efficiency—only the participants in a cartel can benefit from it. The conclusion that most of the resources should finance the combating of cartels is straightforward. Anti-cartel policy has become quite sophisticated, involving hard-core investigative techniques such as dawn raids and wiretapping, lenience programs and settlements. However, not only are these investigative tools resource-consuming (mainly of human resources), they also require a great deal of coordination and capacity building. In many jurisdictions, the use of these tools requires judicial authorization, public prosecutors' and police collaboration, and trained teamwork to sort out relevant documents from within a pile of paper-work or electronic information. The demanding procedure of assuring due process of law must also be followed, otherwise the judiciary will not confirm the decision.

The Brazilian experience has shown that the results of investment in combating cartels are rewarding. However, it took seven years from implementation of the law in 2000 for the first cartel case based on the leniency program to be concluded with a condemnation. The first cartel case using direct evidence collected by dawn raids was completed in 2006, and the first one based on wiretapping in 2005.

In February 2008, the SDE launched the Brazilian Leniency Policy Interpretation Guidelines, and a Model Annotated Leniency Agreement, in order to provide more clarity and certainty regarding the conditions and requirements for leniency in Brazil. Brazil already has a record of effectively detecting hard-core cartels. Up to the beginning of 2008, approximately 10 agreements were signed, and others were being negotiated, 60 per cent of them with members of international cartels.

CADE's statistics do not reflect the priorities put in place by SDE because the cases arrive at CADE after the investigations have been concluded and the defenses presented to be judged. However, it is important to point out that CADE follows the understanding that anti-cartel efforts should be the main focus of the competition policy. Additionally, in May 2007, a new law, Law 11.482, allowed settlements to be made in cartel cases. In September 2007, CADE issued Resolution No 46/2007, establishing the rules for settlement application and negotiation. This represents an improvement in the BCPS, in the sense that early cooperation from the defendants will save public resources, cut down litigation time and expenses for the authorities and the parties, enable early payment of significant sums of money, and provide certainty and transparency for the business community.

Nevertheless, most young jurisdictions, Brazil included, have started fighting against cartels based on indirect economic evidence, using the 'parallelism plus' methodology.[10] Brazil has achieved some cartel convictions based on indirect

[10] Jonathan Baker, 'The Case for Antitrust Enforcement', 17 *Journal of Economic Perspectives* 27–50 (2003).

evidence. Cases based only on this type of evidence depend on a weaker standard of proof, and therefore are less likely to be upheld by the judiciary. Nevertheless, these cases were an important change to the Brazilian competition culture, signaling that the behavior standards of market participants had changed. They also gave legitimacy to the competition authorities' efforts to improve and develop investigative mechanisms and achieve international standards. In total, the fight against cartels has received increasing attention from the Brazilian antitrust authorities, and most of the investigative resources are allocated to this objective.

2. *Unilateral Conduct*

While the combating of hard-core cartels and merger review analysis receive some consensus, there is little convergence in the worldwide treatment of unilateral conduct. There is wide recognition, though, that single-firm strategies are challenging, as it is quite difficult to separate fierce competition on the merits from exclusionary practices. Worse, the condemnation of genuine competition, based on efficient business acumen, can teach dominant firms that it is better for them to generate extra profits from their lower costs than to transfer them, even partially, to consumers. Therefore, given budget constraints, the results of the authorities' activities may be better assessed when efforts are directed towards the combating of cartels, according less attention to unilateral conduct.

CADE's records show that there were nine times as many unilateral conduct cases as cartel cases in 2005. This is not incongruent with the clear priority for cartel combat that the SDE declares itself to have adopted since 2003. The more recent cases have not yet arrived at CADE to be adjudicated, but they are in the pipeline. Nevertheless, in 2007, 50 per cent of the condemnations were in cartel cases, as were the highest fines.

Most cases of single-firm strategy are related to regulated sectors and involve dominant firms that control essential facilities. Most of these firms acquired their dominant position in the privatization process, or are concessionaires of public services, such as in the telecommunications sector or port terminals. A very small number of condemnations are related to exclusive dealings. In the last four years the BCPS has not made any condemnations relating to predatory pricing, tying, resale price maintenance or excessive pricing, all of which are listed by Brazilian Law as examples of conduct falling under Article 20, which defines infractions to economic order.

The SDE has addressed the choice between combating cartels and investigating unilateral conduct through its allocation of time and human resources. CADE has no such choice—all cases have to be adjudicated, according to the law, using the same procedures, ie, first, by the assignment of a reporter Commissioner and, subsequently, by adjudication by the Commissioners at a public hearing. The only possible adjustment to the sequence is the speediness of the decision-making process.

C. Advocacy

CADE has made the judiciary and the Public Prosecutor's Office the main targets of its competition advocacy initiatives. The CADE's Attorney Office, as already mentioned, has started to be more proactive before the judiciary. The President and the Commissioners appear before judges in order to guarantee that CADE is heard before preliminary injunctions are granted, as well as to guarantee that all the reasoning upon which CADE's decision was based is clearly understood. Some positive results have been achieved, and in 2007 CADE won an important decision—the judiciary will require condemned parties to deposit in escrow the amount of any fine imposed in a CADE decision, with interest accumulating, as a prerequisite to granting the right to appeal against CADE's decision.

Over the last few years, CADE members have participated in training programs organized by and for public prosecutors. Since 2005 the subject of 'economic law' has been included in the career tests for public prosecutors. Moreover, some advocacy work has been undertaken before State public prosecutors not only to gain their support in detecting local/regional conduct, but also to redirect local actions that may have an impact in local/regional markets.

IV. Convergence and Prioritization

Convergence and prioritization are not trivial tasks in young jurisdictions, depending as they do on more than just agency leadership and staff. On the contrary, they are multi-institutional tasks, which involve other players, such as the judiciary, the academic community, the legislature, and private lawyers. Even if Brazilian law does not fit international recommendations, the revised law will reflect Brazilian institutional constraints and will be the best one achievable given those constraints. Jurisdictions have different characteristics, levels of economic development, legal regimes, constraints, histories and cultures that make it difficult to achieve a level of convergence based on 'one size fits all'. Harmonization should respect the institutional environments of nations in order to be accepted and enforceable.

This means that the law should provide competition authorities with instruments to impose on mergers remedies that successfully reduce the impact on competition, and with instruments valid to combat anti competitive conduct, to achieve punishment and deterrence. To achieve those purposes, these instruments must address the constraints and limitations that characterize developing economics. Under the BCPS, prioritization is limited by a law that establishes a broad merger threshold, as well as by an institutional design that divides competition authorities into three bodies.

All the efforts related to improving the BCPS have led to improvements in the decision-making process, as measured by some very simple, but useful, indicators of BCPS output. The graphs below show the recent evolution of these measures for the BCPS. The management process requires continuous and comprehensive follow-up of the chosen indicators in order quickly to identify and address undesirable performance. CADE has systematically accounted for the evolution of the number of initiated processes and the number of decisions made, as well as the average time of decision-making.

Graph 1 shows that the annual number of docket processes has declined from an annual average of 534 days in the period 2000–04 to an annual average of 261 days from 2005 to July 2008. Moreover, Graph 2 shows a more important performance evolution regarding merger reviews. The global average time of analysis declined from 252 days in 2005 to 159 days in 2008. If we consider only CADE, the average time taken to reach a decision also declined from 92 days on average in 2000–04 to 81 days in 2005 and 46 days in 2008! The standard deviation has also declined from 122 days in 2005 to 22 days in 2008 (Graph 3).

The standard of performance is not as good with regard to illegal conduct cases. As shown by Graph 4, the overall timeframe is quite long (six years on average) and has not shown a declining trend. After arriving at CADE, however, the decision-making time has declined from 453 days on average to 282 days. Despite all efforts to release the BCPS resources to combat illegal conduct, administrative proceedings account for 7.5 per cent of CADE's decisions. Almost 30 per cent of them resulted in condemnations.

As mentioned before, the effectiveness of the BCPS decisions very much depends on their enforcement. Analysis of performance indicators is also useful in evaluating this result. Graph 5 shows that only 22 per cent of the fines applied were paid from 2005 to 2008. However, this is much better than the mere 5 per cent paid up to 2004. Moreover, the total value collected from 2005 to 2007 was almost double that achieved for the period 2001 to 2004. This was a result both of an increase in the fines applied and an increase in the payment of fines.

The overall evaluation is positive, based on the evolution of the output indicators. Market outcomes (market effects), however, have never been investigated on a regular basis. As a matter of fact, the most important condemnations of illegal conduct, including cartels, were suspended by judicial preliminary injunction. Still, some events reported by important Brazilian newspapers show that the BCPS decisions are being considered in leading firms' strategies.[11]

[11] Rede G Barbosa, 'Wal-mart gives up buying', *Valor econômico*, 9 Sept 2007.

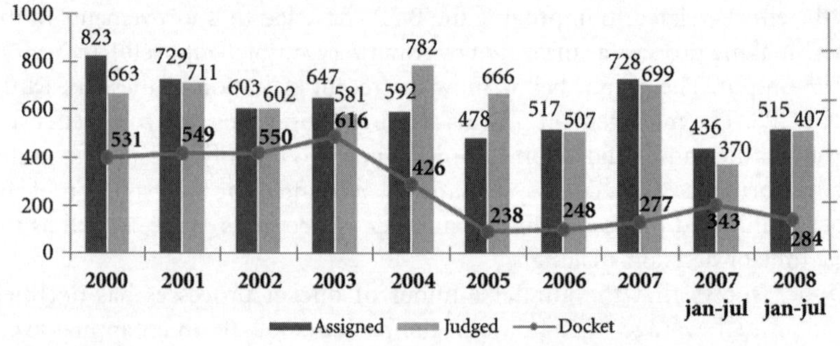

Graph 1 Evolution of judged proceedings x assigned with docket in CADE

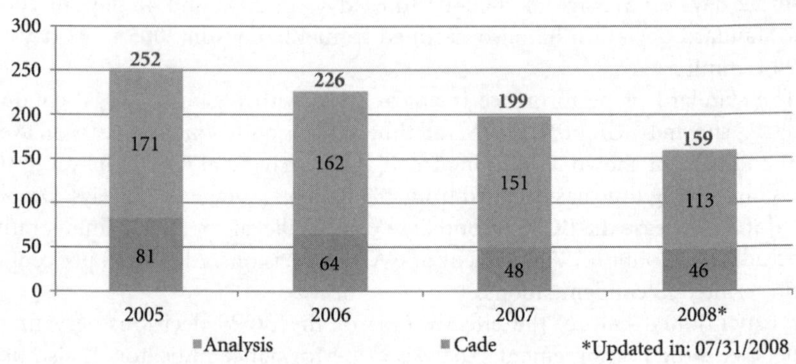

Graph 2 Average time of MRs in BCPS

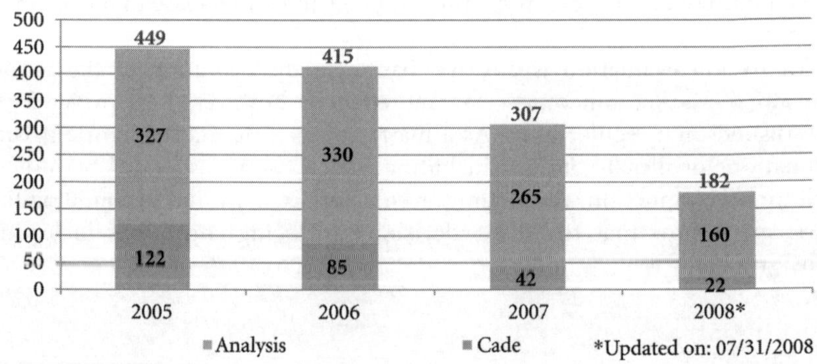

Graph 3 Standard deviation of the MR analysis time (in days)

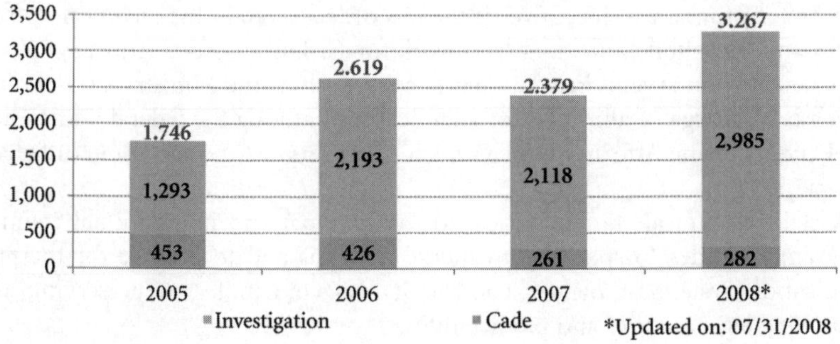

Graph 4 Average time of APs in BCPS

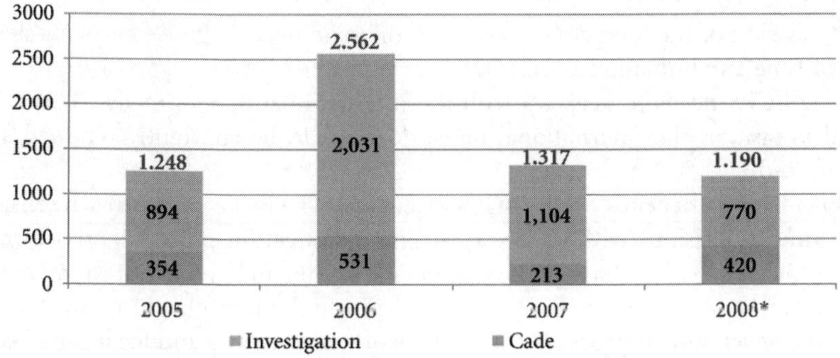

Graph 5 Standard deviation of the AP investigation time (in days)

V. Conclusions: Looking Forward

Brazilian antitrust policy has evolved quickly, improving the effectiveness and efficiency of the competition authorities' performance, supporting the development of the antitrust community, and promoting a new but growing recognition by the judiciary of the importance of BCPS decisions. It has brought about the movement of lawyers, economists, academia, business people, the judiciary and public prosecutors towards a better-informed and better-enforced decision-making process. Nonetheless, we still have a long way to go in this institution-building process.

First, it is critical that the new proposed law be approved soon. The reorganization of the BCPS would improve the efficiency and effectiveness of the competition authorities, and is crucial for preserving the recent achievements.

A better program of incentives is vital in order to retain the technical staff of BCPS and the public attorneys who work for CADE's General Attorney Office. This depends on several institutional players, such as the Ministry of Planning, which is in charge of allocation of technical staff among the federal bodies, and the Union General Attorney Office, which is in charge of the allocation of federal attorneys.

A stable technical staff is critical to the national and international training program, in order to speed up to merger analysis and to prepare for the pre-notification system of merger control. It also contributes to preserving and improving legal security and predictability.

In order to achieve transparency and to reduce the costs of the BCPS, a continuous program of investment in electronic systems and equipment is crucial. The electronic system is also needed to implement the full digital process, which will reduce costs substantially.

A revision of the Merger Guidelines is still pending, though we have invested a lot of time and human resources in it.

The BCPS needs to keep up with the international developments. This is an endless task, as the international network needs to be constantly renewed and reinforced.

Effectiveness depends on the BCPS as a whole. The BCPS cannot reach sensible and timely decisions without a very strong investigation process, and a careful and timely probative phase. This is not a task for one individual but for an entire organization. A strong antitrust policy is built on the interplay of many players, and the development process is full of network externalities and feedback effects.

Chapter IV

Mexican Competition Policy

MARCOS AVALOS BRACHO*

I. Introduction

This chapter describes competition policy in Mexico. Even though a decade has passed since its inception, there are few studies that describe and evaluate how Mexico's competition policy functions. This chapter analyzes the Mexican Federal Law of Economic Competition (FLEC) in its political, economic and social contexts. It examines the main economic principles underpinning the law of mergers and abuse of dominance. The chapter further presents a statistical overview of the Mexican competition policy between 1993 and 2004. Lastly, the chapter analyzes mergers between 1997 and 2001, and offers overall conclusions.

II. Federal Law of Economic Competition

In December of 1992, the Mexican Congress promulgated the Federal Law of Economic Competition (FLEC), which created the Federal Competition Commission (CFC) to promote competition in the marketplace and reduce the scope and mode of government intervention in the Mexican economy.[1] The CFC is the agency in charge of the implementation of competition policy, which includes the investigation of monopolistic practices and the control of vertical and horizontal mergers.

The early years of Mexican competition policy were difficult. The Mexican judicial system had no practical experience in competition regulation and, thus, could not give support for the design and implementation of the new law. Even though the 1857 Mexican Constitution prohibited monopolies, the Government never executed the law in an effective way, and in practice it often would do the opposite. Often the Government protected domestic businesses from external competition. For many government officials, the protection of domestic companies was not

* Professor of Economics, Faculty Economics and Business, CADEN, Anáhuac University. The author would like to especially thank Claudia Schatan. Data and editorial assistance by Daniela Ruiz and Ivan Zuñiga, respectively, are also appreciated. The usual disclaimers apply.

[1] FLEC Mexico. See Official Paper of the Federation (DOF, in Spanish) (Dec 24, 1992).

only part of the development strategy of the time, but also a source of political support. A parallel effect of this was the absence of academic or industry specialists in competition policy law and economics.

Structurally, the CFC is a unit of the Ministry of Economics. However, its decisions may not be reviewed by the Ministry, and the Commission has the authority to create its own budget and submit it directly to Congress. The effectiveness of the CFC depends largely on its budget, the dimensions of the organization, its capacity to implement administrative programs, the rigors of its internal process, the quality of its reports and the efficiency of its 'partner', the judicial system.

The main organizational principle of the competition law is intuitively and theoretically simple. The law promotes the conditions for a competitive market; in other words, it promotes effective competition. Through a series of general indications, the law prohibits certain forms of private commercial conduct and establishes a wide framework to promote economic objectives, thus helping to create an efficient allocation of resources in the economy.

One crucial aspect of Mexican competition policy is the application of the law of competition. In the United States, for example, competition authorities (such as the Department of Justice and the Federal Trade Commission) evaluate the possible anticompetitive aspects of mergers and other practices and take their cases to the judicial power (the courts), which is the ultimate decision maker. However, in Mexico, the courts lack experience in the implementation of competition policy. In general, Mexican judges do not have basic economic training, much less specialization, in areas such as competition and economic regulation. Additionally, the Mexican judicial system has gained a negative reputation for its inefficiency. The creation of courts specializing in economic areas, including competition and anti-dumping, has been proposed, but political[2] and financial obstacles exist.

A. Regulation of Monopolistic Practices

The FLEC divides anticompetitive practices into two types of conduct: absolute (horizontal) monopolistic practices, and relative (vertical) monopolistic practices. Absolute practices are subject to 'per se' treatment. Relative monopolistic practices violate the FLEC only if the firms (in Spanish called 'economic agents' or *agentes económicos*) have substantial power in a relevant market defined through a rule of reason approach.

Article 10 of the FLEC identifies some practices that may be considered an abuse of dominance (exclusive agreements, boycotts), as does Article 7 (predation, distribution exclusivity, price discrimination or sale conditions, crossed subsidies, and growing costs).[3] It has not been easy for the CFC to execute Article 10 with the criteria in Article 7. There is no evidence that the CFC has been successful in sanctioning economic agents based on claims of price discrimination

[2] This judicial entity could acquire an unwanted relative autonomy with regard to the competition authority.

[3] Predation and price discrimination were not explicitly mentioned in the FLEC, possibly because these practices are difficult to prove.

or predation. The CFC has lost all cases based on these claims in the courts. The Mexican Supreme Court considers this disposition unconstitutional, holding

> that it only indicates general criteria about the harm to the competition process and free entry, but it does not establish the necessary guidelines or parameters that the Commission must follow to sanction relative monopolistic practices that are associated with this behavior.[4]

In other countries, price discrimination and predation have been used in a great number of unfounded accusations. Many of the accusations of anticompetitive practices before the CFC in its first years of operation were made by companies asserting that their rivals set prices below average costs or at a level that would push them out of the market. The CFC rejected all such claims due to lack of evidence.[5]

In Mexico, most anticompetitive legislation is concerned with the discriminatory practices which companies can use to obtain or protect monopolistic positions. The evaluation of a 'dominant position' in the 'relevant market' differs substantially in various legislations. For example, in the European Union, a 'dominant position' is defined as established when a company can set prices unilaterally or restrict the supply in the relevant market, and when other companies or distributors cannot challenge such power. In US legislation, a 'dominant position' refers to market power; and a company has 'dominant position' when it intentionally has the object to exclude other agents in the market. According to Amato,[6] the main difference is:

> In the United States it is illegal only when both the exclusion and reduction effects to the consumer appear together (jointly). However, in Europe they are more oriented towards the particular responsibility that dominant companies have in protecting small competitors, and if this is not met, they must identify the possible abuse of dominance and harm to these competitors.

In contrast to European law, Mexican and US practice does not consider a dominant position a violation of the law of competition. In European law, an acquiring firm is monitored continuously from the beginning of a purchase. This monitoring is a protective shield for weak competitors based on a sense of 'justice'. Mexican and US antitrust policy is based more on efficiency than on distribution.

1. *The Decision Process*

The CFC has control over the quality, time and integrity of the investigatory and decision processes in monopolization cases. The decision process has a direct impact on the application of competition policy. Article 30 of the FLEC gives the CFC authority to initiate investigations of potentially illegal monopolistic policies,

[4] The criteria are found in jurisprudence thesis number P./J.11/2004, of the Plenary Session of the Supreme Court, published in *Novena Época* (Judicial Paper of the Federation and its Gazette), vol XIX, p 1162, March 2004. Article 10 of the FLEC is part of an initiative to reform the law that was recently proposed for discussion in the Mexican House of Representatives.

[5] See Annual Reports of the CFC 1994–97, CFC (Comisión Federal de Competencia) (1994–97), *Informe Anual de Competencia Económica, México.*

[6] G Amato, *Antitrust and the Bounds of Power. The Dilemma of Liberal Democracy* (Oxford, Hart Publishing, 1997).

whether originating from an inside investigation or from an accusation made by an economic agent. The CFC has the authority to begin an investigation of any anti-competitive practice (absolute, relative, or a merger) in any sector of the economy, on its own initiative (*de oficio*). Article 5 describes some of the conduct that may be identified as monopolistic. The CFC uses three sources of information to detect these practices: first, indirect sources, such as newspapers, magazines, and Chamber of Commerce bulletins; secondly, suggestions made by the Ministry of Economics (*Secretaría de Economía*)[7]; and thirdly, information provided in accusations by third parties. The CFC gathers information for specific cases but does not have a permanent monitoring or search system for information on monopolistic practices.

In the organizational structure of the CFC, the President and the Executive Secretary have prosecutorial discretion (Articles 22 and 23). Some criteria used in evaluating accusations are: the probability of success; the pursuit of certain anticompetitive practices that firms do not want to denounce; and the number of accusations the CFC can handle. Beginning an internal investigation *de oficio* is extremely difficult, due to imperfect information and a clause in the law that requires that information can be gathered only once an investigation has been initiated formally.

Article 32 of the FLEC establishes that any individual can denounce a monopolistic practice of a company or an economic agent. In the case of relative monopolistic practices, only the allegedly harmed party may bring the accusation. In the first stages of the process, a trial cannot be initiated. Rather, all accusations must be analyzed and evaluated by the CFC. In other words, the CFC initiates and investigates the case and gives its decision. This a fundamental difference from the process in the United States.

The CFC in Mexico has to give a formal response to the accusation within a 10-day period (Article 25). This obligation does not mean that the CFC will investigate the case. Its response may indicate that the case does not violate the FLEC, or that the law does not apply (Article 26). As mentioned above, the decision to investigate an accusation lies exclusively with the President and the Executive Secretary of the CFC (Articles 22 and 23 of the FLEC).

The General Center (Bureau) of Investigations (*Dirección General de Investigaciones*) of the CFC is in charge of carrying out the inquiry. The companies or agents involved are consulted and given the opportunity to present evidence. The Commission, through this entity, has the power to enforce the gathering and presentation of information by the concerned parties. Once the Commission has decided to initiate an investigation, it then publishes a notice in the Official Paper of the Federation (*Diario Oficial de la Federación*).[8] The CFC has to report its decision within a period of no less than 30 days and no more than 90 days. The period can be extended for more than 90 days if it is a difficult case (Article 27).

[7] It is not the general norm for the CFC to receive suggestions from the Economic Ministry. The suggestions tend to occur in specific cases where the Ministry has a special interest in the subject, eg in products such as cacao and beans.

[8] The Commission does not reveal the names of the economic agents subject to investigation. It does mention some characteristics of the relevant market, though, so it is not hard to find out which company is or companies are involved.

The CFC works its cases formally through its Plenary Session[9] via a majority vote, with its President having a deciding vote.

The CFC has the power to impose fines, or to order the suspension or correction of illegal practices. Regarding anti-competitive practices,[10] the CFC uses three types of procedures: preventive, contractual (modifying the terms of the contract), and structural. The resolution on Cintra (the Mexican airline company that merged Mexicana and Aeromexico) was an example of a preventive procedure. The Plenary Session of the Commission decided to monitor Cintra´s behavior in the commercial aviation market continuously. Additionally, the CFC has used extensively a procedure that modified the competitive terms of a contract.

The CFC has the power to impose fines as high as $1.6 million for monopolistic practices. However, it has imposed few, with none reaching the maximum allowed. Graph 1 shows those fines sanctioned for mergers and monopolistic practices. As will be seen, both sets of fines maintained a similar trend from 1997 to 2003.[11] Nearly all fines are imposed without prior notification.[12] Fines have not worked as an effective mechanism to prevent monopolistic practices, since the majority of them have not been collected.

The CFC has a rigorous procedure for the presentation of accusations. Merger cases are evaluated in the allotted time, but accusations of anticompetitive practice require additional analysis.

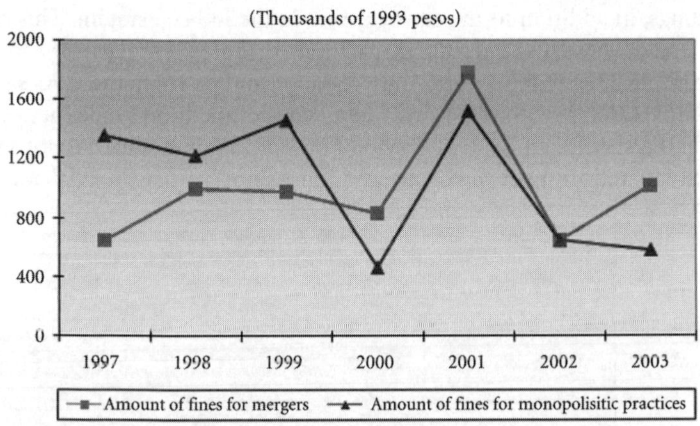

Source: Author, with data based on the Annual Reports of the CFC (2001–04).

Graph 1 Average amount for fines, Mexico 1997–2003

[9] The Plenary Session of the CFC is represented by five commissioners, including the President of the CFC (Art 25).

[10] The same procedures are applied to mergers.

[11] Except for 2003, fines for mergers show an increasing trend while fines for monopolistic practices show a decreasing trend.

[12] See Annual Reports of the CFC (*Comisión Federal de Competencia*) (1997–2003), *Informe Anual de Competencia Económica*, México.

Lastly, Article 39 of the FLEC establishes that after the CFC has ruled on a case, companies can resort to a 'reconsideration petition' (appeal) to reopen the decision. This is an internal process, and only the CFC can review the decision. The CFC President has the power to decide an appeal (Article 10), and the Plenary Session of the CFC can revoke, modify, or sustain a decision. Practically all reconsideration petitions are rejected, the majority of the decisions being ratified. Interested parties usually use the reconsideration petitions to lengthen the investigation period, which takes up a large amount of the time and resources of the CFC.

There are two additional appeal options. First, companies can resort to a 'protection' (*amparo*) trial before the Federal District Court. The Court can challenge the legality or the constitutionality of the CFC decision, but not its substance. Companies have used this constitutional appeal to cause delays in CFC proceedings. Secondly, the parties involved can challenge fines through the presentation of a formal appeal to the Administrative Court, the Federal Tribunal of Fiscal and Administrative Justice (*Tribunal Federal de la Justicia Fiscal y Administrativa*—TFJFA).

Graph 2 shows a rising trend in both types of appeals beginning in 1997, even though protection trials show a small drop in 2002. This indicates that there is a problem in the effective application of fines by the CFC. Not only does the economic agent have the power to contest the fine in the Administrative Court, but the Court can also evaluate the internal proceedings and analysis of competition that gave rise to the fine. The TFJFA has become a forum for review of anticompetitive proceedings, in addition to the ones existing in the judicial system. This causes a vicious cycle, whereby the review carried out by the TFJFA generates additional paperwork, lengthens procedures unnecessarily, and disrupts the CFC system of fines. This creates incentives for firms to violate competition guidelines.

The TFJFA should not be able to review FLEC procedures, since it is not a specialized entity in anticompetitive policies and it does not have any formal authority.[13]

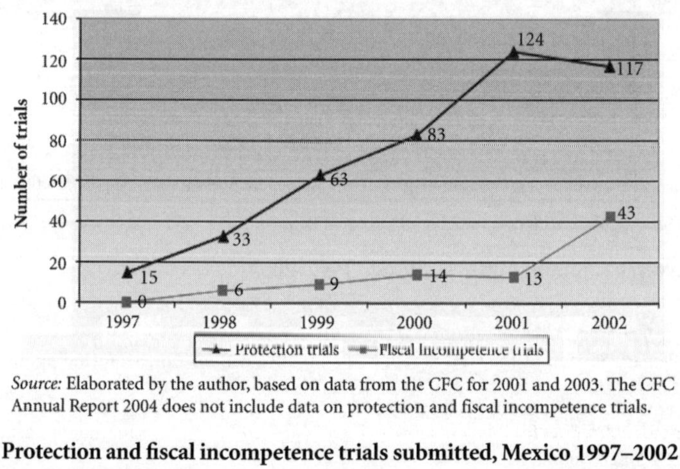

Source: Elaborated by the author, based on data from the CFC for 2001 and 2003. The CFC Annual Report 2004 does not include data on protection and fiscal incompetence trials.

Graph 2 Protection and fiscal incompetence trials submitted, Mexico 1997–2002

[13] Mexican Constitution, Art 28.

The CFC has not taken into consideration in its policy implementation the risk involved in the cases of review by the TFJFA.

B. Merger Regulation

The majority of decisions, notifications and procedures that govern anticompetitive regulation have to do with mergers.[14] The FLEC establishes (as in the United States) that the parties involved in a merger must notify the CFC prior to the transaction if the action falls within the FLEC thresholds established by Article 20. As in the case of monopolistic practices, the FLEC establishes the guidelines that govern merger policy in Mexico. Commissioners vote for the approval, conditional approval, or rejection of a merger based on a formal memorandum. The memorandum contains information provided to the CFC through a notification procedure derived from the FLEC, as well as information developed independently by economists, lawyers and CFC officials.[15]

The criterion for evaluating mergers is efficiency. Article 16 states that

> the Commission will contest (impugn) and sanction those concentrations whose goal is to diminish, harm or prevent competition and the free market of equal, similar or substantially related goods and services.

This approach is similar to the one applied by the US competition authorities under the criteria established by the DOJ/FTC Merger Guidelines. The ability of companies to manipulate prices, or unjustifiably to displace other companies is closely scrutinized by the CFC. Other aspects of competition policy, such as efficiency gains, barriers to entry, competition in imports and elimination of a vigorous competitor, are considered only in special cases.

The most commonly used criteria for analyzing mergers are the Herfindahl-Hirschman (HHI) and Dominance (DI) Indexes. These establish the following classifications:[16]

a) If the HHI index increases less than 75 points or is less than 2,000 points after the merger, the merger will not be contested.

[14] See S Levy, 'Observaciones sobre la Nueva Legislación de Competencia Económica en México' in R L Tovar (ed), *Lecturas en Regulación Económica y Política de Competencia* (México, ITAM, Grupo Editorial Porrúa, 2000), 167–79.

[15] The CFC occasionally relies on external specialists for studies on the relevant markets. An example is the Cintra case. The Plenary of the Commission had to monitor Cintra's relevant market. The CFC hired the consulting firm Serra & Asociados Internacional (SAI), whose main shareholder is ex-Minister of the Mexican Ministry of Industry and Trade, Jaime Serra Puche. As Minister, Serra oversaw Fernando Sánchez-Ugarte, the CFC President at the time.

[16] The CFC published these criteria in the Official Paper of the Federation (*Diario Oficial de la Federación*) on July 24, 1998. The HHI has values from 0 to 10,000 points and is equal to the sum of the market participation squares. HHI indexes are widely used in economic literature and extensively used by competition authorities around the world. The DI index is an alternative concentration index created by an ex-Commissioner of the Mexican CFC. The DI index captures and measures the size of a company relative to others in a relevant market. Under the DI index criteria, a merger does not necessarily increase the index as in the HHI case. For example, when two small companies merge, the index can actually diminish. For more about the DI Index, see P A García, 'Un enfoque para medir la Concentración Industrial y su Aplicación para el Caso de México' 2/57 *El Trimestre Económico* 317–41 (1990).

b) If the DI index decreases or is less than 2,500 points after the merger, the merger will probably not be contested.

The law indicates that other variables, such as sales, number of clients, production capacity or others, will be taken into consideration, as well as concentration indexes to measure concentration levels. Regulations under the FLEC include other elements to determine if the competition process has been substantially damaged:[17]

a) Present or possible effective competition from imports.
b) Availability of substitutes.
c) Any type of barrier to entry, including financial costs, the required amount for investment, regulatory control of entry, and any impact of the merger on barriers to entry.
d) The related ownership of companies or firms that directly or indirectly participate in relevant or related markets.
e) Previous participation of the merged entity in the relevant or related markets.
f) Evaluation of the possible efficiency gains of the merged company. Efficiency gains include economies of scale and scope, the significant reduction of administrative costs, transfer of technology, and reduction of production or costs coming from infrastructure or distribution web expansion.

Concentration and market power are not the only criteria used to evaluate a merger, but the FLEC and its regulations do not accord the same importance or weight to each additional element relative to the concentration index and market share measurements.

III. CFC Administration from 1993–2004

This section provides a statistical review of CFC cases (mergers, monopolistic practices and privatization, among others) for the period 1993–2004. The first official decisions were issued in the middle of 1993. Table 1 below summarizes the CFC's main activities.

The total number of cases considered by the CFC shows an upward trend in the period 1993–2004, moving from 148 cases in 1993–94 to 1,450 cases in 2003. This is a 980 per cent increase. Graph 3 shows a large number of cases involving mergers, except in the period 2002–04, when concessions, permits, privatizations, etc surpassed mergers by 524 cases.[18]

[17] These elements are not mutually exclusive, neither are they classified by order of importance in the FLEC.

Table 1 Federal Competition Commission: Cases Considered 1993–2004[18]

	June–July			2 Terms								
Case	**93–94**	**94–95**	**95–96**	**1996**	**1997**	**1998**	**1999**	**2000**	**2001**	**2002**	**2003**	**2004**
Total	148	175	250	192	499	513	469	529	603	1399	1450	867
Mergers	57	89	109	71	218	195	245	276	311	260	196	194
Anti-competitive Practices	30	16	27	17	52	50	41	63	64	68	38	41
Consultations	14	31	48	14	49	64	41	39	49	40	44	32
Concessions, permits privatizations, declarations of market power and conditions of competition	34	25	31	78	154	164	101	102	104	784	1122	567
Appeals	13	15	35	12	26	40	41	49	75	247	50	33

Source: Annual Reports of the CFC 1993–2004 and Commemorative Document of the First Decade of the CFC.

[18] The number of these type of cases increased because many of them were 'artificial' in the sense than many were only permanent revisions and notifications to the CFC. For example, in cases such as *Natural Gas* (*Natural Gas* Case CNT-106-2000 and RA-36-2000, Aug 31, 2000) and *Coca-Cola* (*Coca-Cola* Case DE-06-2000, Feb 2, 2000), many issues needed to be revised (concessions and permits) by the CFC, but the root of the problem was the same. The same problem was presented under different concepts and was registered under different cases.

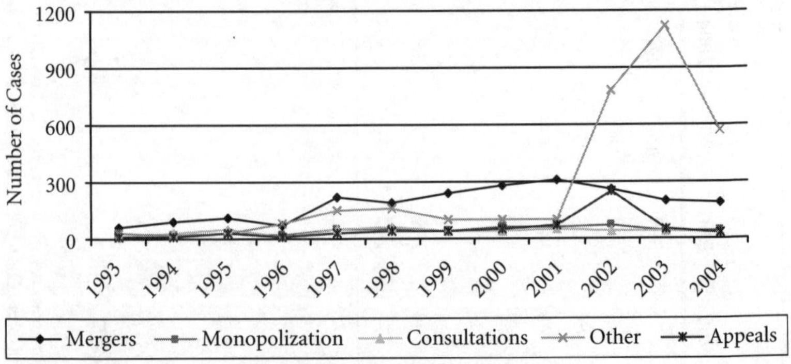

Note: 'Other' refers to concessions, permits, and privatizations, etc.

Source: Based on data from Table 1.

Graph 3 Issues Considered by the CFC 1992–2004

Merger trends can be explained by a number of factors—primarily the restructuring or consolidation of certain industries, economic liberalization, or financial crisis. Investigations of anticompetitive practices have been relatively stable, with an average of 40 cases per year.

According to an OECD report, 20 per cent of the CFC staff analyze regulatory issues, 25 per cent deal with merger and privatization analysis, and 35 per cent with anticompetitive practices.[19] The CFC has financial capacity constraints (for example, from 1994 to 1997 its budget fell 30 per cent in real terms).

A. Monopolistic Practices and Other Restrictions to Competition

Table 2 below illustrates that in CFC's first two years of operation, firms notified it of a large number of anticompetitive practices. The high expectations generated by the creation of the FLEC may explain this. The CFC undertook numerous investigations during that period. The investigations reflect a deliberate policy to legitimate CFC actions. For example, the first investigations that the CFC made were in markets with a strong impact on end consumers, such as credit cards and gasoline stations.[20] It is important to emphasize that the CFC rejected a large number of accusations (65 per cent), which explains why in the first couple of years of existence it focused on investigations. This suggests that many early accusations may have been made by competitors looking to promote their own welfare.

[19] OECD, *Report on Regulatory Reform: Regulatory Reform in Mexico* 2000:25.

[20] CFC Annual Report (1993–94), *Informe Anual de Competencia Económica*, México.

Table 2 Monopolistic Practices and other Restrictions on Competition 1993–2004

	June–July			2 Semester								
Issue	**93–94**	**94–95**	**95–96**	**1996**	**1997**	**1998**	**1999**	**2000**	**2001**	**2002**	**2003**	**2004**
Denunciations	19	6	14	8	25	33	26	55	46	59	33	33
Sanctions and recommendations	4	1	5	0	2	9	3	7	6	20	6	6
Negative resolution of the denunciation	1	1	1	3	1	10	12	33	0	0		
By Article 41 of the FLEC	0	0	0	0	0	1	1	2	2	3	0	3
Closed cases	0	0	2	2	5	2	0	1	17	17	11	9
Other	14	4	6	3	17	11	10	12	21	19	16	15
Oficio investigations	11	10	13	9	27	17	15	8	18	9	5	8
Sanctions and recommendations	6	6	10	2	13	5	6	4	7	3	0	2
By Article 41 of the FLEC	0	0	0	0	0	0	1	0	3	3	0	0
Closed cases	5	4	3	7	14	12	8	4	8	3	5	6
Total	30	16	27	17	52	50	41	63	64	68	38	41
Issue	**1993**	**1994**	**1995**	**1996**	**1997**	**1998**	**1999**	**2000**	**2001**	**2002**	**2003**	**2004**
Denunciations	19	6	14	8	25	33	26	55	46	59	33	33
Oficio investigations	11	10	13	9	27	17	15	8	18	9	5	8
Total	30	16	27	17	52	50	41	63	64	68	38	41

Note: 'Other' includes withdrawn accusations and accusations that do not comply with CFC established criteria.
Source: Annual Reports of the CFC 1993–2004, and Commemorative Document of the First Decade of the CFC.

In the mid-1990s, the number of accusations increased. From 1993 to 2004, the CFC reviewed 507 monopolistic practices cases, of which 357 involved accusations (70 per cent) and 150 were based on operative investigations. It is noteworthy that in 74 per cent of concluded cases, the CFC did not find any violations of the FLEC. Graph 4 shows that operative accusations increased and operative investigations significantly decreased during that period.

Other competition authorities tend not to differentiate between accusations and operative investigations. In the UK, the Monopolies and Mergers Commission (MMC) approaches all cases in the same way, as Davies and Driffield show...[21]

Table 3 shows that the majority of cases have to do with relative monopolistic practices (vertical agreements). More than 70 per cent of them are related to abuse of a dominant position.[22] The emphasis on vertical monopolistic practices investigations shows similarities with investigations in the emerging economies of Eastern Europe. Analyzing the vertical agreements in these transition economies, Fingleton *et al* found that competition authorities take less time defining relevant markets than horizontal agreements.[23]

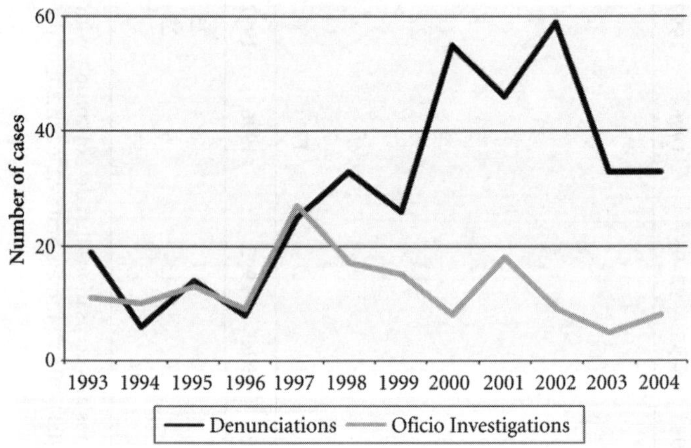

Source: See Table 2.

Graph 4 Monopolistic Practices: Denunciations v Oficio Investigations

[21] S W Davies and N L Driffield, *Monopoly Policy in the UK: Assessing the Evidence* (Cheltenham, Edward Elgar, 1998).

[22] The sample includes 158 decisions made by the CFC regarding anticompetitive practices, included in 10 *Gazettes* (the CFC magazine) in the period 1998–2001 and the Annual Reports of 2003 and 2004. Even though the CFC started to operate formally in the second half of 1993, it was only in the second half of 1998 that it started to publish its decisions officially through the *Gaceta de Competencia Económica* (*The Economic Competition Gazette*) when the FLEC Regulations came into effect. The *Gazette* includes the nature and substance of all CFC decisions.

[23] John Fingleton *et al*, *Competition Policy and the Transformation of Central Europe* (London Centre for Economic Policy Research, 1996).

Table 3 Origin of CFC Decisions and Type of Practices 1998–2004

	Absolute Monopolistic Practices	Relative Monopolistic Practices	Total
Operative	16	21	37
Accusations	17	143	160
Total	33	164	197

Source: Elaborated by the authors based on the *Gacetas de Competencia Económica* (*Economic Competition Gazettes*), Vols 1 to 10, and Annual Reports of the CFC 2002–04.

Table 4 Number of Monopolistic Practices, Decisions and Sanctions 1998–2001

Gazette	Decisions	Sanctions
1	7	5
2	8	2
3	6	2
4	7	1
5	9	1
6	4	2
7	5	2
8	4	2
9	8	2
10	5	3
Total	63	22

Source: Elaborated with data from the *Gaceta de Competencia Económica* (*Economic Competition Gazette*), Vols 1 to 10 in the CFC, 1998–2001.

The majority of horizontal agreements were analyzed through operative investigations rather than following denunciations. Such cases relied on the CFC's capacity to generate its own information. The number of decisions documented by the *Gazette*[24] during the period 1998–2001 was between four and nine, while the number of sanctions was between one and two.

B. Mergers

Table 5 shows that the majority of merger cases come to the attention of the CFC from the notification process. Mergers have been allowed to proceed without any conditions being imposed. In the first 10 years of the CFC's existence, there have only been 18 mergers that have been challenged.

[24] Quarterly publication of the Federal Competition Commission, Mexico.

Table 5 Mergers[25]

	June–July			Half of year							
Issue	**93–94**	**94–95**	**95–96**	**1996**	**1997**	**1998**	**1999**	**2000**	**2001**	**2002**	**2003**
Notifications	n.d.	n.d.	n.d.	n.d.	121	186	188	247	217	219	189
Ex-oficio	n.d.	n.d.	n.d.	n.d.	19	22	10	8	7	1	3
Complaints	n.d.	n.d.	n.d.	n.d.	3	1	1	15	25	9	5
Concluded cases	57	89	109	109	218	195	245	276	311	260	196
Not challenged	52	83	99	99	208	187	220	181	268	238	186
Challenged	0	1	0	0	2	1	3	3	2	2	3
Conditions	5	4	7	7	3	1	6	20	8	5	2
Other	0	1	3	3	5	6	16	72	33	15	5

Source: Annual Reports of the Federal Competition Commission (CFC) 1993–2004 and CFC (2004b).

25 Mergers classified by type of resolution include concluded mergers, desisted mergers , or mergers that did not comply with FLEC criteria.

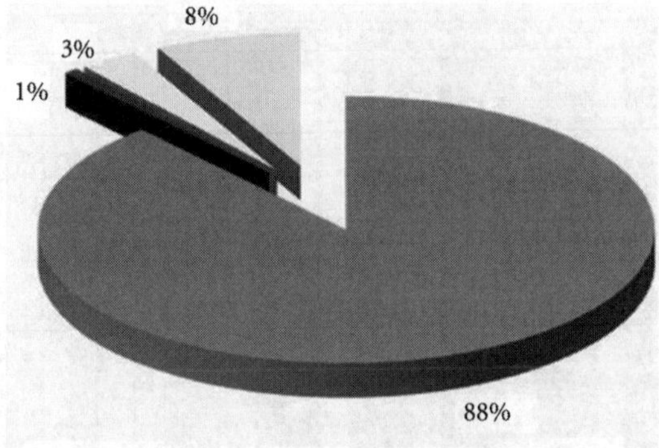

Source: See Table 5.

Graph 5 Distribution by Outcome: 1997–2004

To illustrate the decision pattern of the CFC, Graph 5 shows the range of outcomes. In the period 1993–2004, the CFC challenged 1 per cent of all mergers. Of these, 88 per cent were approved without the imposition of any type of conditions, and 8 per cent were approved with conditions. This decision pattern can be partly explained by the correlation that exists with the threshold levels established by the FLEC. A change would be expected if the threshold levels were increased. The percentages can also be explained by the inconsistencies found in the application of FLEC criteria for the evaluation of mergers.[26]

C. Permits, Concessions, Privatizations and Transfer of Rights

The regulatory framework of various economic sectors requires the endorsement of the CFC so that sector regulators can grant concessions and permits, or authorize their transfer. The issues concerning permits, concessions, privatizations and the transfer of rights reviewed by the CFC are set out in Graph 6. As the graph shows, the pattern of these issues is similar to that applicable to merger distribution (see above). Many of the cases brought before the CFC have generated a favorable opinion without the imposition of any conditions. Graph 6 shows that in the period 1997–2004, only 15 cases were challenged and 17 were subject to conditions.

Graph 7 shows the average value of mergers in constant 1993 prices (pesos). It is interesting to observe that in the period 1997–98, mergers were of little financial value. Starting in 1999, mergers tended to increase in value, reaching an average 1,168 million pesos in the year 2000. The controversial Citigroup Inc/Banamex Accival SA de CV banking merger took place in 2000. In the period 1999–2001, a massive realignment of assets occurred through mergers. The trend decreased after 2001, reaching an average of only 840 million pesos, but it was still higher than the average value for mergers in the period 1997–98.

[26] See section 4.5 of the CFC criteria for evaluating mergers.

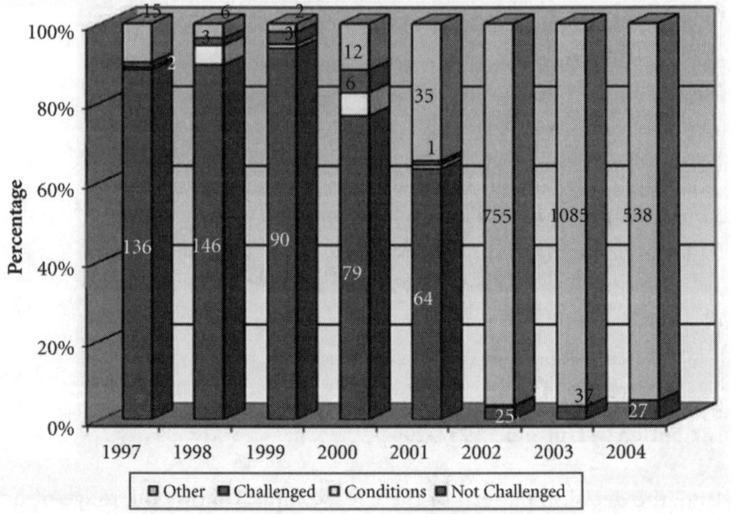

Source: Annual Reports of the Federal Competition Commission 1993–2004 and CFC 2004-b.

Graph 6 Permits, Concessions, Privatizations and Transfer of Rights by Type of Resolution, Mexico 1993–2004

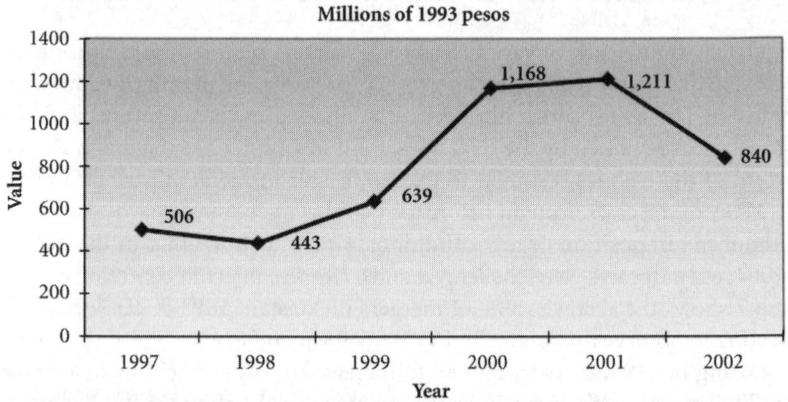

Source: Elaborated by the author based on data from the Annual Reports of the FCFC 1993–2004 and the CFC 2004a. The 2004 Annual Report does not have information regarding the average value of mergers for 2003 and 2004.

Graph 7 Average value of mergers, Mexico 1997–2002

IV. Merger Policy in Mexico 1997–2001

A. Methodology and Database

The objective of the following section is to identify the main elements of the merger competition policy of the CFC in Mexico. Even though a decade has passed since the first merger policies were introduced, this is the first statistical study of the subject. The primary sources of data for this study are official resolutions regarding merger decisions made by the CFC and published in the *Economic Competition Gazette* (*Gaceta de Competencia Económica*), annual reports, and indirect sources such as specialized and general information magazines. The CFC reviewed 881 cases from 1997 to 2001.[27] This study uses only 688 cases, because these are the ones that offered complete information about the entire life cycle of the merger review.

We analyzed each case carefully to extract and classify relevant information. Mergers were classified as 'pure' horizontal mergers or 'administrative' horizontal mergers[28]; and as 'pure' vertical mergers or 'administrative' vertical mergers.[29] Additionally, mergers could be classified as diversified (conglomerate) mergers of three possible types[30]: product extension, diversified in market extension, and pure diversification.[31]

We undertook an analysis of production and service sectors. We applied the merger classifications to be found in the Industrial Classification System for North America (*Sistema de Clasificación Industrial de América del Norte*—SCIAN)

[27] Even though the CFC started to publish its resolutions only from April 1997 onward, an effort was made to build a database for the period 1993–96 which included descriptive characteristics of the merger process and of the companies involved.

[28] Horizontal mergers take place when companies compete for the same market. The potential harm to competition that comes about from this type of merger is the reduction of the number of competitors in the market. However, some of these horizontal mergers can, under certain conditions, increase economic efficiency. A horizontal administrative merger, on the other hand, does not have any effect on the market since it is only an internal company restructuring. See B M S Avalos and N J Melgoza, 'Concentraciones Internacionales y Aplicación de Leyes de Competencia' (2002) *Gaceta de Competencia Económica, Comisión Federal de Competencia* Year 5, 17–51, for more on the subject.

[29] Vertical mergers take place between economic agents that carry out different stages of the production process in the same industry. These operations do not have an impact on the market, even though they can favor relative monopolistic practices. As in the horizontal case, an administrative vertical merger does not have any effect on the market (*ibid*, at 1).

[30] Conglomerate mergers consist of three types. One is the so-called 'product extension' type between companies that make different goods but use similar channels of distribution and marketing, or apply similar productive processes. The second one is the market extension operations type between companies that make the same product but in different geographical markets. Lastly, 'pure' conglomerate mergers exist between companies that have no apparent connection between them, do not participate in related markets, and do not share production technology or distribution systems (*ibid*). Administrative conglomerates, as with all administrative mergers, do not have any repercussion on the relevant market.

[31] The CFC does not establish any classification in its case resolutions.

used by the Mexican Institute of Statistics (INEGI). The SCIAN is the first activities classifier that has been expanded to enable the combined generation and presentation of statistics for Mexico, the United States and Canada.[32] We included a number of qualitative and quantitative variables to capture the factors that determine Mexican merger policy. We arranged variables in two main themes: merger process characteristics, and economic factors the CFC considers when it evaluates factors (that are indicated in official resolutions). The variables reflect the Commission members' criteria. The definition and interpretation of the economic elements are set out in section 3.6. The final data set includes all these variables. We have named this data set the Economic Competition Issues Classifying System in Mexico (*Sistema de Clasificación en Materia de Competencia Económica en México*—SICMAECEM).[33]

B. Behavior Pattern of Mergers in Mexico

As Table 6 shows, merger activity increased in the period 1997–2001. Of total mergers, almost half were 'pure' horizontal mergers (278 cases); and the different types of conglomerate mergers stood out, accounting for 40 per cent of the total (275 cases). Of the conglomerate mergers, pure diversified and market extension mergers were the most dynamic, with 10.9 per cent and 11 per cent shares respectively.

'Administrative' horizontal mergers and vertical mergers were not common in the majority of the cases. Administrative horizontal mergers represented 9.7 per cent of the total 64 cases. These mergers do not have a significant impact on competition policy implementation, since they have no direct effect on the relevant market (they involve only an internal restructuring of the company or group that belongs to the merged company). Pure vertical mergers represented 2.4 per cent of the total, only 16 cases in approximately four years. The administrative vertical mergers were 2.4 per cent more numerous than the pure ones.

Graph 8 shows the pattern of mergers in Mexico from 1997 to 2001. The pattern of horizontal mergers versus vertical mergers is not unique to Mexico. Some annual reports of competition agencies around the world (including those of the United States and the European Union) show a similar pattern. This explains why formal literature on mergers deals only with horizontal mergers, but this tendency has not been well received by competition authority experts. Many of the most complex merger cases deal with vertical mergers or agreements. Economic theory

[32] Classifying mergers with the SCIAN structure has important advantages; if a comparative study is going to be made between Mexico, the United States and Canada, homogeneous information can be generated about mergers at various levels: sector, sub-sectors, and types.

[33] The SICMAECEM is part of a more ambitious project to enlarge the database for other CFC issues, such as monopolistic practices, public biddings, privatizations, etc.

Table 6 Resolutions Made by the Federal Competition Commission by Type of Merger: Mexico, 1997–2001

CFC Resolution	Authorized		Conditioned		Challenged	
	Cases	Percentage	Cases	Percentage	Cases	Percentage
Pure Horizontal	278	42.0	13	76.5	9	100
Administrative Horizontal	64	9.7	0	0.0	0	0
Pure Vertical	16	2.4	0	0.0	0	0
Administrative Vertical	29	4.4	0	0.0	0	0
Pure Diversification	72	10.9	1	0.0	0	0
Administrative Pure Diversification	19	2.9	1	5.9	0	0
Product Extension Diversification	57	8.6	1	5.9	0	0
Administrative Product Extension Diversification	48	7.3	1	5.9	0	0
Market Extension Diversification	73	11.0	1	5.9	0	0
Administrative Market Extension Diversification	6	0.91	0	0.0	0	0
Total Cases	662	100.0	17	100.0	9	100.0

Source: Elaborated by the author with data from SICMAECEM.
Note: In some cases information is incomplete.

must push for more investigation of vertical mergers, and close the gap between competition theory and the application of competition policy.

The CFC did not contest 96 per cent of the cases reviewed; it conditionally approved 2.5 per cent of the cases before it; and it challenged only 1.3 per cent of the cases. Of the 17 conditionally approved cases, 13 concerned horizontal and 4 diversified mergers. Of the challenged mergers, 9 were horizontal.

C. Sector Analysis and Relevant Markets

Analyzing the data in the 688 cases reviewed and classified by sector, 42 per cent concern regulated products controlled through diverse mechanisms by a regulating entity other than the CFC.[34] Table 7 shows the economic sectors with the most

[34] Traditionally, regulating agencies in Mexico control products through price or quantity mechanisms. Other countries are shifting towards regulations that conduct monitoring. For more about

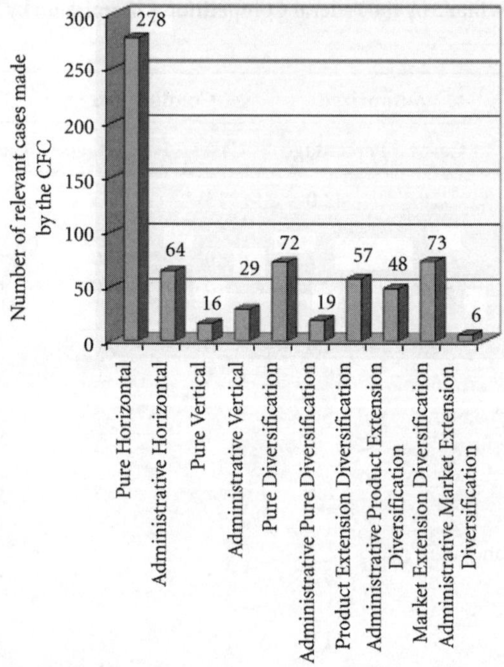

Source: Data from Table 6.

Graph 8 Mergers in Mexico 1997–2001

mergers in the 1997–2001 period. Sectors 31–33 (manufacturing) accounted for 46.7 per cent; sector 51 (financial services and insurance) 13.1 per cent; sector 51 (media) 9.3 per cent; and sector 22 (electricity, water and gas provided to the final consumer) 4.5 per cent. Other sectors saw less merger activity, but are no less relevant: sector 43 (wholesale commerce) 3.1 per cent; sector 46 (retail) 4.1 per cent; and sector 72 (temporary lodgings and food preparation) 4.5 per cent. In the last sectors, as well as in sectors 31–33 (manufacturing), regulated products were not significant.

Sectors that are highly regulated are sector 52 (financial services), sector 51 (real estate services) and sector 22 (electricity, water and gas services), with cases involving regulated products accounting for 88.9 per cent, 81 per cent, and 96.8 per cent of the total cases in each of these sectors, respectively Regulation of these sectors has not always been effective. For Tovar, regulatory and competition policy have been erratic and ineffective in the telecommunications sector

the new theories on competition and regulation policies, see Patrick Rey, Towards a Theory of Competition Policy (2001) *IDEI*, University of Toulouse (unpublished).

Table 7 Regulated Products Participation in Mergers by Sector: Mexico, 1997–2001

	Sector	Merger Frequency by Sector	Frequency by Regulated Products	% of Regulated Cases
11	Agriculture, livestock, gathering, fishing and hunting	5	4	80.0
21	Mining	9	6	66.7
22	Electricity, water and gas provided to end consumer	31	30	96.8
23	Construction	6	3	50.0
31	Foodstuffs, beverages, tobacco, clothing and shoes	5	2	40.0
32	Wood, paper, chemistry and non-metallic chemicals	4	0	0.0
33	Basic metallic industry, metallic products, equipment and machinery, electronics, transportation equipment, furniture manufacturing, and other manufacturing industries	3	0	0.0
31–33	Manufacturing sector	320	71	22.2
43	Wholesale commerce	21	6	28.6
46	Retail	28	2	7.1
48–49	Distribution of Goods	24	16	66.7
51	Media	64	52	81.3
52	Financial services and Insurance	90	80	88.9
53	Real estate services and Rental of Intangible real estate	18	2	11.1
54	Professional, scientific and technical services	15	8	53.3
56	Support services and management and control of remidiation	5	1	20.0
61	Educational services	1	1	100.0
62	Health and social services	2	1	50.0
71	Recreational, cultural and sport services	1	1	100.0
72	Temporary lodging and food preparation	31	3	9.7
81	Other services	2	0	0.0
Total	All economic sectors	685	289	42.2

Source: Elaborated by the author with data from SICMAECEM.

(classified under sector 51).[35] Tovar shows that regulatory responses by both the CFC and the Federal Telecommunications Commission (*Comisión Federal de Telecomunicaciones*—COFETEL) have not modified or altered Telmex's dominant position in fixed telephony.[36] Alberro shows that natural gas price regulation has not aligned prevailing gas prices with competitive environment prices; he contends that the actual prices do not favor the consumer.[37]

There is empirical evidence showing that industry reacts to external shocks through mergers, particularly in the United States. Examples of external shocks are technological innovations, changes in supply (ie oil prices), and deregulation. Andrade and Stafford empirically show that merger activity in the majority of US industries is related to external shocks, particularly deregulation.[38] Mergers in sectors 51 and 52 can be explained by the recent deregulation processes these sectors have experienced.[39] In sector 22 (infrastructure industries) technology changes explain most mergers, as they have experienced limited deregulation activity. Innovations have lowered transportation, communication and administrative costs for companies, thus easing commerce and localization strategies for different geographical locations.[40] Economies of scale and scope have been relevant in this process as well.

Economic sectors where the number of regulated products as well as the number of mergers is low are: sector 32 (wood, paper, chemistry and nonmetallic minerals), sector 33 (basic metallic industry, machinery and equipment, electronic transport equipment, furniture manufacturing, and other manufacturing industries), and sector 53 (real estate services and rentals of real property).

[35] R L Tovar, 'Política de Competencia y Regulación en el Sector Telecomunicaciones' in Comisión Federal de Competencia (ed), *Competencia Económica en México*, 1st edn (México, Editorial Porrúa, 2004).

[36] Tovar uses the 'event analysis' method to prove his hypothesis. The method measures the relationship between a given event and the yield of a certain stock. Tovar proves with statistically significant variables that the implementation of regulatory policies by the CFC and COFETEL is not related to the yield of Telmex stock. *Ibid.*

[37] Alberro argues that the present formula used to fix natural gas prices (the Brito-Rosellon formula, which is the formula that justifies the regulation policy for gas prices) cannot be applied to the inter-temporary maximization problem for which investment and production levels can be determined. The formula does not take into account that PEMEX produces less than under competitive conditions due to the fact that its price is the result of a decision to invest less than it would under competitive conditions. S Alberro, 'Apertura, Competencia y Competitividad del Sector Energético: Electricidad y Gas Natural' in Comisión Federal de Competencia, above n 35.

[38] Andrade and Stafford show that economic sectors that are substantially involved in deregulation processes, such as civil aviation, telecommunications, natural gas, railroads, and banks, were responsible for more than half of the annual average value of total mergers after 1998. G Mitchell Andrade and E Stafford, 'New Evidence and Perspectives on Mergers' 15/2 *Journal of Economics Perspectives* 103–20 (2001). Unfortunately, we cannot follow this line of investigation due to the lack of information regarding the value of transactions. The CFC does not publish the individual value of each merger because it is regarded as confidential information.

[39] The telecommunications and insurance sectors stand out since they have experienced important deregulation processes (laws) in the last couple of years.

[40] The natural gas distribution market shows these characteristics.

Regarding the type of merger, Table 8 below shows that the majority of mergers in these sectors are horizontal. Vertical merger cases stand out only in the manufacturing sector.

It is noteworthy that sectors 22, 43, 46, 51, 52 and 72 have a greater diversity of mergers, where horizontal mergers stand out, as well as pure diversification, market extension and administrative product extension diversification. This shows a clear trend by some companies towards a more dynamic market strategy that increases internal efficiency (see Table 8).

Regarding mergers in relevant markets, the only ones analyzed were those that showed a higher frequency of unchallenged mergers and all conditional or challenged mergers.[41] The most noTable market in terms of mergers approved by the CFC is the credit and savings intermediation service in the financial institutions sector, where 20 cases occurred in sector 303 (see Table 9). Other relevant markets showing high merger activity are sector 348 (pension funds), with 15 approved cases; sector 334 (lodging and connected activities services) with 10; sector 351 (supermarkets and mega markets) with 9 non-challenged mergers; and sector 332 (generation and cogeneration of electric energy services) with 9 approved mergers.

Relevant markets that have obtained conditional resolutions from the CFC are the financial and telecommunication services, as well as two cases in the production, sale, distribution and commercialization of wheat and flour, breads and pastry markets (relevant market 353).

As shown in Table 9, of the mergers challenged by the CFC, half belong to relevant markets in services such as cable restricted television (319), pension funds (348), natural gas distribution in Monterrey and Mexico City (331), and passenger and parcel transportation (2001). The number of challenged mergers (less than 1 per cent of total mergers) is small compared with those of other competition authorities around the world. Countries like the United States and entities like the European Union have made mergers and industrial concentration more difficult under their respective antimonopoly (antitrust) laws. For example, evidence exists that US antitrust policy has made it very difficult for companies to acquire market power.[42] Mexican competition policy has not played a similar role, even though few studies exist to prove the effectiveness of its legislation. Tables 7 and 9 indicate that important concentration levels exist in certain economic sectors and relevant markets.[43]

Table 10 shows the geographical dimension of the relevant market by type of merger. It is noteworthy that horizontal mergers showed a greater market expansion strategy at the national level (60.1 per cent) than at the regional level (22.6 per cent). Only 17.4 per cent of horizontal mergers had an international geographical

[41] The level of desegregation that relevant markets represent is up to the product level. The SICMAECEM database includes the classification of more than 1,000 different markets.

[42] Andrade and Stafford, above n 38.

[43] This can be corroborated using the concentration indexes HHI and DI.

Table 8 Merger of Companies by Sector and by Type of Movement: Mexico, 1997–2001

Type of merger/ sectors	Natural resource explotation	Goods transformation			Manufacturing industries				Distribution of goods		
	Agri-culture, livestock, harvesting, fishing and hunting	Mining	Electric-ity, water and gas provided to the final consumer	Construction	Foodstuff, beverages, tobacco, apparel, and shoes	Wood, paper, chemistry and non-metallic minerals	Basic metallic industry, metallic products, machinery and equipment, electronics, transport equipment, furniture manufacture and other manufacturing industries	Manufacturing sector*	Wholesale commerce	Retail	Goods Distribution
	11	21	22	23	31	32	33	31.33	43	46	48–49
Percentage of the sub-sector in total cases	0.7	1.3	4.5	0.9	0.7	0.6	0.4	46.7	3.1	4.1	3.5
Total cases	5	9	31	6	5	4	3	320	21	28	24
Pure Horizontal	3	5	14	1	1	3	3	140	6	3	11
Administrative Horizontal	1	0	4	1	2	0	0	33	1	4	0
Pure Vertical	0	1	2	0	4	0	0	5	0	2	0

Administrative Vertical	0	0	0	2	0	0	0	15	1	3	1
Pure Diversification	0	1	2	1	0	0	0	37	3	4	3
Administrative Pure Diversification	0	0	1	0	1	1	0	9	1	1	1
Product Extension Diversification	1	0	0	0	0	0	0	33	3	1	1
Administrative Product Extension Diversification	0	1	0	0	1	0	0	22	0	6	1
Market Extension Diversification	0	1	6	1	0	0	0	24	6	4	6
Administrative Market Extension Diversification	0	0	2	0	0	0	0	2	0	0	0

(continued)

Table 8 (Continued)

Type of merger/sectors	**Operations with Information**	**Operation with Assets**		**Professional Services**				**Recreation Services**			
	Information in the media	**Finan-cial and Insurance services**	**Real Estate Services and Rental of Intangible Real Estate**	**Professional, scientific and techni-cal services**	**Business support services and management and control of residual products**	**Education Services**	**Health and Social Services**	**Recre-ational, Cultural and Sports**	**Temporary lodging and food and beverage preparation**	**Other Services**	**Total**
	51	52	53	54	56	61	62	71	72	81	Total
Percentage of the sub-sector in total cases	9.3	13.1	2.6	2.2	0.7	0.1	0.3	0.1	4.5	0.3	100.0
Total cases	64	90	18	15	5	1	2	1	31	2	685
Pure Horizontal	24	53	5	10	2	0	1	0	14	0	299
Administrative Horizontal	7	5	4	0	0	0	0	0	3	0	65
Pure Vertical	3	0	0	1	0	0	0	0	0	0	18
Administrative Vertical	2	1	3	0	0	0	0	0	1	0	29
Pure Diversification	9	4	3	0	0	0	0	1	3	0	71
Administrative Pure Diversification	0	0	2	1	0	0	0	0	2	0	20
Product Extension Diversification	8	4	0	1	1	0	1	0	1	1	56

Administrative Product Extension Diversification	2	17	0	0	0	0	0	0	0	0	50
Market Extension Diversification	7	5	1	2	2	1	0	0	7	1	74
Administrative Market Extension Diversification	1	1	0	0	0	0	0	0	0	0	6

Source: Elaborated by the author with data from SICMAECEM.
Note: includes the following industries: foodstuffs, beverages, tobacco, shoes, apparel, wood and paper, chemical, plastic and rubber, products based on no metallic minerals, basic metallic industries, manufacture of metallic products, machinery and equipment, transport, and other manufacturing industries.

Table 9 Most Dynamic Relevant Markets in Mergers According to CFC Resolutions, 1997–2001

Relevant Market	Approved	Relevant Market	Conditioned	Relevant Market	Objected
303 Intermediation service for savings and credits of financial institutions in national territory	20	302 Jean cotton fabric in its best quality, in every design	1	312 Production and commercialization of tequila in national territory	1
300 Cellular telephony	5	328 Production and commercialization of polyester and other fabrics	1	319 Provisions and sales of cable television service	1
301 Production and commercialization of sugar in national territory	4	347 Distribution and duplication of videocassettes	1	331 Distribution of natural gas in Mexico City and Monterrey	1
302 Jean cotton fabric in its best quality, in every design	2	353 Production, distribution and sales of flour wheat and other mixtures for bread	2	348 Afores and Siefores administration savings for workers who are affiliated with IMSS	1
304 Insurance services for life, accidents and damages	5	361 Provision and sales of restricted satellite television and DHT (direct house television)	1	363 Production and distribution of meat in national territory	1
312 Production and commercialization of tequila in national territory	7	372 Nitrate ammonium fertilizer, diammonium phosphate, triple super phosphate and complex NPK	1	547 Production, distribution and sale of chicken concentrated broth, tomato broth and other soups	1

319 Provisions and sales of cable television service	4	458 Production and commercialization of zippers for clothe, shoes and luggage	1	889 Production transportation and commercialization of carbonated drinks	1
328 Production and commercialization of polyester and other fabrics	5	466 Production, commercialization and distribution of whiskey and vodka	1	2001 Transportation service for passengers and packaging in different routes inside national territory	1
332 Generation and co-generation electric energy in national territory	9	471 Seals with lead-acid storage cells for automotive vehicles	1		
334 Hospitality and activity service	10	502 Production and commercialization of electronic appliances, such as vapor plates	1		
348 Afores and Siefores administration savings for workers who are affiliated with IMSS	15	514 Marine construction for oil infrastructure	1		
351 Mega, hyper and super markets	9	724 Production of conservative vegetables	1		
353 Production, distribution and sales of flour wheat and other mixtures for bread	4	914 Production and commercialization of preventive and nauseous medicines for chemotherapy and radiotherapy, in the treatment to cure cancer in national territory	1		

(continued)

Table 9 (Continued)

Relevant Market	Approved	Relevant Market	Conditioned	Relevant Market	Objected
355 Outdoor publicity service	4	928 Services of the buying bank to the bank issue, transmission of the ATM to the banks system network, the compensation and liquidation of transitions and authorization of transactions	1		
356 Stock market houses service in national territory	4	936 Service of trucking (RMEF) analogical in the band of the 800 MHz in the basic areas of the service (ABS) anticipated by the CO EFETEL in permissions of spectral radio electric	1		
366 Production and fabrication of grills and auto parts	5	946 Service of harvesting, transportation, temporary storage, recycling, thermal treatment and controlled confinement of industrial dangerous or toxics residues in national territory	1		
380 National publicity on TV service (commercial service)	4				
398 Corporate banking	4				

399 Fabrication and Sales of trucks for multiple services, trucks classification 7 and buses in national territory	4
442 Production and Commercialization of wireless national telephony	4
463 Production and development of plastic packages, containers for beverages and food	4
808 Designer, production and distributor of electronic products internationally	4
816 Life insurance	8
817 Insurance service against accidents and diseases	4
834 Mortgage credit service in national territory	5

Source: Own elaboration from the SICMACEM data base.

Table 10 Geographical Dimension of the Relevant Market by Type of Merger: Mexico, 1997–2001

Type of Merger/ Relevant Market	Cases Total	National		Regional		International	
		Cases	Percentage	Cases	Percentage	Cases	Percentage
Horizontal	363	218	60.1	82	22.6	63	17.4
Vertical	45	30	66.7	5	11.1	10	22.2
Diversified*	278	171	61.5	66	23.7	41	14.7
All Cases	686	419	61.1	153	22.3	114	16.6

* Includes various types of diversification.
Source: Elaborated by the author with data from SICMAECEM.

dimension. Vertical mergers were also concentrated at the national level (66.7 per cent), while vertical mergers with international dimensions accounted for 22.2 per cent of the total; the regional dimension for this sector was only 11.1 per cent. Lastly, a large number of diversified mergers were concentrated in relevant markets with national dimensions (61.5 per cent), but the regional market for these sectors was more important than the international sector, with 23.7 per cent and 14.7 per cent respectively.

D. Analysis of Company Characteristics and Strategies

We gathered 685 cases with complete information and analyzed the characteristics of the firms that merged. According to the set of characteristics shown in Table 11, the most frequent are that in 85 per cent of the cases the acquiring company was a multi-product firm, and in 88 per cent of the cases the acquired firm was a multi-product firm. In 61 per cent of the cases, the acquired company was a single product firm, and in 59 per cent the acquiring firm was a single product firm.

The Companies growth patterns can be observed in the type of merger and relevant market. It is useful to analyze the geographic dimensions of the market of the acquiring firm as compared with the geographic dimension of the relevant market following the merger. As Table 12 shows, acquiring firms whose market dimension is regional tend to focus on mergers where the relevant market is also regional, suggesting a regional versus a national strategy. Wal-Mart, Coca-Cola FEMSA, Grupo Carso, Grupo Empresarial Angeles, and Marriot International Inc were among 45 corporate groups that demonstrated this strategy.

If the acquiring firms initially have a national market, they normally prefer a merger strategy that will strengthen only their national presence. Alfa, Molinera de México, Grupo Televicentro, Grupo Nacional Provincial de Pensiones, and Grupo Bimbo were among 165 corporate groups to apply this strategy.

Table 11 Evolution of the Federal Competition Commission by Merger Characteristics: Mexico, 1997–2001

Characteristics reviewed by the CFC	% of cases with characteristics	Frequency of cases	Authorized		Conditioned		Contested	
			Frequency	Percentage	Frequency	Percentage	Frequency	Percentage
If the acquired company is single product producer	14.9	102	95	93.1	5	4.9	2	2.0
If the acquired company is a multi-product firm	85.0	582	563	96.7	12	2.1	7	1.2
If the acquiring firm is single product firm	12.3	84	79	94.0	4	4.8	1	1.2
If the acquiring firm is a multi-product producer	87.7	601	580	96.5	13	2.2	8	1.3
If the acquired firm is a single product firm	60.9	417	405	97.1	10	2.4	2	0.5
If the acquired firm is a multi-product firm	39.1	268	254	94.8	7	2.6	7	2.6
If the acquiring firm is a single product firm	59.6	408	394	96.6	12	2.9	2	0.5
If the acquiring firm is multi-product firm	40.4	276	264	95.7	5	1.8	7	2.5
Cases where a foreign company is participating	73.0	493	477	96.8	11	2.2	5	1.0

Source: Elaborated by the authors with data from SICMAECEM.

Table 12 Geographical Dimension of the Relevant Market of the Merger by the Acquiring Firm's Type of Market: Mexico, 1997–2001

Market Dimension of the acquiring firm	Geographic Dimension of the Relevant Market						
	Cases totals	Regional		National		International	
		Cases	Percentage	Cases	Percentage	Cases	Percentage
Regional	59	45	76.3	12	20.3	2	3.4
National	195	29	14.9	158	81.0	8	4.1
International	425	75	17.6	246	57.9	104	24.5
Total of the acquiring firm	679	149	21.9	416	61.3	114	16.8

Source: Based on data from SICMAECEM.

Companies that have international market dimensions look for mergers in relevant national markets, which indicates their intention to penetrate national markets and strengthen their international relevant markets (see Table 12). Grupo Fertinal, Daw Internacional Inc, Bell Canada International, Dixon, Pearson, and Seagram´s Groups were among 246 corporate groups to have applied this strategy.

E. Evaluation Criteria for Mergers

This section seeks to identify the key quantitative and qualitative criteria which determine the CFC's decision-making regarding the approval, conditional approval, or rejection of a merger.

Numerous studies at the national and international levels have evaluated the implementation of competition policies by various governments. In the United States, a number of studies have focused on the selection process.[44] Coate *et al* found evidence that those political variables, such as the influence of Congress, the weight of FTC decisions, and that these same authorities do not take into account possible efficiency gains when evaluating mergers.[45] The authors also found the lawyers of the FTC have more influence in merger analysis than the economists. In the United Kingdom, probit analysis studies, such as Weir´s evaluation of merger

[44] Richard A Posner, 'A Statistical Study of Antitrust Enforcement' 13 *Journal of Law and Economics* 365–426 (1970); R A Katzmann, 'Federal Trade Commission' in James Q Wilson (ed), *The Politics of Regulation* (New York, Basic Books, 1980); Malcom B Coate *et al*, 'Bureaucracy and Politics in FTC Merger Challenges' 33 *Journal of Law and Economics* 463–83 (1990); Malcom B Coate and Fred S McChesney, 'Empirical Evidence on FTC Enforcement of the Merger Guidelines' 30 *Economic Inquiry* 277–93 (1992).

[45] Above n 44.

decisions by the MMC, are based on criteria established in the 'public interest test' of English competition law.[46] Weir shows that few public interest criteria have any significant impact on the competition authority's decision process. Similarly, Davies *et al* use a probit model to analyze 73 monopolistic practices reviewed by the MMC.[47] Khemani and Shapiro studied mergers in Canada and found that the Canadian Competition Commission has consistently applied the criteria established by the competition authority.[48] Lastly, Bergman *et al* analyzed the European Commission's decisions through a logit model and arrived at similar conclusions to those of Khemani and Shapiro.[49] Until now, no empirical study existed that centered on the decision process of the Mexican competition authority.

F. Investigation Design and Data

The objective of this section is to identify those elements to which the CFC gives most weight in its decisions to approve or to reject a merger. To analyze the criteria used by the CFC in its evaluations, the following questions will be raised:

a) Can the CFC decisions be explained by the elements defined in the FLEC and its regulations?
b) What role do concentration indexes and market participation percentage play in determining the results of an investigation, and are these elements accurate enough?
c) If not market percentage and the concentration indexes, what are the most important elements to the CFC?

To answer these questions we used the probit estimation technique, which we consider the most appropriate since the majority of independent variables are qualitative.[50] The predicted values of the probit models are the probabilities

[46] Charlie Weir, 'Monopolies and Mergers Commission, Merger Reports and the Public Interest: a Probit Analysis' 24 *Applied Economics* 27–34 (1992).

[47] Stephen W Davies *et al*, 'Monopoly in the UK: What Determines Whether the MMC Finds Against the Investigated Firms?' (1999) 47/3 *The Journal of Industrial Economics* 263–83.

[48] R Shaym Khemani and Daniel M Shapiro, 'An Empirical Analysis of Canadian Merger Policy' 41 *The Journal of Industrial Economics* 161–77 (1993).

[49] M Bergman *et al*, 'An Econometric Analysis of the European Commission's Merger Decisions' (2003) *Working Papers Series*, Dept of Economics, Uppsala University.

[50] Preliminary tests were made using the logit model which produced similar results, so this estimation model was no longer pursued. Both the logit and probit models are difficult to distinguish empirically (see D L MacFadden, 'Econometric Analysis of Qualitative Response Models' in Z Griliches and M D Intriligator (eds), *Handbook of Econometrics* (Elsevier Science Publishers, 1984), at 1396–1446. One natural extension of the present study is to try to predict the degree of severity of the sanctions suggested by the CFC. The simple characterization of the CFC's decision process is clearly a simplification, since it varies from continuously reporting the merged company's performance in a relevant market to requiring the disinvestment of important assets. We also estimated an ordered probit model, to vary in ordinal form the degree of severity of the decision. As this approach did not produce any value added to the previous analysis, it was not pursued further.

that the event specifies in the dependent variable[51] that occur in the explicative variables function.[52] We estimated the following model using the formula:

$$Z_i = \beta_1 + \beta_2 X_i$$

Z_i is a non-observed index that represents the decision of the CFC to allow or question a merger; X_i is the explicative variables vector; β is the estimated coefficient estimate.

Z_i indicates the CFC's decision in the following way: when $Y = 1$ it means the merger has been approved, and if $Y = 0$ it indicates that the merger has been questioned. A critical level exists at Z_i^*, such that if Z_i exceeds Z_i^* the CFC approves the merger, while if Z_i^* exceeds Z_i the CFC investigates the merger. Given Z_i^* and assuming that it has a normal distribution, the probability that Z_i^* will be less than or equal to Z_i can be calculated with an accumulative normal probability function:

$$P_i = P_r(Z_i^* \leq Z_i) = F(Z_i) = \frac{1}{\sqrt{2\pi}} \int_{-\infty}^{Z_i} e^{-s^2/2} dS$$

S is a normal standardized variable. The Z_i index is estimated through the inverse of the accumulative normal probability function such that:

$$\begin{aligned} Z_i &= F^{-1}(P_i) \\ &= \beta_1 + \beta_2 X_i \end{aligned}$$

Thus P_i is an estimated value of the conditional probability that the merger will be approved.

A large number of independent variables and models were estimated. The model described was the one that best reflected the CFC decision process, and the one that produced statistically significant results.

The database for this section was constructed from a series of official resolutions (merger decisions) published by the CFC from April 1997 to December 2001. We reviewed a total of 239 cases, which represented the majority of horizontal mergers examined by the CFC during that period.[53] We carefully reviewed each case so that relevant information could be extracted and classified.

We gathered a large number of qualitative and quantitative variables to determine the main factors involved in the CFC's decision-making process. The variables gathered reflect the criteria of CFC analysts. Vector X variables represent analysts'

[51] The dependent variable in this study is permitted or questioned. This last aspect includes cases where mergers have been rejected or conditioned.

[52] G Maddala, *Limited Dependent and Qualitative Variables in Econometrics* (Cambridge, Cambridge University Press, 1983); W H Greene, *Econometric Analysis* (London, Collier Macmillan, 1990), at 662–66.

[53] It is important to mention that the CFC does not keep a complete classification of the different types of mergers for the period analyzed, so we proceeded to classify mergers as horizontal, vertical or conglomerate so that later we could concentrate on the first type of merger.

evaluations, while the final decision for each case (allowed or investigated) is made by the Plenary Session (on the votes of the Commissioners). Table 13 below summarizes the variables used.

The classifications of cases—according to the type of decisions made by the CFC—are also shown in Table 13. The majority of approved mergers (189 out of 239) came without conditions, since the CFC viewed these cases to be those that did not harm the competition process. Only 20 per cent of the mergers were questioned.[54]

The list of explicative variables used, along with their statistical description, is also shown in Table 13. *HHI* and *DI* are the Herfindahl-Hirschman and Dominance Indexes respectively (both measure the degree of concentration after the merger). For 192 cases, the real values of the indexes were not included in the official resolutions, but it was indicated whether the values of the indexes exceeded or did not exceed the thresholds established by the Commission.

To solve this problem in part, hypothetical indexes were calculated with the available information. The *HHI* was included with an average index of 999.5 when the Commission determined that the index was less than 2,000 points (190 cases), while the *HHI* was captured with an average index of 6,000 points when the Commission determined that the index was equal to or greater than 2,000 points (48 cases).[55] In a similar manner, the *DI* registered an average of 1,249.5 when the Commission determined that the value of the index was less than 2,500 points (181 cases), while the *DI* captured was an average of 6,250 when the Commission determined that the value of the index was equal to or greater than 2,500 points (57 cases).

MKT1 and *MKT2* represent market participation resulting from the merger; 25 per cent and 50 per cent were used as critical levels when the dummy variables were constructed from market participation, since a market participation level greater than 50 per cent shows an economic agent has substantial power in the relevant market. A market participation of less than 25 per cent shows the firm has no substantial market power.[56] These variables together with the concentration indexes (*HHI* and *DI*) are used as market structure measures.

Even though the FLEC specifies that concentration levels and market considerations can be taken into account when making decisions, the merger criteria included in the Regulation do not establish classifications for market share, although both are discussed in CFC resolutions.[57]

[54] Forty of these cases were made subject to conditions, while only 10 were rejected.

[55] Index values can also be expressed in decimals (dividing the value by 10,000), so that the value of the index fluctuates between 0 and 1, where 0 indicates a perfect competition scenario and 1 indicates a monopoly.

[56] K Carlsson *et al*, *Konkurrenslagen. en kommentar* (Estocolmo, Norstedts, 1999), at 234–35.

[57] CFC resolutions for some cases include estimates of market participations of merged firms. FLEC makes reference to sale indicators, number of clients and productive capacity; and any element that the Commission considers appropriate may be considered for market participation calculations (see Art 10 of the General Rules for the Relevant Market and Substantial Power Analysis—Regulation of the FLEC (*Reglas Generales para el Análisis del Mercado Relevante y Poder Sustancial*).

Table 13 Definition of Variables and Statistical Description

Decision	Approved	Investigated
Number	189	50
Percentage	79.07	20.92

Explicative variables a ($N = 239$)

		Median	Standard Deviation
HHI:	Herfindahl-Hirschman Index	0.182648	0.175774
DI:	Dominance Index	0.230979	0.205587
Binary dummy variables take the value of 1 when the variable presents itself.			
Variables explicitly presented in the merger criteria in the FLEC and its Regulation			
HIST:	Previous Participation in the Relevant Market	0.058577	0.235325
RELA:	Patrimonial Relationship	0.033473	0.180245
EF:	Efficiency Gains	0.033473	0.180245
IMP:	Import Competition	0.225941	0.419078
EB:	Barriers to Entry	0.255230	0.464862
Variables not included in the FLEC and its regulation			
MKT1:	Combined Market Participation greater than 25% or less than 25%	0.594142	0.492088
MKT2:	Combined Market Participation greater than 50% or less than 50%	0.158996	0.366440
EXT:	Foreign Company Present	0.828452	0.409788

Note: All explicative variables are defined based on the relevant market, which can be local, regional or national.

The remaining variables represent diverse elements that are specified by the FLEC or have been used in cases by the Commission. These variables are qualitative and, when derived from the information, are included in the resolutions. If the resolutions indicated that the variable was present in the decision process and relevant, it was codified with the value of 1. The *HIST*, *RELA*, *EF*, *IMP*, and *EB* variables are elements listed in the FLEC and in the criteria in the regulation of the law.[58] *HIST* indicates whether the company created after the merger had previously operated in the relevant market. *RELA* captures the patrimonial relationship between the firms involved in the merger, or other firms that participate

[58] Together with *HHI* and *DI*; *HIST* and *RELA* are explicitly listed in the Official Newspaper of the Nation (*Diario Oficial de la Federación*, July 24, 1998).

directly or indirectly in the relevant market or other related markets.[59] *EF* captures the level of efficiency gains that result from the merger. The criteria regarding mergers in the FLEC and its Regulation establish that efficiency gains generated through a merger are a relevant and favorable element for firms in the decision process. If no efficiency gains are found, the merger may be rejected.[60] *IMP* reflects the Commission's perception concerning import competition. *EB* indicates whether the Commission perceives that the barriers to entry are high in the relevant market. Quantitative measures concerning barriers to entry are not provided in the resolutions; therefore, the variable was registered with the simple criterion of whether the Commission perceives that barriers to entry exist or do not exist. The last variables, *EXT* together with *MKT1* and *MKT2*, represent the 'other variables' that were mentioned with a certain degree of regularity in the resolutions but are not explicitly established in the FLEC or its Regulation. *EXT* indicates whether at least one foreign company participated in the merger.

1. *Results*

It would be expected that the weight the CFC assigns to each element would be consistent with the FLEC and with Industrial Organization theory. For example, high levels of concentration (*HHI, DI)* and of barriers to entry (*BE*) should increase the probability that the Commission would question the merger, while the presence of import competition (*IMP*) or efficiency gains (*EF*) would reduce it.

Table 14 offers estimates for four alternative specifications using the variables previously described. Regression (1) only includes elements explicitly established in the FLEC and its Regulations (except the *DI* variable). The regression has been estimated excluding the *DI* variable, since a high correlation exists with the *HHI* variable. Introducing the *DI* variable instead of the *HHI* in the restrictive model generates the same effect over the other variables' coefficients (in general terms), but the probability of approving a merger is statistically more significant in the case of the *HHI* index (-1.7 significant at a 1 per cent level) than the *DI* index (-1.3, significant at a 5 per cent level). This result reflects a possible trend in the application of merger policy by the Commission. Even though the implementation of both concentration indexes have different objectives for the Commission, in reality (or in practice) the Commission tends to give more importance to the *HHI* index.[61]

[59] Regressions were estimated considering the variable denominated *IND*, which indicates whether the economic agent that comes about after the merger has or has had a dominant position in other related relevant markets. The coefficients were not robust when these new variables were introduced and it was highly correlated with the *RELA* variable.

[60] The FLEC established that possible levels of efficiency gains must be acknowledged by the firms involved in the transaction.

[61] The *HHI* indicates that the dominant position of a firm depends on its size relevant to its market participation, while the *DI* index reflects the size of the company relative to the rest of the companies in the market.

Table 14 Results*

Variable *dependent: Allowed*	Coefficient Estimates 1	2	3	4
C	1.368	1.345	0.853	0.789
	(8.520)***	(6.936)***	(3.451)***	(3.019)***
HHI	−1.773		−1.837	
	(−3.860)***		(−2.913)***	
HIST	−0.123	−0.188	−0.162	−0.259
	(−0.288)	(−0.415)	(0.371)	(−0.553)
RELA	−1.247	−1.414	−1.041	−1.208
	(−1.942)**	(−2.261)**	(−1.631)*	(−1.931)**
EF	−0.669	−0.997	−0.704	−0.611
	(−1.195)	(−0.997)	(−1.206)	(−1.093)
IMP	0.3382	0.3670	0.386	0.452
	(1.334)*	(1.432)*	(1.475)*	(1.691)**
EB	−0.427	−0.339	−0.379	−0.280
	(−2.041)**	(−1.573)*	(−1.760)**	(−1.261)
MKT1		−0.331		−0.472
		(−1.376)*		(−1.872)**
MKT2		−0.964		−0.978
		(−3.468)***		(−3.425)***
EXT			0.645	0.786
			(2.652)***	(3.077)***
Log Likelihood	−98.90	−96.10	−95.4	−91.3
χ^2	47.35***	52.949***	54.3***	62.5***
McFadden R^2	0.193	0.215	0.221	0.254
% correction level	84.94	85.36	84.52	85.36

Note: The t-values of each variable are shown in parentheses.
* Indicates that the value is statistically significant at a 10% level;
** at a 5% level; and
*** at a 1% level.

As can be seen in Table 14, regression (1) establishes that only three elements presented statistically significant coefficients at conventional levels. The negative variables that were significant (increasing the probability that mergers were questioned) were *HHI* (at a 1 per cent level), *RELA* (at a 5 per cent level) and *EB* (at a 5 per cent level). As was expected, the *IMP* variable had a positive sign but was significant at a 10 per cent level. The *HIST* and *EF* variables were not significant at conventional levels, so they had no relevance in merger decisions made by the Commission.[62] The equation shows a significant prediction rate, greater than 84 per cent in 239 cases.[63]

Regression (2) examines the effect of the market structure introducing the market participation variables (*MKT1* and *MKT2*) in place of the *HHI* variable. The inclusion of these variables had a minimum effect over the coefficients of the other variables. *RELA*, *IMP*, and *EB* remain statistically significant, but the last variable, *EB*, reduces its level of significance to only 10 per cent. Both variables, *MKT1* and *MKT2*, keep a statistically significant negative influence over the probability that the merger will be approved. The first of these variables, *MKT1*, registers a statistically significant level of only 10 per cent, while the second one, *MKT2*, reaches a significance level of 5 per cent, but has slightly less influence than the *HHI* index in the probability that the decision would be to approve the merger. This result shows that the Commission tends to give the same weight to market participation and the *HHI* index. The equation shows a better performance in terms of prediction, because it is greater than 85 per cent in 239 cases.

It is interesting to watch the effect of market share over the *HIST* variable. For example, one could speculate that the change in sign in the *HIST* variable, once the *MKT2* and *MKT1* variables have been included in the equation, is due to the fact that the Commission is very worried about the previous market share of the firms when the participation is very large.[64]

Regressions (3) and (4) also include certain variables that are not explicitly considered in CFC criteria for merger decisions, as is the case of the *EXT* variable. The main result in regression (3) is that the new variable *EXT* has a significant positive effect in the probability that the merger will be approved, at the 1 per cent level. Its inclusion produces generally trivial effects on the rest of the variables; *HHI* and *IMP* remain the same, at the same level of significance. However, even though *RELA* and *EB* remain statistically significant, the first variable reduces its level of significance to just 10 per cent, while the second variable increases its level of significance to 5 per cent. The equation registers a prediction rate greater than 84 per cent.

Equation (3) can be used to predict the probability that the CFC will approve the merger. The equation suggests that when the *HIST*, *RELA*, *IMP*, *EB*, and *EXT* variables are present, the level of the accepTable *HHI* index that allows a

[62] It could be expected that the *HHI* and *EB* variables would show a certain level of correlation, so the same regression was estimated excluding the *HHI* variable. The model was not improved in specification terms, neither did it generate greater changes in the coefficients compared with the regression (1) results.

[63] All signs are 'correct' (except for the *EF* variable, which was not significant). Standard errors and t-values are interpreted in the usual manner.

[64] Nevertheless, no evidence was found of this experiment when the variables were interacted. Due to the lack of significance levels in the *HIST* and other variables, this line of investigation was not followed.

50 per cent probability that the CFC will approve the merger is 1,643 points. But when these variables are not present, the model predicts 4,643 points. The model also predicts that when all the above-mentioned elements are present, the level for the *HHI* index required for the approval of the merger to have an 80 per cent probability is 1,241 points. But when the elements are not present, the allowed level of the *HHI* index for the merger to have an 80 per cent probability of being approved is 2,738 points.

Equation (3) shows a possible inconsistency in the deliberation process of the CFC. Relatively few established elements in merger criteria have an influence on CFC decisions, while some variables that are not explicitly stated in the criteria have a significant impact on the CFC decisions.

Equation (4) replaces *HHI* with *MKT1* and *MKT2* variables as concentration measures. As previously shown in other regressions, the introduction of the *EXT* variable has a positive effect over the *IMP* variable, which becomes more significant. The change in the significance level of the variable *IMP* when the *EXT* variable is introduced shows that for the Commission, the presence of foreign firms (if the *IMP* variable is present) is irrelevant in its merger decision-making. Evidence of this was found in the interactive form of the *EXT* and *IMP* variables in equation (4).[65] Even though the interactive form of the *EXT** and *IMP* variables was positive and significant at a 10 per cent level, the significant statistical level of the rest of the variables was the same, with a prediction rate of 85.3 per cent in 239 of the cases.[66]

2. *Other Experiments*

We experimented with other regressions (besides the ones presented in Table 14 above) but in two different directions.

Interactive Form of the Explicative Variable ***IMP*** and the ***HHI***

We suggest an alternative form of specification for the econometric model. In this model we include the levels of perception in the CFC merger decision, which involves considering jointly the *IMP* and *HHI* variables. High levels of the *HHI* index do not worry the CFC if the import competition is intense. Low levels of import competition together with lower *HHI* index values do not decrease the probability that a merger will be approved. It is important to demonstrate whether these arguments have influenced the Commission's decisions. We have again calculated equation (1), but we have included the interaction of the *HHI* variable multiplied by the *IMP* variable.

[65] Several cases exist showing that the presence of import competition (*IMP*) and of a foreign company in the merger (*EXT*) are crucial elements even when the value of the indices surpasses allowed limits. This was the case in the *AXA SA de CV/Arosa, SA DE CV (Unilever NV)* merger.

[66] We repeated the same exercise in regression (3), but introduced the *HHI* variable instead of the market participation variables *MKT1* and *MKT2*. We obtained the same statistical results with a prediction rate above 83%.

Equation (5) in Table 15 below includes the interactive variable. The statistical instrument known as the *Wald Test* rejects the possibility that these variables could be correlated. The constant term, the interactive variable, *EB* and *HHI* are statistically significant at a 1 per cent level, while the *IMP* variable remains significant at a 10 per cent level. The *EF* variable, like in the previous regressions, is not significant. The R2 and the level of prediction are similar to the ones shown in Table 14 above.

Equation (5) suggests that in cases where only the *IMP*, *HIST*, and *EB* variables are present, the tolerable level for the *HHI* index to ensure the 60 per cent

Table 15 Additional Experiments*

	Coefficients	Estimates
Variable	5	6
Dependent: allowed		
C	1.606	0.782
	(9.178)***	(3.00)***
HHI	−2.648	
	(−5.178)***	
HIST	−0.412	−0.412
	(−0.930)	(0.930)
EF	−0.653	−0.681
	(−1.136)	(−1.249)
IMP	0.503	0.417
	(−1.447)*	(1.591)*
EB	−0.569	−0.318
	(−2.810)***	(−1.469)*
IMP*HHI	3.034	
	(2.777)***	
MKT1		−0.495
		(−1.951)**
MKT2		−0.984
		(−3.452)***
EXT		0.855
		(3.348)***
COLLU		−1.445
		(2.144)**
Log Likelihood	−96.9	−90.7
χ^2	51.2***	63.7***
Mc Fadden R^2	0.208	0.259
% correct predictions	83.68	84.94

Note: T-values are shown in parentheses.
* Indicates statistical significant at a 10% level,
** At a 5% level and
*** At a 1% level.

probability that a merger will be approved has to be 4,615 points.[67] The probability increases to 70 per cent when the *HHI* index level reaches 6,666 points.

Collusive Practices

Normally, collusive practices represent a relevant element in CFC decisions. Equation (6) in Table 15 above shows the effect of this variable (*COLLU*), including it in equation (4). To be able to identify the relative importance of collusive practices in the CFC's decision process, we have excluded the *RELA* variable because it is highly correlated with the *COLLU* variable. As seen in the results, the *COLLU* variable shows the adequate sign and reduces the possibility of a merger approval by the CFC (the coefficient is statistically significant at a 5 per cent level). In general, its inclusion has minimum effects on the coefficients of the *HIST*; *EF* remains insignificant; *IMP*, *EXT*, *MKT1*, and *MKT2* remain significant; and the *EB* variable is significant, but only at a 10 per cent level.[68] Apparently the presence of collusive practices leads the CFC to give more weight to market participation and barriers to entry in its decisions than other variables.

3. *Investigation Conclusions*

The results shown in the probit model suggest that few economic elements (included in the FLEC and its Regulation) have a decisive effect in the evaluation of mergers by the CFC. Only three variables seem to have a significant impact on the results of the evaluations: *HHI*, *EB*, and *RELA*. It was also found that the competition authority considers interactive forms between the variables (for example, the interaction between the *HHI* and *IMP* variables). The logic of this interaction is that significance levels of *HHI* are not sufficient evidence of a lack of competition if there is an open market for imports (measured by the *IMP* variable).

Efficiency gains seem to play an insignificant role in the merger decision process. Even though the CFC acknowledges that mergers improve economic efficiency, it seems efficiency gains do not weigh enough to counterbalance other variables. However, in countries like Canada, the fact that a merger generates efficiency gains (eg, through the reduction of marginal costs) will determine its approval without taking into consideration the concentration levels that it will create. The *EXT* variable, on the other hand, has a significant effect over CFC decisions, even though it does not appear explicitly in the merger evaluation criteria.

[67] This value is above the indices established by the CFC. Many cases exist where the import competition element was crucial in spite of the *HHI* and *DI* index values; eg, the case of the merger between Grupo Industrial Durango, SA de CV/Amcor Paper US, Inc.

[68] In performance terms this equation is not better than equation (4), even though a prediction rate of 84.9% is appreciated in these types of models.

V. Conclusions

This chapter has analyzed Mexico's present competition policy. We conclude that the country has developed adequate institutions and tools to promote competition, that take into consideration the importance of competition conditions in economic development. Even though many legal, institutional and implementation obstacles remain in the path of combating monopolies effectively in Mexico, the Mexican experience offers a relevant reference point for other developing countries for the development of their own competition laws and institutions.

Investigations of monopolistic practices must be improved. There is an immediate need to create an adequate monitoring system for information generation and gathering. The CFC must undertake a proactive rather than a reactive implementation policy regarding monopolistic practices.

Empirical evidence shows that a great number of mergers have clustered merger activity in the utility industries, telecommunications, electricity, water, and gas distribution, and in sectors such as finance, manufacturing, goods distribution, temporary lodging, and beverage/foodstuff preparation. Relevant markets with high levels of concentration were banking, the production and marketing of tequila, hospitality and related service activities, pension funds, various insurance services, electric generation and cogeneration services, and supermarkets.

Little is known about the evaluation criteria and the weight given to each variable in the decision processes of the competition authority. In the present study, we argue that the CFC decision process can be explained by a probit model. The results of the model indicate that few of the merger criteria included in the FLEC and its Regulations influence the competition authority's decision. Only three variables seem to have a statistically significant impact: the HHI, barriers to entry, and patrimonial relationships.

Evidence also was found that the Commission takes into account interactive forms between variables. One such form is the interaction between the HHI variables and the level of import competition, which has a significant positive impact on the probability that a merger will be approved by the CFC. The logic behind the combination of these variables is that a high level of the HHI index is not enough evidence of a lack of competition if the market for imports is open. The efficiency gains criterion, which is positive in mergers, seems to have an insignificant role in CFC decisions. Even though the CFC recognizes mergers that improve economic efficiency, it does not seem consistently to benefit those firms that wish to merge, as the CFC does not have an adequate methodology to quantify future efficiency gains. It is more surprising to find that certain elements (foreign company presence for example) that do not appear explicitly in merger criteria have a more significant statistical effect on the Commission's decisions.

Although Mexico's criteria for merger control state that the HHI and the DI are used as market structure measurements, our empirical results show that the

Commission prefers to use the HHI as a measure of market power. While merger criteria state that market participation is used to measure market structure, the criteria do not establish classifications for these structures. The results indicate that participation levels do have a significant impact on CFC decisions.

Nevertheless, no evidence exists that high levels of the HHI or market participation are a problem for companies that wish to merge. Mergers that surpassed the thresholds established for this index by the Commission had a higher probability of being approved. In most of these cases the import competition variable was the counterweight considered by the CFC when it approved these mergers, even though high levels of concentration were present. This indicates that the CFC is no longer using primarily the HHI in its competition problem analysis.

The study has shown the importance to countries like Mexico of having an international dimension of competition policy. Even though various countries have laws that authorize certain measures against the extraterritorial effects of mergers, many lack coherent criteria and cooperation channels. Globalization of economic activities will increase. This trend will require greater coordination between competition authorities around the world through work groups in international organizations such as the World Trade Organization and the International Competition Network. We expect that in the coming years, corrections will be made in the legal framework to prevent the anticompetitive transnational effects of international mergers. International cooperation models at the bilateral level (such as trade agreements) are important to develop prevention mechanisms between countries. Mexico's trade agreements with several countries, especially the United States and Canada under NAFTA, have increased cooperation, information exchange and modernization, all of which have improved the CFC's performance.

It is difficult to determine whether international mergers have benefited the Latin American region. We lack adequate microeconomic studies that measure the impact on social welfare. Nevertheless, the recent phenomenon of high concentration of foreign firms in the various economic sectors of the Latin American region is a serious issue that should be discussed in different forums. Foreign company presence should be included in the design and implementation of competition policies, especially in OECD member countries.

Chapter V

The Argentine Competition Law and its Enforcement

GERMÁN COLOMA*

I. Introduction

The aim of this chapter is to analyze the basic characteristics of Argentine competition law and its enforcement through the years. First, a short historical note is included, examining the different competition rules that have existed in Argentina since 1933, ending with the enactment of the current legislation (Act No 25,156, approved by the Argentine Congress in 1999).[1] The second section of the chapter contains an analysis of the main features of the current Argentine antitrust system, and its similarities to and differences from the schemes that exist in other countries (especially the United States and the countries belonging to the European Union).

The rest of the chapter contains a review of the main Argentine antitrust cases. There are sections on collusive practices, horizontal exclusionary practices, vertical restraints, and exploitative abuses of dominant position. Lastly, the chapter analyzes several merger cases, both horizontal and vertical, followed by a final section that summarizes Argentine antitrust and develops conclusions.

II. Historical Overview

Antitrust legislation took shape in Argentina in 1933 when the Argentine Congress approved Act No 11,210. United States antitrust law inspired the provisions of the Argentine law, since the two first articles of Act No 11,210 were virtually a translation of Sections 1 and 2 of the Sherman Act.[2] Additionally, the Act contained the enumeration of a series of 'monopoly practices', which were, in

* Professor of Economics, CEMA University.

[1] See the Appendix to this chapter for selected extracts from the Act.

[2] US Sherman Act, 15 USCS §§ 1 et seq.

general, interpreted by Argentine doctrine that had to be included in the general principles established in the first two articles of the Act.

Act 11,210 was replaced by Act 12,906 in 1946. Article 1 of this new Act prohibited practices tending to create or maintain monopolies, while Article 2 included a list of actions that were considered to be special monopoly practices. The interpretation of these provisions was that such practices could be forbidden, although they were not expressly included in Article 1, since many of the so-called 'special monopoly practices' referred to excluded concerted collusive practices not part of the general concept of monopolization. Like its predecessor, Act 12,906 was considered part of the Argentine criminal law, although it established the need to follow an initial administrative procedure under the authority of the Department of Commerce of Argentina. To apply penalties, however, the Secretary of Commerce had to present a claim before the judicial authorities, who ultimately decided antitrust matters.

Both Act 11,210 and Act 12,906 received sparse enforcement, and Argentine case law tracked only four cases that resulted in penalties for breach of these two enactments over a period of 48 years.[3] It was probably because of the lack of enforcement that, in 1980, Congress enacted a new competition law, Act No 22,262, also called the 'Competition Defense Act'.[4] That statute created the first specific antitrust agency in Argentina, which was the National Commission for the Defense of Competition (CNDC). It also implied a movement towards rules that were analogous to European standards, since Articles 1 and 2 of Act 22,262 were clearly inspired by Articles 85 and 86 of the Treaty of Rome (Articles 81 and 82 of the revised Treaty).[5]

With the adoption of the provisions of Act 22,262, Argentine antitrust case law began to evolve, becoming more succinct and coherent. This was largely because the procedures established by the Act were strictly administrative; all the antitrust cases passed before the CNDC. This helped to develop some homogeneous criteria about which practices were anticompetitive and which practices were not. In many ways, those criteria were also compatible with the main international antitrust norms. Decisions made by the CNDC, however, were not enough to resolve antitrust cases. In fact, they were mere opinions that had to be endorsed by the Secretary of Commerce, the true enforcing authority of the Competition Act. During the years of the application of Act 22,262, however, the CNDC's opinions were always endorsed by the Secretary. In fact, there was a complete convergence between the CNDC's opinions and the corresponding decisions of the Secretary of Commerce.

[3] This information appears in Guillermo Cabanellas, *Derecho Antimonopólico y de Defensa de la Competencia* (*Antitrust and Competition Defense Law*), 2nd edn (Buenos Aires, Heliasta, 2005), ch 1.

[4] Argentina's Competition Defense Act of 1980—*Boletin Oficial* del 06-ago-1980, #24474 http://infoleg.mecon.gov.ar/infolegInternet/verNorma.do?id=32636.

[5] Treaty of Rome Treaty Establishing the European Economic Community, 25 March 1957, 298 UNTS 259.

In August 1999, Congress replaced Act No 22,262 with Act No 25,156 as the Argentine competition law.[6] This new statute retained most of the substantive characteristics of its predecessor, especially in the characterization of anticompetitive practices. Dominant Argentine antitrust doctrine, therefore, considers that the case law developed between 1980 and 1999 remains valid. The most important innovation introduced by Act 25,156, however, was the development of a merger notification system. Under this system, the competition authority reviews significant mergers and acquisitions that affect Argentine markets.

Act 25,156 also created a new antitrust agency, the National Court for the Defense of Competition (TNDC). This court was designed to replace the CNDC and to become the only Argentine antitrust agency, with both prosecutorial and adjudicative powers. The main difference between the CNDC and the TNDC is that TNDC decisions do not have to be endorsed by the Secretary of Commerce; this allows for more agency discretion. At the beginning of 2007, however, the necessary organization and infrastructure of the TNDC were still pending. All antitrust cases decided under Act 25,156 have, therefore, been analyzed under the old competition act procedures, involving CNDC opinions endorsed by the Secretary of Commerce.[7] While Act 25,156 and the adoption of the TNDC ensure substantive development of Argentine competition law, the infrastructure and procedural elements have not developed as quickly.

III. Characteristics of the Argentine Competition Law

The Argentine competition law follows the basic antitrust standards set by Articles 81 and 82 of the revised Treaty of Rome. Because of this European influence, the two main offenses under the Argentine competition law are the lessening of competition and the abuse of a dominant position (Article 1, Act 25,156). However, as Cabanellas mentions, the way in which the Argentine Competition Act defines these two offenses allows for some overlap between them.[8] Unlike European Union law, Argentine competition law does not require that the anticompetitive practices that fall under the concept of 'lessening of competition' are concerted practices between two or more economic agents. Therefore, it is possible that a unilateral anticompetitive practice (eg, an exclusionary practice such as predatory

[6] See Appendix to this chapter.

[7] In fact, the secretary in charge of enforcing the Competition Act has changed throughout the years. In the period 1996–99, for example, the CNDC depended on the Secretary of Commerce, Industry and Mining. Between the years 2000 and 2003, it depended on the Secretary of Competition Defense, while in the period 2003–06 the official in charge was the Secretary of Technical Coordination.

[8] Cabanellas, above n 3, vol 2, pp 179–81.

pricing or entry deterrence) may be considered both a lessening of competition and an abuse of a dominant position.

Another requirement that Act No 25,156 includes in its Article 1 is that, in order to be illegal, anticompetitive practices must generate 'damage to the general economic interest'. This concept, which is not directly defined by the Act, has been interpreted by the CNDC and the Argentine courts in different ways. The most widespread interpretation has associated it with the economic concept of 'total welfare'—that is, with the sum of the consumers' surplus and the producers' profit generated in a market.[9] This idea implies that, in order to be illegal, a business practice must be both anticompetitive (in the sense that it implies a lessening of competition or an abuse of dominance) and inefficient (in the sense that it results in a reduction in the economic surplus generated in the relevant market). The concept of general economic interest is also opposed to the concept of private interest, emphasizing the idea that an anticompetitive practice has to affect the market as a whole, not just the distribution of a given surplus between buyers and sellers.

Article 2 of the current Argentine Competition Act contains a list of 14 different types of anticompetitive practices. This list is not exclusive, however, in the sense that other practices can be considered illegal if they fall within the general definition of Article 1. Similarly, a business practice that falls within any of the types enumerated in Article 2 is not considered illegal if it does not comply with the general definition of Article 1 (that is, if it does not imply the lessening of competition or abuse of a dominant position, or does not generate damage to the general economic interest). The Argentine antitrust law, therefore, does not list any anticompetitive practice that is considered illegal per se, and all the offenses to the competition rules must be analyzed under a rule of reason that requires a showing of damage to the general economic interest.

Although the Argentine Competition Act does not define what an abuse of a dominant position is, Article 4 does contain a definition of a dominant position. Under that definition, a person enjoys a dominant position when he or she:

> is the only supplier or buyer in the … market or … when, without being the only one, he or she is not exposed to substantial competition or when, because of the vertical or horizontal degree of integration, he or she is able to determine the economic feasibility of a competitor or participant in the market.[10]

9 That interpretation appears in a document issued by the CNDC, 'Breve análisis económico de la ley argentina de defensa de la competencia' (Brief Economic Analysis of the Argentine Competition Defense Act) (Buenos Aires, Department of Commerce, Industry and Mining, 1997), and it has also appeared in several decisions of the Argentine Court of Appeals on Criminal Economic Matters. In some circumstances, however, the CNDC's interpretation of the concept of general economic interest has also associated it with the consumers' surplus alone. This is particularly true for several merger cases analyzed in recent years.

10 See Appendix to this chapter.

In order to establish whether that standard is fulfilled by a certain undertaking in a specific case, Article 5 of Act No 25,156 establishes that there are three circumstances to be considered:

a) the extent to which the relevant goods or services may be replaced by other goods or services;
b) the extent to which regulatory restrictions limit the access of products or suppliers or buyers to the relevant market; and
c) the extent to which a firm has the power unilaterally to affect prices or to restrict the supply or demand in the market (and the extent to which its competitors are able to offset that power).

Following the European antitrust tradition, the Argentine competition authorities consider abuses of dominant position to be either exclusionary or exploitative.[11] In cases of exclusionary abuses of dominant position, the anticompetitive behavior punishable by law is the use of a dominant position to exclude competitors (either actual or potential). In cases of exploitative abuses of dominant position, conversely, what is illegal is the imposition of prices and commercial conditions that are different from the ones that would exist if there was effective competition in the market.

As was mentioned in the previous section of this chapter, the current Argentine Competition Act introduced a merger notification procedure, which Argentina implemented in 1999. Together with this procedure, the Act established a standard to apply when analyzing whether a merger is anticompetitive, and thus prohibited or subject to conditions imposed by the antitrust authority. That standard is set by Article 7, and it strongly resembles the one that appears in Section 7 of the Clayton Act, which is the analogous US legislation.[12] In order to be prohibited in Argentina, a merger has to lessen, restrict, or distort competition in a manner that may generate damage to the general economic interest. This criterion differs from the one that is used in the European Union, under which a merger is prohibited if it creates or reinforces a dominant position in a market.

Argentine competition law concerning mergers also has a strong point of connection with US law because the Argentine antitrust authorities have issued a set of guidelines very similar to the horizontal merger guidelines issued in the United States by the Department of Justice and the Federal Trade Commission.[13] Following the US precedent, the Argentine guidelines have sections that refer to the definition of relevant markets, the measurement of market concentration, the nature of the firms competing in the relevant markets, the entry barriers,

[11] For a definition of these two classes of abuse of dominance in the European context, see Manfred Neumann, *Competition Policy* (Cheltenham, Edward Elgar, 2001), ch 3.

[12] Clayton Act, 15 USCS §§ 14 et seq.

[13] The Argentine merger guidelines were approved by Resolution 164/01, issued by the Secretary of Competition Defense.

and the efficiency gains generated by a merger. A relatively innovative topic within the Argentine guidelines is an explicit consideration of imports, which is one of the sources of competition that is more frequently analyzed by the CNDC when it deals with horizontal mergers affecting markets in internationally tradable products.

The other distinctive characteristics of the Argentine antitrust law have to do with the procedural aspects of the Competition Act's enforcement. As mentioned in section II of this chapter, the Argentine antitrust system is based on the existence of a single competition agency, which investigates the anticompetitive conduct cases, decides on the merits of those cases, and authorizes and/or prohibits mergers. The decisions of that agency can be appealed before the judicial courts, but all the antitrust processes have to begin with the administrative competition agency.

Unlike most European competition agencies, the Argentine CNDC has not established any procedure of authorization of potentially anticompetitive practices. All cases of anticompetitive conduct are, therefore, analyzed as the result of a complaint by a private party, or are initiated *ex officio* by the CNDC (when that agency believes that a certain economic agent or group of agents is guilty of an anticompetitive practice). Previous authorization, conversely, is required when there is a merger that passes a certain sales threshold (which is currently set at 200 million Argentine pesos) and a certain transaction threshold (which is currently set at 20 million Argentine pesos).[14]

When a person or firm is found guilty of an antitrust offense, the possible penalties established by the Argentine Competition Act are a fine of up to 150 million Argentine pesos,[15] or an order to cease and desist the practice deemed illegal. In some cases, both penalties are applied. The defendant in an anticompetitive conduct case can also offer a commitment to stop the practice under analysis, and the case can end with the acceptance of that commitment by the antitrust agency. Of course, the case can also end with the acceptance of the defendant's explanations by the competition authority, in which case the defendant is acquitted of any anticompetitive practice.

In merger cases, no fines are applied, since mergers are always analyzed before they take place.[16] The possible decisions of the antitrust agency in acquisition cases are the unconditional approval of the merger, the approval of the merger under certain structural or behavioral conditions to be fulfilled by the merging parties, or the complete prohibition of the merger. The most common structural

[14] These are approximately equivalent to US$ 67 million and US$ 6.7 million, respectively (using the average peso–dollar exchange rate of 2006).

[15] These are roughly equivalent to US$ 45 million (using the average peso–dollar exchange rate of 2007).

[16] In fact, merger cases always begin before the mergers take place, but the actual approval or prohibition can occur after the merger has been consummated. This point has been criticized by some commentators.See, for example, OECD, *Competition Law and Policy in Argentina: A Peer Review* (Paris, OECD, 2006) ch 6.

remedies that appear in merger cases are obligations to divest part of the newly merged entity through the sale of a certain number of shares, outlets, plants, commercial brands, or other equivalent assets. The most common behavioral remedies, in turn, consist of prohibitions against discriminating between different customers or suppliers, requirements to give access to certain essential facilities to competitors, and requirements to give customers the option to change their supplier.[17]

IV. Collusive Practices

As in many countries, collusion is one of the main antitrust offenses in Argentina. Article 2 of Act 25,156 characterizes at least six types of conduct that can be considered collusive. These are the ones mentioned in paragraphs a), b), c), d), e) and h),[18] which state that practices such as price fixing, quantity fixing, horizontal market division, bid rigging, horizontal agreements to restrict investments and horizontal agreements to restrict research and development can all be considered anticompetitive, provided that they fall into the general definition given by Article 1.

Although the Argentine antitrust law does not punish any anticompetitive practice on a per se basis, the CNDC and the courts of appeals that have analyzed overt collusion cases have always found price fixing, quantity fixing, bid rigging, and horizontal market divisions to be illegal when they considered that those practices were adequately proved. An early example of that idea can be found in *Buenos Aires Sand Storage v Argentine Sand Company and others*, in which a group of sand manufacturers was fined for establishing production quotas through an agreement that also included the trade unions that represented the shipping workers who transported the sand.[19]

Another significant collusion case is *Lara Gas and others v Agip and others*, in which a group of distributors of liquefied petroleum gas (LPG) was fined for having practiced a market division that restricted competition.[20] This case was particularly important because it reached the Argentine Supreme Court, which had to analyze the question of whether the general economic interest was actually damaged by the agreement among the accused LPG distributors. This Supreme Court sentence is crucial in the Argentine antitrust case law, because it established

[17] The only fines that are sometimes applied in merger cases have to do with situations of late notification, or situations in which firms refuse to give essential information to the antitrust authority.

[18] See Appendix to this chapter.

[19] *Buenos Aires Sand Storage v Argentine Sand Company and others* (1986), Resolution 442/86 from the Secretary of Commerce.

[20] *Lara Gas and others v Agip and others* (1993), Resolution 132/89 from the Secretary of Commerce, Sentence of the Argentine Supreme Court, 23/Nov/1993.

the principle that if it is clear that the market conditions would be more favorable to consumers without the agreement then the general economic interest has been damaged, even though it is not possible actually to measure the amount of that damage.

The most important price-fixing case analyzed by the CNDC, which culminated in a fine to be paid by the defendants, is *AGP v CCAP and others*.[21] In this case, the main stowing companies of the port of Buenos Aires fixed a uniform fee for each container that they stowed.

Lastly, the most important bid-rigging case (which resulted in substantial fines) is *CNDC v Air Liquide and others*, in which a group of oxygen producers was punished for having coordinated their bids in certain auctions organized by several Buenos Aires public hospitals.[22]

If the basic Argentine antitrust doctrine is relatively harsh in cases of overt collusion, it is also relatively cautious in cases of tacit collusion. In *Department of Energy v YPF, Esso and Shell*, for example, the CNDC set the principle that conscious parallelism is not enough to prove collusion.[23] This case involved allegations of price fixing among the three main fuel refiners operating in Argentina. This principle was also applied in several other cases, such as *Fecliba v Roux Ocefa, Rivero and Fidex*,[24] where three pharmaceutical companies were accused of agreeing the prices of their physiological serums, and *Aviabue v American Airlines, United Airlines and British Airways*,[25] where three airlines were accused of jointly reducing the commissions that they paid to their travel agents in Argentina.[26]

A few cases, however, ended in fines when the competition authorities found certain restraints that were capable of facilitating collusion. One of them is *CNDC v Axle and others*, where the main producers of safety valves for LPG bottles were fined for having agreed to use a single marketing company, which was in charge of deciding which firm would sell its product to each customer.[27] Another case, more recent and much more important because of the levels of the fines imposed, is *CNDC v Loma Negra and others*, where the four cement producers that operate

[21] *AGP v CCAP and others* (1996), Resolution 382/96 from the Secretary of Commerce, Industry and Mining.

[22] *CNDC v Air Liquide and others* (2005), Resolution 119/05 from the Secretary of Technical Coordination.

[23] *Department of Energy v YPF, Esso and Shell* (1994), Resolution 99/94 from the Secretary of Commerce.

[24] *Fecliba v Roux Ocefa, Rivero and Fidex* (1998), Resolution 211/98 from the Secretary of Commerce, Industry and Mining.

[25] *Aviabue v American Airlines, United Airlines and British Airways* (2001), Resolution 115/01 from the Secretary of Competition Defense.

[26] This idea about the insufficiency of conscious parallelism to prove the existence of collusion is consistent with the main international antitrust norms. In the US, for example, it was endorsed by the Supreme Court when deciding *Theatre Enterprises v Paramount*, 346 US 537 (1954).

[27] *CNDC v Axle and others* (1997), Resolution 730/97 from the Secretary of Commerce, Industry and Mining.

in Argentina were found guilty of collusion.[28] The main proof for that collusion was the existence of an information system, managed by the trade association of cement producers, through which each firm had detailed information about the sales of the other firms in every urban area of Argentina.

V. Horizontal Exclusionary Practices

In the list of anticompetitive practices that appears in Article 2 of the Argentine Competition Act, there are at least three types of conduct that can be considered horizontal and exclusionary. These are the ones that appear in paragraphs f), l), and m),[29] which state that practices such as entry deterrence, refusals to sell, and predatory pricing can be illegal if they lessen competition or imply an abuse of dominant position, and if they damage the general economic interest.

The first case concerning entry barriers to be decided by CNDC was *A Savant v Matadero Vera*, where the only slaughterhouse in a small city in the province of Santa Fe was found guilty of abuse of its dominant position when it refused to give access to its facilities to a cattle raiser, who also owned a butcher shop that competed with the slaughterhouse.[30] This case is important because it was the first example of use of the so-called 'essential facilities doctrine' in the Argentine antitrust law,[31] and because it was one of the first cases in which a firm was found guilty of abuse of dominance. Another important example of entry deterrence is *Procter & Gamble v Unilever and others*, where the largest powdered soap producer was accused of deterring the entry of its main competitor's new brand of comparable soap onto the same market, through the use of unfair advertising.[32] Although the CNDC found that the practice under analysis was probably designed to harm the plaintiff's interests, this case ended without a penalty, since it was also considered that the means used were not enough to deter the entry of the new powdered soap brand.

Another entry deterrence case that ended without a penalty, and implied an important precedent for future cases, was *Executive Class v Argentine Air Force*

[28] *CNDC v Loma Negra and others* (2005), Resolution 124/05 from the Secretary of Technical Coordination. The total amount of the fines imposed by the Secretary of Technical Coordination was 309,7 million Argentine pesos (approximately equivalent to US$ 100 million).

[29] See Appendix to this chapter, Art 2.

[30] *A Savant v Matadero Vera* (1982), Resolution 78/82 from the Secretary of Commerce.

[31] The essential facilities doctrine was first applied in the history of antitrust law by the US Supreme Court in 1912, in *US v Terminal Railroad Association*, 224 US 383 (1912). In Europe, its use is much more modern. D G Goyder, *EC Competition Law*, 3rd edn (Oxford, Oxford University Press, 1998), for example, cites a case from 1992 as the first application of this doctrine by the European Commission (*B&I v Sealink*, [1992] 5 CMLR 255).

[32] *Procter & Gamble v Unilever and others* (1999), Resolution 884/99 from the Secretary of Commerce, Industry and Mining.

and Manuel Tienda León,[33] where the CNDC set a principle that resembles the so-called *Noerr-Pennington* doctrine.[34] In this case, a taxicab company objected to an agreement between the Argentine Air Force (which was in charge of operating the Argentine airports) and a firm that offered ground transportation services (through both buses and taxicabs), through which the former gave the exclusive right to the latter to offer its services at Buenos Aires international airport. Although the CNDC considered that the practice under analysis restricted competition and was unreasonable (since there were no valid reasons to grant exclusivity when several firms could compete to supply their services of ground transportation between the airport and the city of Buenos Aires), it considered that the practice's origin was a regulation issued by the Government which was exempted from antitrust scrutiny. The competition agency, nevertheless, recommended that such regulation be eliminated. However, the CNDC applied no penalty either to the Air Force or to the accused ground transportation supplier.

The Argentine antitrust case law also contains several examples of horizontal exclusionary practices that were carried out by a group of competitors in order to deter other firms from entering a market. Many of those cases had to do with entities that group together health service providers, such as physicians' associations and hospitals' associations. The first example of this type is *Staff Médico v FeMeBA*, where a private health management organization accused the physicians' association of the province of Buenos Aires of impeding its affiliates from working for the organization, in order to benefit the physicians' own health management organization and to deter the plaintiff from entering the market.[35] This case ended with a fine, and was the first of a relatively long list of cases where physicians' and hospitals' associations which were found to have a dominant position in a certain province or city in Argentina, were penalized for practices aimed at lessening competition.

Very few penalties can be found, conversely, in cases where the plaintiffs alleged predatory pricing practices. One example is *CNDC v Santiago del Estero Bakers' Center and others*, where a group of bakeries was penalized for predatory actions against a competitor.[36] The conduct on the part of the bakers, however, was part of a strategy to manage a collusive agreement in the city of Santiago del Estero.

[33] *Executive Class v Argentine Air Force and Manuel Tienda León* (1998), Resolution 131/98 from the Secretary of Commerce, Industry and Mining.

[34] This doctrine originated in the US as a consequence of the cases *Noerr v Eastern Railroads*, 365 US 127 (1961); and *Pennington v United Mine Workers*, 381 US 657 (1965). It is a principle under which the actions taken to influence government decisions (and any government decisions made as a consequence that influence) are not illegal, even when they are aimed towards lessening competition or damaging competitors. This is because such actions are permitted under other laws and regulations different from antitrust law, and which may therefore have other policy goals different from the defense of competition.

[35] *Staff Médico v FeMeBA* (1982), Resolution 101/82 from the Secretary of Commerce.

[36] *CNDC v Santiago del Estero Bakers' Center and others* (1983), Resolution 319/83 from the Secretary of Commerce.

The cartel members undertook predatory pricing to discipline a baker's shop that had abandoned the cartel.

The most important predatory pricing case that the CNDC has analyzed, *Argentine Chamber of Stationer's Shops v Makro Supermarkets*, concluded with the opinion that the practice was not anticompetitive.[37] The case involved a supermarket chain that sold a stationery product below its wholesale price over a relatively short period of time. Although in this case it was clear that the product was sold below its marginal cost, the CNDC understood that no offense to the competition law existed because the accused supermarket had a very small market share and had no intention or ability to exclude competitors.[38] Its practice of selling the product at a very low price was, therefore, part of a business strategy to attract customers to its outlets, and was aimed at selling all the other products that were offered by the supermarket.

VI. Vertical Restraints

Despite the fact that the Argentine Competition Act characterizes anticompetitive practices by following the European antitrust tradition, the appraisal of vertical restraints by the Argentine competition law has always been closer to the criteria applied in the United States than to the criteria applied in the European Union. This is because the Argentine antitrust authorities have tended to consider vertical restraints less damaging to competition than horizontal restraints, and they have never issued regulations requiring notification or authorization procedures for those practices (as occurs in the European Union and many of its Member States).[39]

The first important case of vertical restraints analyzed by the CNDC, however, ended in a penalty that was later reversed by the National Court of Appeals on Criminal Economic Matters.[40] According to the CNDC, the relevant market in this case was the sale of automobiles of a certain brand (Ford) to government agencies, and the practice was horizontal collusion between the accused car dealers to divide the market between them. The Court of Appeals, conversely,

[37] *Argentine Chamber of Stationer's Shops v Makro Supermarkets* (1997), Resolution 810/97 from the Secretary of Commerce, Industry and Mining.

[38] The standard set by the CNDC in this case resembles the one proposed by Paul Joskow and Alan Klevorik, 'A Framework for Analyzing Predatory Pricing Policy' (1979) 89 *Yale Law Review* 213–70, which is explicitly cited in the CNDC's opinion. It consists of first analyzing the existing market structure, and then appraising the effect of possible below-cost sales only if that structure facilitates the implementation of predatory strategies.

[39] Article 2 of Act 25,156 mentions two kinds of vertical practices that can be seen as examples of anticompetitive conduct (if they fall into the general definition of illegal practices given by Art 1), which are resale price maintenance (para g)) and exclusive dealing (para j) (see Appendix to this chapter).

[40] *CNDC v Acfor and Igarreta* (1983), Resolution 368/83 from the Secretary of Commerce, Sentence of the National Court of Appeals on Criminal Economic Matters, Room 1, 27/Dec/1983.

understood that this behavior was instead a vertical restraint imposed by the car manufacturer. The Court reasoned that such behavior was a reasonable intrabrand restraint to specialize dealers in selling its products to specific customers. The Court also understood that the relevant market was larger than the one originally analyzed by the CNDC, since it included all the automobile suppliers that operated in Argentina at that time (and not only the dealers that sold Ford cars).

After the *Acfor and Igarreta* decision, the vast majority of the cases that involved vertical restraints did not result in penalties. Both the CNDC and the courts considered that the objected-to exclusivity and territorial restraint clauses were in fact means that the firms used to organize their marketing when competing against other firms. A particularly strong application of this criterion appears, for example, in *SADIT and others v Massalin Particulares and others*, where the two main tobacco companies that operated in Argentina were accused of having changed their distribution scheme from a system in which their wholesale cigarette distributors were the same, to another system in which each wholesale distributor became the exclusive dealer of one of the companies, and there was also territorial exclusivity among each company's distributors.[41] In concluding that these practices were not anticompetitive, the CNDC analyzed the business environment in which they took place and found that, in fact, they had been the result of a process aimed at increasing competition between the two main tobacco companies (Massalin Particulares and Nobleza Piccardo). These firms were interested in exerting closer control of their distribution channels so as to compete more aggressively in capturing smokers' preferences. The reduction in the intrabrand competition implied by the practices in question was therefore more than compensated for by an increase in the interbrand competition that was taking place at the same time.[42]

The general tolerance of the Argentine competition law towards vertical restraints also applies to cases of maximum resale price maintenance, which is a practice that was never considered illegal in Argentina. The main example of this doctrine can be found in *FECRA and others v YPF*, in which the CNDC explicitly stated that the setting of maximum resale prices by a fuel refiner meant that the refiner had to compete more effectively against other refiners, and that that implied a benefit (and not damage) to the general economic interest (since it allowed consumers to obtain the fuel products at lower prices).[43]

[41] *SADIT and others v Massalin Particulares and others* (2000), Resolution 281/00 from the Secretary of Competition Defense.

[42] This idea is no doubt inspired by the antitrust doctrine that began with the US Supreme Court decision in the case known as *Continental v GTE Sylvania*, 433 US 36 (1977).

[43] *FECRA and others v YPF* (1995), Resolutions 8, 30–31 and 159–161/95 from the Secretary of Commerce.

Minimum resale price maintenance, conversely, was found to be illegal by the CNDC in *CNDC v TRISA, TSC and others*.[44] There, two sports program suppliers signed an agreement with the three main cable television operators in the city of Buenos Aires, to set a minimum price at which those TV operators would sell the televising of the main national soccer games to their viewers (on a 'pay-per-view' basis). The CNDC understood that the agreement was a way to restrict competition among cable television operators. The result was the creation of a monopoly rent that was mainly appropriated by the program suppliers. The CNDC imposed fines on all those firms that signed the minimum resale price maintenance agreement, but the firms appealed the decision to the National Court of Appeals on Criminal Economic Matters. The Court reversed the administrative decision, arguing that the resale price maintenance at issue did not in fact restrict competition between the accused sports program suppliers and other program suppliers that competed against them. The CNDC appealed the case, but the Argentine Supreme Court decided to uphold the decision taken by the Court of Appeals.

VII. Exploitative Abuses of Dominant Position

The exploitative abuses of a dominant position are a relatively rare cause of antitrust penalties throughout the world. Moreover, in some antitrust systems they are not even considered an offense, since they do not create actual damage to competition but rather a situation in which the lack of competition allows a firm to exert its market power more effectively. Those countries that follow the US tradition of objecting to monopolization practices rather than abuses of dominance, for example, tend to consider that the so-called exploitative abuses of a dominant position are legal, as long as they do not imply exclusionary practices and are not prohibited by other regulatory rules.[45]

Following the European tradition, however, the Argentine competition law considers that an abuse of dominant position can occur either by exclusionary or by exploitative means. This means that a dominant firm can be found guilty of abusing its market position if it establishes prices or commercial conditions that are different from the ones that would exist if there was effective competition

[44] *CNDC v TRISA, TSC and others* (2007), Resolution 28/02 from the Secretary of Competition Defense; Sentence of the National Court of Appeals on Criminal Economic Matters, Room B, 29/Aug/2003; Sentence of the Argentine Supreme Court, 5/Jun/2007.

[45] The doctrine established by the US Supreme Court in *US v Grinnell*, 384 US 563 (1966), for example, considers the two elements that define the offense of monopolization to be the possession of monopoly power in the relevant market, and the willful acquisition or maintenance of that power. More recently, in *Verizon v Trinko*, 540 US 398 (2004), the Court explained that 'the mere possession of monopoly power, and the concomitant charging of monopoly prices, is not only not unlawful, it is an important element of the free-market system'.

in the market (and those conditions generate damage to the general economic interest).[46] The importance of that criterion in current Argentine case law is highly significant, mainly because one of the most notable cases in Argentine antitrust history—*CNDC v YPF*—is just such a case of exploitative abuse of a dominant position.[47]

The case of *CNDC v YPF* is important for two reasons. First, it ended with one of the largest fines ever imposed in an antitrust case in Argentina.[48] Secondly, the penalty from the Secretary of Commerce was affirmed by both the National Court of Appeals on Criminal Economic Matters and the Argentine Supreme Court. The issue analyzed in the *YPF* case was the pricing policy of the defendant concerning its wholesale sales of liquefied petroleum gas (LPG). YPF was the largest supplier of LPG in Argentina, and it was also the largest exporter of that product. The CNDC and the courts that intervened in the case found that YPF had a dominant position in the Argentine LPG market, since the other existing suppliers had very minor market shares and YPF was the firm that controlled the majority of the infrastructure needed to supply the product.

The key factual evidence in the *YPF* case was that, when selling LPG to foreign buyers, the accused firm charged substantially lower prices than those it charged to domestic buyers (for example, local LPG distributors), without having any justification based on cost or quantity differences. The theory underlying the penalty was that YPF was setting an artificially high domestic price, and that it was restricting the local supply by selling its product in foreign markets at a lower price. This created damage to the general economic interest, because the Argentine LPG consumers ended up with higher prices and smaller quantities than they would have had if the objected-to price discrimination had not taken place.[49]

An interesting novelty that the CNDC introduced in the *YPF* case was the way in which it calculated the fine to be applied. In order to do this, it estimated the gap between the domestic prices and the export prices set by the defendant, and multiplied that gap by the total amount of LPG sold by YPF in the local market in the period under analysis. That figure was considered to represent the illegal profit obtained by the defendant as a consequence of its abuse of its dominant

[46] This criterion can also be considered the standard that is applicable in the EU. See, eg, the decision of the European Court of Justice in *European Commission v United Brands* [1978] 1 CMLR 429, where a firm was found guilty of an abuse of a dominant position for having discriminated among customers located in different European countries.

[47] *CNDC v YPF* (2002), Resolution 189/99 from the Secretary of Commerce, Industry and Mining; Sentence of the Argentine Supreme Court, 2/Jul/2002.

[48] The imposed fine was equal to 109 million Argentine pesos, which at the time that it was set by the Secretary of Commerce, Industry and Mining (1999) was equivalent to US$109 million.

[49] Price discrimination is one of the practices cited in Art 2 of Act No 25,156 that can be considered as examples of exploitative abuses of dominant position (para k)). Other offenses that can be included in that category and that are mentioned in Art 2 are abusive pricing (para g)) and tying (para i) (see Appendix to this chapter).

position, which was later increased by 20 per cent in order to set the actual fine that YPF had to pay.

The Argentine antitrust case law also contains a few examples of exploitative abuses of dominant position in which the defendants have been punished for practices that harmed their suppliers rather than their customers. The first case in which this exercise of monopsony power was considered illegal was *General Milking Union v Popular Cooperative of Santa Rosa*, in which the CNDC recommended fining a producer of milk products because of exploitative practices against its milk suppliers.[50] That producer, the only buyer of milk in a certain area of the province of La Pampa, was found guilty of discriminating among its suppliers and setting artificially low prices for the milk that it bought from them. Similarly, in *CNDC v Welbers Industries*,[51] a sugar producer was found guilty of abusing its dominant position against its sugar cane suppliers because it had set artificially low prices that could only be explained by the buying power that it possessed in the relevant market (the Northern area of the province of Santa Fe).[52]

However, in the vast majority of cases involving allegations of exploitative abuses of dominant position, the Argentine antitrust authorities did not impose a penalty. In *A Lafalla v Juan Minetti*, for example, the CNDC found that an increase in the price of cement by the company that had the largest market share in the province of Mendoza was not an exploitative abuse of a dominant position because the defendant had applied the same increase in all the markets where it operated (without discriminating among areas in which it was presumably dominant and areas in which it was not).[53] Similarly, in *N La Porta v Telefonica and Telecom*, the antitrust authority ruled that a price increase by the two monopoly suppliers of local fixed telephony that operated in Argentina (each of them in a separate geographic area) was not an abuse of dominant position because the increase under analysis had been explicitly authorized and decided by the national telecommunications regulator.[54]

[50] *General Milking Union v Popular Cooperative of Santa Rosa* (1982), Resolution 178/82 from the Secretary of Commerce.

[51] *CNDC v Welbers Industries* (1983), Resolution 102/83 from the Secretary of Commerce, Sentence of the National Court of Appeals on Criminal Economic Matters, Room 2, 5/Jul/1983.

[52] Note that, in these cases, prices were considered to be abusive because they were too low. The theory underlying the penalties, therefore, was that those prices were set at a level that was possible only because of the buyer's dominant position. This was considered to be incompatible with the price level that would be expected if that dominant buyer had faced effective competition from other buyers. The *Santa Rosa* and *Welbers* cases, however, were decided in the first years of application of the Argentine Competition Defense Act of 1980. The most recent Argentine case law has never penalized behavior related to abusive pricing, neither in monopoly nor in monopsony situations.

[53] *A Lafalla v Juan Minetti* (2000), Resolution 309/00 from the Secretary of Competition Defense.

[54] *N La Porta v Telefonica and Telecom* (1997), Resolution 337/97 from the Secretary of Commerce, Industry and Mining, Sentence of the National Court of Appeals on Criminal Economic Matters, Room A, 4/Jul/1997.

VIII. Horizontal Mergers

By analyzing the application of Act No 25,156 to merger cases, we can see that in Argentina horizontal mergers are generally prohibited if they create a monopoly in a relevant market. For example, the only two horizontal mergers that have been prohibited by the antitrust authorities since the introduction of the merger notification procedure in 1999 fall into that category. Moreover, in many cases in which the CNDC recommended structural remedies for mergers, its aim was to avoid the creation of a monopoly in a certain product or geographic market.

The first merger that was prohibited by the Argentine competition authorities was *OCA/Correo Argentino*, which, if approved, would have created a monopoly in several postal markets in Argentina.[55] The proposed transaction was in fact the acquisition of the firm that had the concession of the official Argentine post office by its main private competitor. Based on its analysis, the CNDC argued that the two firms were the only two companies that operated in several relevant product markets (the ones involving simple letters, special letters, telegrams, and banking clearing operations). Although both firms also operated in other markets in which they did face competition from other suppliers (eg, package distribution), those markets were relatively unimportant as regards their total revenues.

The other horizontal merger prohibited in Argentina for antitrust reasons was *Teledigital/Esmeralda-Venado Tuerto Television*, which consisted of the acquisition of the assets of two cable television companies by another company that was their only competitor in the city of Venado Tuerto (in the province of Santa Fe).[56] Although in this case the CNDC analyzed the possible competition between the merging parties and the supplier of a substitute good (satellite television), it concluded that such competition was not strong enough because cable television and satellite television were in fact different relevant markets. The efficiency gains generated by the merger (because of the elimination of overlap among the companies' networks) were also considered to be insufficient to compensate for the damage to competition that the creation of a monopoly would entail. Lastly, although the two companies to be acquired operated under bankruptcy protection, the CNDC did not accept the use of a 'failing firm' defense, since it was not the case that the proposed acquiring company was the only candidate to buy the other firms' assets. Indeed, there was another firm that had put forward an offer, though lower, to buy those assets.[57]

[55] *OCA/Correo Argentino* (2001), Resolution 64/01 from the Secretary of Competition Defense.

[56] *Teledigital/Esmeralda-Venado Tuerto Television* (2003), Resolution 32/03 from the Secretary of Competition Defense.

[57] The failing firm defense is an argument that the merging companies can invoke if the most probable alternative to the increase in market concentration generated by a merger is the exit of the acquired firm from the market. This defense is explicitly analyzed in the horizontal merger guidelines issued by the US antitrust agencies, but it does not appear in the Argentine merger guidelines approved by Resolution 164/01.

The idea that horizontal mergers that create monopolies are illegal, however, is highly dependent on the definition of the relevant markets in which the mergers may have effects. In the recent *Multicanal/Cablevision* merger, for example, the CNDC changed its criterion that cable television and satellite television were different relevant markets, and authorized a major merger between the two main cable TV operators of Argentina (which overlapped its activities in several important cities, including Buenos Aires).[58] A similar situation occurred in the *Jumbo/ Home Depot* case, where the CNDC considered that supermarkets that specialized in selling building materials did not constitute a relevant market by themselves, and pooled them together with other kinds of outlets that sold those goods.[59]

These relatively wide definitions of relevant markets contrast with the one used by the CNDC in another recent case (*YPF/Dapsa*), where the CNDC prohibited the acquisition of a gasoline station by the largest Argentine oil refiner (YPF). In that case, the relevant market was defined as five gasoline stations located within a radius of 15 blocks, and therefore the analyzed acquisition implied that YPF would increase its market share from 66 per cent to 88 per cent.[60] If the CNDC had used a wider geographic definition of the relevant market (for example, all the gasoline stations in the city of Buenos Aires) that market share increase would have been much smaller, and the merger would have probably been approved without restrictions.

The principle of avoiding monopoly situations that appears in the merger cases that ended in prohibitions can also be found in a number of situations where the Argentine antitrust authorities have ordered partial divestiture of assets. One example of this is *Telefonica/AC Inversora-Atlántida Comunicaciones*, where the acquiring firm was obliged to sell one of the open television channels that operated in the city of Mar del Plata.[61] This divestiture remedy was in response to concern that the only two open television stations in that city would belong to the merged firm. Similarly, in *Fresenius/RTC*, the acquiring firm had to sell five dialysis centers located in five Argentine cities (from a total of 95 centers controlled by the newly merged firm) because the merger, if approved unconditionally, would create monopolies in those cities.[62]

The CNDC also imposed several structural and behavioral remedies in cases where coordinated effects were feared.[63] In such cases, the merged entities were

[58] *Multicanal/Cablevision* (2007), Resolution 257/07 from the Secretary of Commerce.

[59] *Jumbo/Home Depot* (2002), Resolution 8/02 from the Secretary of Competition Defense.

[60] *YPF/Dapsa* (2007), Resolution 4/07 from the Secretary of Commerce.

[61] *Telefonica/AC Inversora-Atlántida Comunicaciones* (2000), Resolution 53/00 from the Secretary of Competition Defense.

[62] *Fresenius/RTC*(2000), Resolution 83/00 from the Secretary of Competition Defense.

[63] The possible anticompetitive effects of a horizontal merger can be of two types. On one hand, the newly-merged company can exert monopoly power in the relevant market where it operates. This is the main unilateral effect of a merger. On the other hand, an increase in the market concentration provoked by a merger can increase the likelihood of collusion among the firms that remain in the market. This is the main coordinated effect that antitrust law tries to avoid when it requires a procedure of merger notification. For a deeper analysis of these issues, see Germán Coloma, *Defensa de la Competencia* (*Competition Defense*) (Buenos Aires, Ciudad Argentina, 2003), ch 7.

usually required to divest certain assets, the size of which was roughly equivalent to the size of the smallest firm that participated in the merger. In *AmBev/Quilmes*, for example, a Brazilian brewery (AmBev), which had a market share of approximately 11 per cent in the Argentine beer market, bought the largest Argentine brewery, whose market share in Argentina was approximately 70 per cent.[64] The acquisition was approved, subject to the condition that the newly-merged firm divest itself of a number of brands and beer plants, the size of which was approximately equivalent to those that AmBev had in Argentina before buying Quilmes' stock.

Another case in which the CNDC recommended a substantial divestiture was *Telefonica/BellSouth*, in which the second largest cellular telephone company in Argentina (Telefonica) bought the stock of the third largest firm in the same market (BellSouth).[65] Although in that market (cellular telephone services) there were two other firms, the merged company would have had a market share of nearly 50 per cent. The CNDC approved the merger subject to the condition that Telefonica cede its rights to use part of the available radio electric spectrum to a new entrant to the market, whose size was intended to be roughly equivalent to that of BellSouth before it sold its stock to Telefonica.[66]

The imposition of structural conditions for the approval of horizontal mergers, however, is relatively scarce when markets are not highly concentrated, and in cases where the CNDC considers that entry is relatively easy or international competition is relatively strong. Mergers that affect food product markets are emblematic. Among the horizontal mergers that were approved without conditions are *Molinos/Lucchetti*, where there was a large increase in concentration in the dry pasta market, *Arcor/Bagley*, where the main concentration increase occurred in the biscuit market, and *Arcor/La Campagnola*, which implied the creation of a quasi-monopoly in the market for jam products.[67]

IX. Vertical and Conglomerate Mergers

Although the bulk of the antitrust analysis concerning mergers lies in the study of horizontal mergers (that is, mergers among firms that operate in the same relevant market), merger notification procedures are generally applicable to all kinds of mergers, and this includes cases of vertical mergers (that is, mergers among firms that have a real or potential supplier/customer relationship) and

[64] *AmBev/Quilmes* (2003), Resolution 5/03 from the Secretary of Competition Defense.

[65] *Telefonica/BellSouth* (2004), Resolution 196/04 from the Secretary of Technical Coordination.

[66] This requirement was also imposed because of the existence of a specific regulation issued by the Argentine telecommunications' regulatory agency, which prohibited that a single cellular telephone company possessed more than a certain amount of radio electric spectrum in each area of Argentina.

[67] *Molinos/Lucchetti* (2001), Resolution 33/01 from the Secretary of Competition Defense; *Arcor/Bagley* (2004), Resolution 151/04 from the Secretary of Technical Coordination; *Arcor/La Campagnola* (2006), Resolution 11/06 from the Secretary of Commerce.

conglomerate mergers (that is, mergers that are neither horizontal nor vertical). Most of those mergers are approved without conditions of any kind, and this is true in the majority of the countries of the world as well as in Argentina. Argentine antitrust history, however, has seen a few cases of vertical and conglomerate mergers that have been subject to structural or behavioral conditions, and one case of a vertical merger that was prohibited in its entirety.

The only prohibited vertical merger so far in Argentina has been *Aeropuertos Argentina 2000/LAPA*.[68] In this case the firm that held the monopoly license to operate all the Argentine airports (Aeropuertos Argentina 2000) tried to acquire the stock of the second largest Argentine airline (LAPA). The competitive danger that this merger posed, according to the CNDC, was the possibility of a vertical foreclosure, and the possible extension of Aeropuertos's monopoly power from the airport business to the domestic air transportation market. The theory behind the prohibition was that airports are an essential input to supply air transportation services. Therefore, a firm that controls that input, and also has interests in the airline business, has strong incentives to carry out exclusionary practices in order to monopolize the domestic air transportation market. The regulation to which Aeropuertos Argentina 2000 was subject in supplying airport services was relatively lax, and the main competitor of LAPA in the Argentine air transportation market, Aerolineas Argentinas, was in the process of bankruptcy reorganization.

Another important vertical merger analyzed by the CNDC was *Liberty Media-Hicks/Cablevision*, in which the two acquiring firms (Liberty Media and Hicks), which already owned several pay television channels, sought to acquire Cablevision, one of the largest cable TV operators in Argentina.[69] The CNDC's main concern was the possibility of exclusionary practices against other television channel suppliers and other cable television operators. To reduce this possibility, the CNDC approved the merger subject to the condition that the merged firm would provide access to Liberty Media-Hicks' television channels on fair commercial terms to all interested television operators. Similarly, the CNDC requested open access to Cablevision's networks, on fair commercial terms, for all competing television content suppliers.

Most other vertical mergers have posed few anticompetitive concerns because either the acquiring firm or the acquired company had a relatively small share in its relevant market. In those cases, policy seems to be that the Argentine antitrust authorities approve the mergers without imposing any structural or behavioral remedy. Examples of those transactions are *Totalinef/TGN*, which was a partial merger between a natural gas producer and a natural gas transporter, *Maersk/Terminal 4*, which was a merger between an international shipping company and

[68] *Aeropuertos Argentina 2000/LAPA* (2002), Resolution 29/02 from the Secretary of Competition Defense.

[69] *Liberty Media-Hicks/Cablevision* (2001), Resolution 2/01 from the Secretary of Competition Defense.

the firm that had the concession for one of the harbors in the port of Buenos Aires, and *NewsCorp/DirecTV*, which was a merger between a television channel supplier and a satellite television operator.[70]

If vertical mergers are usually unable to distort competition, the same can be said about most conglomerate mergers. In the relatively short history of merger control in Argentina, for example, there are no cases of conglomerate mergers that have been prohibited or substantially conditioned. Among the conglomerate mergers that the CNDC has analyzed, several cases involve market extension mergers (ie, mergers among firms that operate in the same business but in different markets), which were in all cases approved without restrictions. Examples of those cases are *Teledigital/Las Heras Television*, which was a merger between two cable TV operators that were located in different urban areas, *Petrobras/Eg3*, which concerned the acquisition of an Argentine fuel refiner by a Brazilian refiner that had not previously operated in Argentina, and *Pepsi/Quaker*, which involved the acquisition of a cereal producer by a firm that already operated in several food product markets but not in the cereal market.[71]

The Argentine competition law does not contain any provision that establishes a distinction between mergers in which the parties are local firms and mergers in which one or several of them are foreign firms. However, there is one conglomerate merger case (*Petrobras/Pérez Companc*) in which that distinction was analyzed by the CNDC, concerning the acquisition of a firm (Pérez Companc) that controlled the main electricity transportation company of Argentina (Transener) by a Brazilian firm (Petrobras).[72] In that case, although the CNDC explicitly disregarded the argument of nationality as a possible competition problem, the Secretary of Competition Defense accepted a commitment offered by the acquiring firm to sell its share in Transener's stock.

X. Conclusion

The analysis of Argentine competition law and its enforcement carried out in the previous sections may be summarized through a series of concluding remarks. These are as follows:

a) Argentine competition law evolved from a system that was inspired by US antitrust law and was predominantly based on judicial enforcement, to a scheme which is closer to European competition principles and is primarily enforced

[70] *Totalinef/TGN* (2000), Resolution 267/00 from the Secretary of Competition Defense; *Maersk/Terminal 4* (2001), Resolution 17/01 from the Secretary of Competition Defense; *NewsCorp/DirecTV* (2005), Resolution 49/05 from the Secretary of Technical Coordination.

[71] *Teledigital/Las Heras Television* (2000), Resolution 32/00 from the Secretary of Competition Defense; *Petrobras/Eg3* (2001), Resolution 150/01 from the Secretary of Competition Defense; *Pepsi/Quaker* (2001), Resolution 9/01 from the Secretary of Competition Defense.

[72] *Petrobras/Pérez Companc* (2003), Resolution 62/03 from the Secretary of Competition Defense.

by a single administrative agency. This Argentine antitrust system has produced a relatively coherent case law, the standards of which are a combination of US and European criteria.

b) The main distinctive characteristic of Argentine competition law is that anticompetitive practices and mergers may be illegal only if they are able to cause damage to the general economic interest. This concept has been equated to the economic concept of total welfare generated in a market. It also refers to the idea that in the Argentine antitrust system there are no practices that can be considered illegal per se.

c) Most overt collusion practices, however, have been penalized without actually proving the existence of real damage to the general economic interest. Rather, cases in this area suggest that the CNDC and the Argentine courts find that overt collusion always damages consumers' interests.

d) When there are restraints that may facilitate collusion or act as collusive devices, damage to the general economic interest is more difficult to prove because those restraints may be explained by an efficiency rationale. A higher burden of proof must be met in cases of tacit collusion, where it is clear that conscious parallelism is not enough to prove the existence of a collusive practice.

e) Due to the wording of the current Argentine Competition Act, exclusionary practices may be challenged either as resulting in a lessening of competition or as an abuse of dominant position. However, the Argentine case law about such matters is rather conservative, in the sense that both entry deterrence and predatory conduct are punished only if it is clear that there is a practice the sole possible explanation of which is the exclusion of competitors, and there must be an extreme likelihood that such conduct actually excludes competitors from the market. This is probably why the only penalties that we find in Argentine case law due to exclusionary practices are linked to situations that can be explained using a version of the essential facilities doctrine.

f) Argentine competition law has also been very hesitant to penalize vertical restraints, especially in cases of exclusive dealing and exclusive territories. The CNDC, for example, has ruled maximum resale price maintenance legal in all the cases analyzed so far. Minimum resale price maintenance, on the other hand, has been considered illegal when it helped to sustain collusion among downstream competitors and when it helped to extend the upstream supplier's monopoly power.

g) The CNDC has also prosecuted cases of exploitative abuse of dominant position. Although most of them ended without penalties, a few of these cases have resulted in substantial fines. The main rule that can be derived from this field is that price discrimination can be illegal if it is practiced by a dominant firm to enhance its market power, and if it generates damage to the general economic interest that is translated into a price increase that harms domestic consumers, or into a price reduction that harms local suppliers. Abusive pricing, on the other hand, has not been penalized by the Argentine antitrust authority in the last 20 years.

h) In 1999, the Argentine competition system introduced a merger notification procedure, the rules of which are similar to those existing in the United States. Consequently, several horizontal mergers that would have created monopolies in relevant markets have been prohibited or approved with significant conditionality. Mergers that did not create monopolies but substantially increased concentration in markets with large entry barriers, have also been subject to structural remedies, such as the obligation to divest enough assets to compensate for the increase in concentration.
i) These rules regarding the analysis of horizontal mergers, however, are highly dependent on the definition of the relevant market under analysis, and this is a topic in which it is difficult to make accurate predictions based on the Argentine antitrust experience. In some cases the competition authorities have used very wide definitions, while in others they have used extremely narrow ones.
j) Vertical mergers have also been subject to some prohibitions and objections, but only when they involved an undertaking with substantial monopoly power and created a significant risk of vertical foreclosure and market power extension.
k) Lastly, conglomerate mergers have never been prohibited or conditioned by the Argentine antitrust authorities, although there is a case in which there was a 'tacit objection' to the fact that a foreign company bought a local firm that controlled an essential facility in the electricity sector.

Appendix: Excerpts from Act No 25,156[73]

Article 1. Actions and practices related to the production or trade of goods and services that lessen, restrict, or distort competition, or constitute an abuse of a dominant position, in a market, in a manner that may result in damage to the general economic interest, are prohibited and will be penalized pursuant to the rules of this Act.

Article 2. The following practices, among others, to the extent that they configure the hypotheses of Article 1, constitute practices that lessen competition:

a) Fixing, agreeing, or handling either directly or indirectly the selling or purchasing price of goods or services at which they are offered or purchased in the market, as well as exchanging information with the same purpose or to the same effect;
b) Establishing the obligation of producing, processing, distributing, purchasing, or marketing only a limited amount of goods or rendering a limited number, volume, or frequency of services;
c) Sharing horizontally areas, markets, customers, or supply sources;
d) Concerting or coordinating bids in auctions or contests;
e) Concerting the limitation or control of technological development or investments made for the production or marketing of goods and services;

[73] The only official version of Act No 25,156 is the Spanish version. This English translation is therefore unofficial.

f) Preventing, hampering, or obstructing the entry or permanence of persons in a market or excluding them from such market;
g) Fixing, imposing, or practicing, directly or indirectly, in agreement with competitors or individually, any form of price and purchase conditions or of sale of goods, furnishing of services or production;
h) Regulating goods or services markets by means of agreements in order to restrict or control technological research and development, the production of goods, or the furnishing of services, or hindering investments made in the production of goods or services or in their distribution;
i) Subordinating the sale of goods to the purchase of other goods or to the use of a service, or subordinating the furnishing of services to the use of other service or to the purchase of goods;
j) Subordinating the purchase or sale to the condition of not using, purchasing, selling, or supplying goods or services, produced, processed, distributed, or marketed by a third party;
k) Imposing discriminatory conditions for the purchase or transfer of goods or services without reasons based on usual business practices;
l) Refusing, without justified cause, to satisfy effective orders for the purchase or sale of goods or services, under the conditions prevailing in the relevant market;
m) Discontinuing the provision of a dominant monopolistic service in the market to a public utility or public interest service provider;
n) Transferring goods or furnishing services at prices lower than their cost, without reasons based on usual business practices, in order to remove competitors from the market or to damage the image, property, or trademark value of their goods or service suppliers.

Article 4. For the purposes of this Act, it is understood that one or more persons enjoy a dominant position when, for a certain type of product or service, that person is the only supplier or buyer in the national market or in one or several parts of the world, or when, without being the only one, he or she is not exposed to substantial competition or when, because of the vertical or horizontal degree of integration, he or she is able to determine the economic feasibility of a competitor or participant in the market, to the latter's detriment.

Article 5. In order to establish a dominant position in a market, the following circumstances shall be considered:

a) The extent to which the relevant goods or services may be replaced by other national or foreign goods or services, and the conditions and time required for such replacement;
b) The extent to which regulatory restrictions limit the access of products or suppliers or buyers to the relevant market;
c) The extent to which an undertaking has the power unilaterally to affect prices or to restrict the supply or demand in the market, and the extent to which its competitors are able to offset that power.

Article 7. Mergers and other economic concentration transactions, whose object or effect is or may be to lessen, restrict, or distort competition, in a manner that may result in damage to the general economic interest, are hereby prohibited.

Chapter VI

To What Extent Will the Possibility of Executing Agreements with Cartel Members Impact on Brazilian Antitrust Policy?

LEOPOLDO UBIRATAN CARREIRO PAGOTTO*

I. Introduction

The fight against cartels has become the most important issue worldwide in antitrust. As a consequence, antitrust policy, including that of Latin America, has focused on refining the effectiveness of anti-cartel efforts. One such area of refinement is the execution of leniency agreements. The export of leniency from the United States to other jurisdictions has provided positive effects on anti-cartel enforcement, notwithstanding the specific peculiarities of the countries that adopt such institutions.

An additional tool in anti-cartel efforts is a consent decree between a firm and the competition authority in order to conclude cartel investigations swiftly.[1] Though conventional wisdom is that consent decrees are highly advantageous because of their administrability and effective uses of resources, such general conclusions do not hold in the Brazilian context. This chapter utilizes a responsive regulation model to address the limitations of consent decrees and leniency in the Brazilian context. This model holds larger lessons for other countries in Latin America as well.

Levy and Spiller note that local peculiarities and institutional endowments shape the success of regulation.[2] They conclude, 'regulatory systems that demand great complexity as regards its implementation would not work satisfactorily in countries

* MSc in Regulation–London School of Economics and Political Science; LLM in Economic Law–University of São Paulo; PhD Candidate in Economic Law—University of São Paulo.

[1] There are essential procedural differences between consent decrees and plea agreements in the US antitrust system. However, for the purpose of this paper the term 'consent decree' will refer to agreements executed with cartel members before the administrative authorities, but without criminal implications. This is the definition used by the Brazilian Antitrust Law.

[2] Brian Levy and Pablo Spiller, *Regulations, Institutions, and Commitment: Comparative Studies of Telecommunications* (Cambridge, Cambridge University Press, 1996), 1–35.

with weak administrative capacity.'[3] The question that their insight poses is how institutional deficiencies in Brazil and in Latin America could affect or interfere in the level of enforcement of antitrust policy in view of these agreements (including leniency and consent decrees) with cartel members. This chapter uses the responsive regulation model to explore its application to cartel conduct in Brazil.

II. The Responsive Regulation Model and its Application

Responsive regulation has been praised as the new trend for regulators. By replacing unilateral regulatory commands and the absence of market forces with interactive relationships, responsive regulation is said 'to economize motivation, not just virtuous motivation'. Accordingly, it does not rely on 'virtuous citizens' because the 'guns are ready to be fired'. Neither does it undermine virtue (as the gun is kept in the background), nor rely on economically rational actors because 'a variety of forms of persuasion are available'.[4]

The first premise behind responsive regulation is an understanding of what motivates regulated actors. Obviously, what motivates oneself or other individuals, companies and associations will vary, and any attempt to generalize will be flawed. Nevertheless, by understanding the motivations of agents, it is possible to anticipate actions from cartel members and thus define the best response for the antitrust authorities—would a cartel member have incentives to continue the practice even after its detection and punishment?

In order to address the multiplicity of factors that motivate different persons, game theory must be used by regulators. Tit-for-tat (TFT) and vindictive tit-for-tat (VTFT) can be adapted to the regulatory process in advancing the best response of the regulator to the actions of the regulated. Thus, interaction with cartels would be continuous, and the information would be transmitted to the regulated only indirectly, for example by means of disclosure of antitrust decisions, the theory of the revolving door and the relative stability of the small legal and economic community that revolves around antitrust policy. From this perspective, the regulatory process enables the antitrust regulator to foresee the actions of regulated companies and then decide on a course of action.

The second premise of responsive regulation is the use of enforcement pyramids. The first pyramid is formed by layers of sanctions, ranging from the least severe to the most severe, ie from mere notifications to imprisonment. Cooperation between the antitrust regulator and the regulated will be achieved more easily when

[3] *Ibid*, at 2.

[4] Ian Ayres and John Braithwaite, *Responsive Regulation: Transcending the Deregulation Debate* (Oxford, Oxford University Press, 1992), 50.

the former can escalate the sanctions as a response to the resistance of the latter. The idea is to move from compliance to deterrence and, when the latter fails, to incapacitation.[5] The history behind the Bell System divestiture provides an example of continuous escalation towards incapacitation in antitrust enforcement. Moreover, an enforcement pyramid must contain a comprehensive range of sanctions so that each violation does not result in over- or under-deterrence. This comprehensive range of sanctions is probably the greatest challenge to the antitrust authorities, to the extent that they are unaware of the optimum level of punishment in a large number of situations.

Another pyramid consists of layers of strategies, ranging from less intervention to more intervention, ie from self-regulation to command and control regulation. It refers to regulatory strategy, in which rules are established; and if these rules are not followed, penalties are applied. There must be flexibility across choices in the pyramid—the antitrust regulator must have powers to act according to the prescriptions of TFT and VTFT so that it can learn what the appropriate level of sanction and intervention would be over a period of time.[6]

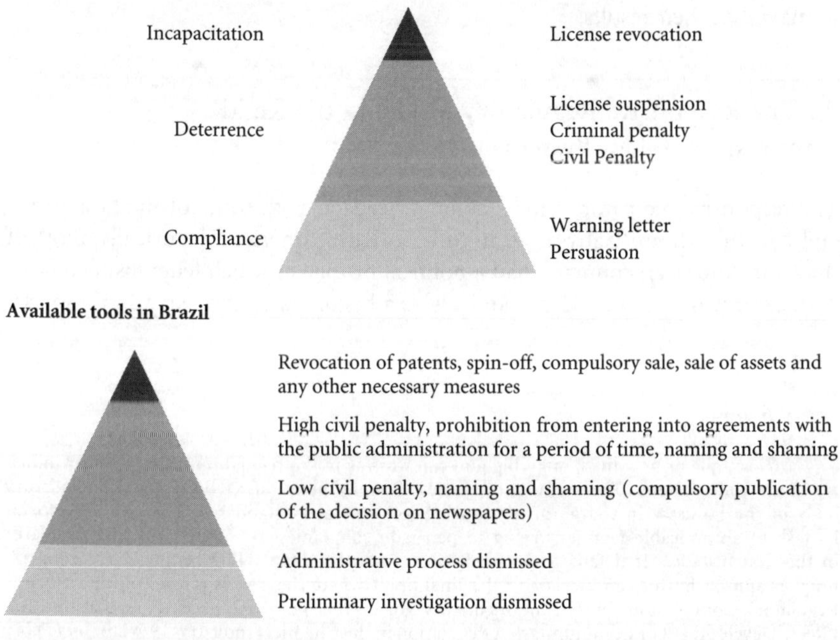

Figure 1 Enforcement pyramind[7]

[5] Christine Parker, John Braithwaite and Natalie Stepanenko, *ACCC Enforcement and Compliance Project: Working Paper on ACCC Compliance Education & Liaison, Strategies* (Canberra, Centre for Competition and Consumer Policy, RegNet, Australian National University, 2004).

[6] Ayres and Braithwaite, above n 4, at 39–40.

[7] *Ibid*, at 35.

The bigger the stick that the regulators carry, the more credibility the regulated will accord regulators and the less regulators need to use their power. Hence, the regulators can speak softly.[8] The existence of 'super-punishments' like compulsory spin-off and sale can also facilitate cooperation from the regulated. Based on this hypothesis, antitrust regulation has a 'benign big gun' of power and punishment. Thanks to the existence of super-punishments, antitrust authorities have been able to use persuasion for the non-formation of cartels in a more efficient and convincing way.

As part of this strategy, the image of invincibility of the antitrust regulator should not be forgotten. The reputation of the antitrust regulator can determine the behavior of the regulated: if the regulator always loses its cases in the courts, there will be an incentive for the regulated to challenge any adverse decisions. Furthermore, punishments should be used within their own appropriate criteria so that the willingness to cooperate is not compromised.[9]

The benign big gun provides a comprehensive guideline for obtaining compliance from the regulated.[10] Although it was initially merely a typology,[11] the concept has evolved into a set of instructions to be followed by regulators who wanted to maximize their results.[12]

A. The Responsive Regulatory Model in the Rigid Administrative Law System

The responsive regulatory model collides head-on with some of the basic principles of the administrative laws in force in Latin America. Historically, most of the Latin American countries had a political history in which federalism collided with centralizing drives. Thus, not only as a historical contingency, but also as a

[8] *Ibid*, at 19.

[9] *Ibid*, at 44–49.

[10] An example of how the benign big gun can work is in the regulation of the nuclear industry in the United States. The Institute of Nuclear Power Operations (INPO) is a self-regulatory body of the industry in charge of monitoring its own safety standards. The INPO performs its task in an amicable manner, trying to persuade companies to comply with the standards in the first instance. If it fails to persuade a nuclear plant, the INPO progressively adopts a tougher approach; this can escalate to the final point where the case is referred to the Nuclear Regulatory Commission (NRC), the regulatory gorilla that enforces the CAC regulations. See J Rees, 'Development of Communitarian Regulation in the Chemical Industry' 19/4 *Law and Policy* 514 (1997).

[11] P N Grabosky and J Braithwaite, *Of Manners Gentle: Enforcement Strategies of Australian Business Regulatory Agencies* (Melbourne, OUP, 1986), 222. For C Currie, *Towards a General Theory of Financial Regulation: predicting, measuring and preventing financial crisis* (Working Paper 132, School of Finance and Economics, University of Technology, Sydney, 2003, <http://www.business.uts.edu.au/finance/research/wpapers/wp132.pdf> (14 June 2008), the authors wished 'to develop a typology to classify the various types of regulatory models of every type of activity'.

[12] Parker *et al*, above n 5, at 12.

political convenience, the French model of administrative law has been largely adopted in Latin American countries.[13]

In these countries, public authorities have a duty to act in the presence of an irregularity, no matter how small or insignificant for the public interest, even if this results in high costs. From the perspective of these legal systems, antitrust enforcement relies mostly on the administrative sphere, which means that the introduction of consent decrees could be seen as subversion of the traditional principle of inalienability of the public interest. Consent decrees and leniency agreements can be set within this context. Both have been imported from the US system based upon a different model and different assumptions of institutional strengths and weaknesses. The adoption of such legal transplants has frequently been employed without analysis and reflection on the peculiarities related to this transplant, and this can cause problems by itself.

The creation of a responsive regulatory model for antitrust in Latin American countries faces specific difficulties caused by the inflexibility of the activities of public authorities. Consent decrees and leniency agreements, which are signed by public authorities, are exceptional within the context of Latin American civil code administrative law. Antitrust law in Latin American countries, which is strongly influenced by the American model, tends to introduce consent decrees and leniency agreements in an unprecedented way—as was the case in Brazil, where similar agreements were prohibited in the administrative sphere prior to the enactment of the Brazilian Antitrust Law.

B. Introduction of Antitrust Laws Within the Scope of the Responsive Regulatory Model

It appears that there are consistent patterns of interaction between competition authorities and companies. In order to identify such patterns, one needs 'to aggregate firms into industry associations'.[14] In antitrust law, this aggregation can be made based on the concept of relevant markets,[15] a methodology that Brazil also follows.[16] Leniency agreements, consent decrees and plea bargains could serve as communication and interaction channels between the authorities and the regulated.

[13] G Marcou, *The Legal and Regulatory Framework of Public Administration* (United Nations Secretariat Paper for the 12th Meeting of Experts on the United Nations Programme in Public Administration and Finance. New York, 1995), <http://unpan1.un.org/intradoc/groups/public/documents/UN/UNPAN000761.pdf>, 7.

[14] Ayres and Braithwaite, above n 4, at 19.

[15] Herbert Hovenkamp, *Federal Antitrust Policy: the Law of Competition and its Practice*, 2nd edn (St. Paul, West Group 1999), 82–84.

[16] See Art 20 of the Brazilian antitrust law, <www.seae.fazenda.gov.br/document_center/legislation/brazilian-antitrust-law.pdf>.

Even if the aggregation of companies into relevant markets is not enough to ensure the presence of responsiveness, one can attempt to broaden the notion of responsiveness to the entire market, because most of the companies subject to close antitrust scrutiny are large ones and are thus organizationally able to comply with regulations. Parker, Braithwaite and Stepanenko implicitly adopt this broader approach in their analysis of the Australian Competition and Consumer Commission.[17]

However, there are other knowledge-spreading mechanisms able to minimize information asymmetry. First, the publicity given to price-fixing investigations by antitrust authorities allows cartel members to analyze the governmental response to collusion. Even though certain details of the decisions issued by the antitrust authorities may remain confidential, the authorities disclose a significant proportion of these decisions to the public—information on fines imposed, conditions for execution of agreements and procedural rules can be easily identified and processed by cartel members. Secondly, the existence of a community specialized in antitrust law refines publicly available information. These experts can transmit this knowledge to cartel members.

For the antitrust authorities, this transmission of knowledge results in the assumption that behavior will be more or less uniform. The actions of investigated cartel members would tend to follow a pattern, as if the cartel member under investigation had recently acquired the knowledge of the cartel members previously investigated, even if the transmission of knowledge was not perfect. The stability of bureaucracy also contributes towards maintenance of acquired knowledge.[18]

Additionally, although cartel members may be replaced in each interaction of the game theory, the antitrust authorities tend to be the same throughout. Thus, antitrust authorities accumulate knowledge about the actions taken by cartel members by means of repeated moves. More than mere maintenance in view of the stability of bureaucracy, there is an accumulation of knowledge, because the antitrust authorities learn from their errors and correct their actions through time. The authorities abandon insufficient criteria and adopt better practices. This asymmetric information benefits the antitrust authorities regarding the use and conditions of consent decrees.

[17] Parker *et al*, above n 5, at 12.

[18] This is not the case in Brazil. See 'Challenges/Obstacles Faced by Competition Authorities in Achieving Greater Economic Development through the Promotion of Competition—Contribution from Brazil (CADE)' (OECD Global Forum on Competition, Jan 6, 2004), <http://www.oecd.org/dataoecd/18/5/23725921.pdf>: 'Optimal efficiency is further hampered by the frequent turnover at the highest levels of CADE, where the President, Commissioners and Attorney General remain for a very brief period in the agency, due to their short mandates (two years which can be politically renewed for another two years).'

Having dealt with the premises behind responsive regulation, this chapter now addresses responsive regulation itself. The responsive process works in the following way. On one side the antitrust authorities make the decisions, while on the other side the large businesses (who are the 'main clients' of the antitrust authorities) respond to such decisions. No company merges with another without paying due attention to the antitrust authorities' response. The major antitrust violators are fully aware that their conduct does not comply with antitrust laws, therefore they try to hide their actions. This assumption is reasonable, since most large corporations have considerable knowledge regarding the legislation of the countries in which they operate. These premises lead to the conclusion that the main players in the market are aware of the antitrust rules. Hence, they are able to interact with the authorities as if they were in a closely regulated market. This is particularly true for companies which operate in concentrated and cartelized markets.

The use of persuasion (one of the main aspects of responsive regulation) in countries whose administrative law follows the French tradition, faces difficulties. Even the wide discretionary powers of antitrust authorities like the Administrative Council for Economic Defense (CADE), which is the decision-making agency among the Brazilian antitrust agencies, must be used in accordance with certain guidelines in order to avoid illegalities. If this were not enough, then persuasion would play a fundamental role in responsive regulation by being the next preferred step in the enforcement pyramid. These factors add somewhat more complexity to the use of responsive regulation.

Brazilian antitrust law contains mechanisms that allow for persuasion of violators to take place. For example, the preliminary investigation of antitrust violations is one such forum. At that stage, the Secretariat for Economic Defense (SDE), the investigative branch of the Brazilian antitrust agencies, has either no or little evidence of wrongdoing, although it may nevertheless be suspicious of some wrongdoing. Under these conditions SDE has to start a preliminary investigation to check whether the alleged violation has any evidentiary support. Meanwhile, direct or indirect persuasion may take place. Even warning letters are an option to persuade violators to comply with antitrust law.

Another mechanism for responsiveness to take place is the Antitrust Certification Program (ACP), a self-enforced method of regulation. This program aims at increasing the level of compliance in the private sector by stimulating companies and associations to enforce their own codes of conduct. The SDE ratifies the voluntary programs, thereby opening communication channels with the companies which can be used as a means to persuade them.[19]

[19] J Black, 'Talking About Regulation', Spring, *Public Law* 77, 97 (1998).

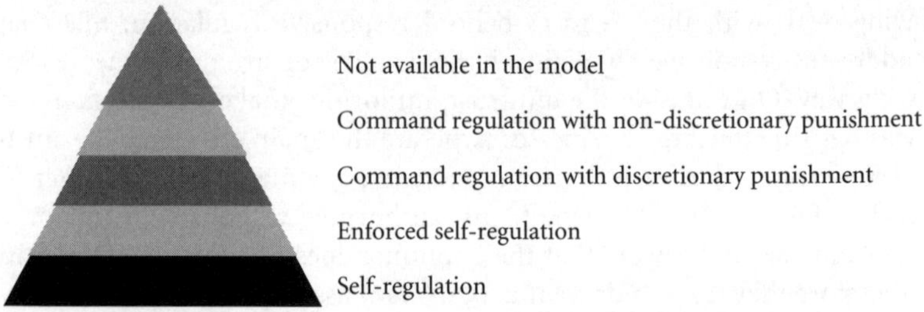

Available tools in Brazil

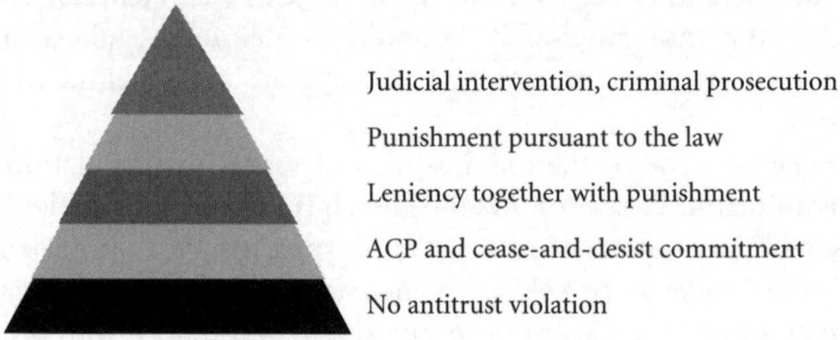

Figure 2 Enforcement pyramind[20]

III. Learning From the Past? Operation of Agreements With Cartels in Brazil

Between 1994 and 2000, Brazilian antitrust law allowed the execution of agreements with cartel members during administrative proceedings in order to halt cartel investigations. The agreements were similar to US consent decrees. However, from the perspective of an anti-cartel policy, the few Brazilian executed agreements conveyed the wrong signals to violators, to say the least. At that time, it was necessary for the defendant neither to be subject to a judgment by default, nor to acknowledge the 'unlawfulness of the practice under analysis'.[21] To make matters worse, the commitments assumed by defendants were not properly monitored, and it was not even mandatory for CADE to request the payment of any fine to execute the agreement. The rare cases of investigated collusive practices came to an end with the execution of these agreements. Until 2000, only one cartel case obtained an adverse judgment, possibly because the strategy of the defense

[20] Ayres and Braithwaite, above n 4, at 39.
[21] Brazilian antitrust law (before the amendments of Law No 10.149/00), Section 53.

did not include the proposal of an agreement.[22] Under such an adverse scenario, it becomes clear that CADE was not following a strategy based on responsive regulation, since there was a problem in the applicable rules involving consent decrees. The agreements executed between 1994 and 2000 were quite different from what is allowed today.

In 2000, Law No 10.149/00[23] amended Brazilian antitrust law, which prohibited the execution of consent agreements for cartel violations. This amendment should be understood in the context of the introduction of leniency, which occurred under the same law. Both amendments led to a potentially more effective anti-cartel policy, since rules would allow the SDE and CADE to investigate and punish cartels. In other words, the new institutional framework allowed responsive regulation to start to take place.

As a result, there was a clear contrast in the number of adverse judgments in comparison with the preceding period, as Table 2 below illustrates. Part of this contrast may be attributed to the improvement of investigative tools at the disposal of the authorities, but it is probable that the new institutional scenario has favored a stronger action on the part of the CADE.

Hence, there is a possible relationship between the mere existence of consent agreements and the number of adverse judgments to cartels.[24] In 2005, the

Table 1 Agreements executed with the CADE (1995–2000)

Year	Executed CCP	Cartel*?
1995	1– Administrative Proceedings 08000.012720/94	Yes
1996	1– Administrative Proceedings 08000.016384/94-11	Yes
1997	1– Administrative Proceedings 49/92	No
1998	0	—
1999	0	—
2000	2– Administrative Proceedings 08000.020849/96-18 and Administrative Proceedings 08012.003303/98-25	One of them is a cartel

* Practices punished under items I, II, III and VIII of Art 21 the Brazilian Antitrust Law are considered collusive practices.
Source: Annual Reports of the CADE.

[22] As of June 2008, the three defendants have neither paid the fine imposed, nor complied with the ancillary determinations imposed by the CADE.

[23] Text available at < http://www.cade.gov.br/legislao/10149lei.asp>.

[24] Other causes are mentioned to explain this relationship, such as the absence of the appropriate regulation for leniency agreements until 2004 and administrative deficiencies in the SDE. Even so, the incentive transmitted to the antitrust community by means of the repeated execution of agreements is paradigmatic: the encouragement to the continuance of a cartel seemed to remain quite high, because the antitrust authorities executed agreements that did not benefit the defendants, even in the few cases in which there was an actual chance of adverse judgment.

Table 2 Adverse Judgments in Cartel Cases in Brazil

Year	Adverse Judgments in Cases Involving Collusive Practices
2000	9
2001	2
2002	6
2003	5
2004	11
2005	11
2006	6

* The practices punished under items I, II, III and VIII of Article 21 of the Brazilian Antitrust Law are considered collusive practices.
Source: Annual Reports of the CADE.

OECD acknowledged in the *Peer Review* that 'this approach, as well as the statutory denial of settlement in cartel cases, reflects sound policy where settlement entails no admission of liability and no penalty.'[25] In May 2007, Law No 11.482/07 reintroduced into Brazilian antitrust law a provision incorporating the possibility of consent agreements with cartel members.[26]

According to the new legislation, the initial submission of the terms of the agreement is incumbent upon the investigated cartel member at any time. However, the wording of the agreement is in principle the responsibility of the Commissioner appointed to analyze the case. The proposal must contain a commitment to cease the collusive practice and to make a payment[27] to a public fund. CADE may analyze the proposal only once, but the practice with both settlement agreements accepted through July 2008 reveals that the initial proposal may be changed to meet the requirements imposed by the Commissioners. Although the Brazilian antitrust law does not contain any provision on the matter, CADE establishes that in cases where the antitrust investigation has been initiated by means of a leniency agreement, the execution of a consent decree will occur only if the defendant pleads guilty. This provision has been widely criticized because it changes the provisions of the Brazilian antitrust law; there is no such differentiation in the law.

The responsive regulation model suggests that one should examine the incentives that make a cartel member decide to apply for leniency rather than waiting for the cartel's detection and then executing a consent decree. In fact, different

[25] OECD Secretary General, IDB, *Competition Law and Policy in Latin America: Peer Reviews of Argentina, Brazil, Chile, Mexico and Peru* (Paris, OECD Publishing, 2006), 168.
[26] Text available at <http://www.cade.gov.br/legislacao/11482lei.asp>.
[27] Brazilian antitrust law does not mention the word 'fine' in this provision.

conditions apply regarding the execution of agreements in those cases in which there was leniency as opposed to cases in which there was no leniency. This situation is extremely delicate in Brazil, because it can directly interfere with the success of anti-cartel policies.

Take the example of a potential party to a leniency agreement. This agent faces the following dilemma: should he make the first move and execute a leniency agreement, or should he wait for the detection of the cartel and then seek to execute a consent decree? The agent will ponder the benefits offered by both possibilities before abandoning the other members of the cartel; and if he decides to abandon them, he will gain an advantage.

Points in support of the execution of a leniency agreement are:

a) the possibility of obtaining complete immunity and avoiding monetary penalties;
b) the chance of gaining a competitive advantage over the competitors through financial unbalancing or as a result of search and seizure; and
c) moral gains, which are merely subjective and which result from satisfaction in complying with the law.

Points in support of waiting for detection of the cartel are:

a) a relatively low risk of detection through any investigations conducted;
b) the tardiness of investigations;
c) the possibility of delaying the payment of a fine for several years in the courts; and
d) the possibility of executing an agreement without pleading guilty.

Therefore, the gains resulting from the possibility of immunity can be reduced if the agents who execute consent decrees obtain significant reductions in fines. In the context of responsive regulation, rational agents would be aware of this possibility. If the penalties agreed to in the consent decree are less than the advantages gained from the cartel, leniency may become an institution without any incentive, because the most rational and maximizing strategy would be to wait for the outcome of the investigations in order to assess the involved risks, in view of the fact that the consent decree would be a 'profitable' alternative. An additional benefit of the execution of a consent decree is that the proposal may be submitted up to the end of investigation.

Guilty pleas by cartel members are a usual requirement in plea agreements executed by the Department of Justice in the United States. However, there is no such requirement under Brazilian antitrust law, so that CADE has wide discretionary power to decide whether to require a guilty plea or not. Lastly, there are no requirements for public consultation regarding the agreement to be executed. CADE's regulations provide that the agreement must be made available on the website within five days of its execution.

Table 3 Institutional Structure

	United States		Brazil
	Consent Decree before the FTC	**Plea agreement before the DOJ**	**Brazilian Consent Decree**
Field	Civil	Criminal	Civil
Is it applicable to cartels?	No	Yes	Yes
Is it possible even in cases initiated by means of leniency agreements?	Not applicable	Yes	Yes, provided there is a guilty plea
Is there a need for public consultation?	Yes	Yes	No
Participation of Public Interest Groups (PIGs)?	Yes	Yes	No

In these potentially adverse institutional circumstances, leniency agreements executed in Brazil could be merely derive from agreements executed in other countries, that is, a company that executes leniency agreements in several jurisdictions would also execute one in Brazil. As a consequence, only international cartels would be affected as a result of the reaction of cartel members to international investigations, since local cartel members would not have incentives to execute leniency agreements due to the low incentives vis-à-vis the low likelihood of detection and punishment of potential candidates. The use of leniency agreements for fighting local cartels should be re-evaluated in order to increase the rate of responsiveness.

IV. Spoiling Responsiveness: Unintended Effects of the Introduction of Consent Decrees in the Antitrust Policy to Fight Cartels

The introduction of a new variable in the regulatory toolkit may not produce the expected effect. In certain scenarios, it is possible to observe the side-effects of an allegedly responsive regulation in a given balance, and any regulatory change may affect the existing balance. A correct understanding of the effects of a rule is indispensable for successful anti-cartel policies, because 'wishful thinking is no substitute for theoretical understanding. Underlying most regulatory failure, ironic or otherwise, is bad science.'[28]

[28] P N Grabosky, 'Counterproductive Regulation' 23 *International Journal of Sociology of Law* 347, 356 (1995).

Win–win games, which are so clearly seen in the case of leniency agreements, become more obscure in the negotiation of agreements with cartel members. What would a cartel member win by accepting a deal under which it agrees to pay a fine? In the US, the clarity of the punishment system, expressed in the US Sentencing Guidelines, shows that the likely advantage of the consent decree is a smaller fine. However, the same cannot be said about systems like the Brazilian system, which lack this predictability. Moreover, what should be said about systems in which actual punishment may remain uncertain even after detection and conviction of the cartel by the antitrust authorities? These scenarios are clearly possible in Brazil, because the execution of only the two consent agreements to date[29] may prove to be insufficient to generate guarantees such as those under the US Sentencing Guidelines. Even worse, uncertainty regarding punishments may signal that a likely punishment under a consent decree will be more than offset by the gains to be won by the activities of the cartel.

By using institutional deficiencies characteristic of a certain country, cartel members are able indirectly to 'change' the quantum of punishment imposed by the antitrust authorities. Alternatively, the quantum imposed by the authorities may actually be less than the amount necessary to dissuade the cartel even if no deficiencies of the system are taken into consideration. As the operation of responsive regulation is linked with each country's institutional endowment, one of the main concerns for an antitrust policy importing leniency and consent decrees is how much the quantum of punishment can be changed by these local peculiarities. This is why simultaneous manipulation of leniency agreements and consent decrees requires a reasonable determination of the monopolistic gains made on the part of the antitrust authorities, so as to establish the optimum level of punishment.

A light punishment deriving from a consent decree could discourage leniency to the extent that all cartel members would continue betting on non-detection; and should they be detected, they would be able to settle the case upon payment of a low fine. This is the worst-case scenario flowing from the undesired effects of the simultaneous use of leniency agreements and consent decrees. Even in the US, probably the jurisdiction with the strictest antitrust enforcement, Connor notes that punishments imposed on cartels were not sufficient to dissuade the formation of global cartels, and he identifies the cause as follows:

> Large discounts on maximum fines are often granted for both legitimate reasons (leniency programs) and for minimal cooperation. Payments of fines and settlements are often made many years after the cartel's monopoly profits were earned, which robs recipients of prejudgment interest. Moreover, by charging smaller subsidiaries

[29] Many companies under investigation filed proposals for executing consent decrees in the first days following enactment of CADE's regulation on the matter. However, as of July 2008, CADE had executed only two agreements, and the analyses of the other proposals had not been decided.

> of parent multinationals and by offering multi-year installment payments, antitrust authorities are reluctant to impose fines that might require a defendant to sell some of its assets.[30]

Within this context, it is not implausible to suppose that a failure in the manipulation of a model that theoretically produces the best outcome actually produces worst results. By looking into certain features of the Brazilian institutional endowment, which are essential for the smooth operation of responsive regulation, this paper will show that the Brazilian antitrust authorities may have underestimated the role of the institutional endowment when consent decrees were incorporated as a tool in the antitrust policy. For this reason, in the Brazilian and probably and in the LatinAmerican scenarios, a institutional structure in which the Antitrust Authorities are empowered to execute only leniency agreements could lead to better global results for the enforcement of antitrust authorities than the fourth scenario in which the Antitrust Authorities.

V. Requisites for the Operation of Responsive Regulation: The Use of Consent Decrees in View of Possible Negative Influence from the Institutional Endowment of Brazil

As Sections 2 and 3 above showed, a number of institutional arrangements in Brazil tend to reduce regulatory responsiveness. There are negative influences from the institutional endowment which may impact on the efficient use of public resources—the point is how to use the resources in accordance with one country's own institutional abilities.[31]

As antitrust agencies gain relevance, they tend to draw the attention of politicians, and swiftly become one of the targets in the political bargaining process. In this scenario, it is worth recalling that

> corruption in developing countries is often believed to arise from the clash or conflict between traditional values and the imported norms that accompany modernization and socio-political development.[32]

[30] John M Connor, *Global Price Fixing* (New York, Springer, 2007) at 437.

[31] Bruce M Owen, *Competition Policy in Latin America* (Working Paper 268, Stanford Law School, John Colin Program in Law and Economics, 2003), at 8: '… when we see countries the size of Costa Rica, Panama, Jamaica or Barbados undertaking to enforce US-style antitrust laws, we have to ask whether these countries' human resources are being allocated rationally'.

[32] M S Alam, 'Anatomy of Corruption: An Approach to the Political Economy of Underdevelopment' 48 *American Journal of Economics and Sociology* 441–56 (1989); D H Bayley, 'The Effects of Corruption in a Developing Nation' 19 *The Western Political Science Quarterly* 719–32 (1966).

Both leniency agreements and consent decrees demand wide discretionary powers for the antitrust authority and are to be used in coordination. Otherwise, responsive regulatory outcomes will not be produced. The limitation is recognized implicitly by Levy and Spiller, who consider that 'regulatory schemes designed to maximize efficiency ... usually require substantial discretion for the regulator'.[33] However, one of the ideas behind restricting discretion (and hence the ability of public administration to negotiate) is that this general prohibition can prevent the formation of illicit arrangements involving the public administration.[34]

Another factor is the institutional capacity of Brazilian antitrust authorities. There is chronic turnover among CADE's administrative staff. There are two main explanations for this: the absence of a specific career path, and low salaries. These limitations may explain why CADE is willing to rely upon consent decrees to reach its goals. High turnover reduces institutional memory vis-à-vis the intelligence of cartel members, and makes regulation less responsive.

Besides the above-mentioned particular features of the Brazilian institutional endowment which impact adversely on the operation of the responsive regulation, there are two others which are analyzed in detail below.

A. Damage to the Image of Invincibility

There are no consolidated statistics about the rate of success of Brazilian antitrust authorities. However, CADE has lost many important cases since 1994. In the price-fixing cases concerning medical associations and unions, CADE won seven cases and lost six; in the appeal court, CADE lost both cases appealed. In the steel cartel cases, CADE lost seven cases and won two; in the appeal court, CADE did better by winning one case. In its attempt to force banks to notify CADE of mergers (in addition to the Central Bank), it similarly lost a number of important cases; only after six years of litigation did CADE manage to succeed in one of the appeal courts.[35]

More telling is that 'successful' cases do not result in large penalties. In 2002, only R$12,770 were actually paid out of the R$2.8 million imposed in fines. In 2003 the same situation continued, illustrating how chronic the problem was; total fines imposed amounted to R$8.3 million, but only R$620,000 were paid to the authorities. In 2005, CADE imposed more than R$5.6 million in fines, though none of this amount was paid. In 2006 and 2007, there was a perceptible change in the trend, but the damage to CADE's reputation (as a regulator that lacks invincibility) had already been done.

[33] Levy and Spiller, above n 2, at 2.

[34] Eugene Bardach and Robert Kagan, *Going by the Book: the Problem of Regulatory Unreasonableness*, 2nd edn (Edison, Transaction Publishers, 2003), at 35.

[35] CADE *Relatório anual 2005* (Brasília, 2005), at 37–60.

Table 4 Fines imposed and paid following violation of the economic order

Year	Assessed	Paid	Percentage paid
2002	R$ 2.8 million	R$ 12,770.00	0.45%
2003	R$ 8.3 million	R$ 620,000.00	7.46%
2004	R$ 5.6 million	R$ 0.00	0%
Total (02/04)	R$ 16.7 million	R$ 632,770.00	3.78%

Source: OECD[36]

One antitrust lawyer, Grinberg, has confirmed this pattern and argued that that only lip service was paid to the so-called priority to fight hard-core cartels.[37] In the period from 1999 to 2003, he argued that none of the 25 antitrust violations punished by CADE was about market division or the limitation of production; instead they concerned price-fixing and fraud in public bids. Further, only two cases concerned the industrial sector (steel and shipyards), five the commercial sector (gas stations) and 18 professional associations. Among these 18 cases, 15 concerned medical associations or unions. Grinberg concluded that there was a great difference between what the authorities said and the reality of the actions that CADE condemned.[38]

Such a serious mismatch between regulatory practice and regulatory rhetoric reduces the credibility of persuasion as a tool. In spite of recent improvements made by CADE's Attorney Office, the success rate of defendants continues to be more than reasonable. Law enforcement has historically encountered problems in Brazil, where cynics say that 'there are laws that are enforced and other that are not enforced'. This makes enforcement an even more serious issue for any Brazilian regulator.

Legal enforcement by itself is said to be detrimental to responsiveness.[39] So what kind of incentive would a recidivist company need in order to obey the law? If it is an organizationally incompetent entity, it will continue to break the law. Would a company be persuaded not to commit a violation, or not to form a monopoly through merger, if it was known in advance that there was a 50 per cent chance of success? Moreover, path dependence problems,[40] in the analyzed case represented by the resistance to stronger competition enforcement, can cause major difficulties in the current attempts by the Brazilian competition authorities to improve the system's performance.

36 OECD, *Competition Law and Policy in Brazil – A Peer Review* (Paris, OECD Publishing, 2005).

37 Mauro Grinberg, 'O CADE, os cartéis e suas condenações' ('CADE, the Cartels and its Condemnations'), *Gazeta Mercantil* (Dec 7, 2004) 1.

38 *Ibid.*

39 Bardach and Kagan, above n 34, at 177–99.

40 Douglass North, 'Privatization, Incentives and Economic Performance' (Working Paper, Washington University, St Louis, 1994), <http://netec.mcc.ac.uk/WoPEc/data/Papers/wpawuwpeh9411002.html>, 11.

In this adverse scenario, executing consent agreements with cartel members could be seen as the least bad institutional alternative. Agreements avoid time- and resource-consuming litigation. The SDE recognizes this aspect, and enthusiastically endorses the policy which uses consent decrees as a regulatory tool.[41] Nevertheless, such an approach ignores the fact that cartel members look to the performance of CADE in the courts when deciding whether to make leniency applications and execute consent decrees instead of litigating. If the success rate of cartels in the courts is high, the antitrust authorities will be forced to negotiate on even less favorable terms in order to dissuade the formation of cartels. To paraphrase Epstein, less is even less.[42]

All of the difficulties have an adverse impact on the operation of the 'benign big gun' by the Brazilian antitrust authorities. Leniency becomes less attractive, because the chances of successfully challenging an adverse final decision increase. Indirectly, this is reflected in a higher inclination by cartel members to wait for detection and not to approach the antitrust authorities in order to execute leniency agreements. There is evidence that changes in the level of enforcement are underway, but it is too early to predict their effect.

B. Lack of Transparency and Public Interest Groups (PIGs)

Transparency is one of the requisites for responsive regulation to take place. In this regard, pressure groups with a focus on the public interest in antitrust enforcement can perform a pivotal role, as they can act as a countervailing force to the risk of capture and corruption in the antitrust community. The PIGs may participate in the decision-making process in three different ways:

a) easy access to information available to the regulators;
b) participation in the negotiations between the regulatory authority and the company; and
c) the possibility of bringing an action against the company in order to enforce, on similar conditions to the regulator.[43]

However, none of these is present in the Brazilian institutional structure.

This scenario, ie the absence of participation of PIGs in the process of executing agreements with cartel members, increases the risks of distortion resulting from the lack of transparency. In spite of the efforts made by CADE, the criteria for

[41] See 'Política da SDE para emitir parecer sobre proposta de TCC em cartéis', <http://www.mj.gov.br/main.asp?View={9F537202-913E-4969-9ECB0BC8ABF361D5}&Team=&params=itemID={597B15F3-5E70-4344-8D2E-1D00D14E5804};&UIPartUID={2868BA3C-1C72-4347-BE11-A26F70F4CB26}>.

[42] Richard Epstein, *Antitrust Consent Decrees in Theory and Practice: Why Less is More* (Washington, AEI Press, 2007) at 2.

[43] Ayres and Braithwaite, above n 5, at 57–58.

deciding when to execute consent decrees are not consolidated, let alone clearly institutionalized—principles laid down by CADE are stated in its two decisions with non-binding effects.

Indeed, the OECD had recommended to Brazil that the execution of agreements should be preceded by public consultation:

> The ability to negotiate for a minimal fine should provide an incentive for firms to settle rather than engage CADE in protracted administrative litigation and judicial review proceedings. CADE could issue an appropriate remedial order (after a public comment period) and impose a small fine, thus effectively restoring competition without the delay and expense associated with litigation.[44]

Thus, the amendment to the Brazilian Antitrust Law was the opposite of what had been recommended. With more transparency, interested parties could play a major role in the maintenance of incentives for the execution of leniency agreements, and such pressure could serve as a form of compensation for the possible lack of effective (ie deterrent) punishment in a consent decree.

The PIGs have certain procedural rights at their disposal, which allow them to bring an action to enforce antitrust laws, but their ability to challenge a final decision issued by the CADE is controversial. This confirms that these procedural rights are limited, especially to the cases of damage suffered by large number of consumers who do not normally hold strong buying power. Thus, only those PIGs that have suffered a loss caused by the cartel are able to bring an action, and it is not clear whether an indemnity can be paid to a PIG's associate members. Furthermore, in view of the low organizational level of the PIGs in Brazil, they do not possess resources and specialists capable of dealing with complex matters. These difficulties are reflected in the small number of private suits for damages.[45]

This unfavorable scenario, in which there are no PIGs directly involved or interested in the outcome of the antitrust policy, is harmful to CADE's autonomy. In order to promote a culture of competition, CADE should encourage the development of independent entities with a focus on antitrust as a way of granting transparency and legitimacy to its own actions. The PIGs could assist the antitrust authorities in promoting competition advocacy, for instance by assisting in more complex court cases.

VI. Conclusion

The increase in the number of successful cartel investigations in Brazil as of 2003 changes one of the variables of the formation of cartel costs: cartel detection has

[44] OECD Secretary General and IDB, above n 25, at 168.
[45] OECD Secretary General and IDB, above note 25, at 125.

increased significantly. After detection of the cartel, the cartel members face more concrete risks of punishment than when the agreement was secret. The responsive regulation model predicts that such a change transforms the reactions of cartel members to cartel enforcement. Decisions of cartel members would depend not only on the nature of the punishment established by the antitrust authorities, but also on the certainty of its enforcement. The precise identity of those factors that may interfere in that enforcement will be known, which will help the antitrust authorities to define the appropriate level of punishment, that is, a punishment that includes both punitive and dissuasive characteristics. This is the Achilles' heel of the Brazilian antitrust authorities.

As widely acknowledged, it is very difficult to establish an institutional model that allows a *Pareto Optimum*. Responsive regulation assumes this premise to be true, and suggests that the best strategy should be based on a case-by-case approach. More than theoretical perfection, those who formulate public policies should concentrate on the adequacy of the institutional endowment of each country. It is not an easy task, and it is unlikely that the legislators will acknowledge that their countries are not able to deal with sophisticated legal structures.

This chapter is not about criticizing the simple introduction of an institutional change to copy the system in force in the United States. On the contrary, the responsive regulation model acknowledges that the possibility of executing agreements with violators is indispensable to successful enforcement. If this increase in efficiency does not occur, however, or if it produces collateral effects, the introduction of consent decrees must be set aside in favor of institutional arrangements that reflect a second best choice.

Given a certain institutional environment, a regulatory structure deemed optimum in another jurisdiction (eg the possibility of executing agreements with cartels to resolve cases rapidly) may present inferior or undesired effects in a sub-optimum environment (eg the impossibility of executing agreements with cartels, which delays resolution of the cases). The great paradox is that the same conditions that enable an optimum regulation also cause undesired effects or consequences.[46] Analysis of the Brazilian institutional endowment suggests that the simultaneous adoption of leniency and consent decrees may lead to this scenario.

[46] Contrarily, OECD seems to ignore the fact that plea agreements can have undesirable effects. 'An objection to leniency, similar to an objection sometimes raised against 'plea bargaining,' is that law enforcement agencies that take less than vigorous action against violations are improperly shirking their duties. In such a conception of jurisprudence, the enforcer has no discretion to moderate the law's application. But few if any agencies could function effectively subject to such expectations. Some prioritising and balancing of costs and benefits in the enforcement process is inevitable. The European Commission addresses this objection directly, finding that 'the interests of consumers and citizens in ensuring that [cartel] practices are detected and prohibited outweigh the interest in fining those enterprises which co-operate with the Commission, thereby enabling or helping it to detect and prohibit a cartel.' A similar statement appears in the UK program. It is likely that overall enforcement effectiveness and compliance will improve, as leniency for a few participants makes it possible to apply the law more thoroughly to others.' OECD, *Fighting Hard Core Cartels: Harm, Effective Sanctions and Leniency Programmes* (2002), 26.

As the Congress is currently discussing a Bill to replace the Brazilian Antitrust Law, legislators should take this matter into account and exclude the possibility of executing consent decrees.

Although there have been visible efforts by CADE and the SDE to overcome these negative characteristics of the institutional endowment, the level of success varies from country to country, and recent Latin American history reveals that regression is common after periods of success. There are forces that tend to distort the use of consent decrees and that, by changing the payoffs expected by the cartel members, could discourage the use of leniency agreements by opportunist cartel members. All these factors could adversely affect the operation of leniency agreements. Notwithstanding the existence of this force that tends to distort the purposes of consent decrees, the outcomes remain uncertain—antitrust authorities should pay attention to these aspects to avoid policy mistakes.

Chapter VII

'Gun Jumping' or Cartel: Is Brazil Prepared for this Analysis?

LEONOR CORDOVIL*

I. Introduction to 'Gun Jumping'

Competition law is a relatively new in Brazil and in a state of evolution.[1] One area in which it is evolving is the intersection of merger control with cartel enforcement. The intersection occurs when there is coordination between companies or economic groups prior to mergers, which is called 'pre-merger coordination' or 'gun jumping'. Both terms describe the acts of information exchange and communication prior to merger. The biggest challenge is to distinguish between when such actions lead to pro-competitive outcomes and when they lead to illegal anti-competitive outcomes.

In some countries, legislation requires the parties involved in a merger to be under close scrutiny during the period while competition authorities review the merits of the merger. The parties cannot exchange information or act to the detriment of competition until the analysis is complete.[2] This system is common in a pre-merger notification system. Brazil presents an anomalous situation in that it has adopted the post-merger notification system. That is, the parties first sign the merger agreement and then notify the competition authorities. Condition precedent is not mentioned in Brazilian law, which means that the companies can adopt any type of practice they consider necessary to the completion of the transaction, even before its approval. However, the exchange of information or practices that eliminate competition among

* The author is a trade and competition lawyer in Brazil and a PhD in International Economic Law and Economic Law in the University of Sao Paulo and the Université Paris 1—Pantheon Sorbonne. The author would like to thank Mauro Grinberg and Natália Lima Figueiredo for their help with ideas and review.

[1] Although competition law concerns can be traced back to the Brazilian Constitution of 1937, the current Brazilian competition policy system (BCPS) has its foundation in 1994's Law # 8.884/94.

[2] In the United States, three laws address this dynamic interaction of pre-merger notification and collusion: section 7A of the Clayton Act, which requires pre-merger notification; section I of the Sherman Act, which prohibits agreements that unreasonably restrict trade; and section 5 of the Federal Trade Commission Act, which forbids unfair competition methods.

companies can be considered under Brazilian law as a collusive activity, which is punishable according to Article 21, I, of Law # 8.884/94.[3] Because of the law's wording and because there are no specific provisions about 'gun jumping' or limits on pre-merger activity, it is difficult to discern where information exchange ends and collusion begins. The current post-notification structure creates particular challenges to an effective Brazilian competition policy system (BCPS).

As a consequence of the limitations of the current post-merger notification institutional design, the Brazilian legislature has introduced a Bill that would change the current system to require pre-merger notification. Bill # 5.877/2005, which aims to revamp the BCPS completely, includes a number of innovations, but does not indicate a reasonable term within which transactions must be kept 'frozen' until approval, or at least until initial authorization by the authority. Additionally, the Bill places no restrictions upon conversations and negotiations between parties. Therefore, it is possible that competition between the merging parties may cease even before notification to the authorities. This proposed approach may be very tempting for companies that simply wish to exchange market information and set strategies, in collusion, without any concern about a future merger.

II. Current Brazilian Standards

Unlike most countries in the world, Brazil currently has a post-merger notification system. A transaction may be submitted to the authorities up to 15 business days after the execution of a merger agreement.[4] The authorities' approval is not mandatory for the completion of the transaction. The parties are free to undertake the transaction, execute all necessary documents and transmit all confidential information, without needing to wait for the authorities' approval.

All mergers involving companies or economic groups that have registered, in Brazil, a turnover of R$400 million (approximately US$ 200 million) or more, and which represent a relevant market of 20 per cent or more, must be reported. In cases of late submission, the applicable penalty ranges from 60.000 to 6.000.000 UFIR (1 UFIR is around R$1.23). In spite of these general provisions, Brazilian antitrust legislation includes no specific provision about 'gun jumping'. There are no guidelines regarding corporate behavior before or after notification, or about information transmitted before or after filing.

[3] Article 21 of Brazilian Antitrust Law provides that setting or offering prices and conditions, in any way, in collusion with competitors, for the sale of certain products and services, will be deemed a violation of the economic order.

[4] Art 54.

Brazilian competition law does address cartel behavior. Article 21 of Law # 8.884/94 establishes that certain behaviors are unlawfully anti-competitive. Two of the unlawful behaviors are:

a) fixing price and sales conditions, or colluding with a competitor in any way; and
b) obtaining or influencing the adoption of uniform or coordinated commercial conduct between competitors.

Sanctions may include penalties set at between 1 per cent and 30 per cent of the company's gross turnover in the year before the previous fiscal year, in addition to any criminal and civil personal penalties against individuals, cartel leaders or anyone who has participated actively in the cartel.

In the last five years, there has been an incredible increase in the number of cartel investigations in Brazil. The first conviction in a cartel case took place in 1999, in the steel sector. In 2002, the Administrative Counsel for Economic Defense (CADE) fined two cartels involving gas stations, penalties equal to 10 per cent of the cartel members' revenues. Investigatory methods have become more and more sophisticated due to stronger integration between antitrust authorities and the police, and because of the use of wiretapping and computer monitoring. In 2003, Brazilian antitrust enforcers undertook their first dawn raid in the crushed stones case.[5] Antitrust enforcers seized documents, agendas and electronic data. This evidence contributed to the companies' condemnation by CADE for price-fixing, which occurred in 2005.

Evidence of cartels is not easy to find. Proof of parallel conduct by companies is not enough to establish a cartel infraction. Additionally, finding formal evidence of collusion is essential, such as evidence that there was a meeting of minds.

Article 30 of Law # 8.884/94 provides that the Secretariat of Economic Law (SDE), which is part of the Ministry of Justice, can initiate preliminary investigations even when the evidence provided by the parties or otherwise currently available is not sufficient to initiate an administrative proceeding. During preliminary investigations, the search and seizure of documents may take place, as well as the collection of evidence which will enable the authorities to decide whether to file an administrative proceeding (since there is no obstacle to such collection in the administrative procedure). If the SDE is convinced that sufficient evidence exists, it can file such a proceeding before CADE.

A. 'Gun Jumping' in Brazil

There is no Brazilian legal provision related to 'gun jumping' or to negotiations preceding a merger. The interested parties are *apparently* free to exchange any

[5] *Crushed stones* [2006] AP no 08012.002127/02-04.

information they wish before the execution of the agreement. After the execution, they have a legal obligation to notify the authorities of the agreement within 15 business days, but they do not need to wait for the authorities' approval in order to close the transaction.

Such legal unpredictability encourages companies to believe that there are no limits to the exchange of information or negotiations, or to the completion of the merger. It is not rare to observe companies in the process of a merger acting as though they are already integrated, even though they have not yet executed the first binding document. If this merger is not completed for any reason, the companies would have already shared a significant amount of information, and would know the strategies, prices and data of their competitors.

Every proposed merger presumes at least one initial meeting between the parties to negotiate the terms of the agreement. It is not unusual to find news reports by the Brazilian media about groups or companies which, wishing to merge, meet in order to negotiate the conditions relating to payment, price, share value and asset value. The media disclose the existence of the meeting but, in many cases, do not know, and hence do not disclose, the meeting's purpose. Most of these companies are unaware of the legal limits to their negotiations and believe that the more information transmitted (especially by the company to be acquired), the higher the price of the transaction will be for the acquiring company. Even if the companies are aware of their limits, they may prefer to take the risk and exchange all relevant information for the transaction. In this case, the transfer of information related to their strategies, prices and commercial advantages would increase each company's value, but it would reduce the real competition in the market, as the second company will know the first company's plans and will act accordingly, leaving the consumer with no choices as regards price, quality and distinct strategies.

Although there is no specific legal provision which protects or regulates the exchange of information at the negotiation stage, any meeting between competitors in which they define a merger strategy which may lead to an intended parallelism of economic conduct that may harm competition, can constitute an infraction and be considered evidence of a cartel (as stated in Article 21, Item I, of Law # 8.884/94).

In order for a merger to be condemned, it is necessary for it to meet at least one of the criteria stated in Article 20, that is, it must have the purpose or effect, even if not achieved, of limiting, restraining or otherwise harming free competition or enterprise, controlling relevant product or service markets, increasing profits on a discriminatory basis or abusing a dominant position. Therefore, Brazil follows American case law, which does not consider the exchange of information a violation per se of the Sherman Act.

Another important requirement for a cartel conviction is the existence of market power in some or all of the companies involved. If there is no market power, the companies will not be able to harm competition or even obtain the economic results of their practices, as other companies, which have market power and are not involved in the cartel, will immediately offer their products in the affected market.[6]

Notification to the authorities of the existence of a signed agreement brings a certain relief and tacit approval of all information already transmitted or all necessary acts carried out, once BCPS is aware that the two competitors are behaving as a single entity. The problem is when the merger is not concluded, which leaves the firms in an extremely fragile position, unprotected by the authorities.

But if the authorities become aware of the meetings and exchange of information between competitors in Brazil, send an official letter to such competitors and receive an answer to the effect that the meetings are part of preparatory acts for a merger, should the authorities be satisfied with such an explanation and not carry out an investigation? And, keeping in mind the provisions of the Hart-Scott-Rodino Act even though there are no similar provisions in Brazil, should the authorities not be worried about the loss of a competitive situation between the agents, which could become even worse if the concentration is not completed?

B. Establishment of 'Gun Jumping' Rules in Brazil

Although there are no cases on illegal 'gun jumping' in the Brazilian antitrust case law, there are many decisions about cartels, discussing the parties' practices and the nature of the information transmitted between them. Therefore, it is possible to know which parameters the Brazilian authority may use when faced with a cartel.

In a proceeding related to private security companies, the condemnation was based on formal evidence obtained by SDE.[7] A search and seizure was made in which many types of documents were found—documents which demonstrated the existence of collusion to the BCPS. The case represented the first use of leniency in Brazil, that is, some of the documents and evidence were provided by a whistle-blower firm in exchange for reduced penalties. Among the documents were:

a) minutes of meetings;
b) electronic data in which exchanges of information and the collusion between the companies and their representatives were recorded;

[6] 'A mere discussion about prices between companies without any market power does not cause any risk to competition, since they are not able to harm competition. In order for a combination of prices between such companies be considered illicit, it is necessary that they have a minimum market power. Without it, the combination does not present any risk and cannot be punished simply because the most probable result is that the companies will destroy themselves, losing market, if they try to increase their prices in view of such agreement' (free translation of SALOMÃO, Calixto. Direito Concorrencial: as condutas, Sao Paulo: Malheiros Editores, 2001, p 268). In Administrative Proceeding 08000.024758/94-44, CADE decided that there would be little incentive for the affiliates of the Potters' Association of the city of Panorama/SP to form a cartel, given their low market share.

[7] *Private security companies* [2007] AP no 08012.001826/2003-10.

c) electronic data with transcriptions of conversations between the parties;
d) agendas and notebooks with comments;
e) documents containing information about the competitors' number of employees; and
f) documents containing information about the competitors' turnover and prices.

In a proceeding involving the liquefied petroleum gas (LPG) sector, CADE analyzed written and oral messages sent by Sinergás, the producers' trade union, to affiliated companies.[8] In another proceeding in which gas stations headquartered in the city of Florianópolis were investigated and afterwards condemned, SDE collected (among others) documents exchanged between the gas stations and newspaper articles pointing out the existence of meetings and similar practices.[9] Again, the authority demonstrated the existence of meetings.

In the case regarding the crushed stone cartel, SDE found minutes of meetings, as well as messages and e-mails exchanged between the parties containing information, statistics and graphics.[10] In this case, there was a special place for the secret meetings—a closed room accessible only by magnetic card. The seized software also evidenced the coordination and contained specific descriptions of the practices.

Some of the documents and actions mentioned above could be found in any merger process, such as exchanged e-mails, graphics, etc. Imagine that two companies, wishing to integrate their activities or create a joint venture, proceed with the exchange of information through e-mails, printed messages, registering information about competitors in their systems, or by meeting in order to discuss the best strategies. These acts are not necessarily illegal, but they can eliminate totally or partially the competition between the companies.

Regardless of the effects achieved with respect to the merger or joint venture, it is certain that, during that preliminary phase, competition will already have been threatened or ceased to exist. Indeed, that in itself would represent important evidence of the existence of an agreement to fix or practice, in any form, prices and conditions related to the sale of goods or services.[11] It is also not difficult to find the effects listed in Article 20 of Law 8.884/94, especially those contained in Item I (relating to the limitation of free competition).[12] Therefore, it would not be impossible for the authority consider the activity as amounting to the creation of a cartel, and not simply as acts preparatory to a merger, although the practices are conceptually distinct.

Some exchange of data between the two companies is necessary, but they can adopt some safety measures, in order to minimize anti-competitive risks, like using

[8] *LPG* [2005] AP no 08012.003068/2001-11.
[9] *Gas stations* [2002] AP no 08012.02299/2000-18.
[10] *Crushed stones* [2006] AP no 08012.002127/02-04.
[11] As stated in Art 21.
[12] Above n 5.

external consultants to deal with this sensitive information.[13] When companies are really in a pre-merger action, they must behave as firms in a pre-merger state, and not as a single company.

In view of such substantial risks to the firms and also to the competition, the establishment of rules about 'gun jumping' in Brazil is necessary and urgent. However, it is impossible to define concrete rules, precise information, or specific documents which cannot be exchanged or sent during the waiting period connected with the authorities' decisions. Such criteria are identifiable only on a case-by-case basis; specific defining of criteria can harm their practical applicability, making them either exaggerated or too superficial. Some definition is to be found in the case law, but it will be applicable in the Brazilian Civil Law tradition only if the obligation to respect a waiting period is clearly stated in the legislation. The rules might also clarify some non-exhaustive guidelines about the behavior and companies' action in the pre-merger period.

C. Cartels and 'Gun Jumping'

Although there are no rules in Brazil about 'gun jumping', in view of what Brazilian case law defines as a cartel, it is possible to differentiate it from normal practices that precede a merger. In the proceeding known as *CSN-Cosipa-Usiminas*, CADE defined a cartel as being an agreement between companies in which the price is generally fixed or the market is divided.[14] However, CADE states that cartels come in other forms too, such as cartels connected to product quality and the launch of new products, among others. Cartels have a pre-established purpose, which is to increase the price to consumers, reducing competition as though there was just one competitor. CADE noted that there are some classic requirements for the creation of a price cartel, such as a small number of competitors, homogeneous products, high entry barriers, the absence of incentives to exit, similar cost structure and stability of market shares.[15]

In the case of the *Crushed Stone* cartel, CADE defined 'hard-core' cartels as secret agreements among competitors with any form of institutionalism, aimed at fixing sales prices and conditions, sharing consumers, defining the production level or preventing the entry of new competitors into the market.[16] CADE stated that this type of cartel operates according to an institutionalized mechanism of coordination, which can involve, amongst other things, periodical meetings, operational guidelines and behavioral principles. That is, the formation of the cartel does not derive from occasional instances of coordination, but from the construction of permanent mechanisms to achieve its aims.

[13] Section III below.
[14] *CSN-Cosipa-Usiminas* [1999] AP no 08000.015337/97-48.
[15] *Ibid.*
[16] *Crushed stones* [2006] AP no 08012.002127/02-04.

Diffuse cartels are another form, one which is distinguishable from the hard-core cartels. They are distinct because their coordination is occasional and not institutionalized. This is the case, for example, when a group of companies decides to meet in order to combine prices and challenge an external event that simultaneously affects all of them, for example they decide to reduce their production in order to increase prices.

Hard-core cartels are illegal per se in most jurisdictions. In Brazil, there is no such automatic condemnation. CADE's general opinion is that cartels should be condemned only if they cause or may cause harm to the market. All the cases mentioned in this section give some guidance as to when the BCPS will deem a cartel to exist. There will usually be the following indications:

a) a pre-established purpose;
b) a small number of competitors;
c) homogeneous products;
d) entry barriers;
e) absence of incentives to cheat;
f) similar costs between the companies involved;
g) stability of market shares; and
h) any form of institutionalism (eg, meetings).

In view of the these indicia, it is possible to conclude that, in Brazil, the practice of 'gun jumping' would not fall within the requirements of Brazilian case law and legislation for the characterization of a cartel. However, the threshold between the preparatory acts of a merger and collusion for price formation and coordinated practices is very narrow. If the competition authorities become aware that preparatory acts precede a transaction, condemnation cannot take place, given that there is no explicit law prohibiting the exchange of information between competitors in a pre-merger proceeding. In such a case, the purpose of exchanging information with a view to a merger must be very clear, and the companies must show that their purpose was not to collude (pre-established purpose), that they could not behave like a cartel because of the relevant number of competitors in the market, that there are differences among their products, that the low entry barriers would permit market contestability from other competitors in other markets, or one of the other cartel requirements described in the last paragraph (letters 'f', 'g', 'h', 'i').

Article 21 of Law # 8.884/94 condemns agreements for fixing prices or sales conditions, which is very different from, for instance, condemning exchanges of information or strategies for a merger. However, whether behaviors are considered to be preparatory acts or illicit agreements is a decision made exclusively by the authority, based on the criteria mentioned above, which will analyze the existing evidence provided by the interested parties. For this reason, the establishment of legal provisions setting limits and penalties for the acts between competitors occurring before a merger is urgent, in order that such preparatory acts can be effectively differentiated from the establishment of a cartel.

D. Competition Bill

One of the most important modifications that Bill # 5.877/2005 proposes is the establishment of a pre-merger notification system. The purpose of such a system is to avoid the costs associated with occasional future divestures[17] of already completed transactions. César Mattos concludes that one potential problem would be occasional delays in the analysis of simple acts, which would have a harmful effect on urgent restructurings in the private sector.[18] In the case of these simple acts, according to Mattos, the parties and authorities could decide to observe different periods of analysis, depending on the transaction's needs. For example, in a very urgent transaction, a maximum period of analysis could be established, within which CADE would have to give its opinion in relation to the continuation of the transaction, based on its preliminary evaluation.[19]

Although the bill # 5.877/2005 does not provides for gun jumping, the necessity of granting urgent 'blessings' to less important acts was recorded, as well as CADE's power to allot a shorter time for certain analyses. Accordingly, apparently simple transactions, which do not raise concerns from a competition point of view, are allowed by the authorities. Given such allowance, the competitors would be free to carry out all the activities related to the transaction and could act as one single player in the market.

III. Guidelines

The identification of what types of information are too sensitive and what acts are ill-advised before and during the waiting period depends on the sector in which the industry operates and its concentration level. Each transaction involves different competitors and sectors. Further, the information that is allowed will vary with time—the nearer the conclusion of the business, the greater the volume of information that can be exchanged.[20]

Normally, avoiding 'gun jumping' includes a prohibition on transmitting the following information:

a) specific information about price, costs, discounts and profits (except historical information);
b) research and development plans;
c) strategic plans;

[17] If the authority decides that the structure of the transaction is not good for competition, it may force the companies to return to the 'status quo ante', to the situation before the structure.

[18] César Mattos, 'Bill n 5.877/2005—Reestruturação do Sistema Brasileiro de Defesa da Concorrência: exposição de motivos'. Exposure of Reasons' (2007). www.econ.pucrio.br/PDF/seminario/2007/Resumo%20Projeto%20de%20Lei%205877.pdf>.

[19] *Ibid.*

[20] *Ibid.*

d) marketing plans;
e) lists of individual consumers;
f) information about the terms and conditions of agreements which are not in the public domain;
g) certain information about suppliers which may grant competitive advantage.

Another important matter to take into consideration when drafting guidelines on 'gun jumping' is that confidentiality agreements, contrary to popular belief, do not really protect the parties. Indeed, once the existence of such an agreement becomes known, it will help to condemn the parties, being seen as evidence of the exchange of information that could not be exchanged. An interesting practice in the United States is the use of 'clean teams'. These generally consist of advisors or external accountants, who provide one company with any required market information about the other company, in order to avoid any direct exchange of information between the two companies. We can use the same recommendations in Brazil, for Brazilian companies and according to Brazilian law. Some companies, in bad faith, may exchange information and, if the authorities decide to investigate them, explain that their practice is a pre-merger coordination. In this case, the practice falls within the concept of collusion, in violation of Article 21, Item I, of Law # 8.884/94.[21]

IV. Conclusion

In countries with the post-merger notification system, such as Brazil, unclear guidance about potential gun jumping has increased businesses' lack of confidence in the BCPS. In Brazil, Law # 8.884/94 states that a cartel means the establishment, in agreement with competitors, of sale prices and conditions, among other elements.[22] Such acts can be confused with the acts preceding a merger process, in which the companies exchange strategic information related to their respective future commercial practices. Likewise, a company investigated for cartel activity can allege, in its defense, that it is merely preparing for a merger.

Brazil faces significant challenges in modifying and improving its notification system. Clear rules must be established concerning which practices are permissible before a merger is reported to the authorities, as well as what is permissible in the interval between the submission of a proposal and its approval. If such rules are not put in place, and a delay of approval occurs, the parties will continue to move forward, carrying out all the informal and tacit acts needed to complete the transaction. By doing this they cease to be competitors, which is exactly the condition the law seeks to avoid.

[21] Above n 5.
[22] Above n 4.

Chapter VIII

Leniency Program in Brazil

MAURO GRINBERG*

I. Introduction

This chapter focuses on the problems of the Brazilian leniency program and its legal aspects that lead some authors to assert that it is not constitutional. The chapter also highlights practical issues concerning amnesty programs that may relate not only to Brazil but also to many other jurisdictions. One of the main thrusts of competition policy is to ensure a continuing fight against collusion and price fixing. Antitrust authorities are motivated by the maximization of social welfare by minimizing the occurrence of collusion among firms.

Antitrust agencies need to determine how best to address and combat cartels. In the design of cartel policy we find richer and more complex mechanisms than those based simply on increasing fines.[1] Accordingly, Brazilian legislation provides for some alternatives to reward undertakings (referred to as 'firms' in the United States) and individuals that cooperate with the enforcement authorities, helping them to detect and punish certain crimes. In this context, leniency programs play an important role in fighting cartels effectively without wasting public resources.

Leniency has changed the landscape of cartel enforcement. The clearest and most complete form of leniency is amnesty from prosecution, but it can also mean a reduction in the penalty compared with what would be sought in the absence of full, voluntary cooperation. Since 1978, the US Antitrust Division of the Department of Justice has allowed for the possibility for guilty parties to avoid criminal sanctions if they meet specific conditions. In 1993, the policy was redesigned and issued as the *Corporate Leniency Policy*.[2] This has proven to be an amazing success and has resulted in a number of leniency applications, which have led to dozens of convictions and to billions of dollars in fines. Many

* Mauro Grinberg is a partner at Barcellos Tucunduva and a former Commissioner of the Brazilian Administrative Council for Economic Defense (CADE). The author wants to thank the hard work of Natália Lima Figueiredo, still an intern but certainly a great future competition lawyer.

[1] Massimo Motta and Michele Polo, 'Leniency Programs and Cartel Prosecution', 21 *International Journal of Industrial Organization* 347–79 (2003).

[2] US Dept of Justice, *Corporate Leniency Policy* 1 (Aug 10, 1993), http://www.usdoj.gov/atr/public/guidelines/0091.htm.

European countries introduced similar policies following the leniency program introduced by the European Union in 1996.

Because cartels are, by their very nature, secret as a practical matter, it is very difficult to detect and investigate them without the cooperation of firms or individuals connected to the illicit activity. Consequently, it is in the social interest to reward firms involved in these types of illegal practices that are willing to put an end to their participation and cooperate in administrative or criminal investigations, independently of the rest of the undertakings involved in the cartel.

A decisive contribution to the opening of an investigation or to the detection of an infringement may justify the granting of immunity from any fine to the undertaking in question. These initiatives have proved to be useful for the effective investigation and termination of cartel infringements, and they should not be discouraged.[3]

II. Brief Introduction to Antitrust in Brazil

The Brazilian competition system comprises:

a) Secretariat for Economic Monitoring (SEAE/MF): SEAE is responsible for the analysis of economic aspects of transactions (mergers) and administrative procedures (conduct cases).
b) Secretariat of Economic Law (SDE): SDE is in charge of the analysis of legal aspects of transactions, monitoring legal entities with significant market power in order to prevent violations, filing administrative procedures involving anti-competitive actions, and producing and analyzing evidence.
c) Administrative Council for Economic Defense (CADE): CADE is responsible for the analysis of the cases and opinions issued by SEAE and SDE, and for the final decisions in all cases related to antitrust law.

Article 35-B of the Brazilian Antitrust Law (Law No 8.884/94) provides for the possibility of granting leniency to corporations and individuals reporting illegal activity, provided that the parties cooperate with the SDE:

> *The Federal Government, through SDE, will be able to enter into leniency agreements, extinguishing the punitive action which could be taken by the government or reducing the applicable penalty by one- to two-thirds pursuant to the terms hereof, for individuals and legal entities that engage in anti-competitive practices, provided that such individuals and legal entities effectively cooperate with investigations and administrative proceedings*

[3] These conclusions, which we share, are found in the EU's *Commission Notice on Immunity from Fines and Reduction of Fines in Cartel Cases* (2006/C298/11). http://ec.europa.eu/comm/competition/cartels/legislation/leniency_legislation.html

III. Brazilian Leniency Program

An amendment to the Brazilian Antitrust Law (Law 8.884/94) introduced leniency in 2000. Since then, there have been a number of leniency applications. As of the time of writing, 12 leniency agreements have been executed.[4] Due to the lack of experience of the Brazilian authorities in executing this kind of agreement, many doubts have arisen with regard to the legal provisions concerning leniency.

A. Requirements for Leniency Applications

According to the Brazilian Antitrust Law, leniency agreements may be executed only by individuals or legal entities that meet certain requirements. First, the applicant must be the first applicant to apply under the program and cannot be the cartel leader or manager. Secondly, SDE must not have amassed enough evidence already, ie at the time of the leniency application, to convict the companies or individuals involved in the cartel. In addition, the company or the individual must have ceased its involvement in the illegal activity as of the date it applies for the program.

After executing the agreement, the party must provide full, continuous and complete cooperation to SDE at his or her own expense. The leniency policy requires full and frank disclosure as a condition precedent to an applicant receiving final leniency. Cooperation with SDE is a continuing obligation, requiring the applicant to provide SDE with expeditious access to individuals and information. Although the execution of the leniency agreement is not subject to CADE's approval, if an applicant does not provide the degree of cooperation expected, CADE may not grant amnesty when judging the respective administrative proceeding.

The amnesty accorded to the applicant may be total or partial, depending on SDE's level of awareness of the underlying anti-competitive behavior. Amnesty will be total if SDE was unaware of the cartel at the time the applicant applied for the program. The requirement that SDE does not know of the existence of a cartel is quite flexible. SDE may not wish to deny an applicant immunity from prosecution and penalty in circumstances where SDE has only very general information pointing to the existence of a cartel. On the other hand, the immunity will be partial where the government already has some substantial knowledge.

Leniency policies generally provide two levels of protection:

a) immunity from prosecution; and
b) immunity from administrative penalty.

[4] Information available at http://www.terra.com.br/istoedinheiro/edicoes/595/cerco-aos-carteisgoverno-intensifica-combate-aos-esquemas-que-prejudicam-a-127060-1.htm.

Brazilian antitrust law, however, does not expressly mention these two kinds of protection. The law merely states that CADE, when judging the respective administrative proceeding and verifying that the leniency agreement was abided by, will:

a) extinguish the administration's power to convict the offender if SDE was unaware of the cartel at the time the applicant applied for the program; or
b) in the remaining cases, reduce the applicable penalties by one- to two-thirds.

B. Leniency for Directors, Officers and Employees

Leniency has become an important part of anti-cartel policy around the world. Part C of the US Amnesty Program states that:

> *Directors, officers, and employees of the corporation who admit their involvement in the illegal antitrust activity as part of the corporate confession will receive leniency, in the form of not being charged criminally for the illegal activity, if they admit their wrongdoing with candor and completeness and continue to assist the Division throughout the investigation.*[5]

Likewise, Brazilian Law 8.884/94 states that the leniency agreement will be extended to managers and directors of the company who qualify for the amnesty program, as long as they execute the agreement collectively with the company. Although the law does not expressly mention officers and other company employees, CADE tends to include in the agreement all individuals who confess their involvement in the illicit conduct. By doing so, CADE provides full protection for those who cooperate effectively, and this makes its corporate leniency policy more effective, transparent and predictable. All employees and corporate executives who execute the agreement will be afforded leniency.

Individuals who approach SDE on their own behalf, not as part of a corporate offer or confession, to seek leniency for reporting illegal antitrust activity of which SDE has not previously been aware, will also be granted leniency, as long as they meet the following conditions:

a) At the time the individual comes forward to report the illegal activity, SDE has not received the information about the activity being reported from any other source;
b) SDE did not have sufficient evidence to convict the corporation or the individual at the time the agreement is proposed;
c) The individual confesses his or her involvement in the illegal activity and provides full, continuing, and complete cooperation to SDE at his or her own expense; and
d) The individual was not the leader of the activity.

[5] Dept of Justice, *Corporate Leniency Policy* (also called 'Amnesty Program'), Part C, 'Leniency for Corporate Directors, Officers, and Employees', http://www.usdoj.gov/atr/public/guidelines/0091.htm.

Note that the Brazilian conditions are very similar to those required in the Department of Justice's Amnesty Program. In Brazil, most of the leniency granted to individuals who have come forward to report illegal activity involves individuals who were dismissed from firms undertaking illegal behavior. Brazilian antitrust authorities do not give any degree of leniency to firms or individuals that cooperate with a certain investigation if they are not the first to request amnesty.

A question that may arise when an individual applies for a leniency program on his or her own behalf is whether there are circumstances in which leniency should be granted to a corporation after an individual (the Brazilian legal term is a 'natural person') has applied for leniency for the same conduct. Under the current legislation, this is not permitted. It would require an amendment to Law 8.884/94. As a matter of policy, there is good justification for granting amnesty in these types of cases. For instance, there may be circumstances in which a natural person qualifies for leniency but has limited knowledge of the cartel and no access to relevant documents, when it will be beneficial to grant amnesty to a firm. In order to gather a sufficient amount of evidence, SDE should allow firms to apply for leniency after a natural person has also applied. This would provide firms with an incentive to turn over information, while simultaneously providing with SDE a cost-effective mechanism by which to find and collect evidence.

C. Amnesty Plus Program

One important element of Law 8.884/94 is that it states that a company which fails to meet the requirements for full amnesty will be able to enter into a leniency agreement related to *another illegal activity*, so long as SDE is unaware of such other anti-competitive activity. This provision of the amnesty program is an incentive to attract applicants to the program because information on other matters will still be rewarded. Thus, even though a firm may not qualify for amnesty in the initial matter under investigation because someone else has beaten it in filing for amnesty, the value of the firm's assistance in disclosing a second cartel will lead to amnesty for a second offense. This, in turn, could translate into a substantial additional reduction (the 'plus') in the calculation of the fine for its participation in the first offense.[6] The plus program creates an attractive inducement to encourage companies who are already under investigation to report the full extent of their antitrust violations.

However, there are limitations to the amnesty plus program. It is very difficult to persuade parties to enroll in it because while SDE is in charge of granting amnesty, CADE is in charge of deciding whether any violations have occurred and the amount of fines to be imposed. Thus, while an application to the amnesty plus program will lead to a discount of a certain percentage of the fine, the amount of

[6] Law # 8.884/94, *Official Gazette of the Federal Executive*, 13 June 1994.

the fine cannot be gauged in advance. This is a major problem, because fines range from 1 per cent to 30 per cent of the annual turnover.

D. Leniency Program v Juridical Security

According to article 35-B of Law 8.884/94, the leniency agreement is entered into between the whistleblower, which can be a firm or an individual and SDE. The problem, however, is that SDE is bound by the Ministry of Justice and therefore is subject to political influence. In addition, SDE members do not have the estability arising out of a term of office. In this sense, it is controverse whether it would have the necessary impartiality to grant amnesty to the whistleblowers as well as to reduce their penalty.[7]

Besides, par. 9 of article 35-B establishes that the terms and conditions of the leniency agreement will be deemed confidential, except if in the interest of the investigations and the administrative proceeding. However, it is difficult to believe that this confidentiality will be kept, considering that SDE members do not have a term of office and that, when they leave SDE, they are hired by law firms which represent companies which may be interested in the contnent of such an agreement.[8]

In this context, the political influence that SDE is subject to and the lack of a term of office contribute to increase the juridical insecutity of the Brazilian leniency program.

E. Brazilian Antirust Bill

A new bill (Bill no. 3937/2004) that aims at substituting the current Brazilian Antitrust Law has been recently approved by the the House of Representatives. If approved, the bill will introduce some important changes in the Leniency Program.

The first significant change will refer to the requirements for applying for the program. The condition that established that the whistleblower could not be the leader or the manager of the cartel will not exist anymore. This will certainly increase the number of applicants and will enable a more efficient combat against cartels.

In addition, the leniency agreement will not be executed by SDE anymore. CADE will enter into the agreement. This will reduce the problems arising out of the suspicious neutrality associated to SDE.

[7] João Bosco Leopoldino da Fonseca (coordinator), *O Cartel. Doutrina e estudo de casos*, Belo Horizonte, Editions Mandamentos, 2008, p 76.

[8] *Ibid*, p 77.

IV. Immunity from Prosecution v Brazilian Single Jurisdiction and Federal System

The main point of the leniency program, immunity from criminal prosecution, has been challenged as unconstitutional. The first problem the leniency program raises in Brazil relates to the fact that, pursuant to the Brazilian Constitution, only court judges are competent to decide criminal questions. Consequently, SDE would not be authorized to exempt the offender from punishment. Secondly, although leniency proceedings include representatives of the Federal or State Public Prosecutor as one of the parties, other Public Prosecutors may not feel bound to honor the agreement for two reasons:

a) another prosecutor may belong to a different jurisdiction and may not feel bound by such an agreement;
b) Public Prosecutors are independent according to constitutional principles and are not bound by agreements made by other prosecutors.

As of the time of writing, CADE had decided only one case involving a leniency agreement. Yet it is most likely that some (if not all) of the parties will, at some point, try to challenge this decision in the courts. This raises an even more important concern—Brazilian judges are usually unprepared for such cases.

A. Public Prosecutors

The Public Prosecutor's Office wants to be seen as the fourth power of the Brazilian Government (along with the legislature, executive and judiciary), given that it is a self-governing body independent from those other branches. There are Public Prosecutors at both the Federal and State levels (the Federal Public Prosecutor and the State Public Prosecutor).

The Brazilian Constitution sets forth two main principles that are applicable to the Public Prosecutors:

a) unity/indivisibility; and
b) institutional independence.

According to to the principle of unity, the Prosecutors may be seen as constituting one single body, given that their views are unbiased and represent the institution of the office of the Attorney-General. The principle of institutional independence, in turn, relates to the independence of each Public Prosecutor, which insures his or her personal and professional dignity.[9] Each Prosecutor may act according to

[9] Cândido Dinamarco, *Instuituições de Direito Processual Civil I*, São Paulo, Editions Malheiros, 2001), vol 1, 683–84.

his or her own conscience without the intervention of any of the three branches (legislative, executive and judicial) or of the organs of government superior to the office of Public Prosecutor. Independence also refers to self-administration.

These principles seems to be contradictory sometimes given that the Public Prosecutor, despite the institutional independence, shoul act in conformity with the Public Prosecutor Office as a whole, following the principle of unity. However, this is not what often happens, as Public Prosecutors are allowed to act according to their own mind and do not need to follow the policy adopted by another Public Prosecutor or the Public Prosecutor Office of their own jurisdiction.

In this context, these two principles have direct impact in the Brazilian antitrust policy, especially in the way the antitrust authorities execute leniency agreements.

If one follows an interpretation that outweigh the principle of institutional independence, then it may consider that although SDE, regardless of any legal requirement, usually include a Public Prosecutor (a Federal one, for example) as a party in the leniency agreement, this Prosecutor is not empowered to represent the entire class of Public Prosecutors. Thus, Public Prosecutors representing other jurisdictions (State Public Prosecutors, for instance) may accuse applicants based on their confessions. As a consequence, even Prosecutors from the same jurisdiction would be able to file a lawsuit against a leniency applicant if they believed the leniency agreement executed was not valid or constitutional. A judge would also be able to convict the leniency applicant, if one strictly considered the principle that only judges can exempt individuals from prosecution. This problem may take quite a long time to be solved, due to the lethargic pace at which the Brazilian judiciary operates.

In order to reduce the risks arising out of that interpretation, SDE usually has both Federal and local Public Prosecutors enter into the leniency agreement.[10] Note, however, that besides the Federal District, Brazil has 26 States. Each State has its own Public Prosecutor Office that is independent from the offices of other States. Each such office has several Prosecutors, with each one theoretically acting independently. Even if a local Prosecutor executes a leniency agreement, one would not represent the other State offices.

Another approach is also possible, following an interpretation that gives more importance to the principle of unity in detriment of the principle of institutional independence. The *unity* and *indivisibility* provisions mean that the Public Prosecutor represents a single body. The plaintiffs or defendants in a lawsuit, or the parties in a leniency agreement, will not be bound by one particular Prosecutor but by the Public Prosecutor Office itself. Hence, when a Prosecutor executes a leniency agreement, he or she represents the entire Office of the Public Prosecutor. In competition matters, it is a little unclear if we have State or Federal cases. As to *institutional independence*, each Prosecutor must act in accordance

[10] In Brazil, there is some controversy in the case law so as to which jurisdiction, Federal or State, is to prosecute cartels criminally. For this reason, even though transaction costs are very high, SDE has always included both Federal and State Prosecutors in the leniency agreement.

with his or her own conscience. Yet this also means that the Prosecutor must act according to the applicable law and not at his or her own discretion. Because the law includes the principle of *unity*, the Prosecutor must respect that, when he or she signs an agreement or represents one of the parties in a lawsuit, he or she is doing so as a representative office of the Public Prosecutor and not on his or her own behalf. Therefore, if a certain individual Prosecutor decides to file a lawsuit, another Prosecutor cannot intervene in the decision, revoke the power of the first, and file another lawsuit or declare the filing null. Similarly, when a Prosecutor executes an agreement, he or she does so as the Public Prosecutor itself, and another Prosecutor cannot just breach the agreement; neither shall the judges accept such a breach.

The inclusion of a Public Prosecutor in the leniency agreement is not mandatory. SDE takes this action merely as a precaution based on legal formality. It is only symbolic, indicating that the Public Prosecutor will not charge the whistleblower. Should an individual Prosecutor take such action, the judge will most likely decide not to convict the leniency applicant. To date, there have been no such actions, and this situation is merely hypothetical.

B. Single Jurisdiction

According to the Brazilian Constitution, 'the law will not exclude the judicial branch from judging injury or threat to right' (Article 5, XXXV).[11] Therefore, any conflict, injury, or threat to right is susceptible to judicial review. Only judges are able to impose final decisions. Only the judicial branch is able to decide certain questions, particularly as they relate to criminal issues. Brazilian administrative agencies lack criminal jurisdiction. For this reason, all decisions made by administrative authorities can be reviewed by the courts. Consequently, it is argued that SDE, which is an administrative body, is not authorized to decide issues that involve the granting of criminal immunity or the reduction of penalties. It is argued that the legal provision relating to leniency agreements should be deemed unconstitutional. Under such an interpretation, it would be necessary to apply the 'legal divisibility theory', according to which it is possible to deem unconstitutional only part of a law, so long as the remaining part can subsist independently and in accordance with its legal scope.

This theory misinterprets the law. According to Article 35-B, § 4th, section I of Law 8.884/94:

> *The execution of the leniency agreement is not subject to CADE's approval. However, if it verifies such agreement was complied with, when judging the administrative proceeding, it shall: I—decree the extinction of the public administration punitive action in favor of the whistleblower if, by the time it applied for the program, SDE had no previous knowledge of the infraction.*

[11] Brazilian Constitution—<http://www.vbrazil.com/government/laws.constitution.html>

The fact that CADE can decide in favor of the whistleblower does not mean it is deciding a criminal issue. As we can see by reading the legal provision above, CADE's power is merely to verify whether the parties duly abided by the agreement, ie whether they provided the authorities with full, continuing and complete cooperation, and whether they complied with other accessory obligations. Once the applicant executes the terms of leniency agreement, the granting of immunity is automatic. It will be terminated only if the whistleblower breaches the obligations stated in the leniency agreement.

The Brazilian Criminal Code sets forth some factors that extinguish the administrative power to punish offenders: statutes of limitations, retroactivity of a law that does not consider the action an offense, and judicial pardon. The situations indicated by the Criminal Code do not represent an exhaustive list. A variety of other Brazilian laws list different factors that can trigger the termination of the public administration punitive action, and can also shield a particular individual from conviction. It is important to highlight that if one of these factors is present, the judge is obliged to grant immunity to the offender, or free him or her from culpability. Accordingly, Law 8.884 is one of those laws that enable an offender to escape from criminal liability. The granting of amnesty is automatic and is a legal provision, not a product of CADE's decision. CADE merely examines whether the applicant abided by all of the contractual obligations; and if there was a breach, CADE may revoke the amnesty. In this context, article 35-C, single paragraph establishes that 'upon the fulfillment of the leniency agreement by the applicant, amnesty will be automatically granted'.

V. Conclusion

This chapter addresses the legal problems raised by the new leniency program under Brazilian Antitrust Law. It also challenges the theory that the leniency program is unconstitutional. Overall, as the Brazilian legal system works through the implications of the leniency program, Brazilian anti-cartel enforcement will continue to operate with a certain degree of unpredictability.

Chapter IX

Building Trust in Antitrust: The Chilean Case

ELINA CRUZ* AND SEBASTIAN ZARATE**

I. Introduction

A. Overview

Chile is among the most economically stable countries in Latin America. In some areas, it is viewed as a pioneer in competition law and policy in the region. In spite of a general market-based economic orientation, the problem of Chilean antitrust is one based on a broad trust in competition, but mistrust in the antitrust system.[1] This mistrust manifests itself in at least two areas: collusion enforcement and institutional design. Some of the problems with competition law and policy that will be discussed in this paper are common to other jurisdictions. However, we believe that there are at least two elements that characterize the Chilean case that are not present in similar countries.

First, the process of trade liberalization, deregulation and privatization started in 1973 was relatively early compared with other countries in the region. In the process of market liberalization, Chilean policy-makers understood the freedom to compete as a core value, and consequently the 1980 Chilean Constitution protects the right to develop any economic activity. This principle of freedom to

* Assistant Professor, Pontificia Universidad Católica de Chile. Center of Competition Law at the Pontificia Universidad Católica de Chile. Associate Researcher, Institute of Regional Applied Economics, Universidad Católica del Norte.

** Assistant Professor, Pontificia Universidad Católica de Chile. Center of Competition Law at the Pontificia Universidad Católica de Chile. We would like to thank Ricardo Jungmann, the Executive Director of the Center of Competition Law at the Pontificia Universidad Católica de Chile, for his helpful comments and suggestions on earlier drafts. Any remaining errors are ours.

[1] The Organization for Economic Co-operation and Development (OECD) suggests the need for greater antitrust enforcement in Chile, stating: '[T]he tradition of caution, including an apparent reluctance to find violations and to impose fines, has in part reflected a view in Chile that economic offences against the public are not serious and that the costs of monopoly may not exceed the costs of competition law enforcement.' OECD and Inter-American Bank, Competition Law and Policy in Latin America: Peer Reviews of Argentina, Brazil, Chile, Mexico and Peru (Sao Paulo, OECD Publishing, 2006), at 192–93.

compete was probably the one that at first inspired Chilean competition law and competition authorities. For example, it explains why, even in the context of a country strongly influenced by Chicago School economics, competition authorities viewed vertical restraints initially as anti-competitive. In this sense, Chilean competition law has gradually moved towards an approach based on efficiency considerations and consumer welfare, but even today freedom to compete and to develop economic activities seems to be a powerful motive. For instance, in February 2008, the Competition Tribunal (TDLC) rejected a large retail merger. The public debate that the decision caused was based not so much on efficiency or consumer welfare, but rather on the questions of whether it was constitutional for the TDLC to reject a merger and whether the TDLC actually had the power to make such a decision without affecting economic freedom and private property. This view of competition as a way to achieve the freedom to compete had a strong influence on each of the practices challenged by the Chilean competition authorities. However, under this view, collusion is naturally a conduct that is given less importance than other practices, which is why its study is particularly interesting.

A second element that shapes the Chilean case is the fact that it is a relatively small economy compared with other countries in the region, and its industries are highly concentrated. While it is generally understood that concentration potentially may be a factor that facilitates collusion, in Chile this has worked as a disincentive towards collusion enforcement. For example, according to the OECD Chilean country review on competition policy, there seems to be agreement that a leniency program could fail because a person who came forward with information about collusion would have trouble finding future employment. The reason for this is that concentration produces little job mobility, and consequently informants would face social sanctions in future employment. We believe that this could be an overstatement, but nevertheless it shows a characteristic of Chilean reality which is not necessarily true about other jurisdictions, and that affects the enforcement of competition policy.

The starting point for this chapter (in section II) is an analysis of Chilean case law on collusion from 1973 until 2007. From this analysis we detect a key finding: the fact that almost no collusion claim has been successful in Chile, and that certainly this topic has not been a relevant focus of competition authorities. Nevertheless, the case study also illustrates the second finding: that after the major amendment of the Competition Act in 2003 (Competition Act 2003), the attitude towards collusion has changed towards a far more proactive approach; and for the first time, stronger infringement decisions have been issued by competition authorities.

From an institutional viewpoint, in section III this chapter analyzes two problems of trust that the Chilean competition system has experienced since the application of the Competition Act 2003. The first one is the lack of effective investigatory tools of the Office of the National Economic Prosecutor (FNE), particularly in collusion cases. This problem, currently subject to parliamentary debate in a proposed amendment, is partly due to confusion with regard to the legal nature of competition infractions under Chilean law. The second problem is more serious, and relates to role of the Supreme Court. Instead of building an appeal process before an upper tribunal composed of experts in the topic, the Competition Act 2003 opted for a review by non-specialized Supreme Court judges. In other words, the Supreme Court has been conceived in the institutional design as the *ultimate decision-maker of the competition system*. As such, the Supreme Court has overruled important decisions made by the TDLC (including specialized reasoning in competition law and economics). This weakness is aggravated by what we consider an ill-defined concept of the review powers of the Supreme Court, ie conceiving the review process, the *Recurso de Reclamación*, as an appeal instead of as a judicial review, which has enormous consequences in the level of deference and scope of control of the Supreme Court. In *the last part of* section III, we propose solutions to overcome these elements of distrust displayed towards competition institutions.

B. Chilean Competition Law and the 2003 Amendment

Chile enacted its first competition law in 1959,[2] but this statute was barely used until 1973, the year in which a new Competition Act came into force (hereinafter the 'Competition Act 1973') in the context of trade liberalization and market deregulation. The Competition Act 1973 made no express mention of its goals (eg, promoting efficiency or enhancing welfare), and its substantive provisions consisted basically in punishing 'any deed, act or contract that prevents, restricts or hinders free competition or tends to produce such effects'.[3]

A list of examples of practices that could potentially harm competition followed this general provision, and such a broad set of examples left most of the development of antitrust to the case law handed down by the competition authorities. Consequently, competition case law was an exception: in the context of a civil law jurisdiction, where generally precedents and decisions are non-binding, the legal community viewed the decisions issued by competition commissions as extremely relevant. This factor also explains why it is useful to study the case law produced by competition authorities. The penalties for violation of competition law consisted of imposing fines, dissolving legal entities, and imposing prison sentences (although the third option was almost never used). Fines, although few were actually applied, were the most commonly used sanction, but their amounts were small, averaging US $13,500.[4]

2 Chilean Law 13,305 (April 6, 1959), <http://www.bcn.cl/lc/bleyes/>.
3 Competition Act of 1973, <http://www.bcn.cl/lc/bleyes/>.
4 OECD and Inter-American Bank, above n 1, at 210.

The Competition Act 1973 created several antitrust institutions, of which the FNE is the only that remains in use. Among other tools, the FNE may undertake investigations and enforcement. The Finance Ministry oversees the FNE but the FNE has budgetary independence. The President of Chile appoints the head of the FNE, the National Economic Prosecutor, who may be removed by her at any time. The Competition Act 1973 set up a Resolutive Commission, which was an administrative body equivalent to an antitrust commission. The Resolutive Commission no longer exists and was replaced by the TDLC. The Resolutive Commission had both judicial and non-judicial powers. Among the former, it deliberated cases brought by the Prosecutor's Office or by private parties, as well as appeals of decisions made by the Preventive Commissions. Among the latter, it could recommend the amendment of laws or regulations that were considered to interfere with competition law. The Resolutive Commission was chaired by a Supreme Court judge, chiefs of service from the Finance Ministry, a law school dean and a dean from an economics department. The decisions issued by the Resolutive Commission were subject to review before the Supreme Court, but this procedure was restricted only to those cases that established the dissolution of a business, the prohibition of a person to hold certain posts, or the imposition of fines. Lastly, there were Preventive Commissions (Central and Regional), which the TDLC also replaced, which mostly had consultative powers. Their main role was to answer questions regarding competition law in Chile, and they had the power to issue orders to stop anti-competitive practices temporarily and to require the intervention of other authorities when they considered that competition law was being affected. Commissions were formed by a member from the Ministry of Finance, one from the Treasury, a law professor, an economics professor and a member of the Local Community Association.[5] The case law developed by the Preventive Commissions was probably the most elaborate, hence its relevance for establishing precedents in competition matters.

While the Government granted the FNE a moderate budget, the members of the Resolutive and Preventive Commissions worked *ad honorem* and met once a week. Given this structure, an amendment seemed necessary to improve the enforcement and application of competition law. In November 2003 a new Competition Act came into force,[6] and by 2004 there was full implementation. The Government sponsored this amendment with the aim of improving competition law and enforcement in Chile through the strengthening of the antitrust authorities. It created a Competition Tribunal, the TDLC, which replaced both

[5] According to Art 1 of the Local Communities Act 1997, a community association is 'a local organization representing the residents of a local community with the aim of promoting community welfare, protecting the interests and rights of its members, and cooperating with the Council and Governmental authorities'.

[6] Between 1973 and 2003, Chile amended its competition law under several regulations: Law Decree 2,760 from 1979, Law Decree 2879 from 1979, Law Decree 3,057 from 1980; and Law 19,336, Law 19,610 and Law 19,806. However, the most important change in this law was made by the Law 19,911—the Competition Act 2003—published in the *Official Gazette* in Nov 2003.

the Resolutive and the Preventive Commissions. In particular, the main objectives pursued by the Government through this amendment were:

a) changing the selection process for members of the competition authority, based on a transparent and open call for candidates to ensure they had the necessary expertise to apply competition law;
b) establishing a salary for the members of the TDLC and increasing the number of sessions of the tribunal;
c) separating the roles of the FNE and the TDLC by granting the latter entity budgetary independence;
d) ensuring the independence of the TDLC from the rest of government; and
e) strengthening the powers given to the TDLC in order to enforce competition law.

While the Competition Act 2003 eliminated criminal penalties (in reality these penalties were almost never used), the new law drastically increased the possible amount of the fines (by December 2007 the maximum fine established by the law was approximately US $16,500,000). Moreover, the Competition Act 2003 allowed settlements between the FNE and the parties (unlike in the previous Competition Act). However, the TDLC must call for conciliation and must later approve the settlement between the parties.

The substantive terms of the new law remained basically the same, but the new Article 1 states the objective of Chilean competition law: 'This law intends to promote and defend free market competition.'[7] Nevertheless, the Competition Act 2003 effectively changed competition enforcement in Chile: the decisions issued by the newly created TDLC reflect the expertise of its members, and the sanctions imposed so far by this authority for anticompetitive violations have been stronger than before, with the TDLC imposing fines of over US $6 million.[8] Yet there were some unintended effects of the amendment. The most important of these has been the role played by the Supreme Court in the new institutional design. Little parliamentary debate (if any) was devoted to this topic, especially considering that until the amendment, the Supreme Court had almost no influence within the competition law system. As explained in section III below, judicial review of the rulings made by the TDLC was no longer restricted to certain types of decisions (ie, those that ordered the dissolution of a corporation, disqualified people from holding certain posts or imposed fines). In other words, the new law allowed all decisions of the TDLC that impose any kind of sanction or punishment to be challenged by judicial review before the Supreme Court. This legal change passed silently in a Congress whose debate focused on the creation of an independent tribunal and the increase in punishments for anticompetitive violations, with no awareness of the unexpected power that was being granted to the Supreme Court in this matter. Moreover, because there was an increase in the sanctions that

[7] Competition Law 2003, above n 6, at Art 1.
[8] *Falabella-Paris*, Competition Tribunal (2008), 63/2008.

could potentially be imposed by the TDLC (in particular the amount of fines) and because enforcement became more effective through this more specialized authority, the incentives for the parties to use judicial review increased as well.

Consequently, through the extension of judicial review plus the increase in incentives to use this review that stem from more active competition enforcement, the Competition Law 2003 granted the Supreme Court the role of the ultimate decision-maker in the competition law system. One of the problems with this role is that the Court does not have the expertise to decide on competition law matters, a problem that is common to other jurisdictions. However, what is perhaps particular to Chile is that because of the interpretation that the Court and the parties have given to judicial review, there is no deference whatsoever from the Supreme Court towards the TDLC in technical competition matters. This explains why (as discussed further in section III) what we propose is not to redesign the competition institutions or to pass another legal amendment, but to rethink the interpretation of the nature of the TDLC and of the judicial review procedure.

Overall, the current institutional model is close to what has been called a 'bifurcated agency model'[9] in which there are two separate bodies—one that conducts investigations and brings complaints before a second body that adjudicates. Under Chilean law, there is no doubt that the FNE is an autonomous administrative agency. The situation of the TDLC is more complex. Some scholars argue that the Tribunal is a judicial body, and as such must be treated as a court of the judiciary.[10] They argue that this is because it is subject to the supervision of the Supreme Court.[11] Our position, however, is that the TDLC is an autonomous administrative agency, exercising adjudicative administrative powers, in dispute and non-dispute cases. The reason that the TDLC is subject to the supervision of the Supreme Court is the constitutional requirement that every public body adjudicating in dispute cases must be supervised by the Supreme Court, according to Article 82 of the Constitution. Nonetheless, in the case of the TDLC, this supervision is limited because it is an autonomous agency and because the supervision is only applicable to dispute cases. Therefore, under Chilean law it is possible to have an autonomous administrative agency adjudicating, with the only consideration being that as far as dispute cases are concerned, they are subject to the limited supervision of the Supreme Court.

[9] M J Trebilcock and E M Iacobucci, 'Designing Competition Law Institutions' 25 *World Competition* 361 (2002).

[10] See, eg, T Menchaca, 'Evolución del antiguo al nuevo sistema' *Revista Anales de Derecho UC. Temas de Libre Competencia* (2007). Another example is the case of the former Senator Augusto Parra, a legal academic who was by then one of the members of the Senate committee that undertook the reform in 2002. He insisted on the judicial nature of the TDLC during the parliamentary debate (see Chilean Senate, Second Report of the Joint Committees of Constitutional Affairs and Finance, Bill No 2.944-03, p 53).

[11] Chilean Constitution, Art 82, first para: 'The Supreme Court is entrusted with the executive, correctional and economic supervision of all the courts and tribunals of the nation. The Constitutional Court, the Electoral Commission, the Regional Electoral Commissions and the Military Courts in time of war are excepted from this norm.'

From this brief account, it can be concluded that the Competition Act 2003 has effectively given an impulse to competition law and enforcement in Chile. However, several issues still need to be resolved. For this reason, there is a Bill currently being debated in Congress that introduces amendments to the Competition Act 2003. The main proposals contained in this Bill[12] are the following:

a) the addition of the term 'or effect' to restrict competition (as explained later) and the extension of the law to cases of collective dominance;
b) the incompatibility between holding the post of member of the tribunal and holding other posts, compensated by a salary increase for members;
c) the introduction of a new mechanism to order the dismissal of the National Economic Prosecutor;
d) the granting of new powers to the FNE (as discussed in section III) and the possibility of reaching extra-judicial settlements through the FNE, as well as the possibility of establishing preventive measures to maintain market transparency; and
e) an increase in fines and the introduction of a leniency policy.

II. Collusion in Chile

This section discusses how the lack of trust in antitrust has been reflected in collusion cases and enforcement. The analysis will be divided into two stages: the past and present of competition law and policy in connection to collusion in Chile. The past will be explained through a time-series study of Chilean case law from 1973 onwards. The present is defined as the events that have taken place since 2004, when the Competition Act 2003 came into force. The future of collusion cases lies in the Bill that is currently being debated in Congress about the introduction of a leniency policy, the strengthening of the powers of the FNE and other amendments.

A. The Past: 1973–2003

As mentioned earlier, Article 1 of the Competition Act 1973 punished in general 'any deed, act or contract that prevents, restricts or hinders free competition or tends to produce such effects'.[13] Article 2 contained a list of illustrative practices that could potentially harm competition. Among these practices, the one closest to collusive agreements was the prohibition against determining the prices of goods and services. However, because Article 2 merely contained a list of examples, any

12 As of Jan 2008.
13 Competition Act 2003, above n 6, at Art 1.

conduct that was considered anti-competitive and was not covered in Article 2, could be prosecuted under Article 1 of the statute.

This was the extent of the substantive legal provisions of Chilean competition law, which meant that the Chilean competition authorities, the Preventive and Resolutive Commissions, were left with the role of developing the principles and ideas of competition in the country. For this reason, the following is an analysis of the cases reviewed by these competition institutions.

In selecting the cases relevant to collusion, we have considered different issues. The period chosen was 1973 to 2003. The year 1973 was used as a starting point for the analysis because this is the date on which the Competition Act 1973 came into force; and in turn the year 2003 saw the last collusion case reviewed by the previous competition authorities (replaced by the Chilean TDLC under the Competition Act 2003).

As for the search mechanisms employed, the main resource used was the FNE's website,[14] which contains a link to all decisions issued by Chilean competition authorities before the change to the Competition Act. The practices searched for, selected from the 28 categories available in the website, were the following:

a) cartels;
b) horizontal agreements regarding prices;
c) horizontal agreements regarding production; and
d) horizontal agreements regarding exclusive markets.

The search produced 15 results for a), 110 for b), 7 for c), and 39 for d). However, some of these results were repeated in more than one category, so the total number of cases actually used in the database was 127.

Each result corresponds to one decision issued by the Resolutive Commission or by the Preventive Commissions. According to the Competition Act 1973, some cases were first decided by the Preventive Commissions and then reviewed before the Resolutive Commission, which had the power to issue a completely new ruling. In these type of situations, which represent 15.5 per cent of the total number of cases contained in the study, to maintain clarity, the database shows two separate decisions (even though they refer to the same matter).

The resource used to find Supreme Court decisions issued before 2003 was *Legal Publishing*, and the criterion used for the search was the quotation of the Chilean Competition Act, commonly referred to as 'DL 211' in the decision. The search produced 35 results. Because of the limited powers of the Supreme Court in the review procedure under the Competition Act 1973, as will be explained in section III, none of these results are relevant in this section. The reason is that in the great majority of cases—all of them when it comes to collusion—the Supreme Court confirmed the decisions of the Chilean competition authorities. Hence, in

[14] www.fne.cl.

this subsection the discussion focuses exclusively on the case law produced by the Resolutive and Preventive Commissions, excluding the Supreme Court. The institutional setting changes dramatically when the Supreme Court appears as a relevant actor in the system.

The most striking fact reflected in the time series data is the relative lack of importance of collusion cases in Chilean case law: only 6.3 per cent of the total number of competition cases from 1973 until 2003 are related to this topic. Graph 1 shows the proportion of collusion cases in relation to total number of cases in each year[15]:

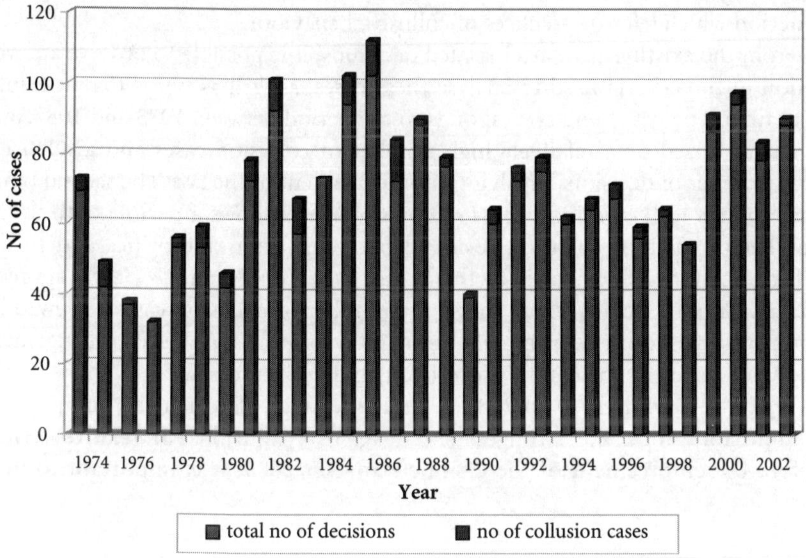

Graph 1 Total number of cases reviewed/number of collusion cases 1974–2003

It is clear from these numbers that a small number of cases from competition case law have been related to collusion. The reason for this may be partly found in the strong focus of Chilean enforcers on the freedom to compete. There is no straightforward set of data which serves as a baseline and shows exactly which proportion of cases corresponds to each of the other potentially anticompetitive practices. However, based on the 2004 OECD *Peer Review of Competition Policy*, in the period 1973–93 the competition authorities focused first on monopolization (abuse of dominance) cases, particularly on infrastructure monopolies, and secondly on vertical restraints.[16] This report categorizes Chile as a pioneer in the

[15] Source: National Economic Prosecutors Office.

[16] OECD (Terry Winslow), *Chile—Peer Review of Competition Policy* (2004), <www.pecd.org/dataoecd/7/41/35908641.pdf>.

field of dealing with infrastructure monopolies as part of the trade liberalization and privatization process carried out since 1973. Vertical restraints cases were initially considered anti-competitive, but the case law evolved and eventually became consistent with the generally accepted view that these practices are pro-competitive. Mergers also followed strong efficiency considerations and, similar to what happens with collusion, the authorities found very few cases to be anti-competitive. Overall, while it is true that the resources devoted to competition enforcement as from 1973 were scarce, and that this area was not a priority for public policy, competition policy developed alongside the process of privatization and deregulation of the economy, having its focus on the freedom to compete; a criterion which left out practices of collusive behaviour.

From the existing 127 cartel-related decisions, it is possible to observe an evolution in the criteria used to analyse these cases, as well as two different trends over time. The first trend corresponds to the period between 1973 and 1987, and is characterized by a relatively high number of collusion cases and a relatively high number of decisions involving an infringement of the law. The second trend corresponds to the period from 1988 onwards, and shows a decline both in the number of cases of collusion reviewed by competition authorities and in the infringement decisions issued by them. These two trends may be clearly appreciated in Graph 2 below, which shows the number of collusion cases reviewed by competition authorities from 1974 until 2003, and the number of infringement decisions issued by the commissions from among these cases.

Period 1 is from 1973 to 1987. This is the stage at which the competition commissions took the strongest stand against collusion (in relative terms) before the enforcement of the Competition Act 2003. It is important to note

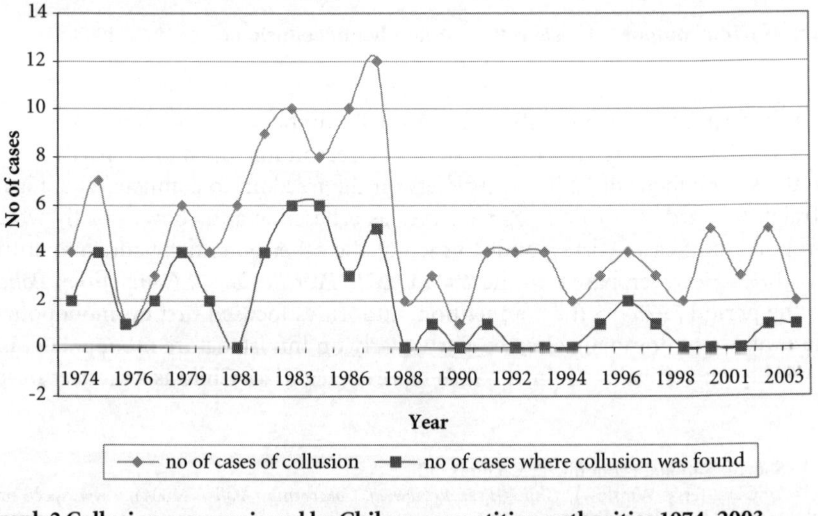

Graph 2 Collusion cases reviewed by Chilean competition authorities 1974–2003

that this stand was not always based on strong legal or economic theory, and that it was not particularly consistent among cases. Despite these difficulties, from the analysis it is clear that there were at least two relevant concepts developed by the competition authorities during this time frame regarding collusion: the prohibition of market sharing agreements, and the 'price identity rule'. Other types of collusion agreements, not based on price or market sharing, received little or no attention, so they must be excluded from this analysis.[17] The prohibition of market sharing agreements is perhaps the only practice that has clearly received strict enforcement by competition authorities. An example of the prohibition of market sharing is *Coca-Cola*,[18] in which the Commission vetoed part of a contract subscribed by the undertaking and its bottlers, which created a geographic division of the country into exclusive territories among the bottlers. Moreover, by 1976 the Central Preventive Commission asserted that market sharing agreements were objectively or 'per se' illegal.[19] This approach towards market sharing agreements has not seen any major changes since then, and it was maintained during the second period (post-1988) as well.[20]

With regard to price agreements, the approach during these early years was also stronger than after 1988, but it was always more inconsistent, and even erratic, when compared with what happened with market sharing agreements. An example of the stronger approach towards price agreements is found in *Airline-Exchange Rate*,[21] in which the Commission issued an infringement decision against airline companies for overcharging an equal amount above the exchange rate to their customers. In connection with price agreements, a primitive 'price identity rule' was developed, establishing that price identity was an indication of collusion.[22] The application and use of this rule varied significantly among cases and within its scope.

The second period is from 1987 to 2003. In 1987, the Resolutive Commission, overturning a decision taken by a Regional Preventive Commission, declared that price identity was not a certain indicator of collusion; rather, price identity may also indicate perfect competition in the market.[23] This was one of the decisions that represented a new approach towards collusion cases: while in the first period 39 infringement decisions were issued, only seven infringement rulings were issued in the second period. Graph 3 below shows a comparison between the number of collusion cases in the first and the second period, as

[17] The other type of agreements reviewed by competition authorities (worth mentioning) were related to collusive tendering or bid rigging, but they amount to a total of 8 cases for the whole period 1973–2003.

[18] *Coca Cola*, Central Preventive Commission (1975), 69-6.

[19] *Aluminio*, Central Preventive Commission (1976), 129.

[20] However, there are very few cases post-1988 that deal with market sharing agreements.

[21] *Airline Exchange Rate*, Central Preventive Commission (1982), 346/792.

[22] See, eg, Concepción Regional Preventive Commission (1974), 5.

[23] *Dirinco con Estaciones de Servicio*, Central Preventive Commission (1987), 244.

well as a comparison of the number of infringement decisions issued in both periods of time:

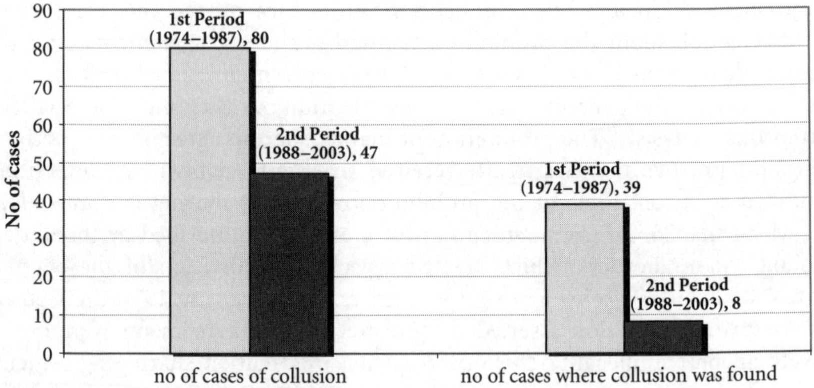

Graph 3 Comparison of no of collusion cases in Chile over two periods: 1974–87 and 1988–2003

From the seven infringement decisions issued in the second period, five of them are related to the public transport industry, and the fines imposed in these cases were insignificant. The remaining two cases refer to different industries: one of them fined pharmacy chains for colluding in retail prices, and the other one fined airlines for colluding to stop entry into the industry using a simultaneous and identical decrease in price.[24] The former decision was accompanied by abundant evidence, including witnesses and confessions. The latter decision is the only precedent for tacit collusion practices, stating that 'it is clear that they acted, at least, tacitly colluded',[25] hinting that the proof of tacit collusion is not as strict as is demanded today by the Supreme Court, as explained below.

Having described the existence of these two periods in the approach of Chilean case law to collusion, we next offer a hypothesis that explains the change in this approach. The hypothesis for the change of criteria in these periods is that we believe that the position adopted from 1973 until 1987 was to a great extent explained by the economic, political and social context of the country during those years. More specifically, as mentioned above, the economy was being liberalized and deregulated, which meant competition authorities needed to deal with industries that were just learning how to react to market forces, and with new law decrees that aimed to govern certain activities in these new circumstances. Hence, during this time, many of the decisions issued by the competition commissions had more to do with contributing to liberalization and adapting to a new

[24] Resolutive Commission (1995), 432.
[25] Consideration 9 of Resolutive Commission (1995), 432.

economic reality than with a strong enforcement against collusion itself. Chile completed the liberalization process for the most part by the end of the 1980s. This led to a more stable market economy. This date coincides with the change of criteria used by competition authorities when reviewing collusion cases.

Some examples of how the economic context influenced collusion cases during the first period, which support our hypothesis, are as follows:

a) Nearly 10 per cent of all collusion cases in both periods are related to the bread industry, and almost 80 per cent of these were reviewed in the period 1973–87. Before the first period, the bread price was fixed by the Government, so the first cases that the competition commissions reviewed were related to structuring cost models for bread without entering into a collusive agreement.[26]
b) Another 10 per cent of all cases (and again 80 per cent of these occurred in the first period) are related to certain law decrees issued by the Government, and their compatibility with competition law and collusive agreements. For example, the commissions reviewed many cases relating to the new laws applicable to the taxi industry and whether these laws facilitated or encouraged collusion practices in the market.[27]
c) During the period 1973–87, 10 per cent of all collusion cases were based on surveys carried out by the DIRINCO. The DIRINCO was the National Bureau of Industry and Trade, created in 1980 in order to preserve market transparency and ensure consumer protection. In 1990 DIRINCO was replaced by the National Consumer Service. The importance of this organization for competition was that it carried out price surveys in different areas of the country, particularly focused on food-related products, and if it found that there was a price identity among sellers, it filed a competition claim. The cases initiated by the DIRINCO constituted an important part of the caseload of the competition commissions during the first period, and these had the advantage of containing some form of pre-prepared evidence like the above-mentioned surveys. The DIRINCO disappeared completely in 1990, which coincides with the change of criteria from competition authorities. In regard to this point, note that the surveys carried out by the DIRINCO were usually limited to a few sellers from a particular region, and on average they referred to three- or four-day periods. Consequently, we believe that any decision issued exclusively according to this evidence was insufficient to establish collusion.

The examples mentioned above show how the decisions issued by competition commissions were strongly influenced by factors related to the economic background of the country, perhaps more than they were influenced by competition concerns. After 1987 most collusion cases seem to fit better into the 'traditional

[26] See Central Preventive Commission (1978), 191/312.
[27] Central Preventive Commission (1981), 5/434-278*bis*.

competition case' scenario, in which a company or the FNE filed a claim against two or more undertakings for engaging in collusive behaviour. It is during this second period when the number of cases of collusion, as well as of infringement decisions, experienced a rather drastic decline and the lack of trust in antitrust in collusion decisions began to show more clearly.[28] Perhaps the exception to this lack of trust is in market sharing agreements, which have produced infringement decisions by competition authorities.

B. The Present: 2003 to Date

The Competition Act 2003 produced dramatic changes in competition law and enforcement in Chile. This amendment encouraged a more active and stronger approach towards potential anti-competitive practices, and collusion has been no exception to this rule. The TDLC meets regularly and has members that specialize in competition matters, which has meant more and better enforcement of competition law in the country. However, while it is true that the TDLC has taken important steps towards a more consistent legal and economic approach to cases, there is still a gap in economic arguments, particularly in the empirical evidence submitted in the cases.

In relation to collusive agreements, the Competition Act 2003 is more explicit than its predecessor in forbidding collusion, punishing:

> [e]xpress or implied agreements between business agents or concerted practices between them having the intent of fixing sale or purchase prices, limiting production or assigning themselves market zones or quotas, abusing the power conferred upon them by such agreements or practices.[29]

Again, the substantive provision of the law is quite short, leaving its exact determination to the case law produced by competition authorities. As of July 2008, there have been seven TDLC decisions regarding collusive agreements, plus three cases that are still pending on this matter. This case load represents just 8 per cent of the total case load of the tribunal, but we believe that this percentage is highly influenced by two facts. First, there is currently a Bill being debated in Congress that introduces a leniency program and gives more powers to the FNE to prosecute cartel cases. It is very likely that potential claimants in collusion cases are waiting for this Bill to be approved. Secondly, there is a strong deterrent in the fact that the Supreme Court has managed to overturn every decision of the TDLC in which collusion was found, as explained below. As discussed below, as a result of the Supreme Court intervention, the TDLC has established that the determination of a collusive agreement is possible only if there is an abuse of dominant position.

[28] Other possible explanations for the cautious approach towards collusion adopted by Chilean competition authorities have been given by the OECD in its *Peer Review*, based on the fact that Chilean case law has focused on infrastructure and natural monopolies, and consequently other anti-competitive practices have been overlooked.

[29] Competition Act 2003, above n 6.

In reality, this new approach to collusion is already having effects: collusion claims are being filed as monopolization (abuse of dominance) cases, and the collusive agreement is treated as a secondary issue.

Despite the encouragement given to competition law by the amendment, once again the lack of trust in antitrust appeared, this time under the form of an empowered player in the competition system—the Supreme Court. The nature of the new powers conferred on this institution will be discussed in detail later; for now, suffice it to say that the Supreme Court can overturn the decisions made by the TDLC. This aspect of the new Act has represented a strike against competition law and policy, particularly since November 29, 2006, the date on which the Supreme Court handed down the first decision to overturn the findings of the TDLC.[30] Moreover, two out of the three overturning decisions made by the Supreme Court (in a six-month period) have been connected to collusion, so the impact has been particularly severe as regards this issue.

As mentioned before, seven cases of collusion were decided by the TDLC in the period of 2004 to January 2008, from which:

— The TDLC rejected three cases; from these three, the Supreme Court permitted one appeal, in which it confirmed the decision taken by the TDLC.
— Two cases involved infringement or violation decisions issued by the TDLC. The Supreme Court overturned both of these decisions. In these two cases, the TDLC had imposed significant fines.
— The TDLC rejected one decision (Isapres), and a decision of the Supreme Court recently confirmed the TDLC's ruling. The difference between this decision and the three rejected decisions already mentioned is that this one shows the influence that the Supreme Court's overturning of decisions has had on the TDLC. Had these overturning decisions had not taken place, the TDLC probably would have issued an infringement decision.
— One decision was an infringement ruling issued by the TDLC, and as of July 2008 it was still pending before the Supreme Court. This decision was based, first, on abuse of dominance and, secondly, on collusion.

Given their importance for this chapter, we will discuss the two infringement decisions overturned by the Supreme Court, as well as the last two cases mentioned above.

1. Asoex[31]

The Chilean National Association of Exporters filed a claim against several shipping agencies (which represent the shipping companies), alleging, among other things, that these agencies had colluded to impose a tariff for an additional

[30] In *James Hardie*, Supreme Court (2006), 3449/2006. This was the first time the Supreme Court overturned a decision made by the Competition Tribunal regarding a predatory pricing case.

[31] *Asoex*, Competition Tribunal (2006), 38-2006; *Asoex*, Supreme Court (2006), 33715.

approval for bills of lading. The TDLC determined that this mandatory tariff was the consequence of a collusive agreement between the shipping agencies. The main factors used to reach this conclusion were the simultaneity in the start of this tariff, as well as the similarity of tariff amounts between shipping agencies. The TDLC also considered the existence of facilitating factors for collusion, such as the fact that exporters had no choice of shipping agencies, the existence of barriers to entry, and market concentration.

A crucial point needs to be made: as in all the other cases to be described, in this one there was no direct or hard evidence of an agreement between the undertakings. However, this lack of evidence should be interpreted cautiously in the context of current Chilean law. The FNE has no powers to inspect the premises of the undertakings; it can only request information from the parties involved in the investigation. In turn, there is no leniency policy to rely on for obtaining further proof of collusion. Considering these two points together, plus the fact that collusive agreements are usually secretive and parties try to hide any evidence of their existence,[32] it could be asserted that it is highly likely that competition authorities in Chile will never be able to obtain direct evidence of collusion agreements. This will be true, however, only until the approval of the Bill that lies in the Chilean Congress, which addresses this issue (among others).

In this context, a lack of direct evidence in a case may signal two possibilities. The first possibility is tacit collusion in the form of conscious parallelism, but the illegality of this practice, according to international competition law, is questionable (for example, in Europe it has been considered that parallel behaviour is punishable only if there are no other alternate plausible explanations for the conduct of the undertakings, among other conditions). In Chile the law is clear: implicit agreements are an offense to competition law. The second possibility is that it may be a function of explicit collusion, but with no direct evidence to prove the agreement. Whatever the scenario, the chances of having the evidence necessary to demonstrate collusion are very low. Keeping this in mind, we describe the Supreme Court decision which overturned the *Asoex* case.

The Supreme Court decision concluded that there was no agreement between the shipping agencies. The main argument used by this institution to reach this result was that there was a lack of evidence. The Court stated that, in a collusion case, the following conditions should be shown:

a) that the behaviour of the undertakings is a result of a concerted practice; and
b) the existence of intent (*mens rea*).

Hence, the standard of proof for collusion was elevated by the Supreme Court. This new standard of proof has produced several reactions in the legal community, which have taken the form of proposals contained in the Bill being debated in Congress.

[32] A Jones and B E Sufrin, *EC Competition Law: Text Cases and Materials* (Oxford, Oxford University Press, 2008).

2. Oxígeno[33]

The FNE filed a claim against oxygen providers for bid rigging in an auction held by the Government to provide oxygen products for the public health system. The TDLC considered this to be a case of collusive tendering for different reasons:

a) the fact that the prices offered by the oxygen providers to public hospitals before the auction were lower than those offered in the auction itself; and
b) that the market incentives existed in the opposite direction (prices should have been lower after the auction).

There was a dissenting vote in this decision from one of the judges, and this is relevant because it anticipates the criteria to be used in the *Isapres* decision (described below). The *Oxígeno* dissenting vote stated that there was not enough evidence to prove the agreement between the undertakings, and that Article 3 of the Competition Act required:

a) an agreement;
b) with an anti-competitive objective; and
c) market power and abuse of this market power.[34]

The vote asserted that condition c) had not been met. This is the first glimpse we get of the new trend followed by Chilean case law towards demanding the existence of an abuse of dominant position to establish collusion. When overturning this decision, the Supreme Court agreed with the dissenting vote, asserting that there was not enough evidence to prove a collusive agreement.

3. Isapres[35]

The FNE filed a claim against several *Isapre* companies (privately run health insurers), accusing them of a collusive agreement which resulted in simultaneously reducing their health coverage from 100–80 per cent (100 per cent of hospital care and 80 per cent of ambulatory procedures) to 90–70 per cent. The Tribunal held that the three conditions mentioned in the minority vote in *Oxígeno* (above) were necessary to establish collusion. The TDLC also analyzed the existence of barriers to entry and other facilitating factors of collusion, such as concentrated markets, frequent interaction between undertakings and information exchange. Despite the fact that all these factors were found to exist, the TDLC decided that there was no agreement among the parties because there might be an alternate explanation for the practice: that of an oligopoly's parallel behavior. This decision was issued with 3 votes in favor

[33] *Oxigeno*, Competition Tribunal (2006), 43-2006; *Oxigeno*, Supreme Court (2007), 5057-2006.
[34] *Oxigeno*, Competition Tribunal (2006), 43-2006.
[35] *Isapres*, Competition Tribunal (2007), 57/2007; Isapres, Supreme Court (2008), 4052-07.

and 2 votes dissenting. This case had abundant evidence (although indirect) to prove collusion, and hence it is likely that the TDLC would have reached a different conclusion if it believed that the Supreme Court would not overturn its decision. Consequently, the effects of the Supreme Court intervention in the system may have had an anticipatory effect in shaping the rulings issued by the TDLC.

The TDLC was right in its anticipation—the Supreme Court recently confirmed its decision by three votes to two.[36] In doing so, it reproduced the conditions required by the TDLC as proof before sanctioning a collusive agreement:

a) the existence of an agreement;
b) the influence of such agreement in a relevant element of competition; and
c) that the agreement should enable the parties to abuse the market power they obtain, maintain or increase through it.[37]

The intervention of the Supreme Court in the competition system has turned out to be particularly damaging to the fight against collusion by the Competition Act 2003. The influence of the Supreme Court is probably related to the fact that the first collusion case was accepted with 5:0 votes, the second one was accepted by 4:1 votes and the third was rejected by 3:2 votes.

However, it is important to note that while the Supreme Court has raised the standard of proof for collusion, the TDLC, perhaps in an attempt to avoid having its decisions overturned, has reacted by developing the theory that collusion cases also need to demonstrate an abuse of dominant position. The effects of the former doctrine might be even more harmful than the Supreme Court intervention if it this is interpreted as the need to add a claim of an abuse of dominant position to the collusion claim. This development is extremely confusing: does this mean that collusion by itself is not enough?

We believe that these questions lead to a lack of clarity as to what practice is being punished (collusion, dominant position or both) and which conditions should be met to evidence them. Moreover, this interpretation leaves no room for a 'per se' approach to collusive agreements, making the evidentiary issue of proof of this conduct more difficult to obtain. The TDLC dissenting vote in *Isapres* (2008) argued that the abuse of a dominant position should not be part of the conditions required by law to establish a collusive agreement. However, the Supreme Court rejected the dissenting vote when it confirmed the TDLC ruling. The result of this new approach towards collusion can clearly be appreciated in the next decision analyzed.

[36] For the first time there was as divided decision from the Supreme Court in collusion matters. The minority vote asserts that the only condition that should be met is that the act has the potential to harm competition in the market (or effectively does).

[37] *Isapres*, Supreme Court (2008), 4052-07.

4. Falabella-Paris[38]

The FNE filed a claim against two big retail chains for stopping their electronic suppliers from participating in a technology fair organized by a banking institution. The allegation was that the retail chains had stopped their suppliers because the terms of sale offered in the fair were better than the ones offered in their retail stores, so these retail chains threatened their suppliers with sanctions if they participated in the fair. The FNE alleged that both retail chains had communicated with each other and jointly agreed to threaten their suppliers. Probably because of the new approach developed by the TDLC, the main allegation of the prosecutor in this case was that there was an abuse of dominance by the retailers. According to the allegation, such abuse was made worse because of the collusive agreement between the parties. The TDLC, following the allegation, condemned the parties for abuse of dominance aggravated by collusion, and imposed the highest fine ever applied in a competition case in Chile, over US $6 million. The TDLC focused its analysis on abuse of dominance, devoting almost no analysis to collusion. This decision seems to show that collusion enforcement is stepping away from a 'per se' approach. In any case, the parties have used the judicial review procedure to file a claim against this ruling before the Supreme Court, which to date is pending.

The Supreme Court's overturning of decisions and the new approach to collusion developed by the TDLC as a response to the Supreme Court have meant that collusion enforcement in Chile has been deterred once again. The role given to the Supreme Court in the institutional design has been particularly damaging for competition law overall and, within competition law, for collusion cases.

III. Institutional Reforms in the Chilean Antitrust System

A. Introduction

Effectively, the Competition Act 2003 has created more powerful institutions to enforce competition policy, but the lack of investigatory tools given to the FNE and the key role granted to the Supreme Court as an ultimate decision-maker both demonstrate that trust has been excessively limited in Chilean competition policy. Also, there are problems as regards the institutional communication between the TDLC and the Supreme Court.

This section will discuss two main points. First, there is a Bill in Congress that proposes granting more powers to the FNE to investigate collusive agreements, which is a signal of trust in this institution. Secondly, these new powers, as well

[38] *Falabella-Paris*, Competition Tribunal (2008), 63/2008.

as the general encouragement given to the law by the Competition Act 2003, may be overshadowed by the institutional design in terms of the role played by the Supreme Court.

However, we believe that the answer to this problem is not the re-design of the system, but rather the correct interpretation given to Chilean competition law and, consequently, to the judicial review procedure. In this sense, the understanding of competition law in Chile as part of Administrative Criminal Law and the categorization of the TDLC as an administrative agency will lead to the conclusion that judicial review, established in competition law, grants the Supreme Court the power to overturn decisions only when due process has not been followed. It does not grant the Supreme Court the right to overturn decisions based on technical issues of competition law and economics. In other words, this interpretation leads the way towards the use of the principle of deference by the Supreme Court towards the TDLC. Moreover, we believe that this deference could be further improved by adequate communication between competition institutions.

Before analyzing this, there are several improvements which have been made in Chile since the Competition Act 2003, worth mentioning as relevant steps towards the development of antitrust enforcement and the creation of a competition culture. There are elements incorporated into the Competition Act 2003 that appear as clear signs of trust in the system, in the sense that they improve the autonomy and expertise of the TDLC. First, it can be observed that one of the most important claims against the structure of the institutions established by the Competition Act 1973 was the lack of personal independence from the Government of the members of the commissions.[39] In the past there have been controversies surrounding members of the commissions appointed by the Government, who at the same time were civil servants or held other posts in the gift of the President.[40] This changed with the Competition Act 2003, and now the members of the Tribunal are appointed after an open process in which anyone meeting the expertise and legal requirements can participate, and civil servants are excluded. An additional aspect in relation to the personal independence of the members of the Tribunal is the fact that they are currently paid, changing the unusual previous situation of serving *ad honorem*.

[39] Menchaca, above n 10.

[40] A case that captured attention was that of the price caps in relation to the incumbent telecom company, in which one of the members of the old Tribunal (the *Comisión Resolutiva*), who also was the energy regulator appointed by the Government, was going to vote against the position expressed by the Government (favoring the telecom company's position). At the time, Mr Espejo, who later served as a Secretary of State of Transport and Telecommunications, resigned from the Tribunal. His resignation was interpreted as a response to the pressure he received from the Government to change his vote. The Chilean Congress investigated this case, and the Deputies approved a non-statutory proposal which recommended that the Government should not impose any pressure or intervention in the regulatory processes.

A second way in which the position of competition authorities has been strengthened is by the fact that the TDLC has been given complete budgetary independence; formerly it was funded by the Ministry of Finance. Moreover, there has been a separation between the TDLC and the FNE, which is a way to mirror the success of the Criminal Procedure Reform implemented in the country in 2000. In this sense, following the institutional typology of Trebilcock and Iacobucci,[41] the current system is close to a *bifurcated model.*

B. Investigatory Powers and Judicial Review Design: Blocking the Trust?

So far, it seems that this has been a happy tale, and that after 30 years of experience in competition policy enforcement, it was time for the institutions to develop and show signs of growth, together with relative economic and political stability. Nevertheless, two problems with the Competition Act 2003 have become evident. Analyzed as a whole, the 2003 Act tries to protect the right to a fair trial by extending the 'appeal'[42] procedure, but it forgets that the nature of the TDLC is highly specialized, and that the Supreme Court is unlikely to have enough knowledge and expertise in competition law and economics. The second issue, mentioned in the next subsection, is that according to the Competition Act 2003, in reality, the investigatory powers given to the FNE have been limited, particularly as regards collusion cases. Overall, the problem has been that both issues of combine to frustrate the efforts of the rest of the team.

The key question here is whether these two problems stem from an imperfect institutional design, or from something deeper. At first sight, the answer seems to be the latter, given the experience with other important reforms implemented in Chile. To take an example, the Criminal Procedure Reform was managed in a similar way, and the result of the whole amendment can be considered to have been fairly successful. In that case, the Congress first approved only the most important provisions changing the former criminal system, including an amendment to the Constitution. It was a year after the approval that it agreed to undertake the further necessary reforms, in what was called the Adaptation Bill. This legislative technique was indeed innovative for Chile in implementing important changes.

Was the intention to follow the same legislative technique for competition policy? There is no mention of this in the discussions of the Competition Act 2003, but it might be arguable that this was the case—after the reformed institutions had been in practice for two years, a new Bill (about leniency policy and others) was introduced.

[41] Trebilcock and Iacobucci, above n 9.

[42] As we will argue later, the existing judicial review procedure has been treated, improperly, as an appeal.

1. *Investigatory powers*

At the time of the Competition Act 2003, it seemed that the powers of the FNE were sufficient for undertaking any investigation about a competition offense. The Competition Act 2003 gave the FNE the power to:

a) require the collaboration of any public servant or anyone employed by municipalities or nationalized industries;
b) require from any person the information or documents necessary for conducting the investigation; and
c) issue subpoenas to those who might have knowledge of the investigated practices.

All of these powers carried the possibility of issuing an arrest warrant if there is a failure to comply with the prosecutor's order. Apart from these, however, there were no further provisions concerning investigatory powers; at the time of the Competition Act 2003, though, these powers were considered proportionate and sufficient for the FNE.

Nevertheless, as discussed above, collecting the evidence has proved to be a difficult task, particularly in tacit collusion cases. Additionally, as has been already mentioned, the TDLC and the Supreme Court have dismissed tacit collusion,[43] which means that under the current legislation they would be unlikely to punish any collusion at all. For this reason, Congress introduced a Bill in 2006, amending various aspects of the Competition Act 2003.

According to this Bill, it would be possible that on certain conditions, in collusion cases, the FNE could make a request to a judge of the Court of Appeal (the one on duty corresponding to territorial jurisdiction). The request would allow the existing police institutions, under the direction of staff members of the FNE, to undertake dawn raids. In this regard, the Bill makes applicable to competition law the conditions and procedure of the Criminal Procedure Act.

These tools were heavily criticized by some people who testified before the Select Committee of Economy of the Chamber of Deputies in the first phase of the Bill's proceedings.[44] For example, a representative of a policy institute linked to right-wing political parties, *Libertad y Desarrollo*, stated that:

> [I]t does not seem convenient to empower the Office of the Economic Prosecutor with faculties that simply belong to a criminal investigation, which—in any case—affect constitutionally protected rights, such as people's privacy and intimacy, and the protection of privacy of forms of communications. ... In any case, the interception of communications does not seem justified.[45]

[43] *Oxigeno*, Supreme Court (2007), 5057-2006.
[44] Chamber of Deputies, Report of the Select Committee of Economy, 2006, Bill No 4324-03-1.
[45] *Ibid*, at 23.

This is indeed a very central point in the way that it focuses the debate on the nature of legal provisions concerning competition enforcement, ie whether they fit into a civil or criminal law category. This is an important consideration, particularly under Chilean law, in which a clear division between these two areas has been vital to the application and enforcement of the entire legal system. This separation causes procedural systems, rights and enforcement to differentiate dramatically, and thus it is critical to investigate the civil or criminal nature of Chilean competition law, not only to analyze the powers granted to the Prosecutor's Office but to deduce further relevant elements that may help to solve other issues.

Some scholars argue that competition offences under Chilean law have a civil nature, or at least that they do not have a criminal connotation. In so arguing, they are mainly influenced by some of the provisions of the Competition Act 2003 that prescribe that in the absence of an express procedural rule, the Civil Procedure Code should be applied. However, these references do not indicate the legal nature of the competition offenses, but rather are procedural rules with a general scope.[46]

We believe that competition offenses under Chilean law are a somewhat special situation, which cannot be classified exactly as civil or criminal in nature. As with other regulatory areas, this is a mixed area, which fits better into the sub-discipline of administrative law or *administrative criminal law*. Indeed, the norms belong to administrative law, because they are enforced by an administrative agency, the TDLC, and the TDLC's function is of an administrative nature. This function consists in responding to binding consultations in non-dispute cases and in deciding dispute cases; and the exact object of this administrative activity is a manifestation of the power of the State to punish offenses: what is called in Chile the *ius puniendi* of the state.

In this regard, the Chilean system of administrative criminal law, the *Derecho Administrativo Sancionador*, applies core principles of criminal law on the grounds that administrative offenses are manifestations of the *ius puniendi* of the State, as the Constitutional Court, the Supreme Court and other national courts of appeals have ruled.[47] Despite the differences between 'truly' criminal law and administrative criminal law, Chilean judicial decisions have not evidenced any lessening in the application of the general principles of criminal law

[46] One of the references of the Competition Act 2003 (Art 22) to the Civil Procedure Act is in relation to the evidence produced: 'There shall be admissible all the evidence indicated in Article 341 of the Civil Procedure Code.' However, this does not imply that this is the only form of evidence admissible, as the Competition Act adds: '... and any other evidence or record that, in opinion of the Tribunal, might be relevant for establishing the facts'. The second reference is a generic one, in relation to the procedure as a whole, filling possible procedural regulatory gaps with the 'General Rules for Judicial Procedures' and 'Ordinary Dispute Resolution Procedure', contained in the Civil Procedure Act.

[47] STC 389-2003, Spanish Constitutional Court (2003), STC 376-2003, Spanish Constitutional Court (2003), STC 479-2006, Spanish Constitutional Court (2006), STC 480-2006, Spanish Constitutional Court (2006), Administradora de Fondos de Pensiones con Superintendencia, Santiago Court of Appeal (2005), 2078-2005, Castillo con Inspección del Trabajo, Temuco Court of Appeal (2007).

to administrative offences. This situation may be compared with that in other jurisdictions, both civil law countries and common law countries, as shown below.

In Spain (another civil law jurisdiction) there has been a slightly different trend in this area. The Constitutional Court and the Supreme Court have ruled that the same set of principles from criminal law must be applicable to administrative offenses, but adapted and attenuated.[48] However, some core principles, such as *mens rea*, are not affected by this attenuation, and it has been ruled that it is against the Spanish Constitution to apply an administrative penalty if the required intent is absent.[49] This is particularly relevant for the Chilean case. As mentioned before, there, *mens rea* is required to the same degree as intent in a criminal offence.

Comparing this area of law in a common law jurisdiction (Canada), it is possible to match this requirement to the decision in *R v Wholesale Travel Group Inc.*[50] One of the arguments behind this decision was the distinction between 'regulatory offences' as opposed to 'truly criminal' ones, the former having a lesser degree of protection than the latter for the purposes of the requirement of *mens rea.* Canadian courts applied the same criteria in another leading case, *R v Nova Scotia Pharmaceutical Society*,[51] which addressed the requirements of collusion.

These references are made with a solely comparative purpose, taking examples from both civil and common law jurisdictions,[52] highlighting that under Chilean law, even if the scholarship has not paid too much attention to the legal nature of competition law infractions, the courts are starting to interpret similar conduct according to the category of administrative criminal law. Under such a label, it has been recognized that there is no less protection than in the case of criminal offences. Particularly in the case of collusion, the Supreme Court has played an important role, requiring the same *mens rea* called for in criminal offenses. We agree with this approach of the Chilean Supreme Court, despite the fact that the Court has not always deferred to the TDLC with regard to the analysis of proof.[53] In other words, we believe that requiring intent for collusion cases, as the Supreme

[48] STC 169/1998, Spanish Constitutional Court (1998); STC 129/2003, Spanish Constitutional Court (2003); STC 18/1981, Spanish Constitutional Court (1981); STC 56/1998, Spanish Constitutional Court (1998); STC 54/2003, Spanish Constitutional Court (2003); STC 9/2003, Spanish Constitutional Court (2003); STC 146/1994, Spanish Constitutional Court (1994); STC 316/2006, Spanish Constitutional Court (2006), among other rulings.

[49] STC 76/1990, Spanish Constitutional Court (1990).

[50] [1991] 3 SCR 154R, Supreme Court of Canada.

[51] [1992] 2 SCR 606, Supreme Court of Canada.

[52] The nature of legal concepts and institutions matters in both common and civil law systems. It has been commonplace to criticize civil law jurisdictions as being too concerned about the nature of institutions, instead of applying them to cases in practice. Here, however, the consideration of whether a public body is an administrative institution or not, or whether a grievance mechanism is properly an appeal or judicial review, changes all the analyses and consequences.

[53] Although the Supreme Court is not the only one to blame for this lack of deference, as the TDLC has not put forward convincing arguments when giving its reasons for accepting the facts as proved.

Court has done, is consistent with general legal principles existing in Chile under administrative criminal law; but this does not mean that the evidence threshold necessary to demonstrate such intent is nearly as high as pretended by the Supreme Court. As long as the TDLC is clear in proving the facts of the offense, the Supreme Court will restrain its control.

Considering that the transgression and the proceedings for investigating and penalizing that conduct are of an administrative criminal nature, this enables the FNE to use a set of tools, ie legal mechanisms, sufficient to undertake its functions.

When the granting of these investigative tools was debated in Congress, it was alleged that giving them to the FNE might affect constitutionally protected rights, ie the right to a fair trial and investigation,[54] and, as in this particular case, those fundamental rights related to the protection of privacy.

These allegations can be interpreted as evidencing an element of distrust in competition enforcement, due to the building of a culture in which these types of illegal conduct have not been perceived negatively as offenses to society. They can also be interpreted as distrust in this kind of institution (FNE), as opposed to the trust shown when dealing with criminal offenses that are handled by the judiciary and the National Criminal Prosecutor.

In Chile, it would not be lawful for the FNE to undertake investigations employing certain investigative mechanisms (eg, intercepting communications) without its being empowered to do so by an Act of Parliament, particularly in the case of the exercise of fundamental rights, according to what Chilean constitutional law calls the doctrine of 'statutory reserve' (*principio de reserva legal*). Therefore, the only realistic way of bringing cases of collusion before the TDLC would be by enhancing the powers vested in the Office of the National Economic Prosecutor.

To sum up this point, it seems that putting into practice the Competition Act 2003 has been positive for building trust. This trust has been tested by the parliamentary discussion of the reform that will extend the powers of the FNE to act in a way similar to the Criminal Prosecutor. More than the discussion of the nature of the offenses contained in the Competition Act, the acceptance that fighting cartels requires more power is indeed a demonstration of a growing confidence in the competition system. However, this somewhat optimistic conclusion cannot compensate for the effects left by the institutional designers in establishing the Supreme Court as the ultimate decision-maker of the system.

2. *Judicial Review: the Recurso de Reclamación*

The new system of judicial review, *Recurso de Reclamación*, established by the Competition Act 2003, has been considerably extended in comparison with the review procedure applicable under the Competition Act 1973. Under the 2003

[54] Chilean Constitution, at Art 19 No 3.

Act, where there is dispute between the parties (non-consultative cases), the TDLC is entitled to:

a) modify or terminate acts, contracts, agreements, systems or arrangements entered into contrary to the provisions of the Competition Act;
b) order the amendment or dissolution of partnerships, corporations and other legal entities of private law involved in acts, contracts, agreements, systems or arrangements referred to in a); and
c) apply fines.[55]

In all these situations it is possible to apply for judicial review of the decision of the TDLC. The standing rules state that the FNE or the parties in the case are the only possible applicants.

The new system also entitles interested parties to seek judicial review in non-dispute cases, in which the applicant requires binding advice from the TDLC (as a preventive mechanism) and[56] the Tribunal's binding response to that consultation consists in meeting certain conditions in order to comply with the Competition Act 2003. Here, the standing rules require that only the FNE and interested parties can apply for review.[57]

Under the Competition Act 2003, the Supreme Court can examine a broader range of decisions. In practice this means that the Supreme Court has tended to analyze every detail of the TDLC's reasoning, without consideration of whether this require any economic or specific legal expertise. In other words, the Supreme Court has been 'invited' to be the ultimate decision-maker in the competition system, and the Court has warmly accepted this invitation. As might be expected, the result is that when the decisions of the Supreme Court are related to the rights of the parties in the proceedings before the TDLC, the Court's rulings have been satisfactory and consistent with legal principles; but in those parts of the decisions involving competition law and economics, the Court has struggled to make sensible arguments.[58]

We estimate that the causes of this failure in design can be traced back to a lack of trust in competition policy by the legislators, together with the ill-defined nature of the TDLC and of the *Recurso de Reclamación* itself. All of the above can be explained if the TDLC is considered a judicial body, with all the characteristics

[55] Competition Act 2003, Art 26.

[56] Function formerly performed by the Preventive Commissions (one in each region of the country, plus the Central Preventive Commission).

[57] The current criterion of the Supreme Court is that the interest will exist when the party is directly affected by the decision of the TDLC. It has been understood that competitors in the relevant market always have sufficient interest to use the judicial review procedure, as does the FNE as guardian of the public interest in this area. However, standing is denied when the interested party seeking judicial review has not acted as an opposing party before the TDLC.

[58] E Cruz, 'Precios Predatorios y Libre Competencia' *Revista Anales de Derecho UC. Temas de Libre Competencia* (2007).

of a court of the judiciary, and not as an adjudicating administrative agency. In this scenario the *Reclamación* is conceived of as an appeal in which there is no deference whatsoever from the Court towards the TDLC. However, we argue that the real nature of the *Recurso de Reclamación* is a judicial review mechanism, established primarily in the Constitution.

It is necessary first to understand the logic behind the *Recurso de Reclamación*, as it is commonly forgotten in this area. The *Reclamación* is intended to cover what is known as 'judicial review'; it is not an appeal procedure: not even an appeal on a point of law is allowed. The Competition Act states that the decisions of the Tribunal described above can be challenged through the *Reclamación*, and apart from the standing rules, the Act does not make any other mention of it. In this sense, since these are decisions from an administrative body principally adjudicating dispute cases (which are the majority of cases, as opposed to binding consultations), they are subject to review through the *Reclamación* originating in Article 38 of the Chilean Constitution, which in the second paragraph declares:

> Any person whose rights shall have been adversely affected by the Administration of the State, the Bodies thereof or the Municipalities, is entitled to file a complaint in the courts established by law, without prejudice to the responsibility which might affect the officer who caused the harm.[59]

The purpose of the judicial action is thus to permit a person who has experienced a violation of his constitutional rights through an administrative act to seek a remedy. In that sense, the Competition Act 1973 was intended to protect constitutional rights whenever there was a risk that the former Resolutive Commission was able to cause such damage. If the three cases in which the affected parties were permitted to seek judicial review are analyzed, it is possible to match each one of them with a possible risk of violation of constitutional rights, as has been shown above.

However, in practice, this constitutional protection by the courts was understood as an appeal procedure, and by the time of the Competition Act 2003, the institutional designers considered that it was necessary to make this 'appeal' procedure available to most of the decisions issued by the TDLC. Unfortunately they did not take into account that the TDLC, as an administrative autonomous body created for an administrative function, was not a court of the judiciary. If the legislator wanted to grant a proper appeal, the two options would have been allowing an appeal before a specialized upper tribunal, or or referring the decision back to the TDLC for an appeal on points of law only.[60]

Again, given the nature of anti-competitive infractions, the difference in names is not a purely terminological issue. The Supreme Court will need to display

[59] Chilean Constitution, Art 38.

[60] The latter was the solution adopted in the Criminal Procedural Reform, in which, because of the costs and time expected for each trial, it was opted not to repeat the trial before an appeal court but instead to permit a review only on points of law.

less deference to the decisions of another body in an appeal-like situation than it would have to show when considering an application for judicial review of an administrative body, as is required in the case of the *Reclamación*. Thus, the attitude of the Supreme Court towards the TDLC has not been in any way deferential, and the Court has entered into the technical competition aspects of the considerations of the TDLC.

This is particularly important, because judicial restraint is part of the generally accepted constitutional principle in Chile of the 'deference of public institutions'.[61] Therefore, if there is no clarity regarding the nature of the TDLC, and if it is treated as a court of the judiciary, the expectation of deference cannot be very high either. Conversely, if it is accepted that the TDLC is an autonomous administrative agency exercising adjudicative powers, and that its decisions are subject to judicial review, the scope, attitude and powers of the Supreme Court change dramatically, and the deference principle is more likely to be applied.

There is certainly agreement that the participation of the Supreme Court has not been in the best interests of the system. This does not mean that Supreme Court judges are exclusively at fault in this matter. As has happened in other areas of constitutional law where the role of the Supreme Court has been crucial, as in the case of the *Recurso de Protección*, another constitutionally regulated action of judicial review, it has been easier to blame the Supreme Court for the constitutional imperfections than to ask for the involvement of the other participants in order to change the situation. Supreme Court judges only speak through their decisions, as it is commonly said, and most of the time they are subject to criticisms from people who do not consider the collective responsibilities of other policy makers and the scholarship on the issue.

In this particular case, the lack of clarity in the scholarship, and to a great extent the Government and the legislature, aggravate the distrust in the system. Supreme Court judges have responded to the unrestrained power given to them in competition cases by 'speaking through their decisions' in these cases, but with their language based on an extensive expertise in civil and criminal law (and the procedural aspects of both) instead of antitrust law or economics. Supreme Court judges are not required to be specialists in antitrust, much less in economics, but the designers of the system trusted them instead of the members of the Tribunal, whose expertise has not been questioned. In the parliamentary debate, it is noticeable that the intention behind this was to protect the right to a fair trial within the Tribunal's proceedings.

Notwithstanding the imperfections introduced into the design, we propose—as a solution to the unintended effect of involving the Supreme Court—the interpretation of the *Recurso de Reclamación* in its original form: as a mechanism for the protection of constitutional rights when they are violated by the Tribunal

[61] P Zapata, *La jurisprudencia del Tribunal Constitucional. Parte general* (Santiago, Biblioteca Americana, 2002).

(Article 38 of the Chilean Constitution). This would mean that the scope of the Court would be limited, as the Constitution states, to remedying the violation of fundamental rights; it would not be able directly to amend the decisions of the Tribunal (in their substantive competition aspects). Using this method, the principle of deference of the public institutions would be upheld.

Chile is arguably a very legalistic country, in which culture mandates that every problem must be solved by an Act of Congress. Sometimes a correct interpretation of current laws is a much more feasible and proportional form of solving institutional problems. Therefore, we are unconvinced that what we need is yet another legal reform; rather, we support better interpretation of the already existing institutions. Indeed, what we have attempted to argue here is that the legal community needs to acknowledge the administrative nature of the TDLC, and to consider the *Recurso de Reclamación* as a judicial review procedure instead of an appeal. The current situation demonstrates that on a strictly legal basis an incorrect interpretation sets up an obstacle in the system. Moreover, beyond the debate of what should be the best interpretation on a point of public law, what lies behind this common understanding among Chilean scholars and the rest of the legal community is distrust in the competition system itself. We believe that strengthening the competition institutions will not be effective if the Supreme Court continues to display a non-deferential attitude towards these institutions.

C. Building the Trust: Effective Communication and Better Interpretation

The designers of the system have shown their distrust in competition by nominating the Supreme Court the 'ultimate decision-maker in competition policy', without being the most expert in competition law and economics. Instead of limiting its functions to the already crucial role of constitutional guardian of fundamental rights, the Supreme Court has been given the principal role of guardian of the competition system as a whole. The result of the current situation is that the Court is overturning the decisions of the TDLC by providing arguments on competition law, but from the perspective of an expert in civil and criminal law.

What is being proposed here is that, without the need for further legal reforms, it is possible to overcome the situation by:

a) interpreting infractions of competition law as breaches of administrative criminal law;
b) restating that the TDLC is an administrative adjudicative body; and
c) ensuring that judicial review is available whenever a fundamental right has been violated by the TDLC.

All of this is a matter of interpretation, but building trust in competition would also mean adopting an effective system of communication between the actors.

The adoption of a common 'code' or 'language' will enhance enormously communication between the actors.

Let us illustrate some of these failures of communication in two important areas. The first is action required before the Supreme Court. There are only two cases—*IP Telephony* (2007)[62] and to a lesser extent *Chiletabacos* (2006)[63]—in which the applicants sought the protection of the Supreme Court on the grounds of constitutional rights. In these cases, the decision of the Court was to dismiss most of the arguments put forward by the applicants. The Supreme Court upheld the TDLC's decision and only agreed to the reduction of the fine. Both cases can be considered an example of the real nature of the debate in a *Recurso de Reclamación.* The remaining applications to the Supreme Court have used the *Reclamación* as a regular appeal, under the general formula of requiring the Court to 'amend the decision of the Tribunal according to the rule of law', which is precisely the legal definition of an appeal under the Civil Procedure Act.[64]

The second area of concern relates to proof of *mens rea* (and proof in general). Under Chilean law, since a competition violation is an administrative offence, constitutional and criminal law require the existence of intent and its proof. Communication between the TDLC and Supreme Court has not been at its best in this regard. The rulings of the TDLC sometimes fail to use the same language the courts employ to refer to the facts and proved elements of the conduct. In this regard, we believe that the problem lies not in the requirement of intent itself, but rather in the interpretation of the proof itself required to demonstrate such intent, as discussed above.

The Supreme Court will show less judicial self-restraint towards the Tribunal regarding issues of general law (criminal, civil and procedural law), for example the reasoning of the TDLC on the legal deductive process as to how the proof of the facts convinced them in order to declare the elements proved. In this area, the TDLC still employs a form of argument that does not really fit with the language used by members of the judiciary (even given that one of the members of the TDLC is a Supreme Court judge). This situation led the Court in *Oxígeno* to criticize the way in which the Tribunal reached its decision, the terminology and the text of the argument being implicitly considered inappropriate by the Supreme Court.

In the most recent decision of the Court,[65] the trend for requiring a correct form of argument from the Tribunal is more evident. In that case, Justice Gálvez (in the majority opinion) is quite severe when referring to the procedural arguments of the TDLC. The Tribunal described different possible scenarios, concluding

[62] *Telefonia IP*, Supreme Court (2007), 6236-2006.
[63] *Chiletabacos*, Supreme Court (2006), 4332-2005.
[64] Civil Procedure Act, Art 186.
[65] *Isapres*, Supreme Court (2008), 4052-07.

that a collusive agreement was unlikely in comparison with other possibilities. In the decision, Justice Gálvez states:

> 11º) That the disquisitions in the last four paragraphs above, seem to have a lack of precision and certainty that is improper of the reasoning that must be adopted by judges of the Republic. Indeed, these statements are vague, ambiguous, contradictory and less enlightening by the time of the definition of whether exactly there is a collusive agreement as it has been argued in this case. It is not enough to mention the concurrence of elements that would eventually be suitable for establishing the facts, but it is necessary to conclude with certainty if they prove this circumstance or not.

One of the most valuable aspects of Justice Gálvez's opinion in this case is that he engages in a dialogue between the TDLC and the Supreme Court. In a way, this ruling opens the door to a more restrained Supreme Court, as long as the Tribunal adopts a more 'judicial style' in writing its decisions and expressing the way it reaches them. By establishing a fluent degree of communication, the Supreme Court, as the *ultimate decision-maker in competition policy*, will veto fewer decisions, and this will help build a richer culture of competition policy between institutions.

D. Conclusion

From a time-series study of collusion case law from 1973 until 2003, it is clear that little attention has been given to these collusive practices, particularly from 1987 onwards, by the Chilean Supreme Court. The Competition Act 2003 initially represented a shift in this trend, producing the first rulings issued against hard-core cartels; these rulings were based on sound economic and legal standards. However, an unexpected problem appeared: the role of the Supreme Court. This institution overturned all the infringement decisions relating to collusive agreements handed down by the newly-created TDLC, leaving in evidence the need for a change in order to detect and punish collusion successfully in the market. Moreover, as a consequence of the Supreme Court intervention, the case law of the TDLC has been altered, requiring an abuse of dominant position on top of a collusive agreement. The effects of this recently developed theory, which is quickly moving away from a 'per se' approach to collusion, are yet to be seen.

We believe that the strengthening of collusion enforcement in Chile requires several conditions. First, following Chilean law, it is essential that the Supreme Court has more flexibility when interpreting the evidence submitted by the parties in these types of cases. Secondly, it would be beneficial to introduce a leniency program and to grant the FNE more powers to investigate collusive behavior; both elements are contained in a Bill currently being debated in Congress. Thirdly, it would be useful to clarify, through case law, that the objectives of competition law are not limited to efficiency and, more importantly, that consumer welfare should be one of its goals.

From an institutional viewpoint, there are elements of the Competition Act 2003 that appear as clear signs of trust in the system, ie the independence and expertise of the TDLC's members, budgetary independence, and complete separation between the tribunal and the enforcement agency. However, in reality there are also signs of distrust: the lack of powers granted to the FNE, and the extension of the procedure of review of TDLC decisions by the Supreme Court. Additionally, there is a serious problem with communication between the TDLC and the Supreme Court.

We believe that the answer to this problem lies not the re-design of the system, but rather in giving the correct interpretation to Chilean competition law and, consequently, to the judicial review procedure. In this sense, the understanding of competition law in Chile as part of administrative criminal law, and the categorization of the TDLC as an administrative agency, will lead to the conclusion that judicial review, established in competition law, grants the Supreme Court the power to overturn decisions only when due process has not been followed. It does not grant the Supreme Court the right to overturn decisions based on technical issues of competition law and economics. In other words, this interpretation leads the way towards the use of the principle of deference by the Supreme Court towards the TDLC.

Moreover, we believe that deference could be further improved by adequate communication between institutions. Paradoxically in order to achieve effective communication, the TDLC must tend towards a more 'judicial' style when weighing evidence and preparing decisions.[66]

Overall, we believe that building trust in antitrust does not require the introduction of new laws to change the role granted to the Supreme Court but, in the context of an already over-legalized country, the proper and better use of existing regulation, and the consequent improvement of competition culture and awareness.

[66] In this process, under the 1973 Competition Act (repealed in this part by the Competition Act 2003), the contribution of the Supreme Court judge who was at the same time the President of the former Tribunal (the Resolutive Commission) was key to achieving such an objective, helping to move this process forward by sharing his expertise in judicial procedures with the other members of the tribunal. In the Explanatory Notes to the Bill containing the current Competition Act 2003, it was stated that the role of the Supreme Court judge would be essential for maintaining the procedural protections of the cases, given his judicial expertise, and for that reason his appointment and position was maintained (it would be the President of the TDLC). However, during the parliamentary debate this was considered inadequate for the independence and role of the Supreme Court itself, and an amendment to the Bill was approved, under which the Supreme Court participates in the appointment process, without appointing one of its members. We agree with the reform on this point, but recognize at the same time the value of the Supreme Court judge as far as importing a judicial style is concerned. See Competition Act 1973, Art 16 (repealed); Explanatory Notes to the Competition Bill (now Competition Act 2003), Presidential Bill No 136-346, p 7; Chilean Senate, Second Report of the Joint Committees of Constitutional Affairs and Finance, Bill 2944-03, pp 17–20.

Chapter X

Quality of Evidence and Cartel Prosecution: The Case of Chile

ALDO GONZÁLEZ*

I. Introduction

The detection of a large number of cartels around the world in the last decade suggests that collusion is a serious problem. Developed countries have reacted to cartels by implementing more sophisticated instruments to prosecute them, and by increasing the penalties for this anti-competitive conduct. Latin American economies, with less experience in antitrust enforcement, are starting to follow a similar path. Brazil and Mexico recently have modified their antitrust legislations, introducing leniency programs and strengthening the power of competition agencies to prosecute cartels. Chile is currently introducing reforms to its Competition Act, to move in the same direction.

Leniency programs (LPs) have played a central role in this new episode of fighting explicit collusion, and have demonstrated their effectiveness in uncovering cartels. One crucial component of the success of LPs is the quality of evidence that is obtained by them, and their effect on the litigation of cases and the application of penalties by the courts. The great revelation of information on the working of cartels achieved by LPs (geographic markets involved, duration of the collusive agreement, companies involved, methods of monitoring and enforcement, etc) makes it easier to establish a case of illegal action before the courts by dispelling any ambiguity about the existence of a cartel. The better quality of information gives greater certainty to court rulings against explicit cartels. With the information revealed through LPs, the likelihood of errors in judgment about explicit cartels has virtually been eliminated. Moreover, the level of fines has been higher due to the application of aggravating circumstances. The evidence shows us that the entry into force of LPs in Europe and the US led to the application of greater sanctions on average than in the previous period. This would imply that although LPs selectively offer a reduction in the sanctions, on average the punishment

* Professor, Economics Department, Universidad de Chile. Email: agonzalez@econ.uchile.cl. I am grateful for the comments of José Tomás Morel and Nicole Nehme.

for cartels is greater now, which undoubtedly strengthens the deterrent effect of such measures. On the other hand, when it is not clear that firms have colluded explicitly, the judicial system is reluctant to sanction them. If the evidence before the courts allows multiple interpretations, besides the collusive one, the courts are hesitant to sanction such alleged cartels.

In Chile, three recent cases of alleged collusion prosecuted by the competition agency and supported only by circumstantial evidence have been dismissed by the courts either at first or at second instance. The inherent ambiguity of the indirect evidence played a key role in the verdicts. The real possibility of obtaining better quality evidence would have reduced the uncertainty about whether the illegal conduct had occurred or not, leading to convictions if the defendants actually colluded and the antitrust agency had acquired the incriminating evidence. Current reforms to the Competition Act in Chile, including a LP and the power to search for direct evidence, will undoubtedly provide more effective tools to fight collusion and to reduce the number of erroneous court decisions.

This chapter is organized as follows: after this introduction, section II presents the different types of evidence employed to prove the existence of collusion. In section III we analyze the relationship between quality of evidence, penalties and deterrence. Section IV describes the Chilean Competition Act and institutions, and discusses the current amendments to the law which are aimed at improving the effectiveness of fighting collusion. Section V presents three recent cases of collusion prosecution in Chile, where the proofs against the firms were indirect or of a behavioral nature. We conclude our analysis in section VI.

II. Circumstantial Evidence v Hard Evidence

There are two known ways to prove the existence of collusion: circumstantial evidence and hard evidence. The first employs the commercial behavior of firms in the market, which is presumed to be explained by an explicit or implicit agreement between the firms. In an industry subject to collusion, firms coordinate their strategies. Thus we should expect to observe a parallel pattern in price movements, types of bids or refusals to deal with some clients. Hard evidence, in turn, corresponds to physical proof, such as documents, minutes, recordings and e-mails that show clearly that there has been direct communication between companies to agree on prices, market sharing, reducing output, or excluding competitors.

Qualitatively the two types of evidence are not the same. The courts tend to give more probative power to hard evidence than to the circumstantial type. The reason is that the former clears any doubts beyond what is reasonable about the existence of the cartel, while the latter always raises questions about whether the allegedly unlawful conduct is actually due to competitive behavior. For example, the parallel conduct in prices could be explained either by the fact that the firms have colluded to adjust their prices simultaneously, or by the fact that some of the fundamentals in the market, such as costs or demand, have changed. Moreover, in oligopolistic markets, where there is interdependence between competitors, it is expected that movements in prices of a firm will be mirrored by the rest of the participants. Thus, in principle, the parallel behavior would be consistent with both explicit coordinated conduct and individual profit-maximizing behavior.

Cases based on circumstantial evidence are sometimes supported by additional factors that facilitate the stability of the collusive equilibrium. The literature on circumstantial evidence mentions exchange of business information between firms, transparency in the pricing system and 'Most Favored Customer' client clauses as possible collusive devices.[1] Structural aspects of the market under analysis, such as the level of concentration, the existence of entry barriers and abnormal levels of profitability of firms, are usually presented as evidence to reinforce the hypothesis of collusion vis-à-vis the competitive.

Courts must weigh, using the available evidence, the error they risk committing by punishing firms that did not act unlawfully (type I error) as against leaving unpunished firms that have been cartelized (type II error). When evaluating these options, courts not only consider the probability that the observed behavior is due to collusion, but also take into account the damage that would be caused to the parties and the working of the market if they punished wrongly. Note that the weaker the support for the hypothesis of collusion by the circumstantial evidence, the greater the likelihood of type I error and the lower the willingness of the court to impose sanctions. This reluctance to apply sanctions based only on behavioral evidence is exacerbated by the fact that in many jurisdictions collusion is a criminal offense. Thus, the requirement of no ambiguity in the evidence becomes more important.

Hard evidence does not suffer from the problem of ambiguity in interpretation. Furthermore, given the 'per se' treatment of an explicit collusion offense in many jurisdictions, the use of a 'per se' rule reduces litigation because the structural and behavioral aspects of the market play a secondary evidentiary role.[2] Although we still may observe sanctions imposed on companies for colluding where decisions are based only on circumstantial evidence, in recent years there has been a tendency in the United States and Europe to apply more stringent standards for condemning firms without material evidence.

Another drawback of circumstantial evidence is that it may reflect only that firms were tacitly colluding, ie agreeing without direct communication. This may be relevant if laws or courts do not deem tacit collusion to be an anti-competitive action. Section 1 of the Sherman Act in the US has been interpreted as forbidding only explicit conspiracies. For instance, in *Interstate Circuit* (1938), the US

[1] Some of these devices may induce higher prices than the competitive level, and strictly speaking are not necessarily collusive in the technical sense of the term, although they are equally harmful.

[2] These elements may play a relevant role if fines are proportional to damages caused to third parties.

Supreme Court condemned the firms based only on circumstantial evidence, but the case was not characterized as one of tacit collusion.[3] Thus, if the judicial standard is not to punish tacit collusion then circumstantial evidence must show that the observed behavior, besides being collusive, is explained and sustained by direct communication among firms.

Many economists also remark upon the legal difficulties that emerge if tacit collusion is declared illegal; it does not seem feasible to force firms to behave against themselves or to act without taking in account what the rivals will do.[4] Whinston warns about the inherent vagueness of a recommendation that induces firms not to behave in their own best interests.[5] Think, for instance, of two firms where each one has monopoly power in its own market. Is it proof of collusion that neither of them wants to enter into the other firm's market? One firm may be reluctant to invade the other firm's market because it may suffer an entry into its own market in response. Both firms are able to understand the risk of having to compete in the two markets, without directly communicating each other.[6]

III. Fines, Quality of Evidence and Deterrence

Under the traditional paradigm of the public enforcement of law, a company compares the benefits of acting illegally versus the costs involved with that action when deciding whether to collude or not. The cost of the illegal action is equivalent to the chance of being detected and punished (**p**) multiplied by the magnitude of the fine (**F**), which amounts to **pF**.

Clearly, higher probability of detection or a higher fine makes the cost of colluding greater. The parameter **p** depends on the effectiveness of the mechanism of prosecution. It is expected that the more resources are devoted to the task of prosecution, the more likely wrongdoers will be caught. On the other hand, increasing the fine, although costly for the transgressor, has no social costs because it is a mere transfer between agents. Thus, the most efficient solution from the social point of view is to allocate the minimum amount of resources to increase **p**, and fix the fine **F** at the maximum level. This insight derives from Becker's seminal work that suggests that in order to deter crimes, it is optimal to set fines equal to infinity.[7] As to the relationship between the two variables **p** and **F**, these variables

[3] *Interstate Circuit v US*, 304 US 55 (1938).

[4] See Massimo Motta, *Competition Policy* (Cambridge, Cambridge University Press, 2004) and Michael Whinston, *Lectures on Antitrust Economics* (Cambridge, Mass, MIT Press, 2006).

[5] Whinston, above n 4.

[6] This was the case of *Soda Ash* in Europe. Commission Decision 91/227 of 19 December 1990, Soda-Ash-Solvay, ICI, OJ 1991, L 152/I. The Commission found the firms guilty of colluding, based on the refusal of domestic firms to enter into rival home markets, as the firms themselves admitted. The verdict allows for an inference that the Commission considered tacit collusion an illegal conduct.

[7] Gary Becker, 'Crime and Punishment: An Economic Approach' 76 *Journal of Political Economy* 169–217 (1968).

are substitutes. In other words, to achieve a certain level of deterrence, we can augment **F** and diminish **p**, or vice versa.

In practice, infinite fines do not exist. Punishments have other purposes beyond deterrence, which do not make it optimal to set maximum fines for every crime.[8] Overall, laws and tribunals tend to fix fines that are proportional to the harm caused to third parties, without having correspondence with the underlying probability of detection. In cartelization, we also observe that penalties are limited by the financial capability of firms. Excessive fines may lead firms to bankruptcy, which may end up hurting consumers, an outcome that goes against the purpose of competition law.[9] For this reason, judges may be reluctant to apply fines that are not congruent with the offenders' ability to pay. The criterion of proportionality of fines is present in the guidelines for collusion practices in both the United States and the European Union. In the first jurisdiction, the base fine must be equal to 20 per cent of the affected commerce during the period of operation of the cartel. In the EU the base fine cannot be greater than 10 per cent of the annual turnover of the offender.

Therefore, the deterrent power of the enforcement system, represented by **pF**, cannot be strengthened only by increasing **F**. Since the fine is upwardly constrained by the reasons explained above, it is also necessary to improve **p** to deter collusive behavior properly. Increasing fines may even be counterproductive if the quality of evidence is not conclusive about the culpability of the accused firms. The traditional enforcement model assumes that a firm detected engaging in collusion will be fined. Relaxing this assumption, Andreoni presents a model of enforcement where the evidence is imperfect, which carries the risk of inducing incorrect decisions.[10] Under this scenario of ambiguous evidence, judges perceive a private cost if they hand down an incorrect sentence.

To explain this reasoning further, we denote as U_1 (X + F) the disutility that a judge (or jury) obtains for punishing a company that has not colluded (type I error), while U_2 is the utility of the judge if he does not condemn a guilty firm (type II error). Both utilities are negative, and U_1 grows in absolute terms (X + F). This subjective utility includes both the social damage caused by an erroneous decision, and the personal cost to the judge when he is perceived as being unfair when applying the rules.

[8] The literature mentions retribution, penitence and readaptation as other goals of penalties. Even Cesare Beccaria (*Dei Delitti e delle Penne* (1764)), who mentions that the main goal of punishment is deterrence, advocates a system of proportional penalties.

[9] Some estimations show that the probability of getting caught in a price-fixing conspiracy multiplied by the real fines applied is far below the benefit of colluding. See Peter Byrant and E Woodrow Eckard, 'Price Fixing: The Probability of Getting Caught' (1991) 73 *Review of Economics and Statistics* 531; Greg J Werden and Marylin Simon, 'Why Price Fixers Should Go to Prison' 32 *Antitrust Bulletin* 917 (1987).

[10] James Andreoni, 'Reasonable Doubt and the Optimal Magnitude of Fines: Should the Penalty Fit the Crime?' 22/3 *RAND Journal of Economics* 385–95 (1991).

In the specific case of collusion, the parameter X may represent the distortion introduced in the market by forcing a company to chill behavior when the behavior is in fact not anti-competitive. This factor is relevant especially when basis for such ruling is indirect or circumstantial evidence. The magnitude of the fine **F** also affects the disutility of a wrong verdict, since the larger the penalty, the greater the injustice being committed on a wrongly condemned accused party.

The quality of evidence is represented by $\boldsymbol{q}$, such that $\boldsymbol{q}$ is a probability that a company has explicitly engaged in collusion given the proof available. Consequently there is a probability $\mathbf{1-q}$ that firms are innocent. A judge decides upon the expected value of the utility of each alternative, so he chooses the option that minimizes the error in expected terms. Thus, a firm is sanctioned if, and only if:

$$(1-q)U_1(X+F) \leq qU_2$$

Which is equivalent to the following condition:

$$q \geq \frac{U_1(X+F)}{U_1(X+F)+U_2}$$

This result, obtained by Andreoni, tells us that in order to condemn, the quality of proof, represented by $\boldsymbol{q}$, must exceed a certain threshold which depends on **F**, the magnitude of the fine.[11] As we can see, the term of the right-hand side is increasing in **F**, which means that a larger fine demands a higher standard of proof by the courts to sentence an offender. An interesting fact that emerges from this result is the relationship of complementarity that would exist between $\boldsymbol{q}$ and **F**, which goes in the opposite direction to the result of substitutability between **p** and **F** predicted by the traditional model of enforcement.

While in this model $\boldsymbol{q}$ is exogenous and depends on the characteristics of the case under analysis, it can be affected by the type of information that brings the prosecutor before the judges. With evidence of high quality, there will be a greater likelihood of condemnation if the firm is guilty, but also there will be more room to increase the fines, which strengthens the deterrent effect of the global mechanism of prosecution. The important lesson to draw is that fines are dependent on the quality of evidence available. Increasing fines without improving the quality of evidence may even be counterproductive, because those who decide may be more reluctant to apply sentences.

Table 1 below shows four scenarios depending on the quality of evidence available and the magnitude of the monetary penalties for the case of cartel prosecution. We have two extreme cases: one in which there is no possibility of detection and monetary penalties are low; and another in which the quality of the evidence is high and the fines are significant. In the latter case, the goal of deterring crime is achieved.

[11] *Ibid.*

Table 1 Relationship between quality of evidence and level of fine imposed

	Quality of Evidence	
Level of Fine	**Poor**	**Good**
Low		Effective Detection No Deterrence Repeated Offense
High	Unlikely Sanction, Impunity	Effective Detection and Deterrence

When the quality of proof is good but the maximum fine is low, companies will choose to collude anyway and then pay the fine once discovered. This may be the case in LPs that are overly generous in granting amnesty. As Spagnolo notes, this scenario, apart from being ineffective, is inefficient, because antitrust agencies must spend resources in the task of obtaining evidence without satisfying the goal of deterring collusion.[12]

In the opposite case—poor quality evidence but high fines—companies will never be punished for colluding due to the impossibility of proving the unlawful act with the available evidence. Increasing fines is not a solution to this problem and, as we have explained above, it may worsen the situation. This scenario may be representative of countries that have severe penalties for collusion but lack the power to obtain direct evidence, either by LPs or by other mechanisms, and where most of cases brought before the court are based entirely on circumstantial evidence.

A. Leniency Programs and the Quality of Evidence

Authors like Motta and Polo, based on an analytical modeling, have highlighted the inherent trade-off between defection and deterrence of LPs.[13] The reduction or elimination of the fine offered by the LP, while destabilizing the formation of cartels, reduces the cost in the expected value of colluding, weakening the deterrent power of the anti-cartel policy. This result is based on the assumption that the fine applied either by direct inspection or by the LP is equivalent in magnitude, which in turn implies that the quality of the evidence obtained by both mechanisms is equivalent as well.

If penalties are dependent on the quality of information that can be extracted about the characteristic of a crime, fines may differ depending upon the mechanism employed to obtain the evidence. Leniency programs have led to the disclosure of a wide range of information on the details of the working of

[12] Giancarlo Spagnolo, 'Leniency and Whistleblowers in Antitrust', in Paolo Buccirossi (ed), *The Handbook of Antitrust Economics* (Cambridge, Mass, MIT Press, 2008).

[13] Massimo Motta and Michele Polo, 'Leniency Programs and Cartel Prosecution' 21 *International Journal of Industrial Organization* 347–79 (2003).

cartels. This includes, amongst other matters, the duration of the agreement, the markets involved, the identity of participating companies, and the turnover of firms. Such a wealth of information enables courts to increase fines by applying the aggravating circumstances. In Europe, the Commission sets fines depending on the number of years during which a cartel is in existence. It also may apply a higher fine to the firm that plays the role of cartel manager. The more information available to the courts, the higher the probability that they can justify an increase in fines.

Although the evidence obtained either by direct inspection or by self-confession using LPs constitutes proof of high quality, it is relevant to ask whether LPs, besides helping in the detection of cartels, produce evidence of higher quality. Is it to be expected that those who defect from a cartel through an LP will provide better information than can be obtained by direct inspection? The answer is yes, since under LPs the potential defecting firm has an incentive to provide as much information as possible when deciding to defect, while under the threat of inspection a firm will tend to hide the evidence. Moreover, LPs introduce additional incentives to amass evidence in the first place—evidence which can be used in the event that one of the companies opts for defection later on.[14] In the absence of an LP, there is no benefit in maintaining information about the characteristics of a cartel because it can be used against the firm itself.

There is evidence suggesting that the introduction of LPs has tended to increase fines on average rather than to diminish them, with respect to the period prior to the introduction of such programs. Brenner obtains results along this line in the case of Europe, indicating that while the LPs selectively reduces fines for certain participants in a cartel, in expected value fines are higher, which would tend to reinforce the deterrent effect of the anti-cartel policy.[15]

IV. Institutional and Legal Framework for Prosecuting Collusion in Chile

The Chilean Competition Law establishes that collusion is an anti-competitive practice. According to Article 3(a) of the Law:

> It shall be considered as a practice that hinders competition and therefore subject to punishment: Any explicit or tacit agreements between traders, or concerted practices

[14] The fact that an employee of a company is rewarded for submitting hard evidence on collusion among firms gives her incentives to keep evidence in the first place. Cécile Aubert, Patrick Rey and William Kovacic. 'The Impact of Leniency and Whistleblowing Programs on Cartels' 24 *International Journal of Industrial Organization*, 1241–1266 (2006).

[15] Steffen Brenner, 'An Empirical Study of European Corporate Leniency Program' (Berlin, Humboldt University, 2005), mimeo.

between them, intended to fix prices of sale or purchase, limit production or allocate areas or market shares, abusing the power that such agreements or practices confer on them.[16]

There are two elements to be highlighted in the text of the Law. First, both types of collusion, tacit and explicit, are illegal. Secondly, the term 'abuse of market power' is included in the offense. The way in which the anti-competitive practice is characterized in the Law, including the concept of abuse of market power, leaves room for multiple interpretations at the moment of prosecuting a case of collusion. On a more permissive view, collusion would not have the status of an offense per se, as it also must be proved that competitive harm occurred in the form of an abuse of market power. From the point of view of prosecuting cases, the competition agency not only must have evidence that demonstrates that the anti-competitive practice occurred, but also must prove that the colluding companies possessed market power and that their actions allowed them to exercise such an abuse of dominance.

The legal definition given to collusion in Chile differs from the 'per se' approach in jurisdictions like the United States and the European Union.[17] As is clear from the text of the Chilean Law, collusion would have a status similar to most of the so-called exclusionary or monopolizing practices. In those cases, along with proof that the practice exists, the agency must demonstrate that it has led or would probably lead to competitive damage. The international norm is for 'per se' treatment for collusion, because it is estimated that situations where collusion is harmless or even beneficial are exceptional and rare. Therefore courts are willing to sacrifice any cases of beneficial collusion for greater clarity and ease of interpretation of the rule.[18] By contrast, theory shows that potentially exclusionary practices, such as bundling, tying, price discrimination or others, are not always harmful from the point of view of competition, and in a number of circumstances even may be beneficial to end consumers. That is why they are analyzed according to the criterion of the rule of reason.

The Chilean Competition Tribunal (TDLC), however, in its latest rulings, has interpreted the Law in a way that leaves collusion at an intermediate stage between the pure 'per se' and the rule of reason. According to the TDLC, firms engaging in collusion are to be condemned if they collectively possess market power, regardless of whether or not their actions led to competitive damage. While in the case of Chile the TDLC is close to internationally applied norms, the lack of clarity in the rule leaves open the possibility of wide variation in the interpretation of the Law. Moreover, we do not know whether the Chilean Supreme Court will endorse the

[16] Chilean Competition Law, Decree with Force of Law No 211 of 1973.

[17] In countries like Canada and Brazil, for instance, collusion is not an offense per se.

[18] According to Robert Bork, *The Antitrust Paradox: A Policy at War with Itself* (New York, NY, Free Press, 1978), if collusion is left to the rule of reason, we will not be able to sanction cartels that are clearly harmful without a lengthy trial about relevant issues such as a market definition or cross elasticities.

approach employed by the TDLC for cases of collusion, or whether it will take a more restrictive interpretation, requiring the demonstration of competitive harm on the part of colluding firms. So far, Chilean jurisprudence has not reached this point because the discussion has focused on an earlier stage, which is the quality of proof presented before the Supreme Court.

Chile has almost no record of successful prosecution of collusion. In general there is a lack of widespread consciousness in the business community that collusion is a serious threat to competition. For example, the president of a medium-size retail grocery company, asked whether he feared anti-competitive actions from its larger rivals, said to the press, 'to deal with this problem I trust more in a frank conversation between competitors, instead of relying on the antitrust institutions'.[19] Neither it is unusual for local government authorities to sponsor agreements among small public transportation operators to raise their fares in order to avoid price wars.

A. Antitrust Institutions

The current antitrust institutions in Chile date back to 2003. The main agencies are the *Fiscalía Nacional Económica* (FNE) and the TDLC. The former is the agency that represents the public interest in competition cases, acting as prosecutor and reporting the cases to the Tribunal. The FNE has investigative powers but cannot impose sanctions upon firms for anti-competitive behavior. The TDLC is a specialized competition tribunal. It is composed of five members: three lawyers and two economists. The decisions of this tribunal can be appealed directly to the Supreme Court.

B. Reforms to the Law

There is a Bill to amend the Competition Law which is currently being discussed in the Congress. Among other things, the reform introduces an LP, and also gives special powers to the FNE to perform searches and seizures for competition infractions. Similarly, it authorizes the FNE to intercept all forms of communications in an investigation.

According to the text accompanying the Bill, both the LP and the power to obtain direct evidence given to the FNE are complementary instruments to make investigations against collusion more effective. As suggested by the earlier discussion in this chapter, it is unlikely that an LP by itself will induce firms to disclose accusatory information, if there is no real threat that the agency will be able to obtain evidence by direct inspections.

[19] President of Rendic Supermarkets in an interview in *La Segunda* (June 2007).

Another important change in the Law is the increase by 50 per cent of maximum fines, from US$16.4 million to US$ 24.6 million.[20] Such an increase, as explained in section III, is consistent with the better quality of the evidence that is expected due to the reforms mentioned above. Also, the concept of competitive damage has been introduced as a reference to fix the level of fines to the condemned firms.

V. Collusion Prosecution in Chile

Between 2006 and 2007 there were three rulings about collusive practices in Chile: *Shipping Agencies*, *Medical Oxygen* and *Health Insurance*. In these three cases, the accused were acquitted, either at first instance by the TDLC, or by the Supreme Court. The critical element of the decisions was the quality of evidence, ie whether the circumstantial evidence demonstrated sufficiently that there was agreement (explicit or implied) between the players in each case. The most important elements of each of the cases are discussed below.

A. *Shipping Companies*[21]

At the beginning of 2003 the Exporters Association filed a complaint against a number of shipping companies regarding an agreement in prices among them and discriminatory practices applied to their clients. The plaintiffs argued that the defendants arbitrarily applied a charge for unsolicited services called 'Integrated Services Documentaries', associated with the processing of export documents.

The main element allegedly indicating a concerted practice was the simultaneity in the application of the new charge by the shipping agencies (between March and April 2002) and the similarity of tariffs among them, which varied between 25 and 27 dollars. The accused firms pointed out that the charges were based on the costs involved in such services. With regard to the similarity of tariff changes among competitors, the firms pointed out that being all in the same market and performing similar functions in a scenario of fierce competition, it is normal to observe such similarity among competitors.

In a unanimous verdict, the TDLC condemned the shipping agencies for collusive behavior. According to the TDLC, the charges applied by the defendants were unjustified, and could be sustained over time only if several companies agreed to fix them at the same time and under similar conditions. The proof employed by the TDLC was the behavior of the accused firms in the market. There was no

[20] Fines are established in Chilean currency adjusted by inflation. The current exchange rate is Ch$500 to 1 US dollar.

[21] *FNE v Ultramar Agencias Maritimas SA, Agencias Universales SA, Sudamericana Agencias SA, Ian Taylor Y Compañía SA and AJ Broom y Cia SAC (2003).*

direct evidence demonstrating that the firms were communicating each other to coordinate their business strategy. For the TDLC, the actions undertaken by the companies, such as the types of charges implemented, and the fact that they were simultaneous and at equivalent levels, were highly unlikely to be the outcome of individual behavior. Therefore, such conduct must be almost exclusively explained by collusive action.

The ruling was appealed to the Supreme Court, which overturned the verdict. According to the Supreme Court, the facts cited as evidence of commercial behavior represented only one hypothesis for collusion. However, such evidence was not conclusive of unlawful conduct. For the Court, collusion required the existence of a joint will and determination to carry out this practice, which could not be demonstrated by the mere similarity and simultaneity of the tariff changes. The parallel conduct, according to the verdict, could just as easily have been explained by the similarity in the type of services provided by the shipping agencies and the competitiveness of the market: factors which led the companies involved quickly to imitate the strategies of competitors.

B. *Medical Oxygen*[22]

In August 2005, the FNE filed an injunction against several companies in the business of supplying medical oxygen, for collusion. Specifically, the FNE accused Air Liquide SA Chile, Indura SA, AGA SA, and Praxair Chile of market division and bid rigging, organized by the agency in charge of the purchases of supplies for hospitals (CENABAST).

In a 4:1 decision, the TDLC found the companies guilty of collusion. The main evidence was the behavior of firms in the bidding process organized by the purchasing agency. CENABAST had devised a complex auction to avoid collusion among participants, because of serious suspicions of collusion among the major providers of oxygen in their direct sales to government hospitals in previous years.[23] Therefore it was crucial to design a collusion-proof bidding process. The process consisted of a sequential descending auction and a reservation price kept secret by the agency. In the first stage, each of the participating firms offered a price for supplying each of the geographical zones. Once firms offered first-stage bids, they were asked successively whether they would be willing to bid Ch$10 per unit less than the lowest bid existing so far. Finally, if prices were above the reservation price, firms were asked whether they were willing to match the reservation price set in advance. During the bidding, the companies offered in both the first and second phase values above the reservation prices that three of them finally accepted.

[22] *FNE v Air Liquide Chile SA, Indura SA, AGA SA and Praxair Chile Limitada (2005).*

[23] The FNE also filed a suit against the same group of companies for collusion, based on the refusal to sell and the disparity of prices for procurement of oxygen by public hospitals in previous years.

For the TDLC, the fact that the initial offers of the participants were almost 50 per cent above the reservation price was evidence of collusive behavior. The absence of bids equal to the minimum acceptable payment, according to the TDLC, was contrary to the self interest of each company and thus, it was indicative of collusion. In the view of the TDLC, the oxygen companies had clear incentives for not being aggressive in their bids during the auction. Offering low prices would introduce a gap with respect to prior prices charged to other customers, and would make transparent a market that was considered opaque at the time. This would transform the market from one that allowed for price discrimination. The transparency that the auction created would induce the clients of the companies (those who had contracts at higher prices) to demand reductions in the rates they had paid. The existence of an implicit 'Most Favored Customer' clause would give an incentive to the firms to soften their behavior in the auction, a strategy, in the opinion of the Tribunal, that would succeed only under collusion.

In the opinion of the TDLC dissenting judge, the conduct of the firms in the auction was insufficient evidence of collusion. Such conduct could be a function of actions of individual companies that operate in an environment where there is interaction between the parties, as is the case in an auction with multiple stages. According to the dissenting opinion of particular importance was the fact that if there was an alleged agreement, it failed, as some firms accepted the reservation price set by the principal. Moreover, the dissenting opinion pointed out that in order to prove a case of collusion, the FNE needed to demonstrate that such agreement allowed those firms to abuse the market power conferred by the collusion. In the opinion of the judge, this abuse could not have occurred because the bidding was successful. The reasoning of the dissenting judge employed in this case suggested a rule of reason approach rather than 'per se' approach to collusion.

The Supreme Court unanimously overturned the ruling of the TDLC, noting that the evidence submitted was inadequate to prove collusion. Moreover, the fact that the auction ended up awarding contracts with the reservation price fixed by the buyer signaled success rather than failure. The Court also pointed out that the participant firms hired experts to advise on how to win the contracts, a fact that would be inconsistent with the hypothesis of a boycott.

With regard to the conduct of the firms in the tender and its relationship to the collusive hypothesis, in a bidding process with multiple stages it is normal that companies would not reveal all the information in the early stages of the process. Even if the auction is designed such that the best strategy from the point of view of each firm individually—the subgame perfect equilibrium in technical terms—is to reveal full information in the first offer, it is also possible that participants may prefer to wait to reveal information if they believe that the other auction participants will do the same, as evidenced by results in experimental games. Moreover, there is no need to collude in order to have incentives to offer high prices at the auction. This is so because individually, and without coordination, each firm loses if it offers a very low price in the tender, as it involves returning money to those clients previously supplied at higher prices. As explained by Cooper, the existence of 'Most Favored Customer' clauses allows firms to sustain higher prices than the competitive level without the need for collusion.[24]

Lastly, invoking the success of the tender from the point of view of the buyers as evidence against the hypothesis of collusion is questionable. The fact that companies have accepted the reference price set by the buyers does not necessarily imply success. For instance, it is plausible that, without the alleged collusion, the companies would have offered lower prices, as noted by the Court's ruling. Note that the reservation price was kept secret by the CENABAST (Supply Center for the Ministry of Health in Chile), and it was intended to be used only in the event that bids were above that value. If the buyers were confident that this price was the competitive one, and there was almost no possibility of having better offers, then there was no point in keeping the price secret.

C. *ISAPRES*[25]

In 2005, the FNE accused five health insurance companies, known in Chile under the name of ISAPRES, of collusion. The purpose of the alleged collusion was to phase out their plans for maximum coverage, known as 100/80, and replace them with others for lower coverage, called 90/70. This replacement of plans, which occurred between 2002 and 2003, was not followed by a reduction in prices, despite the lower level of coverage that was offered to users. Also, in the same period, the profits of the alleged colluding companies increased significantly, some of them by 200 per cent. Additional evidence of concerted behavior submitted by the FNE was the parallel reduction in sales effort and advertising expenditure by the companies during the period when the replacement occurred. This conduct was not followed by other companies, which represented the remaining 20 per cent of the private health insurance market.

The accused firms argued that the change in health plans could be explained by the increase in costs due to the moral hazard problem inherent in the health market, which was exacerbated by having 100 per cent coverage in some services.[26] The insurers also argued that regulatory uncertainty existed at that time and had contributed to the replacement of the plans. Additionally, firms invoked the theory of parallelism of strategies that is intrinsic to competitive markets. They also pointed out that the high turnover of clients among companies was in contradiction to a hypothesis of collusion. Another line of defense employed by the

[24] Thomas E Cooper, 'Most-Favoured Costumer—Pricing and Tacit Collusion' 17 *Rand Journal of Economics* 377, (1986).

[25] *FNE v ISAPRES: ING SA, Vida Tres SA, Colmena Golden Cross SA, Banmedica SA and Consalud SA Health Insurance Providers (2005).*

[26] The accused firms mentioned that people with a plan of 100% of coverage have incentives to overuse the health services when they do not have out of pocket payments.

firms was to discredit the argument that they collectively had market power. The firms argued that the industry had no barriers to entry, and the relevant market was broader and included the public health insurer.

The TDLC, in a 3:2 verdict, found in favor of the health insurers. While acknowledging that there was parallel behavior among the companies, both in the timing and type of the replacement plans and in the reduction of the intensity of competition through the sales effort, the TDLC did not interpret such parallelism as a product of collusion. According to the majority opinion, the parallel behavior could be consistent with either collusive or competitive hypotheses. Thus, the ambiguity of the evidence made it insufficient to condemn the firms.

The minority vote, on the other hand, stated that given the facts of and information in the case, the only plausible explanation for the behavior was collusion among the accused. The dissenting judges were of the opinion that the majority vote did not present a unique explanation of non-collusive conduct.[27] For instance, the judges argued that one must ask about the variations in market conditions that motivated the parallel change of strategies of the accused firms. Assuming that the change was real, why did only some companies, and not others, modify their offer?

The FNE appealed the decision to the Supreme Court, which in a divided verdict upheld the decision of the TDLC. The Court applied similar reasoning to the TDLC. According to the Supreme Court, 'the evidence added to the process is insufficient to prove the existence of collusion'.[28] Later, the decision states that 'the proofs that are intended to demonstrate the existence of collusion in question are not direct because the referred facts can be explained for a variety of reasons'.[29] This decision endorsed the theory of competitive parallel behavior in a competitive market.

VI. Conclusion

The three recent Chilean cases on collusive practices clearly illustrate the inherent difficulty in punishing firms based only on circumstantial evidence. Even if one refines the economic analysis, there will always be doubt that the behavior is a result of collusion rather than individual action. The divergent judgments across the TDLC and Supreme Court on the one hand, and the differences in majority and dissenting opinions within the TDLC on the other, illustrate the complexity of relying upon circumstantial evidence.

[27] This criticism is shared by economists, who submitted a study about the case for the FNE. See Claudio Agostini, Eduardo Saavedra and Manuel Willington, 'Las Fallas del Fallo Isapres', Observatorio Económico No 9, Universidad Alberto Hurtado (2007).

[28] Supreme Court in *FNE v ISAPRES*, above n 25, pp 29 and 30.

[29] *Ibid*, p 28.

The Supreme Court in its three pronouncements has been skeptical about arguments claiming that the observed parallel behavior can be explained only by concerted action of the companies. In two judgments, *Navieras* and *ISAPRES*, the Supreme Court noted that the parallel conduct could have a competitive explanation. Thus, it has rejected appeals on the grounds that the behavioral evidence is not sufficiently clear to apply sanctions, even in cases such as *ISAPRES*, where there was a sound analysis about why the observed conduct of the defendant was unlikely to be the outcome of non-collusion. Such rulings create a high burden of proof for the use of indirect evidence. As a result, it seems unlikely, given the current standard, that firms will be found guilty of collusion based only on behavioral evidence.[30]

Physical evidence would dispel doubts beyond what is reasonable as to whether or not there was collusion between companies. The legal reforms currently under consideration, such as the introduction of a leniency program and the power to obtain direct evidence, will improve the quality of the evidence and of the decisions. This improvement consequently will remove any doubts and likely errors in the decisions made by courts, where the agency gets material evidence for a case.

What standard law should provide for determination of collusion remains an open question. So far the discussion has been focused on the quality of the available evidence. If the amendments to the Law allow the FNE to obtain direct evidence, and the agency submits this material evidence in a case, would it also be required to prove that there has been competitive damage in order to impose sanctions? The TDLC in its most recent verdicts suggest that collusion is anticompetitive per se as long as the involved firms collectively have market power. Nevertheless, it remains unclear if the Supreme Court will take the same approach as the TDLC.

[30] The dissenting opinion of TDLC, in the case of *ISAPRES*, mentions that, given the practical impossibility of having direct evidence—because there are no powers to seize documents or raid offices in search of proof—evidence of conduct constitutes collusion, despite its inherent ambiguity.

Chapter XI

Tacit Collusion in Latin America: A Comparative Study of the Competition Laws and Their Enforcement in Argentina, Brazil, Chile, Colombia and Panama

JUAN D GUTIÉRREZ R*

I. Introduction

Oligopolistic markets are prone to the formation of cartels, even without the existence of explicit agreements.[1] According to Richard Posner, in most cases oligopoly is a necessary condition (but not a sufficient condition) for successful price fixing where antitrust laws are applicable.[2] The markets of Latin America and the Caribbean (Latam) tend towards an oligopolistic structure due to historical, political and economic reasons.[3] Furthermore, oligopolies predominate in all sorts of markets for goods and services, including those markets that have a high impact in terms of poverty and development.

The predominance of oligopolies in Latam's markets poses an important challenge for competition authorities (CAs). First, CAs must enforce competition laws in markets where it is difficult to distinguish between conduct originating in collusive agreements among competitors and the behavior of interdependent firms that take unilateral decisions to adapt to the conditions of the market or anticipate their competitors' decisions. The latter implies a high risk of enforcement errors, either by sanctioning legitimate behavior (false positives) or by failing to detect true anti-competitive practices (false negatives).

* Professor of Law, Universidad Javeriana.

[1] Dennis W Carlton and Jeffrey M Perloff, *Modern Industrial Organization* (Boston MA, Addison Wesley, 2005), 122–25.

[2] Richard A Posner, 'Oligopoly and the Antitrust Laws: a Suggested Approach' 21 *Stanford Law Review* 1571 (1969).

[3] Due in part to the import-substitution policies adopted by Latam countries between the 1950s and the 1980s, and to the small size of their national markets.

Tacit collusion cases imply high costs for CAs, tribunals and private parties. In terms of administrative costs, CAs must spend economic and human resources to prosecute. It is important to stress the fact that Latam's CAs have scarce resources for the enforcement of antitrust, hence their costs must be minimized. Focusing on hard-core cartels (overt collusion, proved through direct evidence) and leniency programs may be less costly and more effective policies to prevent and sanction collusion.

Furthermore, expert testimonies and quantitative methods—which require experienced and robust authorities—are indispensable for any 'conspiracy' case where there is no 'smoking gun' evidence. A court's ability to handle economic evidence is an important question, even for experienced jurisdictions such as the United States.[4] In effect, the use of expert witnesses may generate a principal–agent conflict of interest problem between the adjudicator (who is not a specialized economist) and the expert economists. Moreover, the effects of asymmetric information (adverse selection and moral hazard) may increase administrative costs and enforcement errors.[5]

In sum, 'tacit collusion' is an issue that has inherent complexities and poses an important challenge for Latam's CAs. The objective of this chapter is to analyze Latam's competition rules on 'tacit collusion' cases, and their enforcement by the CAs and the courts. For this purpose, the chapter analyzes the evolution of Latam's case law and compares and contrasts the rules and their enforcement under the spectrum of economic theory and the rules applied in the US (federal level) and the EU.[6]

The analysis of this chapter is deductive and is framed mainly from the point of view of positive economics, describing the law and institutional framework and its possible effects on the agents. However, from the analysis of the case law it is possible, in future studies, to draw conclusions from the point of view of normative economics, especially to assess the negative impact in achieving the aim of poverty reduction in Latam due to tacit collusion.[7]

[4] Cf Richard A Posner, above n 2, at 1583.

[5] See Juan David Gutiérrez, 'Expert Economic Testimony, Economic Evidence and Asymmetry of Information in Antitrust Cases' (2007) CEDEC Competition Law and Economics Working Papers 07-04 <http://ssrn.com/abstract=1023494>.

[6] The analysis takes into account the fact that in theory the same rule in different legal systems should provide similar incentives for the agents subject to its compliance. However, in practice due to social, economic, cultural and institutional differences, the effects of a rule can be completely different. The more a legal rule corresponds to social norms, the more effective it will be and its enforcement will be less costly. See U Mattei, 'Three Patterns of Law: Taxonomy and Change in the World's Legal Systems' 45 *American Journal of Competition Law* 5 (1997) and U Mattei and A Monti, 'Comparative Law and Economics, Borrowing and Resistance' 2 *Global Jurist Frontiers* 1–18 (2001).

[7] Competition law and its enforcement are important both for developed and developing countries, even though different models of application may be applied in the more than 100 nations that have antitrust laws. Eleanor M Fox, 'Economic Development, Poverty, and Antitrust: The Other Path' *New York University Public Law and Theory Working Papers* 57, 104 (2007).

The second section is divided into subsections corresponding to each of Latam's jurisdictions' case law on tacit collusion. Each jurisdiction's antitrust system is described, as is the prohibition on horizontal agreements established by the law. Furthermore, a description of each jurisdiction's case law on tacit collusion includes the following:

a) the burden of proof and the standard of proof applied by the CAs and the courts;
b) attributes of a *successful* defense and of a *successful* prosecution; and
c) evolution of the case law.

The third section concludes, based on the positive analysis presented in the previous section, by contrasting and comparing the different features of the jurisdictions' competition laws and case law.

II. Laws and Enforcement in Latin America

The beginning of the 21st century coincided with the issuance of a third generation of competition laws in Latam and substantial reforms to the antitrust regimes established decades before. Although more than 90 per cent of Latam's Gross National Product of the region is produced in the countries that have competition policies and laws, a number of Latam's countries lack national antitrust legislation.[8]

On the other hand, 18 countries have national competition laws currently in force: Argentina, Barbados, Brazil, Chile, Colombia, Costa Rica, Dominican Republic, El Salvador, Honduras, Jamaica, Mexico, Nicaragua, Panama, Peru, Saint Vincent and the Grenadines, Uruguay, Trinidad and Tobago, and Venezuela.[9] These antitrust systems have different degrees of maturity and the enforcement of the laws is not uniform. Furthermore, the Andean Community of Nations, the Caribbean Community (CARICOM) and the *Mercado Común del Sur* (Mercosur) have enacted supranational competition laws.

Table 1 below contains the statutory provisions on collusion[10] and shows whether there are specific tacit collusion provisions (including additional guidance on tacit collusion such as circumstantial evidence).

[8] This is the case in the following countries: Antigua and Barbuda, Bahamas, Belize, Bolivia, Cuba, Dominica, Ecuador, Granada, Guatemala, Guyana, Haiti, Paraguay, Saint Kitts and Nevis, Saint Lucia and Surinam.

[9] For an inventory of current competition laws in Latam, see: Juan D Gutiérrez, 'La legislación de competencia en América Latina y el Caribe: historia, vigencia, aplicación y reformas' (2007) *CEDEC Competition Law and Economics Working Papers* 07-05, <http://ssrn.com/abstract=1023811>.

[10] The table does not include the decrees that develop the competition laws unless they contain explicit provisions on collusion or circumstantial evidence.

Table 1 Statutory Provisions on Collusion

Jurisdiction	Competition laws	Statutory provisions for collusion	Specific tacit collusion provisions
Argentina	Law 25.156 of 1999 (amended 2001), *Ley de Defensa de la Competencia*	Art 2	No
Andean Community	Decision 608 of 2005, *Normas para la protección y promoción de la libre competencia en la Comunidad Andina*	Art 7	Yes: Art 1[11]
Barbados	Fair Competition Act 2002-19	§13(3) and §§ 33–35	No
Brazil	Law 8.884 of 1994 (amended 2000), *Transforma o Conselho Administrativo de Defesa Econômica—CADE em Autarquia, dispõe sobre a prevenção e a repressão às infrações contra a ordem econômica e dá outras providências*	Art 20[12]	No[13]
CARICOM	Protocol VIII, Treaty Establishing the Caribbean Community	Art 30	No
Chile	Decree Law 211 of 1973 (amended, 1994, 1999, 2002 and 2003)[14]	Art 3	Yes: Art 3(a)[15]
Colombia	**(i)** Law 155 of 1959, *Por la cual se dictan algunas disposiciones sobre prácticas comerciales restrictivas* and **(ii)** Decree 2153 of 1992, *Mediante el cual se reestructura la Superintendencia de Industria y Comercio y se dictan otras disposiciones*	Art 47, Decree 2153	Yes: Art 45(1), Decree 2153[16]
Costa Rica	Law 7472 of 1994, *Ley de Promoción de la Competencia y Defensa Efectiva del Consumidor (LPCDEC)*	Art 11	No

(continued)

[11] Art 1 defines 'agreement', amongst other things, as any coordination among economic agents.

[12] Resolution 20 of 1999 contains the guidelines on the implementation of competition laws. Attachment I of the Resolution defines horizontal restrictive trade practices.

[13] Attachment I of Resolution 20 of 1999 establishes that certain 'structural factors may favor cartelization: high level of market concentration, existence of barriers to the entry of new competitors, homogeneous products and costs, and stable cost and demand conditions'.

[14] The Decree with Force of Law No 1 of the year 2005 contains the restated, coordinated and systematized text of the current law.

[15] Section (a) of Art 3 establishes as a restrictive practice any explicit or *tacit* agreement or concerted practice among economic agents. In relation to the proof of tacit collusion in the proceedings, as will be noted below, the Chilean rules admit the use of circumstantial evidence and presumptions. Art 22 of the Law establishes that all the 'means of evidence indicated in Article 341 of the Code of Civil Procedure shall be admissible as proof, as well as any findings or grounds that, in the opinion of the Court, are fit to establish the relevant facts.'

[16] Art 47 defines 'agreement' as, among other things, any practice that is concerted or consciously parallel among two or more firms.

Table 1 (Continued)

Jurisdiction	Competition laws	Statutory provisions for collusion	Specific tacit collusion provisions
Dominican Republic	Law 42-08 of 2008, *Ley sobre la Defensa de la Competencia*	Art 5	Yes: Art 4[17]
El Salvador	**(i)** Legislative Decree 528 of 2004 (amended 2007), *Ley de Competencia* and **(ii)** Decree 126 of 2007, *Reglamento de la Ley de Competencia*	Art 25, Decree 528	Yes: Art 12, Decree 126[18]
Honduras	Decree 357 of 2005, *Ley de Competencia*	Art 5	No
Jamaica	Fair Competition Act of 1993 (amended 2001)	§§ 17, 34–37	No
Mercosur	Decision 18 of 2006, *Protocolo de defesa da concorrencia do MERCOSUL*	Art 6	No
Mexico	**(i)** Federal Law of Economic Competition of 1992 (amended 2006) and **(ii)** Regulation of the Federal Law of Economic Competition (2007)	Art 9, Federal Law	Yes: Art 5, Regulation of the Federal Law[19]
Nicaragua	**(i)** Law 601 of 2006, *Ley de promoción de la competencia* and **(ii)** Decree 79 of 2006, *Reglamento a la Ley No 601, Ley de promoción de la competencia*	Art 18, Law 601	Yes: Art 17, Law 601[20]
Panama	**(i)** Law 45 of 2007, *Que dicta normas sobre protección al consumidor y defensa de la competencia y otra disposición* and **(ii)** Executive Decree No 31 of 1998, *Por el cual se reglamentan el Título I (Del Monopolio) y otras disposiciones de la Ley 29 de 1 Febrero 1996*	Art 13, Law 45	Yes. Art 7, Decree 31[21]

(continued)

[17] Art 4 defines 'agreement' as 'any meeting of minds expressed through contract or covenant, whether express or tacit, written or verbal, susceptible of aligning the competitive behavior of competitor economic agents'. Art 4 defines 'concerted practice' as 'any voluntary deed among competitor economic agents directed to annul competition among them'.

[18] Art 12 establishes as circumstantial evidence that which indicates the existence of anti-competitive agreements among competitors, among other things, price parallelism over a long period of time that cannot be attributed to price variations in the production factors.

[19] Art 5(ii) establishes as circumstantial evidence anything that indicates the typification of price fixing when two or more competitors establish the same maximum or minimum prices for a good or service.

[20] Art 17 prohibits any conduct, pact, agreement, covenant, or contract either explicit or *tacit*, which has as its object the restriction of competition.

[21] Art 7 establishes as circumstantial evidence anything that indicates the existence of absolute monopolistic practices, among others, whenever there is: 1) parallel behavior (in prices and quantities); 2) coordination managed or sponsored by trade associations or leading firms; 3) exchange of information that is vital for competition; and 4) price dispersion coupled with stable participations.

Table 1 (Continued)

Jurisdiction	**Competition laws**	**Statutory provisions for collusion**	**Specific tacit collusion provisions**
Peru	Decree Law 1034 of 2008, *Ley de represión de conductas anticompetitivas*[22]	Art 11	No[23]
Trinidad & Tobago	Fair Trading Act of 2006	§§ 17–18	No
Uruguay	Law 18.159 of 2007, *Ley de Promoción y Defensa de la Competencia*	Art 4	No
Venezuela	Law to promote and protect the exercise of free competition of 1992	Arts 9–10	No

Those countries with more than a decade of practice and experienced CAs include: Argentina, Brazil, Chile, Colombia, Costa Rica, Jamaica, Mexico, Panama, Peru,[24] and Venezuela.[25] The remaining jurisdictions have enacted their laws only recently, lack the necessary economic and human resources, or simply have not enforced their laws. Furthermore, some of the principal jurisdictions lack case law on tacit collusion. The most notable examples of this lack of case law are Mexico,[26] Costa Rica[27] and Jamaica.

Concerning Mexico and Costa Rica, enforcement has focused on cases of naked cartels and horizontal practices where direct evidence was available.[28] In the case of Jamaica, representatives from the Fair Trading Commission have explained in international forums that parallelism in firms' behavior is very common due to the small size of Jamaica's economy. The Free Competition

[22] Decree Law 1034 of 2008 abrogated the previous competition law, Decree Law 701 of 1991 (amended 1992, 1994 and 1996), *Decreto Legislativo Contra las Prácticas Monopólicas, Controlistas y Restrictivas de la Libre Competencia.*

[23] Art 11 of Decree Law 1034 includes 'concerted practices' among competitors as a form of 'horizontal collusionary practices'. However, the new competition law excluded 'parallel actions', which appeared in Art 6 of Decree Law 701 of 1991 as a form of restraint of free competition.

[24] For a thorough study of the Peruvian case law on tacit collusion and abuse of collective dominance, see Eduardo Quintana Sánchez, 'Abuso de posición de dominio conjunta y colusión tácita: ¿infracciones sin contenido real?' 51 *Thémis Revista de Derecho* (Peru, 2005).

[25] For a thorough study of the Venezuelan case law on collusion, see Gustavo Guevara Inciarte, 'El tratamiento de las prácticas y comportamientos colusorios en Venezuela (1992-2006): problemas teóricos y prácticos' 8 *Revista de Derecho de la Competencia CEDEC* (forthcoming, Bogota, 2009).

[26] Cf D, *Competition Law and Policy in Mexico: A Peer Review* (USA, OECD Publishing, 2004).

[27] Cf Jaime Eduardo Barrantes Gamboa, *Ley 7472 de Promoción de la Competencia y Defensa Efectiva del Consumidor* (Bogotá, Biblioteca Jurídica Dike, 2003) and Comisión para Promover la Competencia, 'Costa Rica's Country Contribution to the "Third Meeting of the Latin American Competition Forum—Madrid, 19–20 July 2005"' (2005).

[28] Cf OECD, above n 26, at 19–21, and OECD, 'Fighting Hard Core Cartels in Latin America and the Caribbean' (2005) *Third Meeting of the Latin American Competition Forum—Madrid*, 19–20 July 2005, <http://www.oecd.org/dataoecd/41/26/38835329.pdf>.

Act prohibits generally uncompetitive practices (section 7) specifically certain horizontal practices, such as price fixing, restraints of production and bid rigging.[29] However, according to David Miller, General Manager of the Jamaican Fair Trading Commission, tacit collusion is not proscribed under the Free Competition Act.[30]

Taking into account the status of Latam's antitrust systems described above, the following subsections describe and analyze the laws, the decisions and the case law on tacit collusion from Argentina, Brazil, Chile, Colombia, and Panama.

A. Argentina

Argentina enacted its first competition law in 1933 (Law No 11.210), which was amended in 1946 (Law No 12.906). However, according to Coloma, the law was scarcely enforced for almost five decades.[31] The replacement of these laws by Law No 22.262 (the Competition Defense Act or CDA)[32] in 1980 marked the beginning of a more rigorous enforcement of competition laws in Argentina and the prolific production of an organized doctrine.[33] The latter may be explained, among other things, by the fact that the new law modified the antitrust system from a judiciary-based system to an administratively-based one.[34] In effect, Law No 22.262 created a competition authority: the National Commission for the Defense of Competition (CNDC),[35] an administrative body which delivered opinions that had to be approved (or disapproved) by the Secretariat of Commerce.[36]

[29] §§ 17, 34–37 of the Fair Competition Act. The Act establishes that agreement 'includes any agreement, arrangement or understanding whether oral or in writing or whether or not it is or is intended to be legally enforceable'.

[30] 'Parallelism in business, where each enterprise when deciding its prices and other market strategies, takes into consideration the likely reactions and counteractions of its competitors to its own moves. To that extent, similarity in prices, movement in prices and other competitive variables could be the result of parallelism or tacit collusion rather than overt collusion. Tacit collusion exists where in the absence of any formal attempts to implement a collusive outcome, firms understand that if each firm competes less vigorously they might all be able to enjoy higher prices and higher profits. This type of collusion is not proscribed under the FCA. (David Miller, 'Fighting Hard Core Cartels' (2005) *Jamaica's Country Contribution to the Third Meeting of the Latin American Competition Forum—Madrid*, 19–20 July 2005, <http://www.oecd.org/dataoecd/41/21/38835255.pdf>, 5.)

[31] From 1933 to 1980 the competition authority decided only four cases. See Germán Coloma, 'The Argentine Competition Law and its Enforcement', ch V in this book.

[32] In Spanish, *Ley de Defensa de la Competencia.*

[33] For a complete legal and economic analysis of Law No 22.262 of 1980, see Germán Coloma, above n 31, and OECD, *Competition Law and Policy in Argentina: A Peer Review* (USA, OECD Publishing 2006), <http://www.oecd.org/dataoecd/36/57/37970045.pdf>.

[34] See Germán Coloma, above n 31.

[35] Acronym according to its name in Spanish, *Comisión Nacional de Defensa de la Competencia.*

[36] According to Coloma, the Secretary of Commerce has systematically endorsed the CNDC's opinions. See Germán Coloma, above n 31.

Argentina enacted its current competition law in 1999 through Law No 25.156.[37] This Law maintained the basic structure of the previous CDA but created a new antitrust authority, the National Court for the Defense of Competition (TNDC)[38] (which has not yet been installed and so the CNDC has been maintained in its place), and included merger review as one of its functions.[39]

The CNDC has a dual role of prosecutor and adjudicator since it may both investigate and decide cases.[40] The investigations are initiated either by a private complaint or *ex officio*.[41] The decisions, products of an administrative proceeding[42] that must start at the CNDC, may be challenged before the courts,[43] in the first instance before a court of appeals and in the second instance before the Supreme Court.[44]

1. *Statutes*

Argentina's CDA and Decree 89 of 2001,[45] which develops the Law, do not explicitly mention tacit agreements or conscious parallelism as forms through which collusion may take place. However, Article 1 of the Law prohibits any act or conduct *manifested in any form* that has the object or the effect of restricting competition or constituting an abuse of a dominant position in such a way that the 'general economic interest' is injured or potentially injured.[46] Moreover, as explained below, according to Argentine case law, parallelism is a form in which anti-competitive practices may take place.

Article 2 of the CDA establishes six types of collusive agreements: 'price fixing, quantity fixing, horizontal market division, bid rigging, horizontal agreements to restrict investments and horizontal agreements to restrict research and development'.[47] Such conduct will be considered to be in restraint of trade[48] if it distorts competition in such a way that the 'general economic interest' may be injured.

[37] See Law 25.156 of 1999 at http://infoleg.mecon.gov.ar/infolegInternet/anexos/60000-64999/60016/texact.htm.

[38] Acronym according to its name in Spanish, *Tribunal Nacional de Defensa de la Competencia*. See Art 17, Act No 25.156.

[39] Germán Coloma, above n 31.

[40] Art 24, Law No 25.156.

[41] Art 26, Law No 25.156.

[42] See Ch VI, 'On Proceedings', Law No 25.156.

[43] See Ch VIII, 'On Appeals', Law No 25.156, and Ch VIII, 'On Appeals', Decree 89 of 2001.

[44] See OECD, above n 33, at 34–35.

[45] See Decree 89 of 2001 at: http://infoleg.mecon.gov.ar/infolegInternet/anexos/65000-69999/65959/norma.htm.

[46] Cf Coloma, above n 31.

[47] *Ibid*. These types are defined in paras a, b, c, d, e and h of Art 2.

[48] In Spanish, *prácticas restrictivas de la competencia*.

2. *Decisions and Case Law*

Argentina's CAs and courts have studied several cases of explicit collusion[49] and tacit collusion.[50] Furthermore, the Argentinian authorities have developed a consistent case law regarding tacit collusion over the past 20 years. The current law is that price parallelism does not provide enough evidence on its own to prove infringement of the competition law.[51]

Most cases of tacit collusion were decided during the period when Law No 22.262 of 1980 was in force. Since the 1999 reform of the law maintained substantial characteristics of the CDA of 1980, especially regarding the types of anticompetitive practices,[52] it is relevant to study the doctrine and case law developed between the years 1980 and 1999. In effect, according to Coloma, '[t]he dominant Argentine antirust doctrine therefore considers that the case law developed between 1980 and 1999 is still valid nowadays'.[53]

Table 2 below lists the analyzed tacit collusion cases.

Table 2 Tacit collusion cases analyzed in Argentina

Case	Product Market	Decision
CNDC v Duperial SA and Compañía Química SA (1985)[54]	Phthalic anhydride	Close investigation
La Casa del Grafito v Rich Klinger y Bruno Cape (1989)[55]	Compressed asbestos slabs	Close investigation
Secretaría de Energía v YPF, Esso and Shell (1994)[56]	Fuels	Close investigation
René Veder Diez v Agip and others (1995)[57]	Bottled liquid gas (LPG)	Close investigation
Alberto Dupuy v VCC and Cablevisión[58] (1995)	Cable TV services	Close investigation

(continued)

[49] Among others, the most important cases of overt collusion are the following: *Secretaría de Comercio*, Resolución 442 de 1986 (*Silos Areneros de Buenos Aires v Arenera Argentina and others*); CNDC, Dictamen No 118 de 1989 (*Lara Gas and others v Agip and others*); *Secretaría de Comercio*, Industria y Minería, Resolución 382 de 1996 (*AGP v CCAP and others*); CNDC, Dictamen No 417 de 2003 (*Cámara Argentina de la Construcción and Delegación Entre Ríos v Cooperativa Entrerriana de Productores Mineros Ltda. and others*); and Dictamen No 510 de 2005 (*CNDC v Air Liquide and others*).

[50] See Germán Coloma, 'Prácticas horizontales concertadas y defensa de la competencia' (2000) <http://www.cema.edu.ar/~gcoloma/concert.pdf>, 28–34.

[51] Cf *ibid*, at 31.

[52] *Ibid*, at 27–28.

[53] Coloma (2007), above n 31.

[54] CNDC, Dictamen 065 de 1985.

[55] CNDC, Dictamen 110 de 1989.

[56] CNDC, Dictamen 160 de 1994.

[57] CNDC, Dictamen 233 de 1995.

[58] CNDC, Dictamen 209 de 1995.

Table 2 (Continued)

Case	Product Market	Decision
CNDC v Axle and others (1997)[59]	Safety valves or bottled liquid gas (LPG)	Sanction firms
Fecliba v Roux Ocefa, Rivero and Fidex[60] (1998)	Physiological serums	Close investigation
Asociación de Agencias de Viajes y Turismo de Buenos Aires v American Airlines and others (2001)[61]	Commercial airlines	Close investigation
CNDC v Loma Negra and others (2005)[62]	Cement	Sanction firms. The defendants appealed the decision and the first instance tribunal's decision is still pending.

Argentina's CA has applied a very high standard of proof regarding tacit collusion from 1985 up to date. Thus far there have been no judicial pronouncements on tacit collusion in Argentina. However, the first instance decision in *CNDC v Loma Negra and others* (2005) is still pending.

Of the nine cases of tacit collusion analyzed, in different markets for goods and services, in only two of them were the firms found guilty. Interestingly, in six cases initiated through private complaints the investigated firms were absolved from the charges, while in two cases initiated *ex officio* by the CNDC the firms were penalized. The most common parallel behavior analyzed by the CNDC has been price parallelism (in nine cases), although the CNDC has investigated market division in at least four of the cases. All the cases occurred in concentrated markets (three cases of duopolies and the rest oligopolies) that were analyzed in detail by the CA in terms of the markets' history and structure, with emphasis on the investigated period.

A detailed economic analysis of the investigated market has always been present in the CA's decisions. However, since *Fecliba v Roux Ocefa, Rivero and Fidex* (1998) there has been explicit inclusion of consideration of the economic theory

[59] Secretaría de Comercio, Industria y Minería, Resolución No 730 de 1997.

[60] CNDC, Dictamen 284 de 1998.

[61] CNDC, Dictamen No 356 de 2001. Two officials from the CDNC who participated in the instruction of the proceeding published a brief account of the case: see Hugo Alejandro Asplindh and Marina Bidart, 'Acuerdo internacional en la industria de transporte aéreo internacional: su tratamiento por la Comisión Nacional de Defensa de la Competencia' (2001)13 *Boletín Latinoamericano de Competencia* 3–8.

[62] CNDC; Dictamen 513 de 2005. For a summary of the case, see OECD, 'Prosecuting Cartels Without Direct Evidence of Agreement' (2006) <http://www.oecd.org/dataoecd/19/49/37391162.pdf>, 80–82.

underlying tacit collusion and international case law (especially from the US, UK and EC). Furthermore, *Asociación de Agencias de Viajes y Turismo de Buenos Aires v American Airlines and others* (2001) included commentary on the so-called 'plus factors' established by US case law. In *CNDC v Loma Negra and others* (2005), the CNDC cited similar cases studied in the UK and the EC.

Lastly, abuse of dominant position was an issue (due to a simultaneous increase of prices) in three of the cases. In each case the definition of the relevant market was an important matter for debate, as well as the market power of the firms. The CNDC assessed collective dominance and its abuse in these cases, although it did not develop the concept explicitly nor its relation with tacit collusion.

Attributes of a Successful Defense

The basic assumption applied by Argentine competition authorities is that parallel behavior, by itself, is not enough to prove an illegal concerted practice. This follows the prevailing economic reasoning and the case law of the US and EU. From the cases of tacit collusion in Argentina's antitrust system, the following conclusions may be drawn regarding the attributes of a successful defense in such a case:

a) The main proof that determined a closure of the investigation was that the conduct of the firms was not simultaneous or similar. In eight of the analyzed cases, the firms proved that their behavior was not parallel through the following facts (among others):
   i) their prices were different due to rebates and discounts;
   ii) the goods of each firm were different (in terms of quality); and
   iii) the payment conditions offered were different.
b) The market structure or exogenous phenomena may legitimately cause parallelism, especially a simultaneous increase of prices. Besides oligopolistic behavior, the CNDC mentioned as possible justifications for parallel behavior various phenomena, such as the following:
   i) the existence of a common cost structure in concurrence with a general increase in production costs;
   ii) a change in consumer preferences;
   iii) an increase in demand that causes scarcity; and
   iv) the fact that all the firms produce at full capacity of utilization.
c) Claims of tacit collusion may be rebutted if the investigated firms do not have a profit motive for concerted action. This was the case in *Asociación de Agencias de Viajes y Turismo de Buenos Aires v American Airlines and others* (2001), where CNDC concluded that since American Airlines and United Airlines did not participate in the route Buenos Aires–London (a relevant market by itself), British Airways would have not profited from coordination with these firms.
d) Claims of tacit collusion may be rebutted whenever there is proof of competitive dynamism of the market. The CNDC identified the following

as competitive elements reflected in the market's performance during the investigated period:

i) tendency of price decreases;
ii) existence of different volume rebates and other commercialization conditions;
iii) variations of market shares and expansion of the market;
iv) markets are not undersupplied;
v) existence of competition through imports;
vi) entrance of new competitors; and
vii) low barriers to entry.

Attributes of a Successful Prosecution

Where firms were penalized due to parallel behaviour, *ancillary restraints* that facilitated collusion (common marketing company or information exchange system) were present. Still, even when the CNDC has proved tacit collusion, it has acknowledged that there is an inherent difficulty in distinguishing firms that participated in the concerted practices from the ones that simply had to follow suit due to an exogenous condition of the market.

Argentina's standard of proof indicates that a successful prosecution in a tacit collusion case must comply with the following attributes:

a) Proof of the existence of parallel behavior among the investigated firms.
b) A highly concentrated market structure with low contestability, characterized by few participants, high barriers to entry, inelastic demand, low levels of or no international trade, or an undersupplied market.
c) Lack of any plausible explanation for the firms' conduct other than the existence of tacit collusion. For example, in *CNDC v Loma Negra and others* (2005), according to the CNDC, the firms' behavior, which eliminated uncertainty regarding their rival's future conduct, allowed them to reduce competitive rivalry.
d) Proof of the existence of practices that facilitate collusion, such as a common marketing company that allocates clients and sets prices, the existence of an information exchange system that allows the firms to coordinate their actions and the hiring of audit firms that monitor any deviation. It is important to stress the fact that in *CNDC v Loma Negra and others* (2005) an information exchange system that allowed the firms to share data regarding vital information for competition was considered, by itself, an infringement of the competition law.

In conclusion, Argentina's standard of proof is close to both the EU and US approach, in the sense that a parallel conduct will constitute an infringement only if collusion is the only plausible explanation for such conduct, and there is evidence of concerted practices represented by contacts among competitors and/or exchange of information about their commercial policy (past, present and future).

B. Brazil

Article 148 of Brazil's 1946 Constitution was the basis for the antitrust system established by Law 4137 of 1962.[63] This Law created the current CA, the Administrative Council for Economic Defence (CADE),[64] and established substantive and procedural rules. However, enforcement of antitrust was not strong until the enactment of a new Constitution in 1988 (Article 173, paragraph 4), especially with the replacement of Law 4137 of 1962 by Law 8884 of 1994.[65]

Law 8884 of 1994 (hereinafter, 'the Law') introduced merger control and reorganized CADE as a federal independent agency with powers of prosecution and adjudication of antitrust cases.[66] Furthermore, the Law established the functions of two complementary agencies with specific enforcement roles: the Secretariat of Economic Law in the Ministry of Justice (SDE)[67] and the Secretariat for Economic Monitoring (SEAE). The SDE monitors markets, identifies possible infringement and initiates investigations *ex officio* or upon request of interested parties.[68]

These three agencies constitute the Brazilian Competition Policy System (BCPS).[69] Proceedings before the CAs are administrative in nature[70] and their decisions may be subject to judicial review before federal courts of first instance if requested by the private litigants. The first instance decision may be appealed before a regional Court of Appeals by private parties or the agencies. Finally, the Court of Appeals' decision may reach the Superior Court of Justice if the private parties or the agencies apply for an appeal.[71] Parallel to the administrative agencies, Brazil's economic crimes law (Law 8137 of 1990) establishes criminal enforcement prosecutors who may file indictments before criminal courts.

[63] Michael Krakowski, *Política de competencia en Latinoamérica: una primera apreciación: un análisis comparativo legal e institucional de las políticas de competencia en Latinoamérica* (Proyecto MIFIC-GTZ, Nicaragua, 2001) 149.

[64] In Portuguese, *Conselho Administrativo de Defesa Econômica.*

[65] See OECD, *Competition Law and Policy in Brazil: A Peer Review* (USA, OECD, 2005), <http://www.cade.gov.br/internacional/Peer-Review-Report-English.pdf> 13.

[66] Arts 2 and 7 of Law 8884 of 1994.

[67] In Portuguese, *Secretaria de Direito Econômico do Ministério da Justiça.*

[68] Arts 13–14 and 30 of Law 8884 of 1994.

[69] In Portuguese, *Sistema Brasileiro de Defesa da Concorrência.*

[70] Title VI ('Administrative Proceedings') of Law 8884 of 1994.

[71] OECD, above n 65, at 65.

The current competition law has been amended on several occasions.[72] One of the most important legislative innovations was the establishment of a leniency program, managed by the SDE, in the year 2000.[73] Furthermore, CADE has issued several resolutions (with guidelines attached) that instruct upon the application of the laws, and Horizontal Merger Guidelines.[74]

1. *Statutes*

Article 20 of the Law[75] establishes as an infringement against economic order any act, *manifested in any way*, intended or able to produce the following effects:

I—to limit, restrain or in any way injure open competition or free enterprise;
II—to control a relevant market for a certain product or service;
III—to increase profits on a discretionary basis; and
IV—to abuse one's market control.[76]

The last subsections of Article 20 establish considerations regarding market control:

a) achievement of market control through efficiency is not illegal;
b) market control occurs when a firm or firms hold a substantive share of a relevant market; and
c) market control is presumed when a firm or firms hold more than 20 per cent of the relevant market.

However, regarding the last presumption, it must be stressed that CADE makes a case-by-case analysis, without invoking the 20 per cent threshold.[77]

A distinctive feature of Brazilian antitrust rules is that the proof of market power is necessary to determine an infringement of competition law, regardless of the type of conduct.[78] Article 21 contains a non-exclusive list (*numerus apertus*) of 24 acts that are 'deemed a violation of the economic order' whenever the hypothesis established in Article 20 is present. A distinctive characteristic of this list, in comparison with other jurisdictions' competition laws, is that it includes both bilateral or multilateral anti-competitive acts (such as cartels) *and* unilateral

[72] Among others, by the following: Law 9021 of 1995, Law 9069 of 1995, Law 9470 of 1997, Law 9781 of 1999, Law 10149 of 2000 and Law 11482 of 2007. See the current competition laws of Brazil at <http://www.cade.gov.br/legislacao/leis.asp>.

[73] Law 10149 of 2000.

[74] See an English translation of the Resolutions and the Horizontal Merger Guidelines at <http://www.cade.gov.br/english/internacional/law8884-94.asp>.

[75] See an English translation of the Law at <http://www.cade.gov.br/internacional/Law-8884-1994.pdf>.

[76] Translation from CADE's English version of the law.

[77] OECD, above n 65, at 20.

[78] Cf *ibid*, at 20.

anti-competitive acts (such as abuse of dominance). Article 21 lists the following types of collusive horizontal agreements:

— Price fixing among competitors.
— Agreement of sale conditions among competitors.
— Adopting or influencing any uniform or concerted business practices among competitors.
— Division of markets of goods or services or the sources of inputs.
— Bid rigging.
— Limiting or controlling technological research, development, investment, innovation of products and services or its distribution.[79]
— Unreasonably increasing prices.

As noted earlier, CADE has issued resolutions to implement competition policy. Resolution 20 of 1999[80] contains two important attachments relevant for the purposes of this chapter. Attachment I defines and classifies restrictive trade practices (horizontal and vertical), and Attachment II establishes the basic criteria for the analysis of the restrictive trade practices listed in the law. The guidelines contained in Attachment I define 'horizontal restrictive trade practices' in the following terms:

> an attempt to reduce or eliminate market competition, whether by establishing agreements between competitors in the same relevant market with regard to prices or other conditions or by adopting predatory pricing. In both cases these practices seek, immediately or in the future, jointly or separately, to increase the company's market power or create the conditions required to more easily exercise such power.[81]

The guidelines classify four categories of horizontal restrictive trade practices:

a) cartels;
b) other agreements between companies;
c) illicit practice of professional associations; and
d) predatory pricing.

According to the guidelines, cartels are

> express or *implied* agreements between competitors in the same market, involving a substantial part of the relevant market, regarding prices, production and distribution quotas and territorial division, in an attempt to increase prices and profits jointly to levels that are closer to monopolistic levels.[82] (emphasis added)

[79] The listed collusive agreements correspond to the numerals I, II, III, VIII, X and XXIV of Art 20.
[80] See an English translation of the law at <http://www.cade.gov.br/internacional/Resolution%2020%20-%201999.pdf>.
[81] Resolution 20 of 1999, at 3. Translation from CADE's English version of the Resolution.
[82] *Ibid.*

Furthermore, the guidelines establish that certain 'structural factors may favor cartelization: high level of market concentration, existence of barriers to the entry of new competitors, homogeneous products and costs, and stable cost and demand conditions'.[83] In tacit collusion cases, as explained bellow, these conditions are verified and comprise important circumstantial evidence for the decision.

In relation to the assessment of conduct by CADE, the guidelines contained in Attachment II establish the assumption that conduct that injures competition requires, as a necessary precondition, 'the use of leverage in one market to attempt to gain market share in another or the search for a dominant position in the relevant market by the party adopting such practice'.[84]

Due to the subsection of Article 20 which established that the attainment of market power through efficiency is not illegal, a balancing test between restrictive effects and efficiency effects is also included in the guidelines' steps for assessing conduct. In the case of cartels, 'CADE assumes that anti-competitive effects exist once the existence of market power is demonstrated'.[85]

Lastly, within the analysis of conduct there must be sufficient evidence of the practice in the case record. The verification of sufficient evidence is not limited to documentary evidence; according to the guidelines, it may also include circumstantial evidence such as meetings, data exchange or 'the absence of economic rationale for adoption of a practice that is not necessarily illegal'. [86]

2. *Decisions and Case Law*

Brazil's enforcement of competition law has focused in recent years on the investigation of horizontal restraints, especially cartels.[87] The authorities were especially active between March 2002 and June 2005, during which period 15 cartel cases were adjudicated.[88] To date, the majority of the cases have been decided on direct evidence of collusion. Although by the early 1990s CADE had started to assess tacit collusion cases,[89] the first major precedent was *SDE v CSN, Usiminas and Cosipa* (1999).[90] Tacit collusion cases are few in Brazil in comparison with Brazil's peers (ie, Argentina, Colombia and Peru).

[83] *Ibid.*
[84] *Ibid*, at 8.
[85] OECD, above n 65, at 20.
[86] Resolution 20 of 1999, at 8. Translation from CADE's English version of the Resolution.
[87] OECD, above n 65, at 21–23.
[88] Roberto Augusto Castellanos Pfeiffer, 'Recent Aspects of Hard Core Cartel Prosecution in Brazil' (2005) *Brazil's Country Contribution to the Third Meeting of the Latin American Competition Forum—Madrid*, 19–20 July 2005, <http://www.oecd.org/dataoecd/40/57/38834958.pdf>, 1.
[89] Coloma mentions *Asbeg v Sitran and others* (1988) and *Codima v Ibemep and others* (1990), where the authority concluded there was not enough evidence to prove collusion. According to Coloma, the basic principle established in these cases was that parallel behavior was not enough to typify a concerted practice. See Coloma (2000), above n 50, at 25.
[90] Administrative Proceeding No 08000.015337/1997-48.

Table 3 below summarizes Brazilian tacit collusion cases.

Table 3 Tacit Collusion Cases in Brazil

Case	Product Market	Decision
SDE v CSN, Usiminas and Cosipa (1999)[91]	Flat rolled steel products	Sanction firms. Confirmed by first instance federal court. Judgment appealed by the firms and the decision is still pending.[92]
CADE decisions over a series of cases in different cities (2002)[93]	Fuel retailing	Closure of investigation/ sanction of firms.
SDE v Varig S.A and others (2004)[94]	Commercial airlines	Sanction firms.
SEAE/MF v Sindicato das Empresas Proprietárias de Jornais e Revistas do Município do RJ and others (2005)[95]	Daily journals of high circulation sold in street kiosks	Sanction firms.

There are several distinctive features of Brazilian law that are relevant for tacit collusion cases. First, according to Article 20 of the Law and Resolution 20 of 1999, CADE requires proof of market power in determining an infringement. Hence, the concept of collusion is explicitly linked with the exercise of collective dominance. Secondly, the guidelines contained in Resolution 20 explicitly list the factors that make markets prone to cartelization: 'high level of market concentration, existence of barriers to the entry of new competitors, homogeneous products and costs, and stable cost and demand conditions.'[96] This list is used as a guide by the three CAs to assess cases. Thirdly, Brazil was one of the first Latin American countries to implement a leniency program, by Law 10149 of 2000.

On the other hand, CADE's decisions have an economic approach rather than a formal legal basis. In effect, in each of the cases mentioned above, the relevant market and its structure is analyzed and explained in detail. Furthermore, proceedings are highly contentious due to the interaction of the different CAs and

[91] *Ibid.*

[92] OECD, above n 65, at 21.

[93] *Ibid.*

[94] Administrative Proceeding No 08012.000677/1999-70. For a summary of the case, see OECD, above n 65, at 85–86.

[95] Administrative Proceeding No 08012.002097/99-81. For a summary of the case see OECD, above n 65, at 86.

[96] Resolution 20 of 1999, at 3. Translation from CADE's English version of the Resolution.

the fact that the investigated firms' present economic expertise to support their defense.

There are common features in the four tacit collusion cases that are pertinent for the purposes of this chapter. First, those features of the markets underlying the cases—the existence of an oligopolistic structure, high market concentration and low contestability due to high barriers to entry. Secondly, the cases are related to price fixing, leaving aside other forms of horizontal collusion such as market division or bid rigging. Thirdly, the defendants employ similar defense strategies, based on the following arguments:

— The existence of a similar cost structure and an increase in their costs due to external factors.
— The interdependence caused by an oligopolistic structure and the existence of 'price leadership' that is followed by the firms, which in turn cause a tendency towards similar prices.
— The fact that the conduct involves not a price increase but rather the elimination of a discount.
— Absence of market power.
— Existence of competitive dynamics such as technological innovation.

Attributes of a Successful Defense

The analysis applied by CADE is influenced by EU and US case law (quoted explicitly), and especially by the latter since the cases explicitly mention 'parallel plus'. Hence, the principle underlying CADE's decisions on tacit collusion, confirmed by the jurisprudence of the courts, is that parallel behaviour is not enough to establish an illegal agreement.[97] The so-called 'plus factors' are indispensable to proving collusion.

From the analyzed cases of tacit collusion and the criteria established by the SEAE to filter price-fixing complaints based on price parallelism, the following are attributes of a successful defense in a tacit collusion case:

a) A plausible explanation for the firms' behavior besides collusion, such as *price leadership* conduct in an oligopolistic structure, the fluctuation of production costs in combination with a similar cost structure, and the influence of government regulations. The *price leadership* justification was a common argument in the investigated firms' defense, which was supported by economic expertise. In the mentioned cases the Brazilian CAs were very careful to assess every alternative explanation[98] for the firms' behavior that could exclude collusion, and made an effort to rebut them in detail.

[97] Cf Castellanos Pfeiffer, above n 88, at 2.

[98] In the studied cases CADE takes into account the possibility that parallel behavior is mere coincidence. However, the probability of coincidence always scored very low statistically.

b) The tendency of the market to discard tacit collusion. According to the criteria established by the SEAE, this is the case when one of the following circumstances is proved:
   i) The firms' profit margin is decreasing.
   ii) There is an increasing profit margin but there is no causal relation between this and parallelism of prices.
   iii) High costs of monitoring, which may be verified when conduct that follows the same pattern is followed by other firms in a large geographical area (eg a State).

Lastly, it is relevant to mention that in the cases mentioned in this document the examples of conduct were simultaneous and similar; hence a defense based on the argument that the firms' conduct was not parallel was absent. However, theoretically this argument would be a valid defense for future cases.

Attributes of a Successful Prosecution

The standard of proof applied by CADE indicates that a successful prosecution in tacit collusion cases includes the following attributes:

a) Proof of simultaneous and identical behavior.
b) Structural factors that make a market prone to the formation of cartels. CADE takes into account the following characteristics[99] that may facilitate coordination: high market concentration, low contestability (due to the existence of high barriers to entry and the absence of imports) and the production of homogeneous goods.
c) The facts and circumstantial evidence must demonstrate that no rational economic explanation for the conduct is plausible other than collusion. The latter has been explicitly endorsed by the federal courts of Brazil. In every case CADE carefully analyzes each of the hypotheses that could explain the conduct, and has the burden of discarding their probability. Among others, CADE excluded the following hypotheses:
   i) The probability that the parallel behavior was mere coincidence was statistically negligible.
   ii) The implausibility of the 'price leadership' justification (eg, when the examples of conduct are simultaneous, the initiative is alternated among the firms or there is contradiction in the firms' arguments).
   iii) An increase in common costs does not justify a joint price increase[100] if cost structures or industrial processes are not identical.

[99] The guidelines establish that certain 'structural factors may favor cartelization: high level of market concentration, existence of barriers to the entry of new competitors, homogeneous products and costs, and stable cost and demand conditions.' (Resolution 20 of 1999, at 3. Translation from CADE's English version of the Resolution.)

[100] Cf Castellanos Pfeiffer, above n 88, at 3.

d) Proof of practices that facilitate collusion, such as the following:
   i) Meetings of firms' representatives before any variation of prices.
   ii) The intervention of a trade association that explicitly facilitated coordination.
   iii) Information exchange systems (eg, of pricing, sales and customers) that allow coordination of the agreement and monitor deviations.

C. Chile

Chile enacted its first competition law, Law 13.305, in 1959.[101] However, competition policy and the enforcement of the law was not strictly applied until the enactment of Decree Law 211 of 1973,[102] which is the current competition law. The Law for the Defense of Free Competition (hereinafter, 'the Law') has been amended on several occasions, among others by Law 18.118 of 1982, Law 19.336 of 1994, Law 19.610 of 1999, Law 19.806 of 2002 and Law 19.911 of 2003. The Decree With Force of Law No 1 of 2005 contains the restated, coordinated and systematized text of the current Law.[103]

Chile's antitrust regime is a judicial-based system.[104] It includes an administrative agency, the National Economic Prosecutor's Office (FNE),[105] which has a prosecutorial role, and a specialized independent tribunal, the Tribunal for the Defense of Free Competition (TDLC),[106] with judicial powers.[107] The decisions of the TDLC may be appealed directly to the Supreme Court.[108]

The National Economic Prosecutor may initiate investigations following private complaints or *ex officio.*[109] If the Prosecutor's Office finds good reason to open a proceeding, it will issue an administrative act[110] that contains the formal charges against the investigated agents.

The TDLC, as a judicial entity, adjudicates the cases brought by the Prosecutor's Office or following private complaints.[111] An important feature of the Tribunal is its composition: two of the five members must be economists.[112] Only the TDLC's final judgments that impose one of the measures contemplated in Article 26 of the Law, or that waive the application of these measures, may be subject to

[101] Cf OECD, *Competition Law and Policy in Chile: A Peer Review* (USA, OECD Publishing, 2004), 15.
[102] *Ibid.*
[103] See the official translation of the Law into English at <http://www.fne.cl/?content=marco_juridico>.
[104] Art 2 of Decree Law 211 of 1973.
[105] In Spanish, *Fiscalía Nacional Económica.* See Arts 33–45 of Decree Law 211 of 1973.
[106] Law 19.911 of 2003 replaced the Competition Commission, also a special court, with the TDLC. In Spanish, *Tribunal de Defensa de la Libre Competencia.*
[107] Arts 5–32 of Decree Law 211 of 1973.
[108] Art 5 of Decree Law 211 of 1973.
[109] Art 39 of Decree Law 211 of 1973.
[110] In Spanish, *requerimiento.*
[111] Art 18 of Decree Law 211 of 1973.
[112] Art 6, section (b), of Decree Law 211 of 1973.

a judicial review[113] requested by the private parties or by the Prosecutor, before the Supreme Court.[114]

1. *Statutes*

Article 3 of the Law establishes a general prohibition against any deed, act or convention, executed individually or collectively, that has the effect of, or that would tend to, prevent, restrict or hinder competition. Moreover, Article 3 contains a non-exclusive list (*numerus apertus*) of deeds, acts or conventions that are considered restraints of competition. Section (a) of Article 3 establishes as a restrictive practice any explicit or *tacit* agreement or concerted practice among economic agents that has as an object price fixing, limiting production or dividing markets, and abusing the power conferred by such agreements.[115]

From the wording of the Article an important question arises: is market power (individual or collective) a prerequisite to an anti-competitive practice? This has been a source of debate even among the members of the TDLC. In *FNE v Air Liquide Chile SA and others* (2006),[116] the TDLC did not focus on the existence of market power, a situation that the dissenting opinion countered with the argument that the proof of dominance was necessary. On the other hand, in the most recent case, *FNE v Isapre ING SA and others* (2007),[117] the majority considered that the proof of dominance was a *sine qua non* for the configuration of an anti-competitive horizontal agreement. The dissenting vote of two members considered that interpretation to be a conceptual error; they argued instead that collusion and abuse of collective dominance are two different forms of infringement of the competition law.

In relation to the proof of tacit collusion in proceedings, Chilean rules admit the use of circumstantial evidence and presumptions.[118] In effect, Article 22 of the Law establishes that all the 'means of evidence indicated in the Article 341 of the Code of Civil Procedure shall be admissible as proof, as well as any findings or grounds that, in the opinion of the Court, are fit to establishing the relevant facts'.[119] Furthermore, according to the last paragraph of Article 22, the TDLC must

[113] In Spanish, *recurso de reclamación*.

[114] Art 27 of Decree Law 211 of 1973.

[115] 'In simple words, according with [*sic*] the law, the hard core cartels are included in the generic form of "collectively [*sic*] agreements between business agents" under [*sic*] an explicit or implicit way. In the first case, the hard core cartels have an explicit agreement (but usually not written) in order to affect or cause distortion on the market. In the second, there is not an agreement, just a common behavior between the competitors that produces the same effect. Both kinds of conducts are illegal under the Chilean competition law. The cartel under an implicit agreement creates a consciously parallel conduct.' (OECD, above n 62, at 87.)

[116] TDLC, *Sentencia No 43 de 2006*.

[117] TDLC, *Sentencia No 57 de 2007*.

[118] 'The economic evidence is particularly relevant in those cases because the cartels and the collusive conducts in general, are not crimes under the Chilean law. Thus, the power of the Prosecutor to investigate is limited by law and cannot consider measures like interception telephones or other ways of communication.' (OECD, above n 62, at 87.)

[119] From the official translation of the Law.

assess the evidence according to due circumspection rules[120] which, as in other 'continental law' jurisdictions, gives 'the judges the opportunity to assign value to every single proof in harmony with the merit of the process and his or her logic and experience'.[121] However, as explained below, the standards of proof in relation to tacit collusion applied by the FNE, TDLC and Supreme Court vary substantially.

2. *Decisions and Case Law*

Enforcement efforts of the TDLC have focused in recent years on cases of abuse of dominant position. According the TDLC's statistics, of 62 total cases adjudicated between 2004 and 2007, seven cases related to collusion (overt and covert), whereas more than half involved the abuse of dominant position.[122] Furthermore, tacit collusion cases have been adjudicated by the TDLC in recent years only after long proceedings[123]. Five cases of tacit collusion decided were between 2004 and 2007 and two reached the Supreme Court.

Table 4 below lists the analyzed tacit collusion cases.

Table 4 Tacit Collusion Cases in Chile

Case	Product Market	Decision
Fiscalía Nacional Económica (FNE) v Nestlé Chile SA and others and *Soproleche and Loncoleche v Preventive Commission* (2004)[124]	Raw milk	Close investigation, but TDLC resolved to establish six preventive measures[125]
FNE v Compañía de Petróleos de Chile SA and others (2005)[126]	Fuel	Close investigation. Confirmed by Supreme Court of Justice

(continued)

[120] In Spanish, *reglas de la sana crítica.*

[121] OECD, above n 62, at 87.

[122] See TDLC; *Base de Datos—Causas Contenciosas al 31 de diciembre de 2007*, available at <http://www.tdlc.cl/DocumentosMultiples/Estadísticas%20Causas%20Contenciosas.xls>.

[123] In the 2007 public accountability audience, the TDLC's president, Justice Eduardo Jara Miranda outlined that the assessment of indirect or circmunstantial evidence in cases where direct proof was not available had been a very important challenge for the TDLC. Available at <http://www.tdlc.cl/UserFiles/P0001/File/CUENTAS%20PUBLICAS%20TDLC/Cuenta%20Publica%202007.pdf>

[124] Tribunal de Defensa de la Libre Competencia (TDLC), *Sentencia No 7 de 2004.* For a summary of the case, see OECD, above n 62, at 88.

[125] The measures imposed conditions on the acts or contracts in the market of raw milk, in general for the whole country, that obliged the plants to 1) maintain a public list of purchase prices that explains the parameters that determines the price; 2) announce, with a month in advance, any change in the conditions of purchase of raw milk; 3) justify any refusal regarding the purchase of milk; 4) keep a registry of the rejected offers and inform the FNE twice a year of the significant changes regarding the purchase of milk; 5) abstain from using the historical margin of deliveries in winter and summer to set the purchase price; and 6) design a system of quality control that guarantees fairness to the all the parties.

[126] TDLC, *Sentencia No 18 de 2005.* For a summary of the case, see Fiscalía Nacional Económica, 'Luchando contra los carteles duros: la perspectiva Chilena' (2005) *Chile's Country contribution to the 'Third Meeting of the Latin American Competition Forum—Madrid*, 19–20 July 2005'.

Table 4 (Continued)

Case	Product Market	Decision
ASOEX and FNE v Ultramar and others (2006)[127]	Maritime agency's services	TDLC sanctioned, but the Supreme Court reversed the TDLC's decision[128]
FNE v Air Liquide Chile SA and others (2006)[129]	Bottled oxygen	TDLC sanctioned, but the Supreme Court reversed the TDLC's decision[130]
FNE v Isapre ING SA and others (2007)[131]	Health insurance	Close investigation. Dissent by Ministers Butelmann and Depolo.

Regarding the prosecution of horizontal collusion, Chile's CA has focused on cases where direct evidence was not available. The five cases above were set in markets with an oligopolistic structure and high concentration. In four of the cases price-fixing charges were studied, in two cases market division charges, and only in one case did the FNE prosecute the firms for bid rigging.

Although Chile's tacit collusion case law has not been as prolific as that of its peers (ie Argentina, Colombia and Peru), the analysis in each case has been thorough (decisions are quite detailed in comparison with the region's usual standards) and the facts and evidence have been the subject of intense scrutiny. Another feature that distinguishes Chile's case law is the absence of explicit reliance on foreign case law, with only one case mentioning EC law.

The FNE and the TDLC apply an economic approach to the assessment of the cases where the market structure and characteristics are explicitly identified. This approach is reinforced by the presence of expert economic testimonies (provided by the plaintiffs and the defendants) in every case, and by the fact that two of the members of the tribunal are PhD economists rather than lawyers. The latter is a unique characteristic of Chile's enforcement system that differentiates it from the other Latam jurisdictions. Perhaps because of this institutional set-up, the economic analysis in the TDLC's decisions contrasts with the strict formalistic approach of the Supreme Court.

Attributes of a Successful Defense

The case law of the TDLC and the Supreme Court both hold that parallel behavior is insufficient to prove tacit collusion. Furthermore, the Supreme Court's concern regarding sanctioning firms that act legitimately or without the intention

[127] TDLC, *Sentencia No 38 de 2006.*
[128] Corte Suprema de Justicia, *Sentencia del 26 de octubre de 2005.*
[129] TDLC, *Sentencia No 43 de 2006.*
[130] Corte Suprema de Justicia, *Sentencia del 22 de enero de 2007.*
[131] TDLC, *Sentencia No 57 de 2007.*

to restrict competition is reflected in its standard of proof, which is close to the position of the European Court of Justice.

The TDLC's case law explicitly deals with the fact that parallel behavior may be explained either by illegal collusion, or by the logic of oligopolistic market structures. Furthermore, the TDLC acknowledges that an increase in prices in a concentrated market, in the absence of barriers to entry, does not create a 'per se' infringement. To discard the possibility of parallelism due to the firms' interdependence or 'price leadership', the TDLC analyzes thoroughly each hypothesis that may justify a firm's conduct on economic grounds. Ultimately, the plaintiff has the burden of proving that there is no economic justification for the firms' decisions besides the existence of collusion.

In summary, the three arguments present in the cases where none of the firms was found guilty are the following:

a) The conduct was not parallel.
   i) The quality of the product is different.
   ii) The prices are not really homogeneous due to the existence of rebate schemes.
b) There was a reasonable explanation for the firms' behaviour besides collusion.
   i) In price-fixing cases:
      1) the prices were raised due to an increase of production costs and their cost structures were similar; and
      2) behavior is normal in the context of an oligopoly where firms are interdependent, transparency of information allows imitation (strategic conduct) and the product is homogenous.[132]
   ii) In market division cases, different conditions of commercialization or distribution explain price dispersion.
   iii) In a case where there is a simultaneous denial to offer a product, the conduct had the objective of reducing a moral hazard and adverse selection problem.
c) The market tendency excludes collusion since there is no dominant position. The following characteristics of the markets were alleged by the defendants:
   i) Market shares were low.
   ii) The profit margins were low, or at least not supracompetitive.
   iii) Barriers to entry are not high.
   iv) There is a high degree of rivalry in the market.

Attributes of a Successful Prosecution

An effect of the Supreme Court's standard of proof for tacit collusion is that there are no cases where firms have been fined for this offense. Since there are no cases

[132] In the case where bid rigging and market division were charged, the argument was the inverse: the quality and commercialization of the good were different.

of successful prosecution for tacit collusion in Chile, its attributes must be inferred from the theoretical considerations of the TDLC and the Supreme Court.

Before analyzing the specific rules for tacit collusion, it is pertinent to discuss the TDLC's case law on collusion more generally. To establish that a horizontal agreement infringes the law and achieve a successful prosecution , the following elements must be proved:

a) the existence of an agreement;
b) on a relevant variable for competition;
c) which allows the firms to attain, maintain or reinforce dominance and abuse from it.

The case law of the TDLC and the Supreme Court, regarding the elements that must be proved to determine the infringement of the law through tacit collusion, may be summarized in the following terms:

a) Concurrence of wills to restrict competition. According to the Supreme Court, the plaintiff must prove the deliberate and joint intent of the firms to adopt an illegal practice.
b) Dominance of the market (individual or collective) and the possibility of abusing it through the agreement.
c) No economic justification exists for the firms' decisions other than the existence of collusion. The Supreme Court has been emphatic as to the following principle: the evidence must allow the adjudicator to go beyond the production of plausible hypotheses; it must be conclusive. Hence, the adjudicator cannot rely exclusively on market evidence to infer collusion. Without losing sight of this principle it is important to mention that according to the TDLC's case law, the following facts, concurrently, may indicate:
   i) Market division:
      1) stable participation of the firms for long periods of time;
      2) high dispersion of prices;
      3) lack of transparency and asymmetry of information regarding prices charged; and
      4) concentrated markets with high barriers of entry.
   ii) Coordination among firms:
      1) existence of high barriers to entry;
      2) high (supracompetitive) profits;
      3) reduction of demand;
      4) few competitors; and
      5) frequent interaction among firms (eg, within a trade association).

Other characteristics of a market have been considered as facilitators of collusion, such as vertical integration which allows the firms to control the final price (which is public and apt for monitoring).

D. Colombia

Colombian competition laws[133] were enacted in 1959 (Law 155) but were not enforced until the mid-1990s.[134] Decree 2153 of 1992 reorganized the CA, the Superintendence of Industry and Commerce (SIC), and established a structured antitrust system. The SIC is part of the executive branch of the Colombian State, under the supervision of the Ministry of Commerce, Industry and Tourism, but with administrative, financial and budgetary autonomy.[135]

The Superintendent of Industry and Commerce is the head of the SIC and issues final decisions regarding the infringement of competition laws.[136] This competence to decide the cases by himself allows the Superintendent to shape competition policy relatively autonomously, including the issue of tacit collusion. Proceedings before the SIC are administrative in nature, and may be initiated via a private complaint or *ex officio* by the SIC. The decision that resolves the case is an administrative act (Resolution),[137] which may be challenged in the courts.[138] First, the parties may file a request for the annulment of the administrative act before a first instance administrative court[139], the Administrative Tribunal.[140] Secondly, the parties may appeal the decision of the Administrative Tribunal before a second instance court, the State Council.[141]

1. *Statutes*

Article 1 of Law 155 of 1959 contains a general prohibition against agreements or covenants that have the objective of limiting competition.[142] Article 47 of Decree

[133] For a complete review and compilation of Colombian competition laws, see Alfonso Miranda Londoño and Juan David Gutiérrez Rodríguez, *Compilación de normas de derecho de la competencia en Colombia Referencias jurisprudenciales, concordancias y anotaciones* (Bogotá, Cámara de Comercio de Bogotá, 2005).

[134] See Alfonso Miranda, *El Régimen General de la Libre Competencia* (Bogotá, Javegraf, 2002) III 'Revista CEDEC' 23–24.

[135] Art 2, Decree 2153 of 1992.

[136] Art 4, Decree 2153 of 1992.

[137] In Spanish, *Resolución.*

[138] See Alfonso Miranda, *El control jurisdiccional del régimen general de promoción de la competencia y practicas comerciales restrictivas* (Bogotá, Javegraf, 2002) III 'Revista CEDEC'.

[139] According to the Colombian Administrative Law Code, Administrative Tribunals have competence to decide at first instance requests for 'annulment of administrative acts and restoration of the rights' whenever the quantum of the suit exceeds 300 times the monthly legal minimum wages (Art 132-3). When the quantum of the suit is below this threshold, an Administrative Judge is competent at first instance (Art 134B-3); the Administrative Tribunal is competent, at second instance, to hear an appeal against the Administrative Judge's decision (Art 133 1). The maximum penalty that the SIC may impose on a firm that infringes the competition law is 2,000 times the monthly legal minimum wages (Art 4-15, Decree 2153 of 1992). To date the requests for 'annulment and restoration of the rights' of a Resolution issued by the SIC have been filed only at first instance before an Administrative Tribunal.

[140] In Spanish, *Tribunal Administrativo.*

[141] In Spanish, *Consejo de Estado.*

[142] Art 1, Law 155 of 1959. Art 46 of Decree 2153 of 1992 contains a similar clause, prohibiting any conduct that affects freedom of competition.

2153 of 1992 contains a non-exclusive list (*numerus apertus*)[143] of 10 types of agreements considered as anti-competitive.[144] Collusive agreements explicitly defined by Article 47 are: price fixing (direct or indirect), fixing conditions of sale, horizontal division of markets, division (quotas) of production or distribution, division or restriction of sources of inputs for production, limits to technological progress, abstaining from producing or affecting the level of production, and bid rigging.[145] It must be stressed that according to the wording of Article 47, these examples of conduct may be considered anti-competitive either because of their effect on the market or due to their objective (potential harm to the market). Article 45(1) defines an agreement as 'any contract, covenant, compromise, or practice that is concerted or consciously parallel among two or more firms'.[146] Hence, it is clear that the Colombian legislation prohibits both explicit mechanisms for collusion and tacit mechanisms such as conscious parallelism.

2. *Decisions and Case Law*

The SIC has frequently dealt with collusion cases, especially price fixing. The explicit prohibition of collusion through tacit means under Decree 2153 of 1992 has been the basis upon which the SIC has initiated several successful investigations. Two cases have reached the State Council, the highest judicial court for administrative proceedings. Additionally, at least seven cases of supposed parallelism have finished due to consent agreements without judicial review. In these cases the SIC does not develop the concept of 'consciously parallel practice'. Instead, the agency focuses on analysis of the viability of the compromise offered by the investigated parties. Furthermore, in comparison with the decisions that impose penalties on the firms involved, these decisions disclose less information regarding the facts of the case and evidence taken into account.

Three different periods may be identified in the enforcement of tacit collusion. This division into separate periods coincides with the appointment and terms of the different Superintendents who decided the cases.[147] It is important to stress the fact that the Superintendent is elected by the President of the Colombia and

[143] It is a *numerus apertus* clause since according to the wording of Art. 47 the agreements listed 'among others' are considered anticompetitive.

[144] For an analysis of each of the anticompetitive agreements established by Art. 47, see Mauricio Velandia, *Carteles restrictivos* (2002) 15 *Boletín Latinoamericano de Competencia* 99–120.

[145] The types of agreements that mentioned correspond to collusive agreements established in sections 1, 2, 3, 4, 5, 6, 8 and 9 of Art 47.

[146] In Spanish, the wording of Art 45(5) is the following: '*Acuerdo: Todo contrato, convenio, concertación, práctica concertada o conscientemente paralela entre dos o más empresas.*'

[147] A first period starts in 1999, when the first cases of tacit collusion were decided by the SIC in the tenure of Emilio J. Archila. A second period between the years 2001–2002 corresponds to the cases decided under the tenure of Monica Murcia. A third period between the years 2002–2007 corresponds to the cases decided under the tenure of Jairo Rubio E. Finally, the proceedings of the cocoa, cement and sugar cases are ongoing and the final decision regarding must be taken by the current superintendent of industry and commerce Gustavo Valbuena Q, whose tenure began in October 2007.

holds office for no fixed term. Hence, the Superintendent may be removed from his post at any time by the President.

Table 5 lists the Colombian tacit collusion cases.

Table 5 Tacit Collusion Cases in Colombia

Case	Product Market	Decision
SIC v Corporación Lonja de Propiedad Raíz de Bogotá and others (1999)[148]	Real estate services	Sanction firms. Administrative Tribunal (AT);[149] State Council (SC) confirmed the decision.[150]
SIC v Cooperativa Lechera Colanta Ltda and Derilac SA (1999)[151]	Milk	Sanction firms. AT annulled initial decision;[152] SC revoked the AT's judicial decision.[153]
SIC v Postobón SA and others (2000)[154]	Soda (soft drinks)	Consent agreement without judicial review.
SIC v Casa Luker SA and Compañía Nacional de Chocolates SA (2000)[155]	Chocolate	Consent agreement without judicial review.
SIC v Alaico and others (2000 and 2001)[156]	Commercial airlines	Consent agreement without judicial review.
SIC v Comunicación Celular SA and others (2001)[157]	Mobile telephone services	Consent agreement without judicial review.
SIC v Ladrillera Helios Ltda and others (2001)[158]	Bricks of clay	Consent agreement without judicial review.
SIC v Continental Airlines and American Airlines (2001)[159]	Commercial airlines	Close investigation.

(continued)

148 SIC, *Resolución 22759 de 1999.*

149 *Tribunal Administrativo de Cundinamarca, Sección Primera, Subsección B, Sentencia de octubre 25 de 2001.*

150 *Consejo de Estado, Sala de lo Contencioso Administrativo, Sección Primera, Caceres y Ferro SA vs SIC. Sentencia del 22 de Noviembre 2002, Radicación No: 25000-23-24-000-2000-0563-01 (7793).* Justice Olga Inés Navarrete Barrero delivered the opinion of the court.

151 *Resolución 22762 de 1999.*

152 *Tribunal Administrativo de Cundinamarca, Sección Primera, Subsección B, Colanta vs SIC. Sentencia del 7 de Febrero de 2002, Exp 000665.*

153 *Consejo de Estado, Sala de lo Contencioso Administrativo, Sección Primera, Colanta vs SIC, Sentencia del 23 de enero de 2003, Radicación No: 25000-23-24-000-2000-0665-01(7909).*

154 SIC, *Resolución 19644 de 2000.*

155 SIC, *Resolución 24206 de 2000.*

156 SIC, *Resolución 25983 de 2000, Resolución 7451 de 2001* and *Resolución 7554 de 2001*

157 SIC, *Resolución 19444 de 2001.*

158 SIC, *Resolución 25153 de 2001.*

159 SIC, *Resolución 36903 de 2001.*

Table 5 (Continued)

Case	Product Market	Decision
SIC v Estación de Servicios Caldas Limitada and others (2002)[160]	Fuel retailers	Sanction firms.
SIC v Mera Hermanos Ltda and others (2002)[161]	Fuel retailers	Sanction firms.
SIC v Estación Terminal de Distribución de Productos de Petróleo de Bucaramanga S and others (2002)[162]	Fuel retailers	Sanction firms. The AT confirmed the decision.[163]
SIC v Silvia Tello Velez and others (2002)[164]	Fuel retailers	Sanction firms.
SIC v Molinos Roa SA and others (2005)[165]	Green paddy rice	Sanction firms. The defendants decision appealed and the AT's is still pending.
SIC v Pavco SA and Ralco SA (2004)[166]	PVC tubes	Consent decree without judicial review.
SIC v Redeban Multicolor SA and Credibanco (2005)[167]	Management of credit and debit card payments	Consent decree without judicial review.
SIC v Cementos Argos SA and others (2008)[168]	Cement	Final decision pending. SIC's first decision sanctions the firms.
SIC v Casa Lúker SA and Compañía Nacional de Chocolates SA (2009)[169]	Cocoa	Final decision pending. SIC's first decision sanctions the firms.
SIC v Ingenio del Cauca SA and others (2007)[170]	Sugar cane	Proceedings ongoing.
SIC v Comunicaciones Satelitales de Colombia SA and others (2008)[171]	Installation of broadband, maintenance and provision of Internet services	Proceedings ongoing.

160 SIC, *Resolución 7950 de 2002.*

161 SIC, *Resolución 7951 de 2002.*

162 SIC, *Resolución 8732 de 2002.*

163 TAC, *Sección Primera—Subsección A, Estación de Servicio la Pedregosa vs SIC, Sentencia del 18 de Noviembre de 2004. Exp 02-0678.*

164 SIC, *Resolución 8027 de 2002.*

165 SIC, *Resolución 22625 de 2005.*

166 SIC, *Resolución 3927 de 2004.*

167 SIC, *Resolución 6816 de 2005* and *Resolución 6817 de 2005.*

168 SIC, *Resolución 51694 de 2008.*

169 SIC, *Resolución 4946 de 2009.*

170 SIC, *Resolución 6381 de 2007.*

171 SIC, *Resolución 19785 de 2008.*

Evolution of Doctrines and Case Law

The definition and the elements of 'conscious parallelism' have not varied substantially during the last decade in the SIC's decisions and the courts' case law. However, there has been a conceptual evolution and modification as regards enforcement in each of the periods analyzed.

In the first period (1999–2001), the development of 'conscious parallelism' in legal terms is incipient, and economic analysis has no major role in the cases. The decisions were based upon an analysis of the price movements and the affidavits of the managers of the firms that were investigated. Furthermore, the SIC established that the existence of 'conscious parallelism' as a form of collusion may be identified by determining the consciousness of the firms regarding competitors' policies and their reiterative imitation, rather than by focusing on the existence of the *will* of the firms. In this period the SIC signed consent agreements on five of the seven cases of tacit collusion, while in two cases the firms were found to be guilty of conscious parallelism.

During the second period (2001–2002), the SIC developed in detail, but still from a formal legal standpoint, the concept, scope and elements of 'conscious parallelism'. For the first time, the authority acknowledged explicitly that 'price parallelism' by itself was not enough to prove the infringement of competition laws. Hence, illegality may be determined with an analysis of the economic justification for the firms' conduct. Furthermore, the SIC established that an awareness by firms of competitors' actions was not illegal per se. A strategy of identifying other firms' actions and policies would be an infringement of competition law when it would tend to distort competition by eliminating competitive factors such as price. In this period the SIC did not settle cases, and it fined firms for conscious parallelism in four cases.

Finally, in the third period (2002–2007), the SIC adopted an economic-based approach rather than a formalist appraisal of cases. The agency took into account the theories regarding the firms' conduct in oligopolies (especially their interdependency) and included a deeper analysis of the relevant markets. The SIC also advanced in the use of different types of proof, besides the analysis of prices and managers' affidavits, by including documents that assess the nature of the market and by taking into account economic expertise presented by the investigated firms.[172] During this period, the SIC signed consent agreements in two of the three cases of tacit collusion, while in one case it found the firms guilty of conscious parallelism.

To date, the doctrine remains ambiguous regarding two issues:

a) the *will* as a necessary element for 'conscious parallelism'; and
b) the criteria used in order to determine that price parallelism of certain firms infringed the law while other competitors, who acted similarly or identically, were not found guilty.

[172] In *SIC v Molinas Roa SA and others*, the opinion of the economic expert referred to oligopolistic pricing and its implications for the green paddy market in Colombia.

The courts, with just one exception,[173] have generally followed the SIC analysis and confirmed the Resolutions fining the firms. So far, in the debate before the Courts, expert economic testimonies have not been included in such cases and it has a pre-eminently formalistic approach.

Characterization of Enforcement

In the 15 Colombian tacit collusion cases analyzed in this chapter, the SIC found in seven of them that the firms had infringed the law; in seven of them the SIC finished the proceedings through consent agreements due to the offering of compromises by the investigated firms; and in only one did the SIC conclude that despite the existence of price parallelism, the firms did not engage in tacit collusion. In four of the cases in which the firms were found guilty, a trade association was involved in the coordination of prices. Most recent cases have focused on markets of primary goods (agricultural) and services, which are almost homogeneous, where markets are duopolistic or oligopolistic and concentrated. In summary, Colombian decisions and case law regarding tacit collusion are characterized by:

a) a sound development, from the legal point of view, of the concept, scope and elements of 'conscious parallelism' as a form of an anti-competitive agreement; and
b) an incipient use of economic analysis and the participation of economic experts.

Attributes of a Successful Defense

The SIC's decisions have established that 'price parallelism' by itself is not proof of collusion through 'conscious parallelism'. In addition, there must be enough evidence to show that there is no economic justification for the conduct of the firms other than collusion. However, there is only one case in which the SIC decided to close the administrative investigation initiated due to supposed tacit collusion.[174] In practice, the SIC has endorsed the following arguments by firms:

a) The firms' parallel behaviour is coincidental.
b) The firms' decisions comprise unilateral commercial policies.

Taking into account the concept of 'conscious parallelism' developed to date, other justifications that the SIC probably would accept are as follows:

a) The behavior is neither parallel nor similar.
b) There is an economic justification for the firms' behavior. To date, the oligopolistic interdependence defense alleged by firms in the proceedings has not

[173] *Tribunal Administrativo de Cundinamarca, Sección Primera, Subsección B, Colanta vs SIC. Sentencia del 7 de Febrero de 2002, Exp 000665.*

[174] The airline industry case: *SIC v Continental Airlines and American Airlines* (2001).

succeeded. However, this does not mean that the SIC refuses to acknowledge that parallel behavior may the product of legitimate behaviour from an oligopolistic market structure.

Attributes of a Successful Prosecution

The SIC has established that there are no specific types of evidence essential in every case to prove conscious parallelism. However, from the seven cases in which the SIC imposed fines for tacit collusion, it would seem that the legal elements that must be proved to determine tacit collusion are the following:

a) Proof of simultaneous and identical behavior. The practice must be reiterative (parallelism manifested by a close imitation of conduct) in such a way that it annuls the firm's autonomous decision-making. The duration of collusion varied, as the SIC found guilty firms that displayed similar or identical conduct over a period of two months (retail fuel cases), six months (green paddy rice case) and three years (milk commercialization case).
b) Parallelism must be 'conscious'; there must be proof of the firms' awareness of the competitor's conduct and policies that leads to a consensus on altering 'normal' conditions of competition. However, mere knowledge of a competitor's strategies is not enough evidence of intention to coordinate actions and collude. This practice will be illegal only when it tends to annul, or effectively annuls, a competitive factor such as pricing.
c) The market structure facilitates coordination. In most cases where the SIC fined firms, the market was highly concentrated, the good was homogeneous, and the information regarding prices was easily verifiable.
d) No economic explanation for the firms' conduct exists other than collusion. The SIC has been very strict in the assessment of firms' justification of their conduct. The SIC analyzes the conduct in light of the market conditions, and determines whether the firms' behavior corresponds to the logic of 'free markets'.

E. Panama

Competition policy enforcement began in Panama after the enactment of Law 29 of 1996.[175] The law was developed further by Executive Decree 31 of 1998 and by agency guidelines.[176] Law 29 of 1996 was amended by Decree Law 9 of 2006, and

[175] For an analysis of Panama's competition laws (history, enforcement and recent amendments), see Juan David Gutiérrez, 'El régimen de defensa de la competencia de Panamá: estructura, aplicación y reformas recientes' (2007) 22 *Boletín Latinoamericano de Competencia* at 84–105. <http://ec.europa.eu/comm/competition/publications/blc/boletin_22.pdf>.

[176] Guidelines for Merger Review (in Spanish, *Guía para el control de las Concentraciones Económicas*) and Guidelines for Analysis of Vertical Restraints (in Spanish, *Guía para el análisis de restricciones verticales a la libre competencia*, Resolución PC-503 de octubre de 2003).

was reorganized by Law 45 of 2007.[177] The new law created a new CA (*Autoridad de Protección al Consumidor y Defensa de la Competencia*—ACODECO),[178] and included substantive and procedural modifications.

The current law establishes a judicial-based system, with an administrative agency (in charge of the defense of competition, consumer protection[179] and price monitoring[180]) that has prosecutorial functions and courts with an adjudicative role.[181] The agency has a right of action before the courts against 'economic agents' (the Spanish term used to refer to firms and individuals) that infringe the law.[182] Additionally, affected persons, consumer associations and reproduction rights organizations ('*entidades de gestión colectiva*') have legal standing to file before the courts suits for infringement of Law 45 of 2007.[183] The decisions of the first instance courts may be appealed before a Tribunal of Appeals,[184] and a final appeal may be taken to the Supreme Courtby the parties.[185]

1. *Statutes*

Article 7 of the current competition law prohibits any act, contract or practice that restricts, diminishes, harms or impedes freedom of competition, or concurrence in the production, processing, distribution, supply and commercialization of goods and services. A specific prohibition against 'absolute monopolistic practices' complements the general prohibition against anti-competitive practices. Article 13[186] of the Law defines 'absolute monopolistic practices' as any act, combination, arrangement, covenant or contract among competitors or potential competitors, or through trade associations, that has as an object or as an effect the following:

1) price fixing[187] (and the exchange of information for that object or effect),
2) limiting the quantity of production, processing, distribution or commercialization of goods and services,
3) division of markets, and
4) bid rigging.[188]

[177] See Law 45 of 2007 at <http://www.gacetaoficial.gob.pa/pdfTemp/25914/7277.pdf>.

[178] The former name of Panama's CA was *Comisión de Libre Competencia y Asuntos del Consumidor* (CLICAC).

[179] Arts 33–82 of Law 45 of 2007.

[180] Arts 199–202 of Law 45 of 2007.

[181] Arts 84–107 and Arts 124–194 of Law 45 of 2007.

[182] Art 87 of Law 45 of 2007.

[183] Art 125 of Law 45 of 2007.

[184] Art 126 of Law 45 of 2007.

[185] Limited to the occurrence of certain conditions established in Art 190 of Law 45 of 2007.

[186] For an analysis of Art 13 (former Art 11), see Claudia Curiel Léidenz, 'El tratamiento de las conductas entre competidores en la legislación Panameña de defensa de la competencia' (2002) 10 *Boletín Latinoamericano de Competencia* 79.

[187] According to the wording of the Article, price fixing may take place through *arrangement*, a *combination*, a covenant or a contract. The last two, according to CLICAC, are forms of tacit agreements. See CLICAC, *Acuerdo PC-020-01 de 2001*, at 7–8 (*CLICAC v Continental Airlines Inc and others*).

[188] The four practices described coincide with the four numerals of the Article respectively.

All these objects or effects of 'absolute monopolistic practices' coincide with the typical collusive conduct.

Although 'tacit collusion' and 'conscious parallelism' are not explicitly defined and prohibited by the law, the doctrine[189] and the case law point out that an 'absolute monopolistic practice' may be configured in these forms. First, according to the case law, explained in detail below, *arrangements* and *combinations* are forms by which tacit agreements may take place. Secondly, the wording of Articles 7 and 13 of Law 45 of 2007, and especially of Article 7 of Decree No 31 of 1998, supports the inference of collusion through indirect evidence. In effect, Article 7 establishes a list (*numerus apertus*) of 'indicative elements' of an 'absolute monopolistic practice' among two or more competitors or potential competitors:

a) When the price structure, market division or other forms of discounts show coordination among economic agents.
b) When the economic agents maintain or vary in the same proportion the prices of similar goods or services, given that this conduct is not due to changes in consumers' preferences or common costs of producers or suppliers.
c) When the economic agents adhere, among themselves, to the prices for sale or purchase of similar goods that are published by a trade association or a competitor.
d) When the trade associations give instructions or recommendations to their associates that entail:
    i) the fixing, manipulation or agreement of purchase or sale prices of similar goods or services; or
    ii) the exchange of information for that object or effect.
e) When the trade associations give instructions or recommendations to their associates that entail obligations:
    i) limiting the quantity of production, processing, distribution, commercialization or purchasing of goods and services; or
    ii) dividing the market.
f) When in public bids there is a pattern of conduct that indicates a possible exchange of information relevant for the prices and quantity offered, or regarding the participation of the agents in the bidding process.
g) When there is price dispersion for identical goods and the market shares are stable for long periods of time in concentrated markets with high barriers to entry.

To summarize, this list contains types of circumstantial evidence that may be used to prove tacit collusion. They include, among others, the following:

a) parallel behavior (in prices and quantities);
b) coordination managed or sponsored by trade associations or leading firms;

[189] Claudia Curiel Léidenz, above n 186.

c) exchange of information vital for competition; and
d) price dispersion coupled with stable participation.

2. *Decisions and Case Law*

Few tacit collusion cases have been decided by Panamanian tribunals and, thus far, all the cases have been resolved under Law 29 of 2006.

Table 6 below lists the tacit collusion cases.

There are several features that distinguish Panama's competition laws and their enforcement from those of other Latam jurisdictions. First, the number of cases in

Table 6 Tacit Collusion Cases in Panama

Case	Product Market	Decision
CLICAC v Gold Mills de Panamá SA and others (2003)[190]	Wheat flour	Sanction. The second instance tribunal[191] and the Supreme Court confirmed the first instance tribunal's decision.[192]
CLICAC v Aceti-Oxígeno SA and others (2004)[193]	Medical oxygen	Sanction. The decision was appealed before a Tribunal of Appeals[194] and the judgment is still pending.
CLICAC v Continental Airlines Inc and others (2001)[195]	Commercial airlines	CLICAC decided to file a suit and the proceedings before the first instance tribunal are still ongoing.
CLICAC v Compañía Texaco Panamá SA and others (2002)[196]	Fuel	CLICAC decided to file a suit and the proceedings before the first instance tribunal are still ongoing.
ACODECO v Nestlé Panamá SA and others (2008)[197]	Purchase of raw milk	CLICAC decided to file a suit and the proceedings before the first instance tribunal are still ongoing.

[190] *Juzgado Octavo de Circuito, Ramo Civil, del Primer Circuito Judicial, Sentencia No 64 del 30 de septiembre de 2003.*

[191] *Tercer Tribunal de Justicia de Panamá, Sentencia de 28 de Junio de 2004.* Justice Luis Camargo V delivered the opinion.

[192] *Corte Suprema de Justicia, Sala Primera, Sentencia del 1 de Diciembre de 2006.*

[193] *Juzgado Noveno de Circuito, Ramo Civil, del Primer Circuito Judicial, Sentencia No 59 del 29 de septiembre de 2004.*

[194] More precisely, before the *Tercer Tribunal Superior de Justicia.*

[195] CLICAC, *Acuerdo PC-020-01 de 2001.*

[196] CLICAC, *Acuerdo PC-368-02 de 2002.*

[197] ACODECO, Resolución DLC-PLP-020-07.

which competition laws are enforced is low (tacit collusion accounting for a high percentage of them) in comparison with Panama's peers. Secondly, Panama's competition law is very detailed and includes a list (specifically, Article 7 of Decree No 31 of 1998) of the type of circumstantial evidence that the agency takes into account in assessing the presence of an absolute monopolistic practice. Thirdly, foreign doctrine and case law from Peru, Spain, Colombia, the EU, the US and Venezuela have been commonly used to support the administrative and judicial decisions. On the other hand, as in the other jurisdictions, in Panama the industries under investigation were oligopolies. Furthermore, tacit collusion was used as a means for achieving price fixing (in most cases), horizontal market division and bid rigging.

Panama's doctrine and case law establish that parallel behavior is not enough to prove collusion: it is only one of the elements that must be present to determine its existence. It must be noted that the *meeting of the minds* for collusion must be proved by its inference from circumstantial evidence. The decisions of the CLICAC and the tribunals have both a consistent economic approach and a formal legal approach. Generally the markets' history and structure are analyzed thoroughly, and the legal concept of tacit collusion is well defined.

Attributes of a Successful Defense

The doctrines of the CLICAC and the tribunals' case law regarding tacit collusion have been aligned so far. According to the established standard of proof, in order to determine the configuration of an absolute monopolistic practice through tacit collusion, three conditions must proved:

a) The existence of a combination or an arrangement.
b) That the investigated firms are competitors or potential competitors.
c) That the conduct has as object or effect the restriction of competition.

Hence, a successful defense should start by refuting one or more of these elements. Since the existence of a combination or an arrangement is inferred from parallelism plus other circumstantial evidence, hypothetically the defendant may prove the following:

a) The behavior is not parallel, or parallelism is merely coincidental.
b) The firms' behavior has an economic explanation, such as the existence of a common cost structure.

Attributes of a Successful Prosecution

The case law establishes that plaintiffs have the burden of proof regarding the three elements that are necessary to infer tacit collusion from the firms' conduct:

a) Proof of parallel behavior among the firms and of other circumstantial evidence, such as:
   i) a market structure which facilitates collusion (absence of substitutes and high barriers to entry);

   ii) close collaboration among competitors (eg joint imports of inputs and offering similar commercial conditions);
   iii) contact between firms' officers or other key employees;
   iv) scarce fluctuation of prices;
   v) different cost structures; and
   vi) no variation of market shares over time.

b) A causal relation between the circumstantial evidence and the monopolistic practice. For example, that the firms' conduct is profitable with cooperation but not if adopted unilaterally (without cooperation), and there is a profit motive for their actions.
c) There is no economic explanation for the firms' behaviour other than collusion. This is also evident when the firms' behavior fails to correspond to a competitive market's 'logic' and their explanation is not credible. This element is manifested by the absence of will to act independently, or by the intention to avoid competition.

The deduction of tacit collusion from the conditions of the market and the firms' conduct may be inferred in other ways besides parallel behavior, according to Article 7 of Decree No 31 of 1998 and the analyzed case law, by other circumstantial evidence such as the following:

— Previous knowledge (awareness) of competitors' future actions.
— Coordination managed or sponsored by trade associations or leading firms.
— Exchange of information vital for competition.
— Excess of idle capacity.
— Absence of independence in firms' decision-making mechanisms.

III. Conclusions

A. Conclusions Based on the Characteristics of the Markets Under Investigation

There are several markets subject to investigation for supposed tacit collusion in more than one jurisdiction. This was the case with the following markets:

a) medical oxygen in Argentina, Chile and Panama;[198]
b) fuel retailing in Argentina, Brazil, Chile, Colombia and Panama;
c) airline ticket distribution in Argentina, Colombia and Panama;[199]

[198] In Argentina the authority fined the firms based upon direct evidence, while in Chile the firms were absolved by the Supreme Court. In Panama the case was based upon indirect evidence.

[199] Furthermore, Mexico's competition authority has brought cases involving price fixing in the airline ticket distribution market (OECD, above n 26, at 21).

d) purchase of raw milk in Chile, Colombia and Panama;[200]
e) bottled liquid gas (LPG) in Argentina, Brazil and Panama.[201]

Moreover, the cases involving the markets in medical oxygen, fuel retailing and airline ticket distribution have a special connection since the investigated instances of conduct:

a) were similar or identical;
b) had similar collusive time frames; and/or
c) were undertaken by the same companies in each country.

In the case of medical oxygen, the accusation was based upon coordination of public bids organized by the State for the provision of hospitals. Four of the accused firms subject to fines in Argentina (Air Liquide, Praxair, Aga and Indura) were also accused in Chile but were acquitted. In Argentina the collusion took place between the years 1997 and 2002, while in Chile the TDLC accused the firms of bid rigging in the year 2004.

The fuel retailing cases have two dimensions: on the one hand the price parallelism exhibited by the owners of the gas stations (Colombian case), and on the other hand the supposed coordination by fuel wholesalers of the prices charged to retailers in Argentina (among others, by YPF, Esso and Shell), Chile (among others, by YPF, Esso and Shell) and Panama (among others, by Esso and Shell).

Lastly, the cases in which the airlines were accused of agreeing on a reduction of travel agents' commissions for the sales of tickets, had the following common features:

a) the reductions occurred close together in time;
b) the conduct involved common firms: in Argentina, among others, British Airways, Continental Airlines and United Airlines; in Colombia, British Airways, Continental Airlines, and American Airlines; and in Panama, Delta Airlines, Continental Airlines and American Airlines; and
c) the same simultaneous conduct occurred: a reduction of the commission paid for the sale of tickets, from 9–10 per cent to 6 per cent.

[200] Moreover, Mexico's competition authority has brought cases involving price fixing on the milk market (OECD, above n 26, at 21).

[201] In Argentina and Panama the cases were based on indirect evidence. In Brazil, the case was decided upon direct evidence: 'A price-fixing case decided in 2004 involved distributors of liquid petroleum (LPG) gas in the city of *São Sebastião*, in the Federal District. CADE fined the participating distributors 15 per cent of their annual revenues and added a fine against the owner of each firm owner equal to 10 per cent of the company's fine' (OECD, above n 65, at 22). Furthermore, in Mexico, 'The CFC continues to monitor recently privatized or deregulated sectors, and recently brought a horizontal collusion case in LP gas distribution market' (OECD, above n 26, at 21).

Interestingly, in different countries, common actions carried out in the same market by the same agents had diverse outcomes before the CAs and the courts. In spite of the fact that Latam's jurisdictions prohibit collusion in similar terms, the different enforcement approaches and standards of proof adopted in each jurisdiction produced dissimilar judgments. This is especially evident in the airline cases:

a) in Colombia the firms were absolved of wrongdoing, since the Superintendent considered the firms' justifications to be credible and that their simultaneous conduct was a mere coincidence;
b) in Panama the airlines were fined, since the authority found no justification, other than collusion, for their conduct; and
c) in Argentina the firms were absolved due to the fact that they did not have a dominant position, their actions involved different relevant markets, or their explanations were plausible.

Another conclusion upon the nature of the markets is that oligopolistic structures predominate in diverse markets of goods and services. In effect, there are cases in the agricultural sectors (milk, sugar cane, green paddy rice, wheat flour and cocoa), in industry (flat rolled steel, PVC tubes, LPG, fuel and asbestos slabs), and in markets for services (cable TV, airline ticket distribution, maritime agents' services, telecommunications and banking services).

Lastly, collusion will have a different effect, in terms of the impact on poverty and development, depending on the market where it takes place. In agricultural markets, energy markets (fuel and LPG) and health-related markets, tacit collusion cases were very common.[202] For example, bid rigging cases were present in the markets for medical oxygen, physiological serums and health insurance services.

There is no doubt of the great harm caused, in those cases where CAs proved collusion, in terms of welfare reduction, for sensible economic sectors. On one hand, harm may be caused to consumers who depend on the good or service and who cannot replace it with a substitute. This is the case as regards hospitals and patients in health-related markets, where the demand for the goods and services is inelastic. On the other hand, harm may be caused to small producers (such as peasants) when a cartel fixes maximum purchase prices for inputs. In effect, the potential damage would have a big impact on croppers in the agricultural cases, where the offer of the good is atomized due to the existence of hundreds of croppers while the buyers are few.

[202] The inelasticity of the demand in these markets might be a plausible explanation and a common feature for this behavior, especially considering the market power of some of the firms involved.

The main conclusions that may be drawn from the comparison of the markets' characteristics in tacit collusion cases are the following:

a) Certain markets have been subject to investigation by several of Latam's CAs.
b) In at least three markets the same firms were investigated due to similar behavior.
c) Although there are cases where the conduct was the same and the market structure was similar, the proceedings had different results in each jurisdiction.
d) Oligopolistic structures predominate in diverse markets.
e) The markets in which tacit collusion was investigated have a high impact in terms of achieving the aim of poverty reduction and development.

B. Conclusions Based on the Proceedings Before the Competition Authorities and Courts

1. *Nature of the Proceedings and Enforcement Results*

Antitrust enforcement systems in Latam are mostly inquisitorial in nature, where the public enforcement by an administrative agency predominates. This is the case in Argentina, Brazil and Colombia, which have a complete and systematized antitrust doctrine due to the prolific adjudication of cases by their CAs. Argentina and Colombia are the countries where the CAs have decided the highest number of tacit collusion cases. Brazil has less case law on tacit collusion, but the concurrence of several authorities in the enforcement of the law makes the proceedings more contentious.

On the other hand, the antitrust enforcement systems of Chile and Panama are adversarial in nature, where public and private enforcement concur. Especially in the case of Chile, the proceedings before the courts are more contentious and complex than the proceedings in jurisdictions with an inquisitorial nature. Taking this into account, it is no coincidence that Chile and Panama have less case law on tacit collusion than their peers (less predominance of their agencies in enforcement). But at the same time, especially in the case of Chile, the proceedings are long and the decisions are well structured.

Table 7 below summarizes each jurisdiction's enforcement results on tacit collusion, which were commented upon above.

Table 7 Results of Enforcement Against Tacit Collusion by Jurisdiction

Jurisdiction	Analysed cases	Judicial Review	Pending Judicial Review	Fines	Fines (%)	No Fines	No Fines (%)	Settlement
Argentina	9	0	1	2	22%	7	78%	0
Brazil	6	1	0	3	50%	3	50%	0
Chile	5	5	0	0	0%	5	100%	0
Colombia	15	3	1	7	47%	1	7%	7
Panama	4	2	2	4	100%	0	0%	0
Total	**39**	**11**	**4**	**16**	**44%**	**16**	**47%**	**7**

2. *Evidence*

The type of evidence assessed by the CAs and the courts is similar in each country; the most common examples provided by the defendants, or brought by the prosecutor or plaintiff, are the following:

a) affidavits of managers of investigated firms;
b) information provided by the investigated firms;
c) testimony of customers of investigated firms;
d) testimony of employees of investigated firms;
e) testimony of managers of competitor firms;
f) documents and information seized during searches of the investigated firms' premises (warranted by a judge);
g) the investigated firms' communications to each other and to their customers;
h) proof of meetings of the investigated firms;
i) press reports;
j) surveys of prices and customer preferences;
k) the investigated firms' invoices and contracts.

Nowadays all the jurisdictions, to different degrees, apply an economic approach in adjudicating such cases. Evolution away from a legal formal criterion towards an economic approach is a common pattern in the CAs' analysis of tacit collusion in Latam. In effect, the decisions include a thorough account of the relevant markets' characteristics, structure and evolution, and consideration of the nature and effects of the investigated conduct.

However, expert economic testimony is not common in the legal proceedings. The exception is Chile, where all cases on tacit collusion decided by the TDLC involved expert economic witnesses brought by the defendants and/or by the plaintiffs. In Argentina, Brazil, Colombia and Panama there was only one case where the investigated firms provided expert testimony as evidence.

3. *Judicial Review*

The courts' review of the agencies' decisions has had diverse effects upon the evolution of the standard of proof in cases of tacit collusion. While in some jurisdictions the courts are aligned with the CA's standard of proof, in other countries they have been reluctant to accept tacit collusion claims. The former is the case in Brazil, Colombia and Panama, where the courts have endorsed the CAs' decisions without introducing substantial changes to the doctrine.[203]

On the other hand, Chile's Supreme Court has had a major role in the shaping of case law. As noted above, the Supreme Court reversed two TDLC decisions,

[203] In Argentina the Supreme Court has not adjudicated any case on tacit collusion, although in *CNDC v Loma Negra and others* the proceedings before the first instance tribunal areongoing.

effectively setting a higher standard of proof, which actually may exclude the prosecution of cases that lack direct evidence of collusion.

4. *Influence of Foreign Case Law and Doctrine*

It is important to stress the fact that Latam's competition laws are equally influenced by the Sherman Act and the Treaty of Rome. Moreover, foreign case law and doctrine have influenced the theoretical framework in almost every case in Latam. Further, as noted below, the so-called 'plus factors' or 'parallelism plus' doctrines developed by US case law have nourished the criteria for adjudication of CAs and courts.

C. Conclusions from the Standard of Proof Applied in the Cases

Although every jurisdiction analyzed in this chapter has established that mere parallelism is not enough to prove tacit collusion, the burden of proof and the standard of proof vary in Latam's case law. Furthermore, the indirect or circumstantial evidence that may be used to determine the existence of an infringement has slowly evolved in each country, especially in Colombia and Chile.

1. *Attributes of a Successful Defense*

The defense employed by investigated firms has tended to focus on arguments that may be classified in the following terms:

a) *Denial of the conduct*
   - The behaviour was not really parallel or simultaneous.
   - There was no agreement among the firms; the decisions were autonomous.

b) *Collusion would not be viable or would be innocuous*
   - Low profit margins of investigated firm.
   - Lack of barriers to entry into the market.
   - High degree of rivalry in the market.
   - Existence of imports.
   - The firms have no dominant (individual or collective) position in the market.
   - High degree of innovation in the market.

c) *Justification of any common pattern in their behavior (alternative explanations for their conduct, other than collusion)*
   - Oligopolistic nature of the market and price leadership induces a common behaviour in firms.
   - Production of a homogeneous good or service (explaining similar prices).
   - Similar cost structure and production process plus an increase in common inputs (explaining simultaneous and homogeneous increase in prices).

— The firms' behaviour was determined by common exogenous factors in the market.
— Different quality of the good, or different commercialization and distribution conditions justified a dispersion of prices while the firms' market shares were stable.

When any of the three types of defense was adequately proved, CAs generally closed the investigations or refrained from filing suits before the courts.

A detailed description of each jurisdiction's attributes for a successful defense is set out in the conclusions of the respective subsections of section II above. However, to illustrate the comparison of the standard of proof in each jurisdiction, Table 8 below identifies the attributes of a successful defense, according to the most recent case law (from the highest ranked authority) in each jurisdiction:

Table 8 Attributes of a successful defense by jurisdiction

Attributes of successful defense	Argentina	Brazil	Chile	Colombia	Panama
1. Behavior is not parallel	x	x	x	x	x
2. Plausible explanation for behavior: market structure or external phenomena cause parallelism	x	x	x	x	x
3. No profit motive for collusion	x				
4. Competitive dynamism in the market	x	x			
5. No dominant position	*	*	x		
6. Conduct does not have as object or effect the restriction of competition					x

* Controversy over attribute

Table 8 shows that among the analyzed Latam jurisdictions there is consensus about two defenses that rule out tacit collusion:

a) the firms' behavior is not clearly parallel and homogeneous (eg different pricing due to the existence of different volume rebates and other commercialization conditions—1. above); and
b) when there is an alternative explanation for the firms' behavior besides collusion (eg oligopolistic interdependence—2. above).

2. *Attributes of a Successful Prosecution*

The highest standard of proof for tacit collusion has been set in Argentina and Chile. In Argentina, the investigated firms were found guilty of collusion in two of the nine cases analyzed in this document. In these cases tacit collusion was determined due to proof of parallel behaviour and of other *ancillary restraints* that facilitated collusion (eg having a common marketing company, or the existence of an information exchange system).

In Chile the Supreme Court has reversed the only two cases where the TDLC fined firms for supposed tacit collusion. The current TDLC's case law (confirmed by the Supreme Court, or at least not overruled) establishes that all alternative hypotheses—explanations other than collusion—must be completely discarded. Hence, the plaintiff has the burden of proof regarding a lack of economic justification for the firms' decisions.

Furthermore, it must be proved that the collusive agreement would allow the firms to attain, maintain or reinforce dominance and abuse resulting from it. According to the TDLC, there are several types of circumstantial evidence that may indicate the existence of price fixing[204] and market division.[205] Nonetheless, the value of indirect evidence ultimately will be determined by the fact that it allows conclusions beyond question. Additionally, the Supreme Court's case law establishes that the firms' deliberate and joint intent to adopt an unlawful practice must be proved.

Brazil, Colombia and Panama have adopted a less strict burden of proof than Argentina and Chile. The Brazilian case law adheres strictly to the *plus factors doctrines* and has established that tacit collusion may be proved when the circumstantial evidence demonstrates that there is no rational economic explanation for the firms' parallel conduct other than the existence of collusion. The indicators of collusion consist of the following:

a) the firms' conduct must be parallel and identical;
b) the existence of facilitating devices (eg information exchange systems and frequent meetings); and
c) a market structure that makes the market prone to collusion (eg oligopolistic, highly concentrated and with low contestability).

As in Argentina, Brazilian case law has identified factors that refute the tacit collusion hypothesis, such as a tendency of decreasing profits and high costs for the firms of monitoring a supposed agreement. The Colombian and Panamanian standards of proof applied by the CAs are less strict. As a consequence, in Colombia half of the cases ended with a settlement, while the in the other half the

[204] As noted before, the following are considered relevant indirect evidence: 1) existence of high barriers of entry; 2) high (supracompetitive) profits; 3) reduction of demand; 4) few competitors; and 5) frequent interaction among firms (e.g. within a trade association). Furthermore, vertical integration may facilitate collusion since it allows the control of the final price.

[205] As noted before, the following are considered relevant indirect evidence: 1) stable participation of the firms for long periods of time; 2) high dispersion of prices; 3) lack of transparency—asymmetry of information—regarding prices charged; and 4) concentrated markets with high barriers of entry.

SIC found the investigated companies guilty of tacit collusion through conscious parallelism. According to the SIC, other than parallel and similar conduct, other indirect evidence must be present in order to prove that there is no economic justification for the conduct of the firms besides collusion.

In the case of Panama, the Tribunal has also established that besides proof of parallelism, other circumstantial evidence[206] (in causal relation to the conduct) must prove that the investigated firms' explanation is not credible. Moreover, as in Chile, the *meeting of the minds* among the firms for collusion must be proved, although it is possible to infer it from circumstantial evidence.

To illustrate the comparison of the standard of proof in each jurisdiction, Table 9 below identifies the attributes of a successful prosecution, according to the most recent case law (from the highest ranked authority) in each jurisdiction.

Table 9 Attributes for a Successful Prosecution by Jurisdiction

Attributes for successful prosecution	Argentina	Brazil	Chile	Colombia	Panama
1. Behavior is parallel	x	x	x	x	x
2. Market structure is prone to cartelization	x	x	x	x	x
2A. Dominance and/or possibility of abuse of dominance	*	*	x		
3. No economic explanation besides collusion	x	x	x	x	x
4. Concurrence of wills to restrict competition			x	x	x
4A. Awareness of parallelism or knowledge of future decisions				x	x
5. Practices that facilitate collusion	x	x			
6. Causal relation between circumstantial evidence and monopolistic practice					x

* Controversy over attribute

[206] As noted before, the following are considered relevant indirect evidence: i) coordination managed or sponsored by trade associations or leading firms; ii) exchange of information that is vital for competition; iii) meetings of officers or other key employees; iv) no variation of market shares over time; v) excess of idle capacity; vi) propensity of the market's structure towards collusion; vii) close collaboration among the firms; vii) the fact that the conduct doesn't correspond to the logic of a competitive market; viii) the fact that the firms' conduct is profitable only under cooperation but not if adopted unilaterally (without cooperation); ix) absence of independence of firms' decision taking mechanisms; x) previous knowledge of competitors' future actions; and xi) no economic explanation for the conduct or no other credible explanation for the conduct besides collusion.

To summarize, each jurisdiction has different criteria for the elements necessary for the assessment of the cases. However, it is possible to identify three basic characteristics, shared by the analyzed countries, of the proof of infringement through tacit collusion:

a) parallel and homogeneous (or very similar) behavior regarding any relevant variable of competition (eg prices and quantity produced—1. above);
b) a market structure that is prone to cartelization (eg close oligopolies—2. above);
c) that the evidence discards any economic explanation for the firms' conduct besides collusion (3. above).

3. *Collective Dominance and Tacit Collusion*

A final topic that distinguishes the conceptual framework of tacit collusion cases in Latam is the relation between collective dominant position and collusive practices. The case law from Chile establishes proof of collective dominance as a prerequisite for the existence of tacit collusion.

In Argentina and Brazil the determination of the dominant position of the firms is assessed by the CAs, but the concept of collective dominance as a necessary element for the configuration of tacit collusion is not explicitly established. In fact, there are several cartel cases in Brazil where CADE has been emphatic that it is not necessary to prove that an alleged collusion produced certain negative effects in the market. Hence, the issue of whether the firms had a collective dominant position, and whether they have the correlative capacity to cause damage, is not necessary to prove illegal conduct. In Colombia and Panama the concept of collective dominance has been treated separately from the concept of tacit collusion, and the proof of dominance is not an issue in the identification of collusive practices.

Ultimately, the discussion is rooted in the definition of what elements determine whether particular conduct constitutes an infringement of the law. In general, due to the wording of the competition laws, Latam CAs and courts (with the noted exception of Chile) have established that a collusive practice will constitute illegal conduct whenever it has the 'object' (subjective—intentional) of producing a certain restriction to competition prohibited by law (eg price fixing and market division), or whenever it has the 'effect' (objective) of producing the prohibited results.

From this point of view, shared by the European Court of Justice, the proof of damage or effect of the practice is not a necessary element for the configuration of the illegal conduct, since the 'intention' of causing the effect is enough, according to the law, to typify the prohibited conduct.

4. *Final Remarks*

Tacit collusion is a complex concept from both the legal and the economic points of view. Its complexity has evident effects on legal proceedings, and poses great difficulties for the competent authorities, specifically in regards to the burden of proof. As a consequence, there are important questions regarding its assessment that remain unanswered, which generates a problem of legal uncertainty that may even lead firms to act irrationally to avoid prosecution.

In this sense, Latam's jurisdictions have assessed similar questions that posed challenges for the proceedings, which are relevant to mention since their answers are still pending:

— How does one distinguish between behaviors that are products of collusion and firms' strategic decisions in an interdependent oligopoly?
— How does one distinguish illegal price parallelism (especially a simultaneous increase in prices) from other phenomena of the market that may cause this behavior, such as a general increase in production costs or an increase in demand?
— Even if tacit collusion is proved, how does one distinguish participants from non-participants?
— Should collective dominance be considered a necessary condition for the configuration of an infringement?
— Should the *intention* of producing the anti-competitive effect be proved? If there is no direct evidence of the *will* of the firms to collude, from which evidence may it be inferred?

Latam's case law on tacit collusion is recent (in comparison to that of the US), and there is still space for its development and evolution. Furthermore, there are great expectations regarding the enforcement of the recently installed CAs, especially in Central America. These inexperienced jurisdictions will have to assess the same questions that have posed complex challenges for the jurisdictions analyzed in this chapter. As stressed above, many of these queries are still waiting for definitive answers by CAs and courts.

An optimal enforcement of antitrust laws requires the minimization of costs borne by the authorities and the parties due to the proceedings, both in terms of administrative costs and enforcement errors. Due to the nature of the concept, tacit collusion cases are prone to these kinds of costs. Hence, it is necessary to evaluate whether enforcement efforts should be channelled towards activities other than the prosecution of firms for supposed tacit collusion.[207] Alternative enforcement policies, such as leniency programs or the focus of enforcement efforts on hard-core cartels, must be assessed and debated among Latam's scholars, enforcers and stakeholders in the near future.

[207] In the future, normative studies based upon cost–benefit analysis could shed light on the effectiveness of the different enforcement strategies in Latam to prosecute cartels.

Chapter XII

The Detection of Cartels and the Blending of Law and Economics

WILLIAM S COMANOR*

I. Introduction

While law is about setting rules to promote the welfare of society, economics is about constructing models to explain the behavior of firms and consumers In many circumstances, economic models are useful aids in the rule-setting process. However, sometimes these models conflict with one another. The question addressed in this paper is how such conflicts can confound the judicial process.

This problem is particularly relevant for the judicial determination of cartel activity. There are two competing models which are relevant for determining whether or not a cartel is present. In order to evaluate the observed behavior of firms in a market, we first need to determine how the member firms would be expected to act in the absence of a cartel. But 'there's the rub', for there are two sets of explanations, each based on a different economic model. These two models are associated with the names of Turner and Posner. And each leads to a very different view of cartel detection, which is an important matter for enforcement practices in all jurisdictions.

The Turner model presumes that firms which compete with a limited number of rivals will invariably find ways to accommodate each other and reach non-competitive outcomes.[1] As a result, one cannot determine the presence or absence of a cartel largely by examining market outcomes. In contrast, the Posner model finds that firms generally reach competitive outcomes even when there are only a small number of firms in the market.[2] In these circumstances, non-competitive outcomes more likely indicate the presence of a cartel Recently, Judge Posner

* Professor of Economics, University of California, Santa Barbara and Los Angeles. I appreciate the very helpful comments on a previous draft by H E Frech.

[1] Donald F Turner, 'The Definition of Agreement under the Sherman Act: Conscious Parallelism and Refusals to Deal' (1962) 75 *Harvard Law Review*, 655–706.

[2] Richard A Posner, 'Oligopoly and the Antitrust Laws: a Suggested Approach' (1969) 21 *Stanford Law Review* 1562–1606.

expanded on his approach in an important Court of Appeals decision.[3] How various forms of firm conduct are evaluated turn critically on which economic model is applied.

In this chapter, I explore the legal implications of both models and derive their policy ramifications. As we shall see, there are wide differences between them, with very different implications for legal standards in regard to the detection of cartel agreements. I then consider how courts have resolved these differences, and pay particular attention to the recent US Supreme Court decision in *Twombly*.[4] This discussion has global implications.

II. The Antitrust Setting

Although cartel agreements are illegal per se under Section I of the US Sherman Act, that fact does not make their detection and prosecution an easy matter. Where there is direct evidence as to the presence of an agreement among rival firms, that evidence can be sufficient to determine the outcome of the matter. However, direct evidence is rarely present.

The available evidence is more commonly indirect or circumstantial in nature. But it is from this type of evidence that the adjudicating body must then determine whether a cartel agreement was present. The critical issue in many cases is what the available circumstantial evidence implies for the presence or absence of an agreement.

An essential feature of this inquiry is that the agreement need not be a written document. What is sufficient to meet the required legal standard is that there must be 'a conscious commitment to a common scheme designed to achieve an unlawful objective'.[5] The issue then becomes what type of circumstantial evidence is needed to satisfy this test. How can a 'conscious commitment' be demonstrated from circumstantial evidence alone?

The answer to this question turns on the economic models that are brought to bear in the proceedings. These models are critical for determining market conditions in the presumed absence of a cartel agreement. When observed market conditions resemble those which are expected absent an agreement, there is little support for finding an agreement. On the other hand, if observed market conditions differ sharply from those which hypothetically would be expected in the absence of an agreement, there is then important evidence for its presence. Under this approach, the critical issue is whether observed market conditions are or are not similar to those which are expected in the absence of an agreement.

[3] *In re High Fructose Corn Syrup Antitrust Litigation*, 295F3d 651 (7th Cir, 2002).
[4] *Bell Atlantic Corp v Twombly*, US Supreme Court, No 05-1126, slip decision, May 21, 2007.
[5] *Monsanto Co v Spray-Rite Serv Corp*, 465 US 752, 768 (1984).

While this approach might appear straightforward, it is challenged by the presence of conflicting models. Indeed, these models are so different that observed market conditions can be similar to projected ones absent a cartel agreement using one model but not the other. In such circumstances, the economic model employed is critical for determining how available evidence should be evaluated.

Note that both models are used to project a counter-factual result when in fact there is a price-fixing agreement. They are both used to determine market conditions absent an agreement, to then be compared with observed market conditions in order to determine the presence or absence of a cartel. For this reason, current observations cannot tell us which model is called for. Indeed, it is the nature of counter-factual applications that they rest on a particular economic model rather than on actual observations.

Our problem is that both models are logically complete, so it is possible to find that the first model more accurately describes market conditions in one set of circumstances while the second more accurately describes conditions in other circumstances. There is no reason to believe that either model is uniformly superior to the other.

III. The Turner and Posner Models of Firm Behavior

Both of these models describe competitive behavior in the absence of an agreement among rivals but where the number of competing firms is relatively small. Both are concerned with how prices are set in oligopolistic markets. Neither model concerns price-setting behavior where the number of rivals is large and exceeds perhaps 10 substantial firms. In such circumstances, competitive outcomes are projected, so finding prices which greatly exceed long run costs offers some preliminary indication of an agreement.

In circumstances where the number of rival sellers is few, there is little agreement between the models as to what pricing patterns to expect. The reason is that there is no consensus as to how rival firms respond to the recognition of their mutual interdependence. Where the number of firms in a market is small, each firm recognizes that its sales are linked to the sales of its rivals. Where rivals' sales increase, perhaps because they set lower prices or develop better products, the firm's own sales will decline; conversely, the firm's own sales will expand when rivals set higher prices that reduce the quantities sold. At its core, the Turner model requires that firms recognize the presence of their mutual interdependence and set prices to maximize joint profits; however, the Posner model requires instead that firms accept the decisions of their rivals as fixed and not responsive to their own actions. In the Posner model, firms do not tailor their decisions to the expected reactions of their rivals but rather act independently.

The implications of the two alternate behavioral rules are readily described through a simple diagram. In Figure 1 below, the firm in question produces a

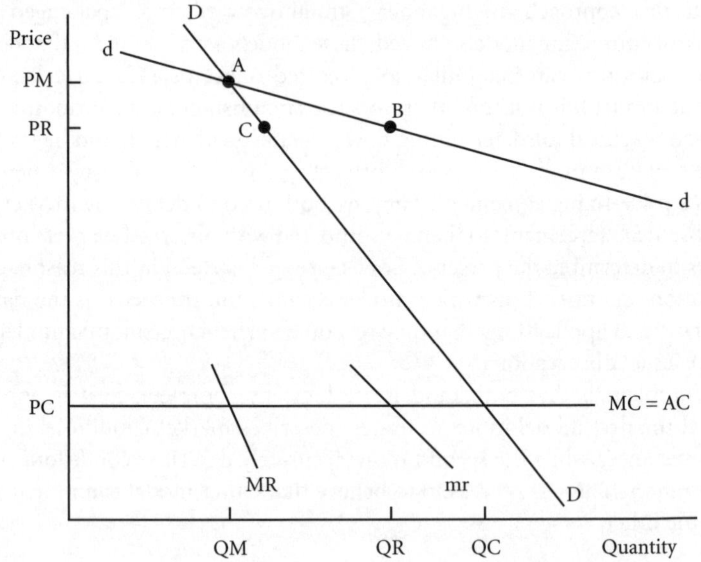

Figure 1

somewhat differentiated product but still competes with a limited number of rivals who do likewise. As a result of its unique product or market characteristics, it faces downward-sloping product demand curves which provide it with some degree of market power. Its prices exceed its marginal and average costs.

In such circumstances, however, the firm faces not one but two relevant demand curves.[6] The first of these demand curves, labeled **DD**, rests on the assumption that all firms change their prices together. They each observe their rivals' prices and shift their own prices upwards or downwards in response to the actions of their rivals. Therefore at each point on this **DD** demand curve, all prices set by the competing firms are the same, and each firm therefore has the same market share regardless of price. This demand curve is termed an iso-market share demand curve, since all market shares are the same along each point on the curve.

Where all firms follow the **DD** demand curve and recognize that their prices vary together, there can be no expectation that one firm can set a price different from its rivals. This demand structure induces a quantity where the marginal revenues associated with the **DD** curve equal marginal costs, and its individual profits are maximized. The optimal price for the firm is, therefore, the current price.

[6] A similar approach was used to explain oligopoly pricing in the US steel industry during the 1960s and 1970s. See Leonard W Weiss, *Case Studies in American Industry*, 3rd edn (John Wiley, 1980) 187–92.

In addition, however, the firm also faces a **dd** demand curve, which rests on the alternate assumption that rival prices remain fixed even while the firm in question changes its prices. It thereby follows a very different behavioral approach, which is that firms act independently and are not destined to follow the actions of their rivals. More formally, this second demand curve requires that rival firms keep their prices fixed at the original level even when the firm in question changes its own price.[7] As a result, the price-setting firm gains market share as it lowers its price, but loses market share as it increases its price, both relative to those of its rivals. This demand curve is more elastic than the prior one since lower prices entice increased sales from two sources: new customers brought into the market by the lower price, and also customers who switch their purchases from the now higher-priced rivals to the now lower-priced seller.

Because the new marginal revenue curve here is more elastic than the prior one, the optimal price is lower than it was previously. Instead of remaining at point **A**, the firm's new optimal price is at point **B**. This alternate rule of firm behavior leads directly to a lower optimal price for the firm.

To be sure, that is not the end of the story. If one rival seeks to expand its market share by undercutting the prices of others, and to move to a new optimal point along the relevant **dd** demand curve, then so should each of them. There is no reason to expect that only one firm behaves in this manner. But if all firms do so, each will actually move along its **DD** demand curve rather than its **dd** demand curve. Although each firm may seek to move to a point like **B**, they in fact will all move to point like **C** on the **DD** demand curve. All prices will decline together, which is the scenario suggested by the Posner model.

Furthermore, following this behavioral rule, the firms in this market will not remain at **C**. A new **dd** demand curve will intersect the **DD** demand curve at point **C**, as it did before at point **A**, and the process will repeat. The common presumption is that this process will continue until all prices approach competitive levels. Both models seek to explain price levels in the absence of an agreement among rival firms. However, they rest on different behavioral assumptions and reach very different results. In the Turner model, firms act on their mutual interdependence and set market values at a point like **A**, where prices reach monopolistic levels; while in the Posner model, firms act independently, ignore their mutual interdependence, and approach a point where prices lie at more competitive levels. The different behavioral assumptions lead to very different results.

The two models have very different implications for the presence of a price-fixing agreement. The Posner model places great importance on the role of an agreement among rivals to achieve non-competitive results, which would not be found otherwise. The Turner model, on the other hand, implies that non-competitive results can be achieved through various other means. Reaching an agreement is not the only, or even the primary, means to achieve that result, so

[7] In the lexicon of economics, these firms follow Bertrand behavior.

that merely observing non-competitive prices says little about the presence or absence of an agreement.

An important element of the Turner model is its reliance on 'rational oligopoly behavior'. What this concept means is that in a concentrated market where there are only a few rivals, firms take the expected reactions of the others into account when setting their own prices. In many circumstances, a firm expects its own price changes to be matched in full. As a result, it recognizes that the **DD** curve in Figure 1 is the relevant demand curve for its own decisions. Firms then adopt a policy of 'conscious parallelism', in which each one acts in a manner similar to its rivals. Each rival does so because that is the rational thing to do even in the absence of an agreement. According to the Turner model, conscious parallelism is inherent in the structure of the market and does not constitute an illegal agreement.

In contrast, the Posner model takes a different view of firm behavior and maintains that even in highly-concentrated markets, firms can benefit by undercutting the prices of their rivals. As a result, firms will continue to expand output towards a price which equals marginal cost. Posner emphasizes that this is not an unprofitable point at which to sell. In Posner's lexicon, tacit collusion describes voluntary behavior and is not an unconscious state, and firms decide on their own pricing rules which are not compelled by market conditions.

There are other conclusions that follow from these alternate positions. The structure of the market and the degree of market concentration are far more important for Turner than for Posner. In the latter's view, prices approach costs even with a small number of firms in the market, so the number of rivals does not have great significance. On the other hand, following the Turner view, prices approach costs only when there are large numbers of competing firms, while prices are often set at high levels when there are few competing firms. Therefore, high concentration is a more important factor for market power in the Turner model than in the Posner model. In contrast, by the Posner approach, collusion is the critical factor leading to market power, where collusion can be either tacit or explicit And, furthermore, collusion of whichever form is not compelled by profit maximization.

IV. Modern Oligopoly Theory

Both of the models discussed above were introduced more than 40 years ago, and economic theory and analysis have continued to evolve. Therefore, an important question is whether this debate has been superseded by more recent developments. In this section, we review the more current approach to these issues.

The most prominent theoretical development during this period has been the application of game theory to the interactions among firms. Some would maintain that its introduction has fully recast the discussion.[8] Economists now explicitly consider payoff structures and equilibrium concepts, where before such matters were largely implicit in the analysis.[9] The terminology has changed. However, there remains the question of whether new conclusions should be drawn.

Game theory provides a means to analyze independent decision-making where the payoffs to each player depend on the decisions of all. In this context, equilibrium is reached when each player makes an optimal decision dependent on his conjecture as to the expected actions of his rivals, and the actions taken on the basis of these conjectures turn out to be mutually consistent.[10] This result, termed a 'Nash equilibrium', is an equilibrium in that no player has a unilateral incentive to depart from it. Applied to the circumstances considered here, it is found where each firm selects a price to charge or a quantity to set where its profits depend on its own actions and also the actions of its rivals, all in the absence of a price-fixing agreement.

In most discussions, the analysis starts with an application of the simple Prisoners' Dilemma game as applied to duopolists. A payoff structure is established where a firm's profits are improved by setting a low price both when the rival sets a high price *and* when he sets a low one. The firm's conjecture, therefore, is that the rival will set a low price, and the firm cuts its price accordingly. When both firms do the same, their conjectures are mutually consistent and a Nash equilibrium is reached under which both prices are lower. Critically, this result is achieved even though the profits of each firm would be greater if both kept their prices at their original high levels.

This application of the Prisoners' Dilemma game provides a further avenue of support for the Posner result. Suppose there is only a small number of firms in a market, and each faces the conditions described in Figure 1. Then, with the payoff structure suggested above, the price **PR** is an equilibrium value for this 'single shot' game. But of course, that is not the end of the story, for the game repeats itself. The process of Bertrand competition continues, and so long as there are no capacity constraints or highly differentiated products, prices approach purely competitive levels, at price **PC** in Figure 1.[11]

A critical issue, however, for the significance of game theoretical results, rests on the distinction between single-shot and repeated games. The former, including the Prisoners' Dilemma game, provide strong results but raise the inevitable question of their relevance in a setting where the players continually interact with one another. And, unfortunately, the implications of repeated games with infinite horizons can be very different from those offered by single-shot games.

[8] Gregory J Werden, 'Economic Evidence on the Existence of Collusion: Reconciling Antitrust Law with Oligopoly Theory' 71/3 *Antitrust Law Journal* 719–800 (2004).

[9] *Ibid.*

[10] See Prajit K Dutta, *Strategies and Games: Theory and Practice* (Cambridge, MA, MIT Press, 1999), 63–71.

[11] Jean Tirole, *The Theory of Industrial Organization* (Cambridge, MA, MIT Press, 1988) 209–12.

The reason for these differences is that the players now have the opportunity to develop strategies that provide each with their share of joint profits, and which are greater than they would receive from actions that are exclusively individualistic. As noted in a recent text, 'the basic intuition for this difference [between repeated and one-time interactions] is straightforward. If players believe that future behavior will be affected by the nature of current interactions, then they may behave in ways that they would not otherwise.'[12] This approach provides further support for the Turner model.

These ideas have been formalized into the so-called 'Folk Theorem' for repeated games, which effectively says that there are an infinite number of possible equilibriums. This conclusion is, as the author of the text notes, 'discouraging from the point of view of predictions'. Indeed, when game theory is extended to repeated games, it is difficult to know just what conclusions should be drawn and how useful is the new theoretical apparatus.

Although it might appear that game theoretical constructs lead directly to the Posner result, that outcome is not required. Indeed, as Phlips points out, 'the Nash equilibrium concept is a general one … [and] an explicit cartel agreement can turn out to be a non-cooperative Nash equilibrium'. He cautions, therefore, to 'make it clear what type of market outcome (competitive, collusive …) a particular non-cooperative Nash equilibrium refers to'.[13]

Whinston makes a similar point:

> The coordination problem [among rivals] arises because typically there are *many* possible subgame perfect Nash equilibrium outcomes. One is always the purely noncooperative … outcome … Frequently, however, a range of more cooperative outcomes is possible, including in some cases the joint monopoly solution. Notably, however, economic theory has relatively little to say about the process of coordination among equilibria.[14]

Still, on the other side of the debate, Werden and others have stressed the significance of the specific equilibrium associated with the Prisoners' Dilemma game, and also its lesson that 'cooperation cannot be expected to just happen'.[15]

Different economists respond differently to this conundrum. Some simply ignore it and rely instead on the strong conclusions that can be drawn from single shot games. That is essentially the position taken by Werden, who argues that 'one-shot oligopoly models are the mainstay of modern economic thinking about competition, even though they are criticized for abstracting from the real-world fact that competitors interact again and again'.[16] Werden also promotes the conclusion 'that repeated game oligopoly models should not be taken seriously by

[12] Dutta, above n 11, at 209.

[13] Louis Phlips, *Competition Policy: a Game Theoretic Perspective* (Cambridge, UK, Cambridge University Press, 1995), 7.

[14] Michael D Whinston, *Lectures on Antitrust Economics* (Cambridge, MA, MIT Press, 2008) 21.

[15] Werden, above n 9, at 728.

[16] *Ibid*, at 759.

antitrust law'.[17] The art, as opposed to the science of economics, turns on the issue of which abstractions are useful for understanding reality, and which are not; and on this point, despite Werden's assertions, there is little consensus.

Although the introduction of game theoretic models has expanded our understanding of pricing decisions in oligopolistic markets, it has not altered the essential issues available for detecting cartel agreements. The conflicting models of Turner and Posner continue to set the stage for the adjudication of antitrust claims under Section I of the Sherman Act. In the discussion that follows, we consider how they are employed in the US context.

V. Current Legal Standards in the United States

For the most part, current US law rests on the Turner model. Where there is no direct evidence of a price-fixing conspiracy, circumstantial evidence can be employed, but it must be 'evidence that tends to exclude the possibility of independent action'.[18] Therefore, the critical questions are what does it mean to exclude the possibility of independent conduct, and what types of evidence can show that result?

The answers to these questions have traditionally included two parts: first, the presence of parallel conduct must be demonstrated, for otherwise there would be no suggestion of collective behavior; and second, certain 'plus factors' must be added to the mix. Mere parallel conduct, even when represented as conscious parallelism, is not sufficient to find a conspiracy under the Sherman Act.[19]

However, even this result is affected by the alternative models of Turner and Posner. Richard Epstein poses this question succinctly when he writes that 'simple parallel conduct among defendant firms in the same industry is not, without more, evidence of collusion, because such behavior is what is expected in all markets, regardless of structure'.[20] Again the question is what type of conduct is expected in the absence of collusion, where the answer depends on the model employed. Parallel conduct is surely projected by the Turner model. That result, however, is less certain in the Posner model, where there is more room for individual decisions and conduct depends less on the structure of the market. This conclusion is thereby less assured than Epstein suggests.

To resolve these matters, current legal standards put forth an array of 'plus factors' to test for the presence of collusion in in the presence of parallel conduct. These include structural, behavioral or historical factors that can support an argument that the observed price uniformity resulted from a price-fixing conspiracy.

[17] *Ibid*, at 763.

[18] *Monsanto Co v Spray-Rite Serv Corp*, 465 US 752, 768 (1984).

[19] *Theatre Enters, Inc v Paramount Film Distrib Corp*, 346 US 537 (1954).

[20] Richard A Epstein, 'Bell Atlantic v Twombly: How Motions to Dismiss Become (Disguised) Summary Judgments' (April 2008), Chicago Law and Economics Working Paper No 403, at 5.

Indeed, many antitrust cases of this genre turn finally on the adequacy of the alleged plus factors. Do they really suggest the presence of an agreement or not? The problem, however, is that the answer to this question often turns on which of the two underlying models of price-setting is employed. Under the Turner model, price uniformity is hardly sufficient to demonstrate the presence of an agreement, and so one must rely on other considerations, such as the specified plus factors. On the other hand, they are much less important in the Posner model. Firms invariably compete via price in this model, so the importance of the plus factors is much less.

VI. The *Fructose* Decision[21]

In 2002, Judge Posner encountered an antitrust case that was directly on point to the issues he had raised more than 30 years earlier in his *Stanford Law Review* article.[22] In the case, the defendants were the four primary manufacturers of high fructose corn syrup, who had been charged by private plaintiffs of secretly agreeing to raise their prices. The trial judge concluded, however, that 'no reasonable jury could find [in the plaintiffs'] favor … without resorting to pure speculation or conjecture',[23] and ruled on Summary Judgment for the defendants. Judge Posner for the Court of Appeals reversed that finding and remanded the case for trial. More relevant for our purposes, he used the occasion to insert his earlier model into the case law on this subject. This decision therefore deserves our consideration.

At the outset of his decision, Judge Posner writes that the statutory language of Section I that forbids:

> contracts, combinations, or conspiracies in restraint of trade ... is broad enough ... to encompass a purely tacit agreement to fix prices ... If a firm raises price in the expectation that its competitors will do likewise, and they do, the firm's behavior can be conceptualized as the offer of a unilateral contract that the offerees accept by raising their prices, or as the creation of a contract implied in fact.[24]

In such circumstances, according to Judge Posner, there is a contract or agreement, 'even though there was no communication between the parties'.[25] Thus, Judge Posner would have tacit collusion be sufficient to invoke the Section I prohibition against price-fixing agreements. In his jurisprudence, tacit as well as explicit collusion would be illegal.

21 Above n 3.
22 Above n 2.
23 *Ibid*, at 2.
24 *Ibid*, at 2.
25 *Ibid*, at 3.

However, Judge Posner acknowledges that 'it is generally believed ... that an agreement involving actual, verbalized communication must be proved in order for a price fixing conspiracy to be actionable under the Sherman Act,'[26] so the rest of his decision follows from that understanding. While he would prefer to see his model of price behavior applied to the circumstances at hand, he recognizes that it is not the current law, so the bulk of his decision elaborates and extends current legal rules.

Proceeding with this approach, Posner observes that the economic evidence presented in such cases is generally of two types: the first is that market conditions are such that price-fixing behavior is feasible, and the second that the market behaves in a non-competitive manner. In effect, the first of these two types of evidence refers to the 'plus factors' that must accompany evidence of non-competitive results. Such factors include the number of rivals in the market and the presence of substantial excess capacity among the major sellers. Another point noted by Posner is that

> the market shares of the defendants changed very little during the period of the alleged conspiracy, which is just what one would expect of a group of sellers who are all charging the same prices for a uniform product and trying to keep everyone happy by maintaining the relative sales positions of the group's members.[27]

These and other factors are probative, Posner writes, of the presence of an agreement among rival sellers.

Judge Posner believes that evidence of non-competitive results is particularly indicative of the presence of an agreement. However, he applies conventional rules in this decision to the issue at hand. In the absence of direct evidence of a conspiracy, the two forms of economic evidence stated above become critical.

What Judge Posner's decision makes clear is that even he is compelled to follow existing legal standards, which rely largely on the Turner model. Evidence of non-competitive behavior is important, but not conclusive. A pattern of similar prices is a necessary condition for an antitrust violation, but not a sufficient one. To a large extent, what we have in this case is Judge Posner applying the Turner standard.

VII. The Problem of Proof

An important text on *Antitrust Economics* is by Blair and Kaserman.[28] In the first edition of their book, these writers describe the opposing views of Turner

[26] *Ibid.*

[27] *Ibid*, at 12–13.

[28] Roger D Blair and David L Kaserman, *Antitrust Economics* Homewood, IL, Irwin Publications, (1985).

and Posner in regard to 'the suitability of the antitrust laws for attacking tacit collusion'.[29] While their discussion is largely similar to that provided above, they reach the following conclusion:

> As a matter of semantics, tacit collusion is a form of concerted rather than unilateral activity. In forbearing to seek short-run gains at each other's expense, in order to share monopoly benefits that require mutual forbearance, the firms act like the parties to a unilateral contract. As far as judicial precedent is concerned, the Supreme Court has declared that Section I does not require proof of express collusion. Finally, we should consider the statutory purpose of the Sherman Act. Section I attacks collusion because it is a joint effort to reap monopoly profits, and tacit collusion has a very similar impact. Thus, Posner's proposal is consistent with the spirit of the Sherman Act.[30]

Thus, these writers essentially accept the Posner position by suggesting that his model should be applied to the detection of cartels.

However, they emphasize that merely employing the Posner model is not sufficient. The problem of proof is not a trivial one, and there is the question as to what types of evidence must be employed to demonstrate mutual forbearance of single-firm opportunities. This matter is sufficiently important, they maintain, that merely accepting the Posner model is not enough to establish appropriate antitrust means for deciding between cooperative and collusive behavior.

To this point we have not focused on the 'problem of proof', which is an important issue regardless of which model is employed, but particularly so for the Posner model. The reason is that this approach relies on proof of non-competitive pricing, which is not so critical when the Turner model is employed. Using the Posner model, proof of non-competitive pricing is particularly relevant.[31]

A conventional approach is to consider price–cost margins or profitability as the primary factor—but this approach can be misleading in various circumstances. First, high profits can be earned when the firms in question have high rates of innovation, which in turn leads to prices that substantially exceed marginal costs even in the absence of collusion. The Posner pricing model emphasizes strategic decisions taken for a fixed menu of products, and is less relevant in circumstances when the menu of products is continually changing under the forces of rapid innovation.

Equally important are circumstances where capacity levels affect pricing decisions. Consider the situation described in Figure 2 below. In that diagram, there is represented a capacity constraint set at **Q*** units of output. Although average and marginal costs can be relatively low at lesser units of output, costs become

[29] *Ibid*, at 201.

[30] *Ibid*, at 205–06.

[31] On this point, Whinston complains that 'Posner's proposal … suffers from a vagueness about exactly what is to be considered tacit collusion'. He continues, 'in the real world firms' strategies are dynamic … [so that] any such determination by a court seems likely to be fraught with difficulty'. Whinston, above n 15, at 54.

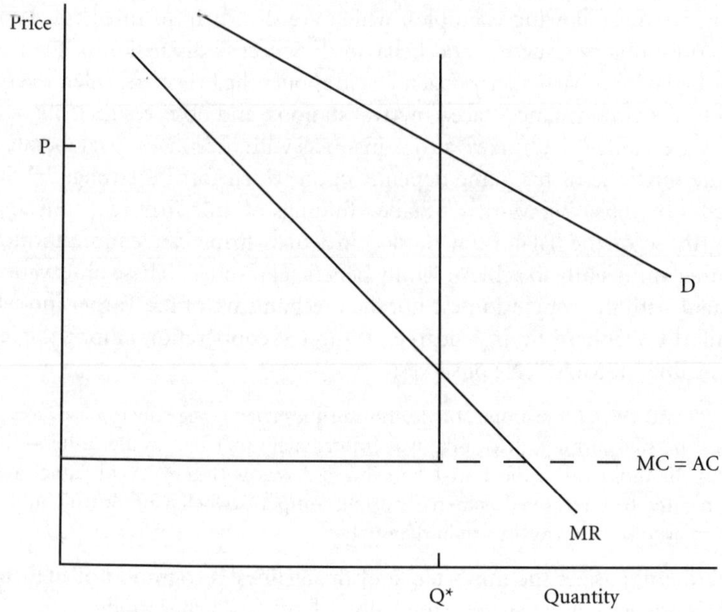

Figure 2

infinite at **Q***, as units beyond this level cannot be produced at any cost. In that case, the monopoly price is set at **P**, but note that it is also the competitive price. Where capacity constraints are binding on the firm's production, then even the competitive price can exceed marginal costs and profits can be quite high, as suggested in this diagram.

Just as the presence of a capacity constraint can lead to high price–cost margins in the absence of tacit or explicit collusion, so can the presence of excess capacity can lead to lower prices. With unused capacity, there is the incentive to increase output by reducing prices, and the failure of sellers to act on this incentive is indicative of the presence of an agreement. In both directions, therefore, evidence of capacity levels is an important factor under the Posner model.

VIII. Some Preliminary Evidence

The presence of competing models does not mean that one is necessarily preferred to the other. Indeed, it is possible and even likely that both are correct. One might expect to find different industries with different pricing patterns and histories. There is no reason to expect that this type of conduct is uniform across the economy.

Consider the following examples, which are drawn from three collections of studies on industry structure and behavior.[32] Scherer's discussion of the gasoline pricing behavior is particularly cogent.[33] He applies the Prisoners' Dilemma pricing model to the circumstances faced by rival stations, and observes that 'oligopolistic rivalries are 'games' that mix rivalrous instincts with incentives to cooperate [such that] the outcome of the game depends upon which force is stronger'.[34] Scherer concludes by repeating Margaret Slade's findings of 'interfirm reactions approximating those of the Tit-for-Tat model', in which firms can 'communicate' with each other sufficiently to achieve jointly beneficial results.[35] These observations are consistent with the conclusions, if not the mechanisms, of the Turner model.

Similarly, Shepherd finds 'a degree of implicit cooperation among the leaders' in the airline industry.[36] He observes:

> In 1998 and 1999, for example, the leading airlines tried repeatedly to raise fares Several times, the first airline's price hike was immediately matched by the others—but not always. In those cases, the initial fare increase was withdrawn. This quick-response action could be interpreted as merely normal competitive behavior. But, it could instead be seen as joint behavior in a tight oligopoly.[37]

Shepherd emphasizes the importance of the airlines' recognition of their mutual interdependence, which again is the hallmark of the Turner model.

Brock's discussion of pricing in the automobile industry stresses the importance of the number and type of rivals for firm behavior.[38] When the industry was dominated by the Big Three US producers, General Motors was the traditional price leader and

> typically initiated general rounds of annual price hikes … when [the] new model line-ups were being readied Ford and Chrysler awaited GM's price disclosures, which they then matched so that the Big Three's prices differed by only a few dollars.[39]

Again, this behavior is more consistent with the Turner model.

However, following the introduction of strong foreign competition, more competitive pricing practices have become the rule. Brock writes:

> Now, prices are continually altered through the year, … [and] competition … compels the companies to constantly adjust their incentives, lease terms, and interest rates on car loans.[40]

[32] For this purpose, I consulted Walter Adams and James Brock, *The Structure of American Industry*, 10th edn (Upper Saddle River, NJ, Prentice Hall, 2001); Victor J Tremblay and Carol Horton Tremblay, *Industry and Firm Studies*, 4th edn (Armonk, NY, M E Sharpe, 2007); and F M Scherer, *Industry Structure, Strategy, and Public Policy* (New York, HarperCollins, 1996).

[33] Scherer, above n 32, at 122–33.

[34] *Ibid*, at 126.

[35] *Ibid*, at 131.

[36] William G Shepherd, 'Airlines', in Adams and Brock, above n 32, at 212.

[37] *Ibid.*

[38] Brock, 'Automobiles', in Adams and Brock, above n 32, at 124–27.

[39] *Ibid*, at 125.

[40] *Ibid.*

The Posner model is currently the more accurate picture of this industry.

There is also Jaffe's discussion of the cigarette industry.[41] He observes that 'despite the high level of market concentration and significant barriers to entry, [pricing] does not approximate the level that would occur if the firms were engaging in joint-profit maximization'. However, he also believes 'there is certainly evidence that cigarette pricing is above competitive levels'.[42] Starting in the 1980s and continuing into the early 1990s, discount brands were introduced. During that same era, the prices of premium brands showed a steady increase, so that by 1992, a price gap of 40 cents per pack emerged between premium and discount brands. As a result, the discount segment grew steadily, with an increasing share that reached 40 per cent in that same year. Finally in 1993, the market leader, Phillip Morris, responded, and on one day reduced the price of its premium brand by 40 cents per pack, effectively eliminating the price differential between premium and discount brands.[43] Industry prices were reduced, and the competitive forces emphasized in the Posner model became prominent.

The study by Cotterill *et al* of pricing in the carbonated soft drink industry is also illuminating.[44] The authors point out that this industry is a dominant duopoly, with Coca-Cola and Pepsi together accounting for 73 per cent of US sales.[45] Despite this fact, the authors find that tacit collusion between these firms has had little effect on price levels and that 'the top two CSD (carbonated soft drink) brands have considerable pricing power due to brand loyalty and their strong consumer franchise [but] only a small amount of exercised pricing power is due to coordinated pricing games'.[46] Their findings are, therefore, more consistent with the Posner than the Turner conclusion.

These few case studies suggest that monopolistic and competitive forces can coexist uneasily in different circumstances, depending not only on the number of rival firms but also on the cultures and traditions of the industry. Indeed, it could well be that both underlying models of firm pricing behavior can coexist in the same or adjacent markets. There is no suggestion here that one or the other of these models is the dominant one.

IX. The *Twombly* Decision[47]

These issues were considered once again by the US Supreme Court in 2007. On May 21, 2007, the Court announced a decision which essentially concerns the

41 Jaffe, 'Cigarettes', in Adams and Brock, above n 32, at 66–68.
42 *Ibid*, at 66.
43 *Ibid*, at 67.
44 Ronald W Cotterill *et al*, 'Soft Drinks', in Tremblay and Tremblay, above n 32, at 205–44.
45 *Ibid*, at 205.
46 *Ibid*, at 236.
47 Above n 4.

distinction between the Turner and Posner models of firm behavior. But on this critical matter, as we shall see below, the Court wanted it both ways.

The posture of the case placed it at an early stage in its proceedings, for it concerned whether a motion to dismiss should be upheld when rival firms were alleged to have 'engaged in certain parallel conduct unfavorable to competition, absent some factual context suggesting agreement'.[48] Because this case considered only allegations rather than factual evidence, it actually offers a more direct consideration of these issues, since there were no factual disputes to be resolved. The distinction between the two models of firm behavior is the critical issue.

Another contextual matter is that the firms at issue were all members of a regulated industry, so that there were regulatory factors in addition to competitive ones that were called into play. Interestingly enough, it was these other factors that provided a final basis for distinguishing between the two models of firm behavior.

At the outset of the Court's decision, it emphasizes that conscious parallelism 'is not in itself unlawful'.[49] And here, Justice Kennedy explicitly cites Turner's article from the *Harvard Law Review*. His discussion then offers a standard restatement of the Turner model of firm behavior as well as the antitrust rules that flow from it.

However, a few pages later, Justice Kennedy comes full-circle when he acknowledges: 'In a traditionally unregulated industry with low barriers to entry, sparse competition among large firms dominating separate geographical segments of the market could very well signify illegal agreement.'[50] That statement is not consistent with the Turner model but rather with the Posner alternative. What he does not acknowledge, however, is its inconsistency with his early discussion. Indeed, if he followed through on the logic of this last point, the antitrust rules for finding collusive behavior in oligopolistic markets would change substantially from what they are now, and become more consistent with the *Fructose* decision.

In making his decision, the tie-breaking fact between the two models was the history of the industry. Kennedy continues: 'A natural explanation for the noncompetition alleged is that the former government-sanctioned monopolists were sitting tight, expecting their neighbors to do the same thing.'[51] If this statement were taken seriously, it would suggest that existing antitrust rules, based on the Turner model, would apply only to previously regulated industries, while rules resting on the Posner model would apply more generally. That distinction, however, is not part of the Court's decision.

What this case points out is the striking ambivalence of the judiciary towards these two models. The fact that both could be mentioned approvingly within

[48] *Ibid*, at 1.
[49] *Ibid*, at 6.
[50] *Ibid*, at 21.
[51] *Ibid*, at 21.

the same decision reflects an unwillingness to choose between them. And the tie-breaking fact applied here was simply a means for the Court to avoid making a decision. While there are other features of this decision which may have applicability for future antitrust jurisprudence, that is not the case for the issue of firm behavior and the detection of price fixing agreements. On this critical issue, the *Twombly* decision does not advance our understanding very far.

X. Conclusions

The problem of detecting collusive agreements among rival firms is made more difficult by the presence of conflicting models of firm behavior. Neither model is easily dismissed, and both have wide support. There is no easy means to choose between them.

Although current antitrust rules rest largely on the Turner model, that result can be explained by the fact that it came first. It also makes it more difficult to find antitrust liability and, therefore, is supported by those who seek to minimize enforcement actions. Whether this reliance on Turner rather than Posner will shift in the future is unclear. Despite the tendency of antitrust enforcement decisions to rely increasingly on Posner-type arguments, that process has not moved very far in the manner by which cartel agreements are detected.

Antitrust rules invariably rest on economic models, and tend to shift when one model is accepted in place of another. In some cases, both models are correct, depending on the market circumstances. There is doubt, however, as to whether workable rules can be fashioned that are sufficiently flexible to deal with this possibility. The problem of applying economic principles in legal proceedings remains exceedingly difficult.

Chapter XIII

Collusion in Convergent Markets

VÍCTOR PAVÓN-VILLAMAYOR*

I. Introduction

Historically, the telecommunications industry was understood as a sector providing voice communication only, so that it was usually differentiated from other related industries such as data communication or broadcasting. During the last years, however, improvements in Internet-based technologies have increased the substitutability between packet- and circuit-switching data transmission. In particular, packet-based data transmission has proved to be an effective substitute for analog transmission in most of the services provided by telecommunications operators. Technological progress has also affected other closely related industries. For example, technological improvements have broadened the service capabilities in the cable industry, in which the joint supply of television, voice and data services has started to become a common practice. The blurring of the market boundaries between industries that stems from improvements in digital transmission technologies has recently been described as a process of convergence. In its account of this phenomenon, *The Economist* has remarked that:

> In applying the 1996 Act, the [US] FCC has sought to make extra distinction between different forms of transmission (copper telephone wire, cable TV, satellite, wireless) and of content (telephone calls, television, data). But the spread of digital technology is making all such distinctions moot. Cable-TV firms carry telephone and internet traffic over their digital networks. Wireless operators pipe e-mail and stream television broadcast. Baby Bell telephone companies such as Verizon, meanwhile, are preparing to enter the television market.[1]

Indeed, the process of convergence has been leading firms in different communication markets to enter adjacent industries either as network operators and/or as service providers.[2] For example, the strong tendency of incumbent fixed-line operators to deliver television services via high-speed Digital Subscriber Lines

* OECD Competition and Regulatory Reform Expert. The author is grateful to Daniel Sokol and his conference's discussant, Germán Coloma.

[1] *The Economist*, 'Face Value' (Jan 22, 2005).

[2] OECD, *Cross-Ownership and Convergence: Policy Issues* (Paris, OECD Press, 1998).

or new purpose-built fibre-optic networks is explained by the emergence of new competitors in their natural markets. Incumbent phone companies are now facing strong competition from cable-TV companies, which are in the position to offer the triple play of TV, broadband Internet and telephony over their networks. In some countries—including France, Italy, Britain and Japan—incumbent operators are also facing competition from over-builders which also offer triple-play bundles over high-speed phone lines. It is then not surprising that incumbents find it imperative to cross their traditional market borders in order to survive within the new competitive environment that convergence has created.[3]

In Latin America, one of the most important processes of market convergence is also occurring in the telecommunications industry, where the fixed and mobile segments of voice communication are in a process of merging into a single market. The most recent trends in telecommunications markets around the world confirm that the number of mobile communication subscribers has been steadily increasing, while the number of subscribers in the fixed-line segment has been contracting. In OECD countries, for example, fixed lines were the dominant access technology until 2000, when the number of mobile phones overtook the number of fixed lines. The most recent figures for the OECD area show that mobile subscribers outnumber fixed-line subscribers by a ratio of more than three to one. This tendency has been inherently linked to a process of substitution between fixed-line and mobile access. As reported by the same source, 'The decrease in these countries is mainly attributable to substitution as mobile phone subscribers give up fixed lines that they may now view as redundant.'[4]

The evolution of the voice communication industry in Latin America has also followed this general trend, as illustrated by Table 1 below.

Table 1 reports for this sample of countries that, on average, 62 per cent and 17 per cent of the Latin American population have mobile and fixed access,

Table 1 Fixed and Mobile Penetration Rates in Latin America, 2006

Service	Argentina	Brazil	Chile	Colombia	Mexico	Peru	Venezuela
Mobile	75%	53%	81%	68%	53%	31%	72%
Fixed Line	22%	19%	20%	17%	19%	9%	14%

Source: Latin American Communications and Mobile Data Markets 2007 Report.

[3] T Bresnahan and S Greenstein, 'Technological Competition and the Structure of the Computer Industry' 47 *Journal of Industrial Economics* 1–40 (1999) have provided a similar account of a process of convergence in the production of computers, and they describe how the presence of strong economies of scope has created incentives for incumbents in one particular segment to enter into new segments of the market. See also Shane Greenstein and Tarun Khanna, 'What Does it Mean for Industries to Converge' in David Yoffie (ed), *Competing in an Age of Digital Convergence* (Cambridge, MA, Harvard University Press, 1997).

[4] OECD, *OECD Communications Outlook* (Paris, OECD Press, 2007), at 95.

respectively. This implies that approximately 45 per cent of the population in the region relies on mobile technology as its only source of voice access. The interesting feature of the table is that this 45 per cent represents the fraction of the population that, in some sense, has substituted away fixed access. This is because had this 45 per cent looked for an alternative means of voice access in the absence of mobile technology, they would have likely chosen fixed access. The data then suggest that the substitution between fixed and mobile services in the Latin American region has not been negligible. Furthermore, it is expected that competition—hence, substitution—between these two technologies will intensify in the years to come, as their degree of service differentiation is reduced. In fact, it is expected that the technologies associated with these two access modes may merge into a single technology:

> The line between fixed and mobile calls is blurring … the emergence of converged devices may necessitate a change in how telephone access paths are counted. For example, several fixed-line operators in the OECD area have introduced devices that place calls over the user's fixed line when the user is at home and over a mobile network when they are away.[5]

The fixed-mobile segment of the voice communication market in Latin America certainly shows features of a convergent market, and it is not the only area where convergence is displaying its technological impact.[6]

The process of market convergence raises important policy issues. For example, the pace and nature of technological change is frequently affected by the regulatory environment in which these changes take place. In particular, one of the critical features of the interaction between technological progress and regulation is that the latter typically displays some degree of sluggishness with respect to the dynamics generated by technological change. This inherent lack of flexibility associated with regulatory surveillance opens the possibility that two initially distinct but converging industries may end up being subject to different regulatory regimes when competing in essentially the same market.[7]

A second topic of policy interest is the extent to which market convergence facilitates collusive behavior. This issue is addressed in this paper through the use of a standard model of product differentiation that characterizes the convergence of two distinct markets over time. In the setting discussed in the following pages, convergence takes the form of an exogenous process of technological change that

[5] *Ibid*, at 97. In particular, the OECD mentions that *KT* in Korea, *BT* in the United Kingdom and *Orange* in France have launched phones that use the mobile network when away from home but can connect to the user's broadband connection via Bluetooth or Wi-Fi at home to place calls at fixed rates. KT's 'OnePhone' , BT's 'Fusion' and Orange's 'unik' networks allow users to roam seamlessly between a mobile network and the Bluetooth connection without disrupting an ongoing call.

[6] Other important areas of convergence in the telecommunications industry are the provision of broadband services through cable-modem and DSL platforms, and the provision of TV content via cable-TV and satellite technologies.

[7] V Pavón-Villamayor, 'La Convergencia y el Principio de la Neutralidad Tecnológica' 74 *El Trimestre Económico* 845–83 (2007).

not only reduces the degree of product differentiation between markets, but also increases the quality of the services associated with them.

On the basis of the analytical treatment of the process of convergence elaborated upon in this paper, this work belongs to the tradition of the economic literature that discusses the effect of product differentiation on collusion. Chamberlin[8] was the first economist to point out that when sellers are few and products are homogeneous, firms have incentives to engage in tacit collusion. The intuition that reaching a collusive agreement is easier when products are more homogeneous has found extensive support in the academic literature (see Posner,[9] Stigler,[10] Asch and Seneca,[11] Levenstein and Suslow,[12] and Raith[13]). In the same vein, Scherer and Ross have claimed that 'cooperation to hold prices above the competitive level is less likely to be successful … the more heterogeneous, complex and changing the products supplied are.'[14]

This intuition has also been the basis of the 1992 US Department of Justice and Federal Trade Commission Horizontal Merger Guidelines, which claim that 'reaching terms of coordination may be facilitated by product or firm homogeneity'.[15]

The argument that lower differentiation increases the likelihood of collusive behavior has, however, been disputed. One of the results that has emerged from the repeated game literature has been that the effect of product substitutability on firms' ability to collude tacitly depends on whether firms compete in prices or quantities. Chang[16] and Ross,[17] for example, discuss a Hotelling model with price-setting firms, and show that increased product substitutability hinders the sustainability of collusion. In a framework more related to the one discussed here—a quantity-setting—Tyagi[18] found that increased product substitutability hinders tacit collusion for the case of linear and concave demand functions, but that product substitutability may either hinder or facilitate collusion for the case of

[8] E H Chamberlin, 'Duopoly: Value where Sellers are Few' 43 *Quarterly Journal of Economics* 63–100 (1929).

[9] Richard A Posner, *Antitrust Law: An Economic Perspective* (Chicago, University of Chicago Press, 1976), at 59–60.

[10] George J Stigler, *The Theory of Price* (New York, Macmillan Company, 1987), at 226–27.

[11] P Asch and J Seneca, 'Is Collusion Profitable?' 58 *Review of Economics and Statistics* 1–12 (1976).

[12] Margaret Levenstein and Valarie Suslow, 'What Determines Cartel Success?' (2002) *University of Michigan Business School Working Paper.*

[13] Raith ('Product Differentiation, Uncertainty and the Stability of Collusion' (1996) *London School of Economics STICERD Discussion Paper EI/16*) in particular, provides the notion that an increase in the heterogeneity of the products leads to a decrease in the correlation of the demand functions of the goods. This is important because, in an environment where a firm cannot observe its rivals' actions but has to infer them from signals, collusion is more difficult to sustain, since discriminating between random demand shocks and deviations from the cartel strategy becomes more difficult.

[14] Frederic M Scherer and David Ross, *Industrial Market Structure and Economic Performance* (New York, Houghton Mifflin Company, 1990).

[15] Guidelines available at <www.ftc.gov/bc/docs/horizmer.htm.>. See section 2.11 of the guidelines.

[16] M H Chang, 'The Effects of Product Differentiation on Collusive Pricing' (1991) 9 *International Journal of Industrial Organisation* 453–69.

[17] T W Ross, 'Cartel Stability and Product Differentiation' 10 *International Journal of Industrial Organisation* 1–13 (1992).

[18] R Tyagi, 'On the Relationship Between Product Substitutability and Tacit Collusion' 20 *Managerial and Decision Economics* 293–98 (1999).

convex demand functions.[19] The analysis contained in this paper supports Tyagi's conclusion, because for linear demand functions, it is found that collusion is more likely the lower the degree of differentiation across markets.

The paper is organized as follows. Section II provides a detailed description of the analytical framework on which the analysis is based. Section III characterizes the equilibrium outcomes in three distinct competitive scenarios, namely: competition, collusion, and coordination break-up. This section provides some comparative statistics of welfare measures across these scenarios. The core part of the paper is contained in sections IV and V, in which the analytical framework is used to discuss the incentives of firms to engage in collusive practices as convergence evolves. Lastly, section VI provides a brief discussion of the implications that the process of market convergence can have for design and the implementation of competition policies in Latin America.

II. The Model

Consider a differentiated duopoly based on the pioneering work of Bowley.[20] The economy contains two sectors. The first sector has two firms providing differentiated services to consumers, while the second is a competitive *numéraire* sector.[21] There is a continuum of consumers of the same type with a utility function separable and linear in the *numéraire* good. Hence, there are no income effects on the first sector and it is possible to perform partial equilibrium analysis. The standard economic argument to justify this assumption is that consumers spend only a small part of their income on the services associated with this industry. The representative consumer then optimizes the program:

$$\max_{x_1,x_2} \; U(x_1,x_2)+\left\{Y-\sum_{k=1}^{2} p_k x_k\right\} \tag{1}$$

where $U(x_1,x_2)$ represents the utility that derives from the consumption of services x_1 and x_2. The term inside brackets describes expenditure in outside

[19] The underlying idea is that higher product substitutability increases both the gains and the costs of engaging in collusion so that the relative magnitudes of these changes—affected by the curvature of the demand functions—determine the net effect of increased product substitutability on collusion. The author found that increased product substitutability increases individual firms' gains from cheating more than their gain from colluding for the case of linear and concave demand functions, which hinders collusion. However, these relative changes can go either way for the case of convex demand functions.

[20] Arthur Bowley, *The Mathematical Groundwork of Economics* (Oxford, Oxford University Press, 1924).

[21] Since the first sector contains exactly two firms and there is no entry or exit, the market structure is exogenous.

goods when the price of service k is p_k and consumer's income is Y. As in Sutton[22] and Symeonidis,[23] it is assumed that utility has the functional form:

$$U(x_1,x_2)=\sum_{k=1}^{2}\left(x_k-\frac{x_k^2}{\left(q_k(\gamma)\right)^2}\right)-2\gamma\prod_{k=1}^{2}\left(\frac{x_k}{q_k(\gamma)}\right)$$

where x_k and $q_k(\gamma)$ stand for quantity and quality of service k, respectively. It is assumed that each firm provides only one variety of the services that are available in the industry. The utility function specified above is just a quality-augmented version of the standard quadratic utility function extensively used in the industrial organization literature, and it has the particular feature that utility is not only increasing in quantities but also increasing in the qualities associated with each of the product varieties (see Dixit[24]; Singh and Vives[25]; Shaked and Sutton[26]). Observe that the parameter $0 \leq \gamma \leq 1$ represents a measure of the degree of horizontal differentiation or substitution observed across markets. It is then possible to characterize—in a sort of inter-temporal framework—the evolution of a process of market convergence by continuously and strictly increasing values of γ. For example, $\gamma = 0$ would characterize a no-convergence regime, since the degree of product differentiation across markets would be so high that consumption of an industry's services would require access to two distinct products or markets. In contrast, $\gamma = 1$ would characterize a total convergence regime, since, when there is perfect substitutability between services at identical qualities, consumption of an industry's services would require access to one product or market only. Therefore, continuously and strictly increasing values in the parameter γ allows for the characterization of a process of market convergence in substitutes.[27]

The framework discussed in this paper also assumes that all firms' strategic decisions are always evaluated within the planning horizon framed by the process of market convergence itself. For example, a firm evaluating whether or not to engage in collusion at time $\gamma = \tilde{\tau}$ will make its cost–benefit evaluation within the planning horizon that spans from point $\gamma = \tilde{\tau}$—the time at which the decision is evaluated—to

[22] J Sutton, 'One Smart Agent' (1997) 28 *Rand Journal of Economics* 605–28.

[23] G Symeonidis, 'Price and Non-price Competition with Endogenous Market Structure' 9 *Journal of Economics and Management Strategy* 53–83 (2000).

[24] A Dixit, 'A Model of Duopoly Suggesting a Theory of Entry Barriers' 10 *Bell Journal of Economics* 20–32 (1979).

[25] N Singh and X Vives, 'Price and Quantity Competition in a Differentiated Duopoly' 15 *Rand Journal of Economics* 546–54 (1984).

[26] A Shaked and J Sutton, 'Multiproduct Firms and Market Structure' 21 *Rand Journal of Economics* 45–62 (1990).

[27] Convergence in substitutes does not exhaust all the possibilities of convergence processes. There is also convergence in complements, which occurs when a new technology opens up the possibility of combining existing technologies to provide a new service. A premier example of convergence in complements is the emergence of the market for handheld computers in the early 1990s. Partly triggered by new advances in handwriting recognition technology, companies from different industries

$\gamma = 1$—the time at which the process of market convergence ends. The feature that firms make their strategic evaluations within finite planning horizons makes the implications of the analysis more tractable and, more importantly, realistic.

One of the most striking characteristics of market convergence in industries such as telecommunications and information services is the rapid pace of innovation. To model this important feature of market convergence, the following assumption is made explicit:

Innovation. The level of quality provided by each service variety is driven by the parameter of convergence γ according to the following specification:

$$q_k(\gamma) = h_k(1+\gamma)$$

for $k = 1, 2$, where $h_k > 0$ represents the initial quality associated with each variety before convergence takes off.[28]

This assumption represents one of the simplest formulations to describe the property that the quality provided by each of the product varieties increases throughout the process of convergence. To see this, observe that when $\gamma = 0$, the level of quality associated with each variety is fixed at the initial level h_k, while as $\gamma \to 1$, quality tends to be twice as large as its base level: $q_k(\gamma) \to 2h_k$. In order to keep the analysis as simple as possible, it is assumed that the initial level of quality provided by each firm is the same, so that $h_1 = h_2 = h > 0$. Note that, since the parameter of convergence γ impacts both markets symmetrically, it follows that $q_1(\gamma) = q_2(\gamma)\ \forall \gamma$. Let us represent this common level of quality as $q(\gamma) = h(1+\gamma)$.

It is worth noting that in the above framework, parameter γ impacts consumers' utility through two different channels. A first channel is the direct impact that stems from the substitutability between services, which decreases utility as γ increases. This substitution effect derives from the fact that consumers derive lower utility from the consumption of the two products due to the increasing substitutability between their functions. The second channel is the indirect impact of γ on consumers' utility through its effect on quality, which increases utility as γ increases. This quality-driven demand effect is the result of the consistent quality improvement that is observed across products throughout the process of convergence.

Finally, the solution to the utility maximization problem described by condition (1) gives the following linear system of inverse demand functions:

$$p_1 = 1 - \left\{ \frac{2x_1}{\left(q_1(\gamma)\right)^2} \right\} - \left\{ \frac{2\gamma x_2}{q_1(\gamma) q_2(\gamma)} \right\}$$

like telecommunications, computers and consumer electronics combined their technologies to offer the first handheld computers in the market.

[28] In section V, a more general representation of the process of innovation in the industry is explored.

$$p_2 = 1 - \left\{ \frac{2x_2}{\left(q_2(\gamma)\right)^2} \right\} - \left\{ \frac{2\gamma x_1}{q_1(\gamma) q_2(\gamma)} \right\}$$

These demand functions will be used extensively in section III. The analysis also assumes that firms compete in quantities and that the production technology is characterized by constant marginal costs which, without loss of generality, are normalized to zero. Formally, the game played at each level of γ is described by two players: the firms operating in the two markets that converge. The set of strategies associated with each firm is to choose a strictly positive level of output while each firm's payoff is explicitly given by:

$$\Pi_j = p\left(x_j, x_i\right) x_j$$

for all $i, j = 1, 2$ but $i \neq j$. One of the advantages of the analytical framework explored in this paper is that welfare measures are extremely tractable, since total and consumer surplus are simply described by $U\left(x_1, x_2\right)$ and $U\left(x_1, x_2\right) - \left(\Pi_1 + \Pi_2\right)$, respectively.

III. Characterization of Equilibrium Outcomes

In this section, the one-shot equilibrium outcomes of three distinct competitive scenarios between firms are explicitly characterized. The first scenario corresponds to a process of standard competition between duopolists; the second scenario—which corresponds to a coordinated outcome or collusion—is modelled as a multi-product monopolist problem; while the third scenario characterizes the equilibrium outcome that derives from the break-up of coordination. Some comparative statistics of welfare measures across these distinct scenarios are also explored.

A. Duopolistic Competition

The one-shot equilibrium outcome associated with competition between duopolists in a converging market derives from the solution to firm's j optimization program, namely:

$$\max_{x_j} \Pi_j = \left(1 - \left\{ \frac{2x_j - 2\gamma x_i}{\left(q(\gamma)\right)^2} \right\} \right) x_j \quad \forall\, i, j = 1, 2\; i \neq j$$

By deriving the first order conditions and by solving simultaneously these best-response correspondences, the following (symmetric) equilibrium quantities and prices are obtained:

$$x_1^* = x_2^* = \left\{ \frac{h^2(1+\gamma)^2}{2(2+\gamma)} \right\} \qquad p_1^* = p_2^* = \left(\frac{1}{2+\gamma} \right)$$

It is straightforward to see that $\partial x_1^* / \partial \gamma = \partial x_2^* / \partial \gamma > 0$, so that the competitive output increases and the competitive price decreases, $\partial p_1^* / \partial \gamma = \partial p_2^* / \partial \gamma < 0$, as the process of convergence evolves. In the following, $\hat{\Pi}_1(\sigma_1 = \sigma_2 = 0)$ and $\hat{\Pi}_2(\sigma_1 = \sigma_2 = 0)$ will denote the equilibrium level of duopolistic profit per period associated with each of the concurring firms. Explicitly, this level of profit is given by:

$$\hat{\Pi}_1(\sigma_1 = \sigma_2 = 0) = \hat{\Pi}_2(\sigma_1 = \sigma_2 = 0) = \frac{1}{2} \left\{ \frac{h(1+\gamma)}{2+\gamma} \right\}^2$$

It is worth noting that $\partial \hat{\Pi}_1(\sigma_1 = \sigma_2 = 0)/\partial \gamma = \partial \hat{\Pi}_2(\sigma_1 = \sigma_2 = 0)/\partial \gamma > 0$, so that competitive profits increase through the process of convergence, regardless of the higher substitutability that is observed across market products.

This result contrasts with a standard Cournot framework with no innovation, $q_k(\gamma) = h_k$, where higher substitutability between products would imply both lower outputs and prices as convergence evolves and, hence, lower profits. It is therefore clear that the driving force behind the result of increasing competitive profits in our framework is the process of innovation underlying the relevant product markets.

B. Collusion

Consider now a scenario in which the concurring firms are able to coordinate the amount of output that is sold in the industry. In particular, assume that this output coordination takes the form of a multi-product monopolist that allocates output quotas across distinct production plants.[29] In this standard multi-product monopolist problem of dependent demands with separable costs, outputs per period are determined through the following program:

$$\max_{x_1, x_2} \Pi = \left(1 - \left\{ \frac{2x_1 - 2\gamma x_2}{(q(\gamma))^2} \right\} \right) x_1 + \left(1 - \left\{ \frac{2x_2 - 2\gamma x_1}{(q(\gamma))^2} \right\} \right) x_2$$

[29] Jean Tirole, *The Theory of Industrial Organisation* (Cambridge, MA, MIT Press, 1998).

The solution to this problem gives the following equilibrium levels of outputs and prices:

$$x_1^{**} = x_2^{**} = \left\{\frac{h^2(1+\gamma)}{4}\right\} \qquad p_1^{**} = p_2^{**} = \frac{1}{2}$$

Note that since $\partial x_1^{**}/\partial\gamma = \partial x_2^{**}/\partial\gamma > 0$, the collusive output also increases as the process of convergence evolves. Also observe that collusive prices always remain above competitive prices. This is not surprising, because when products are substitutes, a multi-product monopolist would find it optimal to increase the prices of substitute products in relation to the prices charged by a duopoly due to the negative externality posed by their substitutability itself.[30] The equilibrium level of profit per period associated with each of the collusive firms is then given by:

$$\hat{\Pi}_1(\sigma_1 = \sigma_2 = 1) = \hat{\Pi}_2(\sigma_1 = \sigma_2 = 1) = \left\{\frac{h^2(1+\gamma)}{8}\right\}$$

which is also strictly increasing in γ. Figure 1 below shows the comparative statistics of the levels of welfare associated with the competitive and the collusive outcomes as a function of the parameter of market convergence γ. The competitive and collusive total surplus in the industry are represented by $U(x_1^*, x_2^*)$ and $U(x_1^{**}, x_2^{**})$, respectively, while the competitive and collusive industry profits are represented by $\Pi_1^* + \Pi_2^*$ and $\Pi_1^{**} + \Pi_2^{**}$, respectively. Figure 1 then illustrates two standard points. First, the implementation of a collusive agreement always reduces total surplus. This is illustrated as a downward movement of the $U(x_1^*, x_2^*)$ schedule to level $U(x_1^{**}, x_2^{**})$.

Secondly, profits in the industry increase as a result of collusion, as illustrated by the upward movement of the $\Pi_1^* + \Pi_2^*$ schedule to level $\Pi_1^{**} + \Pi_2^{**}$. Therefore, Figure 1 implies that the consumer surplus derived from a collusive outcome is always lower than the one associated with competition. To see this, let us assume that the process of market convergence has reached level $\gamma = \tilde{\gamma}$ in Figure 1 above. In competition, consumer surplus is given by the distance AB while, under collusion, it is given by the distance CD, which is smaller.[31]

[30] Massimo Motta, *Competition Policy* (New York, Cambridge University Press, 2004).

[31] Incidentally, note that under a total welfare standard the consumer surplus loss associated with the distance DB would be of no concern for the competition authorities. This is because DB just represents a monetary transfer from consumers to producers with neutral effects on aggregate welfare. In contrast, under a price welfare standard, DB would be computed as part of the welfare loss that stems from collusive behavior.

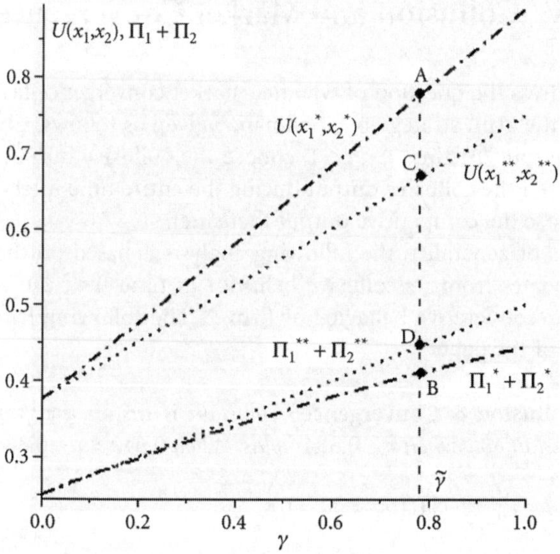

Figure 1 Competitive and collusive welfare as a function of γ

C. Coordination Break-up

To compute the one-shot outcome associated with the breakup of coordination between the colluding firms, assume that firm 1 deviates from its collusive behavior at time $0 < \tilde{\tau} \leq 1$ of the convergence process. Therefore, at time $\tilde{\tau}$, firm 1 chooses its output according to the program

$$\max_{x_1} \Pi_1 = \left(1 - \left\{\frac{2x_1 - 2\tilde{\tau}x_2^{**}}{\left(q(\tilde{\tau})\right)^2}\right\}\right)x_1$$

where x_2^{**} denotes the cooperative output chosen by firm 2 at time $\tilde{\tau}$. The solution to this problem gives firm 1's optimal level of output and associated profit:

$$\tilde{x}_1 = \left\{\frac{h^2(2+\tilde{\tau})(1+\tilde{\tau})}{8}\right\} \quad \hat{\Pi}_1(\sigma_1 = 0, \sigma_2 = 1) = \left\{\frac{h^2(2+\tilde{\tau})^2}{32}\right\}$$

Since $\partial\tilde{x}_1 / \partial\tilde{\tau} > 0$, it follows that the optimal size of the deviating output is larger the lower the degree of substitutability observed across market products. Similarly, the size of the deviating profits is increasing in convergence: $\partial\hat{\Pi}_1(\sigma_1 = 0, \sigma_2 = 1)/\partial\tilde{\tau} > 0$. The following section explores in detail the extent to which collusive behavior is sustainable in markets characterized by convergence processes.

IV. Collusion and Market Convergence

In order to address the question of whether market convergence facilitates collusion, consider the grim strategy of Friedman,[32] given as follows. Choose initially the collusive output. At time $0<\tau\leq 1$, choose the collusive output only if both firms have chosen the collusive output during the entire time interval prior to τ; otherwise, choose the competitive output thereafter.

Without loss of generality, the following analysis is based on the assumption that firm 1 deviates from its collusive behavior at time $0<\tilde{\tau}\leq 1$, triggering the subsequent no- cooperative behavior of firm 2. The following lemma provides the core result of the paper.

LEMMA 1: Collusion & Convergence. *Collusion is sustainable provided* $0<\tilde{\tau}\leq 0.312$ *and unsustainable when* $\tilde{\tau}\geq 0.384$ *holds. When* $0.312<\tilde{\tau}<0.384$ *condition,*

$$\hat{\Pi}_1(\sigma_1=0,\sigma_2=1)\Big|_{\gamma=\tilde{\tau}}-\hat{\Pi}_1(\sigma_1=\sigma_2=0)\Big|_{\gamma=\tilde{\tau}}$$

$$+\int_{\gamma=\tilde{\tau}}^{1}\hat{\Pi}_1(\sigma_1=\sigma_2=0)\exp\big(-\delta(\gamma-\tilde{\tau})\big)d\gamma$$

$$>\int_{\gamma=\tilde{\tau}}^{1}\hat{\Pi}_1(\sigma_1=\sigma_2=1)\exp\big(-\delta(\gamma-\tilde{\tau})\big)d\gamma$$

holds provided $\delta\geq\bar{\delta}$, *so that collusion is only sustainable for* $\delta<\bar{\delta}$, *where* $\bar{\delta}\in(0,1)$ *represents the discount rate at which the discounted value of profit streams when deviating and colluding are equal.*

The left-hand-side of Lemmas 1's inequality expresses the discounted value of the streams of profits accrued to firm 1 when it deviates from its collusive behavior at time $\tilde{\tau}$. In turn, the right-hand-side of the inequality establishes the discounted value of the streams of profits accrued to the same firm when it honors the collusive agreement from time $\tilde{\tau}$ on. In particular, observe that the term $\hat{\Pi}_1(\sigma_1=0,\sigma_2=1)$ appearing on the left-hand-side of the inequality represents the one-off payoff obtained by firm 1 at the time of its deviation $\tilde{\tau}$. Also observe that the third term on the left-hand-side of the inequality computes the present value of the stream of profits, discounted at rate δ, that derives from

[32] J Friedman, 'A Non-Cooperative Equilibrium for Supergames' 38 *Review of Economic Studies* 1–12 (1971).

duopolistic competition from time $\tilde{\tau}$ onwards—the punishment period. A careful examination of this third term leads to the observation that it also includes the no-cooperative profit that firm 1 would have obtained at time $\tilde{\tau}$. This profit should not be included there since it is known that at $\tilde{\tau}$, firm 1 gets the deviating profit instead of the no-cooperative profit. In other words, the correct specification of the discounted value of the streams of profits deriving from deviating at time $\tilde{\tau}$ requires the subtraction of the no-cooperative profit obtained by platform 1 at time $\tilde{\tau}$. This is the reason why the term $\hat{\Pi}_1(\sigma_1 = \sigma_2 = 0)$ is subtracted from the left-hand-side of Lemma 1's inequality.

The core claim associated with Lemma 1, which predicts that cartel stability increases with the degree of product differentiation, can be divided into two parts. First, the lemma claims that the question of whether collusion arises in converging markets can be answered unambiguously—eg, irrespectively of the discount rate—depending on the extent to which product markets are differentiated. In particular, the lemma provides the intuition that collusion is unambiguously feasible (in the sense that the discounted value of the stream of collusive profits is always higher than the one-off deviation profit plus the discounted value of the stream of competitive profits for any δ) during the initial stages of market convergence, and unambiguously unfeasible when convergence has surpassed a minimum threshold.

Figure 2 below illustrates the first of these two scenarios. It shows the discounted value of profit streams—as a function of the discount rate δ—associated with a process of convergence still in its initial phases, $0 < \gamma \leq 0.312$, when the behavioral deviation occurs at time $\tilde{\tau} = 0.30$.

The figure illustrates that in these circumstances deviation from collusive behavior is not optimal, since the discounted value of profit streams associated with collusion are, for any discount rate δ, higher than the discounted value of profit streams that derive from deviating at time $\tilde{\tau} \in 0 < \gamma \leq 0.312$.

The rationale behind this result is simple. When convergence is still in its initial phases, deviation does not increase profits significantly since market products are still highly differentiated. This improves the conditions for having a collusive agreement. At the same time, the size of the punishment associated with a deviation occurring during the initial stages of convergence is not negligible. It is true that in the short run, the size of the punishment cannot be particularly large since differentiation between products is still high. However, in the long run, the process of convergence itself increases the size of the punishment. This is because as products become closer substitutes, the competition intensifies, and this increases the relative size of the sacrificed profits that would have been obtained had the collusive agreement been kept in place. Overall, the size of the punishment outweighs the benefits of cheating, and therefore the conditions for a coordinated outcome are strengthened.

Observe that this is just another instance of the so-called pro-collusive intrinsic effect of demand growth (innovation, in the setting of this paper) on collusion, which establishes that the higher the rate of demand growth, the higher is the

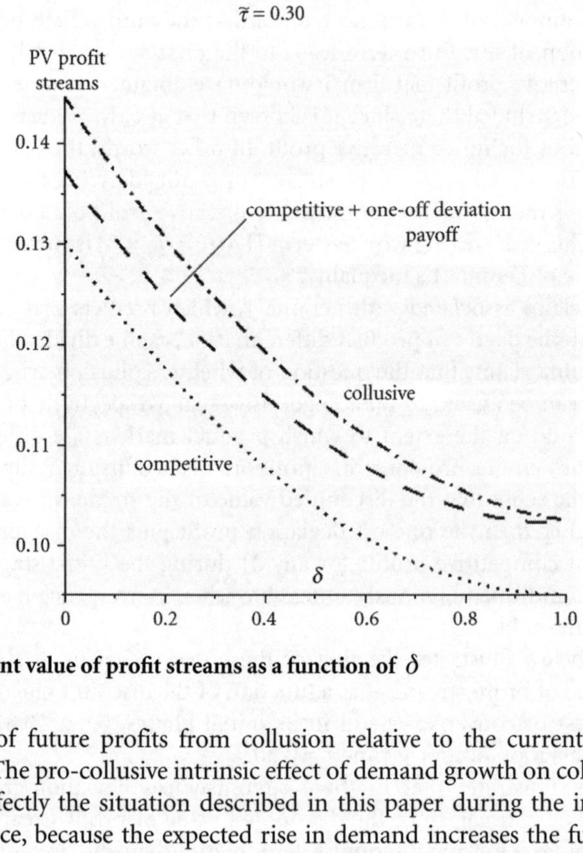

Figure 2 Present value of profit streams as a function of δ

importance of future profits from collusion relative to the current gains from deviating.[33] The pro-collusive intrinsic effect of demand growth on collusion characterizes perfectly the situation described in this paper during the initial phases of convergence, because the expected rise in demand increases the future cost of deviation, which in turn implies that an increase in the market growth (innovation) rate induces an increase in the maximal level of sustainable collusion.

Notwithstanding the similarity between these two conceptual frameworks, the bottom line is that when the process of convergence is going through its initial phases, collusion is sustainable because the short-term gains from deviation are not large enough to compensate for the future loss of profitability derived from a coordinated outcome.

Figure 3 below illustrates the second of the two scenarios described above. It shows the discounted value of profit streams—as a function of the discount rate δ—that derive from a process of convergence that goes through its terminal phases, $\gamma \geq 0.384$, when the deviation in conduct occurs at time $\tilde{\tau} = 0.40$.

In this scenario, collusion is unfeasible because the discounted value of profit streams associated with cooperation are, for any discount rate δ, lower than the discounted value of profit streams deriving from deviation. The rationale behind this result is, as before, the balance between short- and long-run cost and benefits.

[33] H Vasconcelos, 'Sustaining Collusion in Growing Markets' (2008) *CEPR Discussion Paper No 6865.*

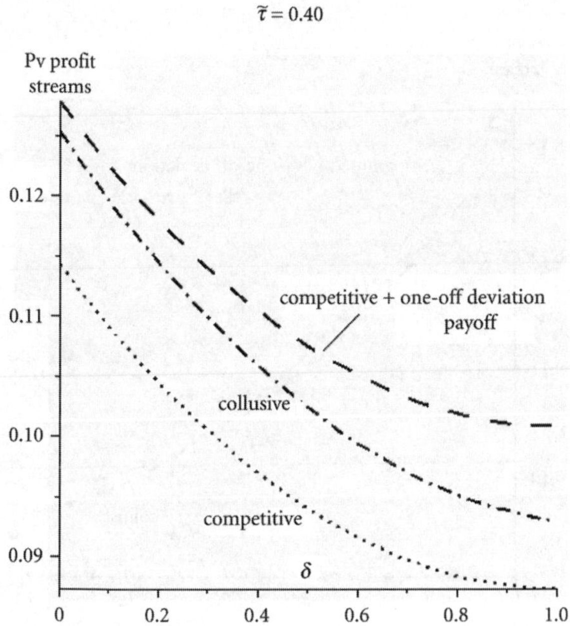

Figure 3 Present value of profit streams as a function of δ

A first observation is that in this case any deviation has the potential to increase profits significantly because the level of market product differentiation is relatively low. This improves the economic incentives for a successful deviation. At the same time, the size of the punishment associated with deviation lowers. It is true that, in the short run, the size of the punishment is large since product differentiation is now relatively low. However, since the process of convergence is evolving through its terminal stages, this large punishment is relatively short-lived. Overall, the incentives for deviation dominate the incentives for maintaining coordination, and this makes collusion unstable. Formally, the pro-collusive intrinsic effect of demand growth (innovation) on collusion is dominated by the incentives to deviate since the expected rise in demand is not particularly high.

The second part of Lemma 1's claim is that, when market convergence evolves through an intermediate range, collusion can be feasible depending on the rate at which future profits are discounted. In particular, the lemma establishes that when convergence evolves through this intermediate period, $0.312 < \gamma < 0.384$, collusion is feasible provided the discount rate is not too high: $\delta < \bar{\delta}$. As before, Figure 4 below illustrates the discounted value of profit streams that derive from a process of convergence that goes through this intermediate period when deviation occurs exactly at time $\tilde{\tau} = 0.35$.

The figure illustrates that the discounted value of profit streams associated with collusion are strictly higher than the discounted value of profit streams

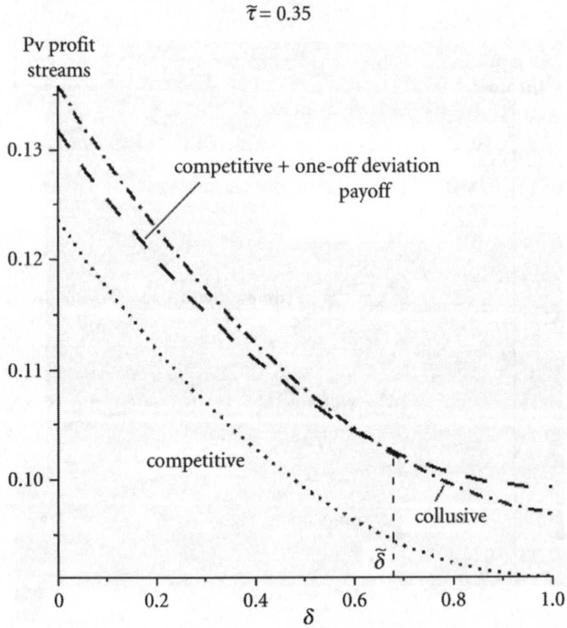

Figure 4 present value of profit streams as a function of δ

that derive from deviation only when $\delta < \bar{\delta}$. The intuition behind this result is as follows. The discount rate represents the weight that firms place on the value of future profits. When $\delta \rightarrow 0$, short run profits are equally valuable as future profits, while when $\delta \rightarrow 1$, profits of the same size are seen as more valuable in the present than in the future. Therefore, collusion is more feasible when δ is low, because only a firm that cares about future profits has incentives to enforce a collusive agreement. In contrast, when δ is high, collusion is less feasible since the attractiveness of earning higher profits now versus tomorrow increases, which makes cooperation more difficult to sustain.

V. Collusion, Convergence and Innovation

One of the most striking characteristics of market convergence in some industries is its pace of innovation. Gambardella and Torrisi,[34] for example, have found that during the period of 1984–92, for the 32 largest US and European electronics

[34] A Gambardella and S Torrisi, 'Does Technological Convergence Imply Convergence in Markets? Evidence from the Electronics Industry' 27 *Research Policy* 445–63 (1998).

firms, higher economic performance was associated with companies that focused on their core business but widened their technological capabilities. This result is somewhat intriguing, as one would expect technological diversification to be encouraged by the prospect of moving into different product markets where these technologies can be applied. The authors argue, however, that the expansion of technological capabilities may also be used to extract greater rents in core product markets by creating more complex products that incorporate distinct technologies. In other words, technological expansion is used not only to enter into different markets, but also to innovate in the functionalities associated with existing products.

The pace at which converging industries innovate has important implications not only for the measurement of welfare, but also for firms' incentives to collude. This is because innovation, by affecting current and future profits, also alters the intertemporal profile of optimal choices underlying the decision whether or not to engage in collusive behavior. In order to explore the impact that innovation has on collusive behavior, assume now that the evolution of the quality level provided by each firm is given by:

$$q_k(\gamma) = h_k(1 + \alpha\gamma)$$

where $0 \leq \alpha \leq 1$ represents an index of the observed degree of innovation in the industry. When $\alpha = 1$, as in the analysis carried out so far, innovation is meant to be maximal, since quality in the industry evolves basically according to the dynamics of the parameter of convergence γ. In contrast, when $\alpha = 0$, the industry is characterized by no innovation, since the quality in the industry remains anchored at its base level h_k. The following lemma illustrates this.

LEMMA 2: Collusion & innovation. *Let $\tau_{\max}$ denote the latest deviation time such that, for any $\tilde{\tau} \leq \tau_{\max}$, condition:*

$$\int_{\gamma=\tilde{\tau}}^{1} \hat{\Pi}_1(\sigma_1 = \sigma_2 = 1)\exp(-\delta(\gamma - \tilde{\tau}))d\gamma > \hat{\Pi}_1(\sigma_1 = 0, \sigma_2 = 1)\Big|_{\gamma=\tilde{\tau}}$$

$$- \hat{\Pi}_1(\sigma_1 = \sigma_2 = 0)\Big|_{\gamma=\tilde{\tau}} + \int_{\gamma=\tilde{\tau}}^{1} \hat{\Pi}_1(\sigma_1 = \sigma_2 = 0)\exp(-\delta(\gamma - \tilde{\tau}))d\gamma$$

holds for any δ. The lower the pace of innovation in the convergent market, the lower the sustainability of collusion since $\tau_{\max}$ is strictly increasing in α.

The content of Lemma 2 is illustrated by Figure 5 below. Lemma 2 claims that the time span—represented in the graph by τ in the vertical axis—over which

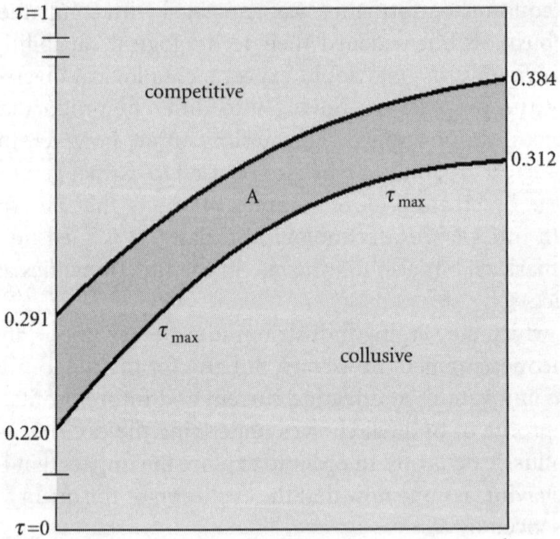

Figure 5 Innovation and the incentives for collusion

collusion is feasible shrinks as the index of the industry's innovation becomes smaller.[35] In other words, collusion is easier to sustain in markets with a high rate of innovation. In principle, this claim would seem to contradict the standard wisdom that in industries characterized by high rates of innovation, collusion is more difficult to sustain.[36]

This standard wisdom is based, however, on the implicit assumption of *asymmetric* innovation. In particular, Ivaldi *et al* have argued that

> innovations, particularly drastic ones, may allow a firm to gain a significant advantage over its rivals. This prospect reduces both the value of future collusion and the amount of harm that rivals will be able to inflict if the need arises.[37]

The intuition seems reasonable. However, when innovation is symmetric and sizeable, the size of the punishment associated with an early deviation increases, since the amount of future profits that have to be sacrificed also increases. Thus symmetric innovation, by increasing the size of the intertemporal punishment, improves the conditions for the stability of collusive behaviour.

[35] The area demarcated by Λ represents the combination of innovation and convergence rates over which the feasibility of collusion depends on the size of the discount rate.

[36] M Ivaldi, B Jullien, P Rey, P Seabright and J Tirole, 'The Economics of Tacit Collusion', *Final Report for the European Commission* (Toulouse, IDEI, 2003).

[37] *Ibid*, at 32.

VI. Implications for Competition Policy in Latin America

The implications of market convergence for competition policy in Latin America are vast. It has been commonly argued, for example, that the blurring of the boundaries between distinct product markets brought about by convergence has eroded the market power of incumbents in many markets. This notion of convergence as a force that encourages market entry has important implications for the case of regulated industries in the region, since it would provide a rationale for the deregulation of markets. Nevertheless, it would be adventurous for the regional competition authorities to initiate a process of deregulation on behalf of this view, since the extent to which convergence encourages market entry is, in its essence, an empirical question.

The main focus of this paper, however, has been on a different area of public policy interest: market convergence as a mechanism that encourages joint dominance. In particular, the paper has presented a framework in which the risk of collusion between symmetric rivals in a converging market is higher, the lower the level of substitutability observed between market products. To illustrate the relevance of this result for competition policies in Latin America, consider the evolution of the process of convergence between the provision of fixed and mobile voice services in the region. As mentioned in the introductory section, fixed-mobile convergence is taking the form of converged devices that allow seamless switching between mobile and local networks for mobile users. It is also likely that the initial provision of these converged services will be dominated by the current major operators of voice communications services—both fixed and mobile—in the region. This would imply that the risk of collusive behavior between the providers of these newly converged services is the highest in cases where the pre-convergence market structure associated with the converging markets is not very competitive.

This argument is particularly relevant for the case of Latin American jurisdictions, because the market structure in the fixed segment of the market in the region has historically been highly concentrated and the mobile segment has been experiencing a strong process of regional consolidation during the last years. Indeed, the regional mobile market is currently dominated by only two firms, *Telefónica* and *Telmex/América Móvil*, which have operations in 26 countries of the region and together have 64 per cent of the regional mobile market.[38] It is precisely in this context of high pre-convergence concentration in the fixed and mobile segments of the market that the analytical framework discussed in this paper takes regional relevance, since the results suggest that there will be a risk of

[38] It is also worth noting that, since entry into the mobile market is restricted by the availability of spectrum, the industry is inherently oligopolistic.

collusion between these dominant operators before these converged services are finally commoditized in the marketplace. The enforcers of anti-collusive policies in the region should then pay special attention to the evolution of recently created markets in industries characterized by high pre-convergence concentration, since there is a risk that anti-competitive agreements will be taking place in those markets.

An additional implication of the model discussed in this paper is that, because collusive behavior is more likely to occur during the initial stages of convergence, widespread uncertainty on whether markets are converging can play in favor of the enforcement of anti-collusive policies. To see this, assume that a firm operating in the initial stages of a convergent market is unsure whether technological change will threaten its market position in future periods. Provided that the likelihood of cartel detection is relatively high, this firm will underestimate the benefits of colluding now since the amount of forgone profits in future periods gets (arbitrarily) smaller. Therefore, uncertainty would lead to a scenario in which, regardless of the fact that structural conditions are given for cartel stability, firms may not collude.

A final implication of the analysis for competition policy in the region is related to innovation. When innovation is markedly asymmetric across firms in a way that a pattern of market dominance can be identified (eg, a firm is in the position to dictate the evolution of the market), competition authorities should be less concerned with the presence of coordinated effects, since the risks of having collusive agreements between the concurring firms is relatively low. This argument has a strong Schumpeterian flavor because, when innovation is markedly asymmetric, strong patterns of market dominance can be identified and this diminishes the chances of successful collusive behavior. Hence, when innovation is asymmetric, a higher rate of innovation is associated with lower chances of successful collusion. In contrast, when innovation is more symmetric in nature, as discussed in this chapter, a higher rate of innovation is associated with higher chances of successful collusion. It is therefore of paramount importance for competition authorities in the region to incorporate into their collusion-related assessments factors that describe the degree of innovation asymmetries observed across firms, since this can provide invaluable information during the process of determining whether collusion is taking place in markets that converge.

Chapter XIV

Latin America and the Control of International Cartels

JOHN M CONNOR*

I. Introduction

Despite the evident antitrust successes in sanctioning international cartels since 1990, many remain skeptical about whether current enforcement regimes are capable of serving the aims of antitrust. A narrow construction on the purpose of antitrust laws limits it to maximizing consumer welfare and efficiency; a broader interpretation gives some weight to income redistribution, small business protection, or dispersion of political and economic power. However, under either stance the aims of antitrust are served by competition policies that deter recidivism. Deterrence is the most commonly accepted legal-economic theory that justifies the passage of antitrust laws, but its role as a practical guide to imposing anti-cartel sanctions across world jurisdictions is doubtful.

While deterrence may have improved marginally in the 1990s, scholars of modern international cartels believe that current competition policies cannot fully deter them because they are 'oriented towards addressing harm done in domestic markets ... [or] merely prohibit cartels without [sufficiently strong] sanctions'.[1] Connor and Lande[2] find that cartel overcharges are so high and conspiracies so durable that current US public and private monetary sanctions provide inadequate deterrence. International cartels—those with international participation—are more difficult to convict yet as a group are even more harmful to customer welfare than domestic collusion. *Global* cartels—those that operate across multi-continental markets—typically reap above-average monopoly profits in jurisdictions with weak anti-cartel enforcement. Moreover, empirical evidence from recent years demonstrates a significant degree of continued cartel formation

* Professor of Industrial Economics, Purdue University.

[1] Simon J Evenett, Margaret C Levenstein and Valerie Y Suslow, 'International Cartel Enforcement: Lessons from the 1990s' 24 *The World Economy* 1221–45 (2001).

[2] John M Connor and Robert H Lande, 'How High Do Cartels Raise Prices? Implications for Optimal Cartel Fines' 80 *Tulane Law Review* 513–70 (2005).

and multiple corporate convictions for price fixing. It would appear that either greater sanctions ought to be applied, or that a multilateral approach should be implemented or both, in order to approach optimal deterrence of international price fixing.[3]

Although studies exist of prosecutions of individual cartels and of anti-cartel efforts in single jurisdictions, few have examined the global effort to deter cartels. The purpose of this chapter is to describe the magnitude of and trends in global antitrust sanctions imposed on modern international cartels, paying special attention to Latin America's anti-cartel efforts. By doing so, this chapter can contribute critical information for the ongoing debate about the effectiveness of global antitrust sanctions in deterring international price-fixing conduct.

The focus of this chapter is on monetary antitrust sanctions that have been imposed on detected private hard-core international cartels between January 1990 and December 2007, and the impact upon Latin America. Monetary sanctions include:

a) *fines* imposed by antitrust authorities on both corporations and individuals; and
b) *payments* made by defendants in private suits to direct and indirect buyers of cartelized products. Payments made by defendants to settle private class action suits usually include the legal fees and costs incurred by plaintiffs in prosecuting their cases.

International cartels are those that have participants from two or more countries; the qualifier does not refer to the geographic scope of the cartel's agreement. *Private* cartels are those that operate without the active involvement of governments or legal protection of national sovereignty. Thus, mandatory agricultural marketing orders are not private, neither are cartels which parliamentary statutes establish (eg, the East India Company), or by treaties among nations (eg, OPEC).

The next section of this chapter presents a broad historical summary of anti-cartel enforcement, followed by a brief literature review and descriptions of anti-cartel laws and policies. The remaining sections lay out the cartel data set, actual enforcement patterns 1990–2007, and measures of effectiveness of sanctions.

[3] One way of increasing sanctions without changing statutes is to extend standing to foreign buyers to permit them to sue for private damages in US courts. On the *Empagram* case, see W Davis, 'US Antitrust Treatment of International Cartels' 17 *Antitrust* 31–35 (2003); John M Connor and Darren Bush, 'How to Block Cartel Formation and Price Fixing: Using Extraterritorial Application of the Antitrust Laws as a Deterrent' 122 *Pennsylvania State University Law Review* 813 (2008).

II. Historical Sketch of Anti-Cartel Enforcement

Nations in nearly every corner of the world have adopted antitrust laws, and virtually all of these laws make price fixing illegal in most circumstances.[4] Prior to World War II, only the United States had an effectively enforced antitrust law, the Sherman Act,[5] but there were few significant US prosecutions of international cartels until the mid-1940s.[6] By the mid-1960s, at least two dozen countries had antitrust laws and 'were engaged in serious efforts to control restrictive practices'.[7] By 1996, 70 countries had adopted competition laws; these countries comprised about 78 per cent of world output and 86 per cent of the value of world trade.[8] With the adoption of an antitrust law in China in 2007, virtually all the world's leading economies have made cartels illegal.[9] Of course, the effectiveness of enforcement of these laws varies widely, as do the legal standards and sanctions available.

Attempts to collude on market prices or output are as old as markets themselves.[10] Most pre-modern cartels were associations whose rules were supported by national courts or the active participation of governments. Formal *private* international cartels, on the other hand, are more recent historical phenomena. The first wave of international cartels began as a consequence of an economic downturn in Germany in the 1870s; the potash syndicate is one of the better studied cartels of this era.[11] Many of the first US-based international cartels began about the same time.[12] Very few if any of these pioneering schemes survived the economic disruptions spawned by World War I, but many were re-established in the early 1920s only to disband again in 1939. Most of these 'interwar cartels' were organized by European companies or national associations allocating exclusive territories to its members—monopolies for domestic commerce and market quotas for international trade to the rest of the world. In the 1930s, nearly 200 private cartels were estimated to have controlled 40 per cent of world commodity

[4] Wyatt Wells, *Antitrust and the Formation of the Postwar World* (New York, Columbia University Press, 2002); ABA, *Competition Laws Outside the United States*, vols I and II (Chicago, American Bar Association, 2002 and 2005 Supplement).

[5] 15 USC § 1–7.

[6] Wendell Berge, *Cartels: Challenge to a Free World* (Washington, DC, Public Affairs Press, 1944); George W Stocking and Myron W Watkins, *Cartels or Competition?* (New York, Twentieth Century Fund, 1948).

[7] Corwin D Edwards, *Control of Cartels and Monopolies: An International Comparison* (Dobbs Ferry, NY, Oceana Publications, 1967).

[8] Mark R A Palim, 'The Worldwide Growth of Competition Law: An Empirical Analysis' 43 *Antitrust Bulletin* 105–45 (1998).

[9] China's new law was passed on Aug 30, 2007 and came into force Aug 1, 2008.

[10] Roman Piotrowski, *Cartels and Trusts* (London, George Allen & Unwin, 1933).

[11] Harm G Schröter, 'The International Potash Syndicate' in Dominique Barjot (ed), *International Cartels Revisited, 1880–1980* (Caen, France, Editions-diffusion du Lys, 1994); Philip C Newman, 'Key German Cartels under the Nazi Regime' 62 *Quarterly Journal of Economics* 576–95 (1948).

[12] Elliot Jones, *The Trust Problem in the United States* (New York, Macmillan, 1900, 1921); William Yandell Elliott *et al*, *International Control in the Non-Ferrous Metals* (New York, Macmillan, 1937).

trade.[13] Participation by Latin American firms in interwar international cartels was confined to a few agricultural and mining schemes.

From 1943 to 1949, the US Department of Justice (DOJ) convicted dozens of international cartels and won nearly all of the criminal cases.[14] From 1950 until 1995, the DOJ launched few cases against alleged international cartels, and the few that it brought to trial mostly resulted in embarrassing losses.[15] The EU began imposing fines on cartels in 1969, with substantial and accelerating fines beginning in the mid-1980s; it principally tended to target intra-EU cartels until about 2000.[16]

Modern international cartels—those detected since 1990—have some distinct characteristics. In recognition of the key industry positions attained by East Asian manufacturers in many lines of business since 1960, most modern cartels have had to include Asian corporations as members. Similarly, a large number of international cartels have sought to control markets in what business marketers call the Triad—North America, Western Europe, and the most industrialized nations of East Asia. Another unique feature is that they were formed by companies that were aware of the antitrust risks. Since the beginning of serious anti-cartel enforcement by the European Union in the late 1980s, international cartelists have had to weigh the benefits of monopoly profits against some probability of being apprehended and punished for collusion in multiple jurisdictions.[17] The antitrust authorities of Canada, the EU and the United States implemented new policies and procedures in the 1990s that are widely believed to have significantly increased the probability of detection. Most obviously, the severity of penalties directed at international cartels has soared compared with the preceding decades. These authorities reallocated enforcement resources toward prosecution of such cartels, increased cross-authority coordination, adopted more effective automatic leniency and 'amnesty plus' programs, imposed higher corporate

[13] Corwin D Edwards, *Economic and Political Aspects of International Cartels* (Washington, DC, US Gov't Printing Office, 1944).

[14] Wells, above n 4, at 96–116, 125–36.

[15] During 1980–94, the DOJ brought only four cases (out of 1,025 criminal price-fixing suits) against international cartels (Joseph C Gallo *et al*, 'Department of Justice Antitrust Enforcement 1955–1997' 17 *Review of Industrial Organization* 75–133 (2000)). See also, John M. Connor, Global Price Fixing, 2nd edition. (Heidelberg, Springer, 2007).

[16] The EU's first two decisions (*Quinine* and *Dyestuffs*) in 1969 involved global cartels, but there were few such convictions until the *Lysine* decision was announced in 2000 (Christopher Harding and Julian Joshua, *Regulating Cartels in Europe: A Study of Legal Control of Corporate Delinquency* (New York, Oxford University Press, 2003), 121–24). See *Amino Acids* (Case COMP 36.545/F3) Commission Decision 2001/418/EC (June 7, 2000) OJ L 152/24; *Quinine Cartel* (Case IV/26.623) Commission Decision 69/240 EEC (1969) OJ L 192/5 (1969); *Dyestuffs Cartel* (1969) OJ L 195/11; *In Re Amino Acid Antitrust Litigation*, 1996 WL 164434 (ND Ill, Apr 2, 1996).

[17] The story of the increasingly effective EU prosecution of cartelists is told in Harding and Joshua, above n 16. Canada, Australia and South Korea have aggressively pursued international cartels since 1990. Opinions vary about the dedication of Japan's FTC to fighting cartels (Harry First, 'Antitrust Enforcement in Japan' 64 *Antitrust Law Journal* 137 (1995); Stuart M Chemtob, 'Antitrust Deterrence in the United States and Japan' Remarks at Competition Policy in the Global Trading System Conference, Washington, DC, June 23, 2000).

fines, and in some jurisdictions applied individual criminal penalties.[18] As the decade of the 1990s progressed, rather than concerned calls for reform in the face of an alarming onslaught of cartels, the speeches of top antitrust officials began to acquire a tone of triumphalism.[19]

III. Literature Review

Analyses of US antitrust prosecutions and convictions of cartels are commonplace, but similar analyses for other jurisdictions are uncommon. Gallo *et al*[20] review the enforcement of the Sherman Act by the US DOJ for the period 1955–97. They describe the number of antitrust cases by type and outcome over time. For per se horizontal violations (a category that corresponds closely to cartels), Gallo *et al* find a total of only 34 international cases during 1955 to 1989, merely 2.3 per cent of all such cases. During 1990–2002, the international rate dropped to 0.4 per cent, but from the late 1990s the rate exceeded 50 per cent.[21] Gallo *et al* find that the average number of defendants per cartel was about four, and that the average size of a cartel's affected sales was 870 million 1982 dollars (about 1,700 million 2007 dollars).[22] The average duration of these US conspiracies was 5.4 years, with no trend over time. Finally, this study determines that the total fines imposed on 2,908 companies during 1955–97 was $305 million (approximately 839 million in 2007 dollars), two-thirds of which was imposed after 1989. In addition, 143 individuals were fined a total of $30 million (83 million in 2007 dollars).

[18] John M Connor, *Global Price Fixing*, 2nd edn (Heidelberg, Springer, 2007); OECD, *Report on the Nature and Impact of Hard Core Cartels and Sanctions against Cartels under National Competition Laws* (DAFFE/COMP (2002) 7), Paris, Organization for Economic Co-operation and Development (April 9, 2002); Wouter P J Wils, 'The Commission's New Method for Calculating Fines in Antitrust Cases' 23 *European Law Review* 252–63 (1998); *Final Report of the International Competition Policy Advisory Committee to the Attorney General*, Washington, DC, US DOJ (2000) (herein 'ICPAC'); Gary R Spratling, 'International Cartels', Speech before the American Conference Institute's 7th National Conference on the Foreign Corrupt Practices Act, Washington, DC (Dec 9, 1999); Donald Klawiter, 'After the Deluge: The Powerful Effect of Substantial Criminal Fines, Imprisonment, and Other Penalties in the Age of International Criminal Enforcement' (2001) 69 *George Washington Law Review* 745–65; William J Kolasky, 'Antitrust Compliance Programs: The Government Perspective', Address at the Corporate Compliance 2002 Conference, Practicing Law Institute, San Francisco, CA (July 12, 2002).

[19] Anthony V Nanni, 'Squeezing the Cartels: Criminal Enforcement Gets Tough' *Legal Times*, April 20, 2002, at 30–35; Scott D Hammond, 'From Hollywood to Hong Kong—Criminal Antitrust Enforcement is Coming to a City Near You', Address at Antitrust Beyond Borders Conference, Chicago, IL (Nov 9, 2001); Mario Monti, 'The Fight against Cartels' Address before EMAC, Brussels, Belgium (Sept 11, 2002), <http://europa.eu.int/rapid...>; R Hewitt Pate, 'The DOJ International Antitrust Program—Gaining Momentum', Speech before the American Bar Association, New York City (Feb 6, 2003); Joel I Klein, Address at the International Anti-Cartel Enforcement Conference, Washington, DC (Sept 30, 1999).

[20] Gallo *et al*, above n 15.

[21] John M Connor, *Price-Fixing Overcharges: Legal and Economic Evidence* ch 4, pp 59–153 in John B Kirkwood (ed), Jan 2007 *Research in Law and Economics* Vol 22 (Oxford, Amsterdam and San Diego, Elsevier).

[22] Gallo *et al*, above n 15.

Russo *et al*[23] compile lists of all cartel decisions taken by the EC from the beginning in 1969 to Spring 2007; Guersent summarizes cartel conduct and EC sanctions taken against 19 international cartels from July 2001 to December 2003[24]; and Harding and Joshua offer an admirable narrative of the evolution of EU cartel enforcement.[25] Levenstein and Suslow survey the economics of cartels, but do not cover legal treatment of cartels.[26]

The Organization for Economic Co-operation and Development (OECD) has an active program for the consideration of a common policy approach towards international cartels. Its report *Hard Core Cartels* presents a unique survey of its member countries' experiences in sanctioning such cartels.[27] In addition, the OECD organizes voluntary annual reporting on competition law developments and enforcement by both its members and non-members; comparable annual reports are available for Argentina, Brazil and Mexico.[28] Particularly valuable are occasional *Peer Reviews* conducted by the OECD upon the request of antitrust authorities; four such reviews have recently been conducted for Argentina, Brazil, Chile and Mexico.[29] The limited literature on Latin American cartel enforcement will be discussed below.

IV. Anti-Cartel Laws and Policies

This section describes the legal basis for antitrust enforcement, the sanctions that can be imposed on cartels, and reasons for successful prosecution in the world's

[23] Francesco Russo *et al*, 'European Commission Decisions on Competition' (ACLE Working Paper 2007–04, Amsterdam Center for Law and Economics, Aug 23, 2007), at 34–96.

[24] O Guersent (ed), 'The Fight Against International Cartels of the European Commission: 19 Decisions in 19 Months between July 2001 and December 2003', Brussels: EC Directorate for Competition (2001) <http://europa.eu.int/indus/competition/antitrust>.

[25] Harding and Joshua, above n 16.

[26] Margaret C Levenstein and Valerie Y Suslow, 'Cartel Contract Duration: Empirical Evidence from International Cartels, in Grossman' in Z Peter (ed), *How Cartels Endure and How They Fail: Studies of Industrial Collusion* (Cheltenham, UK, Edward Elgar, 2004).

[27] OECD (2002), above n 18.

[28] OECD, *Annual Report on Competition Policy Developments in Argentina* (DAF/COMP(2005)33), Paris, OECD (Oct 17, 2005a and previous), <http://www.oecd.org/countrylist/0,3349,en_2649_37463_28325800_1_1_1_37463,00.html>; OECD, *Annual Report on Competition Policy Developments in Brazil* (DAF/COMP(2007)15), Paris, OECD (May 25, 2007a and previous), <http://www.oecd.org/countrylist/0,3349,en_2649_37463_28325800_1_1_1_37463,00.html>; OECD, *Annual Report on Competition Policy Developments in Mexico* (DAF/COMP(2007)14/25), Paris, OECD (May 21, 2007b and previous), <http://www.oecd.org/countrylist/0,3349,en_2649_37463_28325800_1_1_1_37463,00.html>.

[29] OECD, *Competition Law and Policy in Chile: A Peer Review* (Paris, OECD, 2004a)); OECD, *Competition Law and Policy in Mexico: A Peer Review* Paris, OECD, 2004b); OECD, *Competition Law and Policy in Brazil: A PeerReview* (Paris, OECD, 2005b); OECD, *Competition Law and Policy in Argentina: A Peer Review* (Paris, OECD, 2006).

three most active antitrust jurisdictions: the United States, the EU, and Canada.[30] With these three institutions as benchmarks, I then outline the major features of competition-law enforcement in four of Latin America's most active national authorities—Argentina, Brazil, Chile and Mexico.[31]

The choice of these four authorities is not arbitrary. When I last surveyed the antitrust landscape of Europe and the New World in the late 1990s, Argentina, Brazil, Chile and Mexico were already at the forefront in adopting the 'Antitrust Idea'.[32] Since the early 1990s, limitations to effective enforcement were diagnosed by the four nations, several appropriate amendments have been made to national competition laws, and new enforcement policies (many inspired by successes of foreign antitrust authorities) have become standard operating procedures. Public interest in anti-competitive acts still remains highest in these four Latin American nations. Clarke *et al*[32a] show that up through January 2005, the top four nations in Latin America ranked by the number of allegations of anti-competitive activities were Brazil, Mexico, Argentina and Chile; they account for 69 per cent of all such allegations. Moreover, data presented in this chapter confirm that these countries have the continent's strongest record of international cartel enforcement.

A. The United States

'Naked' cartels, those arranged through direct explicit communications between independent firms, are per se violations of US law; no amount of evidence concerning circumstances in the industry or effects of the agreement on markets will be considered evidentiary in determining guilt.[33] More than 90 per cent of detected conspiracies are serious enough and the evidence of intent strong enough that corporations and individuals will be charged by the Antitrust Division of the DOJ as a criminal matter. Unless an investigation is closed, nearly all indicted cartel participants

[30] A Working Paper authored by OECD economist Jens Hoj, 'Competition Law and Policy Indicators for the OECD Countries' (Economics Department Working Paper No 586 (ECO/WKP(2007)28), Paris, OECD, Aug 8, 2007), at 13–16, confirms the leading status of these three jurisdictions in overall competition law enforcement.

[31] In Brazil and Chile, as in the United States, the work of the national competition authorities is supplemented by provincial or State-level competition law authorities; these sub-national authorities are beyond the scope of this chapter.

[32] John M Connor, 'International Convergence of Antitrust Laws and Enforcement (I)' 28 *Law and Economics Review* 17–30 (1997a); John M Connor, 'International Convergence of Antitrust Laws and Enforcement (II)' 28 *Antitrust Law and Economics Review* 73–94 (1997b). See also Jaime Fernandez, 'Antitrust Regulation in Latin America' 30 *The International Lawyer* 521–53 (1996); and Clive S Gray and Anthony A Davis, 'Competition Policy in Developing Countries Pursuing Structural Adjustment' 38 *Antitrust Bulletin* 425–67 (1993). Since then, antitrust activities have begun in earnest in Peru, Columbia, El Salvador and Venezuela. About 10 other Latin American jurisdictions have price-fixing laws.

[32a] Julian L Clarke *et al*, *Anti-Competitive Practices and Liberalizing Markets in Latin America and the Caribbean*. World Economy 28 (2005) 1029–1056.

[33] Herbert Hovenkamp, *Federal Antitrust Policy*, 2nd edn (St Paul, MN, West Group, 1999).

agree to plead guilty.[34] Although the DOJ has a panoply of sanctions that can be imposed on guilty cartelists, by far the most common US Government sanctions are corporate fines, individual fines and incarceration of responsible managers.

The DOJ's notable success in prosecuting international cartels after 1995 may be traced to several amendments to the law and improved investigatory techniques.[35] The Sherman Act's maximum penalties were steadily increased by amendments in 1955, 1974, 1987, 1990 and 2004.[36] In 1974, cartel conduct was made a *felony* for corporations, and prison sentences for individuals were raised from a maximum of one year to three years. To summarize, from 1974 to 1990, the maximum corporate liability from government fines rose from $50,000 to potentially *six times* the cartel's overcharge.

Since 1987, corporate fine calculation has begun with applying the Federal Sentencing Guidelines to the particular defendant's antitrust offense. First, a base fine is calculated by finding 20 per cent of the company's sales of the cartelized product during the conspiracy; in principle the affected commerce could be global in scope, but in practice only US sales are used.[37] Secondly, a pair of culpability multipliers is determined by reference to tabulated values in the Guidelines. Various aggravating factors raise the multipliers (size of company, whether bid rigging was alleged, involvement of top officers, a previous conviction for a similar offense, etc), while mitigating factors lower them (cooperation with the DOJ's investigation, acceptance of responsibility, and the existence of a good antitrust training program). The highest possible multiplier is 4.0, and the lowest is 0.75, which means that a company can be fined as much as 80 per cent of affected commerce. Thirdly, in return for cooperation, a company can request leniency: under DOJ policy the first qualified applicant can receive a 100 per cent discount (ie, amnesty), while the second and third to apply get substantial but progressively smaller discounts. In practice, the cooperation discounts for international cartels average 70 per cent of the maximum fine specified by the Guidelines.[38]

Around 1993 an enforcement policy shift took place in the DOJ that placed a higher priority on investigating international antitrust violations and that instructed the FBI to employ all the tools of their trade to collect evidence. The

[34] About 95% of all formal investigations of international cartels opened by the DOJ end in guilty pleas by at least one company (John M Connor and Gustav Helmers, 'Statistics on Modern Private International Cartels' (Working Paper 07-01, Washington, DC, American Antitrust Institute, Jan 2006), <http://www.antitrustinstitute.org/recent2/567.pdf>). Typically this process takes less than six months. Convictions of companies at trial are rare—less than one per year—but one or two trials of individual managers of cartels do occur each year.

[35] John M Connor, 'Price-Fixing Overcharges: Legal and Economic Evidence' in John B Kirkwood (ed), Jan 2007 *Research in Law and Economics* Vol 22 (Oxford, Amsterdam and San Diego, Elsevier), 59–153; Connor, above n 18; Donald I Baker, 'The Use of Criminal Law Remedies to Deter and Punish Cartels and Bid-Rigging' 69 *George Washington Law Review* 693–720 (2001).

[36] Connor (2007b), above n 18.

[37] Connor and Lande, above n 2, at 559–64.

[38] See John M Connor, *A Critique of Cartel Fine Discounting by the US Department of Justice* (Working Paper), available at SSRN, <http://ssrn.com/abstract=977772>, at 31.

1993 revision of the DOJ Corporate Leniency Program described below was a particularly important investigative innovation. In addition, the DOJ has introduced a number of methods of cooperating with other jurisdictions.[39] Protocols and treaties permit sharing of information on cartel investigations or enforcement actions, subject to restrictions set by national laws on confidentiality. Regular international meetings of enforcement officials have fostered the exchange of effective investigatory techniques.[40]

The Sherman Act authorizes private suits by direct buyers for treble damages and reasonable legal costs in federal court.[41] Besanko and Spulber show that treble damages generally lead to positive welfare increases if the probability of conviction and the multiple of damages recovered is high enough.[42] Since the late 1970s, the largest private cartel cases have been organized initially as class actions and have ended with judicially approved negotiated settlements. Moreover, in about half of the states of the United States indirect purchasers can sue for damages; alternatively, indirect buyers of cartelized products can also receive compensation through suits initiated in federal court by state attorneys general. Therefore, the (theoretical) maximum US liability facing corporate price fixers from government and private prosecutions after 1990 approaches *10 times* its overcharge.

B. The European Union

The European Commission's Directorate General for Competition (DG-COMP) is the world's second most powerful antitrust authority.[43] EU law treats antitrust violations solely as civil infractions by business entities.[44] Individual conspirators are not personally liable for monetary penalties or prison sentences.[45] Corporate members of cartels are subject to maximum fines of 10 per cent of sales in the year prior to the year in which the EC makes its decision. The EC's fines can be based on the *global* sales of an offending firm in *all* its lines of business.

The EU first adopted detailed guidelines in 1998 for calculating firm-by-firm cartel fines.[46] First, the EC considers the 'gravity' of the offense. Although a matter of discretion, cartels are usually placed in the 'very serious' category, which

[39] ICPAC (2000), above n 18; Pate, above n 19.

[40] ICN, International Competition Network Web Page (2007), <www.icn.org>.

[41] Hovenkamp, above n 33.

[42] David Besanko and Daniel F Spulber, 'Are Treble Damages Neutral?' 80 *American Economic Review* 870–87 (1990).

[43] John M Connor, 'Effectiveness of Sanctions on Modern International Cartels' 6 *Journal of Industry, Competition, and Trade* 195–223 (2006).

[44] Besides the USA and Canada, eight other countries provide for criminal sanctions: Austria, Germany, France, Norway, Ireland, Slovakia, Japan and South Korea (Scott D Hammond, 'A Review of Recent Cases and Developments in the Antitrust Division's Criminal Enforcement Program', speech at the Conference Board's 2002 Antitrust Conference, New York City, March 7, 2002). The UK criminalized antitrust in 2005.

[45] Connor, above n 18.

[46] Harding and Joshua, above n 16, at 240–52.

is the highest of three levels of antitrust infringements. Large damages that are geographically widespread add to the gravity. Secondly, to account for disparities in the power of fines to deter, relatively large companies are fined more than smaller participants. Thirdly, fines are increased by 10 percentage points per year for each year the cartel is effective. Fourthly, these three factors result in a base fine (called a 'basic amount') for each company, which is adjusted for culpability—upwards for cartel leaders and downwards for various mitigating factors. Fifthly, under the EU's Leniency Notice, violators are given 10 per cent to 50 per cent discounts for their degrees of cooperation. Since 1996, amnesty has been granted, with a 2001 improved program attracting large numbers of applicants. Lastly, the Commission ensures that the amount of the fine does not exceed 10 per cent of global sales. In late 2006, revised EU fining guidelines were adopted that may double average fines.[47]

There is no provision for private compensatory suits under EU law. However, changes are afoot in the UK, Germany and France.[48] In the UK, which liberalized its rules for launching private suits, at least 21 such actions against cartels resulted in settlements for monetary damages in 2000–05.[49] A handful of EU nations (UK, France, Ireland, Norway) have criminalized price fixing, and the EU seems to be moving slowly in that direction, but instances of incarceration are apparently unknown.[50]

A notable shift in EU enforcement is the devolution of anti-cartel enforcement away from Brussels toward the National Competition Authorities (NCAs) in the 27 Member States. Around 2000, obviously cross-national coordination of cartel investigations began, probably as the result of bilateral sharing of information. As the number of international cartels being detected in the EU outpaced the ability of the EC's DG-COMP to process the decisions, a higher and higher proportion of cartel decisions emanated from the EU's NCAs. The regionalization of antitrust in the EU, already a *fait accompli*, was formalized by the creation in November 2002 of the European Competition Network.[51]

C. Canada

The Canadian Competition Bureau (CCB), together with the Ministry of Justice, enforces criminal laws similar to those in the United States, and its prosecutions of international cartels tend to follow those in the United States by six months to

[47] Cento Veljanovski, 'European Commission Cartel Prosecutions and Fines, 1998–2007: A Statistical Analysis' (London, Case Associates, Sept 2007), <http://papers.ssrn.com/sol3/papers.cfm?abstract_id=1016014>.

[48] Alan Wiseman *et al*, 'Bring On the Private Suits', *Legal Times*, March 19, 2007, at 36.

[49] Barry J Rodger, '*Private Enforcement of Competition Law: The Hidden Story*' (2007), unpublished manuscript.

[50] Harding and Joshua, above n 16.

[51] First reported in *European Report 2002.*

a year.[52] The CCB is a small agency that cooperates closely with the US DOJ on cartels. Hard-core cartel violations are crimes treated in effect as per se illegal acts. Persons can be fined and imprisoned, but this power is used quite sparingly. The CCB imposes antitrust penalties typically close to 20 per cent of Canadian sales during the affected period.

Canada is one of the few jurisdictions outside the United States with effective private antitrust remedies.[53] Private actions usually follow upon government indictments. Introduced in 1976, private suits were little used until Ontario issued formal class action rules in 1992. Now at least four other provinces have such laws, but plaintiffs from any part of Canada may join a provincial suit.

> The situation in Canada increasingly reflects that of the United States and, in the event of a conviction of an international price fixing case in the United States … the commencement of one or more class actions in Canada … is now a virtual certainty.[54]

D. Four Latin American Competition Authorities

The antitrust authorities of Latin America are quite diverse in terms of their histories, legal foundations, and institutional arrangements.[55] In their modern forms, some of the same external conditions in the 1980s and early 1990s seem to account for their births: a return to democracy after a period of dictatorship, the abandonment of formal centralized economic planning and price controls, high rates of inflation, realization of the inefficiencies of many State-owned enterprises, abuse of dominance associated with privatized former monopolies, relaxation of import and foreign-investment restrictions, and the formation of customs unions.[56] In general, they also share a tendency for increasingly intensive and effective cartel prosecutions that dates from the late 1990s. These anti-cartel efforts are pursued in environments where there is little or no popular or business support for antitrust principles, where merger cases or consumer protection vie for agency resources, and where political interference has historically been a concern.

1. *Brazil*

Although antitrust law can be traced to 1962, Law 8884 (passed in 1994) is the principal legislation that forms the basis of modern Brazilian competition law.[57]

[52] Connor (2006), above n 43, at 195–223.

[53] Calvin S Goldman *et al*, 'Private Access to Antitrust Remedies: The Canadian Experience', Address before the Section of Antitrust Law, American Bar Association, April 2–4, 2003.

[54] *Ibid*, at 7.

[55] Ignacio De Leon, *Latin American Competition Law: A Policy in Search of Identity* (The Hague, Kluwer Law 2001).

[56] Connor (1997a), above n 32, at 26–30.

[57] Dallal Stevens, 'Framing Competition Law within an Emerging Economy: The Case of Brazil' (1995) 40 *Antitrust Bulletin* 929–71; John W Clark, 'Competition Policy and Regulatory Reform in Brazil' 2 *OECD Journal of Competition Law and Policy* 193 (2000).

Article 21 of this Law prohibits price fixing, allocation of markets, and other horizontal market restraints.[58] Abuse of market power (private control of prices) can be prosecuted as a criminal or as a civil infraction. In cartel cases, two tests are required for proof: the existence of collective market power from a case-specific analysis, and an agreement to collude in that market.[59] While mention is made of possible efficiency benefits of cartelization, this potentially exculpatory factor is ignored in practice. Unlike many other jurisdictions, Brazil's law has no exemptions for export cartels, 'crisis' cartels, or agricultural cooperatives.

Enforcement is split among three government agencies. Investigations are carried out by the Economic Law Office (SDE) of the Ministry of Justice. If probable cause is established by the SDE, it refers the case to the Administrative Council for Defense of the Economy (CADE), an independent agency reporting to the Prime Minister's office. A third agency, the Secretariat of Economic Monitoring (SEAE) in the Ministry of Finance, contributes non-binding economic analyses of the case to CADE. CADE then decides whether to initiate an administrative law proceeding, decides the case, and announces penalties or other remedies. CADE administrative decisions may be appealed to as many as four levels of federal court, which has created great delays in final outcomes.[60]

In general, practitioners judge Brazil's anti-cartel enforcement to be relatively and increasingly successful,[61] though some critics fault CADE for choosing cases that are the easiest to prove and that have small effects on the economy.[62] In 2000, amendments granted the SDE the power to obtain and serve search warrants at short notice, a change that made 'dawn raids' possible for the first time.[63] In addition, a leniency program similar to the 1993 US program was authorized. Applicants can expect corporate and individual fine reductions of from about 33 per cent to 100 per cent. Both techniques were first implemented in 2003. The SDE and the federal police exercise full powers to search premises, compel oral interviews, and retain evidence. Together with a redeployment of merger specialists, these changes permitted CADE to issue an increasing number of cartel decisions. As of 2007, at least seven cartel investigations are known to have been initiated as a result of leniency applications.[64]

While a few price-fixing defendants have allegations against them dismissed, most cartel decisions result in corporate and individual fines. The former must be in the range of 1 per cent to 30 per cent of a company's total (national and foreign) sales revenues in the year prior to a decision; if indicted, a manager pays

[58] OECD (2005a), above n 28.

[59] Roberto A C Pfeiffer, 'Recent Aspects of Hard Core Prosecution in Brazil' (presented at the Third Latin American Competition Forum, Madrid, 2005), at 2.

[60] Mauro Grinberg, 'Cartels: The Brazilian Experience' (paper at the Global Competition Forum, Toronto, May 2006), at 2.

[61] Barbara Rosenberg and Jose da Matta Berardo, 'Brazil: Cartels and Leniency' *Global Competition Review, Antitrust Review of the Americas*, Special Issue, 2008, at 1.

[62] Grinberg, above n 60.

[63] OECD (2005a), above n 28.

[64] Rosenberg and da Matta Berardo, above n 61, at 2.

from 10 per cent to 50 per cent of his company's fine. There are no specific fining guidelines, but general principles from Law 8884 include:

a) market overcharges or illegal gains to violators as aggravating factors; and
b) cooperation of defendants and their ability to pay as mitigating factors.

Prosecutors appear to be guided by the principle of specific deterrence in setting fines.[65] The first true cartel case, *Flat Rolled Steel*,[66] was filed in 1999 and decided in 2005. Around 1999–2002, most cartel fines tended to be close to the 1 per cent minimum, but by 2005 a few cases (*Liquid Petroleum Gas*[67] and *Crushed Stone*[68]) had concluded with fines in the 10 per cent to 15 per cent range.[69] Several managers have been required to pay personal fines of 0.1 per cent to 1.5 per cent of their company's annual revenues.

The industrial distribution of the 45 cartel convictions made during 1999–2005 is quite different from that in the EU or United States, which tend to be dominated by manufactured industrial material inputs and construction.[70] In Brazil, 69 per cent of the decisions involved localized collusion in the service sector, predominantly bid rigging against medical institutions; only 13 per cent were directed at manufacturing, mining or construction.[71]

A May 2007 proposed amendment (Law 11482) to Brazil's antitrust law will permit cartelists to plea bargain with CADE, ie to receive a reduced fine, immunity for managers, and closure of the investigation in return for inculpatory information about the other cartelists. Like US plea bargaining, this new process of partial leniency will permit rapid disposition of cases because trials and other judicial hearings are avoided. Brazilian antitrust authorities prefer to term this process 'direct settlement'.[72] Indeed, CADE began direct settlements prior to this amendment; the first leniency accord occurred in 2005, followed by six in 2006.[73] The sizes of the fine discounts are not known, but some instances of partial leniency have resulted in substantial fines. In late 2007, a large French company negotiated a fine of $24 million in return for cooperation with CADE and cessation of cartel conduct.[74] In August 2006, CADE announced a leniency accord with orange processors for US $45.9 million to settle allegations of collusion that

[65] Pfeiffer, above n 59; Ana Paula Martinez, Interview, *Global Competition Review* (Sept 7, 2007).
[66] 'Three Brazil steel makers guilty of price fixing', *Globe and Mail* (Canada), Sept 24, 2005, p B7.
[67] *Brazil Liquid Petroleum Gas*—Administrative Proceeding 08012.004860, May 10, 2004.
[68] Juliano Basile, 'SDE julga formacao de carteis no Brasil nos setores industriales; Julgamento do "cartel de britas" marca nova leva de decisoes da SDE', *Valor Economico* (Brazil), Nov 26, 2004.
[69] Pfeiffer, above n 59; OECD (2005a), above n 28, at 50–52.
[70] Connor and Helmers, above n 34.
[71] Grinberg, above n 60.
[72] Martinez, above n 65.
[73] Lorenna Rodriguez, 'Government Closing Circle against Price Fixing'. *Gazeta Mercantil* (Jan 30, 2007) at 1.
[74] 'Lafarge to pay $24USmn in fines', *Business News Americas* (Nov 29, 2007).

depressed fresh orange prices.[75] Because direct settlements substitute for normal judicial findings of guilt, the latter began to decline after 2005.

Several cartel managers have been required to pay substantial personal fines. Criminal proceedings against managers are possible, resulting in up to five years in prison, but no such penalties are known to have been imposed. Private compensatory suits are theoretically possible in Brazil's courts, but few if any have been filed. Legal discussions of Brazil's antitrust scene rarely bother to mention them.

Brazil's antitrust authorities show signs of being overburdened.[76] The federal budget was declining in US dollar terms in 2000–04, employee turnover was high, and there were signs of a chronic shortage of qualified personnel. However, in 2005–06 the budget and number of personnel rose. CADE had a backlog of 738 antitrust cases of all types in 2004. In early 2007, CADE had more than 300 cartel suits underway.[77]

2. *Argentina*

Argentina's antitrust authority began active prosecutions of cartels a few years later than Brazil's, and seemed to be making up for lost time around 2005, but more recently has run out of steam.

Argentina adopted a law similar to the US Sherman Act in 1923, but it was seldom used.[78] Argentina's modern competition law (22,262/1980) was consciously modeled on the EU's law, and established the National Commission for the Defense of the Economy (CNDC). The CNDC can present only advisory opinions to the ministry to which it is attached. To remedy the lack of independence, Law 25,156/1999 created a truly independent oversight Tribunal for the CNDC, but for political reasons the Tribunal was, as of 2008, never constituted. The 1980 law and decisions through 1999 remain the dominant antitrust law in Argentina for horizontal restraints.

Price fixing is unlawful if it harms 'the general economic interest', a legal term that the CNDC interprets as equivalent to consumer welfare. This rule implies that the burden of proof for the CNDC is to show market price effects. Cartel fines cannot exceed AR $150 million (in 2008 about US $49 million) per company and are to be calculated on the basis of the harm caused to victims or the illegal gain to the cartelist. Recidivism can double fines, but cannot exceed the cap, which has not been adjusted since 1999. Argentine law accepts the principle of extraterritoriality and in theory (but not in practice) can impose prison sentences.[79]

The CNDC can participate in dawn raids, but has refrained from many in recent years. Argentina has no leniency program. Merger enforcement takes precedence over anti-cartel activity. While the CNDC opened almost 100 formal

[75] *Tendencias Data* (Aug 1, 2006).
[76] OECD (2005a), above n 28.
[77] Rodriguez, above n 73.
[78] OECD (2006), above n 29.
[79] Ismael Malis *et al*, 'Anti-Cartel Activity in Argentina' (paper at the Third Latin American Competition Forum, Madrid, 2005), at 5.

conduct investigations per year during 2000–05, it closed only 30 per year, leading to a large backlog of cases. An alternative to fines are cease-and-desist orders, of which 35 were issued in 2000–05.[80]

Cartel enforcement began in 2003 with small fines imposed on two municipal conspiracies (LPG distribution and sand).[81] By 2005, 12 cases had been judged, four defendants found guilty, and 30 more cases were under investigation.[82] The two biggest cartel cases (*Cement*[83] and *Liquid Oxygen*[84]) culminated in fines of US $130 million after investigations lasting six and three years, respectively. These decisions and more than 100 others have been appealed; most appeals are brought to a quasi-specialized Commercial Court.[85] In 2006–07, confusion erupted about the proper forum for antitrust appeals.[86]

The absence of an appointed Tribunal makes the CNDC more sensitive to the policies of the national President and the Ministry of the Economy than most other antitrust authorities. Political pressure is most evident in interventions concerning the choice of investigatory targets.[87] The national government's attempts to suppress inflationary tendencies through persuasion prompted several recent CNDC investigations of particular industries.[88]

3. *Chile*

Chile is widely recognized as the Latin American pioneer in implementing an active antitrust law regime.[89] Its first law (13,305) was adopted in 1959 at about the same time the country abandoned centralized price controls. The current competition law (Decree 211) was implemented in 1973 as part of a comprehensive plan to reorganize the economy on laissez-faire principles. It is a criminal statute widely recognized as being modeled on the Sherman Act. Consequently, cartel conduct is viewed by the national antitrust authority as illegal per se. A major amendment (Law 19,610) was enacted in 1999. The current institutional structure was implemented in 2004.

The law is enforced by an independent National Economic Prosecutor (FNE) and 11 non-professional provincial commissions. By the early 1990s, the FNE was recognized

[80] *Ibid*, at 18.
[81] *Ibid*, at 11.
[82] *Ibid*, at 1.
[83] *CNDC v Loma Negra and Others* (2005), Resolution 124/05 from the Secretary of Technical Coordination.
[84] *CNDC v Air Liquide and Others* (2005), Resolution 119/05 from the Secretary of Technical Coordination.
[85] Malis *et al*, above n 79, at 35.
[86] GCR, 'Argentina's Main Appeal Court Is Refusing to Accept Competition Cases', *Global Competition Review* (Feb 9, 2007a).
[87] *Ibid*, at 32.
[88] EIU, Argentina: Competition and Price Regulations, *Economist Intelligence Unit* (July 24, 2007); GCR, 'Argentina Appoints New Antitrust Chief', *Global Competition Review* (May 3, 2006).
[89] OECD (2004a), above n 29.

for its consistency and professionalism.[90] Until May 2004, FNE's recommendations were reviewed by the quasi-judicial, unpaid Antitrust Commission, loosely supervised by the Supreme Court.[91] This Commission met about four hours each week and had no staff or budget. Until 2004 the absence of a staff or budget for the Commission meant that its decisions received little elaboration or justification. The Chilean Supreme Court has overturned a high proportion of these decisions.

The statutory goals of antitrust are economic efficiency and consumer welfare, but in the last decade or so somewhat broader goals, such as economic freedom and non-discrimination, have been enunciated.[92] The FNE and the Commission are extremely reluctant to find antitrust violations, and even more reluctant to assess sanctions. An analysis of 260 FNE decisions during 1974–93 found that the vast majority dealt with monopolization matters; only 37 hard-core cartels were investigated, and only 30 per cent were found to be violations—an extremely small share by international standards. In 2001, out of 55 Commission decisions, only one was a cartel case. In 2004, the FNE had a total backlog of four cartel cases.[93]

In May 2004, because of its 'erratic rulings', the Antitrust Commission was replaced by the Free-Competition Defense Tribunal (TDLC), a competition court that can appeal directly to the Supreme Court.[94] As from 2008, the TDLC will be staffed with full-time, professional commissioners with antitrust expertise who serve six-year terms. It rules on decisions of the FNE or initiates investigations requested by private citizens.

The Antitrust Commission and its successor, the TLDC, have a broad array of remedies at their disposal: fines, cease-and-desist orders, issuing industry rules, restructuring firms, and disbarring individuals or trade associations. Consent decrees and plea negotiations are not employed.

Up through 1998, the FNE had only about 30 employees, but the number doubled in 1999. A parallel budget increase allowed FNE to attract better-qualified professional staff in the early 2000s.[95] In 2003, the maximum antitrust fine was \$230,000.[96] There were no fining guidelines and no leniency program. Fines were few and very small. Out of more than 2000 decisions of the Commission during 1973–2002, only 73 carried fines. Of those decisions with fines, only nine referred to horizontal agreements.[97] The average cartel fine per case was \$51,000. Many antitrust decisions are overturned by the courts or the fines greatly reduced. *Oxygen*, the country's greatest international cartel case, with \$7 million in fines, was dismissed by the Supreme Court in January 2007.[98]

[90] Connor (1997b), above n 32, at 74.
[91] OECD (2004a), above n 29.
[92] *Ibid*, at 18–24.
[93] *Ibid*, at 70.
[94] EIU, 'Chile: Competition and Price Regulation', *Economist Intelligence Unit* (Jan 23, 2008), at 1.
[95] OECD (2004b), above n 29, at 26–27.
[96] *Ibid*, at 30.
[97] OECD (2004a), above n 29, at 71.
[98] GCR, 'Chilean Supreme Court Quashes Antitrust Fine', *Global Competition Review* (Jan 23, 2007).

Chilean antitrust enforcement is, on the whole, weak. A noted analysis of antitrust enforcement in Chile finds four causes:

a) there is little concern by members of the Antitrust Commission for 'white-collar' economic crimes that have such diffuse social harms;
b) Commissioners have strong laissez-faire biases;
c) the FNE is underfunded; and
d) the Commission is composed of part-time amateurs with little economic literacy.[99]

The OECD also seems to be of the opinion that the Chilean criminal antitrust law has not been grafted successfully on to a civil law system.[100]

There have been several positive changes in the law since 2003. Beginning in 2004 the maximum fine was raised to about $17 million, and Congress is likely to pass higher limits in 2008.[101] A leniency program is also being considered. Nevertheless, few high-profile cartel cases have been pursued since the 2004 amendments.

4. *Mexico*

Mexico has the newest antitrust law among the four Latin American authorities covered in this chapter. In the mid-1980s, the Mexican Government began to privatize State-owned corporations, eliminate tariff protections for domestic industry, and end most price controls.[102] Mexico's competition law (the Federal Law of Economic Competition—FLEC) was introduced in 1993, as a condition of its entry into the NAFTA free-trade zone in 1994. At the same time the Federal Competition Commission (CFC) was created to enforce the law. The fundamental purpose of the FLEC is to promote economic efficiency. Petroleum, postal services and a few other 'strategic' industries are exempt from FCC regulation, as is direct price regulation of a few consumer necessities by the Ministry of Commerce. Numerous decisions of the Supreme Court have supported the constitutionality of the FLEC, and the Congress has repeatedly resisted expanding antitrust exemptions for designated industries, yet obtaining effective remedies in the lower courts often eludes the CFC.

The CFC has demonstrated a great deal of independence since about 2000 by attacking some of the country's most powerful business interests. Although nominally part of the Ministry of Commerce, the CFC is guaranteed independence by statute. Importantly, the five Commissioners are appointed by the national President to staggered 10-year terms. A client survey gave the CFC very high marks for its professionalism, honesty, independence and commitment to improving competitiveness.[103]

99 P Serra, 'La Politica de Competencia en Chile' 10 *Revista de Analisis Economico* 63–88 (1995).
100 OECD (2004a), above n 29.
101 EIU (2008), above n 94, at 2.
102 OECD (2004b), above n 29.
103 *Ibid*, at 55.

Conduct that creates or maintains monopoly power, such as hard-core cartel behavior, is illegal per se under the FLEC. There are no efficiency or small-business defenses. The CFC maximum cartel fine is tied to the level of wages; in 2004 the maximum corporate fine was $1.6 million, but in egregious cases the upper limit is 10 per cent of a company's annual sales or assets. There are no explicit fining guidelines, but section 38 of the FLEC says that the CFC must take into consideration the size of the market, amount of damage, recidivism, and ability to pay.[104] Individual criminal charges may be imposed if a cartel affects markets for consumer necessities, or for obstruction of justice. 'In practice … the CFC has not typically imposed severe sanctions in horizontal conduct cases.'[105]

From 1993 to 2002, the CFC handled 428 monopoly or horizontal restraint cases (39 per year), of which 59 per cent resulted in sanctions, recommendations or settlements.[106] Only about 40 of these cases dealt with hard-core cartels.[107] During 1993–2002, the CFC imposed fines on 493 violators totaling $31 million, ie an average of $2.8 million per year or $63,000 per company.[108] The number of such decisions is rising over time, but merger decisions are four times as numerous.[109]

Much of the CFC's enforcement in the 1990s was directed at industry associations. Prior the mid-1980s, these associations had negotiated prices with the Ministry of the Economy, and these habits proved difficult to change. Other CFC cases involved small businesses that had colluded to cope with the power of large firms. In the late 1990s, extraterritorial conduct by the global lysine and citric acid cartels was punished.

The OECD *Peer Review* contained a number of recommendations regarding CFC procedures.[110] Bi-partisan proposals in the Congress in 2005 led to major amendments of the FLEC which became effective in June 2006.[111] The CFC is now empowered to make dawn raids without prior notification. Also, the CFC now has a US/EU-style corporate amnesty program for the first whistleblower to come forward in a hard-core cartel case; later arrivals can receive discounts of 50 per cent, 30 per cent, and 20 per cent on their fines for their additional, significant cooperation. Finally, the upper limit on fines was raised by 400 per cent to $62 million, and for recidivists to 10 per cent of annual sales or assets (whichever is larger).

[104] *Ibid*, at 65.
[105] ABA, above n 4, at 4.
[106] OECD (2004b), above n 29, at 11.
[107] *Ibid*, at 51–52.
[108] *Ibid*, at 47.
[109] *Ibid*, at 49.
[110] *Ibid*.
[111] Jorge A Sanchez-Davila, 'Mexico Takes Important Steps Forward in the Combat of Cartels and Implementation of Leniency Programs' (2008) *Global Competition Review: Antitrust Review of the Americas: Special Issue* 1.

V. Global Antitrust Enforcement Patterns

The previous section discussed the legal authority and procedures to control cartels in general in seven jurisdictions. This section presents original data specifically on prosecutions of *international* cartels, many of them global in scope, in the same seven jurisdictions. The focus is on the actual pattern of anti-cartel enforcement by both government agencies and private suits. These data help to develop a fuller understanding of the potential for effective cartel deterrence in the long run, and of Latin America's role in assisting in that deterrence.

A. Modern Private International Cartels Data

In common with nearly all other empirical studies on cartels, this chapter considers only *detected* cartels. These cartels were clandestine, and their members typically attempted to cover up or destroy evidence of their meetings and communications.[112] Cartel studies generally conclude that only about 10 per cent to 30 per cent of all such conspiracies are detected and punished.[113] Studies that depend on detected cartels may suffer from sample selection bias.[114] Undetected cartels are probably more durable than detected cartels and may differ in some other economic characteristics.

The sample consists of 433 cartels.[115] Seventy-four per cent of these cartels have had several participants indicted or found guilty[116]; the greatest amount of information is available for these cases. Ten per cent of the cartels' investigations have been closed (in some cases because of a statute of limitations), and 16 per cent are still being investigated. All private cartels with international membership that were detected between January 1990 and December 2007 are included in the sample.[117]

The number of companies that have participated in international cartels exceeds 4,800.[118] By far the largest number (3,433 or 72 per cent) are headquartered in Europe. The Netherlands is the world leader, followed by Germany, France, the UK, and Italy. Despite its long history as an antitrust jurisdiction, nearly 500 US companies have been suspected or convicted of price fixing. Next in order of importance are Japan and Korea. Companies from Africa, Latin

[112] Spratling, above n 18.

[113] John M Connor, 'Optimal Deterrence and International Cartels' (paper at the 4th International Industrial Organization Conference, April 15, 2007c), at Table 1.

[114] Andrew R Dick, 'When Are Cartels Stable Contracts?' 39 *Journal of Law and Economics* 241–83 (1996).

[115] John M Connor, 'Latin America and the Control of International Cartels' (SSRN Working Paper, April 14, 2008), at Table 1 (available from the author).

[116] *Ibid*, at Table 2.

[117] John M Connor, 'Private International Cartels' (Spreadsheet, December 2007d).

[118] John M Connor (2008), above n 115, at Table 10.

America and low-income economies seldom participate in international price collusion. More than 200 companies have been participants in multiple international cartels: 53 were convicted in *five* or more, and 17 in *10* or more separate violations.[119]

Approximately 275 executives have been accused or convicted of illegal involvement in international cartels. A large number (180 or 72 per cent) are citizens of countries that have criminal price-fixing laws, ie Australia, Canada, Germany, and the United States; most were cited for national price-fixing violations. Almost all the remaining individuals hail from Japan, Korea, The Netherlands, and the UK; a majority of these persons were convicted because of their involvement in global cartels. In total, cartel managers have paid $192 million in fines and have been sentenced to 764 months in prison; 98 per cent of these penalties were imposed in the United States.

B. General Trends in Enforcement

The acceleration in annual rates of detection of international cartels is quite impressive. Recall that 'detection' is the first date that a formal investigation becomes publicly known, which in some cases is also the date that sanctions are levied. Almost 33 international cartels were detected each year during 2004–07, a rate five times higher than 1990–95.[120] As this chapter will show, Latin American antitrust authorities have also launched an era of notable anti-cartel activism since 2003.

Another trend is the decline in the duration of detected international cartels.[121] In the early 1990s, the average cartels endured for more than 100 months, but longevity has declined steadily to a time barely half as long in 2004–07. The duration of international cartels averages 4.5 years.[122] The longevity of global cartels is much higher, but that of Latin American cartels is particularly brief. With very few exceptions, Latin American authorities have avoided prosecuting global cartels.

The prosecutorial success of the US DOJ and the EC's DG-COMP appears to have encouraged other national agencies to focus more resources on anti-cartel enforcement, to adopt new laws strengthening investigatory powers or raising sanctions, and to reorganize the antitrust authorities. Antitrust authorities have been goaded into action by the disrespect shown by cartelists to competition laws and those who enforce them. Speech after speech by top antitrust officials betrays a visceral antipathy for global price-fixers. The global conspirators are consistently described in highly emotive language as brazen, cold-blooded, contemptuous of the law, disdainful of their customers, and eager to ignore company antitrust compliance policies.[123]

119 *Ibid*, at Table 14.
120 *Ibid*, at Fig 1.
121 *Ibid*, at Figs 5–8.
122 *Ibid*, at Table 9.
123 Hammond (2002), above n 44; Spratling, above n 18; Monti, above n 19.

C. The US Department of Justice

Once the newly-appointed head of the Antitrust Division in 1992–93 recognized the threat of global conspiracies, the agency reordered its priorities fairly quickly. Beginning in the late 1990s, about four-fifths of the DOJ's fines for criminal price fixing have been imposed on non-US firms. The use of personal fines and prison sentences has also escalated, many of them applied to non-US citizens.

During 1990–2007, the Antitrust Division convicted 67 international price-fixing crimes.[124] Starting with *Lysine* in September 1996, the most important US price-fixing convictions have been global conspiracies.[125] Thirty-six such cartels were fully or partially prosecuted during 1996–2007. About 200 companies have been fined by the DOJ for international price fixing since 1995. The DOJ has obtained corporate fines totaling $4.1 billion, of which 90 per cent was from participants in global cartels.[126] It is likely that the future number of international cartel cases will continue to be high. In the early 2000s the DOJ had about 100 grand juries empanelled on price-fixing allegations, of which half were examining international cartels[127]; in 2007 there were 130 such investigations.[128]

In general, the fines collected from individual criminal conspirators are modest compared with their corporate salaries, but prison sentences are becoming more severe. Historically, the DOJ sought prison sentences for individuals in a minority of price-fixing cases; the rate was 23 per cent of all price-fixing cases during 1970–99.[129] But in the case of *global* cartels, the DOJ has obtained prison sentences in about 50 per cent of the cases since 1995. Since 1990, for all types of cartels, more than 300 individuals have been given criminal fines and 260 received prison sentences.[130] During 2000–07, prison sentences averaged 16 months per individual, and half of the prison sentences exceed the felony level of more than 12 months. On average, about three executives plead guilty or are indicted per global cartel, but the number and severity of prison sentences has been increasing since the mid-1990s. This policy reflects an oft-repeated belief by DOJ prosecutors that prison sentences are the most effective tool for deterring cartels.

The conviction and imprisonment of non-US executives for criminal price fixing by US authorities is an extraordinary development in antitrust enforcement history. The US DOJ has arranged guilty pleas from more than 50 top

[124] Connor (2008), above n 115, at Table 5.
[125] *In re Amino Acid Lysine Antitrust Litigation*, 918 F Supp 1190 (ND Ill 1996).
[126] Connor (2008), above n 115, at Table 6.
[127] Pate, above n 19.
[128] Gerald F Masoudi, 'Cartel Enforcement in the United States (and Beyond)' (Speech at the Cartel Conference, Budapest, Hungary, Feb 16, 2007).
[129] Connor (2007b), above n 18.
[130] John M Connor *et al*, 'DOJ Cartel Enforcement: Appraisal and Proposals' in Albert Foer (ed), *The Antitrust Transition* (forthcoming, 2008), at Table 1.

executives who were nationals of about 20 foreign countries.[131] Many of these executives worked in the United States, but some traveled from their residences abroad to submit to the jurisdiction of the US court, plead guilty and pay fines. One reason for foreigners' willingness to serve time in US prisons is that if they reside or even *pass through* countries that have criminal statutes for price fixing, they may be extradited to the United States.[132] The United States has explicit treaties with Canada, Ireland and Japan that permit extradition for antitrust violations, though none of these has yet been invoked.[133] In 2002, Interpol added US antitrust fugitives to its 'Red Notice' watch list for the first time. When foreign executives plead guilty for price fixing, they are frequently granted the right of free passage across US borders for their cooperation.

In summary, the financial penalties applied by the US DOJ to global price fixers in the late 1990s were unprecedented in their severity. Despite an increasing number of amnesties, average corporate fines for members of global cartels after the mid-1990s were many times higher than the fines collected earlier. While individual fines remained modest on the whole, managers of global conspiracies were more than twice as likely to receive prison sentences as managers of domestic conspiracies, and the length of the sentences has risen markedly. The main reasons for the escalation in fines in the late 1990s were the extraordinary rise in the maximum fine levels allowed, the expanded size of the markets affected, the high overcharge rates, the longevity of many of the conspiracies, and, if truth be told, the rising intolerance of the judicial system for 'thieves dressed in expensive suits'. This rise is especially notable in light of the fact that, correcting for inflation, average corporate fines were essentially unchanged for the first 90 years of the 20th century.

D. Canadian Competition Bureau

Canadian cartel-enforcement policy shifted in the mid-1990s. Prosecution of large global cartels began in 1998 with the lysine and citric acid cases.[134] The fines imposed on these two cartels were almost double the amount the Canadian Competition Bureau (CCB) had collected from all other cases in 1990–97. By mid-2007 Canada had collected US $167 million in fines from 20 global cartels, most of which followed quickly after parallel US convictions. In addition, five other international cartel convictions brought the Canadian total to $199 million.

131 Scott D Hammond, 'When Calculating the Costs and Benefits of Applying for Corporate Amnesty, How Do You Put a Price Tag on an Individual's Freedom?', speech at the 15th Annual National Institute on White Collar Crime, San Francisco, CA, March 8, 2001a; Masoudi, above n 128.

132 Nanni, above n 19.

133 In 2004 the first Japanese manager was indicted for a criminal cartel offense.

134 Connor, above n 18.

Only one person, the CEO of a Canadian vitamin manufacturer, has been incarcerated. This sentence of 90 days was the first such punishment in many years. Three more cartel managers, from Germany, Switzerland and Japan, have paid fines for their roles in the citric acid, vitamins and sorbates cartels.[135]

Although Canada has a relatively small national market and many of the convicted firms sold cartelized products only through exporting (thus owning few, if any, assets in Canada that could have been seized in the event of non-payment of fines), it has been able to mount a surprisingly effective anti-cartel campaign using modest enforcement resources and simple rules for fines. Canada is a model for many smaller industrialized countries that have tough anti-cartel laws on their books yet have small enforcement resources. Unlike many other areas of law enforcement, the returns to Canada's treasury far exceed the CCB's budget.

E. European Commission

In 2005, the European Commission surpassed the DOJ in the amount of fines imposed on international cartels. It fined 89 international cartels US $15 billion during 1990–2007, of which 53 were intra-EU and 36 global.[136] Lysine was the first global cartel fined in the 1990s. This fine, of US $110 million, was the fifth largest ever imposed by the Commission. In 2001, decisions were reached in four huge cartel cases with total fines of $1.115 billion—a record amount for any antitrust authority. In 2007 the Commission had a backlog of over 100 amnesty applications, which makes it likely that large fines will continue for the next few years. To handle the backlog, the Commission is about to institute a process of 'direct settlement' with corporate cartelists that is similar to the DOJ's practice of plea bargaining, which exchanges inculpatory information for partial leniency.

F. National Competition Authorities of Europe

This section examines the recent but accelerating number of prosecutions of international cartels by national competition authorities (NCAs) in Europe that are members of the EU-27. Since 1990, each of the members of the EU has enacted competition laws that are compatible with the EU Treaty. All new members have had to have effective NCAs before joining. Some NCAs pre-date the Treaty, but all NCAs have developed increasingly convergent anti-cartel laws and policies. For many years the dividing line between Brussels' anti-cartel activities and those of the NCAs was unclear. Before 1999, an investigation by an NCA that involved some non-domestic firms could be pre-empted by the Commission.

135 *Ibid.*

136 Connor (2008), above n 115, at Tables 5 and 6.

The devolution of the Commission's cartel-prosecution activities to its Member States began in 1999, and became formalized in 2003 with the establishment of the European Competition Network (ECN). Now the NCAs can investigate cartels with significant, but not predominantly cross-Member State sales. Brussels retains jurisdiction over global cartels and those with large cross-national EU market effects.

These NCAs have fined a total of 112 international cartels, issued six cease-and-desist orders and, as of late 2007, were investigating another 20 international cartels.[137] These 138 cartels comprise about one-fourth of the Private International Cartels spreadsheet data set. The NCAs' total fines amount to $6.8 billion.[138] The total amount of fines imposed is larger than in the United States—an impressive amount given the restricted size of these national economies and the relatively few years of active enforcement.

The first international cartel to be fined by a Member State was that in *Glass Containers*, a case reported by the national antitrust authority of Italy in July 1997.[139] Italy has been the most aggressive Member State in prosecuting international cartels—29 in all. The national antitrust authorities in The Netherlands, France, Hungary and Germany have also become energetic in prosecuting international cartels—42 cases with fines. All of The Netherlands authority's cases have been launched since mid-2001, shortly after its investigative powers were strengthened. Much of its work is consumed by a major scandal involving bid rigging by more than 2,000 construction companies.

G. Latin American Cartels and Penalties

In a global context, the antitrust authorities of Latin America are small players in prosecuting international cartels. During 1990–2007, Latin American antitrust agencies investigated or penalized a total of 21 international cartels, most of them in markets for intermediate industrial inputs or services.[140] Of those 21, 16 operated in Latin America proper; they were investigated or prosecuted by Brazil (eight cartels), Argentina (three), Chile (two), and Mexico, Columbia and El Salvador (one cartel each). In addition, two global cartels were fined by Brazil and Mexico (*Vitamins* and *Lysine*).[141] The *Vitamins* conviction by Brazil was the result of a long and difficult investigation.[142] The affected sales of these 21 cartels exceed US $20 billion. As of late 2007, at least three more global cartels were under investigation by CADE: the *Lysine* cartel had global sales of US $1.9 billion and

137 *Ibid*, at Table 5.
138 *Ibid*, at Table 6.
139 AGCM, *Produttori di vetro cavo*, 12 June 1997.
140 Connor (2008), above n 115, at Table 11.
141 See Connor (2007a) above n 6, at pp 379 and 390, respectively.
142 Jorge Nemr, 'Brazil Government Censures Vitamin Cartel' (June 2007) *International Enforcement Law Reporter*.

sales of about US $160 million in Latin America; the *Air-Insulated Switchgear*[143] cartel had about US $1.8 billion in Latin American affected sales; and the huge *Air Cargo*[144] case generated US $30 to US $40 billion in Latin American affected commerce.

In addition to these 21 cartels, another 80 or more global cartels have been detected by other jurisdictions outside Latin America, most of which fixed prices in Latin America. Affected sales in Latin America from global conspiracies were probably $100 to $150 billion. Thus, a total of $150 to $210 billion in affected sales in Latin America can be attributed to *known* international cartels with either regional or global scope. Detection rates are 10 per cent to 33 per cent, so total Latin American affected sales of all cartels is somewhere between $0.5 and $2 trillion.

VI. Assessing Latin American Cartel Enforcement

To assess the enforcement efforts of the four leading antitrust authorities of Latin America, I collected information on the resources available and the enforcement outcomes. Like Hoj,[145] I examined such resources as the budgets and employees assigned to antitrust law activities, the availability of cartel leniency programs and variations on them, and the size of potential and actual monetary and penal sanctions on corporations and individuals convicted of hard-core cartel conduct. In addition, I assembled cross-country data on the number of cartel cases processed annually (with special attention to international cartels), the backlogs of such cases, cartel fines imposed, and the composition of the authorities' professional staffs.[146]

A. Brazil

By nearly all measures, Brazil has the largest and most effective anti cartel authority in Latin America. Antitrust authorities employ almost 400 persons and have by far the largest budgets. However, the proportion of employees with advanced education is relatively low by Latin American norms, and the budgets are quite low relative to Brazil's huge GDP.

CADE and its allied agencies operate under a 1994 law that has frequently been amended to give wider powers and other improvements. Moreover, recently it has overtly emphasized an increased focus on cartel cases rather than merger

143 See Connor, above n 118.
144 *Ibid.*
145 Hoj, above n 30.
146 Connor (2008), above n 115, at Table 13.

control.[147] Dawn raids have been permitted as of 2003, and Brazil was the first jurisdiction to implement an amnesty program (2003) and a partial leniency program (2007). In general, Brazil fines the largest number of hard-core cartels annually, imposes the highest average corporate cartel fines in Latin America, and is the only one regularly to fine cartel managers.[148] Fines are rising over time. Imprisonment is a possible sanction (up to five years), but this option appears never to have been used.

The great majority of cartel cases pursued by CADE consist of highly localized markets, such as gasoline or LPG in one city, or bid rigging on medical services.[149] However, CADE is clearly in the forefront of prosecuting large-scale international cartels organized within Brazil, and is nearly unique in Latin America in prosecuting global cartels.[149a] The highly injurious *Generic Pharmaceuticals*, *Toy Manufacturers*, *Industrial Gasses*, *Blood Products*, and *Sao Paulo Crushed Rock*[150] cases each involved large numbers of well-defended multinational companies; fines in the two decided cases amounted to $120 million. Brazil is the only antitrust authority on the continent to have investigated and convicted members of the vast global *Vitamins* cartel.[151] CADE has also been investigating the global *Lysine* cartel for the past five years or more. In 2007, CADE staged raids on companies suspected of price fixing in two global cartels that are believed to have very large affected sales: *Air-Insulated High-Voltage Switchgear* and *Air Cargo*.[152] Despite a high probability of injuries to their economies, no other Latin American antitrust authority has been reported to have commenced investigations into these two global cartels.

B. Argentina

In terms of budget and employees, Argentina's CNDC is the smallest antitrust authority of the four Latin American countries selected. Even accounting for increases in personnel in the 2000s, the CNDC has the slimmest resources relative to its GDP. It has the ability to launch dawn raids, but has no leniency program.[153] Most of its activities are devoted to merger control. Consequently, the CNDC typically prosecutes only one or two hard-core cartels each year, and imposes negligible cartel fines or sentences of imprisonment.

The year 2005 was a notable exception to Argentina's normally relaxed approach to cartel enforcement. In that year, two vast international cartels—*Cement*

[147] OECD (2007a), above n 28, at 2.
[148] Connor (2008), above n 115, at Table 13.
[149] OECD (2007a), above n 28.
[149a] Connor (2008), above n 115, at Table 11.
[150] See Connor, above n 118.
[151] Nemr, above n 142.
[152] Connor (2008), above n 115, at Table 11.
[153] OECD (2005a), above n 28.

and *Medical Oxygen*[154]—were fined a total of $133 million.[155] These cartels incorporated several powerful multinational companies with long histories of price-fixing convictions in these industries in other jurisdictions. The CNDC expert in charge of these cases was subsequently transferred to another ministry, so comparable high-profile prosecutions may be unique for some time.

C. Chile

Chile's current Competition Law was passed in 1973, making it the oldest in the region. Chile's antitrust authority (FNE) has the second smallest resources of the four Latin American cases examined in this chapter.[156] It is also the only one of the four agencies that does not participate in the OECD's Competition Committee. Yet for the size of its economy, Chile's FNE is almost three times the size of Brazil's three federal agencies.[157] In general, FNE appears to spend the greatest share of its time on merger control rather than cartel activity. A very large proportion of allegations of price fixing result in cases concluded without sanctions, suggesting that there is a high burden of proof on prosecutors in Chile.

The number of decisions on horizontal restraint cases averages two per year, and the average annual cartel fine is a very low $50,000. Until the maximum fine was increased in 2004, Chile's cap was unlikely to provide even minimal deterrence for the typical large-scale international cartel. Without the modern tools of cartel investigation common in other jurisdictions, the FNE is not equipped to uncover or punish international cartels. The one such cartel that was fined was *Medical Oxygen*; participants were fined about $300,000.[158] The only other international case, *Gasoline Distribution*, was closed after many years of investigation.[159] Chile has neither investigated nor punished any global cartels.

D. Mexico

By Latin American norms, Mexico has the largest and best-funded antitrust authority. Relative to national GDP, the CFC's budget is more than four times as high as Brazil's. The CFC appears to have no authority to perform dawn raids. Until 2004, the maximum fine for corporate cartel members was low by international antitrust

[154] *CNDC v Loma Negra and others* (2005), Resolution 124/05 from the Secretary of Technical Coordination; *CNDC v Air Liquide and Others* (2005), Resolution 119/05 from the Secretary of Technical Coordination.

[155] Connor (2008), above n 115, at Table 11.

[156] *Ibid*, at Table 13.

[157] Note that the resources of Chile's extensive regional competition commissions are not included.

[158] *Medical Oxygen Case*; Connor (2008), above n 115, at Table 11.

[159] OECD 'Competition Law and Policy in Chile. A Peer Review (Paris, Organization of Economic Co-Operation and Devlopment, 2004), at 38–40.

standards ($1.6 million), as was the maximum fine for managers ($30,000). Cartel managers have no fear of imprisonment.

Both political parties in the Mexican Congress appear to be prodding the CFC to be more aggressive in fighting cartels; in 2004 the maximum cartel fine was raised to $6.2 million, and in 2006 an amnesty program was authorized. Despite these increased powers, the CFC penalized only 10 hard-core cartels in 2004–06.[160] Rather, the authority seems to be preoccupied with mergers and time-consuming monopoly cases.[161]

For all these reasons, the CFC has done little to attack hard-core cartels in general, or international cartels in particular. It has rendered only four cartel decisions per year since it was founded, and there is no upward trend. The CFC does not publish the level of fines imposed for antitrust violations—the only one of the four authorities that does not. The sole known fine imposed on an international cartelist is about $200,000 for ADM's leading role in *Lysine*.

E. Private Suits

Settlements in private antitrust damages suits are the major form of monetary penalties on international cartels in Canada and the United States. Despite the higher government fines imposed by the EC and the EU's NCAs, because of the near absence of private rights of action, the EU has not been as successful as North America in imposing high monetary penalties on international cartels operating in Western Europe. In the rest of the world antitrust penalties are negligible. Even from an *ex post* point of view, no international cartel has been required to disgorge 100 per cent of its illegal profits.[162] Therefore, absent government fines far in excess of the current legal maximums, private rights of action are essential to achieving optimal (*ex ante*) deterrence of international cartels. This statement applies with even greater force to global price-fixing schemes.

Information on the results of private suits is especially difficult to assemble, because most suits end in out-of-court settlements, many of which are not fully reported; very few involve trials with final published judgments.[163] As a result, relative to government fines, antitrust settlement amounts are significantly

[160] OECD (2007b), above n 29.

[161] David Luhnow, 'The Secrets of the World's Richest Man—Mexico's Carlos Slim Makes his Billions the Old-Fashioned Way: Monopolies', *The Wall Street Journal*, August 4, 2007; Dow Jones, 'Mexico's Anti-Trust Agency Starts Mobile Telephony Mkt Probe', *Dow Jones International News*, Nov 30, 2007.

[162] Connor (2006), above n 43, at 195–223; John M Connor, 'The Great Global Price-Fixing Conspiracy: Sanctions and Deterrence' (Oct 2006a), 4 *Concurrences. Revue des Droits de la Concurrences* 17–20; Connor (2007c), above n 113.

[163] Most large settlements do get reported in the business press or in company financial reports. If the private suit is a class action, there is some information available because many of the opinions of the supervising judges are published on Web-based search engines. The results of suits threatened or launched by firms that opt out of class actions are often unreported in any public source. On the difficulties of gathering information on private antitrust suits, see Robert H Lande and Joshua P Davis,

under-reported. Nevertheless, thorough searches of business and legal news sources turned up satisfactory information on most of the 114 private damages suits against members of international cartels from 1990 to 2007.[163a] All but four of the 114 suits in the sample were filed in US and Canadian courts. Of the 72 US suits, 22 concerned global and 48 regional (NAFTA area) cartels. In Canada, at least 21 global cartels were prosecuted by affected customers, and 13 more international cartels that were regional in geographic scope were prosecuted by Canadian customers. One private price-fixing suit was won by Australian buyers of animal-grade bulk vitamins in 2006—the first such case in Australia's legal history.

Information on settlement amounts is available for 92 of the 114 suits, but a score are still being negotiated. In the United States, private parties have recovered at least $19.7 billion from international cartel defendants.[164] That includes $13.6 billion in the global cartel cases (of which $3 to $5 billion is from *Vitamins* manufacturers) and $6.0 billion to US plaintiffs injured by North American cartels. In Canada the respective amounts are US $164 and $8.7 million. An amazing fact is that private plaintiffs in North America were awarded *about five times* the amount collected in fines by the US and Canadian Governments.

The contrast with international cartel penalties in Europe is stark. In the European Economic Area, the EU and its Member States imposed an impressive $21.3 billion in fines on intra-EU international cartels ($15.8 billion) or on global cartels that affected EEA markets ($5.4 billion). In contrast, restitution or private recoveries in Europe amounted to a paltry $200 million or less.

There is virtually no information about the number or outcomes of private cartel suits outside North America. Private suits are permitted in Japan, Taiwan, Mexico, Australia and several EU Member States, but are rare in practice.[165] These jurisdictions typically permit only single damages, do not allow discovery, disallow class actions and make the plaintiffs pay court costs, have high burdens of proof, and award puny damages to plaintiffs. The absence of private suits outside of North America has a negative effect on deterrence of global cartels, because only 40 per cent of the global injuries caused by such cartels occur there.[166] At present, buyers in nearly all other parts of the world have no recourse to private compensation in their local court systems.

Private suits are legally permitted in two of the four Latin American jurisdictions that are the subjects of this chapter.[167] Except for a small number of cases

'Benefits From Private Antitrust Enforcement: An Analysis of Forty Cases' *University of San Francisco Law Review* (2008).

[163a] Connor (2008), above n 115, at Table 5.
[164] *Ibid*, at Table 6.
[165] Connor (2007b), above n 18.
[166] Connor (2008), above n 115, at Table 10.
[167] *Ibid*, at Table 13.

in Brazil, private antitrust suits are practically unknown in Latin America.[168] The principal barriers to launching such suits are the absence of legal traditions and mechanisms for aggregating large numbers of small claims and of something akin to pre-trial discovery.[169]

F. Empirical Analysis of Cartel Deterrence

Even from an *ex post* perspective, penalties on international cartels are sub-optimal. Because of positive skewness, we focus on the medians of three ratios.[170] The general findings for all regions are: *damages* represented by the price overcharge averaged 19 per cent of affected sales of the cartel in all the jurisdictions in which they functioned; monetary antitrust *penalties* typically represented 3.3 per cent of sales; and penalties recouped 34 per cent of cartel damages.

Three subgroups are of interest. First, let us consider the effectiveness of antitrust penalties imposed in North America, which is widely regarded as having the most effective antitrust enforcement in the world. The median degree of harm (ratio of damages to affected sales) of North American regional cartels was 30 per cent. Private and government monetary penalties accrued to 9.1 per cent of affected sales, which is interesting to some perhaps, but irrelevant for deterrence analysis. The key finding is that the typical penalty recouped only 47.5 per cent of damages in the United States and Canada. On average, cartelization was profitable in the region with the most severe laws and penalty structures in the world.

Secondly, the fines imposed by Latin American antitrust authorities are pitifully low relative to either affected sales (4.9 per cent on average) or to damages (less than 1 per cent). This sub-sample is quite small, but even the highest penalty/damages ratio was only 8 per cent.

Thirdly, the penalties on the sample of global cartels are quite revealing. In general, it was global cartels that were the most severely penalized in 1990–2007, US and Canadian fines alone disgorged 42–49 per cent of jurisdictional damages on average. But then one must add the generally larger settlements obtained by private plaintiffs; for global cartels, North American courts approved median recoveries that amounted to about 103 per cent of Canadian and US overcharges. All told, global cartelists paid penalties that averaged 150 per cent of North American damages. Recovery of greater than single damages is impressive, and from an *ex post* vantage point would appear to provide specific and general deterrence. However, when one considers that global cartels make the great majority of their illegal profits outside of North America, this 'deterrence'

[168] Daniel A Crane, 'Private Enforcement Against International Cartels in Latin America: A US Perspective', ch XV in this book.

[169] *Ibid.*

[170] Connor (2008), above n 115, at Table 8.

is no longer supra-deterrent: only 61 per cent of global cartel profits were disgorged.[171] Moreover, if the probability of detection is indeed in the 13 per cent to 17 per cent range, as most scholars believe, then *ex ante* deterrence is far below optimal.

The absence of high fines or private damages suits outside North America and Europe contributes to the inability of contemporary antitrust regimes to deter international cartels. Although discussions continue, access to treble damages suits in US courts by injured buyers abroad is far off.[172] Improvements in this regard among Asian and Latin American jurisdictions will not only benefit local populations, but also will help discourage the harmful effects of global cartels.

VII. Conclusion

International cartelists face investigations, possible fines, and other monetary penalties in a score of national and supranational jurisdictions. Brazil, South Korea, Australia and several Member States of the EU have increasingly active anti-cartel agencies. However, the world still depends largely on the three jurisdictions with the greatest experience in combating international cartels: the United States, Canada, and the EU. Latin American antitrust authorities play a small role in punishing international cartels, particularly those with a global reach. This is a pity, because international cartels have had large sales in Latin America and cause great economic harm on the continent. Optimal cartel deterrence cannot be achieved without active anti-cartel enforcement in Latin America.

By all measures, of the four Latin American antitrust authorities examined in this chapter, Brazil's CADE has been far and away the most effective in dealing with international price fixing since 1990, and Chile's FNE has been the least effective. The relative success of Brazil is not explained by its age or the quality of its enforcement resources (Chile's and Mexico's authorities rank higher in these regards). Factors that appear to differentiate CADE from the other Latin American competition law authorities are:

— A high degree of independence from ministries that support business.
— Government support for making cartels the highest enforcement priority.
— A critical mass of trained lawyers and economists.

[171] In the absence of pre-judgment interest, the forces of inflation and the time value of money further work against deterrence. For an illustration, see John M Connor 'The Great Global Price-Fixing Conspiracy: Sanctions and Deterrence', *Concurrences: Revue des droit de la concurrences* (Oct 2006) 4: 17–20.

[172] Connor and Bush, above n 3.

— Adherence to the goal of specific deterrence.
— A high limit and objective but flexible rules for setting corporate fines.
— A commitment to punishing individual cartel managers.
— Adoption of modern amnesty, leniency, and other proven cartel-discovery methods.
— A willingness to give weight to domestic harm caused by foreign firms in choosing cases to investigate for cartel conduct.

Continuing high rates of cartel discoveries and evidence of rising cartel recidivism suggest that the need for aggressive cartel enforcement is as high as ever. The phenomenon of historically high and highly-touted monetary sanctions imposed on international cartels in the past decade is obscuring major deficiencies in world anti-cartel efforts. While Brazil's anti-cartel enforcement is on balance the most effective in Latin America, future modifications must be considered to ensure that its goal of optimal deterrence can be reached.

First, CADE is rapidly approaching the maximum permissible price-fixing fine. In any case, by limiting corporate fines to 30 per cent of a company's annual sales, CADE cannot hope to recover all of a cartelist's illegal profits, even in a typical international cartel.[173]

Consideration ought to be given to altering the way in which fines can be calculated, particularly for egregiously harmful cartels. For example, a flexible cap of either 30 per cent of a cartel's affected sales or of treble damages would provide for fines with greater deterrence power. Secondly, increases in the maximum corporate penalties by governments alone may be insufficient to deter cartel formation. The failure of compensatory private suits to take hold outside of North America, and the near absence of large fines in most Latin American jurisdictions, also casts doubt on the power of current penalties to deter recidivism by international cartels. Like the European Union, CADE and other Latin American antitrust authorities should be advocating changes in local court rules that would facilitate private rights of action by the victims of cartels. In order to get the greatest discovery effects, private suits should be allowed to proceed independently from government prosecutions. Thirdly, CADE and its sister agencies can expand the list of available incentives for destabilizing operating cartels. Techniques include

[173] A typical international cartel historically has had a median average overcharge of 31% in the cartelized market and a duration of about six years (Levenstein and Suslow (2004), above n 26; at 59–153). Modern cartels have similar characteristics (Connor and Helmers (2006), above n 34). Therefore, a specialized (single product) participant in a typical international cartel tends to generate illegal monopoly profits equal to 186% (31% × 6) of a single year's total revenues. A maximum Brazilian fine would recoup only one-eighth of the company's cartel profits. Of course, if the cartelist has many lines of business in Brazil or large sales outside Brazil's borders, then the maximum fine rule will not constrain a compensatory fine. On the other hand, one can argue that Brazil's fining rule discriminates against small, specialized firms.

fine surcharges for recidivism and duration, 'Amnesty Plus' fine discounts, and whistleblower payments.[174]

Without significant increases in cartel detection, in the levels of expected fines or civil settlements, or expansion in the standing of buyers to seek compensation, international price fixing will remain rational business conduct for decades to come.

[174] William E Kovacic, 'Private Monitoring and Antitrust Enforcement: Paying Informants to Reveal Cartels' 69 *George Washington Law Review* 766–97 (2001).

Chapter XV

Private Enforcement Against International Cartels in Latin America: A US Perspective

DANIEL A CRANE*

A recent empirical study estimates that from 1990 to the end of 2005, 283 private international cartels were discovered and that the overcharges from these cartels totaled $500 billion.[1] Estimates of the percentage of all detected cartels range from one in six or seven to one in 10.[2] If the one in 10 number is correct, that would mean that overcharges from international cartels in the last 15 years were $5 trillion, or about $330 billion per year. Even assuming that the detection rate is higher today due to the success of the US Justice Department's leniency program and stepped up anti-cartel enforcement around the world, it is clear that international cartels exact hundreds of millions of dollars in illegal overcharges from consumers around the world every year. Indeed, as John Connor shows in his chapter in this volume, international cartels impose overcharges that exceed those of purely domestic cartels.[3]

The United States historically has been the leader in private anti-cartel enforcement. Features that make cartel enforcement in US courts attractive include class actions, broad discovery rights, a judiciary receptive to antitrust claims, a well-developed body of cartel law, liberality in proof of damages, and the treble damages remedy. As long as the US played a dominant role in private anti-international cartel

* Professor, Benjamin N Cardozo School of Law.

[1] John M Connor and C Gustav Helmers, 'Statistics on Modern Private International Cartels 1990–2005', (2006) <http://www.agecon.purdue.edu/working_papers/workingpaper.connor.11.10.06.pdf>.

[2] Sentencing Options: Hearing Before the United States Sentencing Commission (July 15, 1986), available in *United States Sentencing Commission: Unpublished Public Hearings 1986*, at 15 (1988) (Statement of Assistant Attorney General Douglas Ginsburg) (estimating that only one in 10 cartels is discovered); OECD Directorate for Financial, Fiscal and Enterprise Affairs, Competition Committee, *Report on the Nature and Impact of Hard Core Cartels and Sanctions Against Cartels Under National Competition Laws* (April 9, 2002), available at <http://www.oecd.org/dataoecd/16/20/2081831.pdf> at 3, 13 (citing Peter G Bryant and E Woodrow Eckard, 'Price Fixing: The Probability of Getting Caught' 73 *Review Of Economics & Statistics* 531 (1991)) (estimating that one in six or seven cartels is caught and prosecuted).

[3] John M Connor, 'Latin America and the Control of International Cartels', ch XIV in this book.

enforcement, there seemed to be little need to encourage the development of private cartel enforcement in other countries.

However, a recent development in US law makes US courts inhospitable to claims by consumers who made their purchases in a foreign country from an international cartel that also operated in the United States. In *F Hoffmann-La Roche Ltd v Empagran SA*,[4] the United States Supreme Court held that plaintiffs who bought the price-fixed goods in a foreign country cannot sue in the United States unless they can show that their particular claim arises from the cartel's anti-competitive effect in the United States. Although it remains to be seen how the lower courts will interpret *Empagran's* new test, it seems unlikely that US courts will continue to be friendly to claims by foreign purchasers.

This paper explores the need for enhanced private anti-cartel enforcement in Latin America in light of *Empagran* and what we have learned about international cartels from contemporaneous economic scholarship. *Empagran* creates both a need and an opportunity for private anti-cartel enforcement in Latin America. Contrary to the fears of many opponents of private enforcement, however, such enhancement of private antitrust enforcement need not extend beyond cartels or open a 'Pandora's box' of private antitrust litigation abuses.

Part I of the chapter surveys the *Empagran* decision, paying particular attention to the role of *amicus curiae* briefs by foreign governments. Seven foreign governments (Germany, Belgium, Canada, Japan, Great Britain and Northern Ireland, Ireland, and The Netherlands) submitted four *amicus curiae* briefs, all of them urging the Court to adopt a rule restrictive on the rights of foreigners to sue in US courts. Several of the briefs argued that allowing foreign purchasers to sue in the US could stifle the development of private anti-cartel enforcement in other countries. For example, the brief submitted on behalf of Great Britain, Northern Ireland, Ireland, and The Netherlands argued that the institutional distinctiveness of the private anti-cartel enforcement apparatuses emerging in those jurisdictions could be destroyed if foreign plaintiffs were constantly abandoning their home courts to sue in the US. The success of these appeals for space to create a culture of indigenous private enforcement provides motivation for institutional reforms that would enable such a culture to emerge in Latin America.

Part II considers the challenges facing private cartel enforcement in Latin America—which range from the lack of private rights of action to enforce anti-cartel laws, to various administrative, procedural, evidentiary and cultural hurdles. It singles out three issues as particularly important for private anti-cartel enforcement: claim aggregation, access to information, and judicial or administrative competence.

Part III makes the case for at least a limited regime of private anti-cartel enforcement. Although I have written critically about private antitrust enforcement

[4] 542 US 155 (2004).

in the US and its dulling effects on public enforcement,[5] it is important to separate anti-cartel enforcement from antitrust enforcement more generally. If there is ever an appropriate place for private antitrust enforcement, it is against cartels. To be clear, I do not claim that consumers are the *best* anti-cartel enforcers. The most socially costly effect of a cartel's supracompetitive pricing is not that consumers pay more but that some consumers substitute to other products (which creates a deadweight loss); yet would-be consumers of the cartelized products usually will not have standing to assert a claim. So government enforcement should always remain the centerpiece of any anti-cartel program, and it is critical that private enforcement not be allowed to detract from the government's anti-cartel mission. Nonetheless, private enforcement provides a valuable complement to government enforcement and, if properly structured, could redound to the benefit of Latin American consumers.

Private anti-cartel enforcement is not a silver bullet that will instantly and without cost slay the cartels. Private litigation can be distracting and expensive, and foreign observers often rightly react to the excesses of US litigation culture. Creating a system of private antitrust litigation must be part of a larger package of properly balanced institutional choices.

I. The Challenges of *Empagran*

A. The Vitamins Cartel and the Jurisdictional Reach of US Antitrust Law

Beginning in the 1990s, a gigantic and complex international vitamins cartel took shape.[6] It included multinational corporations located in Belgium, France, Germany, Japan, The Netherlands, Switzerland, and the United States. The victims of the cartel, however, did not correspond neatly with the countries in which the co-conspirators were located. One economic study estimated that the 'Vitamins, Inc' cartel (as its own members called it) affected over $34 billion of commerce, that the cartel members earned between $9 and $13 billion of profits, and that 58 per cent of these profits were taken from consumers outside the US, the EU and Canada.[7] In the private litigation that followed, the plaintiffs included vitamin wholesalers from Ecuador, Panama, Australia, Mexico, Belgium, the United Kingdom, Indonesia, Ukraine and the United States.

[5] Daniel A Crane, 'Antitrust Antifederalism' 96 *California Law Review* 1, 40–43 (2008).

[6] I generally adapt the facts recounted here from Alvin K Klevorick and Alan O Sykes, 'United States Courts and the Optimal Deterrence of International Cartels: A Welfarist Perspective on Empagran' in Eleanor M Fox and Daniel A Crane (eds), *Antitrust Stories* (New York, Foundation Press, 2007).

[7] Klevorick and Sykes, above n 6, at 363, citing estimates by John M Connor.

The cartel seems to have been cracked by the US Justice Department, in cooperation with many other antitrust authorities. The Department credited its leniency program, which grants amnesty from criminal prosecution to cooperating defendants in certain circumstances. In particular, the Department cited the cooperation of Rhône-Poulenc, which was the first member of the cartel to cooperate.

Competition authorities in the US, Australia, Canada, the European Union, Japan and South Korea levied substantial fines against the cartel. For present purposes, the interesting aspect of the case concerns the private lawsuit brought under US antitrust law in the US District Court in Washington, DC.[8] The Washington litigation included as plaintiffs both companies that had bought vitamins in the US and companies that had bought vitamins outside the US. The claims of the foreign purchasers raised an interesting and unresolved issue of US antitrust law: can plaintiffs who pay too much money for products outside of the US because of a global price-fixing conspiracy that also harms US consumers sue under the Sherman Act?

Prior to the *Empagran* case, the lower federal courts had resolved this issue in conflicting ways. For example, the federal appeals court in New York had held that people who bought and sold art in the Christies' and Sothebys' auction houses in London could bring claims under federal antitrust law when Christies and Sothebys fixed buyer and seller commissions in both London and New York.[9] The New York court interpreted the relevant federal statute, the Foreign Trade Antitrust Improvements Act (FTAIA),[10] to permit the claims by the foreign purchasers and sellers since the same price-fixing conspiracy also harmed US purchasers and sellers.[11] On the other hand, the federal court of appeals in Texas rejected that position and held that foreign purchasers who did not make their purchases in the US market could not sue under the Sherman Act.[12]

The Supreme Court of the United States accepted the vitamins case for review and sided with the interpretation of the Texas court.[13] The Court's reasoning in interpreting the FTAIA is somewhat technical and dense, and need not detain us here. The upshot is that the Court held that a foreign plaintiff cannot establish that the Sherman Act applies to his claims unless he can show that his injury arose from anti-competitive effects in the US market. In other words, the only way that a foreign purchaser of a price-fixed product could sue under the Sherman Act would be if he established not only that the same cartel that fixed his prices also fixed the prices of US consumers, but additionally that the cartel was *only* able to

[8] *Empagran SA v F Hoffman-La Roche, Ltd*, No Civ 001686 (TFH) (DDC, 2006).
[9] *Kruman v Christie's Intern PLC*, 284 F 3d 384 (2d Cir 2002).
[10] 15 USC § 6a.
[11] Christopher Mason, *The Art of the Steal: Inside the Sotheby's–Christie's Auction House Scandal* (Putnam, 2004) tells an engaging story of the history of the Christie's and Sotheby's price-fixing conspiracy. As with the vitamins cartel, the Justice Department's leniency program played an important role in the detection and prosecution of the cartel's leaders.
[12] *Den Norske Oljeselkap As v HeereMac Vof*, 241 F 3d 420 (5th Cir 2001).
[13] 542 US 155 (2004).

fix the prices in the foreign market because of its success in fixing the prices in the US market.

It remains to be seen whether this test will effectively curtail any suits in the US by foreign purchasers from international cartels. In *Empagran*, the Supreme Court left open the possibility that the plaintiffs could establish US jurisdiction by establishing that their injury was not caused independently of the harm to the US market.[14] On remand, however, the federal appeals court in Washington, DC, construed this potential loophole very narrowly, holding that a plaintiff would have to show 'a direct causal relationship' between the US injury and the foreign injury.[15]

There remains also the possibility that a foreign purchaser could sue in US courts under the law of a foreign country, and hence get the benefit of liberal US discovery rules and the general receptiveness of US courts to private litigation. A few plaintiffs have tried this strategy,[16] thus far without any success.

So it is a good bet to assume that, for all intents and purposes, the US courts are now closed to claims by foreign purchasers who bought from international cartels. Whether this is a good or a bad thing is not the focus of this paper. As we shall see, however, the decision was applauded by a number of non-US governments.

B. The Enforcement Gaps Created by *Empagran*

As noted earlier, the *Empagran* plaintiffs included Mexican, Panamanian and Ecuadorian companies that imported vitamins into Latin America. There is no doubt that the vitamins cartel had a serious negative impact on consumers in Latin America. However, the Court prohibited the Mexican, Panamanian and Ecuadorian plaintiffs from having their claims heard in the United States.

One reaction is 'who cares?' After all, the cartel was discovered, punished by competition officials in the US, Australia, Canada, the European Union, Japan and South Korea, and cartel members paid over $900 million in fines in the US and approximately the same amount in fines in other jurisdictions. Additionally, cartel members paid $2 billion to settle the civil cases. Further, at least 11 individuals received jail sentences.[17]

It is not as if the Mexican, Panamanian and Ecuadorian plaintiffs would have turned around and issued refund checks to their customers if they had received damages. As I will discuss momentarily, anti-cartel enforcement is more important for its deterrent rather than for its compensatory effects. So why is it important

[14] *Ibid*, at 175.

[15] *Empagran SA v F Hoffman-La Roche, Ltd*, 417 F 3d 1267, 1271 (DC Cir 2005).

[16] See, eg, *Information Resources, Inc v Dun & Bradstreet Corp*, 127 F Supp 2d 411 (2000) (rejecting exercise of supplemental jurisdiction over private damages claims arising from alleged violations of Arts 81 and 82 of the Treaty of Rome).

[17] Brief for the United States as Amicus Curiae Supporting Petitioners at 2, *Empagran*, 542 US 155 (2004) (No 03-724), 2004 WL 234125.

for Latin America to allow private rights of action when the rest of the world seems to be doing such a good job at deterring international cartels?

Part of the answer is that Latin America should not assume that the US, EU and other large antitrust enforcers have the interests of Latin American consumers at heart. As Al Klevorick and Alan Sykes have written, 'the United States is largely free to shape its policy toward international cartels to promote the national interest'.[18] And it often does so. For example, the US has a statute called the Webb-Pomerane Act[19] that exempts export cartels from US antitrust law. So long as they do not raise prices in the US, a cartel of US vitamin producers would be free under US law to fix prices for vitamins exported into Latin America.

Why would the US allow such a thing to happen? United States antitrust enforcement officials routinely refer to cartels as a form of theft.[20] Why would the US permit US companies to steal from Latin American consumers? The answer is that what is bad for Latin American consumers may be good for US companies, and indirectly for the US economy.

It is a well-known fact that cartels simultaneously harm consumers and help producers. Cartels benefit producers in two different ways. For one, price fixing allows producers to raise prices above a competitive level and hence transform consumer surplus into producer surplus. But beyond these wealth transfers, there may also be some efficiencies from price fixing. Price fixing may allow producers to engage in better planning, eliminate waste and coordinate activities in a way that helps them to save production costs.[21] It may also allow smaller firms that could not otherwise compete enter the market.[22]

Such efficiency arguments for price fixing are never admissible in US antitrust cases.[23] In Latin America, however, the story is much more nuanced. Some Latin American countries, including, for example, Peru, Colombia and Mexico, follow a rule of per se illegality for price-fixing arrangements.[24] Other countries, like

[18] Klevorick and Sykes, above n 6, at 378.

[19] 15 USC §§ 61–65.

[20] See, eg, Press Release, US Dept of Justice, 'Samsung Agrees to Plead Guilty and to Pay $300 Million Criminal Fine for Role in Price Fixing Conspiracy' (Oct 13, 2005) (quoting Attorney General Alberto R Gonzalez), <http://www.usdoj.gov/atr/public/press_releases/2005/212002.htm> (stating that price fixing 'robs American consumers of the benefit of competitive prices').

[21] The WTO Secretariat has recognized that export cartels may have some associated efficiencies, although it has expressed doubt that this is very often the case. Report by Secretariat, WTO Doc WT/WGTCP/M/21 (2003), at 44.

[22] See generally, D Daniel Sokol, 'What Do We Really Know About Export Cartels and What is the Appropriate Solution?' 4 *Journal of Competition Law & Economics* 967–82 (2008) (arguing that the effects of export cartels are not well understood).

[23] Examples of cases where US courts held that the defendants were not allowed even to argue that their cartel behavior was efficiency justified include *United States v Socony-Vacuum Oil Co*, 310 US 150 (1940) and *Addystone Pipe & Steel Co v United States*, 175 US 211 (1899), *aff'g* 85 F 271 (6th Cir 1898).

[24] Gabriela Mancero-Bucheli, *Competition Law of Latin America and the European Union* (Huntington, NY, Juris Pub, Inc 2001), at 124–31; OECD, *Competition Law and Policy in Latin America: Peer Reviews of Argentina, Brazil, Chile, Mexico and Peru*, OECD Report Nov 9, 2006 (hereinafter *OECD Peer Reviews Report*), at 268.

Venezuela, follow a general rule of per se illegality for price fixing, subject to the possibility of block exemptions for price-fixing behavior.[25] Some jurisdictions, like Argentina and Brazil, reject per se treatment and require proof of economic harm—or at least market power from which economic harm can be presumed—in every case.[26] In some jurisdictions, like Chile, it is unclear whether or not the per se rule applies to cartel behavior.[27]

So, there is far from consensus on whether cartel behavior can ever be justified. But even where the inclination is not to permit cartelists to attempt to justify their conduct in the ordinary case, the justification for per se treatment lies not in the impossibility that a cartel would ever have efficiency benefits. Rather, it lies in the near certainty that cartels will harm consumers and the extremely high probability that whatever efficiencies a cartel may produce will be insufficient to offset the harm. The per se rule is a rule of judicial administrability, not a statement of absolute confidence that cartel arrangements never create efficiencies.

Now suppose that the producer benefits from cartelization are felt only in the domestic market and the consumer harms are felt only in the foreign markets. In that case, from the perspective of the domestic economy, price fixing looks like a good deal. The domestic producers will make more money, and hence create more jobs[28] and pay more taxes in the domestic market. The cartel will affect terms of trade. Moreover, the domestic jurisdiction will not have to internalize the harms of the anti-competitive conduct. Export cartels are just like aiming a giant smokestack across a country's border so that all of the pollution is absorbed by another country. They are a highly effective way to internalize benefits and externalize costs.

The problem with relying on the US and the EU to police international cartels does not stop at export cartels. Suppose that the G7 countries perfect anti-cartel enforcement to the point that they reach a 'Beckerian equilibrium' in G7 markets—that is to say, a point where everyone knows that the expected cost of price fixing (the probability of detection times the penalty) exceeds the profits to be made from price fixing.[29] Now suppose that you are the vitamins cartel and you know that it is economically irrational to fix prices in G7 countries because the expected penalty outweighs the expected benefit. There is still a great deal of money to be made by price fixing in other jurisdictions, including those in Latin America, that do not have nearly as aggressive anti-cartel enforcement. Even if you are caught in one or two of the jurisdictions, the fines that you will pay are far less than the profits you are going to make by price fixing across the region.

[25] *Ibid.*

[26] *OECD Peer Review Report*, above n 24, at 16, 74.

[27] *Ibid*, at 212.

[28] The creation of more jobs is not certain, since the cartel will probably have to lower output when it raises prices. But as it earns more money, the cartel is likely to invest it in other ventures which may create more jobs in the domestic economy.

[29] See Gary S Becker, 'Crime & Punishment: An Economic Approach' 76 *Journal of Political Economy* 169–217 (1968).

The famous US Supreme Court Justice Oliver Wendell Holmes had an interesting approach to legal analysis. He said that we should look at the law from the perspective of the 'bad man', the man who cares only for the legal consequences of his behavior.[30] So think about anti-cartel enforcement from the perspective of the 'bad men' in the cartels. To them, anti-cartel enforcement is just a cost of doing business. As anti-cartel enforcement gets 'better' from the perspective of consumers, the cost of doing business goes up from the perspective of the cartelists. And what happens when the cost of business goes up in one place? Economic theory predicts that, over time, business will tend to shift to lower-cost places of doing business. So if anti-cartel enforcement gets progressively better in G7 countries then one prediction is that more and more international cartel behavior will be directed at countries—including those in Latin America—where the 'costs of doing business' are comparatively lower. This may not be true of industries that are inherently local because of high transportation costs or local market peculiarities, but it is true of many fungible and portable products that have been the subject of international cartels. In other words, the success of international anti-cartel enforcement in the US, EU and Japan may be a magnet for *more* cartel behavior in Latin America.

Thus far, I have only made the case that the *Empagran* carve-out of non-US purchaser claims combined with improved anti-cartel enforcement in G7 countries creates the possibility for *worse* cartel conditions in Latin America. This suggests that there is an imperative to step up anti-cartel enforcement in Latin America. It does not yet establish the case for *private* enforcement. For a perspective on that issue, we now turn to the *amicus* briefs of the foreign governments.

C. The Foreign Government *Amicus Curiae* Briefs

It is customary in US courts—particularly in the Supreme Court—for people, corporations, governments, etc, who are not parties to the case but have an interest in its outcome to file *amicus curiae* briefs urging their view of the case on the Court. When the *Empagran* case reached the Supreme Court, seven foreign governments (Germany, Belgium, Canada, Japan, Great Britain and Northern Ireland, Ireland and The Netherlands) submitted four *amicus curiae* briefs, all of them urging the Court to adopt a rule disallowing suits by foreign purchasers in US courts.[31]

[30] Oliver W Holmes, Jr, 'The Path of the Law' 10 *Harvard Law Review* 457, 459 (1897).

[31] The briefs filed in *F Hoffman-La Roche, Ltd v Empagran, SA*, are Brief for the Government of Canada as Amicus Curiae Supporting Reversal, 2004 WL 226389 (Feb 3, 2004) (hereinafter 'Canada Brief'); Brief for the United Kingdom of Great Britain and Northern Ireland, Ireland, and the Kingdom of The Netherlands as Amici Curiae in Support of Petitioners, 2004 WL 226597 (Feb 3, 2004) (hereinafter 'UK Brief'); Brief of the Government of Japan as Amicus Curiae in Support of Petitioners, 2004 WL 226390 (Feb 3, 2004) (hereinafter 'Japan Brief'); Brief of the Federal Republic of Germany and Belgium as Amici Curiae in Support of Petitioners, 2004 WL 226388 (Feb 3, 2004) (hereinafter 'Germany Brief').

The briefs articulated a number of common themes. All assured the Supreme Court that their native jurisdictions were vigorously engaged in anti-cartel measures and that they did not require supplementary enforcement by private plaintiffs in US courts. All worried that a decision allowing suits by foreign plaintiffs would impede vigorous anti-cartel enforcement in their domestic jurisdictions, for example by discouraging cartelists to seek leniency in exchange for cooperation. The governments all argued that a rule allowing foreign purchaser claims in US courts would violate the sovereignty of the foreign governments, that it would contradict principles of international law, and that it would fail to comport with universally recognized principles of comity.

All of the governments but Japan[32] emphasized an additional point of particular importance here: each jurisdiction allowed private rights of action to recover damages for price fixing. Analytically, this argument was presented with two different emphases.

First, the briefs stressed that allowing foreign purchaser suits in the US would seriously undermine the development of indigenous private enforcement in the *amici* countries because certain features of the US civil litigation and antitrust system—particularly treble damages, contingency fee arrangements, one-way attorney fee shifting, class actions, and liberal discovery rules—would inevitably drive all of the foreign purchaser plaintiffs to the United States. For instance, the UK Brief argued strenuously that allowing foreign purchaser claims would harm the private antitrust enforcement in the governments' own jurisdictions:

> Expanding the jurisdiction of this generous United States claim system could skew enforcement and increase international business risks. It makes the United States courts the forum of choice without regard to whose laws applies, where the injuries occurred or even if there is any connection to the court except the ability to get *in personam* jurisdiction over the defendants. Lord Denning best captured these anomalies when he observed: 'As a moth is drawn to the light, so a litigant is drawn to the United States. If he can only get his case into their courts, he stands to win a fortune.' *Smith Kline & French Labs Ltd v Bloch*, [1983] 1 WLR 730 (CA 1982). Enlarging the prescriptive jurisdiction of the United States to provide a US antitrust remedy to foreign buyers with no cognizable US nexus will attract even more litigants and will increase the number of private antitrust claims filed in United States courts.[33]

The governments also made a second point: in their own national deliberations, they had rejected many of the aspects of US civil litigation that made litigation in US courts so attractive to plaintiffs. For example, the Irish Government pointedly

[32] Although there is a theoretical possibility of private antitrust enforcement in Japan, there appear to be few if any successful private cases. See Wulfgang Wurmnest, 'Foreign Private Plaintiffs, Global Conspiracies, and the Extraterritorial Application of US Antitrust Law' 28 *Hastings International & Comparative Law Review* 205, 213 (2005), n 40 (collecting sources).

[33] UK Brief, above n 31, at *13–14. See also Canada Brief, above n 31, at *14 (noting that the 'policy of the United States permitting recovery of treble damages in civil antitrust actions likely would prove powerfully attractive to most Canadian plaintiffs injured by anti-competitive behavior in Canada').

noted that class actions are not allowed in Ireland.[34] The Canadian Government noted that Canada deliberately rejected the treble damages model because 'punitive sanctions for illegal cartel behavior [may] be imposed only through prosecutions initiated by the Government'.[35] The UK and Northern Ireland, Ireland and The Netherlands also pointed out that none of them would dream of giving cartel cases to juries which are 'swayed by emotional appeals',[36] a comment more notable for its accuracy than its tact.[37] (As a side note, Ireland does in fact give criminal cartel cases to juries. In March 2006, two years after the *Empagran* brief, the Competition Authority secured its first criminal conviction, *by a jury*, against Michael Flanagan (trading as Flanagan Oil), who was fined €3,500 for his participation in a domestic heating oil cartel.[38])

Belgium and Germany made this point about rejecting the US private litigation system even more aggressively. Not only did their governments reject many of the remedial aspects of US private litigation, but they did so in part because of a conscious policy decision to prefer public anti-cartel enforcement to private anti-cartel enforcement. Thus Germany stated that '[w]hile in Germany private parties can also claim damages, see GWB § 33, Germany's focus in obtaining the desired deterrent effect of illegal restraints of trade is on prosecution through its competition authorities.'[39] Similarly, Belgium noted that '[i]n Belgium, although private claims for damages are available in civil courts, the Belgian competition regime primarily utilizes a number of administrative and enforcement bodies to investigate and prosecute violations of the Belgian Act.'[40]

The consensus of the government *amici* briefs on these points should be of interest to Latin American governments. Although the foreign *amici* briefs nominally spoke only for themselves, they clearly intended to convey a unified message about how antitrust enforcers from around the world viewed the importance of private anti-cartel enforcement in their own jurisdictions. We now turn to the relevance of these arguments for anti-cartel enforcement in Latin America.

[34] UK Brief, above n 31, at *5.

[35] Canada Brief, above n 31, at *2.

[36] UK Brief, above n 31, at *15.

[37] I have been similarly critical of the role of juries in antitrust cases, although cartel cases are, of all antitrust cases, the ones in which juries probably perform the best. See Daniel A Crane, 'Technocracy and Antitrust' 86 *Texas Law Review* 1159 (2008). In any event, this point is largely moot in the context of this article, since very few other jurisdictions use juries for antitrust cases.

[38] Global Competition Review, *The 2008 Handbook of Competition Agencies*, available at http://www.globalcompetitionreview.com/reviews/7/sections/16/chapters/161/ireland.

[39] Germany Brief, above n 31, at *11–12. Despite this disclaimer, in 2005 Germany adopted an amendment to its Competition Act that has led to significant enhancement in private party damages claims following on public findings of competition law infringements. ICN, *Interaction of Public and Private Enforcement in Cartel Cases*, Report of Cartels Working Group to International Competition Network Annual Conference (Moscow, May 2007), at 2.

[40] Germany Brief, above n 31, at *13.

II. The Status of Anti-Cartel Enforcement in Latin America

Generalizing about competition institutions in a region as vast and diverse as 'Latin America' is a dangerous undertaking, particularly for an outsider such as myself.[41] The suitability, practicability and relative importance of private anti-cartel enforcement may differ on a country-by-country basis. Nonetheless, there are some general points that can be made. In this section, I make two: first, public anti-cartel enforcement in Latin America is progressing, but only cautiously and sometimes unevenly; and, secondly, there are a number of general obstacles to the success of private anti-cartel enforcement that need to be addressed if private enforcement is to become an effective tool.

A. Anti-Cartel Enforcement and Private Rights of Action—Country Summaries

What is the status of anti-cartel enforcement in Latin America, both public and private? To give what I understand to be a representative taste, I summarize some key findings from a recent *OECD Peer Review Report* on competition policy in five leading Latin American jurisdictions.

1. *Argentina*

The OECD Report commends Argentina for giving its National Commission for the Defense of Competition (CNDC) 'sufficient investigative tools for anti-cartel work'.[42] Recent enforcement actions in the cement industry resulted in record fines of US $106 million, and another US $24 million was imposed for price fixing in the liquid oxygen industry.[43] But despite the existence of adequate procedural tools, such as dawn raids, and the success of some high-profile enforcement actions, the OECD reports that it is suspected that 'cartel activity is rife in Argentina' and that the CNDC may not have the political will to move aggressively against cartel behavior.[44] Private parties can initiate proceedings by lodging a complaint with the Commission, and there is theoretically a private right of action for damages.[45]

[41] There is relatively little academic literature available in the United States on antitrust enforcement in Latin America. The available sources include Thomas W Studwell, 'Latin American Competition Law in the Twenty-First Century: A Practical Guide' 10 *Law & Business Review of the Americas* 747 (2004); Ignacio de León, 'Institutional Analysis of Competition Policy in Transition and Developing Countries: The Lessons from Latin America' 3 *Washington University Global Studies Law Review* 405 (2004); Ignacio de León, 'A Proposal for a New Competition Policy in Latin America' 25 *Brookings Journal of International Law* 275 (1999); Jaime E Fernandez, 'Antitrust Regulation in Latin America' 30 *International Law* 521 (1996).

[42] *OECD Peer Review Report*, above n 24, at 16.

[43] *Ibid*, at 15.

[44] *Ibid*, at 16–17.

[45] Jaime E Fernandez, above n 41, at 525.

2. *Brazil*

Brazil's *Conselho Administrativo de Defesa Econômica* (CADE) has stepped up anti-cartel enforcement in the last decade, particularly since 2003.[46] For example, a 2004 price-fixing decision fined the distributors of liquid petroleum 15 per cent of their annual revenues and imposed an additional fine of 10 per cent of the company's fine on each company's owner.[47] Brazil has adopted an effective leniency program.[48] Under Article 29 of Law 8884, private parties may file damages actions for antitrust violations under the Consumer Defense Code.[49] However, there are no available records of how many such private cases have been filed, and Brazilian authorities believe that the number is small.[50]

3. *Chile*

As noted earlier, there is some uncertainty as to whether cartel behavior is per se illegal in Chile. There have been a few anti-cartel prosecutions, including a 1995 pharmacy case where three incumbent pharmacies were fined about US $80,000 and a fourth new entrant about half that amount.[51] In general, the OECD Report describes the Chilean approach to competition law enforcement as 'cautious'. Chile has a theoretical private right of action for damages for violation of competition law, but such an action cannot proceed until a Commission has found that the defendant violated the law, because a civil court would not be independently competent to make such a decision.[52] Competition authorities do not track the number of private cases filed, and the frequency of such cases is unknown.[53]

4. *Mexico*

Following ratification of the North America Free Trade Agreement (NAFTA), Mexico adopted a Federal Law of Economic Competition (LFCE), which was intended to move Mexico toward more robust market competition.[54] Until the mid-1980s, prices for most goods and services were fixed by law, usually as the result of agreements by 'business chambers' subject to the control of the Ministry of the Economy.[55] In the early years of the LFCE, the competition authorities devoted much of their time to rooting out the old 'business chamber' cartel culture.[56] Since 1998, the pace of such enforcement has slowed considerably. There has been only one criminal enforcement—a 2000 price-fixing case involving tortilla

[46] *OECD Peer Review Report*, above n 24, at 105.
[47] *Ibid*, at 76.
[48] *Ibid*, at 108.
[49] *Ibid*, at 125.
[50] *Ibid*.
[51] *Ibid*, at 218.
[52] *Ibid*, at 210.
[53] *Ibid*.
[54] *Ibid*, at 261.
[55] *Ibid*, at 268.
[56] *Ibid*.

manufacturers.[57] Similarly, anti-cartel enforcement outside the business chamber arena has slowed to a trickle in recent years.[58] The Federal Competition Commission (CFC) feels that it needs enhanced tools, including dawn raid and leniency powers, better to combat cartels.[59] Under Article 39 of the LFCE, when the CFC has found an antitrust violation, private parties that can prove in a Commission proceeding that they suffered damage may sue the responsible party in court for damages.[60] Through 2002, at least, no such actions had been initiated.[61]

5. *Peru*

Competition enforcement in Peru is conducted by the Institute for the Defense of Competition and Intellectual Property (INDECOPI), an autonomous government agency that generally receives good marks for its independence and vigor.[62] In the 1997 landmark 'chicken case', INDECOPI fined a poultry cartel over US $2 million for price-fixing activities.[63] Private parties may initiate INDECOPI proceedings, but the Commission is not authorized to award damages. If the Commission finds a competition law violation, that finding is conclusive proof in any subsequent private action for damages in court, but it is unknown whether any such actions have been filed.[64]

6. *Summary*

The general tenor of the OECD's Report is to praise the enforcement institutions for meaning well and taking some positive steps toward establishing anti-cartel precedents and raising the visibility of the prohibition on price fixing and other cartel behavior. However, an equally important theme is that the victories so far have been largely symbolic, and that many Latin American economies remain rife with unchallenged cartel behavior. As to private enforcement, one can perhaps draw on an analogy that a US court once drew to the Louvre's statue of the Venus de Milo: she is 'much admired and often discussed, but rarely embraced'.[65] While theoretically available everywhere, it seems that private anti-cartel enforcement is a rare occurrence. The next section considers why this may be.

B. Hurdles to Private Enforcement

From a chauvinistic US perspective, it is tempting to say that private anti-cartel enforcement does not succeed in Latin America (as it does not in much of the

[57] *Ibid*, at 269.
[58] *Ibid*.
[59] *Ibid*, at 270.
[60] *Ibid*, at 195–96.
[61] *Ibid*.
[62] *Ibid*, at 334–38.
[63] *Ibid*, at 340.
[64] *Ibid*, at 371.
[65] *McGahee v Northern Propane Gas Co*, 858 F2d 1487, 1495 (11th Cir 1988).

world) precisely because of the absence of most of the characteristics of US civil litigation that drew the ire of the foreign government *amici* in *Empagran*—treble damages, discovery, class actions, juries, joint and several liability, no right of contribution among defendants, contingency fees, attorney fee-shifting, etc. And indeed, the EU's 2005 Green Paper and 2008 White Paper on private antitrust enforcement recognized many of these features as being *possibly* necessary to achieve effective private enforcement.[66]

But other jurisdictions need not mimic the entire US system in order to have effective private antitrust enforcement. Rather, in keeping with the overall perspective of the foreign government *amici*, private enforcement needs to grow indigenously—to appropriate existing institutions and apparatuses rather than to attempt to transplant US features wholesale. With this in mind, I consider three of the most significant obstacles to effective private anti-cartel enforcement that need to be addressed, but which need not necessarily be addressed as they are in the US.

1. *Aggregation of Claims*

As noted earlier, in its *Empagran amicus* brief the Irish Government pointedly noted that class action treatment was foreign to Irish law. Is the availability of class actions necessary to any effective antitrust enforcement? The answer is no, although with some exceptions.

Class actions—or any claim-aggregation procedure—need not be available for private antitrust enforcement to succeed when there is concentrated harm from the anti-competitive conduct. This is particularly true as to monopolization or abuse of dominance, for example, where the most likely plaintiff is an injured competitor. Class actions are not necessary for private enforcement to succeed against Microsoft when firms like Novell and AOL stand ready to jump into the breach.

On the other hand, some form of claim-aggregation procedure *is* necessary when the harm of the conduct is almost entirely dispersed on thousands or millions of consumers, none of whom has a sufficient individual incentive or resources to sue. Unlike in the Microsoft case, where consumers were injured but so were competitors, cartel behavior often does not injure competitors at all. Unless there is some mechanism for aggregation of the claims, the availability of the private right of action may remain a theoretical possibility only.

Paradoxically, even though the US has by far the most liberal class action rules in the world, the need for class actions in cartel cases may be *weaker* in the United States than in much of the rest of the world. This is because antitrust standing rules in the US tend to give standing to large corporate buyers like wholesalers

[66] White Paper, Commission of the European Communities, 'Damages for Breach of the EC Antitrust Rules' (SEC, Brussels, April 2, 2008); Green Paper, Commission of the European Communities, 'Damages for Breach of the EC Antitrust Rules' (SEC, Brussels, Dec 19, 2005).

or retailers rather than consumers—plaintiffs who suffer concentrated harm. The US generally follows a 'direct purchaser' rule, in which the direct purchasers of the price-fixed good have standing to sue even though they may have passed on the overcharge by reselling the good at a marked-up price and hence avoided economic injury.[67] Conversely, injured consumers who pay a higher price but do not purchase directly from the cartelists are denied standing.[68]

But this does not appear to be true in most other jurisdictions that are developing private anti-cartel enforcement. According to a 2007 study of a number of jurisdictions by the International Competition Network (ICN), while the vast majority of the jurisdictions surveyed had not explicitly considered either the direct purchaser rule or the 'passing on' defense, most would probably invoke unjust enrichment principles to deny recovery to a wholesaler or retailer who simply passed on the overcharge.[69] Conversely, the ICN study concluded that the vast majority of surveyed jurisdictions would probably allow suits by indirect purchasers.[70] In other words, in most jurisdictions the parties with standing to sue cartels are often going to be the end users who suffer widely dispersed harm and, hence, have relatively little incentive to sue.

So some form of claim aggregation is important, but it need not mirror the US model. The ICN reports that class actions are available in five of the jurisdictions it surveyed.[71] It also notes that there is a variety of similar models for aggregating claims, including public interest litigation, representative actions, joinder of individual claims and *parens patriae* litigation.[72]

One interesting example is Brazil's Consumer Defense Code (Law 8078), which creates a series of state and local consumer protection agencies called 'Procons' that are located in all 26 Brazilian states, in the Federal District (Brasilia), and in 670 municipalities. The Procons, either upon a consumer complaint or their own initiative, can initiate class action lawsuits for damages on behalf of injured consumers.[73] Similarly, Brazilian law allows non-governmental

[67] *Illinois Brick Co v Illinois*, 431 US 720 (1977).

[68] *Hanover Shoe Inc v United Shoe Machinery Corp*, 392 US 481 (1968). It bears noting that the *Illinois Brick* and *Hanover Shoe* rules apply only in federal lawsuits. In *California v ARC America Corp*, 490 US 93 (1989), the Supreme Court held that federal antitrust law does not preempt state antitrust laws that allow indirect purchaser suits. A number of states have allowed such indirect purchaser suits. Further, the Congressionally appointed Antitrust Modernization Commission recently made a recommendation for legislative reforms that would overrule both *Hanover Shoe* and *Illinois Brick* and allow for removal of state cases to federal court and consolidation of all damages claims as to a particular violation. Report and Recommendation of the Antitrust Modernization Commission Chapter Two (Apr 2007), <http://www.amc.gov/report_recommendation/.chapter3.pdf.>. The court would then make a determination of what the total monopoly overcharge was, treble the overcharge, and allocate the damages pot to the different plaintiffs based on the proportion of their individual injuries to the total.

[69] ICN, above n 39, at 12.

[70] *Ibid.*

[71] *Ibid*, at 24.

[72] *Ibid*, at 24–25.

[73] *OECD Peer Review Report*, above n 24, at 97.

consumer organizations to file antitrust class actions seeking damages.[74] As noted earlier, very few such cases have been filed, but at least there is an indigenous model of claim-aggregation that could be brought to bear on the collective action problems that cartels create.

2. *Access to Information*

A major impediment to private anti-cartel enforcement in many jurisdictions is that private plaintiffs often lack the procedural tools necessary to obtain information about the cartel. Since cartels are usually covert and secretive, amassing the documentary evidence necessary to make out a case often proves difficult.

The United States is often thought to be particularly plaintiff-friendly because of its liberal discovery rules—which essentially allow plaintiffs to demand that the defendants produce any documents that are relevant to the plaintiffs' claims.[75] While depositions of the defendants' executives are also allowed, those may be less available in cartel cases since the individuals may choose to invoke their Fifth Amendment rights against self-incrimination. Nonetheless, US discovery rights tend to be very broad.

Recently, however, the availability of discovery in cartel cases may have been somewhat contracted. In *Bell Atlantic Corp v Twombly*, the United States Supreme Court held that plaintiffs in cartel cases must plead facts which, if true, would directly establish the existence of the conspiracy, and that they may not simply rely upon the existence of parallel behavior by the defendants in the marketplace.[76] This pleading must occur—and be sufficient to satisfy the trial court—before the plaintiffs can get any discovery. In other words, plaintiffs must have some internal evidence of the conspiracy before they can use the process of discovery to search for additional evidence supporting their claim.

Pre-trial discovery is said to be virtually non-existent in many Latin American jurisdictions.[77] As long as this remains true, it is doubtful that a regime of effective private anti-cartel enforcement can emerge. It is not helpful to respond that in many jurisdictions potential private plaintiffs are able to participate in the anti-cartel proceedings brought by the competition authorities and, hence, gather some information that may be useful in subsequent civil litigation. That makes private litigants' access to court entirely dependent on a prior enforcement action by the competition authorities. As I will discuss momentarily, perhaps the chief benefit of private enforcement is to spur the competition authorities to action when they are otherwise disposed to do nothing.

When it comes to international cartels, it might be thought that the best solution for private litigants in jurisdictions without strong discovery rights

[74] *Ibid*, at 125.

[75] Fed R Civ P 26(b)(1).

[76] *Bell Atlantic Corp v Twombly*, 127 US 1955 (2007).

[77] Dante Figuerao, 'Are There Ways Out of the Current Forum Non Conveniens Impasse Between the United States and Latin America?' 1 *American University Business Law Review* 42, 44 (2005).

is to free-ride on discovery efforts in more discovery-friendly jurisdictions, particularly by seeking documents or other information collected in US discovery. But that solution also turns out to be largely illusory. United States courts often impose strict protective orders on the litigants that prohibit them from sharing information learned in discovery, or using that information for any purpose other than the conduct of the case. Similarly, information collected by US antitrust enforcement authorities pursuant to civil investigative demands must be treated as confidential and cannot be disclosed to third parties.[78]

Some form of private discovery in Latin American jurisdictions is thus critical to the success of private anti-cartel enforcement. The obvious problem is that the absence of discovery rights is not peculiar to anti-cartel enforcement—it is a deeply-rooted aspect of Latin American civil litigation culture. Perhaps the *Twombly* decision suggests a plausible model for justifying creating some limited discovery rights in cartel cases: plaintiffs should not be able to get access to documents and other evidence from defendants unless they can assert facts—with a reasonable degree of particularity—evidencing the existence of the conspiracy. Such a threshold requirement for getting discovery would prevent the filing of speculative, harassing or unfounded claims. And what facts might count as sufficient to open the door to discovery? As to international cartels, the fact that the defendant has been indicted on charges of international cartel behavior in another jurisdiction, or that plaintiffs in another jurisdiction have unearthed facts sufficient to survive a motion to dismiss—as disclosed in a court decision—should perhaps count as sufficient (assuming, of course, that the defendant also does business in the relevant Latin American jurisdiction). In this way, facts unearthed in other jurisdictions could serve as an influential threshold showing in Latin American antitrust litigation—a showing sufficient to accord the private plaintiffs their own discovery rights.

3. *Judicial Competence and Acceptance*

The *OECD Peer Review Report* on Latin America notes as to Mexico that the competition authority's (CFC) experience in the district courts before generalist judges does not augur well for private enforcement.[79] It notes that 'the further maturation of Mexico's antitrust environment, especially in the courts, is necessary before private actions can become a significant feature of competition policy enforcement'.[80] Judicial competence to try complex antitrust matters is a serious problem the world over, and may particularly be an issue in Latin America.[81]

[78] 15 USC § 1313.

[79] *OECD Peer Review Report*, above n 24, at 296.

[80] *Ibid*, at 296.

[81] See Edgardo Buscaglia *et al*, *Judicial Reform in Latin America: A Framework for National Development* (Palo Alto, CA, Hoover, 1995).

Fortunately, judicial competence is probably the least serious problem as to cartel cases. Certainly, it takes a judge very knowledgeable about economics and antitrust principles to try an abuse of dominance, rule of reason, merger or price discrimination case. But cartel cases often involve fewer questions of economic policy—after all, the per se rule (in those jurisdictions that follow it) is intended to simplify the plaintiff's proof and avoid difficult balancing questions. Of course, cartel cases are not free from difficult economic questions. An important and complex issue will often be how to calculate and allocate the plaintiffs' damages. But, in general, cartel cases are the easiest of private antitrust cases for generalist judges to handle. They are in many ways much more like traditional fraud or conspiracy cases with which commercially sophisticated judges will be familiar.

There is also the possibility of creating specialized antitrust courts, or allowing the existing competition courts to hear private cases. For example, Canada is cautiously experimenting with opening up its Competition Tribunal—which until recently has been reserved for Competition Bureau enforcement—to private litigants. Similarly, the Indian Competition Commission, which was created by a 2002 overhaul of India's antitrust laws, has the power to award compensation to any person who makes application seeking compensation from any enterprise for any loss or damages caused by a violation of the competition law.[82] Similar moves may be constitutionally barred in jurisdictions that employ a completely administrative—as opposed to judicial—process for competition enforcement. In that case, it may be wise to focus on seminars and other forms of training on private cartel litigation for commercial judges—if not the creation of specialized antitrust courts.

III. The Benefits and Limits of Private Anti-Cartel Enforcement

We come, finally, to the question 'Why?' Why should Latin America look favorably on private anti-cartel enforcement? In this last section, I first make the case for private anti-cartel enforcement (although not necessarily the conventional case). I then acknowledge and examine a key limitation of private anti-cartel enforcement—a limitation that justifies the position of the German and Belgian Governments that private anti-cartel enforcement will always remain secondary to public enforcement. Finally, I try to quell some of the most alarmist suspicions about allowing private anti-cartel enforcement—particularly the view that this

[82] T Ramappa, *Competition Law in India: Policy, Issues, and Developments* 269 (New York, Oxford University Press, 2006).

would be a Trojan Horse, leading to an unbounded, US-style system of private antitrust litigation.

A. The Benefits of Private Enforcement

There has been much talk in recent years about the benefits of private anti-cartel enforcement. In its *Empagran amicus* brief, the UK Government informed the Supreme Court that it recognized the need to enhance private antitrust enforcement in the UK.[83] In 2008, the European Commission produced a White Paper on the need for a more efficient system for bringing damages claims for infringement of EC antitrust law.[84] The ICN's 2007 study on private anti-cartel enforcement noted that 'there have been a number of substantial changes in the last few years in many national legal systems to improve the situation of private plaintiffs'.[85]

But what is the value of private anti-cartel enforcement? In the literature, it is common to hear about two primary objectives: enhanced enforcement because of greater resource commitment, and compensation of injured parties.[86] I will briefly argue that compensation is overrated as a justification for anti-cartel enforcement, that resource enhancement is a good justification, but that there is a third—and even more compelling—justification that has not received sufficient attention.

1. *Compensation*

There is no doubt that it would be *socially* desirable to use antitrust law to compensate the victims of cartels, just as it is good to use the law to compensate people who have been robbed.[87] Unfortunately, antitrust law does a very poor job of this. This is not because courts, agencies and plaintiffs ignore compensation goals. Rather, it goes back to an earlier point in this chapter about the widely distributed nature of cartel harms. If 10 million people have each paid $20 too much for vitamins, the overcharge from the cartel is $200 million, a large sum to be sure. But the cost of identifying each of the 10 million people and issuing them a refund

[83] UK Brief, above n 31, at *15, citing UK Dept of Trade and Industry, 'Real Redress for Harmed Parties' in *A World Class Competition Regime* (Government White Paper, Cm 5233, July 2001), 47–48 (noting recommendation by the Department of Trade and Industry Report to create 'a system in the UK where private actions are less inhibited than at present').

[84] White Paper, Commission of the European Communities, *Damages for Breach of the EC Antitrust Rules*, (SEC, Brussels, Apr 2, 2008).

[85] ICN Report, above n 39, at 2.

[86] See White Paper, above n 84 (arguing that compensation should be the primary goal of private antitrust enforcement and that added deterrence is a secondary goal).

[87] I stress the word *socially* because it hard to justify compensation of injured consumers as an *economic* goal of anti-cartel enforcement. Economics is principally concerned with preventing dead-weight losses caused by anti-competitive behavior, not with any particular distributive theory of market behavior.

check in proportion to their purchases, may well exceed the $20 each person paid in overcharges.

The US experience on this is illustrative. Realizing that the costs of issuing checks to the members of the injured class were often prohibitive, creative lawyers instead invented other ways in which the injured consumers could be compensated. For example, the settling lawyers would have the defendants agree to issue coupons to class members that could be used against future purchases from the defendants. Often, these coupons go unclaimed and unused. Further, they can simply encourage the defendants to raise the price of their products (thus wiping away any compensatory benefit), or can cause inefficient overconsumption by the compensated class.[88] In 2005, the US Congress passed the Class Action Fairness Act,[89] which was designed to rein in perceived abuses in coupon settlements.

I do not claim that the parties injured by cartel behavior are never fairly compensated in private litigation. If the injured party is a large business purchaser that buys the price-fixed item for incorporation into another product (say, for example, a hospital that buys medical supplies, or a car company that buys steel) and faces elastic demand for the downstream product it sells, it may actually absorb a large share of the overcharge and recoup meaningful sums of money through private litigation. Consumers, however, rarely get much valuable *compensation* from private anti-cartel litigation (which is not to say that they do not *benefit* from private anti-cartel enforcement). After lawyers' fees and administrative fees, each consumer's share of the recovery is often negligible, even though the harm across the class is great. Compensation is a much more attainable goal of private antitrust enforcement in cases where the harm is concentrated than in cases where it is widely dispersed.

2. *Resources*

If compensation is a noble but fairly unrealistic goal of private anti-cartel enforcement, adding further resources to the fight against global cartels is both a noble and realistic goal. In the United States, we often refer to the benefits of having 'private attorneys general',[90] private lawyers who perform a public function. One of the chief reasons for having private attorneys general is that the resources of the existing attorney general are often limited. Further, the budgets (not to mention aggressiveness) of public enforcers are usually dependent on the will of the legislature or other organs of government, and hence may ebb

[88] See A Mitchell Polinsky, 'A Damage-Revelation Model of Coupon Remedies' 23 *Journal of Law, Economics & Organization* 653, 653 (2007). Polinsky summarizes the literature critical of coupon settlements, but argues that coupons may be socially efficient if they are designed as an alternative to cash and make the defendant bear costs that better reflect the harms they have caused.

[89] Class Action Fairness Act, Pub L 109-2 (Feb 18, 2005).

[90] See, eg, William B Rubenstein, 'On What a Private Attorney General Is—And Why It Matters' 57 *Vanderbilt Law Review* 21, 29 (2004).

and flow with changes in overall budgetary priorities. Private antitrust enforcers are not dependent on budgetary allocations, and hence provide a steady stream of enforcement regardless of the resources (or politics) of the administration in office.

The amount of money invested in public antitrust enforcement in Latin America seems trivial compared with the challenges of anti-cartel enforcement (much less all competition law enforcement). Argentina's 2005 CNDC budget was less than US $750,000, with only 53 devoted person-years.[91] Chile's National Economic Prosecutor's Office had a budget of US $2.25 million in 2001, but that office has responsibilities beyond antitrust enforcement.[92] In 2003, Peru's INDECOPI had a budget of only US $183,000.[93] Of the five countries surveyed by the OECD, Brazil with US $7 million in competition enforcement resources in 2004[94] and Mexico with a competition law enforcement budget of almost US $16 million in 2002[95] had the most well-funded antitrust enforcers. But even those numbers seem trivial compared with the challenges of anti-cartel enforcement.

To put the Latin American budgetary numbers in perspective, consider the fact that the attorney's fees award made to the primary law firm representing the class of domestic purchasers in the Christie's/Sotheby's commission-fixing case was over $27 million.[96] And, mind you, the auction house attorney's fees award was not some unusually high fluke. If anything, it was lower than many comparable attorney's fees awards, because the federal district judge, Louis Kaplan, submitted the lead attorney role to competitive bidding.[97] In other words, the attorney's fees awarded in a single US cartel case where the judge reined in the attorney's fees exceeded the entire annual competition enforcement budgets of the first, second, third, fifth, and seventh largest Latin American economies combined.

Of course, such comparisons are not entirely fair. A dollar buys you much more enforcement in Latin America, where labor costs are lower, than it does in the US—although, of course, the quality of the services may vary by country. And the attorney's fees awarded to the Boies, Schiller law firm in the auction house cases represented a share of the settlement, not their actual expenses. But still, there is no doubt that the level of resources devoted to public anti-cartel enforcement in Latin America is far too low to do the job adequately. Adding a meaningful system of private enforcement would quickly multiply the resources devoted to protecting Latin American consumers.

91 *OECD Peer Review Report*, above n 24, at 32.
92 *Ibid*, at 244.
93 *Ibid*, at 369.
94 *Ibid*, at 130.
95 *Ibid*, at 300.
96 *In re Auction Houses Antitrust Litigation*, 2001 WL 170792, at *18 (SDNY Feb 22, 2001).
97 *In re Auction Houses Antitrust Litigation*, 197 FRD 71 (SDNY 2000).

3. *Competition for Enforcement*

One benefit of private anti-cartel enforcement that has not received much attention should be obvious to antitrust lawyers: *competition*. Of course, we all hope that better anti-cartel enforcement will produce more competition in commercial markets, but enhancing private enforcement can produce a different kind of competition—competition among antitrust enforcers for more rigorous enforcement.

Part of the problem with relying solely on public enforcement is that public enforcement becomes an institutional monopoly. As with any monopoly, public enforcement monopolies will tend toward lethargy, conservatism (in its worst sense), risk aversion and inaction. Indeed, the prospect of enhanced private enforcement may sometimes draw the opposition of the incumbent antitrust enforcers precisely for the same reasons that State-owned enterprises resist the introduction of private competition. As already mentioned, the *OECD Peer Review Report* noted (with some exceptions) cautious and often inadequate anti-cartel enforcement in Latin America. The introduction of private enforcement would provide incentives for more vigorous public enforcement.[98]

Take, for example, the often-made claim that private enforcement can interfere with public enforcement by altering the balance of incentives that cartelists have to participate in leniency programs or to plead guilty to criminal charges. There is a simple solution to this problem: allow competition authorities to grant immunity—partial or full—from civil liability to cooperating defendants.[99] In order to take advantage of this primacy over cartel enforcement, however, the enforcement agencies would actually need to investigate the case, crack the cartel using leniency programs or other enforcement tools, and reach a resolution with the cartelists. The presence of a vibrant culture of private litigation would give public enforcers greater incentives to pursue cartels vigorously in order to avoid being shown up by private enforcers. From a public choice perspective, governmental enforcers are assumed to maximize advancement of their own careers.[100] It would not look good politically for private enforcers to win case after case that the public authorities had not even investigated.

[98] There are ways in which private litigation could lead to backlash against cartel enforcement. For example, injudicious private enforcers might bring actions against politically powerful interests that the government had avoided prosecuting. However, the net effect of increased private enforcement is likely to be greater transparency and more vigor in anti-cartel measures.

[99] The US has a limited version of this. Under the Antitrust Criminal Penalty Enhancement and Reform Act of 2004, Pub L No 108-237 (2004), defendants that qualify for the requirements of the leniency program receive a reprieve from the harsher aspects of US antitrust civil liability. Plaintiffs are limited to single (as opposed to treble) damages against them, and the cooperating defendant is not subject to joint and several liability.

[100] Roger G Noll, 'Economic Perspective on the Politics of Regulation' in Mark Armstrong and Robert H Porter (eds), *III Handbook of Industrial Organization* (Amsterdam, North Holland, 1989) 1277, 1278.

As noted earlier, the Governments of Belgium and Germany cautioned that private enforcement should always be secondary to public enforcement. Even if that view prevails, it is quite sensible to keep private enforcement as a residual option to give the public enforcers the necessary incentives to do their jobs well.

B. The Limits of Private Enforcement

Having lauded the benefits of private anti-cartel enforcement, I must now take a step back and acknowledge a limit of private enforcement. Indeed, there is an oddity about placing emphasis on the importance of private anti-cartel enforcement. Even if private enforcement were encouraged, the consumers whose injury corresponds mostly closely to the greatest social harm of the cartel behavior would not typically be the parties bringing suit. To understand this, it is necessary to take a quick trip back to the economic foundations of antitrust policy.

When a cartel raises prices above competitive level, it causes at least two distinct kinds of harm. First, some consumers who would otherwise have purchased the product are no longer willing to purchase it at the higher price. Hence, they substitute to a second-best preference—which probably is not sold by the cartelists. We refer to the losses of these consumers as 'deadweight' losses, because they represent a class of forgone transactions that should have, in a competitive market, taken place. Economists identify these deadweight losses as the primary (or, to some, only) *social* costs of cartel behavior. They are a social cost because they result in misallocation of social resources—of customers buying their second-best rather than first-best preferences.

The second class of harm accrues to consumers who continue to purchase the product at the higher price. Their injury is a wealth transfer from consumers to producers. This is not necessarily inefficient in an economic sense, since it merely transfers money from one person to another (as opposed to affecting the deployment of scarce resources directly). There is nothing that can tell us *a priori* that the money is better off in the hands of consumers than in the hands of the producers—for example, if the price-fixed product is a luxury good, the price fixing may work as a progressive tax on rich consumers for the benefit of poor artisans.

For present purposes, it is unnecessary to make a detailed analysis of whether wealth transfers are an important subject of antitrust enforcement. The important point is that deadweight losses are clearly harmful and part of the core—if not the core—of antitrust enforcement. But private parties who sue cartels typically will not be suing to vindicate the interests of the consumers who stopped buying the price-fixed good because it was too expensive. For example, imagine the difficulty of representing a class of purchasers who *stopped* buying vitamins because of the vitamins cartel, or, even worse, who never *started* buying vitamins because of the excessive prices. How would you prove who they were, or quantify their injury? It is much easier to recover damages on behalf of purchasers who made the purchase but paid too much. There, the formula is simply to posit a but-for price and take the difference between the actual price and the but-for price as damages.

Private anti-cartel enforcement tends to focus on a set of purchasers and injuries that are, in my view, secondary in the hierarchy of antitrust concerns. Private enforcement does not seek compensation for or meaningfully analyze the key concern over deadweight losses. On the other hand, public enforcers typically seek penalties, not damages, and do not have to establish standing to sue or make the case on behalf of any particular class of purchasers. Rather, they can focus on the overall social harm of the conduct, and pursue remedies designed to deter and prevent such conduct in the future.

Hence, I am inclined to agree with the German and Belgian Governments that private anti-cartel enforcement is conceptually secondary to public enforcement. This is not a reason to deny private enforcement. Rather, it buttresses my earlier point that perhaps the most important function of private enforcement is to spur the government to action.

C. Private Anti-Cartel Enforcement Need Not Open Pandora's Box

There is a good deal of skepticism in Latin America and around the world about creating US-style mechanisms for private enforcement of antitrust law. One often hears that private litigation in the US is out of control. The example of the woman who recovered $2.9 million from McDonald's after spilling hot coffee on herself is legendary the world over.[101] I have been told by an individual involved in framing a new antitrust law in an Asian jurisdiction that this story is invoked whenever the possibility of private enforcement is mentioned. In its *Empagran amicus curiae* brief, the UK cited a report of the UK Department of Trade and Industry finding that

> many US commentators 'view the number of private antitrust cases in the US as too high' particularly because of 'unscrupulous lawyers . . . quick to file vexatious actions—attracted by the prospect of treble damages'.[102]

Interestingly, even the OECD, which is generally supportive of enhanced competition enforcement, has expressed concern over the availability of a private right of action in the few Latin American jurisdictions where such a right exists. Consider, for example, the following statement from the *OECD's Peer Review Report* on Brazil:

> Private plaintiffs in Brazil may file suit against seeking [*sic*] antitrust damages under Law 8884 and other laws. Just as exposure to prosecution under the Economic Crimes Law

[101] Andrea Gerlin, 'A Matter of Degree: How a Jury Decided That a Coffee Spill is Worth $2.9 Million' *Wall Street Journal* (Sept 1, 1994), at A1.

[102] UK Brief, above n 31, at *15, citing UK Dept of Trade and Industry, above n 83. Despite stressing the need to 'guard against the risks of the US system', the Dept of Trade and Industry Report did recommend changes that would create 'a system in the UK where private actions are less inhibited than at present'.

> can deter pro-competitive behaviour, exposure to private suits for antitrust damages can do likewise. Private damage suits may be commenced in any of Brazil's first instance courts, and there is no information available to determine how frequently such suits are undertaken or how often they result in awards against conduct not properly characterised as anti-competitive. One method for confining private suits to legitimate claims is to amend the law so that such suits may be filed only against parties and conduct that have been subject to a specific finding of illegality by CADE. Such an amendment could include a sunset clause under which the restriction would lapse after a certain number of years unless renewed. Such a clause would provide an opportunity to collect information about and assess the record of private antitrust enforcement in Brazil. If such legislation is not considered appropriate, efforts should nevertheless be undertaken to collect information going forward about the volume, nature, and outcome of private antitrust litigation.[103]

This paragraph strikingly reveals the depths of the antipathy toward private rights of action in antitrust. Despite concluding earlier in the same Report that there have probably been very few private antitrust cases filed in Brazil, the authors of the Report were prepared to recommend at least a temporary moratorium on all independently initiated private antitrust actions so that a study could be done to ensure that the few private cases filed (if any) were not chilling pro-competitive behavior.

I am not unsympathetic to the claim that meritless private antitrust actions can chill pro-competitive behavior. One of the chief criticisms of private antitrust enforcement is that private rights of action lead to abusive suits by competitors.[104] In the United States, about two-thirds of private enforcers of antitrust are aggrieved competitors or other businesses vertically related to the defendant; fewer than 20 per cent are consumers.[105] There is ample evidence that businesses sometimes (and I believe often) abuse the private right of action by filing lawsuits that are primarily designed to harass their competitors and prevent vigorous competition and other efficient practices.

This concern, however, should not deter the creation of a private right of action directed against hard-core cartel behavior. Competitors typically will not have standing to sue the members of a cartel because they are not usually injured by

[103] *OECD Peer Review Report*, above n 24, at 164. Later in the Report, the authors again stress the need for study of private antitrust litigation in Brazil, repeating the concern that private litigation could be 'detracting from effective competition law enforcement'. *Ibid*, at 169.

[104] See, eg, Daniel A Crane, 'The Paradox of Predatory Pricing' 91 *Cornell Law Review* 1, 5–32 (2005); R Preston McAfee and Nicholas V Vakkur, 'The Strategic Abuse of the Antitrust Laws' 2 *Journal of Strategic Management Education* 37, 37–38 (2005); Edward A Synder and Thomas E Kauper, 'Misuses of the Antitrust Laws: The Competitor Plaintiff' 90 *Michigan Law Review* 551 (1991); William J Baumol and Janusz A Ordover, 'Use of Antitrust to Subvert Competition' 28 *Journal of Law & Economics* 247 (1985); Frank H Easterbook, 'The Limits of Antitrust' 63 *Texas Law Review* 1 (1984).

[105] Lawrence J White, 'The Georgetown Study of Private Antitrust Litigation' (1985) 54 *Antitrust Law Journal* 59, 62. White reports that the Georgetown Study conducted on a sample of 2,500 antitrust cases from 1973–83 found that a third of private plaintiffs were defendant's competitors, another 30% were dealers or distributors, and less than 20% were customers or otherwise consumers.

cartel behavior. To the contrary, if the cartel succeeds in raising prices in the market, this will usually redound to the benefit of any firms that do not join the cartel. Indeed, returning for a moment to Oliver Wendell Holmes's 'bad man' perspective, the ideal position of a seller is for his competitors to form a cartel, raise prices artificially high, and implement strict production quotas. The non-participating seller can then make a fortune by 'cheating' slightly on the cartel price and vastly expanding his market share at a lucrative price.

Of course, some cartels can have exclusionary effects—for example, if they not only agree to fix prices, rig bids or divide territories, but also agree to boycott or otherwise impose economic sanctions on non-participating rivals. For example, the 1997 chicken case in Peru noted earlier involved a cartel agreement by poultry producers to limit production, exclude new entry, and even knock some existing producers out of the market.[106] But if abusive suits by competitors of this stripe are a concern, one could limit the reach of the private right of action by specifying that only plaintiffs who have been injured as purchasers from or sellers to a cartel can sue.

The specter of private litigation running amok—of greedy lawyers harassing innocent businesses—is a real concern. But, in this regard, there is a vast difference in incentives and opportunities for abuse between private abuse of dominance litigation and private anti-cartel litigation. Abusive litigation is a comparatively minimal concern if the proposal is to establish a well-tailored program of private anti-cartel enforcement.

IV. Conclusion

This chapter has offered a US perspective on opening up private anti-cartel enforcement in Latin America. Writing from a US perspective comes with both benefits and drawbacks. The benefit is that the US has far more experience with private anti-cartel enforcement than any other jurisdiction. The drawback is that much of the world deliberately rejects many of the features of US civil litigation that make private enforcement so prevalent. Nonetheless, the trend around the world, including in the jurisdictions that filed the *Empagran amici* briefs, is to open up private antitrust enforcement. If there is any place for such measures, it is with respect to cartels, particularly international cartels. Private anti-cartel enforcement in Latin America need not follow a US model. It would be advisable, however, to move in the direction of building indigenous models that are sustainable and effective in bringing the benefits of private enforcement to Latin American consumers.

[106] *OECD Peer Review Report*, above n 24, at 340.

Chapter XVI

The US Federal Trade Commission and Competition Advocacy: Lessons for Latin American Competition Policy

TODD J ZYWICKI* AND JAMES C COOPER**

I. Introduction

Competition regulators in the United States have a variety of tools available to them to execute competition policy. The most prominent are litigation challenging anti-competitive practices and the review of mergers for predicted anticompetitive effects. A less-recognized but often effective tool, however, is 'competition advocacy'. Broadly, competition advocacy involves using persuasion, rather than coercion, to convince government actors to pursue policies that further competition and consumer choice. As the OECD has noted:

> The mandate of the competition office extends beyond merely enforcing the competition laws. ... It must assume the role of competition advocate, acting proactively to bring about government policies that lower barriers to entry, promote deregulation and trade liberalization, and otherwise minimize unnecessary government intervention in the marketplace.[1]

* Professor of Law, George Mason University School of Law; Research Fellow, James Buchanan Center for the Study of Political Economy. Former Director, Office of Policy Planning, Federal Trade Commission. The author would like to thank the Law & Economics Center at George Mason University School of Law for financial support for this project. Both authors are especially grateful to Paul Pautler for generously allowing us to draw on much of his earlier work on the history of competition advocacy at the FTC which appears in James C Cooper *et al*, 'Theory and Practice of Competition Advocacy at the FTC' 72 *Antitrust Law Journal* 1091 (2005), and for helpful comments and suggestions on this chapter.

** Attorney Advisor for Commissioner William E Kovacic and Former Acting Director, Office of Policy Planning, Federal Trade Commission. The views expressed in the essay are the authors' own and do not necessarily represent those of the Federal Trade Commission or any individual commissioner.

[1] Organization for Economic Co-operation and Development (OECD), *Competition Advocacy: Challenges for Developing Countries* (Secretariat Note prepared for the Second Latin American Competition Forum, Paris, 2004) at 1.

Apart from formal attempts to change regulatory policy, the domain of competition advocacy also includes activities that contribute to the establishment of a competition culture, such as seminars, press releases, reports, and other endeavors aimed at educating the public on the benefits of competition.[2] A population that values competition will place indirect political pressure on officials to embrace competition-friendly regulations.

Anticompetitive regulation can result either by design from interest group influence, or as an unintended consequence of otherwise well-intentioned regulation. Regardless of the impetus, public restraints on competition can be as harmful to competition and consumer welfare as private restraints on trade. Indeed, because of the government's greater effectiveness in enforcing its restraints on competition, such regulations may be even more harmful in interfering with the competitive process and reducing consumer welfare than private restraints. Whereas private cartels may collapse over time because of incentives to cheat, and entry or technological change can erode a monopolist's position, public restraints are enforced by the government.

Successful competition policy, thus, must target threats to competition from two fronts, both private and public restraints on competition.[3] Attempting to protect competition by focusing solely on private restraints is analogous to trying to stop the flow of water at a fork in a stream by blocking only one of the channels. Unless competition authorities block both channels of anticompetitive conduct, they are not likely even to slow, much less stop, the flow. Eventually all of the water will simply flow toward the unblocked channel. The same is true of antitrust enforcement. If competition authorities create a system in which private price fixing results in a jail sentence, but blocking competition through government regulation is legal, then parties will simply invest in securing a government-sponsored cartel.[4] Former Federal Trade Commission (FTC) Chairman Deborah Majoras has observed that government-imposed restrictions on competition 'can exist in the daylight, rather than in the shadows, and those who attempt to evade the restraints may receive official punishment.'[5] Interest groups will often mask self-interested restraints in the garb of the public interest, such as consumer protection arguments.

[2] International Competition Network (ICN), 'Competition Advocacy in Regulated Sectors: Examples of Success' in the report of the Capacity Building and Competition Policy Implementation Working Group, April, 2002, at iii.

[3] Todd J Zywicki, 'Competition Policy and Regulatory Reforms: Means and Ends' Japan Fair Trade Commission *CPRC Discussion Paper Series* (2003), *available at* http://www.ftc.gov/speeches/other/031120zywickijapanspeech.pdf

[4] Gordon Tullock, 'The Welfare Costs of Tariffs, Monopoly and Theft' 5 *Western Economic Journal* 224–32 (1967).

[5] Deborah Platt Majoras, 'A Dose of our Own Medicine: Applying a Cost/Benefit Analysis to the FTC's Advocacy Program', speech given at conference on Current Topics in Antitrust Economics and Competition Policy, Charles River Associates, Feb 8, 2005.

But public restraints on competition need not be intentional, or the result of conscious rent-seeking activity by interest groups. Many regulations are animated by the salutary purpose of consumer protection or other social goals. Nonetheless, many such well-intended regulations may have an unintended negative effect on competition, such that the benefits of such regulations are outweighed by the negative effects on competition and consumer choice, or that important social goals could be reached with fewer intrusions on the competitive process.

To address these problems of government-created barriers to competition, the FTC has, for the past 30 years, pursued a competition advocacy program. The purpose of the FTC's program is to study and critique government-created barriers to competition and, where possible and appropriate, to suggest alternative regulatory approaches that can accomplish the same goals at lower costs to the competitive process. This is accomplished through consultations with state and federal regulators to advise them on the economic consequences of their regulatory activities in terms of their effect on competition and consumer welfare. These consultations may be formal or informal, public or private. At the FTC, formal advocacy filings can include filing written comments to other administrative agencies, submitting amicus briefs in litigation, presenting testimony before legislative bodies, or submitting letter comments at the request of appropriate federal and state legislative or administrative bodies. Advocacy activities also can be done informally through conversations with administrative agencies, legislators, or their staffs. Further, advocacy filings can be either positive (supporting a proposed regulatory change, for instance) or negative (opposing a particular regulation or legislation).

Both the success and political support for the program have waxed and waned over time.[6] During this time, the FTC has learned many lessons about what makes for a successful competition advocacy program. Given the extensive governmental regulation of the economy in Latin America, opportunities for a robust competition advocacy program are surely manifest.

This essay distills the lessons of the FTC's competition advocacy program and explains the impact it has had on the American economy and regulatory structure over time, with an eye toward studying the implications of such a program for competition policy in Latin American countries. Some Latin American countries may already have similar programs in place, but we are not aware of any such program as extensive as that of the FTC. An active advocacy program is even more important in the Latin American setting—where additionally the State has been more interventionist in the economy, where consumer interest groups are weaker, where there is less government transparency, and where there is less of a competition culture. It may be easier to import the US lessons in competition advocacy than other areas of US antitrust. Advocacy is about making economic and policy

[6] James C Cooper, Paul A Pautler, and Todd J Zywicki, 'The Theory and Practice of Competition Advocacy at the FTC' 72 *Antitrust Law Journal* 1091–1112 (2005).

arguments, which is easier to transplant than a common law judge-based system in an area that is otherwise civil law-based.

II. Competition Policy in Latin America

Throughout Latin America, competition authorities continue to grapple with the challenges of crafting appropriate competition policy for developing countries. Indeed, a commitment to competition as the organizing principle of the economy is of relatively recent vintage in Latin America. Various forms of economic planning and interventionism historically have characterized modern economic policy throughout the region. The economic legacy of South American colonialism was that of the 'Encomienda', imposed by the Crown for the benefit of Spanish *conquistadores*. The Encomienda system tended toward a high concentration of wealth in a landholding aristocracy, rather than market-based competition.[7] Commerce and competition were subordinated to the institutions and norms of an aristocratic military society.

Independence altered the political institutions of the region but did not radically transform South American economic institutions. Economic theory and policy in the post-colonial era and through most of the 20th century stressed State planning and interventionism rather than market competition, tendencies that were reinforced by widespread acceptance of socialist and Marxist political ideology,[8] as well as economic theories of dependency and import substitution promulgated by, among others, Argentine economist Raul Prebisch. As Professor Ignacio De Leon, former chief of Venezuela's Competition Authority, Pro-Competencia, observes:

> As a result of economic centralization public policy tended to eliminate competition, which was regarded as a dangerous threat to planning development. Economic planning was considered the fundamental means of allocating resources.[9]

Many industries never experienced competition, going from Spanish Crown-imposed monopolies, to local monopolies headed by rich oligarchs, to State-sponsored and/or owned monopolies. Competition was replaced with planning and regulation throughout South America. Many industries were either nationalized or subjected to heavy price controls. Compulsory licensing in many economic sectors stifled competition in services. Protectionist trade policy protected domestic producers from competition from abroad, dampening the incentives

[7] Ignacio De Leon, 'Institutional Analysis of Competition Policy in Transition and Developing Countries: The Lessons From Latin America' 3 *Washington University Global Studies Law Review* 405–28 (2004).
[8] *Ibid.*
[9] *Ibid*, at 421.

to become more efficient and improve quality. Entry and exit into markets was heavily regulated.

During this era, government actively suppressed competition and promoted the development of large industrial enterprises and cartel-type arrangements to encourage economic stability, including widespread professional licensing and other barriers to entry. As De Leon observes, 'Cartels and other forms of competition restrictions were not only tolerated but also openly promoted by the State.'[10] He adds, 'In Latin America, cartels were actively promoted in view of the interest of governments in ensuring the permanence of inefficient domestic producers in the market.'[11] In turn, these large State-owned and State-protected firms and industries were expected to serve as a sort of mini-welfare state, substituting for poorly-funded and politically unstable governments and distributing benefits to their members. The overall effect was to create a cozy relationship between industry and the government that favored economic stability over competition, and the interests of large businesses over those of consumers.[12]

These heavy regulations tend to create substantial regulatory barriers to entry and thereby stifle competition. In turn, by suppressing competition, these high regulatory barriers retard economic growth and spur political corruption.[13] This thicket of regulation makes it almost impossible for legitimate small businesses to enter and remain in business, thereby limiting rivalry to incumbent, often politically well-connected, businesses.[14] Moreover, many countries in Latin America are small economies, in which high levels of industry concentration are more likely to exist—a very different situation from that in the United States.[15] High trade barriers (until post-1990s trade liberalization occurred across Latin America) exacerbated the lack of competition by protecting domestic producers from imported goods as well. This illustrates the need for competition authorities to push for trade liberalization as part of a comprehensive competition advocacy policy (as the FTC did in the United States throughout the 1980s in endorsing more rational anti-dumping rules), a concern that is even stronger in smaller economies such as those in Latin America.[16]

[10] *Ibid.*

[11] *Ibid*, at 422.

[12] Ignacio De Leon, 'An Alternative Approach to Policies for the Promotion of Competition in Developing Countries' 6 *Southwestern Journal of Law and Trade in the Americas* 85–116 (1999).

[13] Simeon Djankov *et al*, 'The Regulation of Entry' 117 *Quarterly Journal of Economics* 1–26 (2002).

[14] Hernando De Soto, *The Mystery of Capital: Why Capitalism Triumphs in the West and Fails Everywhere Else* New York, NY, Basic Books, 2000).

[15] Michal S Gal, 'Size Does Matter: The Effects of Market Size on Optimal Competition Policy' 74 *Southern California Law Review* 1437–78 (2001).

[16] *Ibid.*

III. Competition Advocacy and Competition Policy in the United States

A. The History of Advocacy at the FTC

During the 1970s America suffered 'stagflation', in which the economy simultaneously suffered from low growth (stagnation) and high inflation. American companies became inefficient and unresponsive, consumers suffered, and foreign competitors gained market share. In 1974, in the midst of this era, the Chairman of the FTC, Lewis Engman, gave a speech to financial analysts in which he tied the country's macroeconomic problems to its competition policy.[17] In particular, Engman argued that burdensome federal transportation regulations contributed to the problem of slow growth. Engman explained that the Civil Aeronautics Board, which comprehensively regulated routes and fares in the airline industry, raised prices by limiting the entry of new carriers and controlling the distribution of airline routes. He also noted that the Interstate Commerce Commission's comprehensive rate regulation effectively sanctioned price fixing among freight trucking companies. Misguided efforts to regulate competition in these two industries alone—airlines and trucking—substantially raised transportation costs, which raised prices and hampered economic growth. Over the next decade the federal government moved to substantially deregulate airlines, railroads, trucking and inter-city buses, increasing consumer welfare by tens of billions of dollars annually.[18] During this period, the FTC picked up on Engman's call, using further speeches and formal written submissions to regulatory agencies and legislators identifying the costs of competition-chilling regulations.

Engman's speech effectively launched the modern competition advocacy program at the FTC. Because Engman presented competition policy as a means of addressing the country's pressing economic problems at the time, the speech received substantial coverage in the popular press, including front page coverage in the *New York Times*.[19] It also helped to convince consumers and companies that deregulation was not a zero-sum game, and that by reducing regulatory burdens that raised transportation costs, other industries could flourish.[20]

Moreover, politicians embraced deregulatory and pro-competition policies as a bipartisan initiative, especially in the transportation industries such as trucking and airlines. Senator Ted Kennedy, closely advised by his then-counsel and now Supreme Court Justice Stephen Breyer, held high-profile public hearings in the 1970s that championed deregulation as a mechanism for lower prices, higher

[17] Address by Lewis Engman, Chairman, Federal Trade Commission, before the 1974 Fall Conference of the Financial Analysts Federation, Detroit, Michigan (Oct 7, 1974).

[18] Zywicki, above n 3.

[19] Cooper, Pautler and Zywicki, above n 6, at 1094.

[20] Zywicki, above n 3.

quality and expanded consumer choice. These bipartisan efforts to build popular support for pro-competition policies helped to create a still-strong presumption among the American populace in favor of markets and competition as the primary means of addressing economic issues.

Spurred by this auspicious beginning, throughout the 1980s the Commission continued aggressively to pursue advocacy activities. During this period the Commission repeatedly recognized the valuable role played by the advocacy program in pursuing the Commission's competition policy agenda.[21] By the middle of the 1980s the FTC's advocacy program reached its zenith, with 90 comments issued annually to federal and state regulators. Beginning in the 1990s, however, the advocacy program began to dwindle in importance and resources within the FTC. The reduction in emphasis during this period occurred for a number of reasons, including a general desire by certain FTC Chairs to reduce conflict with other state and federal regulators, as well as a record merger wave in the United States that taxed the resources of the FTC to be able to dedicate assets to the task of competition advocacy activities. Nonetheless, since 1980 the Commission has filed more than 750 advocacy comments with various agencies.

The FTC's continued activity on the advocacy front may be illustrated with a few recent examples. An industry of particular interest has been the regulated professions. Professions, such as attorneys, real estate brokers and optometrists, have a long tradition of self-regulation. Under this type of regulatory regime, groups of competing professionals jointly promulgate and enforce rules that limit entry into the profession and dictate its members' marketplace activities. Although such regulation is often justified in the name of consumer protection, it provides professionals with both the opportunity and the incentive to stifle competition to benefit themselves at the expense of consumers. For instance, in the United States, attorneys have enacted or attempted to enact regulations that restrict advertising of prices and services, proscribe relationships with commercial firms, and expand the list of services that can be provided exclusively by attorneys. Overreaching professional self-regulation can substantially increase the costs of professional services while providing minimal marginal consumer benefits.[22]

As a result of these fears, during the past few years US competition authorities have encouraged the states to adopt pro-competitive professional regulations. For instance, the FTC worked with the Attorney General of Connecticut in commenting before the state opticians board, which was considering whether to require stand-alone sellers of contact lenses (such as mail order or on-line sellers) to obtain state optician licenses.[23] The FTC also has encouraged states to reject proposals that would prevent non-lawyers from competing with lawyers to

[21] Arnold C Celnicker, 'The Federal Trade Commission's Competition and Consumer Advocacy Program' 33 *St Louis University Law Journal* 379 (1989).

[22] Zywicki, above n 3.

[23] Comments of the Staff of the FTC, Intervenor, before the Connecticut Board of Examiners for Opticians (March 27, 2002), <http://www.ftc.gov/be/v020007.htm>.

handle real estate closings, and which would have thereby restricted competition from title companies, out-of-state suppliers of the services and Internet lenders, resulting in higher prices for consumers.[24] Research in the European Union has reached similar conclusions about the welfare effects of overly-extensive professional regulation and can generate support for Member States to ease overly restrictive rules.[25]

Another recent comment that shows the positive effect of the Commission's advocacy program was the FTC's comment filed with the Commodities Futures Trading Commission (CFTC) in January 2004.[26] The comment concerned the application by Eurex, a German–Swiss financial exchange, to establish an all-electronic market in the United States to compete with the Chicago Board of Trade and the Chicago Mercantile Exchange. The incumbent exchanges opposed the application. The FTC's submission to the CFTC noted the theoretical and empirical economics literature that generally found that competition among rival financial exchanges can benefit consumers by leading to lower bid-ask spreads. Moreover, Eurex's innovative electronic exchange would likely reduce costs relative to the traditional exchange, generating technological improvements in the market.

Commissioner Lukken of the CFTC specifically indicated that he had placed great weight on the FTC's analysis in supporting the CFTC's decision to approve another US futures exchange. Subsequent reports in the business press found that the incumbent exchanges did in fact lower their trading fees substantially

[24] See letter from the Department of Justice and FTC to the South Carolina Supreme Court (April 15, 2008), available at http://www.ftc.gov/os/2008/04/v080010sc.pdf; letter from the Department of Justice and FTC to the Hawaii Supreme Court (Jan 25, 2008), available at http://www.ftc.gov/os/2008/01/V080004letter.pdf; letters from the Justice Department and the FTC to the Committee on the Judiciary of the New York State Assembly (June 21, 2006 and April 27, 2007), available at http://www.ftc.gov/os/2006/06/V060016 NYUplFinal.pdf and http://www.ftc.gov/be/V070004.pdf; letter from the Justice Department and the FTC to Executive Director of the Kansas Bar Ass'n (Feb 4, 2005), available at http://www.ftc.gov/be/v050002.pdf; letter from the Justice Department and the FTC to Task Force to Define the Practice of Law in Massachusetts, Massachusetts Bar Ass'n (Dec 16, 2004), available at http://www.ftc.gov/os/2004/12/041216massuplltr.pdf; letter from the Justice Department and the FTC to Unauthorized Practice of Law Committee, Indiana State Bar Ass'n (Oct 1, 2003), available at http://www.ftc.gov/os/2003/10/uplindiana.htm; letter from the Justice Department and the FTC to Standing Committee on the Unlicensed Practice of Law, State Bar of Georgia (March 20, 2003), available at http://www.ftc.gov/be/v030007.htm; letter from the Justice Department to Speaker of the Rhode Island House of Representatives (March 28, 2003), available at http://www.ftc.gov/be/v020013.htm; letter from the Justice Department and the FTC to Task Force on the Model Definition of the Practice of Law, American Bar Ass'n (Dec 20, 2002), available at http://www.ftc.gov/opa/2002/12/lettertoaba.htm; letter from the Justice Department and the FTC to Speaker of the Rhode Island House of Representatives *et al* (March 29, 2002), available at http://www.ftc.gov/be/v020013.pdf; letter from the Justice Department and the FTC to President of the North Carolina State Bar (July 11, 2002), available at http://www.ftc.gov/os/2002/07/non attorneyinvolvment.pdf; letter from the Justice Department and the FTC to Ethics Committee of the North Carolina State Bar (Dec 14, 2001), available at http://www.ftc.gov/be/V020006.htm.

[25] Mario Monti, 'Competition in Professional Services: New Light and New Challenges', Prepared Remarks for *Bundesanwaltskammer*, Berlin, Germany (March 21, 2003), <http://europa.eu.int/comm/competition/speeches/text/sp2003_007_en.pdf>.

[26] Majoras, above n 5.

in reaction to the new competitive threat in the market for US Treasury futures contracts, leading to increases in the volume of trades.[27]

One of the FTC's most notable recent advocacy successes was on the question of the interstate direct shipment of wine. In October 2002, the FTC held several days of hearings on the problem of state regulatory barriers to e-commerce in a variety of industries, including online sales of funeral caskets, contact lenses and wine. Regulation of e-commerce provides a ready example of the failures in the political system that can give rise to anticompetitive regulation. The efficiency of e-commerce flows from the fact that online sellers can service the entire country without the need to maintain high-overhead storefronts in specific geographic areas. Further, because consumers can shop among online sellers more cheaply than offline sellers, online firms are likely to compete more intensely on price than their offline counterparts. As a result, Internet sellers can drive down prices and increase consumer choice.

This business model, however, threatens incumbent bricks-and-mortar sellers, who fear this new competition. Moreover, because the operations of online sellers are diffused all over the country, whereas traditional sellers are located in a specific geographic area, online sellers are politically weaker than local special interests and face the potential obstacle of an array of costly and inconsistent regulations. As a result, just as domestic industries have incentives to seek tariff protection notwithstanding its negative impact on consumers, traditional bricks-and-mortar sellers have the incentive to seek regulations that protect them from out-of-state competitors such as online sellers.

In July 2003, the FTC issued a report on state restrictions on the direct shipment of wine from out-of-state vendors to in-state consumers.[28] In the United States, most alcohol is sold through the 'three-tier' system of producers, licensed wholesalers and retailers. Direct shipment of wine allows the producer to sell directly to consumers using common carriers, such as Fed Ex, to deliver the products. This ability to bypass one or two levels of the 'three-tier' system can reduce prices and increase consumer choice. In addition, because of the rapidly proliferating number of small wineries in the United States, many wineries are unable to find a wholesaler that will distribute their wines for them. Direct shipment thus permits these wineries to distribute their products to consumers it would be impossible to reach by any other means. Research conducted by economists at the FTC found that online sales of wine led to increased consumer choice and lower prices than sales through traditional channels.[29]

Opponents of direct shipment of wine, including most prominently those liquor wholesalers bypassed by direct shipment, raised concerns that permitting

[27] 'Chicago Takes on Europe', *Business Week*, July 5, 2004, at 76–77.

[28] Staff of the FTC, *Possible Anticompetitive Barriers to E-Commerce: Wine* (July 2003) ('Wine Report').

[29] 'Market and Nonmarket Barriers to Internet Wine Sales: The Case of Virginia' 6/2 *Business and Politics* 5 (2004).

direct shipment of alcohol could lead to increased access to alcohol by minors. This is unquestionably a legitimate public concern. But this sort of 'all-or-nothing' approach is unwise as a matter of sound policy-making. At most, it suggests that regulators should attempt to balance the attainment of other social goals against the desire for greater competition, and should seek to attain those social goals with the least restrictive incursions on competition.

The FTC considered these clashing policy concerns in the Wine Report. In fact, the opponents of direct shipping, including state regulators, had expected their expression of concern simply to be taken at face value as the sort of 'trump' described. Rather than simply taking their expression at face value or simply ignoring them, however, the FTC surveyed alcohol regulators in a number of states that had permitted direct wine shipment to discover their opinion on the validity of the underage drinking concerns that had been raised. The FTC found that, in fact, the concerns about underage drinking were largely groundless in practice, due to the economic constraints of direct wine shipment (because of fixed shipping costs, only more expensive wines were less costly when purchased online), the delay involved between order and receipt, and the inherent difficulties associated with online acquisition of alcohol (such as the requirement of a credit card). The experience of state alcohol enforcement officials revealed that alcohol was easily available to most minors through traditional bricks-and-mortar channels, making it unnecessary for minors to incur the additional expense, delay and risk of ordering wine online. Lastly, the FTC found that adopting safeguards, such as checking age identification at delivery, could further address these social concerns without the adverse competitive impact of a prohibition on direct shipment.

The impact of the FTC's Wine Report was felt dramatically a few years later when the United States Supreme Court declared unconstitutional certain state laws that discriminatorily permitted direct shipment to consumers from in-state wineries while prohibiting similar shipment from out-of-state wineries.[30] Under applicable principles of constitutional law, a state law that facially discriminates against out-of-state manufacturers of a good can be justified only if the discrimination is necessary to accomplish a legitimate regulatory purpose and is the least intrusive means of accomplishing the regulatory end.[31] In order to support the regulation, therefore, the state must produce concrete empirical evidence. In striking down the discriminatory state regulations, the Supreme Court in *Granholm* relied extensively on the FTC's findings in the Wine Report, with respect both to the consumer welfare benefits of direct shipping and to the plausibility of the states' justifications for their discriminatory regulatory regime (such as prevention of underage drinking).[32] By contrast, the states offered no empirical evidence

[30] *Granholm v Heald*, 544 US 460 (2005).

[31] Asheesh Argawal and Todd J Zywicki, 'Wine, Commerce, and the Constitution' 1 *NYU Journal of Law & Liberty* 609 (2005); Jerry Ellig, Asheesh Agarwal and Todd J Zywicki, 'Wine Wars: Uncorking E-Commerce?' 27/4 *Regulation* 10 (2004).

[32] *Granholm*, above n 30.

to justify their discriminatory regulatory regimes. As a result, the Wine Report played a pivotal role in the Supreme Court's decision in the case.

As these examples demonstrate, an energetic competition advocacy program can provide an important complement to traditional competition policy tools, thereby generating improvements in consumer welfare. Despite successes such as these, which have increasingly illustrated the benefits of a vigorous competition advocacy policy, the FTC's commitment to the program has waxed and waned over time. Examining the sources of these changing fortunes can provide lessons as to how to maintain the effectiveness of and support for the program.

B. Explaining Variation in Advocacy Activity Over Time

1. *Political and Economic Developments*

Developments exogenous to decisions made within the Commission may explain some of the changing fortunes of the advocacy program over time. In the late 1970s and into the 1980s, over-burdensome regulation of what could otherwise be competitive industries, such as certain transportation markets, was an obvious focal point for advocacy efforts. By the mid-1990s, however, most of those easy de-regulation targets were gone, as regulation of transportation, certain utilities and telecommunications had been altered significantly or eliminated. Thus, there may have been somewhat less need for an advocate for rational analysis of federal regulatory and competition issues at some times. Latin America went through a similar period of liberalization (along with privatization), mostly in the late 1980s and 1990s, but with less successful results. Whereas privatization and deregulation in the United States were combined with aggressive competition policy, in Latin America, privatization often proceeded without deregulation, leading to the replacement of public monopolies with equally insular private monopolies.

Dramatic economic and technological innovations also may create conditions that call forth a higher level of advocacy activity; as new technology displaces existing business models, incumbents often turn to regulators, demanding protection from new competitors. In this vein, the development of the Internet and e-commerce has been a stimulus for advocacy filings, because the Internet creates a new form of competition to established businesses. Various existing laws that have been used to limit competition and consumer choice have now been extended to block competition from the Internet as well. In areas such as direct shipment of wine, Internet casket sales, contact lenses, and in other industries, renewed efforts have been made by entrenched interests to block this new form of competition. In many situations, moreover, the beneficiaries of anticompetitive regulations are in-state merchants, whereas many Internet sellers do a modest amount of business in many states. As a result, in-state merchants have the incentive and influence to lobby effectively for protection, whereas out-of-state sellers lack the ability to compete as effectively in the political market as in the economic market.

2. *Lack of Internal/External Political Support*

The FTC's advocacy program has been controversial from its inception because it cannot avoid offending powerful interest groups and other regulatory authorities on each issue it pursues. Each regulation generally has some identifiable and well-organized political support inside and/or outside government. By contrast, as will be shown in more detail below, consumer interest in increased competition is supported in the abstract, but rarely finds a strong political voice in particular contexts. Some of the political animus toward the program was likely based on disputes over specific policy suggestions, while more general objections may have arisen regarding the proper role (if any) of a federal agency in providing suggestions regarding competition or regulatory policies to a state legislature or regulatory body. Additionally, certain congressional critics also argued that the advocacy program was so resource-intensive that it kept the Commission from aggressively pursuing predation and other non-merger antitrust activities.

This latter concern, however, seems largely unfounded. The resources that the advocacy program consumed were never sufficient to constrain the Commission significantly from pursuing other activities.[33] Advocacy consumed about 3–4 per cent of FTC staff resources (30 to 40 employee work-years) at the 1987 zenith.[34] Advocacy resources were about 2 per cent of FTC resources in 1989, and by 1994 had fallen to less than 0.5 per cent of FTC resources (four to five employee work-years). By 2000, the percentage was so small that the program was virtually invisible—a maximum guesstimate regarding agency-wide advocacy resources would have been two work-years. (The data for that year, such as they are, indicate that less than one work year was devoted to advocacy across the agency.) As of 2002, the total agency work-years devoted to advocacy might have been closer to five.[35] Majoras estimates that resources expended on the advocacy program in 2005 accounted for less than 1 per cent of the FTC's budget, or less than $2 million total.

Although the advocacy program itself is unlikely to have affected enforcement activities negatively, it is possible that internal resources constraints, such as the US merger wave of the 1990s, may have had an indirect effect of slowing the advocacy program. The need to examine the large number of mergers may have drawn off Bureau of Economics resources from the primary research necessary to generate effective advocacies, as well as taxing the small staffs of the individual Commissioners, which remain fixed in size over time. Thus, there are various chokepoints in the advocacy production pipeline that can be affected by resource constraints that are not captured simply by noting the relatively small size of the program.

[33] Celnicker, above n 21.

[34] *Ibid*, at 399 (citing Memorandum from James Giffin, Associate Executive Director, to Andrew J Strenio, FTC Commissioner (July 28, 1987)).

[35] Majoras, above n 5.

C. Relation to Sectoral Regulators

A final question that arises in carrying out advocacy activities is the relationship between agencies that regulate competition generally, such as the FTC, and agencies that regulate particular sectors of the economy, such as the Federal Communications Commission (FCC), the Food and Drug Administration (FDA), the Department of Transportation, or the Department of Agriculture. The mission of competition authorities to promote competition and consumer welfare may come into conflict with the missions of these other sectoral regulators that are responsive to their own constituencies and regulatory goals. Consumer welfare may be one of the goals of sectoral regulators, but it is not their primary charge. For instance, while the Department of Agriculture surely cares about competition and low prices for consumers, its primary political constituency is US farmers and members of congressional agriculture oversight committees, who generally will prefer reduced competition and higher and more stable prices. Given inevitable clashes between interests of consumers and interests of the agency's primary constituencies (here, farmers), the interests of consumers generally will yield. Moreover, competition agencies are much more well-established and internally stronger in the United States than in Latin America. The FTC, for instance, is one of the oldest and well-established agencies in the United States Government, pre-dating many sectoral regulatory agencies by decades. In Latin America, by contrast, sectoral regulators generally preceded the establishment of antitrust authorities, giving them an upper hand in inter-agency 'turf battles' between advocates of greater regulation versus greater competition.

In addition, agencies themselves have their own motivations, and tend to seek to expand their authority, power and budget.[36] As a result, sectoral regulators are chary about sharing their regulatory authority with other agencies, such as a competition authority. Moreover, sectoral regulators tend to have an inherent internal bias towards greater regulation, especially of the command-and-control variety.[37] More detailed and command-and-control style regulation has a higher rate of planned obsolescence built into it, necessitating more frequent amendment and updating. This dynamic creates a natural constituency for the regulator's product, requiring interest groups to exert repeated lobbying efforts to update obsolete regulations in light of changing circumstances. In turn, this boost in demand for the regulator's services is met by a need for larger budgets and regulatory discretion on behalf of the regulators themselves. A competition-based policy, by contrast, is essentially a self-governing system, requiring only minimal oversight

[36] James Q Wilson, *Bureaucracy: What Government Agencies Do and Why they Do It* (New York, NY Basic Books, 1991); William A Niskanen, *Bureaucracy and Representative Government* (Atherton, 1971).

[37] Todd J Zywicki, 'Environmental Externalities and Political Externalities: The Political Economy of Environmental Regulation and Reform' 73 *Tulane Law Review* 845 (1999).

and infrequent intervention to ensure that the system is functioning properly.[38] Absent such malfunctions, no further regulatory activity is needed. By contrast, a regulation-based system requires ongoing maintenance, review and updating, thus creating a steady stream of demand for the regulator's services and recurrent trips into the regulatory pool. Lastly, sectoral regulators may be more prone to the problem of regulatory capture, as their narrow focus and repeat dealings with the industries that they regulate may lead them to adopt the views of such industries, confusing the interests of the regulated industry with the interests of the public at large. Sectoral regulators may also be inclined, by disposition and training, toward the status quo, which is predictable and maintains their human capital. As a result of these various factors, sectoral regulators tend be resistant to intervention by competition authorities, both by mission and by bureaucratic maximization principles.

There is no single correct answer on the proper division of responsibilities between sectoral regulators and competition authorities. Sectoral regulators have greater expertise in a given area or industry. But competition agencies may have better appreciation of the social and economic benefits of competition. Sectoral regulators may lack a background in competition policy and may view industry, rather than the consumer and the competitive process, as their client. Even if they want to promote competition, sectoral regulators may be subject to intense pressure from the industries that they oversee and from the legislators that oversee them, a problem of regulatory capture.

Moreover, sectoral regulators may lack the breadth of knowledge to distinguish between legitimate and illegitimate requests for exemptions from the rigors of the competitive marketplace. Almost every economic sector can plausibly claim that it is somehow 'different' and should be exempt from the competitive process, or sufficiently 'complex' that it should be subject to a unique competition policy. Because of their breadth of knowledge of competition in many economics markets, competition authorities may be better able to distinguish legitimate from illegitimate claims for preferential treatment. Rather than promoting competition and consumer welfare, sectoral regulation often has harmed consumers by imposing needless controls on entry, pricing and new product development.[39] Because of these differences in focus and expertise, competition authorities pursuing advocacy activities may come into conflict with sectoral regulators. These conflicts are unavoidable, although steps may be taken to minimize them.[40]

38 *Ibid.*

39 Timothy J Muris, 'Looking Forward: The Federal Trade Commission and the Future Development of US Competition Policy' 2003 *Columbia Business Law Review* 359–410; Paul L Joskow and Nancy L Rose, 'The Effect of Economic Regulation' in Richard Schmalensee and Robert D Willig (eds), *Handbook of Industrial Organization*, vol II (North-Holland, Amsterdam, Elsevier Science Pub Co, 1989).

40 Zywicki, above n 3.

IV. The Need for Competition Advocacy

A. Advocacy and the Economic Theory of Regulation

Because markets sometimes fail to produce goods or services that consumers value, regulations that restrict competition may arguably be justified. For example, some markets may be so fraught with informational asymmetries between producers and consumers that governmental assurance of quality is warranted. Although regulation in these instances may deprive consumers of the some of the benefits of competition, it may be warranted when the benefits of correcting market failures exceed the opportunity costs of displaced competition.

Regulation, however, also can be used to restrict competition not in order to improve consumer welfare, but to transfer wealth from consumers to a favored industry. It has long been recognized that because of industry's superior efficiency in political organization relative to consumers, consumer interests are often subservient to industry interests in the regulatory process. Beginning with the seminal work of Stigler (later more formally developed by Peltzman and Becker), however, the notion that regulation is produced in a black box to maximize social welfare has given way to what has become known as the economic theory of regulation (ETR).[41] The foundation of ETR is that politicians and constituents are rational economic actors. As such, constituents demand favorable regulation and politicians use the State's coercive power to supply it in return for political support. When adopting a policy, regulators weigh the political support from those who stand to gain against political opposition from those who stand to lose. The interest group most able to translate its demand for a policy preference into political pressure is the one most likely to achieve its desired outcome.

Building on the work of scholars such as Anthony Downs and Mancur Olson, ETR explains why information and organization costs limit the size of effective interest groups.[42] As a threshold matter, individuals must expend resources to gain enough information to recognize their interests. As Stigler notes,

> [t]he costs of comprehensive information are higher in the political arena [than the marketplace] because information must be sought on so many issues of little or no direct concern to the individual, and accordingly he will know little about most matters before the legislature.[43]

[41] Gary Becker, 'A Theory of Competition Among Pressure Groups for Political Influence' 98 *Quarterly Journal of Economics* 371–400 (1983); Sam Peltzman, 'Toward a More General Theory of Economic Regulation' 19 *Journal of Law & Economics* 211–40 (1976); George J Stigler, 'The Theory of Economic Regulation' 2 *Bell Journal of Economics & Management Science* 3–21 (1971).

[42] Anthony Downs, An Economic Theory of Democracy (New York, NY, Harper & Row, 1957); Mancur Olson, The Logic of Collective Action: Public Goods and the Theory of Groups (Cambridge, MA, Harvard University Press, 1965).

[43] Stigler, above n 41, at 11.

Holding constant the size of a wealth transfer, the larger the interest group size, the smaller the per capita benefit; as per capita benefits diminish, the less likely it is that informing oneself on the impact of a regulation makes economic sense.

Secondly, once individuals recognize their interest in the outcome of the regulatory process, they must organize to translate their demand for policy into effective political pressure. Because the benefits from acquiring a desired regulatory outcome are a public good for members of an interest group, however, each member has an incentive to shirk his obligation to the group and free-ride on the contributions of others.

The important implication of this insight is that policies that reduce the welfare of a majority for the benefit of a minority are within the set of feasible outcomes. As Peltzman observes, 'In consequence the numerically large, diffuse interest group is unlikely to be an effective bidder, and a policy inimical to the interest of a numerical majority will not be automatically rejected.'[44] Indeed, one readily can see how consumer interests give way to the interests of a small industry in the regulatory process. Beyond a certain point, per capita benefits from a preferred regulatory outcome are diluted such that it becomes irrational to take part in the political process. A practical consequence of this is that small, concentrated groups with similar interests—like members of a particular industry—can organize political support more effectively than large diffuse groups—like consumers generally. Thus, the equilibrium outcome of the political process is likely to be regulation that harms consumers by protecting a favored industry from competition.

Of course, such regulation seldom will be presented to the public as what it truly is. Instead, proponents likely will cloak their protectionist desires in the robe of 'consumer protection', proclaiming that, left to its own devices, the market will do more harm than good. Indeed, a common criticism of competition advocacy is that competition is not the only value that government should promote, and that there are often other social goals that conflict with greater competition and consumer choice. These sorts of consumer protection concerns are often raised as a sort of 'trump card' against all other public policy goals, such as competition and consumer choice. But because consumer protection concerns may be offered strategically as well as sincerely—special interest groups often raise them as a fig leaf for their own narrow economic benefit—they should not necessarily be taken at face value.

Consider the example of unauthorized practice of law (UPL) rules that prohibit non-attorneys from handling routine tasks associated with the closing of a residential real estate transaction. By protecting attorneys from having to compete against non-attorneys, UPL restrictions raise the prices for legal services. Although proponents of these restrictions tout their necessity in protecting uninformed consumers, empirical examination shows that these restrictions provide consumers with no cognizable benefits in terms of increased protection

[44] Pelzman, above n 41, at 213.

from fraud or incompetence. But consumers are unlikely to mount a challenge. First, bar associations often promulgate these rules, and state supreme courts adopt them through processes of which only members of the bar—the beneficiaries—are likely to have knowledge. Secondly, even if consumers become aware that UPL restrictions are being considered, they would have to expend resources to understand that, despite the rhetoric from the bar associations, these restrictions are almost certain to harm consumers. Lastly, once aware of the costs associated with a proposed UPL restriction, organizing to fight it would be difficult given the expense involved and the collective action problems discussed above.

B. Advocacy as Representing Consumer Interests in the Political Process

The ETR suggests that because consumers are relatively ineffective at representing their interests in the political system, political outcomes may tend to restrict competition and consumer choice more than is economically justified. Tasking a public entity with the responsibility of representing dispersed consumers by promoting the principle of competition in the political process is one way to ameliorate this political market failure. Indeed, because anticompetitive regulation that results from a political market failure can have effects on consumer welfare that are just as pernicious as private conduct that harms competition, there does not appear to be a reasoned justification for the FTC to police the latter but not attempt to ameliorate consumer harm from the former.[45]

By representing consumer interests in the political process, the FTC is able to affect political outcomes through three non-mutually exclusive channels. First, to the extent that a comment informs the public of the way a proposed regulation is likely to affect them, it can spur political action, and thus increase the political costs associated with supporting anticompetitive regulation. In this manner, competition advocacy can move the political equilibrium towards one that is more favorable to competition. Secondly, an FTC comment can provide 'political cover' for public-spirited politicians seeking to benefit consumers but opposed by a powerful industry; regardless of whether an FTC comment increases the political cost of supporting anticompetitive regulations, a politician can claim the FTC comment as an excuse for not supporting a favored industry. Lastly, a comment simply may persuade a politician to oppose a regulation by presenting a compelling case that a certain regulation restricts competition more than is necessary to promote some consumer protection goal, and therefore is not in the public interest.

[45] Fred McChesney *et al*, *Federal Trade Commission, Competition and Consumer Advocacy: Review Session* (1982).

The ETR may also justify tasking a federal agency with carrying out the advocacy function. As noted by James Madison in 'Federalist 10', state and local governments are often the most prone to the sort of faction and interest-group activity that generates anticompetitive regulation.[46] Thus, a particular interest group may be especially concentrated or strong in a particular state, and that group may have undue influence in the political process of that state. In addition, the anticompetitive regulations of one state may have major spillovers, or other externalities, that impose burdens on national markets. As a result, it is appropriate for the advocacy function to rest with a national actor that is less prone to capture by parochial interest groups, but instead is removed from some local political pressures and is able to look out for the national goals of preserving robust economic market competition. In addition, the FTC's status as a bipartisan independent agency may also increase its effectiveness on advocacy issues. Because critics often characterize FTC interventions as 'taking sides', the Commission's status as a bipartisan expert agency may insulate it from some of the attacks that might otherwise be leveled at its advocacy activities.

Despite these justifications for an advocacy program, there are some inherent limits on the benefits that advocacy can provide. First, advocacy can only inform the debate and suggest appropriate action; it cannot compel that action. Although advocacy provides regulators with information concerning the likely economic consequences of a policy choice, the FTC is not a constituent. The Commission's opposition to an unwise or protectionist piece of legislation, therefore, is not the same as constituent opposition, because the FTC cannot provide political support in the form of votes or campaign contributions. In the context of ETR models, by subsidizing the collection and dissemination of information, advocacy increases consumers' efficiency in mounting political pressure.

Another important consideration is that the FTC is itself a regulatory body and may be subject to political pressure from interest groups in much the same manner as federal or state agencies or legislatures. As Timothy Muris, who has served as Chairman and Bureau Director, has observed, 'Congress can, and often does, exert considerable influence over an agency such as the FTC.'[47] Indeed, some studies have found a relationship between the preferences of congressional oversight members' constituencies and FTC policy.[48] And, due to complaints from adversely affected interest groups, in the late 1980s Congress attempted to cripple, if not totally eliminate, the advocacy program.[49] That the FTC is an independent and bipartisan agency, however, is likely to limit the ability of any particular industry

[46] 'Federalist 10 (Madison),' in Clinton Rossiter (ed), *The Federalist Papers* (New York, NY, Signet, 1961) 77.

[47] Timothy J Muris, 'Regulatory Policymaking at the Federal Trade Commission: The Extent of Congressional Control' 94 *Journal of Political Economy* 884–89 (1986).

[48] Barry R Weingast and Mark J Moran, 'Bureaucratic Discretion or Congressional Control? Regulatory Policy Making at the Federal Trade Commission' 91 *Journal of Political Economy* 765–800 (1983).

[49] Celnicker, above n 21.

to capture it. Almost uniformly, the Commission gives unanimous approval for the staff to issue its comments. Because one industry would be unlikely effectively to capture all these Commissioners, the views put forth in advocacy comments are highly unlikely to have resulted from interest group pressure. Further, unlike other agencies with similar structures (eg, FERC, FCC), the FTC deals with a wide range of industries, making it less likely than agencies that serve only one or a few industries to be subject to capture by any single interest group.

V. Assessment of the Competition Advocacy Program

One of the FTC's core goals is to prevent anticompetitive business practices. Competition advocacy furthers this goal by attempting to prevent government action that restricts competition. Important to determining the cost-effectiveness of the advocacy program is examining its efficiency in preventing anticompetitive regulations versus that of FTC enforcement.

A. Factors Affecting the Success of Competition Advocacy

The value of competition advocacy should be measured by:

a) the degree to which comments altered regulatory outcome times; and
b) the value to consumers of those improved outcomes.

For all practical purposes, however, both elements are difficult to measure with any degree of certainty. Although certain advocacy comments almost surely have some effect on final outcomes and others clearly do not, there is no reliable way to determine the marginal impact of a particular comment on the political process. Moreover, even if decision-makers later indicate that they relied on particular evidence or arguments, one can never be sure that such statements are not just after-the-fact justifications.

One study that attempted to assess the advocacy program's impact on regulatory outcomes between 1987 and 1989 found that 40 per cent of comment recipients reported that the comments were at least 'moderately effective', meaning that 'the governmental entity's actions were totally or in large part consistent with all of the FTC's recommendations, and that any action taken was largely or partly because of those recommendations.'[50] The author concedes, however, that this 'does not

[50] Celnicker, above n 21, at 391. Another 11% of the survey respondents found the comments to be 'slightly effective', meaning that 'the governmental entity's actions were to a small degree consistent with at least some of the FTC recommendations, and that any action taken was largely or partly

establish that the FTC effect on those decisions improved them; that is what cannot be measured.'[51] More recently, the FTC conducted a survey of advocacy recipients and sponsors of bills or regulation that the FTC opposed from 2001 to 2006.[52] The study found that 53 per cent of respondents agreed that the outcome of the regulatory process was largely consistent with the FTC position, and 54 per cent of respondents (and 79 per cent of those respondents who had an opinion) believed that the FTC comment influenced the outcome. Further, 81 per cent of respondents responded that the fact that the comment came from the FTC caused them to give it more weight than they otherwise would.

With these caveats in place, we note four factors—two of which flow directly from ETR—that appear to play a role in the likelihood that comments will influence the regulatory outcome. First, comments before executive and independent regulatory authorities generally have met with more success than those before elected legislators. For example, comments to the FCC, National Highway Transportation Safety Administration, Federal Energy Regulatory Commission (FERC), Federal Aviation Administration, FDA and CFTC all appear to have affected regulatory outcomes positively. At the same time, the track record with state regulators appears less successful. For example, although the FTC's efforts to allow entry into taxicab services in the latter 1980s achieved certain successes, for the most part cities chose not to listen to the FTC's advice that free entry, in conjunction with fare competition, would likely provide a better outcome for consumers. These observations are consistent with ETR, which predicts that regulators who are insulated from direct political influence are more likely to act independently based on policy considerations rather than constituent interests.[53] This insight offers an explanation as to why comments may have more effect before non-elected federal regulators than before elected state legislators.

Secondly, the probability of successful competition advocacy rises when one industry (or a subgroup within an industry) is attempting to secure anticompetitive regulation that is designed directly to hinder a rival industry's ability to compete. This prediction follows from ETR, because comments supporting a position taken

because of those recommendations' (*ibid*). Additionally, the author found that 47% of respondents gave the comment 'substantial weight because it came from the FTC' (*ibid*, at 322). In 1989, a virtually identical survey was sent by the Director of the FTC's Advocacy Office to recipients of comments dated June 1, 1987 through June 2, 1989. The responses to this second survey were consistent with those from the first. (Results on file with authors.)

[51] Celnicker, above n 21, at 400.

[52] See *United States Note for OECD Roundtable on Evaluation of the Actions and Resources of Competition Authorities* (May 25, 2007), available at http://www.ftc.gov/bc/international/docs/eval auth.pdf.

[53] Joseph Kalt and Mark Zupan, 'The Apparent Ideological Behavior of Legislators: Testing for Principal–Agent Slack in Political Institutions' 33 *Journal of Law & Economics* 103–31 (1990); Thomas H Hammond and Jack H Knott, 'Who Controls the Bureaucracy?: Presidential Power, Congressional Dominance, Legal Constraints, and Bureaucratic Autonomy in a Model of Multi-Institutional Policy Making' 12 *Journal of Law Economics & Organization* 119–66 (1996); Thomas H Hammond and Gary J Miller, 'The Core of the Constitution' 81 *American Political Science Review* 1155–74 (1987).

by another industry rather than only by consumers are more likely to be successful, given industry's superior comparative political organization ability. Casual empiricism provides some support for this hypothesis. This may be the case because organized industry groups are able to publicize FTC comments to achieve maximum effect. It may also be because an industry group is more likely than consumers to mount successful opposition to a regulation regardless of FTC intervention.

Thirdly, empirical substantiation for a position is important; if a comment can point to careful empirical work, demonstrating that the regulation in question is likely to harm consumers, it generally proves more persuasive to regulators and the public. This may be why comments with a substantial empirical component tend to meet with greater success.

Lastly, comments involving issues at the interface between competition and consumer protection policy appear to be more successful. The Commission's dual expertise in competition and consumer protection will often enable it to speak with great force and credibility on those issues. In these areas, the FTC's input can be especially valuable in debunking consumer protection rationales for anticompetitive regulations, or in recommending less restrictive alternatives to a proposed regulation. In most debates on trade protectionism, by contrast, questions of competition and consumer welfare play little or no role; thus, the FTC's expertise may not be desired in those debates.

Of these factors, whether the FTC's position is touted by a politically organized group may be the most important. For example, recent FTC comments opposing legislation that would have regulated pharmacy benefit managers' (PBMs') contractual relationships with health plans and pharmacies have appeared to have had an impact. Pharmacy benefit managers and major health plans, which have powerful lobbies, opposed such legislation as well. Comments and amicus briefs opposing UPL restrictions that would bar non-attorneys from performing certain real estate settlement tasks (eg title searching, performing closings) have been relatively successful, perhaps in part because the title company industry is affected directly by these restrictions. By contrast, although the FTC staff undertook extensive investigations of trade restraint issues from the mid-1970s through the early 1990s, with many of the filings containing new empirical and conceptual work, two decades of work did not observably alter policy or individual decisions on tariff or trade policy.[54]

The FTC's relative impotence in affecting trade policy, moreover, may be due in part to the fact that trade barriers are the quintessential example of restrictive regulations that provide substantial benefits to specific industries and impose smaller per capita costs widely upon consumers and other industries. The lack of organized opposition to restraints on competition may also offer a partial explanation for the lack of success in taxicab advocacies. Those who might gain from taxi deregulation are unorganized consumers and small, would-be taxi entrepreneurs.

[54] Fred McChesney *et al*, *Federal Trade Commission, Competition and Consumer Advocacy: Review Session* (1982).

B. Efficiency of Competition Advocacy Versus Enforcement

An additional benefit of competition advocacy is that in the American system, advocacy is almost certainly a more cost-effective means than enforcement to attack state-imposed barriers to competition. Moreover, despite the obvious political conflicts created by advocacy filings, overall advocacy may be less prone to conflict and more susceptible to compromise than enforcement through litigation. Because of various exceptions to the American antitrust laws such as the *Noerr-Pennington* doctrine and the State Action doctrine, the imposition of a governmentally-created restraint on competition is largely immune to subsequent antitrust challenge. The *Noerr-Pennington* doctrine immunizes most attempts to use the political system to effect anticompetitive regulation,[55] and the State Action doctrine shields certain anticompetitive conduct from federal antitrust scrutiny when the conduct is:

a) in furtherance of a clearly articulated state policy; and
b) actively supervised by the state.[56]

Thus, FTC enforcement may be unable to reach some anticompetitive regulations, leaving advocacy as the only tool available to prevent consumer harm.

Even for cases where a court finds immunities not to apply, the high costs and inherent uncertainty of litigation, and the extremely small amount of resources needed for advocacy, suggest that advocacy is a more efficient vehicle than enforcement to attack state restrictions on competition. Further, by preventing or ameliorating anticompetitive restraints *before* they are imposed, advocacy can avoid, or at lease attenuate, consumer harm. To a greater extent than litigation—which often can involve idiosyncratic issues—the FTC often can amortize the cost of advocacy activities over subsequent comments on similar issues; once the fixed costs of analyzing a restraint have been incurred, the marginal cost of each subsequent filing on the same or similar topics is often minimal.[57] Lastly, although advocacy is politically controversial, it may be less politically controversial and prone to conflict than litigation under the State Action doctrine, which requires the competition agency to sue the state or an agent of the state alleging anticompetitive conduct. Overall,

[55] *Eastern Railroad Presidents Conference v Noerr*, 365 US 127 (1961); *United Mine Workers v Pennington*, 381 US 657 (1965); *California Motor Transport Co v Trucking Unlimited*, 404 US 508 (1972).

[56] See *California Retail Liquor Dealers Ass'n v Midcal Aluminum, Inc*, 445 US 97 (1980); *Parker v Brown*, 317 US 341 (1943). See also the Report of the State Action Task Force (Sept 2003), http://www.ftc.gov/os/2003/09/stateactionreport.pdf, for a discussion of the problems that have arisen with respect to overbroad application of the State Action doctrine to immunize anticompetitive actions. Similar to the State Action doctrine, federal legislation that conflicts with federal antitrust laws is said to enact an 'implied repeal' of the antitrust laws. See *Gordon v New York Stock Exchange, Inc*, 422 US 659 (1975).

[57] A C Pritchard and Todd J Zywicki, 'Finding the Constitution: An Economic Analysis of Tradition's Role in Constitutional Interpretation' 77 *North Carolina Law Review* 409 (1999).

then, it may be that 'an ounce of prevention' through competition advocacy may be worth a 'pound of cure' in terms of subsequent remedial litigation.

VI. Lessons of the FTC's Competition Advocacy Program for Latin America

The FTC's experience with competition advocacy provides guidance and an example for similar programs throughout Latin America. Given the history of extensive economic regulation in Latin America, the marginal benefits of robust competition advocacy could be substantial. Moreover, extensive interventionism generates problems of rent-seeking and political corruption by interest groups seeking favorable regulation.[58] Ignacio De Leon has been a particularly energetic advocate of the use of competition advocacy in Latin America. As he writes:

> Competition advocacy is particularly important in Latin America because of the former experience of misled government intervention in the region, which is responsible for the current competition and innovation problems.[59]

State-imposed barriers to competition are a substantial obstacle to economic growth and are a source of political corruption in the developing world. Encouraging competition by clearing away some of these obstacles to entry could be extremely effective at the margin in benefiting those economies. Indeed, De Leon observes, 'Regulatory reform is probably the single most important contribution that a competition authority can make to the transition process.'[60] Given the expense and other obstacles associated with litigation as a strategy for executing competition policy, low-cost strategies such as advocacy may be a more practicable and efficient means for carrying out competition policy in less-wealthy countries. Former FTC Chairman Kovacic, for example, has written that newly-minted competition authorities should adopt a 'gradualist' approach to implementing competition policy.[61] A centerpiece of this approach is to develop a competition advocacy program prior to embarking on extensive enforcement. An early step in the development of a competition enforcement regime would include research to reveal the major government policies that suppress competition. Once identified, the nascent competition authority would use already-developed education and publicity activities to advocate for the removal of such policies.

[58] Ignacio De Leon, 'An Alternative Approach to Policies for the Promotion of Competition in Developing Countries' 6 *Southwestern Journal of Law and Trade in the Americas* 85–116 (1999).

[59] Ignacio De Leon, 'A Proposal for a New Competition Policy in Latin America' 25 *Brooklyn Journal of International Law* 275–308, at 302 (1999).

[60] De Leon, above n 7, at 408.

[61] William E Kovacic, 'Getting Started: Creating New Competition Policy Institutions in Developing Countries' 23 *Brooklyn Journal of International Law* 403–08 (1997).

At the same time, implementing an effective competition advocacy strategy may be more difficult in Latin America than in the United States. The United States has a political culture that embraces competition and free markets, as well as political and legal institutions that provide greater protection for private property and place some limits on arbitrary governmental action. The FTC's competition advocacy program taps into this culture and builds on the traditional commitment to free markets as an organizing principle of the American economy.[62] In turn, the FTC's insistence on weighing the virtues of competition and consumer welfare in the regulatory balance helps to reinforce this culture of competition. Thus, investments in advocacy activities can not only improve specific policy outcomes, but can also help to create and nurture a culture of competition that both increases the efficacy of future such activities and helps to instill the ethos of competition into regulators and the public more generally. Further, because it entails detailed analysis of competitive effects, successful advocacy also depends on expertise. The FTC has a large staff, highly trained—through both academic programs and on-the-job experience—in competition law and economics.

A competition culture and expertise in competitive analysis are luxuries that most developing countries lack. Indeed, the reliance of successful advocacy on a competition culture and a highly-trained staff helps to explain why in most developed countries, competition advocacy programs have begun long after rigorous enforcement programs. The interdependence between advocacy and enforcement, then, presents a sort of 'chicken-and-egg' problem for successful advocacy. As the OECD notes, 'a competition agency's reputation will be built largely upon its record in enforcing the competition law, and this reputation will significantly affect its influence as an advocate in other forums.'[63]

Most Latin American countries lack a deep historical commitment to and faith in the virtues of competition. Extensive regulation is both more tolerated and expected in Latin American countries, reinforcing the perception among citizens that economic liberty and property rights depend on the opinions of governmental officials rather than being grounded in the rule of law. In turn, this worldview leads citizens to seek protection of their rights through efforts to influence political officials instead of before courts or independent (and usually non-existent) competition authorities, which further reinforces the perception that economic freedom resides in political discretion rather than legal right. The soil for growing a culture of competition is somewhat rockier in Latin America than in the United States. How, then, does a young competition authority with limited resources engage in successful advocacy if it lacks the requisite expertise and reputation, and if there is no culture of competition on which to draw? Further, Evenett questions OECD and ICN calls for nascent competition authorities to prioritize developing

[62] Zywicki, above n 3.

[63] OECD, above n 1, at 9.

competition advocacy programs over enforcement.[64] Particularly, he makes three observations: first, ETR predicts that politicians' self-interest serves as a check on the anticompetitive effect of regulations; secondly, the efficacy of advocacy will be limited due to the inability of the competition authority directly to influence politicians with contributions and other political support; and, lastly, there is a very little empirical support that advocacy actually works.

One answer to these problems may be to pursue a mixed strategy, where enforcement is not eschewed altogether but rather is focused on the 'low-hanging fruit' of per se violations (eg, price-fixing cartels) and major mergers. Cartel and merger enforcement typically do not entail economic analysis as complex as rule of reason or dominance cases, and thus will not require as much expertise. Government restrictions on competition through the granting of formal licenses and permits are also easily identifiable as reducing economic welfare. Further, such cases provide large and obvious benefits to consumers, thus easily enhancing a reputation and instilling the benefits of competition.

Competition authorities can also focus on advocacy where the decision-makers are also the beneficiaries of the regulations. For example, in the United States, most state real estate commissions are made up of practicing real estate brokers and are charged with regulating the state's real estate industry. In these cases, the self-limiting principles that Evenett identifies will be at their weakest because the governmental actors benefit directly from regulations with increased income rather than only indirectly with political support.[65] To the extent that regulations issued by such bodies are more clearly protectionist, moreover, they will require less expertise to analyze.

The FTC's experience with competition advocacy also may provide some pragmatic lessons as to how Latin American competition authorities can craft an effective competition advocacy program. First, the FTC's status as an independent regulatory agency insulates it from many of the political pressures that might otherwise hamper efforts to engage in competition advocacy. Competition advocacy efforts will face constant pressures to intervene or refrain from intervention at the behest of particular competitors and politically influential interests. Although political independence may not be a necessary condition for competition advocacy, in the United States it generally has served to make the FTC more effective. The FTC's advocacy efforts are often directed at more political bodies, and the FTC's ability to speak as a relatively neutral or bipartisan body provides it some degree of disinterest and authority in these relationships. On the other hand, relative to other agencies, this independence also somewhat removes the FTC from the authority of a close working relationship with the President, thus depriving the agency of some of its political clout in inter-agency affairs. Despite

[64] Simon J Evenett , 'Competition Advocacy: Time for a Rethink?' 26 *Northwestern Journal of International Law and Business* 495–514 (2006).

[65] *Ibid.*

these drawbacks, on net political independence seems to have strengthened the FTC's hand in advocacy filings.

Secondly, if regulators desire to vest primary regulatory authority over a given industry in a sectoral regulator, they should increase their consciousness about promoting an appropriate balance between competition and sectoral regulators, such as by providing for shared jurisdiction, expressly requiring consultation with competition authorities before enacting new regulations, or requiring that any regulations enacted are the least restrictive means of achieving a given regulatory objective. In fact, some countries have gone beyond merely requiring consultation with competition authorities before enacting anticompetitive regulations. Costa Rica, for instance, formally empowers competition authorities to challenge judicially anticompetitive regulations enacted by governments.[66] In practice, concern about regulatory comity and accommodation means that these formal powers are rarely exercised. Nonetheless, such powers may give competition authorities greater leverage to require consultation than would otherwise be the case.

Thirdly, essential to the FTC's success is a clear definition of its mission to pursue the goals of competition and consumer welfare, rather than fuzzy appeals to the 'public interest'.[67] At first glance, vague objective standards, such as the 'public interest', would seem to enlarge the power and discretion of a regulatory authority. In the context of competition policy, however, such a vague standard weakens a competition authority's ability to intervene forcefully in the name of competition and consumer welfare, as flaccid appeals to the 'public interest' can be used to justify almost any regulatory restraints on competition. Thus, the adoption of a clear mission by the competition authority that its goal is the promotion of consumer welfare can make the agency a more powerful voice for that objective in dealing with legislatures or other regulators.

VII. Conclusion

Each country in Latin America faces different challenges and inherits different cultural and legal traditions and institutions. These differences are important in determining the precise form that competition advocacy efforts may take from one country to another. Nonetheless, Latin America generally shares a tradition of economic regulation and interventionism that is skeptical of competition and its benefits. Thus, there is a need for political and economic education in these countries to defend the principle of competition resolutely and to demonstrate the benefits that such efforts may bring about over time.

[66] De Leon, above n 7.
[67] Zywicki, above n 3.

Chapter XVII

Determinants of the Fares in the Chilean Airline Market: An Empirical Approximation to the Case of LAN CHILE*

ROY COSTILLA† AND JAVIER VELOZO‡

The aim of this chapter is to analyze the fare determinants in the Chilean Airline Market. Using data from 1998 to 2007, we estimated a reduced equation of prices so that the main factors that influence fares in the local market are identified. The data comprise a panel of semi-annual data that contains the number of passengers and prices of LAN CHILE's flights over nine destinations within Chile.

Given the type of data used, all the analyses are made taking into account two different fare classes, the highest and lowest available in the database. Throughout the chapter we have identified both as business and coach fare class, respectively. It is also necessary to make an assumption of symmetry between destinations: that all airlines segment their markets similarly in such a way that, for example, the segment of the market which buys coach fares is the same for all. This condition is used by diverse authors for studies of the European and Brazilian airline markets.

Amongst the main findings we have is that traffic influences the lower fare class negatively and the higher fare positively. That is, given a higher proportion of passengers traveling in lower fare classes, density economies may exist. In addition, the effect of fuel prices on fares is positive. In particular, the pass-through rate is found to be lower in the segment of the market with the lower fare. In other words, increases in the price of the fuel are never transferred completely to the users, and even less to the segment of market with the greater elasticity. In relation to the effect of competition on price levels in markets, it is found that in monopolistic markets, and/or where inter-modal competition is very low, companies take

* The authors would like to acknowledge the *Junta de Aeronautica Civil* (JAC) of Chile for kindly providing us with data; Kyle Stiegert; and the conference participants for their helpful suggestions. As usual, the analysis and conclusions are our exclusive responsibility.

† M. A. in Economics, ILADES-Georgetown University. E-mail: roycostilla@gmail.com.

‡ Doctor en Economía de las Instituciones, Universidad Complutense de Madrid E-mail: jvelozoa@gmail.com.

advantage of their market power to increase price levels in the inelastic demand segment.

Lastly, although these results are in line with the existing literature, they must be taken as preliminar, because there is a need for more detailed data yields to make a stronger case.

I. Introduction

The objective of this chapter is to analyze the determinants of the fares in the Chilean airline market. Many of the national routes are covered only by LAN CHILE holding and LAN Express (formerly Ladeco), companies that merged in 1995 and have maintained more than 80 per cent of the national market in recent years. In such a concentrated market, an assumed abuse of dominant position is a usual claim.

Many studies analyze the airline markets, and most of them focus on the United States. Key contributions to this analysis include: Borenstein,[1] Brueckner *et al*,[2] Evan and Kessides,[3] and Berry *et al*,[4] among many others. These studies use data sent by the airlines to the Bureau of Transportation Statistics, a quarterly random sample which includes information from 10 per cent of all domestic flights in the United States. In particular, this sample collects data on capacity, fares, frequency and yields for each flight. Unfortunately, the case of the United States is an exception—such data are not available for any other country in the world. Due to this, the methodologies developed and used in the literature previously mentioned cannot be used without making additional assumptions.

The Chilean airline market is not an exception. As a result, other than the Quiroz[5] and Agostini[6] studies, there are no studies which analyze the Chilean market empirically. One of the main reasons for this is the lack of information necessary to undertake studies of this kind. Unlike the United States, companies in Chile are not required to pass detailed data on their operations in the sector to government agencies.

[1] S Borenstein, 'Hubs and High Fares: Dominance and Market Power in the US Airline Industry' 20 *Rand Journal of Economics* 344–65 (1989).

[2] J K Brueckner, N J Dyer and P T Spiller, 'Fare Determination in Airline Hub-and-Spoke Networks' 23 *Rand Journal of Economics* 309–33 (1992).

[3] W N Evan and I Kessides, 'Localized Market Power in the US Airline Industry' 75 *Review of Economics and Statistics* 66–75 (1993).

[4] S Berry, M Carnall and P T Spiller, 'Airlines Hubs: Costs, Markups and the Implications of Customer Heterogeneity', NBER Working Paper 5561 (1996).

[5] J Quiroz, 'Estudio de los Niveles Tarifarios en el Mercado del Transporte Aéreo', Consultoría para la Junta de Aeronáutica Civil, Ministerio de Transportes y Telecomunicaciones, Chile (2005).

[6] C Agostini, 'Organización industrial del transporte aéreo en Chile' 23/1, *Revista de Análisis Económico* 35–84 (2008).

II. Literaturc Rcview

Diverse studies exist of both European markets and the Brazilian market which do not use yields of operation for the airline companies. Given this type of data, it is necessary to make a further assumption: there is symmetry between destinations and companies so that all airlines segment their markets similarly. This condition is raised by Holmes[7] and Marín,[8] and applied later by Dresner and Tretheway,[9] Nero,[10] Schipper *et al*[11] and Fageda,[12] among others.

Although uniformity between the objectives, explanatory variables and instruments used in each study does not exist, all estimate a reduced equation of prices by Minimum Least Squares in Two Stages (MLST).[13] In particular, as one does not count the yields used in these studies as dependent variable diverse fares, but rather as the lowest, highest, and average. Table 1 below summarizes the main effects considered by the analyzed studies.

Table 1 Estimations of Previous Studies

	Dependent Variable						
	Unique Fare Class	**Lowest Fare Class**				**Average Fare Class**	**Higher Fare Class**
Independent Variable	Oliveria (2003)	Dresner & Tretheway (1992)	Marín (1995)	Schipper *et al* (2002)	Nero (1998)	Fageda (2006)	Carlsoon[14] (2004)
Traffic	1.39*	0.79*	0.08*	−0.42	−0.06*	−0.00015*	−0.21**
Distance			−0.33*	−0.40**	−0.48*	0.16**	−0.74**
Wage			0.16*				
Average Cost	−29.51**			0.29*	0.10**		
N	58		197	170	244	190	130
R^2	0.81	0.78	0.52	0.83	0.75	0.74	0.69

* Significant at 5%.
** Significant at 1%.

[7] T Holmes, 'The Effects of Third-Degree Price Discrimination in Oligopoly 79 *American Economic Review* 244–50 (1989).

[8] P L Marín, 'Competition in European Aviation: Pricing Policy and Market Structure' 43 *The Journal of Industrial Economics* 141–59 (1995).

[9] M Dresner and M W Tretheway, 'Modelling and Testing the Effect of Market Structure on Price: The Case of International Air Transport' 26 *Journal of Transport Economics and Policy* 171–84 (1992).

[10] G Nero, 'Spatial Multiproduct Pricing: Empirical Evidence on Intra-European Duopoly Airline Markets' 30 *Applied Economics* 465–75 (1998).

[11] Y Schipper, P Rietveld and P Nijkamp, 'European Airline Reform: An Empirical Welfare Analysis' 36/2 *Journal of Transport Economics and Policy* 189–209 (2002).

[12] X Fageda, 'Measuring Conduct and Cost Parameters in the Spanish Airline Market' 28 *Review of Industrial Organization* 379–99 (2006).

[13] See study details in Appendix 1 to this chapter.

[14] F Carlsoon, 'Prices and Departures in European Domestic Aviation Markets' 24 *Review of Industrial Organization* 37–49 (2004).

First of all, notice that in general, the effect of traffic on the fare depends on the type of market analyzed. When the lowest available fare is considered, except in the case of Nero,[15] it is found that the traffic has a non-negative effect on the fare.[16] That is to say, increases in traffic are associated with increases in the lowest available fare. On the contrary, if the highest available fare is considered, the traffic has a negative effect on the fare; increases in traffic generate reductions in the highest available fare. In other words, these results could be thought of as showing that, depending on the market segment considered, companies are operating on different zones from the function of costs: in the business segment density economies exist because of the small number of passengers transported, whereas in the coach segment the opposite holds true.

Some caveats are in order. One word about Oliveira,[17] who examines the Brazilian market. This is a special case because it addresses the Air Shuttle Market[18] between Rio and Sao Paolo, where price discrimination does not exist. In this context, he found a positive effect of the traffic on the fare, which indicates that the zone of non-economies of density has been reached, which is congruent with a high flow of passengers in relation to the supplied capacity. Secondly, it is observed that in general, except in the case of Fageda,[19] the distance has a negative effect on the fare, that is to say that distance economies exist. This means that longer-distance trips have a lower cost per passenger per kilometer. Lastly, cost variables, wages and the average cost of operation have significant effects on fares. In particular, this effect is positive and less than one in the lowest fare.

On the other hand, there are two studies that analyze the determinants of the yields in the Chilean Airline Market, Agostini[20] and Quiroz,[21] which use monthly yields for companies in the international airline market, including Chile, between April and June 2004. Both studies find evidence of distance economies, –0.38 and –0.49 respectively; that is to say, statistically significant reductions in yields before increases in the distance traveled. Secondly, Agostini finds that yields increase with the traffic, 0.06; whereas Quiroz finds that they diminish with the occupation factor, –1.14.[22] Lastly, Quiroz finds that yields in the Chilean market are not statistically different from those found in the international air market.[23]

15 Above n 10.

16 Notice that the coefficient estimate for traffic of Schipper *et al*, above n 11, is not significant.

17 A Oliveira, 'The Impacts of Liberalisation on a Brazilian Air Shuttle Market', *The Warwick Economics Research Paper Series (TWERPS)* 676, University of Warwick, Department of Economics (2003).

18 Also known as Air-Bridge because passengers arrive at the airport directly to take the flights and it has many flights every day with a fixed scheduled, ie one flight every half-hour. See definition and details in Oliveira, above n 17.

19 Fageda, above n 12.

20 Agostini, above n 6.

21 Quiroz, above n 5.

22 Agostini, above n 6; Quiroz, above n 5.

23 Quiroz, above n 5.

III. Model

This section presents a model of a market with differentiated products with two companies ($F = A, B$) and two segments ($i = w, s$): coach (w) and business (s) class. It is assumed that both companies compete on prices, with constant and equal marginal costs and without capacity restrictions. Also, that for each firm the segment w has greater price elasticity; that is, the consumers who buy coach tickets are more willing to change in case of a price increase. Following the proposition of Holmes[24] and Marín,[25] we further assume that:

(S1) For each market segment a unique equilibrium exists in which both companies fix the same price. Calling this price the industry price for each segment, the industry price elasticity is defined as the change in the demanded quantity of the industry as a consequence of the industry price.

Let $y_i(p) \equiv x_i^A(p,p)$ be the demand function of the industry for the segment i, then the industry price elasticity in the segment i is given by:

$$(1) \qquad e_i^I(p) \equiv -p \cdot \frac{2dy_i(p)/dp}{2dy_i(p)} = -p \cdot \frac{dy_i(p)/dp}{dy(p)}, \qquad i = w, s.$$

(S2) There is symmetry in the demand function for each company. In particular, in the context of two companies and two markets, the demanded quantity that a company can get given its own price p and its competitor price q is equal for its competitor if both prices are interchanged, for all possible combinations of p and q.

$$(2) \qquad x_i^A(p,q) \equiv x_i^B(q,p), \qquad i = w, s.$$

Based on the previous assumptions, Holmes[26] expresses the firm price elasticity $e_i^F(p)$ as the sum of two components in each market segment: the industry price elasticity $e_i^I(p)$ and the crossed-price elasticity $e_i^C(p)$[27]. Additionally, one can express the equilibrium price for each market segment in terms of price elasticity:

$$(3) \qquad \frac{p_i^* - c}{p_i^*} = \frac{1}{e_i^F(p_i^*)} = \frac{1}{e_i^I(p_i^*) + e_i^C(p_i^*)} \qquad i = w, s.$$

Given the previous assumptions, the business fare class is determined on the basis of the coach class fare plus a constant margin.

[24] Holmes, above n 7.
[25] Marín, above n 8.
[26] Holmes, above n 7.
[27] It is assumed to be positive, that is to say that both products are substitutes.

Also, there are two additional implications for the equilibrium prices. First, since the coach segment has greater price elasticity than the business one: $e_w^F(p) > e_s^F(p)$, the equilibrium price in the first is lower than the later: $p_w^* < p_s^*$. Secondly, for both segments the equilibrium price in a monopolistic regime is greater than the one of a non-monopolistic regime, as in the former substituted goods do not exist so that crossed-price elasticity is zero. This is one of the implications that can be tested, and therefore it will be included in the empirical specification. Particularly, for each segment the equilibrium price under a non-monopolistic regime is given by:

(4) $$p_i^* = \left(1 + \frac{1}{e_i^I(p_i^*) + e_i^C(p_i^*)}\right).c \qquad i = w, s.$$

Lastly, we make an assumption to allow the existence of different destinations. *(S3) For each segment, the price elasticity of the demand is stable throughout all destinations.* It is the price elasticity of the firm $e_i^F(p)$, it does not depend on the analyzed destination but only the segment in demand ($i = w, s$). In other words, companies discriminate prices in the same way for all destinations. This assumption is necessary because the data used are not yields but rather the prices and the number of passengers.

IV. Econometric Specification

Even though the object of the present work is to estimate a reduced price equation, we first characterize the demand and price simultaneous system, in such a way to assure us that it is suitably identified.[28] The structural equation of prices by route k and period t is given by:

(5) $$\begin{aligned} P_{kt} = \alpha_0 + \alpha_1 \mathrm{Q}_{ikt} + \alpha_3 \mathrm{Distance}_k + \alpha_3 \mathrm{Fuel}_t + \alpha_3 \mathrm{Wage}_t \\ + \alpha_3 \mathrm{Competition}_{kt} + \alpha_3 \mathrm{D1000}_k + u_{1ikt} \end{aligned}$$

Where:

P_{kt}: Fare per kilometer on the route k and period t.
Q_{ikt}: Number of passengers (traffic) on the route k and period t transported by the company i.
$\mathrm{Distance}_k$: Kilometers covered on the route k.
Fuel_t: Price average of fuel (dollars by gallon) in the period t.

[28] Formally, the order and range conditions have to be met. Informally, the first one requires that both demand and price equations do not depend exactly in the same variables. It is that there have to be some variables that only appear on one of the equations. Regarding the second one, it requires that both equations have different slopes.

Wage_t: Wage in the period t.
Competition_{kt}: Dummy that indicates if more than one company is operating on the route k during the period t.
D1000_k: Dummy if route k is greater than 1,000 km.

On the other hand, the structural equation of demand is given by:

$$\text{(6)} \qquad Q_{ikt} = \beta_0 + \beta_1 P_{kt} + \beta_2 \text{Distance}_k + \beta_3 \text{Population}_{kt} + \beta_4 \text{IAE}_{kt} + \beta_5 \text{High}_t + u_{2ikt}$$

Where:
Population_{kt}: Population in the region holding the destination of route k in the period t.
IAE_{kt}: Index of Economic Activity of the region holding the destination of the route k in the period t.
High_t: Dummy that indicates if the period t is high season (November–February) or not.

As can be seen, Population and IAE appear only in the demand. On the other hand, as we are considering both supply relation and a demand, both should have a different slope. Therefore, the equation of prices is identified correctly, so that it is possible to use Population and IAE as instruments for traffic in the reduced price equation. In all, the empirical specification for (4) is given by (5).

Given the type of data used, all the analyses are made taking into account two different fare classes, the highest and lowest available in the data base. Throughout the chapter we have identified both as business and coach fare class, respectively. As usual, all the variables are in logarithms but the dummies.

We now describe the expected effects of the variables. First, one expects that the effect of Distance, Competition and D1000 is negative. In particular, the D1000 variable tries to capture the possible competition of other means of transport in the case of routes smaller than 1,000 km. On the other hand, one hopes that Combustible and Wages have a positive effect on the prices.

The effect of the number of passengers deserves a special mention. On one hand, a positive signal is expected if the company is operating in the rising part of the curve of marginal costs. Nevertheless, in the presence of economies of density and/or natural monopolies the opposite case can also occur. As a consequence, this effect cannot be determined a priori.

Last but not least, given the panel structure of the data, we follow McGuirk *et al*[29] and check the existence of autocorrelation in the observations. First of all, the test for serial correlation in the idiosyncratic errors of a linear

[29] A M McGuirk, P Driscoll and J Alwang, 'Misspecification Testing: A Comprehensive Approach' 75 *American Journal of Agricultural Economics* 1044–55 (1993).

panel-data model, discussed by Wooldridge[30] and implemented by Drukker,[31] is performed.[32]

In a case of rejection of the null hypothesis a Generalized Method of Moments (GMM) regression with Newey-West standard errors will be estimated.[33] This method provides us with Heteroscedasticity and Autocorrelation Consistent (HAC) variance estimators.[34]

V. Description of the Data

The study uses a semi-annual panel of nine destinations in the Chilean airline market between 1998 and 2007. Even though the information relating to the number of passengers is monthly, the prices do not cover all months in a year, so that the data are averaged semi-annually according to high (November to February) and low season (March to October).

The main source of information is the Junta de Aeronáutica Civil (JAC), the civil aviation authority in Chile in charge of setting forth the guidelines for the aeronautical activities and of supervising and managing air policies. In particular, the number of passengers by firm and destination; prices by fare class, company and destination; and the distance between destinations come from this source.

Secondly, data on population, the Index of Economic Activity (IEA), and wages are provided by the Instituto Nacional de Estadísticas (INE), the Chilean Bureau of Statistics. The information on population is annual and is disaggregated at the regional level. The IAE data are represented by the Index of Regional Economic Activity (INACER) and are calculated quarterly by the INE for each region. The third item of information, remuneration data, is monthly and is aggregated at the national level.

Lastly, data on fuel prices are taken from the Bureau of Transportation Statistics (BTS) of the United States. This information represents a monthly average price (dollars by gallon) of a schedule jet fuel price (jet_fuel_sch).

The main characteristics of the variables can be found in the appendix 2.

[30] J M Wooldridge, *Econometric Analysis of Cross Section and Panel Data* (Cambridge, MA, MIT Press, 2002). Chapter 10. Basic Linear Unobserved Effects Panel Data Models.

[31] D M Drukker, 'Testing for Serial Correlation in Linear Panel-Data Models' 3 *Stata Journal* 168–77 (2003).

[32] Under the null of no serial the residuals from the regression of the first-differenced variables should have an autocorrelation of −.5. This implies that the coefficient on the lagged residuals in a regression of the lagged residuals on the current residuals should be −.5. The procedure performs a Wald test of this hypothesis.

[33] See L Hansen, 'Large Sample Properties of Generalized Method of Moments Estimators' (1982) 50/3 *Econometrica* 1029–54; and W K Newey and K D West, 'A Simple, Positive Semi-definite, Heteroscedasticity and Autocorrelation Consistent Covariance Matrix' (1987) 55 *Econometrica* 703–08 for details.

[34] W Manuela, Jr, 'Airline Liberalization Effects on Fare: The Case of the Philippines' 60 *Journal of Business Research* 161–67 (2007) provides an empirical application for the airline sector.

VI. Results

Table 2 below summarizes the main findings of the estimation of (5), our reduced price equation using population and the index of economic activity as instruments for the traffic.

First of all, it is shown that the effect of the number of passengers on the fare is significant, and its direction depends on the fare class considered. When considering the highest fare class a positive effect is found, that is to say, increases in the number of passengers generate increases in the price of the highest fare class. In particular, an increase of 10 per cent in the traffic generates an increase of 1.4 per cent in the fare. On the other hand, when considering the lowest fare class the effect is the opposite, so that increases in the traffic generate a decrease in fare. An increase of 10 per cent in the traffic generates a decrease of 1.5 per cent in the lowest fare class price.

These differentiated effects are found because we are not using yields but extreme fare classes. In other words, for each regression we act as if all passengers belong to the fare class considered. Since passengers distribute themselves between different fare classes, it is expected that the effect of the traffic on the yield lies between the estimated effects, ie between –0.15 and 0.14. In particular, it is expected that effect lies closer to the lower limit for the smaller quantity of passengers in the more expensive fare class. Therefore, although actual availability of data does not allow the determination of the existence of

Table 2 Reduced Price Equation

	Highest Fare Class	Lowest Fare Class
traffic	0.140	–0.152
	(2.32)*	(2.36)*
distance	–0.598	–0.441
	(9.21)**	(7.28)**
jet_fuel_sch	0.644	0.348
	(20.97)**	(6.79)**
competition	–0.308	0.124
	(3.30)**	(1.15)
D1000	0.324	–0.035
	(2.93)**	(0.30)
Constant	7141	8044
	(14.97)**	(22.11)**
Observations	112	86
R-squared	0.77	0.76

t-statistical (robust) between parentheses

* Significant at 5%.

** Significant at 1%.

economies of density in the Chilean airline market, it can be said that this is a possible result.[35]

Secondly, we find evidence of distance economies because route distance has a negative impact on both fare classes. A route with a 10 per cent higher distance is found to have a 5.98 per cent and 4.41 per cent lower fare, for the lowest and highest fare classes respectively. Further, this result goes in the line of the literature reviewed: stronger distance economies in the highest fare class.

Thirdly, and in reference to the costs, it is found that the effect of wages is not significant, which is why it is not reported here. This could be due to the proxy used, a wage index for the whole Chilean economy. It may be the case that this proxy is not representative of wages in the airline sector.

Also, the effect of fuel prices on fares is positive and significant in both cases. In particular, it is found that this effect is larger in the highest fare class, 0.348 versus 0.644. This fact is coherent with a maximization behavior of the firms, in the sense that they transfer less of the price increases to the most elastic segments of the demand to minimize the decrease in the number of passengers carried. On the other hand, we can expected that the pass-through rate of fuel cost to prices would be near the inferior limit of the interval, [0.348, 0.644].

Lastly, we have the dummies that measure the effect of competition in the market. Again, one verifies that the effect of variables depends on the fare class used, although this time the effects are only significant in the case of the highest fare class. In this last case, in markets where there is more than one firm, the highest fare class is 30 per cent lower than the highest fare class under a monopoly. Also, for routes with more than 1,000km distance, the highest fare class is greater by 32 per cent. Again, this is an indicator that in markets where inter-modal competition is weaker (because of availability of alternative transport means, such as trains, buses, etc), the firms exercise their market power in the inelastic segment of the demand.

The last step is to check for the existence of autocorrelation given the panel structure of the data. The test results,[36] indicate that the null hypothesis of no first-order autocorrelation is strongly rejected[37] for both highest and lowest fare classes.

Given this result, GMM estimation with Newey-West Standard Errors[38] of the reduced price equation (5) is performed. The results are presented in Table 3 below.

[35] This result is coherent with the non-existence of restrictions of capacity in this market. An opposite example is the Spanish case where, due to the strong flow of tourists, these restrictions are an essential part of the market. See Fageda, above n 12.

[36] See n 30 and 31 above.

[37] The F statistics are 35,208 and 10,874 in the highest and lowest fare class, respectively.

[38] This estimation uses the implementation developed by C F Baum, M E Schaffer and S Stillman, 'Enhanced Routines for Instrumental Variables/GMM Estimation and Testing', *Boston College Working Papers in Economics No 667* (2007). Also, it is performed assuming an autocorrelation of order 1 and applying small-sample corrections.

Table 3 GMM Reduced Price Equation with Newey-West Standard Errors

	Highest Fare Class	Lowest Fare Class
traffic	0.154	−0.149
	(1.81)+	(1.87)+
distance	−0.618	−0.442
	(8.51)**	(5.66)**
jet_fuel_sch	0.630	0.347
	(18.82)**	(5.66)**
competition	−0.327	0.116
	(2.28)*	(0.90)
D1000	0.338	−0.031
	(2.56)*	(0.21)
Constant	7145	8024
	(12.14)**	(17.31)**
Observations	103	77
R-squared	0.76	0.75

Robust t statistics in parentheses
+ significant at 10%;
* significant at 5%; ** significant at 1%

As can be seen, these results do not change the previous findings. With the exception of the effect of traffic on the fares now being statistically significant at 10 per cent, the rest remain unchanged. That is, the new estimated effects of traffic, distance, fuel, competition and intermodal competition on both highest and lowest fare classes are very close to those effects estimated before.

VII. Conclusions

In order to analyze the determinants of the fares in the Chilean Airline Market, the present chapter estimates a reduced price equation for the case of the main operator of this market, LAN CHILE. To do so, the price equation is identified and then estimated by Two-Stages Minimum Squares using a balanced panel of nine destinations in the period between 1998 and 2007.

Due to limitations in the database, and following Holmes[39] and Marin,[40] we assume symmetry between destinations so that price discrimination is equal between them. Individual price equations are estimated for both the highest and lowest fare classes to analyze the sensitivity of the estimates. The effect of

39 Holmes, above n 7.
40 Marin, above n 8.

auto-correlation due to the panel structure of the data has also been taken into account, but does not change the results. All variables maintain their size and direction.

Under these assumptions, we find that the effect of the traffic on the fare is positive in the case of the highest fare class and negative in the case of lowest fare class. In particular, an increase of 10 per cent in traffic generates an increase of 1.4 per cent and a decrease of 1.5 per cent in the highest and lowest fare classes respectively. While the dataset does not allow us to determine with certainty the presence of economies of density, it is still a possible result given that only a minority of passengers travel on high fare classes, ie business class.

Secondly, we find evidence of distance economies because route distance has a negative impact on fares. A route with a 10 per cent higher distance is found to have a reduction of 5.98 per cent and 4.41 per cent on the lowest and highest fare classes respectively.

Thirdly, and with regard to the variables of costs, it is found that the effect of the fuel price is positive and significant. In general, pass-through rates are smaller than one: 0.348 and 0.644 for the lowest and highest fare classes, respectively. In other words, companies do not transfer all changes in fuel costs to consumers. Notice also that changes are more readily transferred to the highest fare class passengers; it is the more inelastic segment. When changes in fuel costs are transferred, this is done differentially in a way that minimizes loss in passengers' numbers.

In relation to the effect of the competition in prices, we find that in monopolistic markets and/or long distance routes where the intermodal competition is very low, the operator takes advantage of their market power to increase fares in the inelastic segment of the demand. In particular, the fares of the inelastic segment are 30 per cent more expensive in monopolies and are 32 per cent higher in routes with distances greater than 1,000 km.

Lastly, we provide a final word of caution. Although these results are in line with literature findings, they must be taken as preliminary evidence, because there is a need for more detailed data yields to make a stronger case.

Appendix 1
Details of the Analyzed Studies

	Marín (1995)	Dresner and Tretheway (1992)	Nero (1998)	Schipper et al (2002)	Fageda (2006)	Oliveria (2003)	Carlsoon (2004)
Data	Annual data for 35 unidirectional routes in 1982 and 1989 in Europe	Data for routes in the Atlantic of the North in 1976 and 1981	Data for 34 bidirectional routes between 1988 and 1992 in Europe	Data for 34 bidirectional routes between 1988 and 1992 in Europe	Semi-Annual data for 67 unidirectional routes in the 2001–2002 for domestic markets in Spain	Monthly data for the Air-Shuttle market between Sao Paolo and Rio de Janeiro between January of 1997 and October of 2001	Data for 172 bidirectional routes in the 2001 for domestic markets in Europe
Level of Desegregation	Route and firm	Route	Route and firm	Route	Route and firm	Route and firm	Route and firm
Specification Reported		Coach fare class	Best adjusted (Likelihood Ratio).		Model 2. Non-monopolistic routes	Varig	Non-monopolistic routes of Model 2

Appendix 2
Main Statistics of the Variables

	mean	sd	min	max	N
Highest Fare Class (chilean pesos)	89,333	37,464	29,900	177,900	126
Lowest Fare Class (chilean pesos)	56,590	18,173	20,000	94,900	100
Distance (Km)	2,230	1,091	858	4,342	226
Traffic (people)	14,479	8,582	840	37,508	226
Population (people)	727,805	513,704	149,784	1,996,099	223
INACER index (1996 = 100)	140.13	25.62	97.49	210.00	226
Jet fuel (US$/gallon)	1.05	0.49	0.43	2.09	226
Wage index (2006 = 100)	87.69	10.88	71.51	110.65	226

Chapter XVIII

Mergers, Prices and Concentration in the Supermarket Industry: The Case of Chile

ANDRÉS GÓMEZ-LOBO* AND ALDO GONZÁLEZ**

I. Introduction

There is a world-wide tendency towards higher levels of concentration in the retail industry. Related to this trend, retail outlets seem to be growing in size and in the scope of products offered, as well as becoming multinational operations. The supermarket industry is no exception.

In Europe, for example, the supermarket five firm concentration index rose from 40.7 in 1993 to 48.9 in 1999.[1] In Spain and Portugal the increase was quite marked, from 21.6 to 40.3 in the case of Spain, and from 36.5 to 63.2 in the case of Portugal. In the United States, Elickson reports that store sizes have increased by 1,000 square feet per year in the last three decades.[2] In Latin America, the largest Chilean retail chains have gone on a shopping spree across the region, buying retailers in Peru, Colombia and Brazil.

Most attribute these tendencies to an increase in the economies of scale due to technological change, particularly in distribution and logistic activities. Elickson argues that as markets grow, supermarket firms start investing in logistical software and technology.[3] As a result, these endogenous fixed costs imply that markets do not fragment as they grow. Instead, the minimum efficient scale in this industry grows in tandem with market sales, implying a lower bound for concentration (four to six firms per market according to Elickson).[4]

* Associate Professor, Department of Economics, University of Chile.
** Assistant Professor, Department of Economics, University of Chile.

[1] Paul Dobson and Michael Waterson, 'Countervailing Power and Consumer Prices' (1997) 107 *Economic Journal* 418–30.

[2] Paul B Elickson, 'Does Sutton Apply to Supermarkets?' 38/1 *RAND Journal of Economics* 43–59 (2007).

[3] *Ibid.*

[4] *Ibid.*

In addition, as supermarket firms grow they have more negotiating power against suppliers. These countervailing powers, as Galbraith defined them, will reduce the market power of large suppliers, thus decreasing input costs.[5] To the extent that these savings are passed on to final prices, then consumers may eventually benefit from higher retail concentration.

In Chile, the supermarket industry has become increasingly concentrated through growth, acquisitions and mergers. In 1998, the two main supermarket chains (Cencosud and D&S) represented 29.3 per cent of sales at the national level. By early 2006, their market share was 62.5 per cent. These figures hide marked regional variation in the level of concentration, however. In many cities, the expansion of these two chains has reduced the level of concentration and the market power of incumbent regional chains.

Recently, several proposed mergers that would have increased even further the level of concentration have been checked by the antitrust authorities. This possible limitation to further consolidation in this industry has generated an intense debate. Economists hired by the main retail chains have argued that economies of scale justify further concentration and that this would benefit consumers.[6] On the other hand, a study contracted by the antitrust authority (Fiscalía Nacional Económica, or FNE) indicates that for food products—the main items sold by supermarkets—prices are higher in more concentrated markets.[7]

In this chapter we critically examine the case for further mergers and acquisitions by the two leading chains in the supermarket industry in Chile, particularly based on the argument of economies of scale. First we present a conceptual discussion regarding economies of scale and merger policy, present several arguments against further consolidation, and briefly discuss the merger cases analyzed recently in the retail and supermarket industry in OECD countries. We then present the history of the supermarket industry in Chile, the available empirical evidence relating to prices, mergers and concentration in this industry, and estimate a model that tries to identify the impact of past mergers and concentration on prices.

[5] John K Galbraith, *American Capitalism—The Concept of Countervailing Power* (Boston, Massachussets, Houghton Mifflin, 1952).

[6] See Loreto Lira, Magdalena Ugarte and Rodrigo Vergara, 'Economías de Escala, Concentración, y Precios en la Industria de Supermercados' (2007), report written on behalf of D&S, at 9–17; A Galetovic and R Sanhueza, 'Un análisis económico sobre competencia y supermercados' (2006), report prepared for *Cencosud*, at 27; and Patricio Rojas and Susana Jiménez, 'Informe Económico Fusion Falabella–DyS' (2007), report prepared for D&S and Falabella, at 6.

[7] Andrés Gómez-Lobo and Aldo González, 'La relación entre los precios de los alimentos y la concentración de los supermercados en Chile: evidencia de un modelo dinámico de panel y análisis de impacto de fusiones propuestas en la industria' (July 2007), *Working Paper Series No 249*, Departamento de Economía, Universidad de Chile. The institutional set-up in Chile is as follows. The FNE, similar to the FTC in the United States, is a governmental agency in charge of investigating antitrust cases and presenting charges to a specially created tribunal (Tribunal de la Libre Competencia). This Tribunal is composed of five members, two of whom must be economists, the rest lawyers. Two lawyers and the two economists are chosen through a mechanism that involves the autonomous Central Bank, while the Chilean Supreme Court chooses the fifth member. The ruling of the Tribunal can be appealed only to the Supreme Court.

We believe the results of this analysis are important for the rest of the region in view of the fact that mergers and concentration in the retail industry will probably be a hotly debated issue in many other Latin American countries, given the current wave of acquisitions (many of them by the largest Chilean retail firms).

II. Merger Policy and Economies of Scale

Advocates for further mergers in the Chilean supermarket industry have explicitly or implicitly stressed the existence of unexploited economies of scale as justification for these operations. In these reports, changes in the technological nature of the industry towards a larger minimum efficient scale are used as a theoretical justification for a complete disregard of the potential negative impacts that further concentration could have on consumers. According to Galetovic and Sanhueza, since concentration is due exclusively to the underlying technological changes and endogenous fixed costs, further concentration is inevitable.[8] Furthermore, it would not only increase economic efficiency, but would also benefit consumers, since the cost savings would be passed on in the form of lower prices. These arguments have no limit and would seem to justify any merger, even if it implies finishing with two firms in the market.

The widespread use of endogenous fixed costs models as a justification for further mergers in the Chilean supermarket industry is surprising, and is not in line either with the mainstream economic analysis employed in merger control or with antitrust practice around the world.[9] Models like Sutton's describe how concentration changes as markets grow, but the bounds approach used does not address welfare considerations and is thus somewhat insufficient for antitrust discussions.[10] Similar to the perfect competitive paradigm, these models do not provide useful guidance for merger control. The only lesson for antitrust purposes that Sutton's model provides is that no merger control should exist, since by construction, firms in the long run cannot obtain supranormal profits. Thus, any merger must be interpreted as a natural movement from one long-term equilibrium to another long-term equilibrium. Clearly, this paradigm overlooks several factors that the literature considers relevant for the welfare analysis of mergers, such as the existence of dominant firms, the timing of entry, and the endogeneity of anticompetitive entry barriers.

[8] Alexander Galetovic and Ricardo Sanhueza, above n 6.

[9] As far as we are aware, in no other country are the ideas of Sutton used in discussions surrounding merger cases. John Sutton, *Sunk Costs and Market Structure* (London, MIT Press, 1991).

[10] *Ibid.*

A. Economies of Scale

The defenders of further mergers in Chile ignore the existing theoretical literature on economies of scale and mergers, not to mention US merger guidelines and the international jurisprudence concerning this issue, particularly in the retail sector.

Farrell and Shapiro express caution about the use of economies of scale as a sufficient justification for a merger.[11] They stress the point of the specificity to the mergers of the economies of scale, and mention that unless the economies are due to synergies between the merging firms' capital stocks, then these economies, if they really exist, would probably be exploited without the merger anyway. The bigger the economies of scale, the more likely it is that firms will attempt to exploit them unilaterally if not allowed to merge.

The US merger guidelines reflect these ideas.[12] Efficiencies will be considered as a possible benefit of a merger only if they are merger specific. That is, they cannot be achieved through any other means (eg, through internal growth or the purchase of assets in the market). The FTC was successful in opposing a merger of the major pharmaceutical wholesalers in the mid-1990s by showing that the economies of scale that supposedly would be achieved through this operation could just as easily be exploited through continued competition among the firms in the market.[13]

Even if we accept that there are economies of scale associated with the merger, a reduction in the number of competitors must be taken into account. This reduction in competitors may well push final prices up, as explained first by Williamson[14] and formalized later in different models of imperfect competition such as those of Farrell and Shapiro,[15] and Deneckere and Davidson.[16]

The presumption given by the supporters of mergers—namely that cost efficiencies from economies of scale will be fully pass-through to consumers—assumes an underlying model of competition *á la* Bertrand, a very extreme case of competition where all rents are dissipated and transferred to consumers in the form of lower prices. This assumption is at odds with the existing empirical literature on the retail industry that suggests that mergers and higher levels of concentration in this industry increase prices for consumers.[17] Research in this area shows that

[11] Joseph Farrell and Carl Shapiro, 'Improving Critical Loss Analysis' (2007) Competition Policy Center, Paper CPC07-079, University of California Berkeley. See also J Farrell and C Shapiro, 'Horizontal Mergers: An Equilibrium Analysis' 80/1 *American Economic Review* 107–26 (1990); and David Spector, 'Horizontal Mergers, Entry, and Efficiency Defences' 21 *International Journal of Industrial Organization* 1591–1600 (2003).

[12] US Federal Trade Commission 1992 Horizontal Merger Guidelines, with 1997 Revisions, <http://www.ftc.gov/bc/docs/horizmer.htm>.

[13] *FTC v Cardinal Health, Inc*, 12 F Supp 2d 34 (DDC 1998).

[14] Oliver E Williamson, 'Economies as an Antitrust Defence: the Welfare Trade-offs' (March 1968) 58 *American Economic Review* 18.

[15] Farrell and Shapiro, above n 11.

[16] Raymond Deneckere and Carl Davidson, 'Incentives to Form Coalitions with Bertrand Competition' 16 *RAND Journal of Economics* 473–86 (1985).

[17] See Howard W Smith, 'Supermarket Choice and Supermarket Competition in Market Equilibrium' 71/1 *Review of Economic Studies* 235–63 (2004); Todd Sharkey and Kyle Stiegert,

supermarkets compete not only in prices but also in location and product variety.[18] Physical distance to competitors is a relevant factor when firms choose prices, since consumers face costs in moving to stores less convenient to them. This locational differentiation allows stores to exercise some local market power, which gives support to the presumption that mergers between supermarket chains that operate in the same area may increase prices.

Entry barriers are another relevant element to consider in merger analysis. The groceries market report submitted by the Competition Commission in the UK recognizes the risk of land-banking as a strategy to impede entry by competitors due to the scarce locational space in consolidated areas.[19] In Chile, the most eloquent proof of this phenomenon is a paragraph contained in the Annual Report and Financial Statements of D&S (one of the leading Chilean supermarket chains) which states:

> One of the strengths of the firm, is to own properties considered to be key to Santiago's and other cities' urban development and that act as a *barrier to entry* for potential competitors.[20]

The CEO of Falabella, one of the largest retail chains that recently entered the supermarket industry by buying a small regional chain (San Francisco) in 2004, declared that it is very costly to start a chain from scratch.[21] This implies that the most feasible way to enter the supermarket industry from now on is to buy an existing chain. If the largest chains are allowed to buy the smaller chains, then this industry will effectively be closed to new entrants.

Furthermore, the claim that large firms are able to exploit economies of scale implies that entry by new firms is a more risky business. In order to compete properly with the large established firms, an entrant will need a higher level of investment in specific capital, such as logistics, advertising and its own store brands. As McAfee *et al* mention, although economies of scale by themselves are not an entry barrier, they comprise an ancillary mechanism that exacerbates the

'Impacts of Nontraditional Food Retailing Supercenters on Food Price Changes' (Feb 2006) 20 *FSRG Monograph Series*; Ron W Cotterill, 'Market Power and the Demsetz Quality Critique: An Evaluation for Food Retailing' 15/1 *Agribusiness* 101 18 (1999); Marcus Asplund and Richard Friberg, 'Food Prices and Market Structure in Sweden' 104/4 *Scandinavian Journal of Economics* 547–66 (2002); and Pedro Barros, Duarte Brito and Diogo de Lucena, 'Mergers in the Food Retailing Sector: An Empirical Investigation' 50/2 *European Economic Review* 447–68 (2006), as a sample of the most recent studies. A complete list of studies can be found in section 3 of Gómez-Lobo and González, above n 7.

[18] See Competition Commission of the United Kingdom, 'A Report on the Supply of Groceries From Multiple Stores in the United Kingdom' (2000), <http://www.competitioncommission.org.uk/rep_pub/reports/2000/446super.htm#full>; and Yesim Ohrun, 'Spatial Differentiation in the Supermarket Industry' (2005) *Working Paper*, Haas School of Business, University of California at Berkeley.

[19] The firm may keep the land undeveloped or to lease to a third party with restrictive covenants, such as one prohibiting the tenants from building a supermarket.

[20] D&S, *Memoria Anual y Estados Financieros* (2006) section 4.1, at 127. Translated by the authors. Emphasis added.

[21] 'Gerentes de D&S y Falabella detallan sus estrategias de internacionalización', *Diario La Tercera*, August 25, 2007, at 54.

importance of other entry barriers such as the sunk investments needed to operate in the industry.[22]

Thus, it is highly likely that the number of competitors in the long run will be determined by the court's ruling on current or future merger operations. As an example, in 2007, Cencosud, the second largest supermarket, sought to buy a declining medium-size chain called Unimarc. The opposition of the FNE and the resulting court consultation process were instrumental in blocking the operation and allowing a new investor to buy the chain and enter the supermarket industry. This third actor now accounts for 13.5 per cent of the market. With the recent blocking of the merger between D&S and Falabella by the Competition Tribunal, there is some likelihood that a new relevant actor may emerge in the industry if the latter firm decides to expand its supermarket branches (Tottus and San Francisco).[23] Without the merger revision it is probable that there would be only two—instead of three or maybe four—supermarket chains in the country.

Within OECD countries there are several cases of supermarket mergers that have been challenged by the antitrust authorities. In the UK in 2003, the Competition Commission (CC) did not allow any of the three largest supermarket chains to buy the failing firm Safeway. The agency decided to avoid ending up with a highly concentrated market structure with only three dominant operators. According to the CC's ruling, such a scenario would substantially reduce competition in the groceries retail market. Only the merger with Morrisons, the fifth chain at that time, was deemed not to be detrimental to competition in the industry. The CC explicitly stated that it preferred to have a market with four equivalent firms instead of three with a potential dominant player.

In 1996, the European Commission rejected the merger between Kesko and Tuko, which affected the Finnish groceries market.[24] The former firm was at that time the dominant chain in Finland with 40 per cent of the market, while the latter had 20 per cent of the market. The Commission feared that the merger would consolidate a dominant firm in the domestic market without an equivalent rival that could offset the exercise of market power. Furthermore, the Commission concluded that the dominant character of Kesko would make it highly unlikely that the entry of new rivals would be observed after the merger.

More recently, in 2007, the antitrust agency of New Zealand opposed the purchase of one of the two large supermarket operators (The Warehouse Group) by the biggest department stores company (Woolworths Limited). The central argument against the operation, as expressed by the agency, was the suppression of the main potential competitor's ability to challenge the existing duopoly in the supermarket industry.[25]

[22] P McAfee, Hugo M Mialon and Michael A Williams *et al*, 'What is an Entry Barrier' (2004) 94/2 *American Economic Review Papers and Proceedings* 461–65.

[23] On January 31, 2008, the Tribunal rejected the merger between D&S and Falabella.

[24] European Commission (1996) Case No IV/M.784—*Kesko/Tuko*.

[25] Woolworths Limited Proposed Acquisition of 22 Action Stores and Development Sites, Commerce Commission of New Zealand: Foodstuffs, Woolworths and the Warehouse Group Limited, Commerce Commission Decision 606/607, 2007.

In June 2007, in the US, the FTC decided to block the acquisition of Wild Oats by Whole Foods. The agency considered both grocery chains, which specialize in natural organic food, to be part of a separate market from the traditional supermarket stores.[26]

III. The Evolution of the Supermarket Industry in Chile

As in other market economies, the Chilean supermarket industry has shown a marked trend towards higher levels of concentration at the national level. During the last decade, the landscape has evolved from a rather dispersed market structure towards a kind of duopoly, with the two largest operators jointly having close to 65 per cent of the market.

Cencosud started with a hypermarket (large supermarket) format called 'Jumbo', which in 1994 had just 6 per cent of the market. This group entered in the smaller format segment of the industry, buying two national medium-size supermarket chains—Santa Isabel in 2003 and Las Brisas in 2004. The group D&S, with its known branch 'Lider', grew mostly through endogenous growth, with a diversified portfolio of stores, including hypermarkets and medium- and small-size supermarkets. The main acquisition of this group was the purchase of the stores of Carrefour in Santiago. The French giant supermarket operator decided to leave Chile after a few years of activity in the country.

In the middle of 2006, both chains engaged in a process of purchasing regional supermarkets, inducing the FNE to ask for a preventive measure requiring authorization from the Tribunal to proceed with any acquisition by these two chains. This petition was accepted by the Tribunal.[27]

Triggered by the preventive ban on future acquisitions imposed on the two largest chains, a new group emerged in the industry—Saieh—buying Unimarc and merging with the regional chain Deca-Rendic. At time of writing, this group has bought other small- and medium size chains—Montserrat, Bryc, Mayorista 10 and El Loro—becoming the third operator in the industry at the national level with the 13.5 per cent of the market. None of these last operations has been contested by the national antitrust agency (FNE).

The first empirical paper on the supermarket industry in Chile was by Lira, Rivero and Vergara.[28] They show that food prices fall when a new hypermarket

[26] The district court dismissed the FTC's claims. On appeal, the DC Circuit overturned the lower court ruling.

[27] Chile does not have a compulsory merger notification system. Firms may voluntarily ask for a revision of the deal, or may go through the merger process risking that the FNE will oppose the operation in the courts.

[28] Loreto Lira, Rosario Rivero and Rodrigo Vergara, 'Entry and Prices: Evidence from the Chilean Supermarket Industry' (2005), Segundo Borrador, PUC.

Table 1 Mergers in Retail in Chile 2003–08

Date	Acquiring	Acquired	Geographical impact
July 2003	Cencosud	Santa Isabel	National
December 2003	D&S	Carrefour	Santiago
January 2004	Cencosud	Las Brisas	National
March 2004	Deca-Rendic	Atacama	III Region
August 2004	Cencosud	Montecarlo	Santiago
May 2006	Cencosud	Infante	II Región
June 2006	D&S	El Pilar	VII Region
August 2007	Unimarc	Deca-Rendic	National
January 2008	Deca-Rendic-Unimarc	Bryc-Mayorista10	National

Source: A González, 'Efectos Competitivos del Aumento en la Concentración en el Mercado de la Venta de Alimentos al Detalle. Un Análisis Conceptual' (2006), Report prepared for FNE, Santiago, Chile, and press reports.

opens up in a regional city.[29] This fall precedes the opening of the new venue, indicating that existing firms react before the opening of the new store.

Gómez-Lobo and González[30] reinterpret the results of Lira *et al*[31] indicating that a fall in prices is to be expected when a new competitor enters a local market. They estimate the same model as Lira *et al* but substitute their entry variable for a local market concentration index. As expected, the lower concentration is associated with lower food prices. Thus, it is natural that as a new hypermarket opens in a city, food prices will fall, but the merger implications of this phenomenon are very different from what Lira *et al* intended. In this case, mergers that significantly reduce the number of competitors in a city should not be approved.

Lira, Ugarte and Vergara counter the above criticism by re-estimating their model, including both a local concentration variable and the dummy indicating the entry of a hypermarket in a city.[32] The results indicate that both of these variables are statistically significant and have the expected sign. However, the coefficient on entry is larger than the coefficient of concentration. The merger implications of these results are not clear. Higher levels of concentration increase prices, but by marginal amounts (the estimated elasticity of concentration on prices was between 0.01 and 0.02). The authors, on the other hand, interpret the coefficient on entry as a proxy for the expansion of the two largest chains and the transfer of the economies of scale of these operators to consumers.[33] However, this last interpretation is

[29] Average food prices by city are the only data available to study this issue. As mentioned further below, almost 80% of supermarket sales are food products. However, the National Institute of Statistics (INE) also collects food prices in some cities from open street markets and small convenience stores, thus the price index in some cities does not exclusively reflect food prices of supermarkets.

[30] Gómez-Lobo and González, above n 7.

[31] Lira *et al*, above n 28.

[32] Lira *et al*, above n 6.

[33] *Ibid.*

not very convincing. If the two largest chains have a cost advantage over competitors and they pass these efficiencies to final consumers, then it is the identity of supermarkets in each local market and their expansion that matters, not just the new entry of these chains to a new regional market. Therefore, the model estimated by Lira *et al* suffers from an omitted variable problem.

In this chapter we further analyze this debate by estimating a model that includes both concentration levels and dummies controlling for past mergers. We explore the effects that past mergers had on prices. Due to the time period of our data we can explore the impact only of the first five mergers in Table 1 above. We believe this model will shed more light as to the impact that mergers have on prices in Chile compared to previous studies.

A. The Model

We estimate a partial adjustment model for food prices in each city. This model is similar in spirit to those used in the Staples–Office Depot merger analysis in the United States.[34]

At each moment of time, equilibrium prices are given by:

$$P_{it}^{*} = \alpha + + \beta' \cdot X_{it} + \gamma \cdot S_{it} + \mu_i + \lambda_t + \nu_{it} \qquad (1)$$

where i denotes the city and t denotes the time period. P_{it}^{*} is the equilibrium price, which depends linearly on a vector of explanatory variables, X_{it}, market concentration, S_{it}, a fixed effect for each city, μ_i, a time effect, λ_t, and a well-behaved random shock, ν_{it}.[35] On the other hand, α, β and γ are parameters (or vector of parameters) to be estimated.

It is important to emphasize that the individual fixed effect, μ_i, will control all time-invariant factors specific to each city: for example, systematic differences in transport and logistical costs, land and property values, and wages. Although many of these variables are not time invariant, they are unlikely to vary much between cities during the time span of the data of this study.

The equilibrium price, P_{it}^{*}, of equation (1) is contingent on market conditions at time t. However, firms do not adjust prices instantaneously to this equilibrium

[34] See Jonathan B Baker, 'Econometric Analysis in FTC vs Staples' 18/1 *Journal of Public Policy and Marketing* 11–21 (1999); Orly Ashenfelter *et al*, 'Econometric Methods in Staples' (2004) *Princeton Law and Public Affairs Working Paper No 04-007*, Princeton University, Spring Semester. The available data preclude the estimation of a structural model such as used by Ivaldi and Verboven ('Quantifying the Effects from Horizontal Mergers: Comments on the Underlying Assumption' 23 *International Journal of Industrial Organization* 699–702 (2005)) in the proposed Volvo–Scania merger in Europe, since we do not observe individual supermarket prices but only average food prices in a given city. For the same reason we are unable to use 'critical loss' analysis, which has figured predominantly in recent supermarket merger cases in the United States (Kevin Murphy and Robert Topel, 'Critical Loss Analysis in the Whole Foods Case' (March 2008) *Global Competition Policy Magazine*); see also the discussion by Farrell and Shapiro, above n 10. In section V below we discuss the available data.

[35] In the empirical application all continuous variables are transformed to their natural logarithm.

level. Rather, the effective price in period *t* is price quoted in the last period plus a proportion of the adjustment required to reach the new equilibrium price:

$$P_{it} = P_{it-1} + \theta \cdot \left(P_{it}^{*} - P_{it-1}\right) \tag{2}$$

In this last equation, the parameter θ ($0 \leq \theta < 1$) measures the speed of adjustment of prices to their long-run equilibrium. If this parameter is close to one, the adjustment is almost instantaneous. With monthly data, a value close to one implies that prices adjust to their new long-run equilibrium within a month. If θ is close to zero, prices adjust very slowly to their long-run equilibrium.

Why is it reasonable to specify a partial adjustment model for supermarket prices? First, the data strongly suggest such a specification, as will be shown further below. Secondly, both the theoretical and the empirical literature support a partial adjustment model for prices in the supermarket industry.

The main theoretical argument in favor of a partial adjustment model is the existence of 'menu costs' for retailers, an idea well developed in the macroeconomic literature to explain aggregate price dynamics.[36] The intuition is that firms, especially in the retail sector such as supermarkets, face significant fixed costs of changing prices. As a result, prices are not updated continuously but, rather, at discrete time intervals. Even when a firm's current prices are not at their equilibrium level, it may be optimal to wait some time before prices are changed.

Empirical studies seem to confirm the existence of 'menu costs'. For the supermarket industry in the United States, Levy *et al* and Slade estimate that menu costs are significant.[37] Furthermore, they generate price dynamics similar to those generated by the partial adjustment model used in this chapter. Slade also introduces the idea that supermarkets do not adjust their prices immediately (or completely) when economic circumstances change in order to maintain the 'good will' of their customers.[38]

The equilibrium price of equation (1) is not observable by the econometrician. However, this equation can be substituted into equation (2) to obtain the following model for observed prices:

$$P_{it} = (1-\theta)\cdot\alpha + \theta\cdot P_{it-1} + \theta\cdot\beta'\cdot X_{it} + \theta\cdot\gamma\cdot S_{it} + \theta\cdot\mu_i + \theta\cdot\lambda_t + \theta\cdot\nu_{it} \tag{3}$$

[36] See, eg, the seminal contributions to this literature by Robert Barro, 'A Theory of Monopolistic Price Adjustment' (1972) 39 *Review of Economic Studies* 17–26; Eytan Sheshinski and Yoram Weiss, 'Inflation and Costs of Price Adjustment' 50 *Review of Economic Studies* 513–19 (1997); and Andrew S Caplin and Daniel F Spulber, 'Menu Costs and the Neutrality of Money' 102/4 *Quarterly Journal of Economics* 703–25 (1987).

[37] Daniel Levy, Mark Bergen, Shantanu Dutta and Robert Venable, 'The Magnitude of Menu Costs: Direct Evidence form Large US Supermarket Chains' 112/3 *Quarterly Journal of Economics* 791–825 (1997); Margaret Slade, 'Optimal Pricing with Costly Adjustment: Evidence From the Retail-Grocery Prices' 65 *Review of Economic Studies* 87–107 (1998).

[38] Slade, above n 37. It must further be noted that sales and marketing campaigns can also restrict the velocity by which supermarkets can change prices.

By redefining some parameters, the above equation can be expressed as:

$$P_{it} = \tilde{\alpha} + \tilde{\theta} \cdot P_{it-1} + \tilde{\beta}' \cdot X_{it} + \tilde{\gamma} \cdot S_{it} + \tilde{\mu}_i + \tilde{\lambda}_t + \tilde{v}_{it} \qquad (4)$$

In equation (4), $\tilde{\gamma}$ measures the short-run impact of concentration on prices. The long-run impact is:

$$\gamma = \frac{\tilde{\gamma}}{(1-\tilde{\theta})}. \qquad (5)$$

This long-run impact of concentration on prices can be readily obtained from the parameter estimates of equation (4).[39] The closer $\tilde{\theta}$ is to zero, the faster prices adjust to their long-run equilibrium.

1. *Econometric Considerations*

Equation (4) is a dynamic panel data model. Several well-known econometric problems arise if this model is estimated using conventional estimators (ie, OLS). The main difficulty is that P_{it-1} is correlated with μ_i, generating a classical endogeneity problem. Several estimators have been proposed in the literature to estimate consistently the parameters of dynamic panel data models. Table 2 below, inspired by a similar table contained in Benavente *et al*, summarizes the available options.[40]

When the number of cross-section observations (*N*) is large and the number of time series observations (*T*) is also large, the data can be pooled and the model can be estimated by OLS or other conventional estimators. When *T* is small and *N* large (as in household survey data), the GMM estimator of Arellano and Bond or its extension by Blundell and Bond are popular options.[41] On the other hand, if *N* is small but *T* is large, the with-in group estimator is a good choice, since this estimator is consistent as the number of observations grows in the temporal dimension.[42]

What happens if T and N are relatively small? This is the case in our study, where $T = 51$ and the number of cities is equal to 24 ($N = 24$). Several Monte

[39] In some specifications of the model estimated further below we allow current prices to depend on two lags of prices. That is prices in period last month (*t-1*) and two months ago (*t-2*). It is trivial to derive for the two-period lag model equations analogous to (4) and (5). See José Miguel Benavente, Alexander Galetovic, Ricardo Sanhueza and Pablo Serra, 'Estimando la demanda Residencial por Electricidad en Chile: El Consumo Sensible al Precio' (2005) 42 (Mayo) *Cuadernos de Economía* 31–61 for details.

[40] *Ibid.*

[41] Manuel Arellano and Stephen Bond, 'Some Tests of Specification for Panel Data: Montecarlo Evidence and an Application to Employment Equations' (1991) 58 *Review of Economic Studies* 277–92; R W Blundell and S Bond, 'Initial Conditions and Moment Restrictions in Dynamic Panel Data Models' (1998) 87 *Journal of Econometrics* 115–43. With a balanced panel, which is not the case of this study, the with-in group estimator with bias correction proposed by Kiviet ('On Bias, Inconsistency and Efficiency of Various Estimators in Dynamic Panel Data Models' 68 *Journal of Econometrics* 53–74 (1995)) can be used. The Monte Carlo simulations presented in Kiviet show that the corrected with-in group estimator has very good small-sample properties.

[42] Stephen Nickell, 'Biases in Dynamic Models with Fixed Effects' 49 *Econometrica* 1417–26 (1981). The with-in groups estimator is identical to a fixed effects panel data model.

Table 2 Available estimators for dynamic panel data models

	T small	$T \rightarrow \infty$
N small	With-in groups estimator (Judson and Owen, 1999; Galetovic *et al* (2005))	With-in groups estimator (Nickell, 1981)
$N \rightarrow \infty$	Arellano and Bond (1991) Blundell and Bond (1998)	OLS or other conventional estimators

Source: Adapted from Benavente *et al.*[43]

Carlo studies suggest that in this case the with-in groups estimator is the preferred choice. Judson and Owen recommend this estimator for unbalanced panels when $T \geq 30$.[44] Benavente *et al*, using Monte Carlo simulations, show that the with-in groups estimator has the lowest bias among available estimators for dynamic panel data models.[45] They use generated data very similar in structure to ours, with $N = 20$ and $T = 100$. Based on these results, in this chapter we use the with-in groups estimator, although we also estimate the model using the GMM estimator of Arellano and Bond in order to check the robustness of our results.[46]

B. The Data

1. *Prices*

We do not have access to supermarket price data. However, the National Institute of Statistics (INE) collects average monthly food price data for 95 products in 24 Chilean cities, including the capital, Santiago. We could not include other goods sold by supermarkets because there is no public information available for the prices of such goods. However, food products represent close to 80 per cent of supermarket sales.[47] Another potential problem is that, in some cities, INE collects food prices not only from supermarkets but also from small vendors and open street markets.

The use of average price information at the city level implies making several assumptions regarding the size and scope of each market. First, at the geographical level we have to assume that each city is an integrated market. This is unlikely to be too far off from reality, as most of the 24 cities are small. However, it is an optimistic assumption for larger cities such as Santiago, Valparaíso and Concepción. Secondly, at the product level we have to assume that products sold through different channels (supermarkets, open markets and small vendors) are

43 Benavente *et al*, above n 39.

44 Ruth A Judson and Ann L Owen, 'Estimating Dynamic Panel Data Models: a Guide for Macroeconomists' 65 *Economic Letters* 9–15 (1999).

45 Benavente *et al*, above n 39.

46 Arellano and Bond, above n 41.

47 Lira *et al*, above n 28.

close substitutes. These assumptions imply relevant markets larger than those recommended by the available international evidence and literature.

Our data cover the period from January 2002 through March 2006. Price data are available from January 1998, but only for 16 cities and 52 products. In addition, the aggregate supermarket sales in each city are available only from January 2002.

We use a price index of 95 products available for all cities during the period from INE's Annual Price publications.[48] These products were aggregated into a single price index using the weights from the Consumer Price Index. There are three cities without price data for some goods at the end of 2005. Therefore, the price index series for these cities is incomplete.[49] In Appendix 1 we present graphs of the evolution of the price index for each city during the period.

2. *Evolution of Industry Structure*

The number and size of supermarkets in each city comes from the Supermarket Directory compiled monthly by INE. This Directory registers venues that sell one or more products at the retail level, using a self-service format and with three or more cash registers.[50]

The information from the Supermarket Directory, which contains information on the opening and closure of each store and the number of cash registers, was cross-checked and complemented with information provided by the National Economic Prosecutor (FNE), the web pages and Annual Reports of the main supermarket chains, and press reports found on the Internet.

3. *Aggregate Sales and Concentration Index*

Monthly aggregate sales data for each city were obtained from INE. This information is in nominal Chilean pesos, and was deflated using the Consumer Price Index (IPC). Unfortunately, this information is available only at the aggregate level and not by supermarket chain. Therefore, it was necessary to use a proxy variable for the market share of each company in order to construct a concentration index, as discussed further below.

As a measure of concentration we use the Hirschman-Herfindahl concentration index (HHI):

$$HHI_i = \sum_{j=1}^{N} (s_{ij})^2$$

[48] Instituto Nacional de Estadisticas de Chile, <http://www.ine.cl/>.

[49] In Rancagua there are no price data for long-life tomatoes in October 2005; in Linares there are no price data for long-life tomatoes and lettuce in October and November 2005; and in the city of Los Andes there is no price registered for long-life tomatoes in October and December 2005.

[50] Once again, this may imply too wide a market definition. However, small convenience stores, which may not belong to the same relevant market as supermarkets, will have a very small influence on the concentration index since their market share will be very small.

where s_{ij} is the market share of firm j in city i. The advantage of using this index over other concentration indices is that it incorporates the two dimensions considered relevant in order to determine the competitive level of a market: the number of firms and their relative size.

We consider all chains belonging to the same owner as part of the same firm. For example, Jumbo and Santa Isabel are considered as part of one firm after these two chains merged in 2003.

In order to construct the HHI it is necessary to know the market share of each firm. This information is not available from INE, but the FNE has some information on sales for some chains. Unfortunately, however, this information is not available for all firms in the sample and therefore cannot be used to construct the concentration index. In this chapter we follow Barros, Brito and de Lucena and use a proxy for sales.[51] They use the surface area of each supermarket. Since we do not have information on the surface area for all firms in our sample, we use another variable highly correlated with sales, the number of cash registers, as a proxy for this variable.

Table 3 below presents the correlation coefficient between sales, surface area, and the number of cash registers for the years and firms where these data are available.[52] The correlation coefficient between cash registers and sales is 0.83 on average. This figure is almost identical to the correlation coefficient between sales and surface area (0.82). Therefore, using the number of cash registers as a proxy for sales seems to be just as good as using the surface area of the supermarkets of each firm.

The HHI based on the share of cash registers of each firm was multiplied by 10,000. Therefore, this index has a range between 0 and 10,000. The graphs of the evolution of this index by city are presented in Appendix 2 to this chapter.

Table 3 Correlation coefficient between sales, surface area and number of cash registers for selected firms

	Cash registers	Sales area (m^2)	Sales 2003	Sales 2004	Sales 2005
Cash registers	1.0000				
Sales area (m^2)	0.9453	1.0000			
Sales 2003	0.9103	0.8780	1.0000		
Sales 2004	0.8070	0.8006	0.9598	1.0000	
Sales 2005	0.7639	0.7712	0.9221	0.9707	1.0000

Source: Own calculations based on information provided by INE and FNE.

[51] Barros *et al*, above n 17.

[52] The information on sales and surface area is available for: D&S, Montserrat, Economax, Cencosud and Rendic.

4. *Mergers*

Dummy variables were constructed for the first five mergers described in Table 1 above. These variables take a value of one in the cities where the merger had an effect starting from the month after the date presented in Table 1 until the end of the time period of the data.

C. Results

Table 4 below presents the estimation results. Specifications (1) and (2) were estimated using the with-in groups estimator (Fixed Effects panel data model), while specifications (3) and (4) were estimated using the Arellano-Bond GMM estimator.[53] In each case a time-specific monthly dummy was also included, but due to space limitations the results for these variables are not presented in Table 4.

The first thing to note is that the results are very consistent across specifications. There is clearly a lagged response of prices to lagged values of this variable. The aggregate value of sales in each city was not statistically significant in specifications (1) and (3). This is probably due to the city-specific fixed effects which are already controlling for differences in market size across cities. The growth of sales in each city is probably correlated across cities due to macroeconomic effects, and most of this variation is probably being controlled for by the monthly time-specific dummies. As a result, we estimate specifications (2) and (4) without the aggregate sales variable.

Table 4 Estimation results

	Ln(Price)			
	(1)	(2)	(3)	(4)
Ln(Price)t-1	0.5678645	0.5676639	0.5586158	0.5320572
	(19.08)***	(19.10)***	(18.69)***	(17.73)***
Ln(Price)t-2	0.2239459	0.2238251	0.216095	0.1930947
	(7.46)***	(7.47)***	(7.18)***	(6.42)***
Ln(IHH)t-1	0.0087843	0.008628	0.0084755	0.0116748
	(2.61)***	(2.72)***	(2.45)**	(3.17)***
Ln(Aggregate sales) t-1	0.0007428	–	0.0019289	–
	(0.14)		(0.34)	
Merger dummies:				
Cencosud-Santa Isabel	–0.0012416	–0.0012119	0.0004893	0.0020301
	(–0.56)	(–0.55)	(0.21)	(0.73)

(continued)

[53] Arellano and Bond, above n 41.

Table 4 (Continued)

	Ln(Price)			
	(1)	**(2)**	**(3)**	**(4)**
D&S–Carrefour	–0.0044767	–0.0044402	–0.0040555	–0.0044384
	(–0.64)	(–0.63)	(–0.57)	(–0.58)
Cencosud-Las Brisas	–0.0001913	–0.0044402	–0.0009592	–0.0022301
	(0.08)	(–0.09)	(–0.41)	(–0.75)
Rendic-Atacama	–0.0147806	–0.014668	–0.0160396	–0.0196504
	(–2.63)***	(–2.64)***	(–2.77)***	(–3.15)***
Cencosud-Montecarlo	–0.0015513	–0.0015845	–0.0017126	–0.0022062
	(–0.22)	(–0.22)	(–0.24)	(–0.30)
Estimation method	**Within**	**Within**	**Arellano-Bond**	**Arellano-Bond**
R2 overall	0.93	0.93	–	–
R2 within	0.63	0.68	–	–
Sargan test of overidentifying restrictions	–	–	Prob > chi2 = 0.3522	Prob > chi2 = 0.1238
Number of obs	1171	1171	1146	1146
Number of cities	24	24	24	24
	Price-concentration elasticities			
Short-run	0.009	0.009	0.008	0.012
Long-run	0.042	0.041	0.038	0.042

Notes: The Arellano-Bond estimator used up to 12 lags of instruments and dependent variables. The Z statistic is presented in parentheses below each coefficient. * indicates variable statistically significant at 10% confidence level, ** indicates variable statistically significant at 5% confidence level, *** indicates variable statistically significant at 1% confidence level. Monthly time dummies were also included but results are not presented in this table.

The HHI index is positive and statistically significant in each model. This implies that more concentrated markets are associated with higher food prices. This is not due to different market sizes, since we control for city-specific fixed effects and include in some specifications the aggregate value of sales in each city. The results of this model are very similar to those of Gómez-Lobo and González, who use a longer data set (from 1998 to March 2006) but include a price index of only 52 food items.[54] The long-run elasticities of food prices to concentration are presented at the bottom of Table 4.

[54] Gómez-Lobo and González, above n 7.

The most interesting results are those for the merger dummy variables. Of the five mergers included in the model, four are not statistically significant.[55] The most important merger during this period is the purchase of Santa Isabel by Cencosud. However, there is no discernible effect of this operation on prices.

The only merger that seemed to have lowered prices was where Rednic, a relatively small regional chain in the north of the country, purchased another small regional chain (Atacama). One can only speculate as to the reason why in this case the merger seems to have had an effect on prices. One possibility is that economies of scale are stronger for smaller chains, and their merger generates sufficient efficiencies to lower final prices. Another possibility is that the purchased chain was grossly inefficient in this case.

What seems to be clear from the results, however, is that there is no evidence to indicate that the two big chains (Cencosud and D&S) have passed on any cost savings as a result of acquisitions they have made in the past. Either there were no economies available from these operations, or if cost savings resulted these were not passed on to final consumers. Given the importance placed on economies of scale as a justification for further mergers in this industry, these results are troubling.

IV. Conclusion

It is evident that technological change has spurred increased levels of concentration in the retail sector, including the supermarket industry. To some extent, higher levels of concentration may not be bad for consumers. However, once an industry is very concentrated, the benefits of increased concentration for productive efficiency may well have to be balanced with the added competitive risks.

If higher levels of concentration are achieved through endogenous growth of individual firms competing in the market, then to some extent this tendency is inevitable. The true policy dilemma comes about when concentration is achieved not through organic growth of each successful firm, but through a process of mergers and acquisitions.

In this chapter we have presented several arguments that call for caution when analyzing further mergers in the Chilean supermarket industry. The current situation is already troubling, with what amounts to a national duopoly in this industry. As a result of a more proactive antitrust stance by the competition authorities and the Competition Tribunal, some recent mergers which would have further concentrated the industry have been blocked. This has allowed a third actor to enter the industry.

[55] To be fair, the two mergers in Santiago (D&S–Carrefour and Cencosud–Montecarlo) were minor mergers involving the acquisition of only a few stores. It is unlikely that price changes as a result of these operations would be registered in a city-wide food price index for such a large city as Santiago.

In recent merger cases, advocates of these operations have stressed the existence of economies of scale in this industry and the efficiency benefits that would come about through more mergers. In this chapter we critically analyze these arguments and show that, in general, both the academic literature and international practice indicate that further mergers and acquisitions by the two main supermarket chains are probably against consumers' interest. We also estimate a dynamic price-concentration model using monthly food price data for 24 cities between 2002 and 2006 to show that, contrary to common belief, there is no evidence that past mergers by the two main supermarket chains have led to lower consumer prices. We do find evidence that higher levels of concentration are associated with higher prices. These findings lend evidence in favor of recent court rulings against further mergers by the leading actors in this industry.

Appendix 1
Price Index Evolution by City

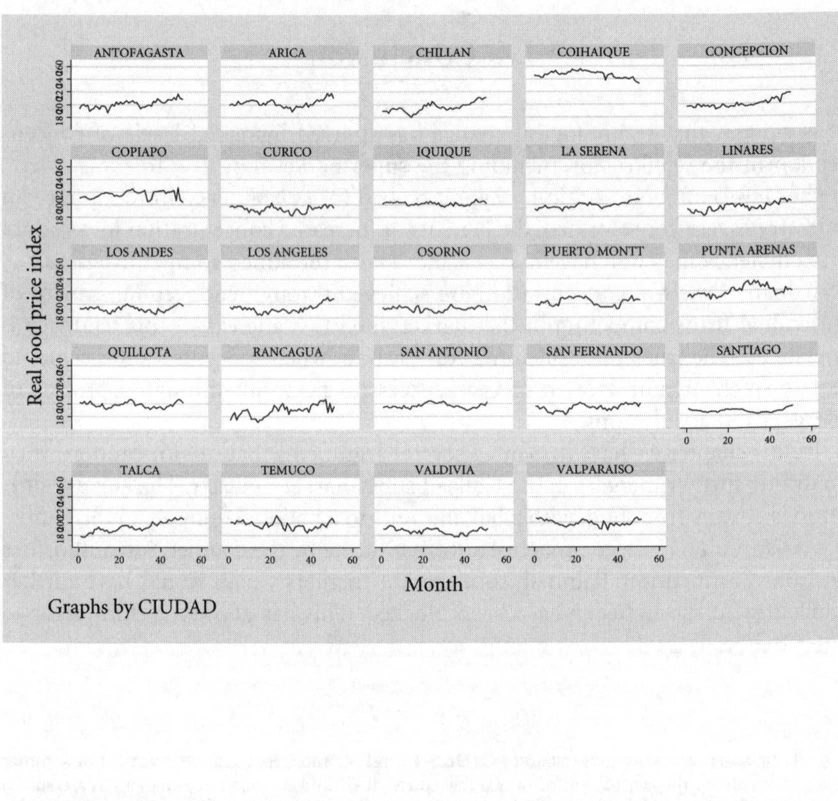

Appendix 2
HHI Index Evolution by City

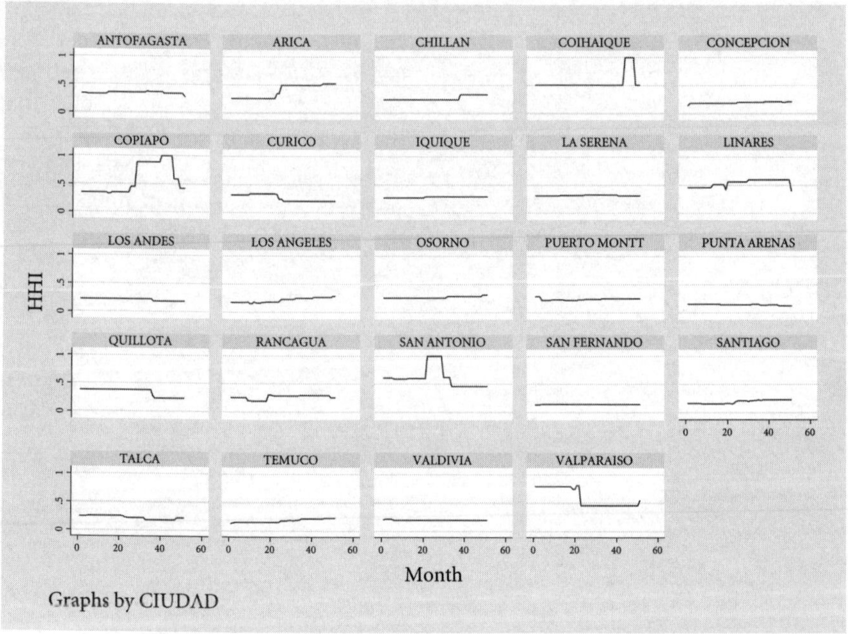

Chapter XIX

The Agricultural Sector and Competition Policy in Colombia

RICARDO ARGUELLO* AND MARÍA CLARA LOZANO ORTIZ DE ZARATE**

I. Introduction

In this chapter we review competition policy and law in Colombia, with an emphasis on the agricultural sector. For this analysis, we first visit the legal and institutional structure of competition policy and its implementation from a historical viewpoint. Then we examine the legal and institutional relationships between competition law and agricultural policy, as well as the role of competition policy in agricultural development. This chapter examines a number of cases investigated by the *Superintendencia de Industria y Comercio* (the Colombian competition agency, the Superintendency of Industry and Trade or 'SIT') to illustrate the main issues involved in implementing competition policy in the agricultural sector.

After several decades in a dormant state, competition policy in Colombia has received a major shake-up, with the opening up of the economy and the revamping of competition law and institutions. During the last 15 years there has been a substantial increase in the use of competition policy. Several high-profile cases have tested both the adequacy of competition law and the legitimacy and capability of the relevant authorities. With the passage of time and the increase in the number of cases investigated, the SIT has gained experience and enhanced its expertise for promoting a competitive environment in Colombian markets.

The use of competition policy in regulated or quasi-regulated sectors is of particular interest. Even though currently there is no extensive governmental intervention in the agricultural sector, the State intervenes in important ways in the functioning of agricultural markets. Several policy instruments have been put in place that effect competition. Moreover, more open markets and the increasing involvement of the Colombian agricultural sector in a market environment have made competition issues arise in important ways. Competition issues affect

* Professor of Economics, Universidad del Rosario.
** Law Faculty, Universidad Javeriana, and Lozano & Asociados.

not only relatively complex organizational and property structures, typical of a modern economic sector, but also truly atomistic and dispersed producers more akin to a peasant economy.

Disciplining the market, in the sense of guaranteeing its competitiveness, has different implications for different agents. As we shall see, it can mean curbing the appetite of oligopsonists for determining purchase prices, and therefore protecting the primary producers, or it may mean teaching primary producers that they cannot collude to hurt consumers. This ample range of market outcomes provides the environment in which competition and agricultural policies interact.

The relevance of examining the agricultural sector is further highlighted if we take into consideration that it accounts for about 14 per cent of GDP and 23 per cent of total employment in Colombia. These shares may well triple if we include sector linkages upstream and downstream. Furthermore, there is another important aspect to Colombian agricultural development: its dualistic nature. As in other developing countries, the agricultural sector has historically been characterized as having two distinct segments. On one side there is a modern, technologically developed segment that is fully linked to the market; on the other there is a relatively backward, technologically stagnant segment only partially linked to the market.

This characterization has become fuzzy with the development of the Colombian agricultural sector and with improved technology diffusion and adoption. As a result, the technologically and market-based dualism has tended to shift to a size-based dualism, in which issues such as effective access to credit, to new technologies, and to marketing circuits are the dominant features determining market outcomes. For several products, scale economies and minimum efficient scale in handling and processing determine market entry. A number of sectors, among them cocoa processing, sugar production, rubber processing, tobacco processing, snack production, rice milling and dairy processing, show moderate to high concentration levels in Colombia.

In these circumstances, having competitive markets is essential to agricultural development. Competitive markets provide the most efficient way to bridge the gap between large and small producers. Competition policy has an obvious and key role to play in generating and keeping markets competitive. It also has an important role in safeguarding domestic agents against international anti-competitive practices, whether they originate abroad or at home. In the face of increasing concentration in key international markets, and in view of evidence of anti-competitive behavior, greater openness and market deregulation do not substitute for competition policy.

II. Competition Law in Colombia

Colombia has the oldest competition law among Andean countries. Issued in 1959, Law 155 provided the first attempt to promote competition in Colombia.

The law addresses three antitrust areas: interlocking of positions in boards of directors[1] and administrative offices, traditional restrictive business practices, and mergers and acquisitions. Regarding restrictive business practices (RBPs), Law 155/59 contains a general statement prohibiting all conduct intended to restrain competition. However, it does not provide specific examples of anti-competitive conduct. This may be one reason why there were practically no cases brought before the authorities until the 1990s, when the Colombian Congress amended the competition policy legislation. This Law also provides some criteria in order to identify companies with market power.

At the same time, Law 155 of 1959 gives the Government the power to allow agreements that, although they may be considered anti-competitive, are deemed necessary for stabilizing an economic sector that is regarded as 'basic' to the economy.[2] The definition of 'basic' sector is found in another piece of legislation, dated 1964, and is so broad that practically any economic sector may qualify as such.[3]

Regarding mergers, the Law establishes a mandatory pre-merger notification procedure. By this, firms whose combined assets are worth more than 20 million Colombian pesos (about US $10,000 at the 2007 exchange rate, an adequate figure for 1959) must submit to the authorities any plan for merging in order to obtain prior approval. As will be explained below, this threshold has been changed twice in recent years. The measure is intended to evaluate the likelihood that the proposed merger may restrict competition. The Law does not give any specific content to this concept, and the antitrust agency has applied different criteria for judging different cases in this area.

The liberalization of the Colombian economy from the late 1980s to early 1990s necessitated an updated Colombian competition law and policy. The Colombian Political Constitution, amended in 1991, provided in Article 20 transitory[4] the authorization to give a new structure to the Colombian State. Following this constitutional disposition, the executive branch of the Colombian Government issued Decree 2153 of 1992, which contains substantial dispositions regarding

[1] This is a prohibition on an individual simultaneously serving on more than one board, or being an administrative officer in more than one unrelated firm in the same industry.

[2] There is an interesting discussion regarding who is the authority in this case. In its Circular Unica (General Statute) issued in 2001, the SIT indicates that the competition agency is the only one that can grant the exception. However, there is a legal definition of 'Government' in the Colombian Constitution: the Government is the President and the corresponding Minister. Therefore, as Law 155/59 provides that the Government is the grantor of the exception, there would be a seeming contradiction as to whether the SIT can effectively grant it.

[3] Art 1 of Decree 1302 from 1964 defines as a 'basic sector' any economic activity that has, or may have in the future, significant importance for the rational structuring of the economy and for providing goods and services necessary for general welfare. It also lists in a non-exclusionary manner some sectors that fulfill these characteristics, eg the production or distribution of food, clothing, health services, housing, financial services, education, transportation, energy, water, telecommunications and insurance.

[4] Transitory constitutional articles were set to give time to the administrative branch of the government to adequate its structure to be able to guarantee the new set of rights issued.

antitrust matters and the corresponding new structure of the Colombian antitrust agency.

Decree 2153 supplemented Law 155 and reinforced the powers of the competition agency, while significantly reducing the degree of governmental discretion in competition issues. The Decree created specific prohibitions and provided for a more objective assessment of violations through the establishment of a set of specific standards. It also provided a clear definition of the basic antitrust concepts related to conduct and structure, and a list of specific exceptions to the application of Colombian competition law, such as R&D agreements. Another exception is made on efficiency grounds in merger cases. However, to date, the SIT has yet to approve a merger based on an efficiency exception.

The definition of the term 'agreement' provided by Decree 2153 does not make any difference between horizontal and vertical agreements. Therefore, the specific prohibitions of Articles 47 and 50 of the Decree must be scrutinized to determine if they apply to horizontal or vertical conduct. An open question in enforcement is whether to use 'per se' or rule of reason standards. This question is before the Council of State (Colombia's top administrative authority) and a decision on the matter is still pending. Regarding unilateral conduct, the Colombian Political Constitution (as amended in 1991) provides that it is illegal to abuse a dominant position in a market.

Decree 2153 set the current institutional structure of Colombian competition policy. It created a new structure for the already existing SIT, which the Decree charged with the enforcement of competition law, other than that related to specifically regulated industries The SIT is a body independent of the executive branch, headed by a Superintendent. In addition to its competition policy function, the SIT oversees consumer protection and management of the intellectual property rights system, and supervises the chambers of commerce.

Regarding competition policy, a Deputy Superintendent for the promotion of competition is charged with investigations and merger analysis. His or her office conducts investigations and analyzes proposed mergers, prepares investigation reports, including conclusions of law, and submits them to the Superintendent for final adjudication. During the adjudication process, the Superintendent has the obligation to consider recommendations from an Advisory Committee, created by Decree 2153, but does not have to abide by them. The Superintendent adjudicates the cases on the basis of his or her own discretion, and may even depart from the conclusions put forward by the Deputy Superintendent on whether to impose sanctions and fines. The SIT's decisions may be reviewed only by the administrative courts.

In addition to its enforcement function, the SIT has a competition advocacy role. Among other activities, it can advise other government agencies on matters related to regulations affecting market entry and competition issues in natural monopolies and privatizations. Remedies used by SIT for enforcing competition include: orders to rectify or cease any conduct contrary to law; fines of up to 2,000 times the minimum legal monthly wage (approx US $440,000) on companies involved and of up to 300 times the minimum legal monthly wage (approx US $65,000) on individuals. Importantly, the Colombian Political Constitution of 1991 declares the right to competition to be a collective right. This allows, besides private rights of action, antitrust class actions.

Sector regulators are the primary enforcers of competition in regulated sectors.[5] The Superintendency of Domestic Public Services ensures competition in the supply of domestic public services. However, the SIT investigates restrictive trade practices in non-residential telecom services. The Financial Superintendency is charged with investigating antitrust issues in the banking and insurance sectors. Regarding TV services, the National Television Commission (CNT) is the relevant authority. Nevertheless, there has been a recent interesting agency case where the SIT has claimed authority to review a merger (Telmex—Cablecentro—Supercable[6]; all providers of TV cable services) due to the fact that the companies renounced their licenses in order to perform the operation. According to SIT, at the moment the firms renounced their licenses the CNT lost (while the SIT gained) jurisdiction to review the merger.[7]

III. Competition Policy Implementation

During the first three decades of competition law in Colombia—due, among other things, to the fact that there was only one general prohibition plus the exception previously mentioned—the SIT never prosecuted a case.[8] This also appears to be partly the consequence of there being infant industry and import substitution protectionism, which allowed the consolidation of monopolies and oligopolies in almost every industrial sector. The intricate relationship that followed between powerful firms and conglomerates, on the one hand, and government officials and politicians, on the other, was not the best environment for an effective competition policy. Furthermore, the general prohibition set out in Law 155 refers to the need for 'unfair' prices to develop as a consequence (potential or actual) of the anti-competitive conduct, a difficult concept to define and use within an investigation procedure. Lastly, as mentioned above, the Law did not lay down examples of anti-competitive conduct. This left the application of competition law in a regulatory vacuum.

[5] Sometimes there is overlap between sector regulators and the SIT. In other cases, the SIT lacks authority to act because the sector regulator has sole responsibility for the promotion of competition in the given sector.

[6] See SIT's Resolutions 17651 and 17652 of June 14, 2007.

[7] There was no need to renounce to the licenses. Apparently the firms decided to do so to perform the merger; and once this happened, the SIT claimed jurisdiction.

[8] Jatar, Ana Julia and Luis Tineo, 'Competition Policy in the Andean Countries: A Policy in Search of its Place' (Washington, DC, Organization of American States, 1997), http://www.ctrc.sice.oas.org/compol/Articles/cpandea.asp#*.

Since 1992, when the SIT began operations under the new legal framework, a number of important cases have been investigated. As in other Andean countries, the emphasis has been on behavior rather than structure, a feature that is credited with making the enforcement of competition policy less traumatic for the economy than trying to correct market structure (in terms of number of competitors or degree of concentration). The emphasis on behavioral remedies (though not to the exclusion of structural remedies) is particularly important given the uncertainty of determining the optimal size of firms in the market.

The Superintendent has the power to close a competition investigation if the defendant enters into a sufficient guarantee (similar in concept to a consent decree) that it will cease or amend the conduct under investigation. As collateral for compliance with the remedies offered, companies must take out an insurance policy for the SIT's benefit. Whenever the SIT considers that there has been a failure to comply with the required commitments, it can initiate a process to prove such lack of compliance and bring into effect the insurance policy. The insurance company is allowed to bring a legal action against the company undertaking the policy for its non-compliance. The ability to create guarantees has led to the settlement of a significant number of cases.

Though guarantees have led to swift settlement of cases, such settlements prevent the SIT from issuing final decisions, which limits the development of much-needed jurisprudence and enforcement precedents. Furthermore, having the discretion to settle in this way even cases involving violations that are analyzed as 'per se' restrictions in other jurisdictions, seems contrary to the development of a competition culture. Moreover, consumers cannot recover the social cost caused by certain restrictive practices and have no participation in the negotiating process that determines the guarantees (and therefore no assurance that the guarantees respond to their interests). The social cost argument is twofold: first, neither the plaintiff nor consumers take part in the negotiating process, and this seems to undermine transparency and culture formation; secondly, the practice under investigation is presumed to have an economic (welfare) effect, and society does not recover any of this cost since there are no fines or income receipts accruing to the Government.

Compliance with guarantees has been an issue in recent years. When the SIT has found non-compliance it has imposed fines and has made effective the corresponding insurance policies. One recent example of non-compliance is the SIT's[9] claim against the insurance policy issued on behalf of CEMEX, by which the latter obtained the closing of an earlier investigation. The insurance policy was set to guarantee the SIT that CEMEX would stop colluding with other firms for fixing cement prices. As part of CEMEX commitments, the company was obliged to keep detailed documentation supporting any decision regarding price changes and to produce and keep minutes detailing the main criteria by which prices were modified; documents that must be made readily available to SIT. Upon a visit by

[9] See SIT's Resolution 26360 of 2006.

SIT to CEMEX, the former found evidence that the firm was not in compliance with these commitments and decided to claim the insurance policy.

Merger control is a large part of the SIT's antitrust enforcement. The Circular Unica (General Statute) from the SIT, issued in 2001, established the notification requirements for potential merging parties. Merging parties had to receive prior approval from the agency when they had at least 20 per cent of market share or jointly had assets of a value equivalent to 50,000 times the monthly legal minimum wage. Later, Resolution 22195 of 2006 raised the threshold for prior approval to 100,000 times the monthly legal minimum wage (more than US $22 million) for combined annual operational revenue or combined total assets, without mentioning any threshold regarding market share. The long-awaited measures were intended to rationalize the review process; the now-inadequate threshold established in Law 155 tended to clog up SIT's operational capability. According to the SIT, the market share threshold was eliminated due to its lack of objectivity and legal uncertainty.

In non-merger enforcement, the vast majority of cases relate to agreements regarding price fixing, output restraints, and market allocation. Cases related to resale price maintenance conduct and the refusal to deal have also been prominent and very complex.

IV. The Agricultural Sector and Competition Policy Law

Colombia's competition legislation is fully applicable to the agricultural sector. However, Article 65 of the Colombian Political Constitution provides for special protection regarding food production. Moreover, Decree 2478 of 1999, establishing the structure and procedures of the Ministry of Agriculture, includes an article that addresses competition issues.[10] The latter allows the Ministry to regulate domestic agricultural markets, determine price policy for these goods and their inputs when there are market failures, and to submit to the relevant agencies requests for the issuance of policy measures aimed at correcting the internal competition environment. The Agricultural Ministry has used this power in only one case, as discussed further below.

Even though there are a number of areas within agricultural policy in need of greater attention as regards competition, the SIT has undertaken little competition advocacy in the agricultural sector. This in spite of the fact that a number of sector policy instruments have clear effects on competition and that the legislation that created them lacks any mention of competition law. There is frequent potential tension between sector policy and competition policy, because sector policy is

[10] Article 3 (15).

often aimed at protecting rural income (or the income of certain rural groups) through direct or indirect price setting and other mechanisms, among them indirect monetary transfers from some economic agents to others or market regulation. The 'disconnect' that used to exist between the Ministry of Agriculture's policies and the SIT created a vacuum that proved a barrier to enhancing competition in the agricultural sector, as well as to implementing sector policy successfully in the long run.

An example showing this disconnect between the Agricultural Ministry and the SIT is a Concept[11] from the Chief of SIT's Legal Advisory Office (Concept 25623 of 2000), created in response to a consultation[12] as to whether Resolution 321 of 1999 from the Ministry of Agriculture could be in violation of competition law. The Resolution involved a price system and framework for the operation of dairy markets in Colombia (implementing parts of a Competitiveness Agreement for the Dairy Sector, brokered by the Ministry of Agriculture between private agents from the sector and the Government in 1999). Although there is a general prohibition against anti-competitive behavior, there is also (in the same article) an exception. This exception applies in the case of basic sectors, such as agriculture. In the above case, the Ministry of Agriculture provided an exception to competition law without reference to the SIT. The agency strongly argued that antitrust exceptions are under its sole jurisdiction. The Concept asserts that the Competitiveness Agreement was issued in July 1999, before the issuing of Resolution 321, and that there is no document in the files of the SIT proving that the agency had conceded or had been asked to grant an authorization to issue the above-mentioned Agreement.[13] Therefore, if there were any provision in the Competitiveness Agreement that could be in violation of competition law, the Ministry of Agriculture's Resolution would be protecting conduct that was contrary to Constitutional principles and law. Nonetheless, the Concept highlights the fact that the Ministry's Resolution is an administrative act protected by a presumption of legality, and that unless suspended or declared null by the administrative courts, this presumption would have to be taken into consideration when assessing the Resolution's legality. This example underscores the difficulties inherent (from the legal and economic points of view) in providing a regulatory framework for agricultural activities and the promotion of competition. As the issue has not been revisited, it is not clear which agency would legally prevail.

The 'disconnect' between the two agencies already mentioned now seems to be less severe. The Ministry of Agriculture has begun to intervene *explicitly* in competition matters in its sector. Moreover, coordination between the

[11] Under Colombian law, a concept is a non-binding interpretation of law issued by an authority.

[12] A consultation is a concept asked by a particular to an authority in order to clarify the extent or scope of a regulation. Consultations are not binding for the issuing authority.

[13] An unsurprising fact given the ambiguity that exists as to who is the relevant authority for granting an exception in order to stabilize a basic sector. However, competitiveness agreements similar in scope and depth to the one mentioned above, exist for agricultural sectors that clearly are not in need of special stabilization measures.

Ministry and the SIT has increased. One apparent cause is the push by private organizations[14] and their members in the food system regarding potential and actual anti-competitive practices in this sector. There is an international element to this concern regarding international cartels. As a function of improved inter-governmental concern in this area, the Colombian Government, particularly the Ministry of Agriculture, has started to intervene to correct alleged anti-competitive practices, internal or international in origin, in several subsectors. An additional factor pushing greater competition has been the proposed free trade agreement with the United States. These factors led private agricultural organizations to propose that the Ministry of Agriculture should issue competition guidelines for the sector. Though this effort ultimately failed, it exemplifies a shift in orientation on competition in agriculture in Colombia.

Partly as a consequence of this effort, in 2005 the SIT and the Ministry of Agriculture started an ambitious program related to the establishment of an agriculture competition group inside the SIT: the Interinstitutional Agricultural Follow-up Group. The intent was to have a specialized technical group to study mergers and acquisitions, and to carry out RBP investigations in this sector. The Ministry of Agriculture funds the agricultural competition group of the SIT. It consists of seven staff members, most of them with two bachelor degrees.[15] In terms of the human capacity of the agency, this educational background means that the members of staff lack graduate qualifications but have, for example, both an economics and a law degree.

In July 2005, the Ministry of Agriculture, under its authority from Decree 2478, issued Decree 2513 to define the term 'unfair price' (required for the application of the ambiguous general prohibition contained in Article 1 of Law 155) as it applies to the dairy sector. Decree 2513 also established that the Ministry would consult the SIT in cases in which the Ministry suspected anti-competitive practices or unfair price setting in the raw milk market. However, this definition was temporary in its nature and remained in place for only about a year.[16]

In September 2005, the Ministry of Agriculture issued Decree 3280. Decree 3280 refers to how the SIT should handle requests for agreements aimed at agricultural stabilization of food production and distribution. In particular, the Decree provides that the power to authorize such agreements belongs to the SIT, but that the Superintendent should ask for a Concept from the Ministries of Agriculture and Trade. The Concept must refer to the need for sector stabilization. It also provides for previous and non-binding Concepts from these Ministries in cases in which the Superintendent analyzes the possibility of finishing an agreement for considering that the sector has already been stabilized.

[14] Such as farmers' cooperatives and the Colombian Farmers Association.

[15] SIT's competition promotion branch consists of 14 people besides the agricultural group.

[16] This was a temporary policy, but it illustrates two important points: first, the difficulty of using the general prohibition due to its ambiguity; and, secondly, that this was a clear 'intrusion' of the Ministry into the realm of SIT.

A further development in inter-institutional cooperation relates to the issuing by the Ministry of Agriculture of Resolutions 00128 and 00125 of June 2006. The first provides policy guidance for determining prices for agrochemical products, while the second subjects the market in these products to vigilance by the Ministry (a controlled freedom regime[17]). According to the Ministry of Agriculture, the measures address old complaints from agricultural producers to the effect that agrochemical plants and distributors make use of anti-competitive practices, price fixing in particular. The controlled freedom regime was extended to other agrochemical and agricultural inputs in November 2006 (Resolution 00302) and April 2007 (Resolution 0092). Firms in the agrochemical sector[18] are now required by the Ministry to submit information on prices, production costs, sales, goods and distribution (a power the Ministry has under the controlled freedom regime).

The implementation of price controls has not been an easy issue in Colombia. This case was no exception. In view of the fact that a number of firms did not comply, or did so in an incomplete fashion, the Ministry asked the SIT to request information on compliance directly, making use of a feature of the controlled freedom regime and the power of SIT to impose sanctions on those who do not comply with SIT requests. Based on this request, in June 2007 the SIT required 300 firms that were not complying to submit the information within a 20-calendar-day window (by July 10). Non-compliance[19] would entail a fine of up to 2,000 monthly legal minimum wages (about US $437,000). The measure has a precedent in a previous Resolution by SIT, issued in March 2007, by which the agency fined five agrochemical firms for not fulfilling their obligation to report market and price information to the Ministry of Agriculture. At the end of July, it was clear that a number of cases of failure to report were due to non-operating firms having closed without fulfilling all legal procedures. Other cases were due to mistakes in reporting on the part of the firms. Lastly, a number of cases, about 100, were effectively cases of lack of or misrepresentative reporting.

The Ministry increasingly has made use of policy instruments to increase competition in the sector. One such example is the so-called 'absorption accords' created in 1995. These accords were agreements brokered by the Ministry of Agriculture, the Ministry of Trade and the Ministry of Finance between private agents, by which the right to import under preferential arrangements was made conditional on the purchase of domestic product, for which a purchase price was agreed.[20] However, in this case, as in other cases, legislation creating the policy made no explicit mention of either competition policy or of a role for the SIT.

[17] A situation in which firms are allowed freely to set their prices, but are obliged to inform the authorities in writing about their variation and the way in which they are determined, in accordance with a methodology determined by the authorities.

[18] This included producers, mixers and importers.

[19] A similar situation occurred in the banking sector, where five banks that refused to send information were recently fined by the SIT.

[20] This instrument is no longer used, since it was replaced by a system for auctioning import rights based on purchases of domestic product.

V. The Role for Competition Policy in Agriculture

Even in a developing country such as Colombia, the agricultural sector tends to be significantly market oriented. Having a dynamic agricultural sector, in the sense of increased productivity, is vital not only for improving social conditions in rural areas, but also for economic development in general. Competition policy affects the way agents in agricultural production behave as much as how they relate to other sectors in the economy, and may prove to be an important tool in helping develop a dynamic agricultural sector.

For producers, having the capacity to substitute inputs with relatively elastic supplies for inputs with inelastic supplies is a key factor in improving efficiency and returns. However, market structure may tend to hinder this possibility. By far, markets for agricultural products, such as corn, fruits and vegetables, and many others, are much less concentrated than markets directly related to the sector, such as agrochemical products, agroindustry, and massive retail sales. Although market concentration does not necessarily lead to anti-competitive behavior, it favors the development of market power and creates conditions favorable for asymmetric bargaining power. Of course, there is a trade-off between fairness and efficiency, especially evident when there are economies of scale in a market. But nonetheless, asymmetries between the more competitive agricultural production and other markets that integrate the whole food and raw materials chain could be of concern.

There are several potential forms of market power in the agricultural sector. The scale of operation of firms with which agricultural producers relate (upstream and downstream) and the degree of concentration in these markets may tend to favor sustained price fixing at levels lower than the competitive one. Vertical integration or coordination may also lead to producers losing their economic surpluses, as some research in the context of developed countries has tended to show. Non-competitive contracting is usually the means for this. Asymmetric information, barriers to entry, conditional access to technological innovation, and even agency capture, are also ways in which market power may be exerted. Even though none of these forms has been documented as happening in Colombia, there is always the potential for them to develop, as the market becomes more and more complex and competition intensifies, making firm survival more challenging.

From the above, it is clear that there is a potentially important role for competition policy in helping foster agricultural development. However, the right mix between agricultural and competition policies cannot be determined a priori. The particular conditions that prevail in a market must be considered on a case-by-case basis so that the trade-off between the two policies may be assessed. The non-economic objectives pursued by agricultural policy, such as food security and social policy, must be taken into account. There is also a clear need for a better understanding of the international context, and its relation and influence on national markets.

The Ministry of Agriculture has demonstrated its concern regarding some of these related markets. Such is the case as regards agrochemical products production and distribution, a sector that shows a relatively high degree of concentration. The Ministry's concern relates to the potential influence of agrochemical agents' behavior on the agricultural chain of production, especially on the way it may affect farmers' capability for taking advantage of more productive inputs.

The marketing and distribution sector is also undergoing an accelerated concentration process, at least at the higher end of the chain. The SIT has investigated large retailers such as Carrefour, Exito (Casino's French Group), Carulla and Olimpica[21] for:

a) violation of the general prohibition of Article 1 of Law 155/59;[22]
b) anti-competitive discrimination;
c) exploiting suppliers;
d) threatening suppliers with withdrawing their products; and
e) abuse of collective dominant position against suppliers.[23]

The investigation ended with the giving and receiving of guarantees.[24] One guarantee comprised an Agreement on Good Practices and Consumer Protection (AGPCP),[25] signed by the main associations of suppliers and distributors of Colombia.[26]

Recent mergers and acquisitions in the supermarket segment have led to dominance of the market by three big players. In conducting a review for a proposed merger between two of the biggest supermarket chains in the country (Exito and Carulla), the SIT imposed conditions on its granting approval. To neutralize

[21] This investigation was opened by Resolution 24180 of 2002.

[22] A number of types of conduct fall within this prohibition, among them selling below the cost of acquisition.

[23] Conduct investigated as a violation of Art 50 of Decree 2153 included: predatory pricing; discrimination; tying; non-compliance with agreed terms for payment; mandatory supply of free products for new stores; unjustified rejection of products; undue pressure to attain the same conditions granted by the seller to other hypermarkets; mandatory and frequent request of products for promotional activities; threat to withdraw products from the supermarket as a negotiating tool with suppliers; unilateral determination by the supermarket of the logistic operator with which the supplier has to do business.

[24] Resolution 13466 of 2004.

[25] The AGPCP is a binding 35-page long document that provides regulation as regards the following aspects: (i) predatory pricing; (ii) commercial agreements and payment terms; (iii) unilateral charges by the hypermarket; (iv) negotiation and execution of commercial agreements; (v) promotion campaigns; (vi) exhibition of products in the hypermarket; (vii) devolutions; (viii) deceptive information; (ix) acceptance of products and suppliers (requirements); (x) proper trademarks; (xi) withdrawing of products or suppliers; (xii) breach of conditions in promotions; (xiii) information for suppliers; (xiv) prohibition of the obligation that similar conditions had been given previously to another hypermarket; (xv) opening of new sale points; (xvi) conditions for the suppliers; (xvii) sales people of the supplier in the hypermarket; (xviii) retaliation. Additionally, the AGPCP provides a procedure for private resolution of conflicts between hypermarkets and suppliers before having recourse to the SIT.

[26] One of the authors negotiated the AGPCP.

competitive concerns as regards the merged firm's negotiating power vis-à-vis its suppliers, the SIT made its approval of Exito-Carulla conditional on:

a) compliance with the AGPCP;
b) acting according to the following restrictions applying to raw and processed consumption products deemed important:
   i) elimination of exclusivity;
   ii) elimination of preferential clauses;
   iii) elimination of exclusivity clauses in technology and manufacturing contracts;
   iv) no ability to request competitors' prices or discounts;
   v) non-discrimination of suppliers;
   vi) no retaliation against the refusal of a supplier to provide information on prices and terms given to other competitors;
   vii) no retaliation against suppliers that have granted different terms (eg, pricing) to competitors, or to tie these terms to the ones given to Exito-Carulla; and
   viii) not making the acceptance of price increases conditional on there having been previous negotiation of a price with competitors.

The SIT also imposed a structural condition: the merged company must divest itself of 11 stores (Resolution 34904, December 2006).[27]

Some markets in the processing sector have become increasingly concentrated. One such market is the dairy sector. As mentioned earlier, government intervention has been warranted in order to provide a definition of 'unfair' prices—the first time the term has been defined under Colombia's competition law. The Government also established a price-setting mechanism for raw milk, at a high cost in terms of implementation, monitoring and resistance from affected parties.

Increased trade openness and the need to secure supplies and solve coordination issues have been the reasons behind the surge of different forms of vertical coordination and integration. Integration may be of concern, as agents may act as sellers or buyers of agricultural produce, giving them more leverage on the market. In the same direction, as vertical integration develops, markets for raw materials and intermediate inputs tend to lose depth, and price signals weaken.

VI. Illustrative Cases

This section discusses a number of representative cases which provide an overview of the key issues in competition policy and law pertaining to the agricultural sector.

[27] The SIT approved the sale of the 11 stores to Olimpica in 2007.

A. Price-fixing and Market Allocation Agreements in the Agrochemical Industry

As mentioned above, the agrochemical industry has been under scrutiny from the Ministry of Agriculture for several years now. In a related case, by Resolution 15847 of 2006, the SIT opened an investigation against two of the largest firms in the fertilizer industry: Monomeros Colombo Venezolanos, and Abonos Colombianos. The conduct under investigation comprised price fixing and market allocation of six types of fertilizer, all of which were put under the controlled freedom regime by the Ministry of Agriculture. While under investigation, both firms offered the SIT guarantees that they would cease their conduct and provide the SIT with information on compliance.

Under Resolution 3119 of 2007, the SIT accepted the guarantees, which included commitments by the firms to:

a) independently determine their prices;
b) establish a Production and Marketing Committee for marketing policies to deter anti-competitive behavior and adopt criteria for pricing; and
c) inform to the SIT of any anticipated price changes and the motivation for such changes.

The SIT accepted similar guarantees regarding market allocation (in terms of production and imports). The SIT also required the firms to obtain insurance policies with a value equivalent to 100 per cent of the maximum fine that it could charge the firms and their legal representatives (approximately US $440,000 and US $65,000, respectively).[28]

B. Price-fixing, Market Allocation, Conditioned Sales and Obstruction of Market Entry Agreements in the Sugar Sector

By Resolution 12305 of 2001, the SIT opened a cartel investigation against a set of 11 sugar producers (the bulk of the Colombian sugar industry) and a marketing company (Dicsa). The marketing company was created by the sugar producers, with the aim of commercializing and promoting the consumption of sugar and molasses in the national market. The firm had a contract with the sugar producers under which it sold in the market molasses provided by the sugar producers. The preliminary investigation led to the opening of an investigation to consider whether Dicsa had exclusivity in trading; the sale price was the same for each

[28] Under Colombian law, when an 'economic agent' (typically a firm) offers guarantees, it does not accept any liability in the case. The SIT's final decision in an enforcement matter that has a guarantee only covers the sufficiency of the guarantee to amend or eliminate the conduct that raises competition concerns in the specific case.

sugar producer; Dicsa, according to the contract, had to assign to sugar producers the sale of molasses in an equitable fashion and to inform them about the conditions of sales; and that in the sales contracts the molasses buyers had to commit to using molasses as an input for feedstock only (no human consumption). Dicsa had the power to inspect and impose economic penalties in the case of breach.

The firms under investigation offered the SIT guarantees in order to close the investigation. The offer included an end to price fixing for sugar and molasses, and a commitment to inform the SIT with respect to any variation in the prices of these products. Additionally, the sugar producers committed to not granting Dicsa exclusivity in the trade of raw sugar and molasses. They also committed to modifying the sales contracts in order to eliminate the conditions objected to by the SIT.

The SIT accepted the guarantees and required the firms to obtain insurance policies for a value equivalent to 40 per cent of the maximum fine that it could impose on them and on their legal representatives (the firms had offered to take insurance policies for an equivalent of 10 per cent of the maximum fine). It also required the firms to determine, at the level of the board of directors, explicit procedures for the determination of sugar and molasses prices, and to ensure that these procedures would be followed at all times.

C. Price-fixing (for Ethanol Production Purposes and Sugar Production) and Market Allocation Agreements in the Sugar Sector

In March 2007, by Resolution 6381, the SIT opened an investigation against 13 sugar processors for price fixing, following complaints by sugar cane producers. The alleged practices took place between May 2005 and February 2007. Preliminary evidence points towards the existence and use of a unique formula to determine the price of sugar cane for ethanol production on the part of the sugar processors. The facts also signal that sugar cane producers do not have the freedom to choose the sugar processor to which to sell. The case remains open.

D. Price-fixing Agreements in the Pasteurized Milk Market

In January 1997, the president of the Association of Independent Milk Processors made a statement in the press declaring that, starting that day (January 25), the price of a one liter milk bag would be COLP$600 on the Bogota market. By February of the same year, 11 milk processors and distributors had indeed fixed a sale price of COLP$600. In April 1997, the SIT decided to open an investigation for price fixing against these processors and plant owners. The SIT closed the case in 2000 under Resolution 27762. The SIT established that there was price-fixing behavior on the part of at least two processing plants. It ordered the two guilty producers to cease this behavior, and fined the firms.

E. Abuse of Dominant Position: Discriminatory Conditions, Conditioned Sales, and Obstruction of Market Entry in the Milk Sector

In 2002, the National Association of Entrepreneurs (ANDI) laid a complaint before the SIT against a milk cooperative (Colanta), for abuse of its dominant position in the milk market against milk producers from whom Colanta bought raw milk. According to the ANDI, Colanta made the entry of new members to the cooperative conditional on the purchase of Colanta's feedstock. In response, the SIT opened an investigation. It found no connection between buying feedstock from the cooperative and being a member on terms for raw milk sales. On the contrary, the conditions applying to milk sales were deemed objective and responsive to the market environment. It also found that there was no conditionality related to the purchase of feedstock from the cooperative or of acceptance as a cooperative member. Under Resolution 588 of 2003, the SIT ruled that even though the cooperative had a dominant position in the relevant market, it had not exerted market power or abused its dominant position.

F. Abuse of Dominant Position in the Coffee Export Market

In 2001, through Resolution 30616, the SIT opened an investigation against the National Federation of Coffee Growers (Fedecafe) and two private coffee exporters' associations, for abuse of dominant position. Fedecafe has acted for a long time as a marketing board for coffee, controlling an important share of the market both as a buyer in the domestic market and as an exporter. The case was brought by SIT on several counts. First, the SIT considered the allegation that the allocation of export quotas and agreements for exclusive supply to certain international buyers (that have to register before Fedecafe) may have resulted in limited access to other exporters and hindered free trade. According to SIT's analysis, Fedecafe and the two associations agreed to assign export quotas in a 3:7 proportion, to the detriment of new entrants or of non-affiliated exporters, especially small ones. Furthermore, the three associations appeared to have participated in an agreement for setting buying prices for coffee in periods in which coffee was in short supply. The SIT suspected that the participants in the agreement would abuse their joint dominant position by excluding competitors.

The associations offered guarantees to the SIT to:

a) terminate the conduct in question;
b) not enter into agreements with each other or with individual exporters that might imply export quota allocations or quotas for buying exportable coffee;
c) not fix prices; and
d) provide non-discriminatory conditions for buying or exporting coffee for non-affiliated firms.

As usual, the associations committed to supply the SIT with information necessary to monitor compliance with the guarantees, and the SIT accepted insurance policies as collateral for the offer (the amount was fixed at 50 per cent of the maximum fine that the SIT could have imposed on the associations and their legal representatives). The guarantees were accepted by the SIT under Resolutions 3361 and 19923 of 2003.

G. Price-fixing Agreements in the Rice Sector

In 2000 two rice producers' associations complained to the SIT of purchase price fixing by five rice-milling companies. The SIT opened an investigation on the matter (Resolution 2249 of 2000). The rice millers offered guarantees to cease the price fixing. The SIT accepted the guarantees and closed the investigation (Resolution 15645 of 2001). Subsequently, the rice producers filed an additional complaint of price fixing. The SIT concluded that the purchase price set by the millers was similar across a 591-day period, and that occasional price variations were graduated in such a way that average prices were identical between millers. In view of this, the SIT issued Resolution 7347 of 2003, which nullified Resolution 15645 of 2001 and opened a new investigation. The SIT attempted to enforce the guarantees, giving rise to a series of legal procedures that have not ended yet.

In September 2005, as a result of a new investigation instituted because of another complaint by rice producers, the SIT issued Resolution 22625 against two of the same milling companies for price fixing on paddy rice purchases in the central part of the country, and imposed heavy fines on the firms and their legal representatives (based on their past history of price fixing). The firms offered guarantees to stop this behavior, which the SIT accepted under Resolution 15645. In December 2005, the firms asked the SIT to void Resolution 22625, based on the SIT's violation of due process and the right to defense,[29] and the SIT's lack of consideration of relevant evidence. The SIT contested the firms' arguments and upheld Resolution 22625 in its entirety.

H. M&A: Breach of the Obligation to Report a Merger in the Poultry Sector

Under Resolution 11030 of 2002, the SIT opened an investigation against four poultry producers and an agricultural firm created by them, for not filing for

[29] In this particular case, the investigated party claimed that its right of defense was violated by the SIT because: (a) the latter rejected the request to consider void a recourse previously presented by the investigated party (given that it was signed by the attorney formerly representing the party); (b) the SIT did not consider evidence provided by the party in another request; (c) the SIT considered as not pertinent a request to declare void its previous decision; and (d) the SIT upheld the totality of its previous findings and decisions.

pre-clearance of a merger under Colombia's merger review process. The SIT concluded that the firms competed in the relevant product market for the purchase of maize and soybeans for feedstock, in both domestic and export geographic markets. The SIT viewed this as a case of vertical rather than horizontal integration, and that, given the value of the combined assets of the poultry producers, this necessitated merger review. The SIT closed the case under Resolution 8315 of 2003 and imposed fines. We argue that this case involved a collaboration agreement among competitors and not a merger between the poultry firms, that it was not a vertical integration, and that the SIT's reasoning is problematic.

I. M&A: Breach of the Obligation to Report a Merger in the Banana Sector

In July 2002 (Resolution 25186), the SIT opened an investigation against a banana trading company, a holding company and a set of eight banana producers, for failing to report a merger for review. The investigation established that the trading company had acquired from a third party (another holding company) all of the assets of the holding company under investigation. The latter had control over the eight banana producers. With the acquisition the trading company indirectly took control over the banana producers. The SIT found that the trading company, the holding company that was acquired by it, and the banana producers should have notified the SIT of the acquisition in advance. By Resolution 21820 of 2004, the SIT determined that the firms had a duty to get prior approval for the merger. Though the firms disputed the need for pre-merger clearance, the SIT prevailed on the merits and Resolution 28515 of 2004 upheld Resolution 25186 almost in its entirety.

J. Abuse of Dominant Position: Predatory Pricing in the Mushroom Sector

The SIT opened an investigation in 2002 (Resolution 20893) against a mushroom producer for predatory pricing. The case contains a lengthy discussion about the relevant market, in terms both of the product and of the geographical market. The SIT determined that the firm's size, market share and production level, as well as the sunk costs that other incumbents or new entrants in the market would have to incur in order to increase supply, demonstrated a dominant position by the producer. However, in reviewing the case, the Office of the Superintendent partially departed from the conclusions of the competition promotion branch of the SIT. After examining the behavior of the firm's prices (among other relevant factors during the period analyzed), and taking into account marketing costs (which the competition promotion branch had ignored), the SIT concluded that there had been no predatory pricing, under Resolution 30835 of 2004.

K. Wholesale and Supply Rcstraints in the Scallions Market

The 2003 OAS Report on Development and Enforcement of Competition Policy and Laws in the Western Hemisphere reports a case of market allocation and supply restraint in the scallions market in Bogota. The Report asserts that a complaint was made to the SIT by a trader against three other traders and Bogota's wholesale market (Corabastos). The complaint alleged the dividing-up of markets among distributors and agreements that affected the level of production of the good. The SIT carried out an investigation to determine whether Corabastos and the traders had signed an agreement, known as the *Acta de Transaccion*, by which they sought to achieve output and territorial restrictions.

In its investigation, the SIT uncovered the agreement and evidence of its implementation. The fourth clause of the agreement indicated that Corabastos would not authorize the wholesale distribution and selling of scallions on the premises of the warehouse market. As a consequence, sellers who leased stores in Corabastos were forced to sell their scallions to the leaseholders participating in the agreement. The SIT fined Corabastos and the other investigated parties.

Another price-fixing case in the scallion market occurred in 2007, when local media reported on a practice by scallion producers of restricting supply during the largest harvest season. Scallion production supplying Bogota's market comes almost entirely from a town in a neighboring department (Aquitania, Boyaca). The vast majority of producers are small farmers, cultivating no more than 2 or 3 hectares. Due to the rain pattern, the biggest harvest occurs during November. Bogota's market has a well-known absorption level for this product, and prices drop sharply when it is surpassed. To avoid price declines, producers colluded to restrict the number of trucks leaving Aquitania for Bogota to limit output. In view of the news, the SIT decided to open an investigation against several of the leaders of the community for restricting supply. The investigation is currently underway.

VII. Conclusion

Counting on competitive markets in the first stages of the value chain is an important factor in the quest for a dynamic agricultural sector—this ensures the enhancement of technological innovation and adoption. An elastic supply of high productivity inputs is needed to ensure that benefits stay in the agricultural sector, and higher returns drive further technological change. Gains in productivity may be threatened by market power and asymmetries in the interplay between primary producers, on the one hand, and processors, distributors and retailers, on the other.

Therefore, having competitive markets at the primary producers' level, as well as in markets where they interact with other segments of the value chain (input producers, processors, traders and retailers), is critical for agricultural and economic growth. Hence, competition policy can play an important role in helping secure favorable conditions for agricultural development. However, there are inherent tensions between agricultural and competition policies. These derive from the fact that agricultural policy often seeks to tilt the balance in favor of specific rural groups, and tends to do so by intervening in the market in ways that may be anti-competitive. Striking the right balance between agricultural and competition policies is therefore at the cornerstone of governmental intervention in the sector.

After decades of neglect, it seems that agricultural and competition policies in Colombia have begun to interact explicitly and intentionally. The participation of the private sector appears to be a principal motivation for this interaction. Increased openness to international markets, a greater degree of concentration in key industries, and better information on competition policy seem to be among the driving forces for private sector activism.

We can draw a number of lessons from Colombian competition policy in the agricultural sector. Even though the cases are meant to be illustrative, they show the richness that agricultural and agriculturally-related markets have in terms of competition policy enforcement. The cases range from the analytically simple cases of lack of prior reporting and approval of a merger, to elaborate and complex conduct (and firms' intertwined property) in the sugar or banana sectors. Cases also range from firms in oligolopolistic markets attempting to abuse their dominant position, to small producers trying to protect their incomes by avoiding price decreases.

Cases have been brought at the request of affected parties, or by SIT itself.[30] The former originate in private agents' knowledge of competition policy and the rights and protections it gives them. The latter originate in SIT's organizational mission to promote efficiency and the competitive process. While both help to bring greater competition to agricultural markets, they clearly differ in spirit, as the former may be regarded as the product of a competition culture that seems to be slowly but firmly growing, whereas the latter form part of the process of creating such a culture. The former also potentially may be abused, as competitors attempt to have the SIT open investigations as a business strategy to increase the costs for firms under investigation.

There is no doubt that agriculture has been an active field in Colombian competition policy in the last decade. Though late to enforcement in the agricultural sector, competition policy has become significant and effective. A mixture of market developments and governmental intervention against anti-competitive practices, both inter-institutionally across government agencies and on the part of the SIT, is the basis for this development.

[30] In Colombia administrative investigations are addressed by the SIT (there are no private rights granted in these investigations). After the SIT issues its final resolution, the affected party can go to the judge and ask for damages for breach of law. There are also class actions that admit consideration of damages, but they are not addressed by the SIT.

A multidimensional learning process has been taking place in Colombian competition policy. The SIT has gained experience and has started to develop a still limited but unprecedented knowledge of domestic agricultural markets. It has (implicitly) recognized, though, that maintaining a competitive agricultural sector demands a level of expertise that the SIT has yet to develop. Private agents in the sector have learned (and continue to do so) about competition policy concerning their rights and obligations. Governmental agencies, in particular the Ministry of Agriculture, have seemingly learned the importance of inter-agency coordination and support for competition policy enhancement. There is also learning at more complex levels. With experience, the SIT has gained greater political legitimacy and capability in handling sensitive cases, such as the coffee case. Still, a fully-developed competition culture is a long way away.

Even though positive in general terms, the lessons from competition policy implementation in the agricultural sector are not all rosy. From the standpoint of implementation, at least two issues merit attention. First, it is important to examine the role of guarantees in antitrust procedures. Even though it seems to be an adequate tool for attaining the goals of a SIT investigation, recourse to negotiating and offering guarantees has tended to be taken for granted, as past experience illustrates. Moreover, compliance with commitments under guarantees has not always been strong. To date, the SIT has opened several investigations regarding non-compliance with guarantees, and has made claims on the offenders' insurance policies. Nevertheless, as cases of repeated non-compliance tend to show, there is the possibility that the guarantee system may open the door to undermining law enforcement and weakening the development of a competition culture. Adding to the complexity of guarantees is the fact that the procedure for offering and negotiating guarantees is not subject to explicit rules, which exposes the process to the risks of uncertainty. This calls for greater transparency.

Secondly, even though there has been important progress in inter-agency coordination, a systematic examination of the competitive effects of sector policy instruments needs to be undertaken. The main issues involved, no doubt, will be put on the table sooner or later, as new cases will be brought for investigation; some of the cases currently underway directly or indirectly touch upon this area. However, from the point of view of the private sector seeking greater predictability, clearly it is undesirable for sector policy to collide with competition policy. This possibility is detrimental to both sector and competition policies, and may have a negative impact in creating a competitive environment.

In sum, recent developments in competition policy and its implementation, as they apply to the agricultural sector, show an important dynamic in Colombia. As a result, a positive environment for developing a competition culture has arisen in the sector, and a multidimensional learning process is taking place. Inter-agency coordination has increased and a body of jurisprudence is beginning to develop. However, the country still has a long way to go to achieve a fully-fledged competition culture for this sector (and the economy at large). A review of the role that guarantees play in policy implementation and enforcement, and a systematic review of the potential competitive effects of some sector policy instruments, are among the more important tasks that need to be undertaken to enhance the process currently underway.

Chapter XX

Merger Policy in Latin America

JOSEPH KRAUSS*

I. Evolution of Convergence in Antitrust Law in Latin America and Selected Case Studies

A. Introduction

Mergers and acquisitions, and the competition authorities' review of such transactions, are a key—and perhaps the most important—area in the development of antitrust law in Latin America. There is a variety of reasons that support this conclusion, including:

a) the constantly increasing number of transactions that require antitrust review in the region;
b) the richness in terms of cross-country analysis of merger reviews, which allows for a regional perspective; and
c) the general agreement in favor of merger coordination across jurisdictions, the prevalence of coordination and cooperation across jurisdictions, and the widespread support for common best practices.

In recognition of these factors, this chapter considers the general approach towards the review of mergers and acquisitions in the Latin American region as compared to the United States and the European Union. To provide context for this analysis, the chapter concludes with a review of specific case studies in which companies faced competition review by Latin American authorities. It also focuses on the necessity and the possibility of convergence between US, Latin American and EU competition agencies. However, the chapter recognizes the fundamental distinctions between their antitrust enforcement philosophies, and the reality that significant divergences can occur even where philosophies are similar. Even among mature regimes that have emphasized the need for convergence (ie, the United States and the European Union), historically there have been differences in approach.

* Partner, Hogan & Hartson, Washington, DC.

This issue is increasingly important as companies find themselves subject to competition review by multiple countries' competition authorities. Over 90 jurisdictions now have merger filing requirements, and many have preng filing requirements. As was the case in the review of Kimberly-Clark's acquisition of Scott Paper, it is not uncommon for a merger to be subject to review by antitrust authorities simultaneously in numerous jurisdictions. Kimberly-Clark's acquisition was reviewed in the United States, Canada, Mexico and the European Union.[1] In some cases, 'the application of merger control rules may appear to be influenced by [national] political or industrial policy objectives'.[2]

The potential for merger review in numerous jurisdictions can have a significant impact on the filing parties. First, even the initial determination of where parties are required to execute competition-related filings can involve significant initial effort and cost. Additionally, the actual preparation of these filings in multiple jurisdictions can be time-consuming and expensive. Consequently, merging parties must adopt some semblance of a strategy to coordinate filings in anticipation of potential investigations by multiple competition authorities. For example, parties will sometimes stagger filings, and may file with the agency from which the parties expect to receive the greatest degree of scrutiny first.[3]

Perhaps more significant than the effect of multi-jurisdictional filings on the individual parties is the general effect on transnational mergers and acquisitions. Despite the positive aspects of the globalization of antitrust enforcement,[4] a key difficulty is the potential for widely divergent competition analyses across jurisdictions. This situation creates uncertainty and may discourage consolidation, even where it is desirable for efficiency and societal advances. The multiplicity

[1] William E Kovacic, 'Merger Enforcement in Transition: Antitrust Controls on Acquisitions in Emerging Economies' 66 *University of Cincinnati Law Review* 1075, 1082 (1998) (addressing increasingly expansive views of extraterritoriality).

[2] Andre Fiebig, 'A Role for the WTO in International Merger Control' 20 *Northwestern Journal of International Law and Business* 233, 244 (2000); see also William H Page, 'Antitrust Review of Mergers in Transition Economies: A Comment with Some Lessons from Brazil' (1998) 66 *University of Cincinnati Law Review* 1113, 1118 (asserting the danger of antitrust enforcement based on ideological and financial concerns rather than the actual effect of the transaction on the economy, and pointing to the EU's review of the Boeing–McDonnell–Douglas merger, which raised concerns that it was driven by a desire to protect Airbus rather than protect competition generally).

[3] But see Alan Ryan and Karine Faden, 'Managing Antitrust in Latin America' *Global Competition Review: Special Report 2008 The Antitrust Review of the Americas* (stating the importance of planning a transaction so that events happen nearly at the same time in each jurisdiction so that one authority will not feel pressured into making an early decision in advance of others).

[4] Cf Eleanor M Fox, 'Toward World Antitrust and Market Access' 91 *American Journal of International Law* 1, at 1, 3 (1997) (indicating the need for the internationalization of antitrust laws because of the increased potential for foreign conduct to have domestic effect, where the goal of competition law is to enhance consumer welfare by breaking down barriers to trade and preventing the misuse of corporate power); Kenneth J Hamner, 'The Globalization of Law: International Merger Control and Competition Law in the United States, the European Union, Latin America, and China' 11 *Journal of Transnational Law & Policy* 385, 403 (2002) ('[T]he globalization of business has blurred the lines between domestic and international business, thus creating the need for extraterritorial jurisdiction as well as convergence within separate bodies of competition law.').

of antitrust regimes may also lead to political conflict between politicians in one country that approves a transaction and politicians in another country that rejects the same merger.[5] Additionally, the globalization of merger control imposes significant costs on the regulatory agencies themselves.[6] To avoid these problems, the United States and other countries with mature antitrust regimes have committed to the convergence of global competition policies and laws.[7] The European Union authorities have adopted a more rigorous economic approach like that traditionally seen in the United States. The benefit of convergence, or

> achieving consistency in antitrust law, policy, processes, and economic theory across jurisdictional lines, [is that] global firms spend less time and money on compliance and can devote more of those resources to the business of competition and innovation. Moreover, when global rules are predictable, business[es] feel greater freedom to forecast, take risks, innovate, and compete.[8]

The issue of convergence has come increasingly to the fore as transitional economies like those in Latin America have begun to regulate competition through indigenous antitrust regimes. In Latin America, many of these regimes have come into force within the last 20 years—Brazil in 1994, Colombia in 1992, Costa Rica in 1994, Mexico in 1992, Panama in 1996, Peru in 1991, and Venezuela in 1991.[9] These countries have increasingly flexed their regulatory muscles and extended their laws extraterritorially. The real danger in the broad application of the antitrust laws of countries with transitional economies is that '[a]s these countries move to an open economy, antitrust enforcement against mergers may take on the characteristics of nationalist controls on direct investment'.[10] To the extent that these countries in Latin America have competition laws that vary in fact or as applied, the additional layer of scrutiny of a deal with multinational consequences may make companies wary of even positive business combinations. This further suggests a need for the convergence of antitrust laws internationally.

[5] See Fiebig, above n 2, at 244.

[6] See *ibid*, at 243 (quoting Mario Monti, former European Commissioner for Competition Policy, who indicated the European Commission would strive to achieve efficient antitrust enforcement by focusing on '"cases which have a real Community interest"'; Robert Pitofsky, former Chairman of the FTC, similarly indicated merger review placed a severe strain on the agency's budget).

[7] See eg, 'International Competition Network Presents Report on Unilateral Conduct & Announces Merger Convergence Report', Press Release (June 1, 2007), < http://justice.gov/opa/pr/2007/June/07_at_397.html> (quoting Assistant AG Thomas Barnett, '"Multijurisdictional mergers are an important part of global commerce ... With the growing number of jurisdictions active in merger review, ... it is important for the ICN to work towards consensus on substantive merger analysis."').

[8] Makan Delrahim, Deputy Assistant AG, Antitrust Division, DOJ, Presentation Before the American Bar Association, Section of Antitrust Law Conference on Antitrust and Intellectual Property, 'International Antitrust & Intellectual Property, Challenges on the Road to Convergence' (May 21, 2004), <http://www.usdoj.gov/atr/public/speeches/205629.htm>.

[9] Hamner, above n 4, at 398.

[10] Page, above n 2, at 1119 (indicating the potential for this reaction stems from the 'resentment in developing countries among those who view the market-based reforms of donor organizations as a form of imperialism that opens their economies to dominance by multinational corporations').

B. Background Framework

Many of the divergences in antitrust laws from one country to the next stem from differences in the philosophies underpinning these regimes. The antitrust approach in the United States is based on the desire to maximize consumer welfare. The Supreme Court, in a famous antitrust case that summarizes the goal of the US policy, asserted that the antitrust laws are aimed at

> preserving free and unfettered competition as the rule of trade. [They rest] on the premise that the unrestrained interaction of competitive forces will yield the best allocation of our economic resources, the lowest prices, the highest quality, and the greatest material progress.[11]

Also, in recognition of these goals, the Department of Justice (DOJ) and the Federal Trade Commission (FTC) have focused on preventing anticompetitive practices such as price fixing and cartel formation.[12]

The emphasis on consumer welfare manifests itself in the United States' willingness to tolerate some concentrations of power if they are intended to have and do have the effect of enhancing economic efficiency, particularly in the area of merger review.[13] When conducting a merger review, the FTC and the DOJ will consider the efficiencies that result from the aggregation. However, not just any efficiency will do. The Merger Guidelines state that US agencies will consider only those efficiencies that are specific to the proposed transaction and that could not be accomplished via other, competitively less restrictive means.[14] Under the DOJ/FTC Merger Guidelines, 'efficiencies are most likely to make a difference in merger analysis when the likely adverse competitive effects, absent the efficiencies, are not great'.[15] Nevertheless, efficiencies almost never justify a merger that creates a monopoly or near monopoly in the relevant market.

By comparison, the competition laws in transitional economies like those in Latin America, (although sometimes drawing specifically on the American

[11] *Northern Pacific Railroad Company v United States*, 356 US 1, 4 (1958).

[12] Shanker A Singham, 'Shaping Competition Policy in the Americas: The Scope for Transatlantic Cooperation' 24 *Brooklyn Journal of International Law* 363, 365 (1998).

[13] Antitrust enforcement in the US has been largely political over time, and heavily influenced by the prevailing economic theory in place. Early US cases sought to prevent the growth of monopolies in their incipiency in order to protect and nurture the growth of small business. Later economic theory, however, reversed the idea that monopolies were inherently bad and postulated some aggregation in the market might be justifiable to realize economies of scale. Therefore, the agencies' determinations rest upon an examination of a merger's actual effect on the market as a whole and its effect on the prices consumers pay for goods. See Singham, above n 12, at 368.

[14] US DOJ and FTC, 'Horizontal Merger Guidelines' (amended April 8, 1997), reprinted in 4 *Trade Reg Rep* ¶ 13104 [('The Agency will consider only those efficiencies likely to be accomplished with the proposed merger and unlikely to be accomplished in the absence of either the proposed merger or another means having comparable anticompetitive effects.').

[15] *Ibid.*

tradition) tend to lean toward the European model,[16] which emphasizes the prevention of monopolistic behavior and abuse of dominant positions.[17] Also like the European model, countries in Latin America place 'comparatively greater emphasis on the use of merger policy to achieve industrial policy objectives and a number of political and social goals beyond enhancing economic efficiency'.[18] For instance, certain sectors of the economy are exempt from competition laws altogether.[19] Additionally, in terms of merger policy for example, Brazil, Colombia and Venezuela consider 'the allocative efficiencies a merger might produce and weigh this against the anticompetitive effects when approving mergers and acquisitions'.[20] These countries also accept the so-called 'failing company defense', even if the merger has nothing to do with efficiency.[21]

Despite the apparent diversity of approaches among Latin American countries themselves, convergence has increasingly occurred through the coordination of antitrust authorities in the region. The Andean Community Commission (CAN) in Decision 608 adopted a regulatory regime for free competition in the Andean sub-region, 'whether exercised within the territory of one or more Member Countries, or of a country outside the Andean Community, and whose real effects are felt in one or more Member Countries.' This regime does not apply to anti-competitive practices that originate in or affect only a single Member Country. Members of the Andean Community include Colombia, Peru and Venezuela. In connection with these efforts, CAN may also allow for the possibility of joint filings in the region in the future.

In addition, membership of Mercosur (also called the Southern Common Market) requires Argentina, Brazil, Chile, Paraguay and Uruguay to cooperate on antitrust issues, as stated in Mercosur's *Understanding on Cooperation between Competition Defense Authorities of Member States of Mercosur for the Enforcement*

[16] Hamner, above n 4, at 398 ('With the exception of Costa Rica, Panama, and Mexico, which model their competition laws after those of the US, most Latin American countries are modeled after EU statutes which penalize the abuse of a dominant position rather than an attempt to monopolize.'); see also Kovacic, above n 1, at 1086 ('Compared to US jurisprudence and the policy, the EU model of antitrust is more likely (1) to define relevant markets narrowly; (2) to find substantial market power at lower market-share thresholds; (3) to reflect solicitude for the well-being of individual competitors, rather than focusing more single-mindedly on a transaction's effect on the choices available to users generally; and (4) to adopt a more expansive definition of dominant firm behavior that will be considered unlawfully exclusionary.').

[17] Singham, above n 12, at 390 ('The view of the Organization of American States (OAS) is that laws in the region target the promotion of freedom in industry and commerce, equitable participation of small and medium sized enterprises, and the decentralization of economic power.').

[18] Kovacic, above n 1, at 1090, 1087 ('Transition economies might prefer the more egalitarian nature of EU competition standards over the stronger efficiency-orientation of US antitrust policy.').

[19] Singham, above n 12, at 390 (asserting that Mexico does not apply its competition laws to petroleum, natural gas, or export cooperatives; Chile does not apply its laws to mining or petroleum; and Colombia excludes household public services and the financial and insurance sectors).

[20] Hamner, above n 4, at 398–99.

[21] Singham, above n 12, at 393 ('The analysis includes the possibility that the merger took place purely to strengthen certain companies, and not necessarily to boost efficiency.').

of National Competition Laws.[22] The enforcement agreement aims to promote cooperation in the execution of national competition laws and technical cooperation between national competition authorities. In accordance with the agreement, antitrust authorities must, in some circumstances, inform the others of any prohibited practices or economic concentration proceedings initiated in their jurisdictions.[23]

The United States has also pursued a cooperative strategy through the establishment of bilateral agreements with two key Latin American countries, Brazil and Mexico. These agreements help harmonize competition policies and contribute to increasing business certainty.

Signed in 1999 and entering into force in 2003, the US agreement with Brazil is designed

> to promote cooperation, including both enforcement and technical cooperation, between the competition authorities of the Parties, and to ensure that the Parties give careful consideration to each other's important interests in the application of their competition laws.[24]

The agreement includes notice, enforcement cooperation, and coordination provisions. It also includes provisions related to the 'avoidance of conflicts', and states that each country

> shall, within the framework of its own laws and to the extent compatible with its important interests, give careful consideration to the other [country's] important interests throughout all phases of its enforcement activities, including decisions regarding the initiation of an investigation or proceeding, the scope of an investigation or proceeding, and the nature of the remedies or penalties sought in each case.[25]

The agreement has proven useful both for the United States' provision of technical assistance to Brazil and for the exchange of substantive information, including 'investigation strategies, views on relevant market definition, theories of anticompetitive harm, [and] potential remedies.'[26] Additionally, since the inception of the agreement, Brazil has amended its laws based on its own enforcement experiences and its interactions with competition authorities in the United States and elsewhere via international bodies like the International Competition Network. One key change Brazil made to its competition laws was raising the threshold for mandatory merger notification. Prior to 2005, merger notification was required

[22] Ryan and Faden, above n 3.

[23] *Ibid.*

[24] 'Agreement between the Government of the United States and Brazil Regarding Cooperation between their Competition Authorities in the Enforcement of their Competition Laws', <http://www.usdoj.gov/atr/public/international/3776.htm> (last accessed May 28, 2007).

[25] *Ibid.*

[26] 'The Brazilian Recent Experience with International Co-operation', submitted to UNCTAD's Seventh Session of the Intergovernmental Group of Experts on Competition Law and Policy, Geneva, 30 Oct to 2 Nov 2006, 4. <http://www.unctad.org/TEMPLATES/Download.asp?docid=7638&lang=1&intItemID=3980>.

for transactions involving parties with a turnover of R$400 million globally; now, notification is necessary only where parties have a turnover of R$400 million in Brazil. This change reduced the number of filings in Brazil significantly. The two countries have also notified one another of mergers that may have cross-border implications, and have coordinated on investigations that involve firms in the other country.[27]

Similarly, the agreement with Mexico, signed in 2000, is intended in part to 'avoid conflicts arising from the application of the [United States' and Mexico's] competition laws.'[28] Like the US agreement with Brazil, this agreement includes notice, enforcement cooperation, and coordination provisions.[29] In addition, the agreement states that either country's 'interests may be affected at any stage of enforcement activity'. and that both countries 'recognize the desirability of minimizing any adverse effects of their enforcement activities on each other's important interests, particularly in the choice of remedies.'[30] Accordingly, the agreement states that the United States and Mexico agree to consider each other's interests in fashioning any remedy. The US–Mexican bilateral agreement codified previous antitrust coordination between the two nations and formalized future cooperation.[31] An example of the kind of cooperation envisioned by this type of bilateral agreement may been seen in the 1997 approval (with conditions) of the Guinness and Grand Metropolitan merger by the countries' competition authorities. The agencies developed similar remedies, which included divestitures in both nations. This case study is addressed in more depth in section II of this chapter.

Although cooperation and bilateral agreements have established similarities between US antitrust laws and those of countries in Latin America, differences in approach remain. One American official, speaking at the annual conference of the International Competition Network, asserted

> that while there has been cooperation and consensus in both the substance and procedure of merger review, there have been 'notable differences' in outcomes or analysis that reflect the need for more dialogue and a better understanding about the law and economics of modern merger analysis.[32]

[27] See *ibid*.

[28] 'United States and Mexico Sign Antitrust Cooperation Agreement'. Press Release, July 11, 2000, <http://www.ftc.gov/opa/2000/07/mexico.shtm> ('The purpose of the agreement is to promote cooperation and coordination between the competition authorities in each country in order to increase the effectiveness of each nation's antitrust enforcement as well as to avoid conflicts arising from the application of competition laws.').

[29] 'Agreement Between the Government of the United States and Brazil Regarding Cooperation Between Their Competition Authorities in the Enforcement of Their Competition Laws', http://www.usdoj.gov/atr/public/international/3776.htm (last accessed March 9, 2009).

[30] Ryan and Faden, above n 3.

[31] The North American Free Trade Agreement (NAFTA), entered into in 1994, included competition provisions prior to entry into the bilateral agreement between Mexico and the United States specifically addressing competition concerns. North American Free Trade Agreement, US–Can–Mex, Dec 17, 1992, 32 *ILM* 605 (1993).

[32] Erin Marie Daly, 'US Sees Obstacles to Merger Review Convergence', *Competition Law* 360, online (May 31, 2007).

These similarities and differences are revealed in the case studies that follow in section II of this chapter. The Bayer and Aventis merger and the Guinness and Grand Metropolitan merger demonstrate the similarities between countries in merger analysis and the possibility for the convergence of merger policy. By contrast, the beer companies' joint venture and the Coca-Cola and Cisneros Group joint venture demonstrate where merger analysis can go wrong and the results can diverge dramatically.

II. The Possibilities for Convergence Contrasted With the Realities of Divergence in Merger Analysis

The following section offers case studies that describe and analyze historic, and more recent, US, EU and Latin American agency review of mergers. These studies illustrate some of the differences and similarities between Latin American competition authorities and the other countries' review of the same transactions. Three of the cases studied consider reviews by some of the most important countries in terms of the development of competition law in the region—Brazil, Argentina and Mexico. These countries were early adopters of modern antitrust regimes, and have evolved in their approach over time.

The case studies also demonstrate that early merger review in Latin America has sometimes relied on more simplistic merger analysis that is typical of regulatory regimes in their infancy and similar to the historic approach of the EU authorities. However, as these regimes have matured and evolved, more sophisticated analysis has been observed, and increased convergence in the analysis (as well as result) is likely.

A. Argentina: Bayer and Aventis CropScience

The 1999 Defense of Competition Act introduced merger control laws into Argentina's antitrust regime. This Act applies to individuals and businesses conducting economic activities in Argentina, as well as to individuals and businesses conducting activities outside of Argentina that have an effect inside the country. Substantively, the Act prohibits 'economic concentrations that have the purpose or effect of reducing, restricting, or distorting competition in a manner that could damage the general economic interest'.[33] Parties must report economic combinations that have a business volume in Argentina of more than 200 million Argentine

[33] Thomas W Studwell, 'Latin American Competition Law in the Twenty-First Century: A Practical Guide' 10 *Law and Business Review* 747, 750 (2004). An economic concentration is defined as an acquisition of control of a business entity via merger, transfer of a going concern, transfer of a substantial number of shares giving acquirer control over issuer, or any other agreement that transfers assets or control of one enterprise to another. *Ibid*, at 750–51.

pesos (though there are exemptions to this requirement).[34] If a qualifying transaction has not been reported to the National Competition Tribunal, it will have no legal effect between the parties or with respect to third parties.[35] Parties are also subject to a fine of up to 1 million pesos per day. The Tribunal requires information such as financial and background information about the parties, terms of the proposed deal, description of relevant product and geographic markets,[36] substitute products, and manufacturing information.[37] Penalties include cease-and-desist orders, fines and divestitures.[38]

The Bayer and Aventis CropScience merger faced review by the antitrust authorities of multiple nations because of the global scope of the companies' operations. Argentina's analysis, as compared with that of the United States or the European Union, superficially appears to be quite divergent; nevertheless, upon closer analysis, the approaches are more similar than they are different.

In November 2001, Bayer and Aventis CropScience notified Argentina's National Commission for Competition Defence (CNDC)[39] of Bayer's planned acquisition of Aventis CropScience. Although the United States and the European Union had already cleared the deal, in November 2002 the CNDC issued an order requiring more significant divestitures than those required by the United States and the European Union.[40] The CNDC found the transaction would create a dominant position in 15 markets comprising broader categories of nematicides, defoliants, fungicide seed treatment products, and insecticides and insecticide seed treatments. The agency found the companies held 16 per cent of the country's agrochemical business sales.[41] The CNDC required divestment of:

a) intellectual property rights over the active ingredients before named;
b) right of use of trademarks related to the active ingredients before named;
c) sanitary permits and requests or petitions regarding the active ingredients before named;
d) documents and components needed to produce the active ingredients to be divested; and
e) inventory of the active ingredients to be divested.

[34] This converts to approximately $69,444,000.

[35] Studwell, above n 33, at 751.

[36] This includes a detailed quantitative analysis of market shares, supply and competitive studies, strategic plans and reports, profitability information, qualitative market data and projections, costs and expected efficiency gains. *Ibid.*

[37] *Ibid.*

[38] *Ibid*, at 752.

[39] The CNDC was created under the previous antitrust law, and will continue to enforce and monitor compliance until the National Competition Tribunal (TNDC) can be created. The TNDC will be an autonomous agency, governed by seven presidentially-appointed members who will sit for six-year terms. Siro P Astolfi and Javier Rodriguez Galli, 'Antitrust Law in Argentina', *The Control of Anticompetitive Practices in Latin America* 7, Affinitas Antitrust Group (ed), Sept 2006.

[40] Ryan and Faden, above n 3.

[41] OECD, 'Competition Law and Policy in Argentina' (2002), <http://www.oecd.org/dataoecd/22/11/34830440.pdf> (last accessed June 5, 2007).

By contrast, the United States and the European Union required simply the sale of three Aventis insecticides and a Bayer herbicide.[42]

Nevertheless, the differences between the competition analysis of each authority and its results may be less dramatic than they appear. The United States evaluated four broad categories or product groups:

a) new generation insecticide products;
b) research, development, manufacture and sale of new generation insecticide ingredients and technologies;
c) grass herbicides; and
d) cotton defoliants.

The US divestitures concentrated on key insecticides, because of concern that a Bayer–Aventis merger would eliminate actual and potential competition in the market, where the only other producer of the new generation insecticides exclusively allowed by the EPA was Syngenta.[43]

The European Commission's analysis focused on 130 specific product markets that make up the broader categories of crop protection, professional pest control, and animal health products. Its approval was subject to the divestment of a group of insecticides, both new generation chemicals and fungicides together, to a single purchaser.[44] The Commission's decision also required divestment of another new generation insecticide as well as beet, potato and vegetable herbicides. The companies also gave both Europe-wide and country-specific exclusive licenses for the formulation of certain products.

However, the four broad product markets the United States identified encompassed virtually all of the products specifically mentioned by the European Union and the CNDC. In this way, all three competition agencies reached similar results, even though they defined product markets very differently.

Since this merger was effectuated, the CNDC has struggled with the development of Argentine competition law. The CNDC has experienced severe budget cuts and high employee turnover, which has correlated to low levels of expertise among agency staff.[45] In addition, the independence of the agency has been challenged, most recently by Resolution 26/2006, which, in July 2006, established that the Argentina Secretary of Technical Co-ordination of the Ministry of Economy

[42] 'Bayer: Conditions of Acquisition: Aventis CropScience' (June 10, 2002) *European Chemical News* 7.

[43] 'Addressing Competitive Concerns in Core Markets, FTC Approves Bayer AG's Acquisition of Aventis CropScience Holdings SA', Press Release, May 30, 2002, <http://www.ftc.gov/opa/2002/05/bayeraventis.shtm>.

[44] This included two insecticides, both from the new class of chemicals called pyrazoles, and five fungicides that are part of Aventis's highly specialized seed treatment business. In this industry, only Aventis, Bayer and Syngenta have significant activities. 'Commission Clears Bayer's Acquisition of Aventis CropScience, Subject to Substantial Divestitures', Press Release, April 17, 2002.

[45] 'Competition Law and Policy in Argentina', Policy Brief, OECD Observer, Oct 2006.

would have the authority to decide whether the CNDC must analyze a merger.[46] It remains to be seen whether the Argentinean authorities can recover from these setbacks, particularly in light of the country's overall economic pressures.

B. Mexico: Guinness/Grand Metropolitan

Mexico's Federal Competition Commission (FCC) regulates and monitors Mexico's antitrust regime. The country's 1992 Federal Law of Economic Competition restricts economic concentrations 'having the purpose or the effect of diminishing, damaging, or impeding competition in identical, similar, or substantially related goods or services'.[47] The factors the Commission evaluates to determine whether there has been a violation are market power and whether the newly-formed entity is able to fix prices. The Commission may condition approval on restructuring, or undo the combination altogether. Parties must notify the Commission of any transaction valued at 12 million times the daily minimum wage (DMW) for the Federal District, or those involving the accumulation of more than 35 per cent of the assets or shares of an entity with assets or sales exceeding 12 million DMW, or those involving entities whose assets or sales exceed 48 million DMW and an accumulation of assets or capital exceeding 4.8 million DMW.[48] The Commission requires parties to submit information including a description of the transaction, financial statements, a description of the transaction's objectives, information about the goods and services involved, including their market shares, and the names and market share of both Mexican and international competitor products.[49] For violations, the Commission can fine parties, order divestitures, and issue cease-and-desist orders. Parties are also subject to both civil and criminal liability. Mexican law provides for a private cause of action as well.[50]

Guinness and Grand Metropolitan announced their $36 billion merger in April 1997. This merger would create the seventh largest food and drink company in the world. Because of its global reach, the merger was subject to review in multiple jurisdictions, including Mexico, the United States, the European Union, Canada and Australia.

In Mexico, consideration of the merger concerned the links between Guinness and its Mexican subsidiaries[51] and Metropolitan-controlled Jose Cuervo tequila. The FCC, in evaluating the competitive effects of the merger, looked at the concentration in the markets for whiskey, gin, vodka, tequila, brandy, cognac, rum, liquors and wine. The agency determined that as a result of merger, United

[46] 'Argentina: Competition and Price Regulations'. TMCnet.com, available at <http://latinamerica.tmcnet.com/news/2007/07/27/2818940.htm>.

[47] Studwell, above n 33, at 761–62.

[48] *Ibid*, at 762.

[49] *Ibid*.

[50] *Ibid*.

[51] Guinness's Mexican subsidiaries are United Distillers de Mexico and Importadora, Distribuidora Inter.

Distillers de Mexico, Importadora and Jose Cuervo would collectively have a 64.9 per cent market share in whiskey. The merger would also concentrate distribution of premium brands, because Jose Cuervo, previously distributed internationally by Metropolitan, would be able to use Guinness's channels of distribution as well. This would result in a foreclosure of Guinness's distribution channels to other producers, which would be offset to some degree by the existence of other large international distributors. Based on these considerations, the agency found that the merger would give the new entity substantial power in each of the relevant markets and thus could facilitate monopolistic practices. Subject to the divestiture of the J&B whiskey brand, the agency allowed the merger.[52]

In the United States, the FTC's analysis was similar and resulted in a conditional approval subject to the divestiture of its most popular premium liquor brands. The FTC asserted that Grand Metropolitan and Guinness are competitors in the sale and distribution in the United States of premium Scotch and premium gin. The FTC's primary concern was that the proposed merger would eliminate substantial competition between the companies, and increase concentration in the already-concentrated market for premium liquors. In the United States' market for premium Scotch, Guinness was the largest competitor with a 68 per cent share. In this same market, Grand Metropolitan had the second largest share with 24 per cent. Combined, the companies would control 92 per cent of the market. The market shares of Guinness and Grand Metropolitan were similar in the premium gin market, where Guinness had 58 per cent of the market, and Grand Metropolitan was the third largest with a 15 per cent share. In this market, the combination would have yielded 73 per cent control. The FTC required the worldwide divestiture of Dewar's Scotch, Bombay original gin, and Bombay Sapphire gin brands as a condition of approval of the merger.[53]

In reaching its opinion, the FTC worked closely with competition agencies in Europe,[54] Canada, Mexico and Australia to determine the agreement's terms. Both the FCC and the FTC focused on the elimination of competition in the market for premium liquors. Their shared concern was that increasing concentration in already highly-concentrated markets would facilitate monopolistic practices in the markets for gin and Scotch in the United States, and whiskey and the distribution of tequila in Mexico.

[52] 'OECD Country Data: Mexico 1998', <http://www.oecd.org/dataoecd/7/55/1806858.pdf > (last accessed May 30, 2007).

[53] The FTC would also require the divestiture of other assets, including the companies' Scotch distilling capacity, but only if the acquirer of the divested assets needs the distilling capacity to compete effectively. Additionally, the FTC suggested it might also require the companies to produce gin for the acquirer if the third party that currently produces gin for them does not want to continue in this arrangement with the acquirer. FTC, 'Dewar's Scotch, Bombay Gin and Bombay Sapphire Gin to Find New Corporate Homes Under FTC Agreement'. Press Release (Dec 15, 1997). <http://www.ftc.gov/opa/1997/12/scotch.shtm>.

[54] The EU similarly found the merger gave rise to substantial antitrust concerns, and required divestitures in the gin and whiskey markets too, as well as divestitures in distribution capacities.

C. Brazil: Anheuser-Busch/Antarctica and Miller/Brahma Joint Ventures

Brazil's competition authority, the Administrative Council of Economic Defense (CADE), though in existence since 1962, has actively enforced its antitrust laws only since 1994, with the enactment of Law 8884. The Law requires

> that any acts that may limit or restrain free competition or result in the control of a relevant market, be submitted to CADE for review. This includes acts intended to increase economic concentration, such as mergers, acquisitions, and joint ventures ...[55]

Transactions that result in an entity controlling 20 per cent or more of the relevant market, or those in which either party has an annual turnover in Brazil of at least R$400 million, are subject to mandatory notification. Jurisdiction extends to acts performed in Brazil or partially in Brazil, as well as to acts committed outside of Brazil with effects within the country.[56] Parties must submit power of attorney, relevant binding agreements, and any later agreements if the transaction is fairly straightforward. If complex, CADE requires detailed financial and background information about the companies involved, the transaction, and the relevant product markets. CADE may order such acts as a reversal of the deal, divestiture and an end to activities violating the antitrust laws. CADE may also order fines, which can be doubled for repeat violators.[57]

In 1997, both Anheuser-Busch and Miller were seeking local partners to enter the beer market in Brazil. Alone, the American companies were unable to capture even 1 per cent of the market. At the time of the proposed joint ventures, Brahma had 47 per cent of the market, Antarctica had 32 per cent, and Kaiser had 17 per cent.[58] Anheuser-Busch hoped to create a joint venture with Antarctica, and Miller with Brahma. The joint ventures were designed to allow the American companies to compete in Brazil's market, and would have increased the number of choices available to consumers.

[55] Studwell, above n 33, at 754.

[56] *Ibid.* ('Consequently, the law would be deemed to apply to a merger or acquisition involving two non-Brazilian companies, if one or both of them have subsidiaries, branches, or business operations in Brazil, so long as one of the parties meets the revenue threshold.')

[57] In addition to CADE, there are two other agencies with merger control responsibilities in Brazil—the Economic Law Office (SDE) in the Ministry of Justice, and the Secretariat for Economic Monitoring (SEAE) in the Ministry of Finance. While CADE is the most important of these because it has adjudicative authority, SDE has the principal investigative role and the authority to issue non-binding opinions, and SEAE is primarily responsible for providing economic analysis of mergers and acquisitions. A typical filing will be reviewed by SEAE, SDE and CADE, in that order, with the final decisions being issued by CADE. In 2003, the Joint Administrative Act No 1 of SDE and SEAE created a 'fast track' for cases that, because of their simplicity, and as a result of a determination by SDE and SEAE, cannot potentially harm competition. The fast track requires SDE and SEAE to issue their opinions within 15 days.

[58] Kaiser was actually backed by Coca-Cola. Singham, above n 12, at 381.

CADE concluded in 1997 that both deals would negatively impact competition in the beer market. CADE determined that the joint ventures would raise anticompetitive concern under the *American* concept of potential competition, which 'implies that a firm not participating in a market may affect competition in an oligopolistic or monopolistic industry'.[59] More specifically, because of the American companies' size, greater efficiency, global dominance in the beer industry and well-known strategies of targeting emerging economies for entry, CADE determined that Miller and Anheuser-Busch were able to influence prices. The agency indicated that 'far from rendering the market more competitive, [the companies'] consolidate[d] [their] structures and even crystallized the shared dominant position between Brahma and Antarctica'.[60]

Under CADE's adopted potential competition theory,[61] joint ventures like those proposed by Miller and Anheuser-Busch could be anticompetitive because they prevent one of the partners from entering into the market *de novo*. CADE's analysis under this doctrine was problematic for a number of reasons. First, CADE did not have enough of the specific evidence required under its statutory authority to bring a potential competition case. To apply this doctrine, the challenger of the merger must demonstrate that the market is concentrated, that other potential competitors exist, that there is reasonable probability that the potential competitor will enter the market independently, and that the potential competitor's entry would have significant pro-competitive benefits.[62] CADE's analysis provided very little evidence of any of these elements.

Secondly, CADE's opinion was based on the assumption that concentration is always a problem. However, in this case the degree of concentration in the beer market at the time of the proposed merger was actually an improvement on years past, demonstrating that 'there is substantial competitive threat to the leading firms from existing competitors'.[63]

Thirdly, aside from focusing on concentration in the market, CADE failed to present specific evidence on why the American companies posed the greatest threat of entry into the market. CADE's assertion that the companies, specifically Anheuser-Busch, had focused on entering the markets of developing economies under the United States' interpretation of the potential competition theory,

[59] A E Rodriguez and Malcolm B Coate, 'Merger Pitfalls in Practice: Three Case Studies' 20 *University of Pennsylvania Journal of International Economic Law* 793, 812 (1999).

[60] *Ibid*, at 813.

[61] The potential competition theory is divided into two approaches: (i) perceived potential competition; and (ii) actual potential competition. In the United States, actual potential competition analysis is disfavored because of the difficulty in demonstrating the elements necessary to show that a firm is an actual potential competitor. As contrasted with the actual potential competition approach, applying the perceived potential competition doctrine is relatively easy as it requires only that the challenger show proof that the acquirer had the capability and incentive to enter into the market; it must also be one of the few firms with these characteristics. See Singham, above n 12, at 382.

[62] See Singham, above n 12, at 382.

[63] Rodriguez and Coate, above n 58, at 814.

'would only be useful in inferring its entry intentions, but without evidence that it was precluding other entrants, no violation occurs'.[64]

A final problem with CADE's analysis was that it ignored the efficiencies the joint ventures would have brought to consumers in the form of new brands in the marketplace. The agency 'trades a very certain immediate efficiency benefit to Brazil's consumers for a chance of a somewhat greater future benefit' in the form of a future *de novo* entry into the market by either of the firms.[65]

D. Venezuela: Coca-Cola/Cisneros Group Joint Venture

Venezuela's antitrust authority is the *Superintendencia para la Promocion y Proteccion de la Libre Competencia*, also known as ProCompetencia. This agency is charged with

> promot[ing] and protect[ing] the exercise of free competition and efficiency to the benefit of producers and consumers, and … prohibit[ing] monopolistic, oligarchic conduct and practices and other measures that could impede, restrict, falsify, or limit the enjoyment of economic freedom.[66]

Mergers are governed by Article 11 of the Antitrust Law. Venezuela does not require pre-merger notification like many other jurisdictions. Below a certain threshold, approximately US $1,457,700, mergers are not subject to review; nevertheless, large or controversial parties will file anyway to avoid any fines or reversal of the transaction if the agency determines, after the transaction has been finalized, that it violates the law. The information required for notification includes information about the parties and the transaction, a description of the relevant markets involved, market shares, and information about major competitors. ProCompetencia's fines can be levied at 10 per cent or 20 per cent of a violator's sales; this jumps to 40 per cent for repeat offenders.[67]

In August 1996, the Cisneros group terminated its long-running exclusive bottling deal with Pepsi to join forces with Coca-Cola and enter into two joint ventures with the group, one which owned bottling and distribution assets and another which held the trademarks for soft drinks. As part of the deal, Coke acquired 50 per cent of Cisneros's business.[68] Prior to the agreement, Pepsi held 42 per cent of the carbonated soft drink (CSD) market; Coke lagged with only 10.8 per cent of the market.[69] After the joint ventures were formed, Coca-Cola increased its share to 53 per cent, while Pepsi retained a 40 per cent share, the

64 *Ibid*, at 815.
65 *Ibid*.
66 Studwell, above n 33, at 765–66.
67 *Ibid*, at 768.
68 The business included 18 bottling plants and a number of soft drink brands. A E Rodriguez and Mark D Williams, 'Recent Decisions by the Venezuelan and Peruvian Agencies: Lessons for the Export of Antitrust' 43 *Antitrust Bulletin* 147, 158 (1998).
69 Rodriguez and Coate, above n 58, at 806.

next largest competitor.[70] As an attempt to avoid antitrust liability, Coca-Cola had divested its Coke-owned bottling and distribution assets in Venezuela, offering Pepsi a short-term lease on the assets (to enable continued production) and the right of first refusal to purchase the assets.[71]

In December 1996, ProCompetencia challenged the proposed Coca-Cola and Cisneros Group's joint venture, asserting a violation of Article 11 of the Antitrust Law that 'prohibits mergers that restrict competition or strengthen a dominant position'.[72] The Agency asserted that the transaction would substantially increase concentration in the CSD market, based on the assumption that the divestiture of Coke's bottling assets would not be sufficient to avoid anti-competitive effects.[73] The agency did not dismantle the Coke–Cisneros transaction or impose heavy fines, both of which would have been permissible; rather, the agency imposed modest fines and required a divestiture of local CSD flavors that Cisneros controlled.[74]

ProCompetencia's decision was flawed in a number of ways, particularly because the joint venture would have reduced concentration in the market, 'transform[ing] the relevant industry from a near-monopoly [by Pepsi] into a competitive duopoly'.[75] The decision's primary defect was in its analysis of barriers to entry. The agency evaluated the difficulties a *de novo* entrant into the market would face, rather than those an existing player in the market would face. Two leading commentators assert that the key difference between these two situations is that where a *de novo* entrant is concerned, the primary hurdle it must face is the cost of advertising to develop name recognition. In this case, they noted that after the transaction between Coke and Cisneros, there would be no diminishment in Pepsi's brand-name recognition, making it easy to re-enter the market once it obtained access to bottling facilities.[76] Therefore, 'the chief flaw in ProCompetencia's decision [was] its failure to account for the possibility (indeed the likelihood) of re-entry by Pepsi into the Venezuelan soft drink market'.[77]

Although this case study does not directly implicate merger activities outside of Venezuela, it likely had transnational implications for the companies involved. Coca-Cola had taken steps, in anticipation of potential anticompetitive effects of the joint venture, to divest its bottling assets. Yet despite Coke's actions, the agency was able to thwart Coke's lawful joint venture based on antitrust analysis

[70] Michael Byowitz, 'Post Privatization in the Americas: Competition Law Policy and the Alternatives' 6 *Southwestern Journal of Law and Trade in the Americas* 81, 82 (1999).

[71] Rodriguez and Coate, above n 58, at 806. Later that year, Pepsi responded by forming its own joint venture with Empresas Polar, the nation's largest beer producer.

[72] *Ibid*, at 805.

[73] *Ibid.* After the divestiture of Coke's assets, the joint venture would have lowered the HHI from 6870 to 4410. Excluding the divestiture, however, the combination would have significantly increased the HHI to 8746. ProCompetencia argued that Coke controlled 93.4% of the bottling facilities in the country.

[74] Byowitz, above n 69, at 84.

[75] Kovacic, above n 1, at 1107.

[76] Rodriguez & Coate, above n 58, at 810; see also Rodriguez & Williams, above n 67.

[77] Kovacic, above n 1, at 1107.

that is largely inconsistent with the US approach, in that it exceeded what the US antitrust enforcement agencies would be expected to do in the same situation.[78] Indeed, FTC Commissioner William Kovacic noted that 'ProCompetencia's decision … revealed the power of transition economy antitrust laws to affect the business plans of American firms doing business in transition economies'.[79]

E. Recent Merger Analysis

Two recent mergers—between the News Corporation and Hughes Electronics in 2003, and between Procter & Gamble and Gillette in 2005—provide additional reference points for comparing merger analysis across jurisdictions.

In 2003, the News Corporation aimed to expand its satellite network to cover the United States, and purchased 34 per cent of Hughes Electronics, which provides the DirecTV service, the nation's largest direct broadcast satellite provider, for $6.6 billion. The Federal Communications Commission (FCC) approved the acquisition and, based on this decision, the DOJ did not challenge the merger.[80] The DOJ agreed with the terms proposed by the FCC to conclude that the combination did not pose anticompetitive concerns, as long as the new entity met the condition that the network carry local channels.[81] Additionally, the FCC required News Corporation to provide its cable channels to cable operators at the same price at which the channels were offered to DirecTV and News Corporation. This requirement was designed to arbitrate programming disputes between cable and satellite providers rather than allow service interruptions and private negotiations that could contribute to price increases for the consumer.[82]

The Brazilian competition authority, CADE, found that the proposed transaction could raise competitive issues because News Corporation's Sky Latin America competes in Brazil with DirecTV, and the proposed combination would give News Corporation control of 95 per cent of the satellite television market in Brazil. Brazil's domestic provider, Tecsat, would be left with a mere 5 per cent of the market. However, at the time of the proposed deal Sky controlled 19.7 per cent of the market and DirecTV had an 11.3 per cent share of the market.[83] Nevertheless, CADE finally approved the merger, subject to certain

[78] Byowitz, above n 69, at 84 (suggesting the fines were improper because of Coca-Cola's attempt to avoid violation via the divestitures, and that the divestiture of the local flavors was improper because the transaction did not increase concentration but rather reduced it at the syrup level).

[79] Kovacic, above n 1, at 1076.

[80] DOJ, 'Justice Department Will Not Challenge News Corp's Acquisition of Hughes Electronics', Press Release (Dec 19, 2003), <http://www.usdoj.gov/atr/public/press_releases/2003/201918.htm.>.

[81] Geoffrey Drake, 'Old Man and the Sky: The Brazilian Antitrust Implications for Rupert Murdoch's Expansion of the Sky Global Satellite Network' 37 *Vanderbilt Journal of Transnational Law* 1147, 1150–51 (2004).

[82] *Ibid*, at 1166–67.

[83] *Ibid*, at 1152.

restrictions, in May 2006.[84] Some of the restrictions included an end to exclusive contracts for the airing of soccer championships, and a prohibition on News Corporation's charging different rates for access to its programming between its own stations and others.[85]

A review of the authorities' actions in this matter reveals that CADE and the FCC followed a similar analysis when they imposed requirements on the parties. In both countries, the key concern was with the merged entity's ability to discriminate on price between its own network stations and those stations of other providers, thereby limiting the amount of programming available and raising the price of existing programming to consumers. Consequently, while the agencies imposed requirements that were appropriate for their national markets, the competition approach was compatible.

In another case, the competition agencies of the United States, Mexico, the European Union and Canada coordinated and cooperated to approve Procter & Gamble's 2005, $57 billion acquisition of rival Gillette. Mexico's FCC identified the relevant markets for men's and women's deodorants and antiperspirants, mouthwashes, toothpastes, and electric and battery-operated toothbrushes. The Mexican FCC found an increase in market concentration that exceeded Mexican anticompetitive thresholds in the market for electric and battery-powered toothbrushes. The Mexican agency determined this situation was not anticompetitive because:

a) the market in Mexico was still developing;
b) there had been significant shifts in market shares in the preceding years; and
c) Procter & Gamble's market share was declining.

Similarly, the United States upheld the merger, but required divestitures in product markets where the two companies competed. The FTC found anticompetitive effects in the market for home teeth-whitening products,[86] battery-powered toothbrushes,[87] rechargeable toothbrushes[88] and men's antiperspirant/deodorants.[89]

[84] Business Information Systems, 'CADE Approves Sky-DirecTV Merger' (May 26, 2006) *Business Information Systems*.

[85] Juliano Basile, 'Julgamento parcial do Cade aprova restrições à fusão Sky/DirecTv', *Valor Economico* (May 25, 2006).

[86] Together, Procter & Gamble's products and Gillette account for over 80% of sales in the market for home teeth-whitening products. *In re Procter & Gamble Co and Gillette Co*, Docket No C-4151 (FTC, Sept 2005).

[87] In the adult battery-powered toothbrush market, both companies accounted for over 85% of the market. *Ibid*.

[88] Gillette and Philips Oral Health Care, Inc are the only significant suppliers in the market for rechargeable toothbrushes. Procter & Gamble and Philips are engaged in a joint venture to sell the first integrated toothpaste/toothbrush combination. The acquisition would result in Procter & Gamble acquiring the only significant competitor to its joint venture partner, Philips. *Ibid*.

[89] Both Procter & Gamble and Gillette account for more than 50% of sales in the market for men's antiperspirant/deodorants. Following the acquisition of Gillette, Procter & Gamble would be the dominant supplier in that market. *Ibid*.

In addition to the increased market concentration in these markets, the FTC determined the barriers to entry in these markets were significant because of advertising costs, brand name recognition, and patents and other intellectual property barriers. Although permitting the merger, the FTC required divestitures of specific products, including Gillette's Rembrandt home teeth-whitener, Procter & Gamble's Crest SpinBrush battery-powered and rechargeable toothbrushes, and Gillette's Right Guard men's antiperspirant/deodorant business.

Significantly, although the Mexican and US authorities defined the relevant markets similarly, each competition authority considered the combination in terms of the specific circumstances of its domestic market. In Mexico, despite increases of concentration in the market for battery-powered and electric toothbrushes, the FCC considered the surrounding context of the merger—that Procter & Gamble was losing market share and that there had been frequent fluctuations in market shares because it was a new industry. This kind of analysis contrasts significantly with the analysis CADE used to evaluate the beer companies' proposed joint ventures.[90]

Even as agencies in the region converge in their antitrust analysis, divergent antitrust decisions will arise. Most recently, Brazil, Mexico and Colombia reviewed Mexichem's March 2007 purchase of Amanco's subsidiary PAVCO for US $600 million. Mexichem is the largest producer of PVC resin and compounds in Mexico, and PAVCO is one of its main customers and the leading manufacturer of PVC pipes in Latin America. Brazil and Mexico cleared the transaction, but Colombia's Superintendency of Industry and Commerce (SIC) blocked the transaction in a decision issued on July 16, 2007.[91] The SIC concluded that Mexichem and PAVCO have dominant positions in their respective markets, and their vertical integration would harm competition. The SIC also determined that the relevant markets had high barriers to entry that would be even higher if the transaction was approved, particularly in the commercialization of the plastic tubes market, where other market participants would have limited access to the raw materials needed for manufacturing the plastic tubes. Notably, Colombia faces an unusually high custom tariff to import vinyl resin, and PAVCO is the only manufacturer of vinyl resin in Colombia. These factors illustrate that even if countries converge with respect to their underlying antitrust analysis, there will be country-specific issues that will influence the outcome of an antitrust review.

[90] See section II.C. above. CADE's faulty analysis of the beer companies' proposed joint ventures did not take into account that the joint ventures would actually increase competition in the previously concentrated market rather than decrease it. Additionally, CADE did not recognize that the market's current concentration was an improvement over past degrees of concentration. Mexico's analysis, however, does take into account historical data about the market to provide a broader context in which to view the merger.

[91] Ministerio de Comercio, Industria Y Turismo, Resolution No 021345 (July 16, 2007). Notably, when they conducted their analysis, the Colombian authorities cited to the US DOJ's and the European Commission's respective Non-Horizontal Merger Guidelines.

III. Conclusion

The case studies set out above are just a few examples in Latin America of the current state of merger analysis in the increasingly global antitrust enforcement landscape. While some of the older cases, such as Bayer–Aventis CropScience and the Guinness–Grand Metropolitan mergers, appear to have been based on superficial analysis (although arriving at the same result as a more in-depth approach), these older decisions are reflective of young antitrust regimes. In the future it is likely that there will be fewer decisions based on this type of analysis, and a greater level of convergence can be expected within Latin America and with the US and EU antitrust authorities. This is particularly true (as we have witnessed in countries such as Mexico and Brazil) as Latin American competition authorities work with the ICN and other nations to develop their antitrust laws. Other countries, such as Argentina and Venezuela, appear to be less advanced in their approach, but that may result from larger economic pressures. The remainder of the region falls in between, but there is a movement in favor of convergence. Indeed, at a recent Merger Working Group meeting during the Sixth Annual ICN Conference, Assistant Attorney General Thomas O Barnett, Chief of the DOJ's Antitrust Division, noted that the absence of public controversy signified 'the silent success story of international convergence around sound merger analysis'.[92]

Even established antitrust regimes with reasoned guidelines to govern their review engage in analysis that confounds observers. Convergence is not a guarantee that companies can rely on merger guidelines when considering the competition barriers to, and cost of, a merger. Companies will always face the risk that any nation's competition authority will thwart their proposed transactions and inhibit their merger plans. As companies are forced to engage in multiple filings in multinational mergers, this risk increases.

[92] Bureau of National Affairs, 'DOJ Official Says ICH Merger Working Group is Setting the Stage for Analysis Convergence' (June 15, 2007), *Antitrust & Trade Regulation Daily*.

Chapter XXI

Downloading Competition Law from a Regional Trade Agreement: A Strategy to Introduce Competition Law in Bolivia and Ecuador

FRANCISCO MARCOS*

I. Introduction

Bolivia and Ecuador are the only Andean Community countries without competition legislation. Different reasons explain this situation. Although several initiatives have tried in the last decade to provide these two countries with competition laws, and significant resources have been poured on the process by the respective governments and by foreign donors and international organizations, no success has been achieved so far.[1] No relevant competition rules have been adopted by the legislature, or by any of the administrative branches of the government. Political instability and institutional weakness are the main explanations behind this outcome.[2] A conscious disregard for the virtues of a competitive market, small size of domestic markets and widespread poverty are other factors that have so far contributed to the blockade of all the draft competition laws.

* Director of Competition Service, Madrid Regional Antitrust Court; Professor of Law, Instituto de Empresa Business School, Madrid (Spain). The author gratefully acknowledges the comments by Albert Sánchez Graells and Ainhoa Veiga. Daniel Sokol read a prior version of the chapter and has greatly enhanced the final draft with his comments and questions. The usual disclaimers apply.

[1] See Rodrigo Urquieta Arias, 'Bolivia', in Pradeep S Mehta (ed), *Competition Regimes in the World. A Civil Society Report* (Jaipur, CUTS International, 2006), at 547; Gesner Oliveira, 'Ecuador', *ibid*, at 577–78.

[2] See Francisco Marcos, 'Do developing countries need Competition Law and Policy?' presented at the 23rd EALE Conference, Sept 2006, Madrid (WP-Instituto de Empresa Business School, available at http://www.ie.edu/). It is true that there are other countries in the region suffering similar institutional weakness, and yet which have adopted competition rules and established competition authorities. Even if there is no evident explanation of why the evolution in Bolivia and Ecuador has been different, one can guess that institutional malfunctions are more severe in these two countries, but there is no clue about why this should be.

II. The Andean Community and Andean Community Law

The Andean Community (CAN) was established in 1969 as a Regional Trade Area initially comprising the South American countries of Chile, Bolivia, Peru, Ecuador and Colombia. Venezuela entered the agreement in 1973, and Chile withdrew in 1976. Recently Venezuela has announced its withdrawal, although formal requirements may delay its effectiveness for some time.

The CAN was originally conceived as a Free Trade Area and Customs Union, with a common external tariff and a uniform external trade policy, especially regarding foreign investments.[3] The CAN was created to enhance the standard of living of the population of the Member States through the establishment of a common market and the promotion of:

> "[T]he balanced and harmonious development of the Member Countries under equitable conditions, through integration and economic and social cooperation; to accelerate their growth and the rate of creation of employment; and to facilitate their participation in the regional integration process, looking ahead toward the gradual formation of a Latin American Common Market [...] to reduce external vulnerability and to improve the positioning of the Member Countries within the international economic context; to strengthen sub-regional solidarity, and to reduce existing differences in levels of development among the Member Countries."[4]

In accordance with the objective of regional market integration [and as it is usual in other Regional Trade Agreements (RTA)], the CAN also establishes a principle of collaboration and a positive obligation by Member States to adopt measures necessary to secure the fulfilment of Andean Community objectives, along with a commitment not to adopt or use measures that might go against those rules or that could endanger the enforcement of Andean Community rules.[5]

[3] For some reflections on the origins of this policy (which apparently strongly deterred foreign investment), see Antonio R Zamora, 'Andean Common Market-Regulation of Foreign Investment: Blueprint for Future?' 10/1 *International Lawyer* 153–66 (1976); Dennis L Greenwald, 'The Multinational Enterprise in the Context of Latin American Economic Integration: The Andean Agreement Model' 11 *San Diego Law Review* 245 (1973). In the last decade the attempt to revitalize the Andean Community has been founded on a different approach, more benign to foreign investors; see Thomas Andrew O'Keefe, 'How the Andean Pact Transformed itself into a Friend of Foreign Enterprise' 30/1 *International Lawyer* 811 (1996). A recent view on the 'achievements' of the Andean Community in terms of integration can be seen in Comunidad Andina (Secretaría General), *Estado de la integración andina. Instituciones, mecanismos y disciplinas relacionados con el comercio*, SG/di 666, 12 Oct 2004.

[4] Art 2 of the Cartagena Agreement (1969).

[5] Art 4 of the Treaty Creating the Andean Court of Justice, codified by Decision 472 (*Official Gazette of the Cartagena Agreement*, no 483, 17 Sept 1999, at 5–12): 'Member States are obliged to adopt measures that are necessary to guarantee the observance of the legal rules that belong to the legal order of the Andean Community. They also commit themselves not to adopt or use any measure that may be contrary to those rules or that in any manner may hinder their implementation.' Similar words, though related to the limited scope of Decision 608, are contained in Art 36. See also the interpretation of this commitment in Preliminary Ruling 5-IP-89 of 26 Oct 1989 (section 1.1).

Over the years the CAN has never fulfilled its aim of economic integration. However, it has developed some vigorous and strong institutions, like the Andean Court of Justice, which have proved their effectiveness in the matters of their competence. One of the achievements of the CAN has been the establishment and development of a body of law, Andean Community Law, built around the founding charter of the Andean Community, the Cartagena Agreement,[6] the aim of which is to provide an adequate legal background for economic and market integration within the CAN.

Through the last four decades, especially after 1985, when the Andean Court of Justice began its activities, a new body of law has been consolidated and enforced.[7] The basic elements of Andean Community Law are the Treaties and Protocols signed by the Member States (primary sources), and the rules adopted by the different Andean institutions (secondary sources): the Decisions of the Andean Council of Foreign Ministers, the Decisions of the Andean Commission, and the Resolutions of the Andean Community General Secretariat. All these rules, which ultimately are based in the Cartagena Agreement or any of the treaties adopted thereafter, deal with the matters and competencies that the Member States have transferred to the CAN, and are directly applicable and enforceable in the Member States. Moreover, Andean Community Law enjoys supremacy over Member States national laws.[8]

The *direct applicability or direct effect* of Andean Community Law on each of the Member States' legal orders is legally recognized in Article 3 of the Treaty creating the Andean Community Court (1979).[9] The Andean Community Court declared the *supremacy* of Andean Community Law over national law of the Member States in 1990, with remarkable parallelism with European Community law.[10] In sum,

[6] Decision 406 codifies the Cartagena Agreement (*Official Gazette* no 273, 4 July 1997, at 1–33).

[7] The Andean Court of Justice was formally created in 1979 and is located in Quito. On its activities, see the reports by Nicolás de Pierola, 'The Andean Court of Justice', *Emory Journal of International Dispute Resolution* 2 (1987), at 11–37; Edwin P Lochridge, 'Note: The Role of the Andean Court in Consolidating Regional Integration Efforts', *Georgia Journal of International and Comparative Law* 10 (1980), at 351–83.

[8] See Jorge A Quindimil López, *Instituciones y Derecho de la Comunidad Andina* (Valencia, Tirant Lo Blanch, 2006), ch 2. Note the clear parallelism with some of the basic traits of European Union law and institutions.

[9] It reads: 'Decisions of the Andean Council of Foreign Ministers or of the Commission and Resolutions of the General Secretariat shall be directly applicable in Member Countries as of the date they are published in the Official Gazette of the Agreement, unless they indicate a later date. … When their text so stipulates, Decisions must be incorporated into national law through an express act stipulating the date they will enter into effect in each Member country'. See also Judgment of 24 March 1997, Procedure 03-AI-96, *Gazzete* no 261, 29 March 1997, and Roberto Salazar Manrique, 'El Derecho Comunitario Andino: De la teoría jurídica a la realidad actuante del Derecho', *Revista Jurídica de la Universidad Católica de Santiago de Guayaquil* 9 (1994), at 257–59.

[10] The Court purposely has followed the path of the European Court of Justice in its judgments in *Costa/ENEL* (1964) and *Simmenthal* (1978), which were even expressly mentioned by the Andean Court in its first opinion on this matter; see Preliminary Ruling 2-IP-90 of 20 Sept 1990 (section 1: 'In the matters in which the regulation corresponds to Community Law, following the founding or basic rules of the Community Law, the competency is automatically displaced from the

from the perspective of a citizen, Andean Community Law can be directly alleged before, and its application is mandatory for, national courts and administrative authorities. Furthermore, national rules contradicting Community rules are null and void.

III. The Andean Community Competition Rules

The Cartagena Agreement contains references to the necessity for signatory States to adopt rules against anti-competitive agreements and practices within the CAN.[11] The General Secretariat is the institution within the CAN in charge of combating CAN-based anti-competitive business practices that damage the functioning of the Andean Common Market under the Cartegena Agreement.[12] The Cartagena Agreement expressly gives the General Secretariat the power to enforce the antitrust rules adopted by the Commission of the Andean Community. The resolutions of the General Secretariat applying Andean competition rules may be appealed before the Court of Justice of the Andean Community.[13]

A. 'Soft' Andean Competition Rules (1971 to 2005)

For many years, existing antitrust rules within the Andean Community Law lacked effectiveness, as they consisted of simple recommendations or mere

National legislature to the Community legislature. It can be said that the Organized Community invades or occupies the National legislative ground for reasons of the matter regulated, displacing in this manner National Law. Community Law does not abrogate national laws, which are subject to the national legal order: it only makes them inapplicable it they go against it').

[11] Similar rules exist in the Southern Cone Common Market (Mercosur), not in force yet, and lie at the foundation of a common Latin-American framework of cooperation in the fight against anti-competitive practices in the region; see Aladi/Comunidad Andina/Mercosur, *Convergencia Comercial de los países de América del Sur hacia la comunidad sudamericana de naciones. Política de competencia*, 14, 2006.

[12] See Art 105 of the Cartagena Agreement, which places the Andean Commission in charge of adopting rules that confer powers on the Andean General Secretariat to prevent or correct practices that may distort competition within the Andean Community ('The Commission, before December 31, 1971 and at the General Secretariat's proposal, shall adopt the essential provisions to guard against or correct practices that may distort competition within the Sub-region, such as dumping, improper price manipulations, maneuvers to upset the normal supply of raw materials, and others with a like effect. In this respect, the Commission shall consider the problems that could be created by imposing duties and other restrictions on exports. … It shall be the General Secretariat's responsibility to ensure the application of those provisions to the particular cases that are reported').

[13] Art 17 of the Treaty Creating the Court of Justice of the Cartagena Agreement (Amended by the Cochabamba Protocol). This nullity action may be brought by any person against a resolution that 'affect[s] their subjective rights or their legitimate interests' (Art 19).

declaratory rules without teeth.[14] That was the situation with the Commission's Decisions 45 (adopted 18 December 1971), 230 (adopted 11 December 1987[15]) and 285 (adopted 21 March 1991[16]). Only the last of these has some record of enforcement that deserves comment.

When Decision 285 entered into effect in 1991 there was no competition culture reflected in the Member States' legislation. Only one of the Andean Community Members had a competition law (Colombia).[17] This fact partially explains why the CAN framework provided by Decision 285 embodies recommendations aimed at preventing trans-border anti-competitive trade and dumping practices (which were also applicable to practices originating in third countries that affected more than one Andean Community Member State). For that reason, one of the main weaknesses of Decision 285 was that its standard for a determination of harm was similar to that of trade law and anti-dumping provisions, rather than antitrust harm.[18]

Whenever there was a trans-border spill-over of a potential anti-competitive business practice or decision, the rules provided by Decision 285 charged the Secretariat of the Andean Community with investigating anti-competitive conduct. If the Secretariat found a violation, Decision 285 gave the Secretariat powers to issue cease-and-desist orders, to impose retaliatory trade-related remedies, or to issue mere recommendations to the parties aimed at ending the infringing conduct.[19] In conducting an investigation and analyzing the practice in question, the Secretariat applied a rule of reason standard. Decision 285 did not include a merger review procedure, neither did it give the Secretariat any sanctioning powers. The record of implementation of Decision 285 shows only decisions related to trans-border trade and dumping practices.[20]

Due to the defects in the design of competition rules and the lack of sanctioning powers by Andean institutions in charge of applying them, no major anti-competitive measures introduced by Member State governments or undertaken by business firms were detected or sanctioned during that time.[21]

[14] A review of this regulation is given in Bruno Ciuffetelli, 'Venezuela: role of antitrust law in Latin American integration' 26/11 *International Business Lawyer* 522–25 (1998). However, this is not peculiar to the CAN; the same situation is found in other RTAs and Preferential Trade Agreements (PTAs), especially in Latin America. D Daniel Sokol, 'Order Without (Enforceable) Law: Why Countries Enter into Non-enforceable Competition Policy Chapters in Free Trade Agreements' 83 *Chicago Kent Law Review* 231 (2008).

[15] Rules to prevent or correct practices that may distort competition within the Sub-region (*Official Gazette of the Cartagena Agreement* no 26, 18 Dec 1987).

[16] Rules to prevent or correct the distortions in competition raised by restrictive practices of free competition (*Official Gazette of the Cartagena Agreement* no 80, 4 April 1991, at 14–17).

[17] Law155/1959 of 24 Dec 1959, adopting several rules regarding restrictive commercial practices (*Official Journal* no 30.138, 22 Jan 1960).

[18] See Art 13 of Decision 285.

[19] See Arts 16 and 17 of Decision 285.

[20] Jorge Castro Bernieri, 'La regulación de la competencia en la Comunidad Andina', *Gaceta Jurídica de la CE y de la Competencia* 207 (May/June 2000), at 61–63.

[21] Gabriel Ibarra Pardo, 'La política de competencia en la Comunidad Andina de naciones', *Revista de Derecho de la Competencia*, CEDEC V, 2004, 315–25.

B. 'Hard' Andean Competition Rules (2005 to present)

Andean Commission Decision 608 was adopted on 29 March 2005. This Decision established new rules to protect and promote free competition in the Andean Community.[22] The rules forbid collusive agreements to restrict competition, as well as the abuse of dominant position by firms that may affect trade among Member States.[23] The Decision also contains some rules addressing competition advocacy, aimed at spreading competition culture in the Andean Community and preventing the introduction of anti-competitive restraints by Member States.[24] However, it does not establish a merger review system for *ex ante* control over business mergers and acquisitions that may impair market competition later on.

Decision 608 limits its scope of application to conduct restricting competition that affects business activities among CAN Member States. Cross-border effects are required. Therefore, the Decision applies to those practices that take place in the territory of one or more Member States and have effects in one or more Member States, or those that take place in the territory of a non-Member State and the effects of which are felt in one or more Member States. Practices with origins and effects in a single Member State are excluded from its scope of application.[25] Different from its predecessor, this rule authorizes the General Secretariat to impose heavy sanctions for the violations of the Decision's prohibitions. The General Secretariat can initiate an investigation on its own initiative, or at the request of national authorities of the Member State or at the request of any person if there is evidence of behaviour that could unduly restrain competition. The General Secretariat and national competition authorities of the Member State jointly undertake the first phase of the investigation, with the latter being in charge of most of the inspections to be performed and of adoption of any precautionary measures. Once the investigation is concluded, the General Secretariat prepares a statement of objections, which is made available to the parties and to

[22] *Official Gazette of the Cartagena Agreement* no 1180, 4 April 2005, 1–9.

[23] Arts 7, 8 and 9 establish the material prohibitions. For a description, see Ramón García and Dolores Domínguez, 'La reforma de la norma de competencia en la Comunidad Andina', *Boletín Latinoamericano de Competencia* 20 (junio 2005), 44–53. For criticism, see Gabriel Ibarra Pardo, 'Análisis de la Decisión 608 en el estado actual de la Comunidad Andina de Naciones', mimeo 2006.

[24] Arts 36 and 37 of Decision 608. See above n 5. For one of the cases in which it has been applied, see CAN General Secretariat Report 01-2007, of 26 March 2007, against the Republic of Colombia for an aid program for the agriculture and flower industry. See also, Procedure 87-IP-2002, *Telecel c Sirese* (*Official Gazette* no 868, 2 Dec 2002), 4.2, paras 7–8 .

[25] Art 5 of Decision 608. Javier Cortázar Mora, *Rev Derecho de la Competencia*, CEDEC VI, 2/2 (2006) 127–31, underlines how the interpretation of the 'effects clause' (which, at the end, is mirrored on EC antitrust law) is key to the future and credibility of the new rules. For the first interpretation, which, compared with that predominant in the EU, is rather narrow and strict, see CAN General Secretariat Report 01-2007, of 26 March 2007, against the Republic of Colombia for an aid program for the agriculture and flowers industry, 11–13 (arguing that this program merely had domestic effects and it could not be considered that it distorted competition in the Andean Sub-region).

the Andean Committee on the Defence of Free Competition.[26] This Committee in turn delivers a recommendation to the General Secretariat, which is the body that undertakes the final decision.

Decision 608 establishes corrective measures and fines that the Secretariat may impose for violations of the prohibitions (with a cap on the fines of 10 per cent of the value of the total gross income of the violator in the previous year).[27] Following the general rules of Andean Community Law, the General Secretariat resolution may be appealed before the Court of Justice of the Andean Community.

The weakneses of CAN and of Andean legal system and its path dependence may well drag future developments. The poor experience with the CAN anti-trust rules enacted prior to Decision 608 has been inherited as part of the new system, and it is not easy to foresee where its enforcement will lead and what the effects of Decision 608 will be. The first two years after its adoption proved these doubts to be well founded. To date, no enforcement record exists. Apart from the weaknesses of the CAN itself, and the lack of resources of the General Secretariat that may hinder application of Decision 608, there is considerable asymmetry in Member States as to how widespread competition culture is in their economic systems and laws,[28] which reflects different institutional settings and market cultures.

IV. Downloading Andean Rules to National Legal Systems

Decision 608 is based on European Community competition law. Following the European model, it sets a simple but effective framework to further economic integration and competition in CAN markets. Indeed, its adoption is the result of a CAN–EU cooperation and assistance program. The European experience in enforcing Articles 81 and 82 of the EC Treaty provides a clear path to follow, and it may reveal the weaknesses and strengths involved in the process. Moreover, the European experience is also key in assessing how enforcement of CAN competition rules will undoubtedly affect the development and implementation of domestic competition law and policy of Member States. CAN competition rules (ie, Decision 608) provide a powerful potential deterrent against anti-competitive

[26] The Andean Committee on the Defence of Free Competition (*Comité Andino para la Defensa de la Competencia*) was created by Decision 608 and is made up of one high-level representative from each Member State (see Arts 38–41).

[27] Art 34. The Member States in which the sanctioned firms are located or have their main place of business are the ones responsible for executing the measures or the fines imposed (see Art 35).

[28] Ranging from countries familiar with competition law, like Colombia, Peru and Venezuela, to countries like Ecuador and Bolivia that do not have competition law at all; see Javier Cortázar Mora, *Rev Derecho de la Competencia*, CEDEC VI, 2/2 (2006) 134.

practices affecting trade among Member States. Besides, they may also influence the enforcement of national rules, and even lead to a modification of national rules.[29]

One of the singularities of the system enacted by Decision 608 explains this book chapter and its title: Andean competition rules (Decisions 608 and 616)[30] empower Bolivia and Ecuador to apply the prohibitions and sanctions contained in Decision 608 in their domestic setting as a transitory device until they adopt their respective national rules.[31] Indeed, this possibility was designed as a way of helping these countries to adopt their own national competition rules, which may well be inspired by Decision 608. For that possibility to be effective, both countries were asked to designate the national institution in charge of applying Decision 608 in their domestic setting.[32]

Metaphorically, I have referred to such an approach as constituting the capability of Ecuador and Bolivia directly to 'download' legal rules from the 'host legal system' of Andean Community Law to their respective 'client (domestic) legal systems'. Following the 'downloading' procedure, Andean legal rules would be transferred from their supranational setting to the national setting, much as downloading occurs in the computer context.

A. The 'Downloading' Alternative

In deciding which parts of Decision 608 to download, Bolivia and Ecuador can choose any of the rules contained in the Decision that 'may be applicable'. The wording of this clause is open to interpretation.[33] It is not clear whether national authorities may freely choose which of those rules contained in Decision 608 they want to transfer to their legal system. A flexible interpretation seems preferable. Certain accommodations, adaptations or modifications may be necessary to the rule to be downloaded and to the client legal system and institutions, to permit the downloading to proceed and for the downloaded rule to be fully operative and enforceable.

[29] *Ibid*.

[30] Decision no 616, of 15 July 2005, regarding the entry into force of Decision 608 in the Republic of Ecuador (*Official Gazette* no 1221, 25 July 2005, 3).

[31] See Art 49 of Decision 608. See also Art 1 of Decision 616. There have been some suggestions that this device may be useful in other Regional Trade Areas in which Member States do not have national competition laws, eg, COMESA (Common Market for Eastern and Southern Africa); see George K Lipimile and Elizabeth Gachuiri, 'Allocation of competences between national and regional competition authorities: The case of COMESA', in Philippe Brusick, Ana Maria Álvarez, Lucian Cernat (eds), *Competition provisions in regional trade agreements. How to assure development gains* (New York and Geneva, UNCTAD, 2005), at 408.

[32] See Art 50 of Decision 608 and Art 2 of Decision 616.

[33] See, eg, Maria Clara Lozano, 'La Decisión 608 de la CAN y sus implicaciones en Bolivia', *Boletín Latinoamericano de Competencia* no 21/1 (Feb 2006) 47–48. In the Ecuadorian case one question that has been raised is whether the national authority *de facto* downloading Decision 608 (ie, CONATEL) could change the definitions and rules included in the Andean rule.

Of course, downloading Decision 608 may require that some of its rules remain inapplicable and that some of them need be adapted to the specific national procedures, rules and institutions in force in Ecuador or Bolivia. However, Decision 608's spirit of promoting competition has to be respected as part of the localized download. Accepting other approaches would probably run counter to the obligations that Bolivia and Ecuador have as Member States of the Andean Community.[34]

Other treaties, such as that of the European Union, have enabled Member States' institutions to apply supranational competition rules. This decentralization occurs only in situations when the conduct at issue had anti-competitive effects on trade between the Member States. Indeed, the downloading alternative provided by recent CAN competition rules has nothing to do with the decentralization of EC competition law enforcement (which has its corollary in EU Council Regulation 1/2003, of 16 December 2002). The downloading is not conceived as a decentralization tool(as enforcement of Decision 608 is to be exclusively done by Andean institutions). In the EU there exist both European and national competition rules that coexist and are applicable to different practices (impact on trade between Member States being the key point to determine which of the rules is applicable).[35] The only innovation under Regulation 1/2003 was the power awarded to national competition authorities and national judges to apply directly and in full the EU substantive competition prohibitions (Articles 81 and 82).[36] In the Andean Community the application of CAN competition rules by two of the Member States (Bolivia and Ecuador) is a provisional and transitory solution, to allow these two countries to use Andean Rules *as if they were* national rules only because they do not have national competition rules. This peculiar device *does not* allow Ecuadorian or Bolivian authorities to apply Andean competition rules *as such*, that power remaining embodied in the CAN General Secretariat. The downloading alternative is a device aimed at giving Bolivia and Ecuador the chance to enforce the basic substantive competition rules they have not been able to provide for themselves.

The argument in favour of this downloading device is to give Ecuador and Bolivia the possibility to overcome the difficulties faced in adopting competition rules at a national level. Initially, allowing them temporarily to use supranational rules until they adopt national rules seems to be a good idea. In the short term, it is true that it circumvents the impediments and obstacles to the adoption of their

[34] See Art 4 of the Treaty Creating the Andean Court of Justice, reproduced above n 5. Similar words, though related to the limited scope of Decision 608, are contained in its Art 36.

[35] See para 4 of the European Court of Justice's judgment of 13 February 1969 (*Walt-Wilhelm*, 14/68, 1969 ECR 1), where the Court accepts the simultaneous application of national and EC law to certain practices (the so-called 'double barrier') but that the supremacy of EC law needs to be respected in any case.

[36] Moreover, according to Art 3 of Regulation 1/2003, national law cannot prohibit practices that would be permitted according to EC law.

own domestic antitrust rules, and it may help in building a competition culture. In the long term, it may also put pressure on national legislators to speed up the adoption of national competition rules. Additionally, downloading antitrust rules may even help the implementation of Decision 608 itself at the supranational level. The compliance and enforcement of the downloaded rules may spread knowledge about Decision 608 and about the sanctions that may be imposed by the General Secretariat for anti-competitive practices in trade among CAN Member States.

However, the downloading tool may also prove to be problematic. The rules contained in Decision 608 may be difficult to implement at the national level for several reasons. First, the very same reasons that explain the lack of national competition rules may impede the enforcement of the downloaded Decision 608 at the national level. If the addressees of competition rules have successfully opposed the adoption of national rules (this may be one of the very reasons why they do not have them yet), one may guess that they could also be successful in preventing the implementation of downloaded Decision 608. Secondly, problems may arise in adapting the downloaded rules to the national setting. The drafters of Decision 608 had different institutional and procedural framework in mind, and the adjustment to the national setting may not be easy, with difficulties likely to arise in designing the procedures and institutions in charge of implementing the downloaded rules nationally. Additionally, downloading may also endanger the enforcement of Decision 608 at the Andean level if contradictory decisions are delivered by national and Andean institutions in applying the same rule to similar situations. It is true that the comparability of decisions will be limited due to the different scope of the downloaded rules (which are applicable only to purely domestic violations). However, if the conflict ever arises, the downloading device does not provide a system for solving such conflicts.

Further problems may arise due to the fact that Decision 608 provides a framework of competition rules for a RTA and is undoubtedly concerned with other goals apart from promoting competition to benefit consumers and efficient business firms. Indeed, as it clearly sets out in its preamble, the CAN is also aimed at furthering economic integration and free trade among Member States of the Andean Community. Interpretations of Decision 608 by the Andean institutions will be made with that background in mind, and if they are used later within the downloading process, national authorities should also bear that in mind to avoid any interference on the national settings to which the Decision 608 is being downloaded and later on will be applied. Following the European model, Decision 608 purports not only to deter anti-competitive behaviour, but also to further Andean market integration. This latter aim is not meaningful for the implementation of the downloaded rules, which will be concerned with punishing standard antitrust violations in national or infranational markets.

B. 'Downloading' in Practice

Decision 608 requires Ecuador and Bolivia to designate the national authority that will be in charge of applying the downloaded rule at the national level. Identification of the local authority or authorities responsible for domestically implementing the downloaded rule is key to starting the download and to monitoring the downloading process. Mandatory authority designation is aimed at preventing distortions in the transfer process due to conflicts among different Member States' national authorities, which may fight among themselves for the power to implement the downloaded rule at the national level.

1. *Ecuador: 'Downloading by an Active Regulatory Agency'*

The Ecuadorian Constitution of 5 June 1998 expressly recognizes freedom of enterprise (Article 23.16),[37] and it has generally been understood as requiring the adoption of a competition law that provides the framework for free competition without distortions in Ecuadorian markets. However, despite several attempts to adopt a competition law in the last few years, to date none has succeeded.[38] The lack of rules against anti-competitive practices in Ecuador (aside from rare specific rules for regulated industries) provides a fertile setting for the downloading of Andean Decision 608.

The National Directorate for External Trade Policies in the Ministry of External Trade, Industrialization, Fisheries and Competitiveness has been designed as the national competition authority in Ecuador with power to apply Decision 608. However, unexpectedly, the National Telecommunications Council (CONATEL) adopted a resolution on 13 October 2005, expressly recognizing the possibility of applying Decision 608 to the telecommunications sector and proposing the drafting of a regulation that would provide for the procedures and bodies in charge of its application.[39]

In Ecuador, CONATEL is empowered to protect, promote and guarantee competition in the telecommunications sector by the Special Law of Telecommunications. This Law provides the power to draft regulations. CONATEL shares investigative powers with the National Secretary of Telecommunications (SENATEL). The Super-Agency of Telecommunications is charged with sanctioning powers. In view of the CONATEL initiative, which was not free from problems and difficulties,[40]

[37] See Official Registry no 1 of 11 Aug 1998.

[38] See Francisco Marcos, '¿Una política de competencia para la República de Ecuador?' 21/2 *Boletín Latinoamericano de Competencia* 93–94 (Feb 2006).

[39] Resolution 416/15 CONATEL 2005, of 13 Oct (Official Registry no 142, 10 Nov 2005, 15–16).

[40] The self-attribution by CONATEL of the power to draft rules to make Decision 608 applicable in Ecuador was questioned due to lack of legislative empowerment. The same argument applies to the sanctioning powers attributed to the Super-Agency of Telecommunications.

the possibility is open for Andean rules to be downloaded from a regulatory industry perspective. CONATEL and the Super-Agency of Telecommunications are regulatory authorities of an industry with specific problems (natural monopoly, public goods, etc), and have functions which, if fulfilled, may conflict with the aims of the general competition rules of Decision 608 that they would also have to apply (should CONATEL's proposal be implemented).[41]

CONATEL prepared a draft Regulation downloading Decision 608 at the national level.[42] This was met with great opposition by firms operating in the telecommunications industry. These firms filed comments questioning the CONATEL initiative and the specific rules that had been drafted. Apart from transferring the bulk of Decision 608 at the national level for the telecommunications industry, the draft Regulation includes certain rules and provisions of a regulatory nature. That may be controversial, as competition and regulation objectives potentially are at odds. Furthermore, such download by sector regulators was something the Andean competition rules did not foresee. The sector download may aggravate the difficulties for other initiatives aimed at providing Ecuador with a general competition law.

On the other hand, CONATEL's approach leaves open the issue of how its download of Decision 608 would affect other industries not covered by the telecommunications Regulation. Downloading was meant to be effected for all markets and economic sectors simultaneously, and the attempted partial download by CONATEL would split or endanger the necessary consensus that would be needed for the download to be useful (ie, it would not lead to the adoption or instalment of a fully-fledged system of competition rules).

2. *Bolivia: 'The European Way of Downloading'*

Bolivia also recognizes freedom of enterprise and commerce in its Constitution (Article 7.d). In recent years, several attempts have been made to draft a competition law for Bolivia, but all of them have been unsuccessful. This leads to a situation in which (aside from certain rules sanctioning anti-competitive practices in regulated sectors) downloading CAN Decision 608 may provide a tool to combat anti-competitive restraints in Bolivia.

The Vice-Ministry of Industry, Commerce and Exports was designated as the institution in charge of applying Decision 608 at the national level in Bolivia. Subsequently, a complete and exhaustive legal framework was drafted, which would create a National Council for the Promotion and Defence of Competition

[41] See, with references, UNCTAD Secretariat, *Best Practices for defining respective competences and settling of cases which involve joint action of Competition Authorities and Regulatory Bodies*, 15 Sept 2005.

[42] See *Proyecto de reglamento de aplicación de las normas para proteger y promover la libre competencia en el sector de las telecomunicaciones*, undated (made public on 31 Jan 2006). A public discussion process was opened twice after the draft was first made public, and a explanatory note of the regulation was prepared (to deal with some of the complaints against the draft) and made public in May 2006.

[*Consejo Nacional de la Promoción y Defensa de la Libre Competencia* (CPDLC)], and provide detailed procedural rules for the actions of this new organ and of the other Bolivian authorities taking part in the investigation of and decisions on violations of the new competition rules.[43] Nevertheless, no provision was made regarding the possibility of exemption or authorization of anti-competitive practices at the domestic level.[44] Moreover, care was exercised in adequately inserting the new procedures—mirrored on those provided by Decision 608—in Bolivian administrative law (Law 2341/2002 on administrative procedures).[45] In the Bolivian download, the prohibitions contained in Decision 608 are left intact and no reference is made to what elements the National Council will use in deciding disputes. This may cause some trouble due to the lack of experience and tradition of Bolivian authorities. However, it is reasonable to assume that they will follow the precedents set by the CAN General Secretariat in applying Decision 608.

The Bolivian Draft Law contains rules regarding sanctions, further developing those provisions contained in Decision 608.[46] Two additions are worth noting: the Bolivian Draft Law allows private damage claims (although no further reference is made to how they may operate), and there is a provision regarding fines.[47] The Draft Law also establishes some rules on investigation of anticompetitive offenses by Bolivian authorities and on their cooperation under the procedures initiated by the General Secretariat of the Andean Community in enforcing Decision 608.[48]

C. Why 'Downloading' May not Work

1. *Lack of System Compatibility*

The download may be difficult if the national legal system contains peculiarities that prevent some of the Andean rules from being integrated into domestic law.

[43] See *Proyecto de Decreto Supremo, Reglamento de la Ley de Procedimiento Administrativo para procedimientos en materia de defensa de la competencia, en particular los procesos de investigación en materia de defensa de la competencia*, undated. The Draft Law makes great efforts to separate the investigative and prosecutorial function and the adjudicative process of antitrust rules enforcement: see Art 4. Allegedly, the inclusion of regulatory authorities (SIRESE and Super-Agency of Enterprises) in the investigation phase is aimed at profiting from their knowledge and experience in business competition issues within their corresponding industries; see Maria Clara Lozano, 'La Decisión 608 de la CAN y sus implicaciones en Bolivia', *Boletín Latinoamericano de Competencia* no 21/1 (Feb 2006), at 44 and 49.

[44] Art 6 of Decision 608 provides for Member States to apply to the Commission for authorizing exceptions or exclusions to the prohibitions in certain circumstances.

[45] Clara Lozano, *Consultoría sobre el ambiente institucional y guías de procedimiento, Proyecto de Competencia*, CAN-UE, 2005, 32–42.

[46] See Arts 65–75 of the Draft Law (inspired by Arts 34–35 of Decision 608).

[47] Inspired by *Reglamento de Sanciones y Procedimientos Especiales por Infracciones, Decreto Supremo no 25950*, 20 Oct 2000 (Super-Agency of Telecommunications/SITTEL). See Lozano, above n 45, at 42.

[48] See Arts 76–80 of the Draft Law.

However, if this problem arises, it will likely be solved through the use of the provisions in Andean Community Law that oblige Member States not to adopt rules that contradict or go against the aims of the organization or of Andean Community Law.[49] The supremacy of Andean Community Law will necessarily lead to the abrogation of any national rules contrary to it. Although these potential conflicts may exist or arise, overcoming them is essential if the Andean integration process is to keep going.

2. *Conflicts with other National Rules and Institutions Affecting Competition*

Lack of competition law in Ecuador and Bolivia does not mean that these countries lack rules and institutions that affect or regulate competition more broadly, especially within regulated industries.[50] Moreover, the State plays a significant role in economic activities, and intervenes in the functioning of the market through several policies. Indeed, some of the national rules that may contradict the downloaded Andean competition rules will undoubtedly need to be abrogated or, at least, modified and adapted. However, problems may arise in coordinating the new legal framework with the former one. Of course, this problem is also faced by other nations where competition rules are also included in regulated utilities frameworks; it is not peculiar to Ecuador or Bolivia.

For example, in Bolivia, the SIRESE Supreme Agencies (Sistema de Regulación Sectorial) will be in charge of investigating practices that may constitute a violation of Decision 608 whilst also being a violation of Law 1600 of 28 October 1994 (Law SIRESE) which the SIRESE Supreme Agencies apply.[51] Apart from the obvious conflict of interest and lack of independence, this makes it easy to confuse competition and regulatory policies, which are aimed at different (and not always complementary) tasks and objectives.[52]

3. *Risking Credibility of Andean Competition Rules*

The Andean Community has never had a powerful system to fight against anticompetitive practices or market restraints. Decision 608 provides an instrument potentially to correct that shortcoming. The implementation of this rule is a challenge for the Andean Community due to its lack of experience and possible problems with enforcement. One of the difficulties that may be faced is related

[49] See Arts 15 ff of Decision 608. See also above nn 5 and 37.

[50] Lorena Otero, 'El derecho de la competencia en Bolivia', *Rev Derecho de la Competencia*, 2 VI, 21–27 (2006), ed. Centro de Estudios de Derecho de la Competencia, Pontificia Universidad Javeriana (Bogotá); Arias Rodrigo, 'Bolivia', in Pradeep S Mehta (ed), above n 1, at 548.

[51] See Art 4.II.a) of the Draft Law. Both roles may be confused, see Lozano, above n 45, 21, 43.

[52] UNCTAD, *Fortalecimiento de Instituciones y Capacidades en el Área de Políticas de Competencia y Protección al Consumidor. Casos de Bolivia, Costa Rica, El Salvador, Honduras, Guatemala, Nicaragua y Perú*, COMPAL Program (2004), 92–93.

to the lack of a widespread market competition culture, and Andean Community institutions and national authorities will have to devote resources to help change that.[53]

The downloading experiment may make the job harder for Andean institutions and for national authorities, especially in Ecuador and Bolivia, due to the possible confusion caused by transferring Andean rules to be applied in the domestic setting. It may not be clear for market agents when original Andean rules or downloaded Andean rules are to be applied, and this may be a vital issue when differing interpretations of the rules are made by national and Andean authorities (in practice, however, it would not easily occur). This may add confusion to the process of consolidating clear-cut case law and doctrine on Andean Community competition law. Bear in mind that one of the more controversial questions regarding Decision 608 has to do with its scope of application. Decision 608 applies when a practice has 'real effects' on trade among Member States. Interpretation of this rule may be controversial, as conflicts may occasionally arise between Andean law and national laws regarding which law is applicable. In the Bolivian and Ecuadorian case, once the download is complete, the conflict would be between Decision 608 in its original Andean version and in its downloaded version, and making distinctions will be impossible.

4. *Dangers for Prospects of Adopting a National Competition Rule*

Downloading competition rules from the Andean Community Law raises the problem, as the Spanish say, of 'bringing through the window what did not enter through the door'. If the national level has proven inhospitable to competition law, there may be many and powerful explanations behind that outcome. Obtaining competition law through a download helps to overcome some of the political or institutional difficulties that have so far managed to prevent Ecuador and Bolivia from having competition laws. However, those same problems undoubtedly will appear in a different guise later on, when identifying the institutions in charge of the implementation of the downloaded rules, drafting the national application procedures, and in the enforcement activities themselves. For example, institutional weakness explains the difficulty encountered in the appointment of the institutions in charge of applying the national competition rules (be they nationally drafted or downloaded from Andean Community Law). The Ecuadorian example illustrates the problems of a 'volunteering' institution (CONATEL), while Bolivia illustrates a compromise among all possible interested institutions where a final solution may be too complex. However, if the download is successful, presumably this may help in the adoption and consolidation of a set of national competition rules in the future.

[53] Frédéric Jenny and Pierre Horna, 'Modernization of the European Legal System of Competition Law Enforcement: Lessons from other Regional Groupings', in Brusick et al, above n 31, at 302–03.

V. Conclusion

The efforts to provide Ecuador and Bolivia with national competition rules are in stasis. The downloading alternative provides an interesting way to overcome the impasse regarding national initiatives aimed at installing competition laws and policies in these two countries. This option is not free of problems. However, in spite of its shortcomings, it provides a solution to the institutional and political deadlock found in these countries that has prevented the adoption of national competition laws. Once the necessary adaptations and accommodations are in place, the implementation of the downloaded rules may enrich the soil in which a solid competition policy may grow in the future.

Chapter XXII

Promoting Competition Policies from the Private Sector in Latin America

JULIÁN PEÑA*

I. Introduction

The purpose of this chapter is to analyze how competition policy has been and may be promoted from the private sector in Latin America. There are a number of different public, private and academic initiatives throughout the region that have improved Latin America's anemic competition culture. First, it is necessary to provide some context. Historically, Latin American countries have had weak competition cultures.[1] One contributing factor has been the historically significant role of the State in the economy. Even though most Latin American countries had free market ideals in their independence movements in the 19th century, a period of very active State intervention in the markets followed in the 20th century.

For decades, most Latin American countries had economies led by State-owned monopolies, price controls, anti-competitive and discriminatory government regulations, and other protectionist measures. Prices were determined by government officials and not the market. These policies led to a private sector more used to rent-seeking through lobbying government officials than market competition. In a shift from this situation, during the 1990s, countries in the region underwent a series of reforms influenced by a series of guiding principles imposed by Washington-based international financial institutions. These policies, known as the 'Washington Consensus', gave birth to a drastic change in the paradigm of State intervention. The Washington Consensus favored the market and market-facilitating institutions over State intervention. As a consequence, during the 1990s, many Latin American countries opened their economies, privatized many public service companies and liberalized regulation to make it more market friendly. Although not all Latin American countries implemented the Washington

* Partner, Allende & Brea. Professor of Competition Law, Graduate Program of the University of Buenos Aires. Founder and Moderator of ForoCompetencia.

[1] See also Julián Peña, 'Competition Policies in Latin America, Post-Washington Consensus', in Philip Marsden, *Handbook of Research in Trans-Atlantic Antitrust* (London, Edward Elgar, 2006).

Consensus in a similar manner, this pendulum shift introduced new rules, expectations and disappointments.

One of the emblematic changes as part of the period of liberalization was the introduction of competition laws within the region. Until the 1990s, only Argentina, Brazil, Chile, Colombia and Mexico had any kind of competition legislation. However, there was little enforcement or effect of these laws. During the 1990s, these five countries introduced significant changes to their legislation, and countries such as Costa Rica, Panama, Peru, Uruguay, Venezuela and the Andean Community enacted new competition regimes.

Since the late 1990s, Latin American countries have faced a backlash to the Washington Consensus as a consequence of unfulfilled development promises. Presently, Latin American countries are trying to define a new paradigm on the role of the State in the market that is somewhere between the historic State interventionism and Washington Consensus-based neo-liberalism. Some countries have returned to a strong State presence in the economy through nationalization of private companies, price control regimes and new protectionist measures. Another group of countries have made some changes in their discourse but have not made significant changes in the enforcement of their legislation.

However, not all recent developments are so grim. In spite of the backlash towards the policies of the so-called Washington Consensus, no country has abolished its competition laws. In fact, countries have undertaken revisions to reform the existing laws (Argentina, Brazil, Chile, Mexico, Peru, Venezuela and Uruguay), or have intended to introduce competition laws where none previously existed (El Salvador, Honduras, Nicaragua, Dominican Republic, Ecuador and Paraguay). As of the date of publication of this chapter, the Congresses of Chile, Dominican Republic, Mexico, Uruguay, Honduras, Peru, Nicaragua and El Salvador have already approved their respective Bills. It is within a context of nascent competition regimes, a lack of competition culture, economic fragility, insufficient economic development, institutional weakness and resentment towards the Washington Consensus-related policies that private competition advocacy in Latin America should be analyzed.

II. The Sinuous Path of Competition Policies in Latin America

A. Competition Policies before the Washington Consensus

Although most Latin American countries supported free market ideals after their independence in the 19th century, a completely different paradigm was followed throughout the region during most of the 20th century. Strong protectionism and interventionism have been present for decades in the vast majority of Latin American countries. State control in the economy manifested itself through large State-owned enterprises, regulatory barriers, and mechanisms of price and exchange control. Until the 1990s, the governments of most Latin American countries determined the prices of many products. They created some specific agencies to deal with the prices of products such as sugar, grains and meat. Foreign competition was kept away with high trade and non-trade barriers that promoted the establishment of the protectionist import substitution model, and also created legal limitations to foreign investments. As a result of these policies, there were low levels of Foreign Direct Investment (FDI) flows. This situation was representative of most Latin American countries from the 1920s until the 1980s (the latter known as the 'lost decade'). As a result, the region developed many obsolete and uncompetitive industries. Due to these economic policies, Latin American governments ended up highly indebted, which resulted in a full-blown regional financial crisis.

B. Competition Policy During the Washington Consensus

The foreign debt crisis experienced by most of Latin America led the economist John Williamson to give a famous speech in Washington in 1989, the content of which has become known as the Washington Consensus. This speech pointed out a series of policy recommendations given to Latin American countries in order to re-establish their credibility with Washington-based international financial institutions. These recommendations to Latin America included a series of financial measures to be taken, as well as some pro-market regulatory measures. The implementation of these policies transformed the role of the State in the market.

During the Washington Consensus years most Latin American countries have, without a proper transition:

- — deregulated their highly regulated economies;
- — privatized the State-owned enterprises;
- — eliminated some government incentives;
- — experienced the acquisition of many local companies by multinationals;
- — received important FDI inflows; and
- — liberalized their foreign trade.

As a consequence of the opening and deregulation of their economies, there was a proliferation of competition laws during the 1990s.

New competition agencies were created and the previously existing ones were rebuilt. There was not a common pattern in the types of institutional frameworks adopted. For instance, some of the Latin American agencies were created as collegiate bodies in the form of Commissions, while others had a single individual in charge, and some jurisdictions had more than one administrative agency intervening in competition law enforcement. Among the agencies created by the new competition laws, some are assigned only antitrust-related issues, while others deal with broader objectives such as consumer protection, intellectual property and/or anti-dumping. In their competition laws, most Latin American countries (eg, Argentina, Brazil and Peru) took inspiration from the European competition law model, both in substance and in procedure. However, a growing American influence can be found in the economic reasoning underlying competition policy.

C. Competition Policy Post-Washington Consensus

Though most Latin American countries implemented the policies of the Washington Consensus, the results disappointed. As a consequence, disenchantment with the Washington Consensus began to materialize throughout the region. The turning point for these policies had its origins in the Mexican crisis of 1994 and the subsequent economic deterioration throughout the region. Since then, most Latin American countries have voted for presidential candidates who took an anti-Washington Consensus position. The path each Latin American country has taken after the demise of the Washington Consensus paradigm differs. Yet all share a vision that the Washington Consensus model failed to solve the region's historical development problems, and that it lacked a sense of equity and social awareness.

There are at least as many alternative paths as there are countries in Latin America. The role of State intervention in the market is a crucial issue that has recently been interpreted in different ways throughout the region. However, a common response to the crisis of the Washington Consensus in the region is characterized by a greater presence of the State in the market. The difference across countries, however, is the degree of return to State interventionism. Some of the policy changes in the post-Washington Consensus era could be summarized as follows:

— a return by the State as an active player in the market either through expropriation of private companies, or through nationalization of formerly privatized companies or the creation of new State-owned companies;
— government influence on pricing through the establishment of price and exchange controls;
— international trade conflicts among Latin American countries increasingly being solved through government-promoted cartels; and
— a greater role for government intervention in public services regulation.

The enforcement of competition laws in Latin America in the post-Washington Consensus era has seen, in a number of countries, the introduction of non-traditional concepts, a weakening of the institutional framework and, therefore, a more politically-driven enforcement. These factors, together with the lack of a competition culture, have been critical in the setback of competition policy in the region. Furthermore, as a consequence of the results of the implementation of the Washington Consensus policies, competition policies have lost some political support in various countries throughout the region.

III. Creating a Competition Culture

The International Competition Network has defined 'competition advocacy' as:

> Those activities conducted by the competition authority related to the promotion of a competitive environment for economic activities by means of non-enforcement mechanisms, mainly through its relationship with other government entities and by increasing public awareness of the benefits of competition.[2]

In other words, it is the government, through its competition agencies, that should promote the creation of a competition culture.

Given the long decades of non-competition culture in most countries within the region, the struggle to promote competition values has been a tough task. There has been backlash by market participants and from other parts of government. Within this context, competition advocacy undertaken by most Latin American competition agencies has been inconsistent and insufficient. However, there have been a number of private sector initiatives to promote competition policies within the region, from private professionals as well as from academia. These initiatives have helped both the technical development of competition law in the region and the competition agencies in their competition advocacy mission.

A. The Need for an Interdisciplinary Debate

1. *Public/Private/Academia/Judiciary/Media*

A key element in the development of competition advocacy in Latin America should be the interdisciplinary interaction between government officials, private parties, academia, the judiciary and the media. All five are key players in the process of establishing a competition culture. Without this interconnectivity, any individual effort is insufficient. Government involvement in competition advocacy is crucial. Without it, any effort would be limited, and possibly even senseless. Competition agencies can undertake advocacy in different manners, either to undertake initiatives of their own or to support the work of others. There are plenty of competition advocacy activities that a competition agency can undertake, but the limited resources most Latin American competition agencies have make it necessary for them to focus on certain key activities. Given this resource limitation, the two pillars of competition advocacy on which the competition agencies should be focused are the transparency of their enforcement activity and the promotion of a pro-competitive regulatory framework.

Transparency of the competition agency enforcement activity is necessary in order for the private sector to see competition law as a predictable tool. A lack of transparency creates business uncertainty and reduces accountability. There are

[2] ICN, *Advocacy and Competition Policy*, Report of the Advocacy Working Group (2002).

a number of different ways to reach greater transparency. One important one is the Internet. This has become a tool to facilitate communication between competition agencies and the public as to what is going on within the walls of these agencies and how their work benefits society.

The other task competition agencies should focus on, given their limited resources, is the promotion of a pro-competitive regulatory framework. This role is crucial in order to avoid inconsistencies in the government's approach towards competition. Regulatory legislation sometimes does not contemplate competition principles, thus creating contradictory rules that damage competition.

In other areas of competition advocacy, competition agencies should rely on and support private initiatives. These initiatives could come either from the private sector or from academia. The different perspectives and interests held by companies (or their lawyers and economists), and by intellectuals who study the development of competition law and policy both in their countries and abroad, can combine in a constructive interaction with the competition enforcers and result in very fruitful outcomes. The synergies created by the association of these three legs of the competition advocacy tripod are countless. The interrelation between these three also aids each in a better understanding of the others, thus improving the effectiveness of the work each one does.

Academic forums have proven to be the best place for players from these three sectors to interact. However, the interaction between the public, private and academic members should not be limited to these forums. Competition agencies should realize that the more they interact with civil society, the better the outcome for competition advocacy.

The two other key players in the creation of a competition culture within the region are the judiciary and the media. Most of the competition-related activity within the region is focused on the government, the private sector and academia. However, the ones who have the final say in all competition cases are the judiciary. The involvement of members of the judiciary in competition-related activities is still relatively marginal within the region. One reason why the judiciary does not get as involved in competition-related activities is that most Latin American countries lack specialized competition courts. An understanding of competition policy is not a priority for judges who have other kinds of cases and whose caseload of competition-related cases is relatively low. However, given the fact that the intervention of the judiciary in all competition cases is growing, it is crucial that these judges get involved as much as possible in the peculiarities of handling a competition case. In order for this to occur, the involvement of representatives of the judiciary in the activities organized by the public, private and academic sectors is highly recommended.

The news media form the channel through which civil society monitors competition enforcement activity. In order for the media to understand what is going on, their members need to become as specialized as possible. Their major task is to explain to civil society what competition agencies are doing. In order to carry out this mission, the media need to have interlocutors—not only in the competition agencies, but in the private and academic sectors as well—who can explain to them what is really going on. In past years, many of the region's competition agencies have modernized their websites, making it possible to obtain a growing amount of information from them. It is worth noting in particular the case of CADE, one of the Brazilian competition agencies, which allows the public to follow its weekly council meetings online through its website.

2. *Legal/Economic*

Competition law is perhaps one of the few fields where legal and economic analyses coexist intensively. It is not possible to understand competition cases in full from either a legal or an economic perspective alone. Therefore, the interaction between lawyers and economists is crucial for the development of competition law in the region. Traditionally the two have mistrusted each other. However, the greater complexity in competition cases calls for a better understanding of both fields. In order for this to happen, it is necessary to promote the economic preparation of lawyers as well as the legal education of economists. This is a task where the academic has a crucial role.

B. Latin American Experiences

1. *The Public Sector*

Competition advocacy in Latin America, especially during the 1990s, has been heavily supported by international organizations through technical assistance programs. The international organizations that have been most intensively active in competition advocacy work in Latin America have been the UNCTAD, the OECD, the World Bank, the Inter-American Development Bank, the Organization of American States and the European Commission. Other national agencies have also cooperated with their Latin American counterparts, such as the US Department of Justice and Federal Trade Commission, Spain's *Tribunal de Defensa de la Competencia* and France's *Conseil de la Concurrence*, among others. This assistance in competition advocacy has been reflected by the training of many enforcers through conferences, courses and publications, among other activities. The *Boletín Latinoamericano de Competencia*, an electronic newsletter created in 1997 by Juan Antonio Riviere-Marti at the European Commission, deserves special mention. The *Boletín*, over its first decade, has turned into a vehicle for Latin American regulators and professionals to share their unique experiences on competition policy.

In recent years, a series of new regional forums, such as the *Foro Iberoamericano de la Competencia* and the OECD/Inter-American Development Bank Latin American Competition Forum, have been created for competition agencies to meet and discuss topics of their concern. The *Foro Iberoamericano de la Competencia* was launched in Spain in 2002, and the Latin American competition agencies, along with their Spanish and Portuguese counterparts, attend annually. The *Foro* also created the Iberoamerican Competition School in order to train Latin American agencies' staff members. At roughly the same time, the Inter-American Development Bank and the OECD created the Latin American Competition Forum. This annual forum gathers the Latin American competition agencies and other agencies to 'promote dialogue, consensus building and networking between competition policymakers and law enforcers, and the identification and dissemination of best practices in competition law and policy in a collegiate setting'.[3] The Forum has implemented a 'peer review' system, in which the experiences of a particular country are analyzed by the rest of the region's agencies. So far the Forum has made in-depth analysis of the competition regimes in Chile, Peru, Brazil, Mexico and Argentina.

2. *The Private Sector*

The private sector in Latin America has become increasingly involved in cooperating with competition advocacy in the region. There has also been, in the past few years, a growing number of competition-related institutions appearing in different countries such as Argentina, Brazil, Peru and Colombia, as well as stronger media coverage of antitrust issues, especially in Argentina and Brazil.

IBRAC

The pioneer in promoting competition policy from the private sector in Latin America is the Brazilian Institute of Studies on Competition, Consumer Affairs and International Trade—IBRAC. It was established in December 1992 as a non-profit private entity to foster the development of research, studies and debates involving competition law issues. In its first 15 years, IBRAC has played an active role in the promotion of events such as the annual International Seminar on Competition Law, where representatives of the private, public and academic sectors of Brazil meet. Competition experts from Europe, North America and Latin America are regular speakers at IBRAC events.

The Institute has also played an important role in the development of technical assistance, through a series of technical cooperation agreements with the Brazilian antitrust authorities *Conselho Administrativo de Defesa Econômica* (CADE), *Secretaria de Acompanhamento Econômico do Ministério da Fazenda* (SEAE), *Secretaria de Direito Econômico do Ministério da Justiça* (SDE) and a number of other (non-governmental) institutions.

It has also become a nexus for Brazilian academia by having a permanent university extension course in São Paulo. Leading competition professionals and authorities teach this course. Additionally, IBRAC promotes the involvement of undergraduate and graduate students in competition-related issues by holding an annual essay contest on Competition Issues sponsored by Esso Brasileira de Petróleo. The contest receives submissions from students from over 45 Brazilian universities. Since 2004 IBRAC has also held an annual Contest of Monographies

[3] OECD, First Latin American Competition Forum—Background Note (Paris, April 7–8, 2003).

for graduate students and professionals on the subject of competition vis-à-vis the illegal market, which is co-organized with ETCO—the Brazilian Institute on Ethics in Competition.

Internationally, IBRAC has promoted official visits to foreign entities and agencies such as the Federal Trade Commission, the US Department of Justice's Antitrust Division, the European Commission and the World Trade Organization, among others, and has participated as a Non-Governmental Advisor at the ICN Conferences. Additionally, among its publications, IBRAC has published a competition journal called *Revista do IBRAC* since 1993. This is the only newsletter in Brazil that serves as a vehicle for CADE rulings, articles and essays. It also has a weekly newsletter called *Clipping do IBRAC* which covers relevant press clippings and resolutions published in the Official Gazette. IBRAC also covers issues on consumer protection and international trade, playing a leading role in Brazilian society.

ForoCompetencia

ForoCompetencia is a discussion group that was created in October 2001 for the purpose of analyzing different competition regulation issues from an interdisciplinary perspective. It is also now a network of more than 400 lawyers and economists from over 25 different countries, mainly from Latin America and Europe. The members of ForoCompetencia include competition and regulation specialists from the public, private and academic sectors of Argentina, Belgium, Brazil, Chile, Colombia, Costa Rica, Ecuador, El Salvador, France, Germany, Guatemala, Holland, Mexico, Nicaragua, Panama, Paraguay, Peru, Spain, Switzerland, the United States, Uruguay and Venezuela, among others.

ForoCompetencia is a virtual network. It sponsors debates held electronically through an e-mail listserve. Topics are proposed on a monthly basis by different members of ForoCompetencia. The debates last an average of one week. To date, ForoCompetencia has held over 50 debates, which have covered an important variety of topics such as general economic interest, the exploitative abuse of dominant positions, the relationship between anti-dumping and competition, competition and intellectual property, the effects of the informal economy on the definition of a relevant market, the failing firm defense in developing countries, institutional structures and the role of efficiencies in antitrust analysis.

ForoCompetencia has also developed an information-sharing network on competition issues named *FC-News*, and also publishes a yearbook containing all of the group's activities and debates. It also organizes bi-annual colloquia. The first event was held in 2003, with 70 participants from seven countries. The second colloquium was held in 2005, with nearly 100 participants from six countries. At the third colloquium, held in 2007, members from 10 different countries participated.

In June 2005, ForoCompetencia launched its website (www.forocompetencia.com) with the aim of promoting its activities, providing its members with access to previous debates and publishing news regarding future activities. ForoCompetencia has been a truly interdisciplinary experience. In its debates, professionals from different countries and from different backgrounds give their perspectives on a wide variety of competition-related topics. These debates, which are later compiled in the yearbooks, have become a reference source for competition law in Latin America, since the debates reflect the economic, legal and political peculiarities of the region. Locally, ForoCompetencia has held over 80 breakfast debates in Argentina, attracting the attendance of members from the competition agency, the judiciary, and private lawyers and economists. In these monthly meetings, both issues and cases have been discussed in open-minded interdisciplinary debates.

Other Organizations

There are a number of other private organizations with intense competition-promotion activities. With a broader scope, there is the *Centro de Estudio de Derecho de los Mercados* (CEDEMERC) in Colombia and the *Grupo de Estudos de Direito Econômico* (GEDECON) in Brazil. Their scope also covers related areas of interest, though an important part of their activity is in regard to competition issues. The *Ordem dos Advogados de São Paulo* (OAB) is another group that has a very active competition committee which has organized a variety of events.

3. *The Academic Sector*

Since the 1990s, a large number of Latin American universities have introduced competition law into their curricula, at both the undergraduate level and the graduate level, especially at law schools, where the subject, for the most part, did not previously exist. Perhaps the university where the most intense competition-related academic activity has taken place is the Universidad Javeriana in Bogotá, Colombia. Its *Centro de Defensa de la Competencia* (CEDEC) was created in 1995 by its Law School. This center has organized a wide variety of activities on competition-related topics. The CEDEC has introduced at different graduate programs competition courses such as commercial law, communications law and economic law. It has also organized different seminars, discussion forums and monthly meetings, and owns one of Colombia's most complete document centers on competition issues. The publications of the CEDEC include a yearly journal called *Revista de Derecho de la Competencia CEDEC*. Other academic institutions have also had important competition-related activity in the region. For instance, Argentina's Universidad Argentina de la Empresa has its *Centro de Economía de la Regulación* '(CEER)', which holds a three-week-long graduate program twice each year on the economics of public service regulation and competition.

4. *The Judiciary*

A greater 'judicialization' of competition enforcement is taking place in Latin America, especially in Argentina and Brazil. There is a growing number of cases in which the courts are intervening, not only to control but also to replace the competition agencies. For instance, due to the delay by the Argentine Government in establishing the independent competition tribunal created by competition law in 1999, a number of federal judges have intervened in merger control cases. They held that the *Comisión Nacional de Defensa de la Competencia* lacked the legal right to act as competition authority. In one case, the intervention of a federal judge delayed the divestment process necessary to obtain clearance from the competition agency by three years. In another case, a series of contradictory rulings by the same federal judge delayed the Commission's merger review of a transaction by more than three years. Finally, in a third case, a judge forbade the Commission to issue injunctions during the investigation process of a merger case. Indeed, there have also been cases in which competition law was interpreted by administrative, commercial or even labor courts.

In Brazil, it is in the anticompetitive conduct cases where the judicialization is most evident, though the courts are intervening in a greater number of merger cases as well. Brazilian competition experts foresee the judiciary taking an increasingly important role, and some have even considered that CADE will become dedicated to assisting judicial enforcement.[4] Finally, though some legislation provides for private antitrust enforcement, this has not occurred in Latin America, and it is not likely to occur significantly in the near future.

5. *The Media*

The news media have increasingly taken notice of different competition-related issues. As never before, press coverage has taken competition issues to the front pages of important newspapers. Television programs interview competition officials, journalists regularly follow competition law developments, and newspapers publish periodic opinion columns on the subject.

It is in Brazil and Argentina, in that order, where competition issues get the most press coverage. Newspapers such as the *Folha de São Paulo* have different columnists who periodically write on competition-related subjects. In Argentina, for instance, *Infobae Profesional* is a newspaper that closely follows the activity of the *Comisión Nacional de Defensa de la Competencia* and of the courts on competition cases, and also publishes the most important court rulings.

There are not yet, as is the case in developed countries, a large number of full-time competition journalists, primarily because there is not currently enough activity in any of the Latin American countries to justify such dedication. However, the trend is to see competition issues in the media more often.

IV. Conclusion

In order to determine how better to promote competition from the private sector in Latin America, it is first necessary to have knowledge of the political context.

[4] José Inácio Gonzaga Franceschini, 'Private Competition Enforcement: is there room for CADE?', May 2005—1st Antitrust Spring Conference.

Within the region there is a lack of competition culture, due to decades of strong State intervention in the markets.

Although some competition agencies have been active in competition advocacy, the work has been inconsistent and insufficient. It is within this context of incipient competition regimes, lack of competition culture, economic fragility, insufficient economic development, institutional weakness and resentment towards the Washington Consensus-related policies that private competition advocacy in Latin America ought to be analyzed.

No matter how actively involved the private sector gets in competition advocacy work, without government involvement any effort would be limited and possibly even senseless. In order to promote the creation of a competition culture, it is crucial that an interdisciplinary interaction exists between government officials, private parties, academia, the judiciary and the media. They each play a key role in competition advocacy.

Since most competition agencies have limited resources, they should focus on greater transparency of their enforcement activities and promote a pro-competitive regulatory framework. The private and academic sectors can produce significant synergies when their efforts are combined with competition agencies for fruitful discussion. However, the discussion cannot be limited only to these parties, since the judiciary and the media also play important roles. In the end, the courts are the ones that have the final say in all competition-related cases, and the media provide the channel of communication with society.

Secondly, the interaction between lawyers and economists is crucial for the development of competition law in the region, since competition law is one of the few fields where legal and economic analysis coexist intensively. Greater economic preparation of lawyers and legal education of economists needs to be promoted, especially by the universities.

Different non-governmental competition advocacy projects have been launched in Latin America. Some of them, such as IBRAC and ForoCompetencia, have been private initiatives; others, such as the CEDEC and the CEER, have been academic initiatives. They all have in common the promotion of competition in the region through interdisciplinary interaction between the government, the private sector, academia, the judiciary and the media. It is through this open-minded constructive dialogue that a competition culture must be built in a socio-political context that is sensitive to the idea of pro-market initiatives, especially considering the lessons of the shortcomings of the Washington Consensus.

INDEX